CALIFORNIA
THE ULTIMATE GUIDEBOOK
SECOND EDITION

"The text is bright with lots of information."
—*Los Angeles Times*

"Provides excellent coverage."
—*Gourmet*

"Casts a critical eye on the best the state has to offer."
—*San Francisco Examiner*

"Good, straightforward guide."
—*San Diego Union*

"Superlative 500-page work."
—*Las Vegas Sun*

"Comprehensive guide to the Golden State."
—*Rocky Mountain News*

"Has everything..."
—*The Oregonian*

"Offers insights into this unique state."
—*Publishers Weekly*

"Worth packing. Riegert is a good read."
—*Detroit News and Free Press*

"Competent, useful, clear, well-organized and far-reaching."
—*Houston Chronicle*

"Captures the imagination."
—*San Jose Mercury News*

CALIFORNIA
THE ULTIMATE GUIDEBOOK
SECOND EDITION

Ray Riegert

LESLIE HENRIQUES
Executive Editor

JUDITH KAHN
Editor

TIMOTHY CARROLL
Illustrator

ULYSSES PRESS

Published by: Ulysses Press
Post Office Box 3440
Berkeley, CA 94703

Library of Congress Catalog Card Number 91-65093

ISBN 0-915233-33-9

Printed in the U.S.A. by the George Banta Company

10 9 8 7 6 5 4 3

Managing Editor: Claire Chun
Research Associates: Jan Butchofsky, Marty Olmstead, Judy Wade,
    Phil Abrams, Jennifer Postlewaite
Designer: Steve Renick
Maps: Phil Gardner
Index: Sayre Van Young
Cover Photography: Galen Rowell/Mountain Light (front cover);
    Lee Foster, Ed Simpson, Michael Helms (back cover)

Distributed in the United States by Publishers Group West, in Canada by Raincoast Books, and in Great Britain and Europe by World Leisure Marketing

Printed on Recycled Paper

To Leslie,
whom I love and admire

Acknowledgments

The person who deserves the most heartfelt thanks is my wife Leslie. She not only endured the frenetic schedule but worked on every aspect of this marathon project. As always, she willingly contributed her rare combination of intelligence, talent and spirit.

Judith Kahn did a brilliant job editing endless stacks of manuscript pages. Claire Chun kept everything on track, performing wonderfully in dozens of different roles.

Steve Renick contributed a dynamic design motif and Tim Carroll once again created a series of compelling illustrations. I also want to thank Marty Olmstead and Judy Wade for their help with the manuscript and Phil Gardner for his cartography.

Special recognition belongs to Sayre Van Young for the index and Jan Butchofsky, Phil Abrams and Jennifer Postlewaite for editorial assistance. Galen Rowell, Ed Simpson, Lee Foster and Mike Helms also receive a tip of the hat for their cover photography.

Charlie Winton and everyone at Publishers Group West deserve special mention, as does Bill Julius of Banta Company.

On the home front I want to thank Mignon for her advice and Keith and Alice for their love and patience.

Contents

Maps

Ray Riegert's Best of California

ADVENTURES

Skindiving Santa Catalina *(Santa Catalina, page 119)*
Horseback Riding in Death Valley *(Page 219)*
Sailing the Channel Islands *(Santa Barbara, pages 226–27)*
Sea Kayaking in Monterey Bay *(Monterey, page 283)*
Hiking the Lost Coast *(Page 419)*
Llama Pack Trips *(Pages 424–25)*
White-water Rafting *(Page 443)*
Skiing Squaw Valley *(Page 450)*

BEACHES

Santa Monica State Beach *(Santa Monica, page 108)*
Point Mugu State Park *(Ventura, page 228)*
Point Sal State Beach *(Guadalupe, page 240)*
Stinson Beach Park *(Stinson Beach, page 407)*
McClure's Beach *(Point Reyes, page 408)*
Sonoma Coast State Beach *(Sonoma, page 411)*

BED & BREAKFAST INNS

The Venice Beach House *(Venice, page 100)*
Carriage House *(Laguna Beach, page 133)*
Bed and Breakfast Inn at La Jolla *(La Jolla, page 160)*
Mill Rose Inn *(Half Moon Bay, page 279)*
East Brother Light Station *(Point Richmond, page 369)*
Harbor House *(Elk, page 413)*
Mine House Inn *(Amador City, page 439)*

CALIFORNIA EXPERIENCES

Hot Air Ballooning *(Del Mar, page 188)*
Train Ride Along the California Coast *(Page 238)*
Watching Elephant Seals *(Año Nuevo, page 278)*
Houseboating on the Sacramento Delta *(Page 370)*
Touring a Family Winery *(Wine Country, page 382)*
Whale Watching *(Page 409)*
Exploring a Redwood Forest *(Page 423)*

COASTAL DRIVES

HISTORIC SIGHTS

HOTELS

MOUNTAIN DRIVES

MUSEUMS

Los Angeles County Museum of Art *(Los Angeles, page 39)*

Huntington Gallery *(San Marino, page 68)*

J. Paul Getty Museum *(Malibu, page 109)*

Timkin Gallery *(San Diego, page 173)*

M. H. De Young Memorial Museum *(San Francisco, page 328)*

Asian Art Museum *(San Francisco, page 328)*

NATIONAL PARKS

Santa Monica Mountains Nat. Rec. Area *(Malibu, page 108)*

Cabrillo National Monument *(San Diego, pages 178)*

Joshua Tree National Monument *(Pages 208–209)*

Death Valley National Monument *(Pages 213–17)*

Golden Gate Nat. Rec. Area *(San Francisco, pages 337–41)*

Point Reyes National Seashore *(Point Reyes, pages 402–04)*

Redwood National Park *(North Coast, page 423)*

Yosemite National Park *(Pages 457–60)*

PARKS

Griffith Park *(Los Angeles, page 75)*

Heisler Park *(Laguna Beach, page 135)*

Balboa Park *(San Diego, pages 172–73)*

Living Desert *(Palm Desert, page 202)*

Golden Gate Park *(San Francisco, pages 328–30)*

PLACES TO GO WITH CHILDREN

Los Angeles Children's Museum *(Los Angeles, page 24)*

Disneyland *(Anaheim, pages 139–140)*

Sea World *(San Diego, page 164)*

San Diego Zoo *(San Diego, page 174)*

Monterey Bay Aquarium *(Monterey, page 268)*

Santa Cruz Beach Boardwalk *(Santa Cruz, page 276)*

Exploratorium *(San Francisco, page 338)*

PRESERVES AND SANCTUARIES

RESORTS

RESTAURANTS

ROMANTIC PLACES

SHOPPING

Rodeo Drive *(Beverly Hills, pages 59–60)*
Main Street *(Santa Monica, page 106)*
Fashion Island *(Newport Beach, page 131)*
Horton Plaza *(San Diego, page 170)*
Palm Canyon Drive *(Palm Springs, pages 206–207)*
El Paseo *(Santa Barbara, page 237)*
Union Square *(San Francisco, pages 295–96)*

STATE PARKS

Malibu Creek State Park *(Malibu, page 111)*
Crystal Cove State Park *(Laguna Beach, page 136)*
Torrey Pines State Beach and Reserve *(La Jolla, pages 162–63)*
Anza-Borrego Desert State Park *(Pages 209–11)*
Montaña de Oro State Park *(Morro Bay, page 248)*
Point Lobos State Reserve *(Carmel, page 260)*
Calaveras Big Trees State Park *(Page 436)*

UNIQUE PLACES

Watts Towers *(Los Angeles, page 35)*
Queen Mary *(Long Beach, page 90)*
Venice Boardwalk *(Venice, page 100)*
Madonna Inn *(San Luis Obispo, page 246)*
Hearst Castle *(San Simeon, page 249)*
Tassajara Zen Center *(Big Sur, page 258)*
Locke *(Sacramento Delta, pages 369–70)*
Mono Lake *(Page 453)*

VISTAS

Point Fermin Lighthouse *(San Pedro, page 91)*
Zabriskie Point *(Death Valley, pages 216–17)*
Old Coast Road *(Big Sur, page 252)*
Golden Gate Bridge *(San Francisco, page 339)*
Mt. Tamalpais *(Marin County, pages 400 and 402)*
Chimney Rock Overlook *(Point Reyes, page 403)*
Emerald Bay *(Lake Tahoe, page 450)*
Glacier Point *(Yosemite National Park, page 460)*

ONE

The Golden State

It seems a wonder of nature and human invention that the most popu-   **1**
lous state in the United States is also the most popular. California,
which adds a phenomenal 600,000 people to its census each year (a
number greater than the entire population of Vermont), is also one of
the top tourist destinations in the country.

The reason, quite simply, is that the Golden State is not a state at
all. With a thousand miles of beaches, vast deserts, 14,000-foot mountains and breadbasket interior valleys, California is in fact a nation
unto itself. How else to explain a region that boasts the sixth largest
gross national product in the world?

In *California: The Ultimate Guidebook*, each of California's "states"
is treated in an individual chapter. There's *Los Angeles*, a mere mark on
the map at the turn of the century, that today is a global economic
power; and the *Los Angeles Coast*, where surfers have created a culture
based on physical prowess and the last wave. *Orange County*, the birthplace of Disneyland, has not only established a personal identity but
its own fantasy world as well.

San Diego, as large in area as the state of Connecticut, lays claim to
75 miles of beachfront real estate and a history dating back to the first
Spanish missionaries. *The Desert* is truly a place apart, an endless expanse where elevations climb from below sea level to over 11,000 feet
and temperatures vary from below freezing to over 130 degrees.
California's *Central Coast* extends for 350 miles, encompassing everything from the sea cliffs of Big Sur to the spires of Hearst Castle.

Northern California, which many contend is another nation entirely, centers around *San Francisco* and the *Bay Area*. The nearby *Wine
Country* vies with France's most famous vineyards in producing fine
wines. The *North Coast*, that indescribable realm of redwood forests
and Mendocino saltboxes, is simply one of the most beautiful places in
the world.

Comprised of ore-laden rivers and sun-bleached mining towns, the *Gold Country* is where the Old West staged its most colorful history. Rising above this foothill region is the *Sierra Nevada*, an awesome granite range formed by a single block of earth 430 miles long and 80 miles wide.

Together they constitute California, the nation-state where the 21st century begins. With a multicultural population approaching 30 million and a leadership role among Pacific Rim nations, it resides on that tumultuous edge where the present gives way to the potential. Of course new ideas have never seemed all that new out at the edge of the continent. California has always symbolized freedom, promise and the hope for a fresh beginning.

During the Gold Rush thousands of '49ers poured into the Sierra Nevada intent on fulfilling a personal destiny. Later, middle-class Midwestern "pioneers" journeyed to the promised land of Southern California, where oranges and lemons, if not money, hung on trees. Eventually miners and ranchers were supplanted by the high-tech inventors and aerospace engineers who fueled California's rise to world prominence.

Indeed, the promise of California, its ability to conjure dreams and then fulfill them, is the theme of this book. *California: The Ultimate Guidebook* deals with the best of the California experience. Each locale is described individually, with details on local history and culture, hotels, restaurants, sightseeing, shopping and nightlife.

The focus throughout is on quality and value, the exemplary and the unique. You will find a five-star dining room next to a mom 'n pop cafe or a world-class resort together with a funky mountain cabin simply because each represents the very best of its kind. Since California's most remarkable features are natural, I have included ample information on state and national parks. Special attractions like these often are given pronounced attention in the many highlighted articles added to the text.

The place that novelist Wallace Stegner called "America only more so" has always defined its own borders, placed its imprimatur on a personal culture. If not a state, California is a state of mind. This is where movie moguls and pot growers, surfers and ranchers, gays and grandmothers, environmentalists and entrepreneurs coexist in a frenzied state of creativity that sets the agenda for much of the United States.

It's a land where smog, traffic and impossible real estate prices have cast a shadow over paradise, where the threat of a major earthquake is a daily reality. America only more so. Ponder these threats to the environment and your thoughts turn inevitably to California. Its problems, its potential have become those of the United States; the California mythology has been appropriated by the rest of the country.

Envision an orange, plump, round and spilling over with the promise of good health, and your thoughts turn to California. Think of political conservatism, the presidencies of Richard Nixon and Ronald Reagan, or of radicalism, the Free Speech Movement and the antiwar demonstrations, and the nation's western fringe will flash to the fore. Or conjure a picture of Mexican culture, saturated with sentimental imagery, and your daydreams will lead inevitably to the far edge of the Sunbelt.

California is living out its own legend, embellishing on the myth as it moves forward. It's a place where fiction and fact are often inseparable and where you'll eventually find yourself swept along not by the reality but the romance of the region. It is the spirit of California that entices and enthralls us all, holding us prisoner in paradise. It is in this spirit that this book is written.

History

DISCOVERY AND EXPLORATION   Naturally, it began as fiction. California, according to an old Spanish novel, was a mythical island populated by Amazons and filled with gold, a place "very near to the terrestrial paradise." The man who set off to pursue this dream was Juan Rodríguez Cabrillo. The year was 1542, and Cabrillo, a Portuguese navigator in the employ of the Spanish crown, sailed north from Mexico, pressing forward the boundaries of empire. Although Cabrillo found no fabulous gilded cities, he had discovered a new land, Alta California, which he promptly claimed for the Spanish crown.

Of course, the area was already inhabited. Before the advent of Westerners, as many as 300,000 Indians lived in California in 50 separate groups. Along the southern coast were the Dieguño and the Chumash; the areas north of San Francisco were home to Miwoks, Pomos, Athabascans and Yuroks. They were hunter-gatherers, exploiting the boundless resources of the ocean, picking wild plants and stalking indigenous animals. In the state's southern desert, Agua Caliente Indians had found healing powers in the local mineral springs; in the northern interior, Maidu, Washoes and Paiutes stalked the heights of the Sierra Nevada.

Sixteenth-century world powers, however, were not famous for their understanding of native peoples. They proceeded to battle each other over this newly "discovered" territory. The British, determined to thwart Spanish conquests in the New World, harried the Spanish and encouraged privateers to plunder their galleons. Sir Francis Drake, the most famous of these adventurers, happened upon the coast in 1579, possibly landing at Point Reyes and, naturally, claiming the territory for England.

This outpost of empire, known to the British as Nova Albion, proved more significant to the Spanish. Since their ships, laden with luxurious goods from the Philippines, passed California en route to Mexico, they began seeking ports of call. In 1587 Pedro de Unamuno anchored at Morro Bay. Eight years later Sebastian Rodríguez Cermeño, a daring seaman, swept down the coast past Cape Mendocino, lost his ship to a ferocious storm in Drake's Bay, then pressed on with 70 men in an open launch.

The next *adelantado*, or merchant-adventurer, to take up the California challenge was Sebastian Vizcaíno, who charted and named much of the coastline and so grossly exaggerated the harbor of Monterey that his mapmaker was eventually hanged.

THE MISSIONS   In fact, all California seemed like one grand exaggeration. It was a region that promised rich gold discoveries but delivered none, was rumored to contain a Northwest Passage but did not, and that was desolate, dangerous and difficult to reach. The British virtually ignored it, and the Spanish took more than two centuries to begin colonizing the place.

Then in 1769, as Juan Gaspar de Portolá and Padre Junípero Serra ventured north to establish the first mission in San Diego, the California dream began. Portolá continued on to Los Angeles and, following a route that would become the fabled El Camino Real, reached San Francisco Bay, perhaps the first explorer to discover the site. Later, Captain Juan Bautista de Anza opened the territory farther north.

But it was Father Serra, the hard-driving Franciscan missionary, who wrote the early chapter in the history of the state. Between 1769 and 1823, he and his successor, Padre Fermín Francisco de Lasuen, established a chain of 21 missions from San Diego to Sonoma. Fortified with presidios, they became the backbone of Spain's colonial empire.

Serra's dream of a New World became a nightmare for Native Americans. Devastated by European diseases, they were forcibly converted to Catholicism and pressed into laboring on the missions. While their slaves were dying in terrible numbers, the Spanish, dangerously overextended, were plagued with other problems throughout the empire. In 1821 Mexico declared its independence and Alta California, still numbering only 3000 Westerners, was lost.

MANIFEST DESTINY   Abandoned and ignored for centuries, California was becoming an increasingly vital area. British ships had re-entered the Pacific in force, and by 1812 the Russians, lured by the region's rich fur trade, built Fort Ross on the Sonoma coast. More important, the United States, asserting itself as a commercial power, was despatching New England harpooners in pursuit of California gray whales. Whaling stations were built in San Diego, Palos Verdes and farther up the coast in Monterey and Bolinas.

Meanwhile the Mexican government secularized the missions in 1833, distributed the land to early settlers and ushered in the era of the *ranchos*. These generous land grants, often measuring 75 square miles and lining the narrow coastal strip once occupied by the missions, became huge cattle ranches. Merchants from New England traded pewter, copper and jewels for animal skins as a lucrative trade developed. Hides became known as "California banknotes," and Richard Henry Dana, sailing along the coast in 1834, immortalized the industry in *Two Years Before the Mast*.

Gazing round him at the rich ocean and undeveloped shore, Dana remarked that "In the hands of an enterprising people, what a country this might be!" The thought was occurring increasingly among Americans, who tried unsuccessfully to buy California from Mexico. Manifest Destiny was on the march, wagon trains were crossing the Sierra Nevada with pioneers and even the interior valleys were filling with Americans.

Not all of the state-to-be proved hospitable to incoming adventurers and settlers, however. When explorer Jedediah Smith crossed the Mojave Desert in 1826, he called it a "country of starvation," a barren land of no use. (Smith's words were far from prophetic—the desert turned out to be a treasure of minerals, including borax, gold, silver and zinc.) The beautiful mountains to the north could be equally harsh on the unprepared. In the terrible winter of 1846–47, a group of pioneers, the Donner Party, were stuck in 22-foot-high snow in the Sierra Nevada near present-day Truckee. During that winter, many of the group died or went insane, and others resorted to cannibalism to survive.

But the state filled with settlers nonetheless. In 1846, the "California Trail" over the Sierra was crossed by 500 pioneers. That was also the year Americans finally decided to grab the state from the Mexicans. With assistance from the United States government, a group of American settlers fomented the Bear Flag Revolt. Colonel John Charles Fremont seized San Francisco, while Commodore John D. Sloat took Monterey. Just two years before precious metal was finally found in Spain's fabled land of gold, the stars and stripes flew over California.

THE GOLD RUSH   On January 28, 1848 a hired hand named James Marshall discovered gold in the Sierra foothills, revealing how near the Spanish had come to their gilded vision. The California dream was realized. For anyone with courage and ambition, it represented a chance to blaze trails and become rich in the flash of a lucky find. Gold became the currency of Manifest Destiny, drawing 100,000 people across an implacable land and creating a civilization on its western fringes.

San Francisco became its de facto capital. The town's population exploded with prospectors, and a wild Barbary Coast ghetto grew along the bay. Over 500 businesses sold liquor; gambling, drugs and prostitution were rampant; gangs roamed the boom town and iron-fisted vigilance committees enforced law and order. Sailors were shanghaied, and failed prospectors committed suicide at the rate of 1000 per year. By 1850, about 500 ships, whose crews had deserted for the gold fields, lay abandoned in San Francisco Bay. Some were used as stores, hotels, even lunatic asylums; others became landfill. Speculators wildly divided the city into tiny plots.

The North Coast, filled with lumber needed in the gold mines, also flourished. Mills and settlements by the hundreds were established, and every cove became a shipping port. Mendocino, Fort Bragg, Eureka and other timber towns soon dominated the area.

The Gold Rush not only brought prospectors and loggers to Northern California: American writers found the area a literary gold mine. Mark Twain arrived during the 1860s, as did local colorist Bret Harte. Ambrose Bierce excoriated everyone and everything in his column for William Randolph Hearst's *Examiner*. Robert Louis Stevenson explored the Bay Area, and Jack London spent much of his life in Northern California, setting many of his adventure tales there.

THE INDUSTRIAL AGE   By the time the transcontinental railroad connected California with the rest of the country in 1869, Southern California trailed far behind its northern counterpart. Los Angeles, the largest town in the region, numbered 6000 people. During the 1870s the South began to rise. The Southern Pacific railroad linked San Pedro and Santa Monica with the interior valleys where citrus cultivation was flourishing. Southern California's rich agriculture and salubrious climate led to a "health rush." Magazines and newspapers romanticized the region's history and beauty, leading one writer to proclaim that "if the Pilgrim fathers had landed on the Pacific Coast instead of the Atlantic, little old New York wouldn't be on the map."

San Diego, Santa Monica and Santa Barbara became fashionable resort towns, and the port of San Pedro expanded exponentially, making Los Angeles a major shipping point.

When oil was discovered early in the 20th century, Southern California also became a prime drilling region. The Signal Hill field in Long Beach, tapped by Shell Oil in the 1920s, became the richest oil deposit in the world, and Los Angeles became the largest oil port.

Little wonder that by 1925, flush with petroleum just as the age of the automobile shifted into gear, Los Angeles also became the most motor-conscious city in the world. The Pacific Coast Highway was completed during the 1930s, "auto camps" and "tourist cabins" mushroomed and motorists began exploring California in unprecedented numbers.

MODERN TIMES   Meanwhile San Francisco, long since recovered from the horrific 1906 earthquake that shattered the San Andreas fault and rocked Northern California, was developing into a major financial center. The California coast became the state's most precious commodity, and political battles surrounded its use. During World War II the Navy developed port facilities in San Diego. Coastal defense bases grew at Camp Pendleton, Point Mugu, Vandenberg, Fort Ord and in Marin County.

This rush to protect the coast turned into a kind of social mania in 1942 when the United States government, in one of the most racist acts in its history, ordered the "relocation" of 93,000 Japanese-Americans. Stripped of their rights, they were removed from coastal regions where, it was charged, they could aid the Japanese empire. In fact the only attack on the coast occurred when a lone submarine lobbed a few shells at an oil field near Santa Barbara, doing minor damage to a wooden pier.

After the war, development became the order of the day. Homes and businesses sprouted up along the entire coastline. Los Angeles became the nation's second largest metropolis, and California became the most populous state.

Also during this period, California solidly established its reputation for quirkiness, creativity, and political commitment. The Beats invaded San Francisco's North Beach district during the 1950s, followed by the hippies of the Haight-Ashbury neighborhood during the next decade.

The state became a center for revolt in the 1960s. Berkeley launched the Free Speech Movement in 1964. Within a few years, confronted by a conservative governor in the person of Ronald Reagan, it also became a staging ground for the anti-Vietnam War movement. Meanwhile the Black Panther Party was established in Oakland and César Chavez's United Farm Workers struck the growers of the Central Valley.

The 1970s and 1980s witnessed a massive influx of Hispanics and Asians into the state, adding to California's multicultural diversity and promising to transform it into a pluralistic society by the early part of the 21st century.

Throughout these decades the environmental movement remained an integral factor in the equation of state politics. Unbridled development, combined with the 1969 Santa Barbara oil spill and plans for a controversial nuclear power plant in Diablo Canyon, led in 1972 to the creation of the California Coastal Commission. Established by the voters, this watchdog agency began a long crusade to slow development and preserve the natural beauty of the shoreline.

By the time the conservation movement began to flex its muscle, however, California had already demonstrated—through its tourism, ports, oil deposits, aerospace business and high-tech industries—that the gold sought centuries before by Spanish explorers did indeed lie in this land, a region whose natural treasures proved equal even to the excesses of the old myths.

Climate

California stretches over 850 miles from Mexico to Oregon and almost 200 miles from east to west. Within that broad expanse lies the Pacific coastline, a wide interior valley, the lofty Sierra Nevada, arid deserts and a weather pattern that varies as dramatically as the terrain.

Generally, there are four different climatic zones. The Pacific coast enjoys mild temperatures year-round, since the coastal fog creates a natural form of air conditioning and insulation. The mercury rarely drops below 40° or rises above 70°, with September and October being the hottest months and December and January the coolest.

Spring and particularly autumn are the ideal times to visit. During winter, the rainy season brings overcast days and frequent showers. Summer is the peak tourist season, when large crowds can present problems. Like spring, it's also a period of frequent fog; during the morning and evening, fog banks from offshore blanket the coast, burning off around midday.

Since most winter storms sweep in from the north, rainfall averages and the length of the rainy season diminish as you go south. Crescent City receives 70 inches of rain annually, San Francisco averages about 20 inches and San Diego receives only 10 inches. Inversely, temperatures vary from north to south: Eureka ranges from an average of 47° in January to 57° during August, while San Diego rises from 55° to 70° during the same months. The ocean air also creates significant moisture, keeping the average humidity around 65 percent and making some areas, particularly Northern California, seem colder than the thermometer would indicate.

The seasons vary much more in the interior valleys, creating a second climatic zone. In the Wine Country, Delta and Gold Country, summer temperatures often top 90°. There's less humidity, winters are cooler and the higher elevations receive occasional snowfall. Like the coast, this piedmont region experiences most of its rain during winter months.

The Sierra Nevada and Cascade Range, the third zone, experience California's most dramatic weather. During summer, the days are warm, the nights cool. Spring and autumn bring crisp temperatures and colorful foliage changes (which the coastline, with its unvarying seasons, rarely undergoes). Then in winter, the thermometer plummets and enough snow falls to make these mountain chains spectacular ski areas.

It's no secret that the fourth climatic zone, the desert, is hot in the summer, with temperatures often rising well above 100°. Spring is a particularly pretty time to visit, when the weather is cool and the wildflowers are in bloom. Autumn and winter are also quite pleasant.

Calendar

JANUARY

Los Angeles   The **Tournament of Roses Parade** kicks off the **Rose Bowl** game in Pasadena on New Year's Day.

The Desert   Snow willing, the **Annual Sled Dog Races**, a cross-country competition in the mountains outside Palm Springs, attracts teams from the United States and Canada. Celebrities and pros gather in Palm Springs for the annual **Bob Hope Desert Chrysler Golf Classic.**

Central Coast   The **AT&T at Pebble Beach Pro-Am Golf Championship** swings into action.

San Francisco   During late January or early February, the **Chinese New Year** features an extravagant parade with colorful dragons, dancers and fireworks.

FEBRUARY

Orange County   Arts and crafts displays highlight the **Laguna Beach Winter Festival.**

The Desert   The **Riverside County National Date Festival** at Indio Fairgrounds features camel races and a diaper derby.

North Coast   The **World Championship Crab Races and Crab Feed** takes place in Crescent City; if you forgot to bring your own, you can rent a racing crab.

MARCH

Orange County   The **Fiesta de las Golondrinas** commemorates the return of the swallows to Mission San Juan Capistrano. Meanwhile along the coast crowds gather for seasonal **grunion runs.**

Central Coast   Stars and stargazers gather for **Santa Barbara's International Film Festival**. Monterey presents the **California Wine Festival**, with winetasting, gourmet food stands and cooking demonstrations.

San Francisco   Bands, politicians and assorted revelers parade through the city on the Sunday closest to March 17, marking **St. Patrick's Day**. The **San Francisco International Film Festival** offers a wide selection of cinematic events.

North Coast   Mendocino and Fort Bragg celebrate a **Whale Festival** with whale-watching cruises, lighthouse tours, art shows and winetasting.

Sierra Nevada   The **Snowfest and Winter Carnival** in Truckee and along Lake Tahoe's North Shore is a spectacular celebration with ski races, dancing and concerts.

APRIL

Los Angeles   **Easter Sunrise Services** are marked at the famed Hollywood Bowl. In Little Tokyo **Buddha's Birthday** is celebrated; along nearby Olvera Street the Blessing of the Animals, a Mexican tradition, is re-enacted.

Los Angeles Coast   Race car buffs train their binoculars on the **Long Beach Grand Prix**.

The Desert   The **Peg Leg Liars Contest**, a tall-tale competition, takes place in Borrego Springs. The **Ramona Pageant** in Hemet depicts early California history with Indian rituals, music and dance.

San Francisco   Japantown's **Cherry Blossom Festival** is a time for parades, tea ceremonies, theatrical performances and martial arts displays. **Opening Day on the Bay**, occurring on the first day of Daylight Saving Time, launches the yachting season with a flotilla of sailboats and powerboats.

Wine Country   The entire town of Sebastopol turns out for an **Apple Blossom Festival**, staging exhibits and parades.

MAY

Los Angeles   Dancers, revelers and mariachi bands around Olvera Street and East Los Angeles celebrate **Cinco de Mayo**, Mexico's Independence Day. The **UCLA Mardi Gras** offers games, entertainment and food.

San Diego   In Old Town, mariachis and Spanish dancers highlight the **Fiesta de la Primavera**, a spring celebration, with an art show and historical exhibits. The **Wildflower Festival** blossoms in Julian.

Central Coast   San Luis Obispo observes **La Fiesta** with a parade, carnival, arts and crafts exhibits and chili cook-off.

San Francisco   Over 100,000 hearty souls (soles?) run the **Bay to Breakers** race, many covering the seven-and-a-half-mile course in outrageous costumes.

Bay Area   San Jose marks **Cinco de Mayo** with fiestas, parades and costumed dancers.

Wine Country   Winetasting becomes serious sport at the **Russian River Wine Festival** in Healdsburg.

Gold Country   Musicians from around the globe jam at Sacramento's **Dixieland Jazz Jubilee**, the largest such festival in the world. Up in Angels Camp, the **Jumping Frog Jubilee**, immortalized by Mark Twain, includes not only frog-jumping contests, but a carnival, air show, rodeo and county fair as well.

Sierra Nevada   A parade, steer-roping contest, barbecues and crafts displays mark **Mule Days** in Bishop.

JUNE

San Diego   The **National Shakespeare Festival** starts its summer run at the Old Globe Theater.

Central Coast   A parade and other festivities highlight Santa Barbara's **Summer Solstice Celebration**, while Lompoc sponsors an annual **Flower Festival**. The **Ojai Music Festival** includes classical and new music concerts.

San Francisco   **The Gay Freedom Day Parade**, with its colorful floats and imaginative costumes, marches to the Civic Center.

JULY

Los Angeles   **The Hollywood Bowl Summer Festival** explodes with a Fourth of July concert.

Los Angeles Coast   Surfers hang ten at the **International Surf Festival** in Hermosa, Manhattan and Redondo beaches.

Orange County   **The Festival of Arts & Pageant of the Masters**, one of Southern California's most notable events, occurs in Laguna Beach.

The Desert   Big Bear Lake remembers **Old Miners Day** with burro races, parades and dances.

Central Coast   Santa Barbara is busy with its **Greek Festival**.

San Francisco   Here and throughout California, firework displays commemorate the **Fourth of July**. The **San Francisco Marathon** begins in Golden Gate Park, then winds for 26 miles to the Civic Center.

Bay Area   San Jose sponsors the **Great American Tapestry Art Show**, one of the nation's largest sidewalk art displays.

AUGUST

Los Angeles   Little Tokyo's **Nisei Week** honors Japanese-American culture with parades, dances, music and martial arts demonstrations.

San Diego   Crowds sprout up at the Julian **Weed Show** for an artful display of native plants.

Central Coast   Santa Barbara rounds up everyone for the **Old Spanish Days Fiesta, Rodeo and Stock Show**. Santa Cruz hosts the **International Calamari Festival**, Salinas celebrates its **Steinbeck Festival** and Pebble Beach sponsors the **Concours d'Élégance**, a classic auto show.

San Francisco   The **County Fair Flower Show**, at the Hall of Flowers in Golden Gate Park, features thousands of blooms.

Gold Country   The capital city of Sacramento hosts the **California State Fair**.

SEPTEMBER

Los Angeles   **Los Angeles County Fair**, the nation's largest county fair, offers music, food, carnival rides, livestock competitions and just about everything else you can imagine.

San Diego   The **Cabrillo Festival** in Point Loma commemorates the discovery of the California coast.

Central Coast   Ojai applauds **Mexican Independence Day** with a grand fiesta. Solvang celebrates **Danish Days** with food, music and dance. It's also the magic month for the internationally renowned **Monterey Jazz Festival**.

San Francisco   This month for music is marked by the opening of the **San Francisco Opera** and the **San Francisco Symphony**, as well as the annual **Blues Festival** and **Opera in the Park**.

Gold Country   The **Gold Country Fair** in Auburn features a harvest festival, parade, livestock auction and country music.

OCTOBER

San Diego   The **Festival of the Californias** presents concerts and crafts exhibits. Julian celebrates its harvest with an **Apple Festival**.

The Desert   An arts and crafts fair, barbecue and parade mark the Borrego Springs' **Desert Festival**. Parades, parties and gunfights commemorate **Calico Days** in Calico Ghost Town.

Central Coast   Food, exhibits and dancing highlight the **Fiesta Italiana** in Santa Barbara. The **Art and Pumpkin Festival** in Half Moon Bay features food booths, crafts exhibits and pie-eating contests.

San Francisco   **Columbus Day** is marked by a parade, bocci ball tournament and the annual blessing of the fishing fleet.

NOVEMBER

Los Angeles   Santa arrives early at the **Hollywood Christmas Parade** and is joined by television and movie stars. In Pasadena, the rollicking **Doo Dah Parade** parodies the city's staid Rose Parade.

The Desert   The **Death Valley Annual Encampment** honors desert pioneers with gold panning contests, liars' competitions, sing-alongs and historical programs.

San Francisco   Several fairs and festivals kick off the holiday season. These include the **Folk Art International Exhibition and Sale** and the **KQED Wine and Food Festival**.

North Coast   Mendocino hosts a **Thanksgiving Festival** complete with musical performances and crafts exhibits.

DECEMBER

During December   Several coastal communities mark the season with **Christmas Boat Parades**. Hispanic communities in Los Angeles, San Luis Obispo, San Diego and throughout California celebrate the Mexican Yuletide with **Las Posadas**.

San Francisco   The **Dickens Christmas Fair** and **Sing-It-Yourself Messiah** commemorate the season. There are also **Christmas Parades** in towns throughout California.

Visitor Information

Several agencies provide free information to travelers. The **California Office of Tourism** (1121 L Street, Suite 103, Sacramento, CA 95814; 916-322-1396) will help guide you to areas throughout the state. The **San Diego Convention and Visitors Bureau** (1200 3rd Avenue, Suite 824, San Diego, CA 92101; 619-232-3101), **Los Angeles Visitors and Convention Bureau** (515 South Figueroa Street, Los Angeles, CA 90071; 213-624-7300) and **San Francisco Convention and Visitors Bureau** (201 3rd Street, Suite 900, San Francisco, CA 94103; 415-974-6900) are also excellent resources. For information on the North Coast counties between San Francisco and Oregon, contact the **Redwood Empire Association** (Spear Street Tower, 1 Market Plaza, Suite 1001, San Francisco, CA 94105; 415-543-8334). Also consult local chambers of commerce and information centers, which are mentioned in the various area chapters.

Packing

There are two important guidelines when deciding what to take on a trip. The first is as true for California as anywhere in the world—pack light. Dress styles here are relatively informal, and laundromats and dry cleaners are frequent. Remember, the airlines allow two suitcases and a carry-on bag.

The second rule is to prepare for cool weather, even if the closest you'll come to the mountains are the bluffs above the beach. While the coastal climate is temperate, temperatures sometimes descend below 50°. Even that might not seem chilly until the fog rolls in and the ocean breeze picks up. A warm sweater and jacket are absolute necessities. In addition to everyday garments, pack shorts year-round for Southern California and remember, everywhere in California, except the desert, requires a raincoat between November and March.

Lodging

Overnight accommodations in California are as varied as the state itself. They range from highrise hotels to bed-and-breakfast inns to luxury resorts. One guideline to follow with all is to reserve well in advance. California is a popular destination, particularly in summer, and facilities fill up quickly. In *The Ultimate Guidebook* I have chosen the best or most unusual accommodations the state has to offer. To help you decide on a place to stay, I've organized the accommodations according to price.

Budget hotels are generally less than $50 per night for two people; the rooms are clean and comfortable but lack luxury. The *moderate* hotels run $50 to $90 and provide larger rooms, plusher furniture and more attractive surroundings. At a *deluxe* hotel you can expect to spend between $90 and $130 double. You'll check into a spacious, well-appointed room with all modern facilities; downstairs, the lobby will be a fashionable affair, and you'll usually see a restaurant, lounge and a cluster of shops. If you want to spend your time in the very finest hotels, try an *ultra-deluxe* facility, which will include all the amenities and price above $130.

Restaurants

It seems as if California has more restaurants than people. To establish a pattern for this parade of dining places, I've organized them according to cost. Each restaurant entry describes the establishment as budget, moderate, deluxe or ultra-deluxe in price.

Dinner entrées at *budget* restaurants usually cost $8 or less. The ambience is informal cafe-style and the crowd is often a local one. *Moderate* price restaurants range between $8 and $16 for a dinner entrée and offer pleasant surroundings, a more varied menu and a slower pace. *Deluxe* establishments tab their entrées from $16 to $24 and feature sophisticated cuisines, plush decor and more personalized service. *Ultra-deluxe* dining rooms, where $25 will only get you started, are gourmet gathering places where cooking (hopefully) is a fine art form and service a way of life.

Camping

The state oversees 285 camping facilities. Amenities at each campground vary, but there is a standard day-use fee of $5 per vehicle, plus $14 per campsite (more along the coast in Southern California). For a complete listing of all state-run campgrounds, send $2 for the *Guide to California State Parks* to the **California Department of Parks and Recreation** (P.O. Box 942896, Sacramento, CA 94296; 916-445-6477). Reservations for campgrounds can be made by calling 800-444-7275.

For general information on federal campgrounds, contact the **National Park Service** (Western Regional Office, Fort Mason, Build-

ing 201, San Francisco, CA 94123; 415-556-0560). To reserve campsites call any local **Ticketron** outlet.

In addition to state and national campgrounds, California offers
numerous municipal, county and private facilities.

Camping and hiking in the wilderness and primitive areas of national forests require a permit. They are free and issued for a specific
period of time, which varies according to the wilderness area. Information is available through the **U.S. Forest Service** (630 Sansome
Street, San Francisco, CA 94111; 415-556-0122).

Family Travelers

Visiting California with kids can be a real adventure and, if properly
planned, a truly enjoyable one. To ensure that your trip will feature
the joy rather than the strain of parenthood, remember a few important guidelines.

Use a travel agent to help with arrangements; they can reserve
spacious bulkhead seats on airlines and determine which flights are

---

CALIFORNIA MARINE MAMMALS

*Few animals inspire the sense of myth and magic associated with the marine mam-
mals of California. Foremost are the ocean-going animals like whales, dolphins and
porpoises, members of the unique Cetacea order that left the land 30 million years
ago for the alien world of the sea. Six species of seals and sea lions also inhabit the
coast, together with sea otters, those playful creatures that delight visitors and be-
devil fishermen.*

*While dolphins and porpoises range far offshore, the region's most common
whale is a regular coastal visitor. Migrating 12,000 miles every year between the
Bering Sea and Baja Peninsula, the California gray whale cruises the shoreline
each winter (see the "Whale Watching" section in Chapter Eleven).*

*The seals and sea lions that seem to loll about the shoreline are characterized
by small ears and short flippers equipped for land travel. Fat and sassy, they have
layers of blubber to keep them warm and loud barks to inform tourists who is king
of the rookery.*

*Even people who never venture to the ocean have seen California sea lions,
those talented circus performers. Occupying the entire coast, particularly around
Santa Barbara, they stay offshore for months at a time, landing only during breeding season.*

*Harbor seals differ from these showmen in an inability to use their hind flip-
pers for land travel. Not to be upstaged, they sport beautiful dark coats with silver*

least crowded. Bring everything you need on board—diapers, food, toys and extra clothes for kids and parents alike. If the trip to California involves a long journey, plan to relax and do very little during the first few days.

Always allow extra time for getting places. Book reservations well in advance and make sure the hotel has the extra crib, cot or bed you require. It's smart to ask for a room at the end of the hall to cut down on noise. Also, many bed-and-breakfast inns do not allow children.

Even small towns have stores that carry diapers, food and other essentials; in larger towns and cities, **7-11** stores are open all night (check the Yellow Pages for addresses).

Hotels often provide access to babysitters. Also check the Yellow Pages for state-licensed and bonded babysitting agencies.

A first-aid kit is always a good idea. Ask your pediatrician for special medicines and dosages for colds and diarrhea.

Finding activities to interest children in California couldn't be easier. Especially helpful in deciding on the day's outing are *A Kid's Guide to Southern California* (Gulliver Books), *Places to Go with Children in Northern California* (Chronicle Press) and *Weekend Adventures for City Weary People* (Carousel Press). The calendar sections of the major newspapers often have special listings for children's events.

---

and white spots from which they borrow their second name, leopard seals. Like other pinnipeds, harbor seals feed on fish, shellfish and squid.

Largest of all the pinnipeds are the northern elephant seals, those ugly but lovable creatures that grow to 16 feet and weigh three tons. Characterized by a huge snout, they come ashore only to molt, mate and give birth. Breeding season, beginning in December, is the best time to watch these waddling characters. The males wage fierce battles to establish who will be cock of the walk. A few weeks after the males finish their tournament the females arrive.

Every California visitor's favorite animal is the sea otter. A kind of ocean-going teddy bear, it is actually a member of the weasel family, weighing up to 85 pounds, measuring four feet and characterized by thick fur, short paws used for feeding and grooming and webbed hind feet that serve as flippers.

Smart critters, sea otters are capable of using tools, rocks with which they pry tenacious shellfish from the ocean bottom and hammer open shells. They are also voracious eaters, feeding on abalone, sea urchins and crabs and consuming 25 percent of their body weight daily.

Inhabiting kelp beds where they are difficult to spot, these sleek animals can best be seen during feeding time in early morning and late afternoon. Watch for the sea gulls that circle kelp beds in search of sea otter scraps. Then look for a reddish-black animal, relaxing on his back, tapping a rhythm with a rock and abalone shell, his mouth curved in a cunning smile.

Disabled Travelers

California stands at the forefront of social reform for the disabled. During the past decade, the state has responded to the needs of the blind, wheelchair-bound and others with a series of progressive legislative measures.

The **Department of Motor Vehicles** provides special parking permits for the disabled. Many local bus lines and other public transit facilities are wheelchair accessible.

There are also agencies in California assisting disabled persons. For tips and information about the San Francisco Bay Area, contact the **Center for Independent Living** (2539 Telegraph Avenue, Berkeley; 415-841-4776), a self-help group that has led the way in reforming access laws in California. Other organizations on the coast include the **Westside Center for Independent Living** (12901 Venice Boulevard, Los Angeles; 213-390-3611) and the **Community Resource Center for the Disabled** (2864 University Avenue, San Diego; 619-293-3500).

The **Society for the Advancement of Travel for the Handicapped** (26 Court Street, Penthouse Suite, Brooklyn, NY 11242; 718-858-5483), **Travel Information Center** (Moss Rehabilitation Hospital, 12th Street and Tabor Road, Philadelphia, PA 19141; 215-329-5715), **Mobility International USA** (P.O. Box 3551, Eugene, OR 97403; 503-343-1284) and **Flying Wheels Travel** (143 West Bridge Street, P.O. Box 382, Owatonna, MN 55060; 800-533-0363) offer helpful information. **Travelin' Talk** (P.O. Box 3534, Clarksville, TN 37043; 615-552-6670), a networking organization, also provides information. Or consult the comprehensive guidebook *Access to the World—A Travel Guide for the Handicapped*, by Louise Weiss (Holt, Rinehart & Winston).

Be sure to check in advance when making room reservations. Many hotels and motels feature facilities for those in wheelchairs.

Senior Travelers

California is an ideal spot for older vacationers. The mild climate makes traveling in the off-season possible, helping to cut down on expenses. Many museums, theaters, restaurants, and hotels offer senior discounts. Be sure to ask your travel agent when booking reservations.

The **American Association of Retired Persons**, or AARP, (1909 K Street Northwest, Washington DC 22049; 202-872-4700) offers members travel discounts and provides escorted tours. For those 60 or over, **Elderhostel** (80 Boylston Street, Suite 400, Boston, MA 02116; 617-426-7788) offers educational programs in California.

Be extra careful about health matters. Bring any medications you use, along with the prescriptions. Consider carrying a medical record with you—including your current medical status and medical history, as well as your doctor's name, phone number and address. Also be sure to confirm that your insurance covers you away from home.

Foreign Travelers

PASSPORTS AND VISAS   Most foreign visitors are required to obtain a passport and tourist visa to enter the United States. Contact your nearest United States Embassy or Consulate well in advance to obtain a visa and to check on any other entry requirements.

CUSTOMS REQUIREMENTS   Foreign travelers are allowed to carry in the following: 200 cigarettes (or 100 cigars), $400 worth of duty-free gifts, including one liter of alcohol (you must be 21 years of age to bring in the alcohol). You may bring in any amount of currency, but must fill out a form if you bring in over $10,000 (U.S.). Carry any prescription drugs in clearly marked containers. (You may have to produce a written prescription or doctor's statement for the custom's officer.) Meat or meat products, seeds, plants, fruits and narcotics are not allowed to be brought into the United States. Contact the **United States Customs Service** (1301 Constitution Avenue Northwest, Washington, DC 20229; 202-566-8195) for further information.

DRIVING   If you plan to rent a car, an international driver's license should be obtained *before* arriving in California. Some rental companies require both a foreign license and an international driver's license. Many car rental agencies require a lessee to be 25 years of age; all require a major credit card.

CURRENCY   United States money is based on the dollar. Bills come in six denominations: $1, $5, $10, $20, $50 and $100. Every dollar is divided into 100 cents. Coins are the penny (1 cent), nickel (5 cents), dime (10 cents), quarter (25 cents). Half-dollars and dollar coins are rarely used. You may not use foreign currency to purchase goods and services in the United States. Consider buying traveler's checks in dollar amounts. You may also use credit cards affiliated with an American company such as Interbank, Barclay Card and American Express.

ELECTRICITY   Electric outlets use currents of 117 volts, 60 cycles. For appliances made for other electrical systems you need a transformer or other adapter.

TWO

Los Angeles

If California is the land of dreams, Los Angeles is the dream factory, that worldly workshop where the impossible takes form. Since its founding as a pueblo in 1781, the city has continually recast itself as a promised land, health haven, agricultural paradise, movie capital and world financial center.

Second largest city in the country, it rests in a bowl surrounded by five mountain ranges and an ocean and holds within its ambit sandy beaches, tawny hills and wind-ruffled deserts. At night from the air Los Angeles is a massive gridwork, an illuminated checkerboard extending from the ink-colored Pacific to the dark fringe of the mountains.

Today, with a population numbering three-and-a-half million (almost nine million inhabit Los Angeles County), the city is truly a multicultural metropolis. In Los Angeles minorities are becoming the majority. Hispanics, for instance, now number almost 40 percent of the population and include the largest concentration of Mexicans outside Mexico. The area is also home to large numbers of blacks, Koreans, Chinese and Japanese.

The place they inhabit will be the world's twelfth largest city by the turn of the century. Once a pastoral realm of caballeros and señoritas, greater metropolitan Los Angeles now leads the nation in aerospace, boasts the country's largest concentration of high-tech industries and possesses the fastest growing major port in the world. In raw economic terms it is the eleventh largest "nation" in the world, with a gross national product higher than Australia, Switzerland and India. A schizophrenic among cities, Los Angeles is comprised of many facets, many cities. In fact, Los Angeles County includes 82 towns as well as 1500 miles of freeways.

To simplify matters, this chapter divides the city into 11 geographic sections. Creating an arc around central *Downtown* are several neighborhoods: *Olvera Street, Chinatown* and *Little Tokyo, Exposition Park* and the *Elysian Park–Silver Lake Area.* The *Wilshire District* forms a narrow corridor along Wilshire Boulevard, running west from downtown toward the ocean. *Hollywood* and *Beverly Hills* require little introduction; both border the *Westside*, an upscale area comprised of Universal City, Westwood and Bel Air. To the northeast, bounded by mountains and desert, lies the San Gabriel Valley, whose cultural center is *Pasadena*. Northwest of Los Angeles is the *San Fernando Valley*.

Put all these sections together and you'll find in the end that L.A. is a city that you will come to love or scorn. Or perhaps to love *and* scorn. It is either Tinseltown or the Big Orange, Smogville or the City of Angels. To some it is the Rome of the West, a megalopolis whose economic might renders it an imperial power. To others Los Angeles is the American Athens, an international center for cinema, music and art.

Culturally speaking, the sun rises in the west. L.A., quirky but creative, sets the trends for the entire nation. It has been admired and self-admiring for so long that the city has swallowed its own story, become a reflection of its mythology. Beautifully crazed, pulsing with electric energy, Los Angeles is living its own dream.

Downtown

Contrary to the opinion of Los Angeles bashers, the city does indeed possess a center. Ever since the town was settled in 1781, the focus of the community has been near the Los Angeles River.

While there's barely enough water in the river these days to cause a ripple, the downtown district is inundated with people. About 20,000 people live in this vital neighborhood, and more than 200,000 commuters arrive daily. Adding to the smog and congestion, they also make downtown the center for politics, finance and culture.

Art and politics have always been odd bedfellows, but they make a cozy couple around the Los Angeles Civic Center in the heart of downtown Los Angeles. Here an impressive group of government buildings combines with an array of museums to create a complex well worth touring.

The centerpiece of the ensemble is **City Hall** (200 North Spring Street; 213-485-4423), a vintage 1928 building. Rendered famous by the old "Dragnet" television show, this pyramid-topped edifice has a tile-and-marble rotunda on the third floor that's a study in governmental architecture. But the most impressive feature is the **observation deck** on the 27th floor, from which you can enjoy a 360° view of Los Angeles' smog banks.

Those who report on City Hall reside across the street at the **Los Angeles Times Building** (202 West 1st Street; 213-237-5000). One

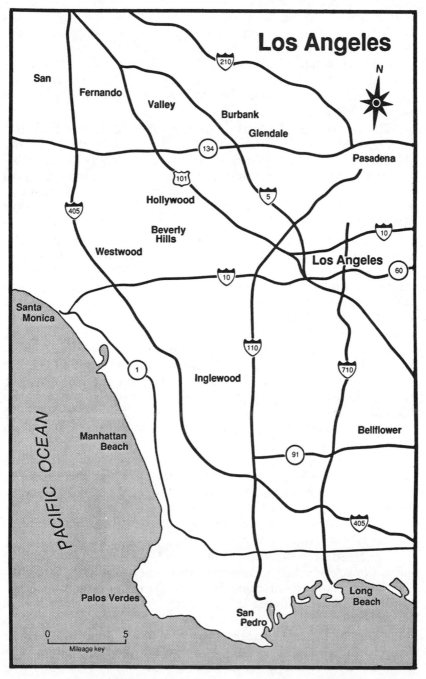

of the nation's largest and finest newspapers, the Times sits in a classic 1934 moderne-style building that is open to guided tours.

Cultural counterpoint to these centers of power is the nearby **Music Center** (Grand Avenue between 1st and Temple streets; 213-972-7211). Gathered into one stunningly designed complex are the Dorothy Chandler Pavilion, a marble-and-black-glass music hall that hosts the opera and symphony; the Mark Taper Forum, a world-renowned theater that presents contemporary and experimental drama; and the Ahmanson Theatre, where traditional plays are staged. Guided tours are available.

The **Museum of Contemporary Art** (250 South Grand Avenue, 213-621-2766; admission), affectionately dubbed "the MOCA," is an ultramodern showplace designed by Japanese architect Arata Isozaki. It's an exotic mix of red sandstone and pyramidal skylights with a sunken courtyard. The galleries consist of expansive open spaces displaying a variety of traveling exhibits and the works of Mark Rothko, Louise Nevelson and others.

It's the noisiest museum in the world. The **Los Angeles Children's Museum** (310 North Main Street; 213-687-8800; admission), with countless hands-on and hands-all-over-everything exhibits, is probably the happiest as well. There's an ambulance and police motorcycle for kids to ride, an X-ray table and dentist chair for practicing future professions, plus video cameras for children to tape their own antics.

While social classes may be miles apart culturally, their neighborhoods often stand shoulder to shoulder. Midway between the Los Angeles centers of political and financial power sits **Broadway**, a vibrant Hispanic shopping district. A cross between New York's 42nd Street and the boulevards of Mexico City, this multiblock strip is crowded with cut-rate clothing stores, swap meets and pawn shops.

Start at the South 300 block and wander uptown. The first place you'll encounter is **Grand Central Public Market** (317 South Broadway), a fresh food bazaar in the tradition of Mexico's *mercados*. Produce stands, vendors, butchers and fresh fish shops line the aisles. More than 30,000 people pass through every day, making it one of the city's most vital scenes.

The **Bradbury Building** (304 South Broadway; 213-624-2378) across the street, while unassuming from the outside, is a turn-of-the-century masterpiece inside. It boasts an extraordinary courtyard, winding stairs surrounding an open cage elevator, and flourishes of marble and brick.

Today the focus of finance in Los Angeles is found in a highrise district between Grand Avenue and Flower, 3rd and 5th streets. Here the **Security Pacific Headquarters** (333 South Hope Street) rises

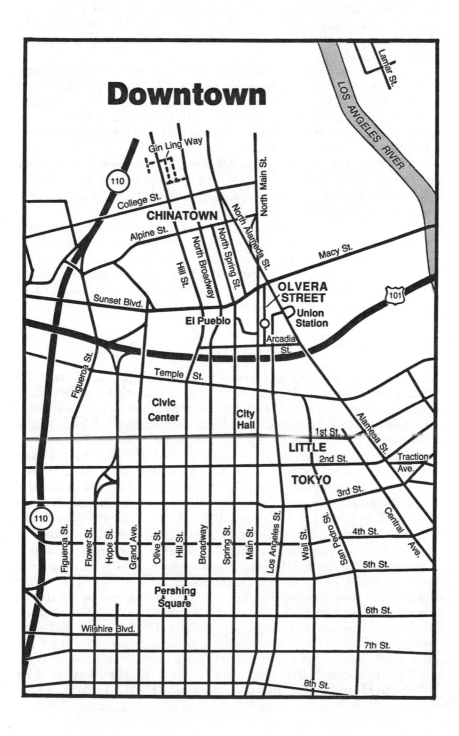

Downtown

Gin Ling Way

110

College St.

CHINATOWN

Alpine St.

North Main St.

North Alameda St.

North Spring St.

North Broadway

Hill St.

Macy St.

Sunset Blvd.

OLVERA
STREET

101

El Pueblo

Union
Station

Arcadia
St.

Figueroa St.

Temple St.

Civic
Center

City
Hall

1st St.

Alameda St.

LITTLE

2nd St.

Traction
Ave.

TOKYO

3rd St.

110

Figueroa St.

Flower St.

Hope St.

Grand Ave.

Olive St.

Hill St.

Broadway

Spring St.

Main St.

Los Angeles St.

Wall St.

San Pedro St.

Central Ave.

4th St.

5th St.

Pershing
Square

6th St.

Wilshire Blvd.

7th St.

8th St.

LOS ANGELES RIVER

Lamar St.

55 stories. Across the street at the **Wells Fargo History Museum** (333 South Grand Avenue; 213-253-7166) you can view displays re-creating more than a century of Western history. The **World Trade Center** (333 South Flower Street), another architectural extravaganza, looms nearby.

Not far from these towering symbols of tomorrow stands an emblem of the past. The **Los Angeles Central Library** (5th and Hope streets; 213-612-3200), built in the 1920s, incorporates Egyptian, Roman and Byzantine elements into a Beaux-Arts design. Unfortunately the interior was gutted by fire in 1986, and the library is not scheduled to reopen until 1993.

The **Greater Los Angeles Visitors & Convention Bureau** (695 South Figueroa Street; 213-689-8822) is the city's main information center. Here you'll find maps, leaflets and a friendly staff to help point the way through this urban maze.

For a view of blue-collar Los Angeles, depart central downtown for the wholesale **Flower Market** (Wall Street between 7th and 8th streets), where for an entire block the air is redolent with fragrant merchandise. Over at the **Produce Markets** (Central Avenue and 7th Street; or San Pedro and 11th streets), the bounty from California's interior valleys goes on the block early every morning.

DOWNTOWN LODGING

In the moderate price range it's hard to top the **Figueroa Hotel** (939 South Figueroa Street; 213-627-8971). A 1927 Spanish-style building, it offers a beautiful lobby with tile floor and hand-painted ceiling. The palm-fringed courtyard contains a swimming pool, jacuzzi and lounge. The rooms are very large and decorated with wallhangings.

Catering largely to an international clientele, the **New Otani Hotel & Garden** (120 South Los Angeles Street; 213-629-1200) is a 448-room extravaganza with restaurants, shops, lounges, spa and a tranquil half-acre Japanese "garden in the sky." Conveniently located in Little Tokyo, the hotel offers small guest rooms, many decorated in traditional Japanese style with *shoji* screens. Deluxe to ultra-deluxe.

What can you say about a place that became a landmark as soon as it was built? To call the **Westin Bonaventure** (404 South Figueroa Street; 213-624-1000) ultramodern would belittle the structure. "Post Future" is a more appropriate tag. Its dark glass silos rise 35 stories from the street like a way station on the road to the 21st century. Within are five levels of shops, 1474 rooms, 17 restaurants and a revolving cocktail lounge. Guest rooms are small and pie-shaped but offer good views of the surrounding financial district. Ultra-deluxe.

The past rests safely ensconced a few blocks away at **The Biltmore Hotel** (506 South Grand Avenue; 213-612-1575). Here the glamor and elegance of the Roaring '20s endure in a grand lobby replete with stately pilasters and floor-to-ceiling mirrors. The 700-room Biltmore conveys an Old World ambience with hand-oiled wood panels, frescoes and ornamental molding. The moderate-sized bedrooms feature contemporary artwork and traditional French furniture. Ultra-deluxe.

A welcome addition to downtown Los Angeles is the European-style **Checkers Hotel** (535 South Grand Avenue; 213-624-0000). This 187-room luxury hostelry originally opened in 1927 as the Mayflower Hotel, one of the most strikingly beautiful buildings of its time. A massive renovation has restored it beyond even its original elegance. Posh rooms come complete with original artwork, marble bathrooms and three telephones. Ultra-deluxe.

DOWNTOWN RESTAURANTS

To dine in the true style of Mexico the place to go is not a restaurant at all. **Grand Central Public Market** (317 Broadway), a block-long produce market, features stands selling Mexican finger foods. Try the *chile rojo* (pork in red chile sauce) and *lengua* (tongue). If you're really daring there's *rellena* (blood sausage) and *tripas* (intestines). *Mucho gusto!* Budget.

Casey's Bar and Grill (613 South Grand Avenue; 213-629-2353) is one of those marvelous old dining lounges with dark paneling, trophy cases and graying photographs. Lunch consists of hamburgers and entrées such as prawns over black pasta. For dinner there are pasta dishes, sea bass and steak Diane. Moderate.

The Original Sonora Cafe (445 South Figueroa Street; 213-624-1800) is a chic Southwestern restaurant with blond wood furnishings and *vega* ceilings. The fare includes fajitas, duck tamales and steak dishes. Moderate to deluxe.

Incomparable is the perfect adjective to describe **Rex II Ristorante** (617 South Olive Street; 213-627-2300). Set in a landmark art deco building and modeled after a 1930s Italian luxury liner, it represents one of Los Angeles' loveliest restaurants. This Italian dining room is enhanced by a sweeping staircase that curves up to a black marble dancefloor. The cuisine is exceptional, the wine list one of the most formidable in the country. The ultimate dining experience is the fixed-price menu, a stunning six-course meal. Ultra-deluxe.

It is, quite simply, Everyperson's Eating Place. **The Original Pantry** (877 South Figueroa Street; 213-972-9279), short on looks but long on soul, has been serving meals 24 hours a day since 1924 without missing a beat. It consists simply of a counter with metal stools and a formica dining area, with the cuisine a culinary answer to heavy metal—ham hocks, navy bean soup and standing rib roast. Budget-priced and bound to stay that way.

Another of downtown Los Angeles' funky but famous restaurants is **Gorky's** (536 East 8th Street; 213-627-4060), a Russian-American café open 24 hours on the weekend. This plastic-chairs-and-exposed-pipes eatery mixes all-American with all-Soviet cuisine. That means bacon and eggs versus *pelmeni* (meat-filled pasta) and roast beef sandwiches versus *shchi* (beet and cabbage soup). Budget to moderate.

DOWNTOWN SHOPPING

Shopping in downtown Los Angeles has blazed back to life with the development of malls like the **Atlantic Richfield Shopping Center** (ARCO Plaza, 5th and Flower streets), where 60 shops and restaurants create one of the largest subterranean shopping centers in the country.

In a space age linkup, this mall connects via glass footbridge with the **Westin Bonaventure Shopping Gallery** (404 South Figueroa Street), where three levels of stores surround the Bonaventure's vaulting atrium lobby. Among these elegant shops are **August Moon** (213-626-4395), with a beautiful selection of Oriental arts and jewelry, and **Arias International Boutique** (213-687-4406), which boasts an intriguing array of men's and women's accessories.

Broadway Plaza (700 South Flower Street), at the heart of the downtown shopping hub, features **The Broadway** (213-628-9311) department store as well as a galleria of specialty shops.

A charming European-style center, **Seventh Market Place** (Citicorp Plaza, 735 South Figueroa Street; 213-955-7150) contains dozens of shops and restaurants in an open-air setting. The emphasis is on fashion.

At the **Los Angeles Flower Mart** (754 Wall Street) you can usually buy directly from the wholesalers. Get there early, however; the action is over by 9 a.m.

DOWNTOWN NIGHTLIFE

Traditionally, downtown bars catered to an after-work crowd, but the trend these days is toward later nights and more live entertainment.

Mariachi music and margaritas draw folks to **La Golondrina** (213-628-4349) on Olvera Street in a historic adobe building.

The Genji Bar (120 South Los Angeles Street; 213-629-1200) at the New Otani Hotel is a restful piano bar in the heart of Little Tokyo.

Housed in the Japanese American Cultural and Community Center in Little Tokyo, the **Japan America Theatre** (244 South San Pedro Street; 213-680-3700), presents traditional and contemporary Japanese productions.

Located next to the Dorothy Chandler Pavilion, **Otto Roths-child's Bar & Grill** (135 North Grand Avenue; 213-972-7322) is *the* place to meet before and after the theater. Sixty years of theatrical photos cover the walls.

A lovely place for evening cocktails, **Bonavista** (404 South Figueroa Street; 213-624-1000) offers a revolving 360° panorama of the city from the 34th floor of the Westin Bonaventure Hotel. One floor

---

L.A.'S BEST BUYS

In trendsetting Los Angeles, you can blow several inheritances shopping in the high-fashion boutiques and ultrachic megamalls. But you can also find bargains if you know where to look. Try starting with these value-filled shops scattered around the downtown area.

The city's old jewelry district (Hill Street between 5th and 7th streets) still houses a variety of shops selling goods at competitive prices. Historic St. Vincent Jewelry Center (650 South Hill Street; 213-629-2124) is reputed to be the world's largest jewelry outlet, covering an entire square block. Here and at the International Jewelry Center (550 South Hill Street), another mammoth complex, you'll find items in every price range.

As in many urban areas, warehouses and industrial districts around Los Angeles have become home to young artists seeking low rents. Among the small galleries that have resulted are the Woman's Building (1727 North Spring Street; 213-221-6161), which exhibits the work of women only, and Cirrus Gallery (542 South Alameda Street; 213-680-3473), where contemporary works by Los Angeles artists are displayed. Los Angeles Artcore (652 South Mateo Street; 213-617-3274) is a nonprofit art organization where you'll find outstanding modern works. Another nonprofit gallery, the Los Angeles Contemporary Exhibitions (LACE) (1804 Industrial Street; 213-624-5650), also provides space for performance art, video productions and film forums.

You can literally shop until you drop in Los Angeles' bustling Garment District. Known as a major manufacturing center since the 1930s, the district today lies concentrated along Los Angeles Street between 4th and 10th streets. The Cooper Building (860 South Los Angeles Street) offers eight floors of name brand clothes and accessories, with prices as much as 70 percent below retail. And there's the bargain hunter's delight, The Alley (between Santee Street and Maple Avenue). Boxes, bins and mannequins line the two-block-long alleyway where hawkers and vendors vie for your attention.

Also consider Bronsons LA Action (1101-A South Maple Avenue; 213-749-3320), a manufacturer's outlet with prices 50 percent below retail, and Bell of California (1018 South Santee Street; 213-748-5716), which displays a beautiful selection of women's silks and cottons.

up, the lounge at the **Top of Five** restaurant also sports a tremendous view and live piano entertainment.

The **Grand Avenue Bar** (506 South Grand Avenue; 213-624-1532) offers an all-star jazz lineup weeknights until 9 p.m. in the stately Biltmore Hotel. For piano music, check the hotel's **Rendez-vous Court**.

Located below street level, **Casey's Bar and Grill** (613 South Grand Avenue; 213-629-2353) may well be the most popular downtown bar. A comfortable pub filled with sports memorabilia, it draws business people on weekdays until 10 p.m.

At **Vertigo** (333 South Boylston Street; 213-747-4849), another upscale restaurant and nightclub, the doorman decides who is sufficiently chic to enter. A giant dancefloor pulsates with top-of-the-chart tapes and live bands nightly. Cover; reservations a must for dinner.

The **Los Angeles Theater Center** (514 South Spring Street; 213-627-5599), a complex of four small theaters, offers avant-garde dramatic productions, as well as dance, music and poetry programs.

The most prestigious performing arts complex on the West Coast, the **Music Center** (135 North Grand Avenue; 213-972-7211) consists of three major theaters:

The elegant **Dorothy Chandler Pavilion**, home to the Los Angeles Philharmonic Orchestra, is a spectacular 3000-seat facility. The concert hall also hosts performances by the Joffrey Ballet, Los Angeles Master Chorale and Los Angeles Civic Light Opera.

The 2000-seat **Ahmanson Theatre** presents classic dramas and comedies as well as West Coast premieres.

The more intimate, 700-seat **Mark Taper Forum** is ideal for contemporary dramatic and musical performances. Tickets for Dorothy Chandler Pavilion performances are available through Ticketmaster (213-486-3232). Ticketron (213-410-1062) handles reservations at the Ahmanson Theatre and the Mark Taper Forum.

An upbeat dinner theater located several blocks from the Music Center, **Itchy Foot Ristorante** (801 West Temple Street; 213-680-0007) boasts its own Itchy Foot Cabaret performing lively theater-in-the-round. Cover.

Olvera Street

The historic heart of the city is El Pueblo de Los Angeles, a 44-acre outdoor museum centered around Olvera Street. In 1781 a few dozen Spanish settlers established hardscrabble farms and built adobes, breaking ground for what eventually became one of the world's largest metropolitan areas.

Today, buildings dating to the 18th century have been preserved, along with the noisy, colorful atmosphere of a Mexican marketplace. Olvera Street's brick-paved walkways are lined with shops selling Mexican artwork and handicrafts. Food vendors serve homemade *maza* (cornmeal) tortillas and tempting *nopales* (fresh diced cactus candies). The area provides a window on early Los Angeles.

The **visitor center** (622 North Main Street; 213-628-1274), dispensing maps, brochures and walking tours, sits in one of the pueblo's vintage buildings, an 1887 brick-faced Victorian called the Sepulveda Block.

Heart of hearts is the **Plaza** (North Main Street and Paseo de la Plaza), a tree-shaded courtyard adorned with statues and highlighted by a wrought-iron bandstand that's a frequent site for fiestas and open-air concerts.

Anchoring one corner of the plaza is **Firehouse No. 1** (134 Paseo de la Plaza), Los Angeles' original fire station, built in 1884. Today it's a miniature museum filled with horse-drawn fire wagons and other memorabilia.

The plaza's most prestigious building, **Pico House** (Paseo de la Plaza and North Main Street) was built in 1870 by Pio Pico, the last Mexican governor of California. Italianate in style, it represented the grandest hotel of its era.

Old Plaza Church (535 North Main Street), first established as a chapel in 1784, also faces the square. The city's oldest Catholic church, it is unassuming from the outside but displays an interior that is a study in wrought iron and gold leaf, with ceiling murals and religious canvases adorning the place.

Among the antique buildings bordering narrow Olvera Street is the **Avila Adobe**, a classic mud-brick house constructed around 1818. The oldest building in Los Angeles, it has undergone numerous incarnations, serving as a private residence, boarding house and restaurant and surviving numerous earthquakes. Today it's a museum, fully restored and filled with period pieces.

Nearby **Union Station** (800 North Alameda Street), one of the country's great train depots and an embodiment of the romance of travel, has been a Los Angeles landmark since 1939. With a Spanish-Mexican exterior, the station is a cavernous structure boasting marble floors, a beam ceiling 52 feet high and walls of inlaid tile.

The **San Antonio Winery** (737 Lamar Street; 213-223-1401) represents the last of a disappearing breed. Years ago vineyards dotted the San Gabriel foothills. Somehow this family-operated facility remained in spite of Los Angeles' urbanization, situated surprisingly close to the center of the city. Today second- and third-generation members of the Riboli clan lead tasting tours through the vintage 1917 building.

OLVERA STREET RESTAURANTS

Olvera Street is a prime place for Mexican food. Tiny **taco stands** line this brick-paved alley, dispensing fresh Mexican dishes at budget prices. There are also bakeries and candy stands, where old Mexican ladies sell *churros* (Mexican donuts) and candied squash.

La Golondrina (West 17 Olvera Street; 213-628-4349) provides something more formal. Set in an 1850-era home built of fired brick, it features an open-air patio and a dining room with stone fireplace and *vega* ceiling. The bill of fare includes a standard selection of tacos and enchiladas as well as specialties such as sole sautéed in white wine. Moderate.

Across from Union Station stands one of the city's most famous cafeterias. **Philippe's Original Sandwich Shop** (1001 North Alameda Street; 213-628-3781) has been around since 1908, serving pork, beef and lamb sandwiches in a French-dip style. With sawdust on the floors and memories tacked to the walls, this old-style eatery still serves ten-cent cups of coffee. Budget.

EAST LOS ANGELES

The spirit of Mexico is alive and shimmering in the barrio of East L.A. With a population that is 90 percent Latino, this sprawling neighborhood contains the country's largest concentration of Hispanics.

Brooklyn Avenue, a major thoroughfare in the Boyle Heights district, represents "Little Mexico," a region rich in Mexican restaurants and family shops. If Brooklyn Avenue is the heart of the barrio, Whittier Boulevard is the spine, a neon ganglion charged with electric color. Lined with discount stores, tacquerías and auto body shops, Whittier is the Sunset Strip of East L.A.

The life of the barrio is also evident at El Mercado (3425 East 1st Street), an indoor market with shops selling everything from cowboy boots to Spanish-language videos. The signs are bilingual and the clientele represents a marvelous multicultural mix.

Of course the full flavor of the Hispanic community is found among the murals that decorate the streets of East Los Angeles. Exotic in design, vibrant with color, they are a vital representation of the inner life of the barrio.

The greatest of all East L.A.'s Mexican restaurants is El Tepeyac Cafe (812 North Evergreen Avenue; 213-268-1960), a hole-in-the-wall with so much soul people migrate across the city to feast on its legendary burritos. The place serves everything from machaca to huevos con chorizo. The food is delicious, the portions overwhelming, the price budget. What more can I say?

Chinatown and Little Tokyo

Back in 1870, when the Chinese population numbered perhaps 200, Asians were sequestered in a rundown neighborhood southeast of the original plaza. As that area was torn down during the 1930s to build Union Station, they moved in increasing numbers to modern-day Chinatown, the cultural and commercial center for Chinese throughout the city.

For an authentic view, stroll the **600 block of North Spring Street** past the herb shops and fresh fish stores. Here local residents buy goat meat and fresh produce and choose from among the racks of roast ducks that hang forlornly in store windows.

Don't miss **Kong Chow Temple** (931 North Broadway; 213-626-1955), a tiny chapel with gilded altars tucked away on the second floor of an assuming building. Crowded with elderly Chinese, the place is heavy with incense and handwoven tapestries.

The commercial heart of the district lies along Broadway and Hill Street. Connecting these two thoroughfares is **New Chinatown** (Gin Ling Way), a two-block-long pedestrian mall. Traditional gates with swirling outlines mark the entranceways to this enclave. Figures of animals and ceremonial fish adorn the buildings, and dragons breathe fire from the rooftops.

The Japanese response to Chinatown is Little Tokyo, a discrete neighborhood bounded by Los Angeles Street, Central Avenue, 1st Street and 3rd Street. At the heart of the district is the **Japanese American Cultural and Community Center** (244 South San Pedro Street; 213-628-2725), a stoic plate-glass-and-poured-concrete structure designed by Buckminster Fuller and Isamu Noguchi.

Follow the brick paving stones from the cultural center through **Japanese Village Plaza**, a two-block shopping mall adorned with fountains and sculptures. At the end of the plaza stands Little Tokyo's tile-roofed **fire tower**, an ornamental but practical structure that has become a local landmark.

Another cultural gathering place is the lovely **Higashi Hongwanji Buddhist Temple** (505 East 3rd Street; 213-626-4200). With its tile roof and golden dragons, the temple represents pagoda architecture adapted to a Western cityscape.

The **Temporary Contemporary** (152 North Central Avenue; 213-621-2766; admission), a branch of the Museum of Contemporary Art, sits on the outskirts of Little Tokyo. At the cutting edge of the modern art scene, it contains changing exhibits from all over the world. The focus is on the post-World War II era with artwork ranging from abstract paintings to wildly imaginative sculptures.

For a taste of the truly avant-garde, be sure to visit the **Museum of Neon Art** (704 Traction Avenue; 213-617-1580; admission). One of the city's most unusual showcases, it specializes in neon, electric and kinetic art. A wonderfully bizarre place.

CHINATOWN AND LITTLE TOKYO RESTAURANTS

The carved ceilings, ornate posts and elaborate decorations at **Hong Kong** (425 Gin Ling Way; 213-628-6217) certainly convey a sense of Chinatown. The menu is as multifaceted as the decor: it contains over 100 Szechuan and Cantonese entrées. Budget to moderate.

One of Chinatown's finest dim sum dining rooms, **Ocean Seafood Restaurant** (747 North Broadway; 213-687-3088) is a voluminous, sumptuous second-floor establishment. The dim sum service is only during lunch. At dinner there's a comprehensive Cantonese menu. Moderate.

An anomaly in an Asian neighborhood, **Little Joe's** (900 North Broadway; 213-489-4900) is a throwback to the days when Italians in the area outnumbered Chinese. This sprawling restaurant, with six dining rooms, is covered with murals of Italia. The menu mixes pasta dishes with specialties such as veal piccata and butterflied halibut. Moderate.

The most elaborate of Little Tokyo's addresses is **Horikawa** (111 South San Pedro Street; 213-680-9355). This beautifully appointed establishment serves meals in four separate locations—a sushi bar, a dining room, a *teppan* room where meals are prepared at your table and a luxurious teahouse where guests are served a 14-course meal in private rooms. The dining and *teppan* rooms are deluxe; the teahouse rooms are ultra-deluxe and require a seven-day advance reservation.

Tokyo Kaikan (225 South San Pedro Street; 213-489-1333) is a warren of woodframe rooms, each decorated with lanterns and masks. Dinner includes several dishes cooked at your table as well as specialties such as *wafu* steak and king salmon. One of the district's most popular restaurants. Moderate to deluxe.

CHINATOWN AND LITTLE TOKYO SHOPPING

Ornate Chinese-style roofs in reds and greens adorn **Chinatown Plaza** (900 block of North Broadway), where gift shops offer everything from imported trinkets to very fine, very ancient antiques and artworks.

A treasure trove of antique stores dot nearby Chung King Road. **Fong's** (943 Chung King Road; 213-626-5904) and **The Jade Tree** (957 Chung King Road; 213-624-3521) are two of the finest.

Mandarin Plaza (970 North Broadway) is a modern pedestrian mall housing stores like **Kay's Asiatic Imports** (213-625-7597), which carries the largest selection of kimonos and silks in Chinatown, and **Asian Craft Imports** (213-626-5386), which sells import gift items.

In the heart of Little Tokyo, **Japanese Village Plaza** (327 East 2nd Street) is a commercial expression of the sights, sounds and flavors of Japan. Here **Pony Toy Go Round** (213-687-0853) features battery-operated creatures from Japanese monster movies.

Weller Court (South Onizuka and 3rd streets), a modern tri-level shopping arcade, boasts among its tenants **Matsuzakaya America, Inc.** (213-626-2112), a branch of Japan's oldest and largest department store. Conveniently, the mall is connected via walking bridges to the **New Otani Hotel Shopping Arcade** (110 South Los Angeles Street), where specialty shops showcase everything from fine jewelry to tourist trinkets. The center features **Kinokuniya Book Stores of America** (213-687-4447), with a complete selection of books on Japan.

Exposition Park Area

Home to impressive architecture, major museums, an athletic palace and one of the city's fine universities, the Exposition Park area lies just southwest of downtown Los Angeles.

Minutes from the ultramodern city center sits the spacious, Romanesque campus of the **University of Southern California** (bounded by Jefferson Boulevard, Vermont Avenue, Exposition Boulevard and Figueroa Street; 213-740-2311). Lined with sycamore and maple trees, this red-brick-and-ivy enclave features a parklike setting filled with historic buildings.

WATTS TOWERS

*Los Angeles' most spectacular folk-art creations, the result of an individual artist with an uncommon vision, are the **Watts Towers** (1765 East 107th Street, in Simon Rodia State Historic Park). Fashioned by Simon Rodia over a three-decade period, these delicate, curving towers, inlaid with objets trouvés, rise over 100 feet above Los Angeles' black ghetto. Encrusted with tile shards, stones and more than 70,000 seashells, they form a work of unsettling beauty, a kind of icon to a personal god. After half a lifetime of work, Rodia finished the sculpture in 1954, gave the property to a neighbor and left Los Angeles, refusing to ever talk about the towers again.*

The movie location for everything from *The Hunchback of Notre Dame* to *The Graduate*, it's an ideal spot for a stroll. Among USC's many features are the **Fisher Gallery** (213-740-8229), with an excellent collection of European and New World art, and the **Hancock Memorial Museum** (213-740-0433), containing the furnishings of an 1890 mansion modeled after the Villa de Medici.

The **Skirball Museum** (3077 University Avenue; 213-749-3424), part of Hebrew Union College, sits across the street from USC. Devoted entirely to Judaica, the displays include exhibits on the Torah and the Jewish holy days as well as archaeological displays.

Exposition Park (Figueroa Street at Exposition Boulevard) is long on exposition and short on park. There *is* an enchanting **sunken garden** with a fountain, gazebos and almost 20,000 rose bushes. Otherwise the park blooms with museums and sports arenas.

The **California Museum of Science and Industry** (213-744-7400) is one of those hands-on, great-for-kids-of-all-ages complexes. Over in the **Aerospace Complex** there are planes, jets and space capsules suspended from the ceiling in mock flight.

The **Los Angeles County Museum of Natural History** (213-744-3466; admission), reputedly the largest and most popular museum in California, is a world (and an afternoon) unto itself. Among the three-dozen galleries are dioramas of bears, wolves and bison; set pieces from the American past, including a cutaway Conestoga wagon demonstrating life on the frontier; and, of course, the dinosaur skeletons required of every self-respecting natural history museum.

Prettiest of all the buildings in this museum park is the **California Afro-American Museum** (213-744-7432) with its glass-roofed sculpture court and bright, airy galleries. Devoted to black culture and history, the center displays the work of artists from around the world.

Surprisingly enough, Exposition Park's most notable architectural achievement is not the museum buildings, but rather the **Los Angeles Memorial Coliseum** (213-747-7111; admission), a 91,000-seat, classic-style arena built in 1923. One of the most beautiful stadiums in the country, it was site of the 1932 and 1984 Olympics.

Elysian Park–Silver Lake Area

North of downtown lie several suburban neighborhoods set along sloping hillsides and separated by parks and eucalyptus groves. This hill-and-dale district—which features mountain roads and tile-roofed houses—is now inhabited by an intriguing mix of blue- and white-collar workers. The heights above Silver Lake, with their curving mountain roads, jogging paths and city vistas, are also popular with artists and young professionals.

For the outdoor-minded, 575-acre **Elysian Park** (near the intersection of Routes 110 and 5), the city's second largest park, is a forested region of rolling hills and peaceful glens, exotic palm trees and nature trails offering views of central Los Angeles and the San Gabriel Valley.

Nearby **Echo Park** (Glendale Boulevard and Park Avenue) features a palm-fringed lake complete with footbridge and ducks, and rental boats to explore the water. That circular structure with the imposing white columns across the street is **Angelus Temple** (1100 Glendale Boulevard; 213-484-1100). Modeled after Salt Lake City's Mormon Tabernacle, it served the congregation of spiritualist Aimee Temple McPherson during the 1920s and 1930s.

The nearby neighborhood of Angelino Heights was the city's first suburb, built during the 1880s. Today the once elegant borough, ragged along the edges, still retains vestiges of its glory days. Foremost is the **1300 block of Carroll Avenue**, where a string of gingerbread Victorians have been gussied up in the fashion of the Gay Nineties. The street is an outdoor museum lined with turrets, gables and fanciful woodwork. For further information, call 213-250-5976.

MOUNT WASHINGTON

If an entire neighborhood could qualify as an outdoor museum, the Mount Washington district would probably charge admission. Here, just northeast of downtown, are several picture-book expressions of desert culture within a few blocks.

*The **Lummis House** (200 East Avenue 43; 213-222-0546), or El Alisal, is the work of one man, Charles Fletcher Lummis, whose life is inextricably bound to the history of the region. A devotee of Southwestern culture, he built this stone house himself, using granite from the nearby arroyo and carving the doors by hand.*

*Perhaps Charles Lummis' most important role was as founder of the **Southwest Museum** (234 Museum Drive; 213-221-2163; admission). Set in a Mission-style structure, this important facility contains exquisite jewelry, weaving and other handicrafts from Pueblo Indian tribes. California's Indians are represented by their pottery, weapons and decorative beadwork. There are also bead papooses of the Plains Indians and totem poles from the Pacific Northwest tribes.*

*The museum's **Casa de Adobe** (4605 North Figueroa Street; 213-225-8653), a replica of an 1850s hacienda, represents the Southwest's other vital cultural strain. Built around a central courtyard, each room is decorated in the style of the period.*

*That antique neighborhood on the other side of the Pasadena Freeway is **Heritage Square** (3800 North Homer Street; 818-449-0193; admission), an eclectic collection of historic buildings. Several impressive Victorians, a Methodist church and the old Palms Railroad Depot rest here. Open only on weekends and most major holidays.*

ELYSIAN PARK–SILVER LAKE AREA RESTAURANTS

Your Colombian connection is **Los Arrieros** (2619 West Sunset Boulevard; 213-483-0074), a fresh, bright cafe with tile floors and wall murals. Entrées range from shrimp in garlic sauce to *carne asada*. Budget to moderate.

Combine dining and art at **L.A. Nicola** (4326 West Sunset Boulevard; 213-660-7217). The cuisine at this exposed-pipe-and-tracklight dining room is as contemporary as the canvases adorning the walls. The deluxe-priced menu offers shrimp with tequila, steak on garlic baguette and seabass with leeks. A scene at either lunch or dinner.

Seafood Bay (3916 West Sunset Boulevard; 213-664-3902) is the best type of seafood restaurant, one with an adjacent fish market, ensuring freshness. Just a naugahyde cafe with formica tables, it offers swordfish, trout and practically everything else that swims. Priced budget to moderate.

ELYSIAN PARK–SILVER LAKE AREA NIGHTLIFE

The **Dresden** (1760 North Vermont Avenue; 213-665-4294), a stately brick-and-stained-glass restaurant, hosts an elegant piano bar.

They'll serenade you tableside with operas and show tunes at **La Strada** (3000 Los Feliz Boulevard; 213-664-2955), a Northern Italian dinner club.

The Bavarian-style **Red Lion Tavern** (2366 Glendale Boulevard; 213-662-5337), a friendly German rathskeller, serves lagers in two-liter schooners. The German bartenders double as accordion players and initiate impromptu sing-alongs, especially after games at nearby Dodger Stadium.

There are two small theaters of note in the Silver Lake area. **Colony Studio Theatre Playhouse** (1944 Riverside Drive; 213-665-3011) hosts classic dramas, musicals and new plays. The **Celebration Theatre** (426 North Hoover Street; 213-666-8669) presents gay and lesbian productions.

Wilshire District

Extending from downtown all the way to the Pacific Ocean, Wilshire Boulevard reaches for 16 miles through the western heart of Los Angeles. In its course the grand avenue passes Jewish, Korean, Southeast Asian, Filipino, Mexican and Central American neighborhoods. Originally an Indian trail leading from the Elysian Park area to the La Brea tar pits, the boulevard was developed during the 1890s by H.

Gaylord Wilshire, a socialist with an ironic knack for making money in real estate.

Within the Wilshire District stands the modern West's money center. Smaller and more sedate than its New York counterpart, the **Pacific Stock Exchange** (233 South Beaudry Avenue, 12th Floor; 213-977-4500) nevertheless conveys a sense of financial drama. You can view all the action from the visitors' gallery.

One of Los Angeles' truly exquisite structures, **I. Magnin Wilshire** (3050 Wilshire Boulevard; 213-382-6161) is a 1929 art deco extravaganza marked by a solitary tower and boasting several tiers of thin, fluted columns.

Not to be outclassed, the residential architecture of **Hancock Park** (between Wilshire Boulevard and Melrose Avenue, centered around the Wilshire Country Club) includes posh 1920s estates once owned by the Crocker, Huntington and Doheny families.

Back in the 1920s and 1930s the showcase for commercial architecture rested along the **Miracle Mile** (Wilshire Boulevard between La Brea and Fairfax avenues). The magnificent art deco towers that lined the strip still survive, particularly between the 5200 and 5500 blocks of Wilshire, but the early glory has faded.

The West's largest museum is a multibuilding complex with an international art collection. Providing a thumbnail tour of the entire history of art, the **Los Angeles County Museum of Art** (5905 Wilshire Boulevard; 213-857-6111; admission) ranges from pre-Columbian gold objects and African masks to post-World War II minimalist works. Included are works by Rembrandt, Cézanne, Monet, Magritte and Chagall. The Pavilion for Japanese Art houses the famous Shin'enkan collection of paintings as well as screens, ceramics and sculpture. The entire complex is beautifully laid out around a central courtyard adorned with terra cotta pillars and a four-tiered waterfall.

Beauty gives way to the beast at the adjacent **George C. Page Museum** (5801 Wilshire Boulevard; 213-936-2230; admission). This paleontological showplace features displays of mammoths, mastodons and extinct camels. Together with over 200 varieties of other creatures, they fell victim to the **La Brea Tar Pits**, which surround the museum. Dating to the Pleistocene Era, these oozing oil pools trapped birds, mammals, insects and reptiles, creating rich fossil deposits. Today you can wander past the pits, which bubble menacingly with methane gas and lie covered in globs of black tar.

Another tiny but intensely powerful exhibit is the **Martyrs Memorial & Museum of the Holocaust** (6505 Wilshire Boulevard; 213-852-1234). Devoted to the tragedy of World War II, it is filled with images from the Nazi extermination camps. Many of the docents are Holocaust survivors with personal stories to recount.

Nearby **Fairfax Avenue** (between Beverly Boulevard and Melrose Avenue) is the center of the city's Jewish community. It's filled with delicatessens, bakeries and kosher grocery stores. A favorite gathering place here is the intersection of Fairfax and Oakwood avenues. One corner supports a **mural** depicting Jewish life in Los Angeles, and another contains **Al's Newsstand**, a 24-hour outdoor vendor reminiscent of the early 20th century when Jews first occupied the area.

WILSHIRE DISTRICT LODGING

The **Mayfair Hotel** (1256 West 7th Street; 213-484-9614), near downtown, is a 306-room deluxe hostelry. Built in 1928 and beautifully refurbished, it offers a touch of luxury at a price lower than the five-star hotels. There's a restaurant and lounge as well as an attractive skylit lobby.

Another 1920s-era art deco building, the **Wilshire Royale Hotel** (2619 Wilshire Boulevard; 213-387-5311) has been fashionably transformed into a contemporary 200-room facility. The lobby is a beamed-ceiling affair with piano and upholstered armchairs. Guest rooms have tile baths. Pool and spa. Moderate to deluxe.

The **Sheraton Town House** (2961 Wilshire Boulevard; 213-382-7171) conveys a sense of old-time ease in its 272-room facility. Practically an urban resort, the 1929 complex features a large pool and patio area complete with shade trees, spa, restaurants and tennis courts. The hardwood-furnished guest rooms represent some of the largest accommodations in the city. Deluxe.

Wilshire Crest Inn (6301 Orange Street; 213-936-5131) is one of those terribly modern hotels with track lighting, black trim and fabric wall coverings. The 34 rooms, built around an interior patio, are done in oak and furnished with platform beds. There's a dining room and plush sitting area. Moderate.

Salisbury House (2273 West 20th Street; 213-737-7817), one of the city's rare bed-and-breakfast inns, is a marvelous 1909 Craftsman bungalow with hardwood floors and leaded-glass windows. There's a formal dining room as well as a living room with fireplace. The five guest rooms (two with shared bath) are nicely furnished with antique pieces. Moderate to deluxe.

WILSHIRE DISTRICT RESTAURANTS

Elegance 24 hours a day in a restaurant on wheels? At **Pacific Dining Car** (1310 West 6th Street; 213-483-6000) 'round-the-clock service is provided in dark wood surroundings. Modeled after a plush old-style railroad dining car, this destination has been a Los Angeles landmark since 1921. The cuisine is well-heeled all-American: breakfast includes eggs Benedict and dinner features wild game dishes as well as some of the best steaks in the city. Deluxe to ultra-deluxe.

The reason for the balcony at **La Fonda** (2501 Wilshire Boulevard; 213-380-5055) becomes stirringly evident every evening when Los Camperos, one of the city's best mariachi bands, strikes up a Spanish song. Besides the music, diners enjoy Veracruz-style shrimp, steak *picado* and chicken *flautas*. Moderate.

Well-known for its Siamese cuisine, **Chan Dara** (310 North Larchmont Boulevard; 213-467-1052) is a modern restaurant with mirrored bar and brass-rail dining room. The specialties vary from spicy barbecue to vegetable entrées. Moderate.

Angular beam ceiling, pipe sculpture aquarium and candles. Sound chic? That's **Muse** (7360 Beverly Boulevard; 213-934-4400), a California-cuisine restaurant with the feel of an offbeat art gallery. They serve pasta dishes as well as a changing repertoire of entrées such as salmon over mixed beach lettuce with *macedoine* of avocado. It's the only menu I've ever seen written in English but still requiring translation. Deluxe.

Also out along the edge is the **Nowhere Cafe** (8009 Beverly Boulevard; 213-655-8895), an upscale vegetarian restaurant decorated in Southwestern fashion. The bill of fare includes sizzling vegetables and Tex-Mex burritos (with pumpkin seeds, black beans and green peppers). Moderate.

WILSHIRE DISTRICT SHOPPING

The city's burgeoning Koreatown is a warren of small shops and markets, each brightly painted in the calligraphy of the East. The **Korean Shopping Center** (3300 West 8th Street), a small arcade housing quality shops, features two exceptional boutiques, **Marie France** (213-480-0013) and **Michelle**.

A spate of new art galleries and restaurants has attracted a flood of shoppers to the **La Brea corridor**, as the area along La Brea Avenue

---

L.A.'S MOST FAMOUS DELI

L.A.'s best-known delicatessen lies at the heart of the Jewish neighborhood around Fairfax Avenue. Canter's (419 North Fairfax Avenue; 213-651-2030), a casual 24-hour restaurant, doubles as local landmark and ethnic cultural center. As you might have guessed, lox and bagels, hot pastrami and matzo ball soup are the order of the day. When in doubt, go kosher. Moderate.

between Wilshire Boulevard and Melrose Avenue has come to be called. Among those featuring unique art exhibits are **Jan Baum** (213-932-0170) and **Garth Clark** (170 South La Brea Avenue; 213-939-2189), **Wenger** (828 North La Brea Avenue; 213-464-4431) and **Jack Rutberg Fine Arts** (357 North La Brea Avenue; 213-938-5222).

Scene of the Crime (3764 Wilshire Boulevard, in the Wiltern Building; 818-981-2583) evokes images of Sherlock Holmes' library. You won't need a detective to tell you this bookstore specializes in mysteries.

In the gift shop at the **Los Angeles County Museum of Art** (5905 Wilshire Boulevard; 213-857-6146), you'll find art books, photographic items and graphic reproductions. Further down Wilshire Boulevard, contemporary folk art is the theme at the **Craft and Folk Art Museum** (6067 Wilshire Boulevard, 4th floor; 213-937-5544).

Farmers Market (6333 West 3rd Street; 213-933-9211) is a giant shopping complex covering nearly 20 acres. It's a European boulevard, Oriental bazaar and Mexican market all in one. In addition to fruit and vegetable stands, there are crafts stores, clothing outlets and sundry shops.

Journeying from the ethnic to the futuristic, you'll arrive at the **Beverly Center** (8500 Beverly Boulevard; 213-854-0070), a neon-laced, eight-acre shopping mall with signature clothing stores and world-class restaurants. Among the center's 200 international shops and restaurants are the **Irvine Ranch Farmers Market** (213-657-1931), an expansive gourmet place with some of the prettiest produce in town, and **Following Sea** (213-659-0592), a gift shop selling many items you didn't know you wanted and a few that you didn't know existed.

WILSHIRE DISTRICT NIGHTLIFE

City Restaurant (180 South La Brea Boulevard; 213-938-2155), a high-style, high-tech warehouse, features a dynamic bar with a streetfront patio.

The Mexican food may be good at **El Cholo** (1121 South Western Avenue; 213-734-2773), but the famed margaritas really draw the crowds to this lively bar scene.

Tom Bergin's (840 South Fairfax Avenue; 213-936-7151), a traditional Irish pub dating to the 1930s, was voted one of the top 100 bars in the United States by *Esquire* magazine. Judging from the 5000 patron-inscribed shamrocks mounted on the walls, the crowd agrees.

Actors, musicians and writers meet in the small **Coronet Bar** (370 North La Cienega Boulevard; 213-659-4583), a comfortable and unpretentious spot.

The Hard Rock Cafe (8600 Beverly Boulevard; 213-276-7605), a wildly popular gathering place, features loud music and rock memorabilia including Madonna icons and walls covered with Beatles artifacts.

The **Wiltern Theater** (3790 Wilshire Boulevard; 213-380-5005), a 1931 art deco masterpiece, is a center for classical music, drama and opera programs.

A beautiful 1927 Renaissance-style building, the **Wilshire Ebell Theatre** (4401 West 8th Street; 213-939-1128) is the setting for television specials and live theater, opera and dance.

The **Coronet Theatre** (366 North La Cienega Boulevard; 213-652-9199) houses the Serendipity Theatre Company, which performs family and youth-oriented theater.

Hollywood

It was farm country when Horace and Daeida Wilcox first moved to Cahuenga Valley. Originally part of the Rancho La Brea land grant, the dusty hills lay planted in bell peppers, watermelons and citrus trees. Then in 1887 Horace had a brainstorm: he subdivided the family farm, Daeida christened the spread "Hollywood," and they put lots on the market for $150 an acre.

By 1910, the cow town's population had grown to 4000 middle-class, god-fearing souls drawn predominantly from Midwestern stock. Then came the deluge. The fledgling movie industry—attracted by warm weather and natural locations—began relocating to Hollywood. The first studio arrived in 1911. By the 1920s the movie industry had become a billion-dollar business, with Hollywood its capital. Picture palaces mushroomed along Hollywood Boulevard beside glamorous restaurants and majestic hotels, and by 1930 the population totaled 150,000.

Hollywood's glory days lasted until the 1960s, when development gave way to decline. Today the area is in the midst of a renaissance. The commercial districts are being refurbished and West Hollywood has developed into a center for gay lifestyles.

Regardless of the changes, seemingly in spite of itself, the place remains Hollywood, tawdry and tragic, with all its myth and magic. The town that F. Scott Fitzgerald said "can be understood ... only dimly and in flashes" is still an odd amalgam of truth and tinsel, promise and impossibility, conjuring images of big studios and bright stars.

It was 1918 when Alice Barnsdall, an enchantingly eccentric oil heiress, purchased an entire hill in Hollywood, planted the 36 acres with olive trees and christened the spot Olive Hill. She next hired Frank Lloyd Wright to design a family home and adjoining arts center.

Olive Hill subsequently became **Barnsdall Park** (4800 Hollywood Boulevard), an aerie studded with olive and conifer trees, from which visitors can survey the entire sweep of Hollywood. Wright's masterwork became **Hollyhock House** (213-485-4580), a sprawling 6200-square-foot home built in the form of a Mayan temple. Guided tours are available.

The last of the great studios to remain in Hollywood, **Paramount Studios** (5555 Melrose Avenue; 213-956-5575; admission) first shone brightly during the silent era. The production company signed stars like Rudolph Valentino and Clara Bow in the 1920s, Gary Cooper and Marlene Dietrich during the 1930s and later headlined Dorothy Lamour, Betty Hutton, Bob Hope and Bing Crosby. Weekday tours are available.

Many of these same legends lie buried just north of the studio in **Hollywood Memorial Park Cemetery** (6000 Santa Monica Boulevard). Surrounded by high walls and shaded with palm trees, the 65-acre greensward is crowded with Greek statues and Egyptian temples. Among those at rest here are Rudolph Valentino, Tyrone Power and Cecil B. DeMille.

For a tour of the truly macabre there's **Graveline Tours** (P.O. Box 931694, Hollywood, CA 90093; 213-876-0920). From your resting place in a Cadillac hearse you'll see the hotel where John Belushi died, the spot where George "Superman" Reeves shot himself, and the sites of other infamous Hollywood deaths. Heavy, man.

Looking back, no one can quite figure how Movieland's most famous address became so prominent. Most of the action occurred elsewhere, but somehow the corner of **Hollywood and Vine** has come to symbolize Hollywood.

Maybe it's the many radio studios that lined the thoroughfare during the 1930s, or perhaps because the **Pantages Theater** (6233 Hollywood Boulevard) is just down the street. One of the nation's finest art deco theaters, the Pantages was built in 1930 and housed Academy Awards presentations from 1949 to 1959.

Gazing down on all the commotion is the **Capitol Records Tower** (1750 Vine Street), a building you have seen in countless photographs. Resembling a squadron of flying saucers piggy-backed on one another, the 13-story structure was actually designed to look like a stack of records with a stylus protruding from the top.

In a tribute to the great studios once occupying the area, **Home Savings of America** (1500 North Vine Street) adorned its facade with the names of hundreds of stars and added a tile mural depicting the most noteworthy. The interior contains a marvelous stained-glass window with scenes from Hollywood's early movies.

During the halcyon days of the 1920s, as silent movies gave way to talkies, Hollywood Boulevard was door-to-door with mansions. The

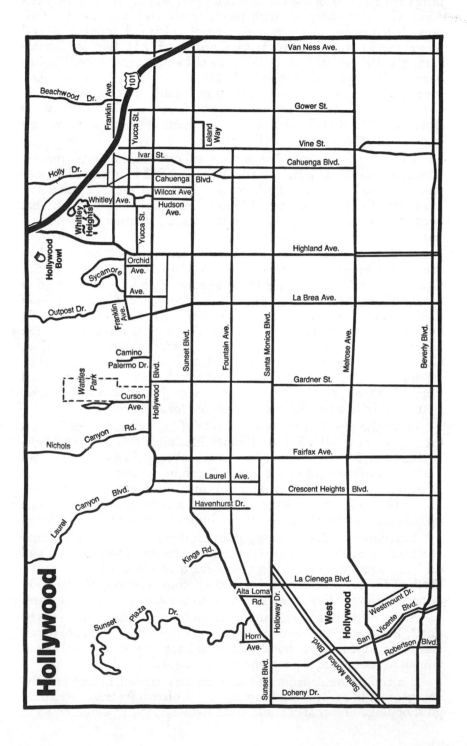

Janes House, one of the last of this long-vanished breed, is a Queen Anne Victorian complete with turret, gable and stained-glass windows. The grande belle rests at the end of a plastic shopping mall and houses the **Visitors' Information Center** (6541 Hollywood Boulevard; 213-461-4213). Perhaps they can tell you where to find the lost beauty of Hollywood. Today, Hollywood Boulevard has been taken over by taco vendors, cut-rate video stores and T-shirt shops.

Then there's the **Hollywood Wax Museum** (6767 Hollywood Boulevard; 213-462-8860; admission), a melancholy place where you can "see your favorite stars in living wax."

Two relics from those days of yore still cater to the town's movie-hungry populace. The **Egyptian Theater** (6712 Hollywood Boulevard; 213-467-6167) was built by Sid Grauman in 1922, after the discovery of King Tut's tomb. Much of the original architecture has been lost to mindless remodeling, but some Egyptian elements endure.

Far more famous and better preserved is **Mann's Chinese Theater** (6925 Hollywood Boulevard; 213-464-8111), also built by Sid Grauman in 1927. This fabulous movie palace is fashioned in a kind of Oriental Baroque style with pagoda roof, stone guard dogs and Asian masks. Though the architecture is splendid, the theater is actually known for its sidewalk. Embedded in the cement forecourt are the handprints and footprints of Hollywood's greatest stars. Jean Harlow, Cary Grant and Jimmy Stewart have left their signatures in this grandest of all autograph collections. Not every celebrity simply signed and stepped—there are also cement images of Jimmy Durante's nose, Betty Grable's leg and the webbed feet of Donald Duck.

Of all the places in Hollywood, one of the best retrospectives on the stars is at the **Max Factor Beauty Museum** (1666 North Highland Avenue; 213-463-6668). The great make-up man's former studio has been converted into a showplace for an important Hollywood art form. There are celebrity make-up rooms, antique tools of the trade and an impressive photo gallery. They have even managed to dredge up hairpieces worn by George Burns, Jimmy Stewart and John Wayne.

Throughout this area—extending for three and a half miles along Hollywood Boulevard from Gower Street to Sycamore Avenue and on Vine Street between Sunset Boulevard and Yucca Street—is the **Walk of Fame**, a star-studded terrazzo commemorating almost 2000 notables from the film, television, radio, theater and music industries.

After completing the grand tour of Hollywood Boulevard, stop by **C. C. Brown's** (7007 Hollywood Boulevard; 213-464-9726) for an ice cream sundae. This traditional malt shop, around since 1929, is famous for hot fudge sundaes and its own candy.

If a time traveler from the 21st century landed in our era, the voyager would easily feel at home along **Melrose Avenue**. He could go shopping. The chic corridor is door-to-door with designer stores purveying space-age fashions. What Beverly Hills' Rodeo Drive is to classical fashion, Melrose has become to the avant-garde.

Then he could dine. The restaurants lining this strip are tile-and-copper cafes with bare-duct ceilings and Post-Midnight Modern architecture. They serve sushi and whip up recipes on file at the U.S. Patent Office.

If you need a landmark to lead you through this tony part of town, consider a whale. The "Blue Whale" to be precise; that's the nickname for the blue-glass monstrosity on Melrose Avenue and San Vicente Boulevard. Formally known as the **Pacific Design Center** (213-657-0800), it's a mammoth mall catering to the interior design industry. Since opening in 1975, it has spawned a Green Whale next door. Rumor has it that Moby Blue is pregnant with a Red Whale, due sometime in the 1990s.

As God no doubt willed, Melrose Avenue ends in **West Hollywood**, the first city in the nation to be governed by avowed homosexuals. Much more than a gay city, West Hollywood is a free-form laboratory for social experiment, a place where the spirit of the '60s is transformed into the art form of a later era.

The street scene centers along Sunset Boulevard, a flashy avenue studded with nightclubs and restaurants. During the 1930s and 1940s, the section between Crescent Heights Boulevard and Doheny Drive formed the fabled **Sunset Strip**. Center of Los Angeles night action, it was an avenue of dreams, housing nightclubs like Ciro's and the Clover Club, where starlets bedecked with diamonds went with their leading men.

Today, the two-mile strip is chockablock with the offices of agents, movie producers and music executives. The street's most artistic achievement is the parade of **vanity boards**, outsize billboards advertising the latest movie and record releases. Representing the work of the region's finest sign painters and designers, they are often done in three dimensions, with lights and trompe l'oeil devices.

The lower slopes of the nearby Santa Monica Mountains contain some of Los Angeles' most fashionable addresses. Known as the **Hollywood Hills**, these rugged foothills are divorced from the glitter of Hollywood by serpentine roads and provide a pricey escape valve from the pressures of Tinseltown. But for those with a car and an afternoon, it costs little to explore Hollywood's vaunted upcountry.

Beachwood Canyon (Beachwood Drive), one of the town's prettiest residential areas, is a V-shaped valley with 1920s- and 1930s-era homes on either side. First developed as "Hollywoodland" by *Los Angeles Times* publisher Harry Chandler, the neighborhood is now popular with screenwriters.

To advertise "Hollywoodland" the developer erected a huge sign on the hillside. Eventually "land" was removed, the fixture was refurbished, and Chandler's billboard became the **Hollywood Sign**, a

45-foot-tall, 450-foot-long landmark that is now the foremost symbol of Movieland.

For stars living in **Whitley Heights** during the 1920s, life was much as it is in Beverly Hills today. This hilltop neighborhood, with its tile-roofed Mediterranean homes, was the premier residential area for the silent-movie set, including Rudolph Valentino. To explore the landmark neighborhood, drive up Whitley Avenue to Whitley Terrace and Wedgewood Place.

One of Hollywood's most enduring symbols is the **Hollywood Bowl** (2301 North Highland Avenue; 213-850-2060), a concrete band shell built in 1929. Situated in a sylvan glade called Daisy Dell, the concert hall is an amphitheater within an amphitheater, surrounded by a circle of wooded hills. The adjacent **Hollywood Bowl Museum** (213-850-2058) features listening rooms and hosts a changing series of exhibits on the culture of music.

A part of Hollywood's history stands just across the street. Back in 1913, a young director named Cecil B. DeMille found a farm town called Hollywood with an empty barn he could convert into a studio. Eventually moved to its present site, the historic building became the **Hollywood Studio Museum** (2100 North Highland Avenue; 213-874-2276; admission), a silent film era showplace.

The real spirit of the Hollywood Hills resides in the deep canyons that climb from Hollywood Boulevard into the Santa Monica Mountains. **Nichols Canyon** (Nichols Canyon Road), a chaparral-coated

---

HOLLYWOOD IN ACTION

The tram is filled with innocent people, a random collection of folks from all walks, some with little kids in tow. Suddenly it is blasted by aliens and highjacked onto a giant spaceship. As the Cyclons prepare to destroy the tram, a laser battle of galactic proportions breaks out.

*Sound like Hollywood? Actually it's the **Universal Studios Tour** (100 Universal City Plaza, Universal City; 818-508-9600), a Disneyesque introduction to one of the nation's biggest motion picture and television facilities. Founded in 1912, Universal is a mammoth 420-acre complex complete with 36 sound stages, a 15-story administration building and a staff of over 10,000 filmmakers.*

More like an amusement park than an authentic studio tour, Universal's adventure offers visitors an ersatz introduction to Hollywood. The tram passes the locations for classic films like My Little Chickadee *(1940) and modern ones like* The Sting *(1973) and explores the backlot with its street sets of Europe, Texas, New York and Mexico. If Hollywood is one step away from reality, the Universal Tour is two steps. It's a staging of a staging, a Hollywood version of Hollywood.*

*The **NBC Studio Tour** (3000 West Alameda Avenue, Burbank; 818-840-3537) provides a similar view of the television industry. Though only 75 minutes*

valley adorned with million-dollar homes, represents one of the toniest parts of town. Possessing the same cachet and even greater fame, the rustic **Laurel Canyon** (Laurel Canyon Boulevard) became known as a hippie hideaway during the 1960s.

Both Nichols and Laurel canyons rise sharply into the mountains, eventually reaching the rim of Los Angeles, a 50-mile-long country road called **Mulholland Drive**, which extends from Hollywood to Malibu. Tracing a course along the ridge of the Santa Monicas, Mulholland is a spectacularly beautiful road, curving through forests, climbing along sharp precipices and offering magnificent views.

HOLLYWOOD LODGING

One of Hollywood's best bargains is found at the **Magic Hotel** (7025 Franklin Avenue; 213-851-0800), a 40-unit establishment next to the famed Magic Castle, a private club for magicians. Spacious suites with kitchens are furnished in oak and decorated (presto!) with magic posters. Pool and sun deck. Moderate.

The first Oscars were presented at the **Hollywood Roosevelt Hotel** (7000 Hollywood Boulevard; 213-466-7000). Built in 1927, the Spanish revival building has been completely refurbished and now offers 400 rooms, plus restaurants, lounges and a palm-studded courtyard with pool and sauna. Priced below the five-star hotels, this classic

---

*long (in contrast to Universal's half-day extravaganza), it takes in a special-effects center and visits a mini-studio where visitors participate in a mock game show. The wardrobe area, set-construction shop and make-up room are also on the itinerary. Here and at **CBS Ticket Information** (7800 Beverly Boulevard, Los Angeles; 213-852-2624), free tickets to television shows are available.*

*The **Burbank Studios** (4000 Warner Boulevard, Burbank; 818-954-1744), by contrast, takes you behind the scenes to see the day-to-day activities of a multimedia complex. Home to Warner Brothers and Columbia Pictures, the studio accepts only small groups, showing them sound-effects techniques, the wardrobe and property departments and the set-construction mill. Guides discuss the entire process of production, providing a thumbnail course in filmmaking and sometimes taking visitors on the set while television shows are taping.*

*For a personal introduction to the practices and personalities of Hollywood, there's nothing like being there. If you're interested in finding out where movies and television shows are being filmed around town, the **Motion Picture Coordination Office** (6922 Hollywood Boulevard, Hollywood; 213-485-5324) issues a daily shoot sheet for a nominal fee.*

That's Hollywood!

caravansary has many features of the finest hostelries, including a luxurious lobby. Deluxe to ultra-deluxe.

The traditional Hollywood rest stop is **Château Marmont** (8221 Sunset Boulevard; 213-656-1010), a Norman-style palace built in 1929. Formerly home to Jean Harlow and Howard Hughes, the hotel still lures Hollywood luminaries such as Robert DeNiro, Dustin Hoffman and Diane Keaton. They come for the privacy and quirky charm of the place, which offers rooms, suites and cottages at deluxe and ultra-deluxe prices.

L'Ermitage Hotels, a group of several hotels within a ten-block radius, represents one of the most innovative hotel chains in the country. The hallmark of the streamlined Mondrian, Bel Age, Le Parc and Le Dufy hotels is the artwork, which hangs seemingly everywhere.

The **Mondrian Hotel** (8440 Sunset Boulevard; 213-650-8999) is a stylized tribute to the Dutch painter Piet Mondrian. The exterior of this 12-story highrise has been painted sherbet colors by a contemporary artist, while the interior is filled with works of modern art. Restaurant, lounge, spa and fitness center. Ultra-deluxe.

Somewhat more offbeat is the **Bel Age Hotel** (1020 North San Vicente Boulevard; 213-854-1111) in West Hollywood. It offers similar amenities in an all-suite complex positively laden with artwork. Ultra-deluxe.

Another chic Hollywood resting spot, the **Sunset Marquis Hotel and Villas** (1200 North Alta Loma Road; 213-657-1333) is a Mediterranean-style hotel frequented by beautiful people with big purses. Guest rooms, which surround a terrace pool, range from standard facilities to lavish villas. High in snob appeal, the hotel offers complete amenities. Ultra-deluxe.

The elegant **St. James Club** (8358 Sunset Boulevard, West Hollywood; 213-654-7100) treats guests to an upper-crust British club atmosphere. Completed in 1931 as Sunset Towers and now restored to its art deco magnificence, the Club once was home to screen luminaries from nearby studios. To get around its "private club" status yet fill its 74 rooms and suites, it allows $8-per-night temporary memberships. Ultra-deluxe.

HOLLYWOOD RESTAURANTS

La Poubelle (5907 Franklin Avenue; 213-465-0807), a small candlelit restaurant, serves up delicate French cuisine with a style (and a local following) all its own. Dinner and Sunday brunch at moderate rates.

Popular with entertainers from nearby studios, **Columbia Bar & Grill** (1448 North Gower Street; 213-461-8800) is the last word in sleek, from its brick patio with topiary trees to the pullman booths and green-glass shades. The American regional cuisine includes fresh fish, pasta and assorted steaks. Moderate to deluxe.

Hollywood's oldest restaurant, **Musso and Frank Grill** (6667 Hollywood Boulevard; 213-467-7788) is a 1919 original with dark paneling, red leather booths and a clubby atmosphere. Among the American-style dishes are cracked crab, prime rib and roast lamb. A slice of tradition at a moderate price.

Hampton's (1342 North Highland Avenue; 213-469-1090) may be the world's only hamburger joint with valet parking. This well-known noshing spot has transformed the art of hamburger cooking to a science, preparing over two dozen varieties. You can order one with sour plum jam or creamed horseradish. Moderate.

The celebrity photos covering every inch of **Formosa Cafe** (7156 Santa Monica Boulevard; 213-850-9050) tell a tale of Hollywood that reaches back to the 1940s. This crowded cafe, originally fashioned from a streetcar, has seen more stars than heaven. Today it's a budget-to-moderate-priced Chinese-American restaurant covered with autographs, a kind of museum with meals.

Hollywood's prettiest restaurant is a re-created Japanese palace called **Yamashiro** (1999 North Sycamore Avenue; 213-466-5125). Dine here and you are surrounded by hand-carved columns, *shoji* screens and Asian statuary. The courtyard garden contains a waterfall, koi pond and miniature trees. They serve a complete Japanese menu and Western entrées; moderate to deluxe.

Melrose Avenue, where the fashion-conscious can dress to dine and then shop for their next dinner outfit, has vaulted to prominence as one of L.A.'s leading restaurant rows. Among the more savvy gourmets, many squeeze into **Citrus** (6703 Melrose Avenue; 213-939-5354), a white-wall-and-track-lighting dining room highlighted with fresh flowers. The theme is California cuisine (what else?), with a focus on fresh fish. Deluxe.

Modern art and pastel walls are also standard issue in the neighborhood's best Chinese restaurant. **Genghis Cohen** (740 North Fairfax Avenue; 213-653-0640) serves gourmet dishes to an appreciative crowd at its multiroom complex. Not your ordinary Asian restaurant, specialties here are "scallops on fire" and "no-name" duck. Deluxe.

Southwestern in decor, nouvelle California in cuisine, **Trumps** (8764 Melrose Avenue; 213-855-1480) has received critical acclaim for both. Burlap banquettes and square cement tables create an air of nonchalance. For dinner they serve entrées like smoked baby back ribs and steamed salmon with wild rice pancakes. Moderate to deluxe.

La Toque (8171 Sunset Boulevard; 213-656-7515), a nouvelle French restaurant with a bold reputation, is one of the places that put West Hollywood on the culinary map. Nightly the chef prepares venison medallions, saddle of lamb and salmon with blood orange sauce.

While the building is Southwestern in design, the elegant dining room has a distinctly European feel. Deluxe.

A favorite celebrity-watching restaurant, **Dan Tana's** (9071 Santa Monica Boulevard; 213-275-9444) is small and crowded, making reservations a must. The fare is Italian, pricey but excellent. Dinner only, deluxe to ultra-deluxe.

Duke's (8909 Sunset Boulevard; 213-652-3100) is another legendary watering hole, especially popular with music industry figures. A crowded coffee shop bedecked with posters, it also attracts West Hollywood's underground population. People with purple hair pile into the communal tables, order meat loaf or Chinese vegetables and settle down for the day. A real scene. Budget.

With the possible exception of Berkeley's Chez Panisse, **Spago** (1114 Horn Avenue; 213-652-4025) is California's most famous restaurant. Owner Wolfgang Puck helped originate California cuisine, which achieves its pinnacle at his West Hollywood restaurant. The dining room is dominated by an open-view brick oven. The furnishings are informal, and everything that can be painted is painted white. Among the entrées are duck with apricot ginger sauce and squab with parsnip pancakes. Dinner only; reservations required. Deluxe to ultra-deluxe.

L'Orangerie (903 North La Cienega Boulevard; 213-652-9770) possesses all the pretensions you would expect from one of Los Angeles' finest, most expensive French restaurants. The dining areas are appointed with oil paintings and outsized wall sconces; fresh flowers and the scent of money proliferate. Food, decor, service, all are the finest. The *foie gras* and seafood are flown in fresh from France. Dinner only; reservations required. Ultra-deluxe.

HOLLYWOOD SHOPPING

Hollywood Boulevard probably has more bookstores than movie theaters. **Larry Edmonds Book Shop** (6644 Hollywood Boulevard; 213-463-3273) claims to have the world's largest collection of books and memorabilia on cinema and theater. If any place can challenge their claim, it is **Collectors Book Store** (1708 North Vine Street; 213-467-3296), with its museum-quality inventory of stills, posters, books and scripts. **Universal News Agency** (1655 North Las Palmas Avenue; 213-467-3850) has newspapers and magazines from around the world.

Frederick Mellinger started a tiny mail order company in 1946 based on the philosophy that "fashion may change but sex appeal is always in style." Today, **Frederick's of Hollywood** (6608 Hollywood Boulevard; 213-466-8506) continues to entice and enrage onlookers with its fantasy lingerie.

A bigger-than-life mural of Marilyn Monroe marks **Cinema Collectors** (1507 Wilcox Avenue; 213-461-6516). Selling film and television collectibles from every period, they have over 18,000 movie posters and two million photos.

Amid the billboards along Sunset Strip is a series of star-studded cartoon characters signaling the way to **Dudley Do-Right Emporium** (8200 Sunset Boulevard; 213-656-6550). Jay Ward's cartoon characters come to life at this Bullwinkle enthusiast's mecca.

Hollywood's chic leather crowd frequents **North Beach Leather** (8500 West Sunset Boulevard; 213-652-3224), where original designs attract a celebrity clientele.

Sunset Plaza (Sunset Boulevard between Sunset Plaza Drive and Sherbourne Drive), a two-block cluster of shops, offers some of the most luxurious shopping on the Strip.

Ultramodern shoppers make a beeline for **Melrose Avenue** (between Sycamore Avenue and Ogden Drive), the smartest street in all L.A. Peopled by visionaries and voluptuaries, it's sleek, fast and very, very chic.

Of course the most futuristic element of all is the past. At **Chic-A-Boom** (6905 Melrose Avenue; 213-931-7441), the "Mother Lode" of vintage retail, you'll find such shards of American history as World War II propaganda posters and a Twiggy-fashion tote bag. If it's rock-and-roll memorabilia you're after, a few doors away the same owners opened **The Rock Store** (6817 Melrose Avenue; 213-930-2980), filled with collectibles.

Off The Wall (7325 Melrose Avenue; 213-930-1185) is known for "weird stuff" and unusual antiques.

Ever wonder what it would be like to stand in John Travolta's shoes or Cher's boots? At **A Star Is Worn** (7303 Melrose Avenue; 213-939-4922), you can browse through the wardrobes of celebrities, who donate their old clothes to charity through this shop.

Displaying in-house designs and one-of-a-kind creations are **Tiziana** (7369 Melrose Avenue; 213-653-5203) and **New Kid In Town** (7429 Melrose Avenue; 213-653-0590). Olivia Newton-John's **Koala Blue** (7366 Melrose Avenue; 213-655-3596) showcases Australian-inspired designs.

Occupying an entire block, **Fred Segal** (8100 Melrose Avenue; 213-651-3342) is a series of stores within stores. Seeming to specialize in everything, this consumer labyrinth has clothes, luggage, electronic gear and cosmetics.

Designer's Row, near the Pacific Design Center, consists of classy interior design shops and high-ticket antique stores. **John Good Imports** (8469 Melrose Avenue; 213-655-6484) is an elaborate antique showroom, with beautiful displays.

Clustered nearby around Robertson Boulevard are several prestigious art galleries. At **Margo Leavin** (812 North Robertson Boulevard and 817 North Hilldale Avenue; 213-273-0603), two large buildings house an impressive collection of work by painters of regional and national renown. Artworks in ceramic and bronze are displayed in a delightful outdoor sculpture garden at **Asher/Faure** (612 North Almont Drive; 213-271-3665). Another constellation of galleries lies along the 600-to-800-block stretch of North La Cienega Boulevard.

HOLLYWOOD NIGHTLIFE

Reminiscent of the 1930s, the Hollywood Roosevelt Hotel's sophisticated, deco-style **Cinegrill** (7000 Hollywood Boulevard; 213-466-7000) is putting glamor back into Hollywood nightlife. Crème de la crème cabaret entertainers perform. Cover.

Famous jazz, blues and swing artists appear regularly at **Vine Street Bar and Grill** (1610 North Vine Street; 213-463-4375), an art deco dinner club with a solid reputation. Cover.

For sunset panoramas, nothing quite matches **Yamashiro's** (1999 North Sycamore Avenue; 213-466-5125). Set in a Japanese palace, the lounge overlooks gracious Oriental gardens from a perch in the Hollywood Hills.

Club Lingerie (6507 Sunset Boulevard; 213-466-8557) is a bare-walls dance club packed to the rafters with trendy Hollywood crowds. A prime place for hot, live rock-and-roll, reggae and blues. Cover.

The lounge at **The Roxbury** (8225 Sunset Boulevard; 213-656-1750) is a rendezvous for record company executives and show business figures.

The level of talent at the **Comedy Store** (8433 West Sunset Boulevard; 213-656-6225) is evident from the celebrity signatures covering the building's black exterior and photo-lined interior. The Main Room features established comedians, the Original Room showcases new talent, and the Belly Room presents female comics. Cover.

In fickle Hollywood, **Nicky Blair's** (8730 Sunset Boulevard; 213-659-0929) was hot the minute it opened to a star-studded crowd and still hasn't cooled off. The bar is packed shoulder-to-shoulder every night with beautiful people dressed to kill.

The Central (8852 Sunset Boulevard; 213-652-5937), a small, casual club, is known for live rhythm-and-blues. Many celebrity musicians sit in on Tuesday night jam sessions. Cover.

Three long-standing rock clubs dominate Sunset Strip. **Whiskey A Go Go** (8901 Sunset Boulevard; 213-652-4202) had its heyday in the '60s and is still popular with younger dance crowds. **The Roxy** (9009 Sunset Boulevard; 213-276-2222) headlines known rock and jazz performers in an art deco-style room. **Gazzarris** (9039 Sunset Boulevard; 213-273-6606), the oldest rock club on the Strip, offers a stage for dancing. Cover charge at all three clubs.

La Cage Aux Folles (643 North La Cienega Boulevard; 213-657-1091), an outrageous cabaret, is overrun by female impersonators who would have you believe that show biz's biggest stars—Dolly Parton, Diana Ross, Marilyn Monroe—are men. Great entertainment. Cover.

Nucleus Nuance (7267 Melrose Avenue; 213-939-8666) is an art deco nightclub with pizzazz. Well-dressed singles stand three-deep at the bar; quiet tables on the patio offer romantic privacy; live jazz is on tap nightly. Cover.

Who would imagine that a neighborhood saloon could survive the gentrification of Melrose Avenue? **J. Sloan's** (8623 Melrose Avenue; 213-659-0250), with its sawdust floor and old movie props, has not only survived but flourished in the shadow of Melrose's chrome-and-tile nightspots.

There are often as many comedians in the bar as on stage at the **Improvisation** (8162 Melrose Avenue; 213-651-2583). This spacious brick-walled club, patterned after the New York original, draws top-name comics as well as local talent. Cover.

One of the hottest trends in Hollywood nightlife is the coffee-house. With plump armchairs, weatherbeaten tables and walls covered by contemporary art, places like **Java** (7286 Beverly Boulevard; 213-931- 4943), **The Living Room** (110 South La Brea Avenue; 213-933-2933) and **Bourgeois Pig** (5931 Franklin Avenue; 213-962-6366) serve cappuccino and light meals until 4 a.m. Poetry readings, performance art, music and an edge clientele are also on the menu.

Theater in Hollywood varies from tiny storefront establishments to famous stages. In a city filled with actors, the playhouses inevitably are loaded with talent. Professionals from local television and movie

---

THE GAY SCENE

Nowhere is West Hollywood's gay scene more out front than in its cabarets and nightclubs. Some of the city's top entertainment spots are concentrated within this avant-garde neighborhood.

Grecian columns are incongruously combined with high-tech appointments at **Studio One** *(652 North La Peer; 213-659-0472), a popular gay disco. In the adjoining* **Backlot Theater** *(657 North Robertson Boulevard), the club's cabaret and live male acts range from the sublime to the raucous. Cover.*

The **Rose Tattoo** *(665 North Robertson Boulevard; 213-854-4455) attracts a gay and straight crowd to its pink-and-white cabaret. Cover.*

Rage *(8911 Santa Monica Boulevard; 213-652-7055) is a spacious dance club that spills onto the sidewalk; inside there are outrageous videos plus sounds ranging from rap to rock. Cover on weekends.*

The "videotainment" program at **Revolver** *(8851 Santa Monica Boulevard; 213-550-8851) means color monitors on every wall. With two bars, an espresso bar and a lively crowd, the place is hot. Cover.*

studios continually hone their skills on stage. The **Hollywood Arts Council** (P.O. Box 931056, Hollywood, CA 90093; 213-462-2355) offers seasonal calendar listings of all Hollywood theaters.

Beverly Hills

Back in 1844 a Spanish woman named Maria Rita Valdez acquired controlling interest over 4500 acres of sagebrush and tumbleweed. But the land was of little worth; plans for wheat cultivation, oil drilling and a community of German immigrants failed.

Finally in 1912 a group of entrepreneurs, struggling to sell this barren real estate, happened on the idea of building a big hotel to publicize their new housing development. Then in 1920, when the undisputed King and Queen of Hollywood, Douglas Fairbanks and Mary Pickford, built their palace on a hill above the hotel, the community's future was secure. The dusty farmland, now a town named Beverly Hills, had finally blossomed.

It's a rags-to-riches town with a lot of Horatio Alger stories to tell. The world capital of wealth and glamor, Beverly Hills is a place in which driving a BMW makes you a second-class citizen and where the million-dollar houses are in the poorer part of town. It is one of the few spots outside Texas where flaunting your money is considered good taste. Still, it's Beverly Hills. The town has style, history and an indomitable sense of magic.

It seems only fitting that the gateway to this posh preserve should be along **Santa Monica Boulevard** (between Doheny Drive and Wilshire Boulevard), a greenbelt with an exotic array of plant life on each block. Most impressive of all is the landscape of cactus and succulents between Camden and Bedford drives.

Rising near the center of the promenade is **Beverly Hills City Hall** (North Crescent Drive and Santa Monica Boulevard), an ornate 1932 Spanish baroque structure capped with a tile cupola. A contemporary commentary on City Hall, the adjacent **Beverly Hills Civic Center** features a stepped design in Spanish deco style.

By contrast the **U.S. Post Office** (9300 Santa Monica Boulevard) is an Italian Renaissance structure of brick and terra cotta. Built in 1933, the interior contains WPA-type murals popular during the Depression.

To help find your way around the winding streets of this hillside community, the **Beverly Hills Visitors Bureau** (239 South Beverly Drive; 213-271-8174) provides printed information. And the classic-style **Beverly Hills Trolley** (213-271-8174) at Rodeo Drive and Dayton Way provides free guided tours of the posh downtown area.

Regardless of its famous faces and stately residences, Beverly Hills has a single address that symbolizes the entire community. **Rodeo**

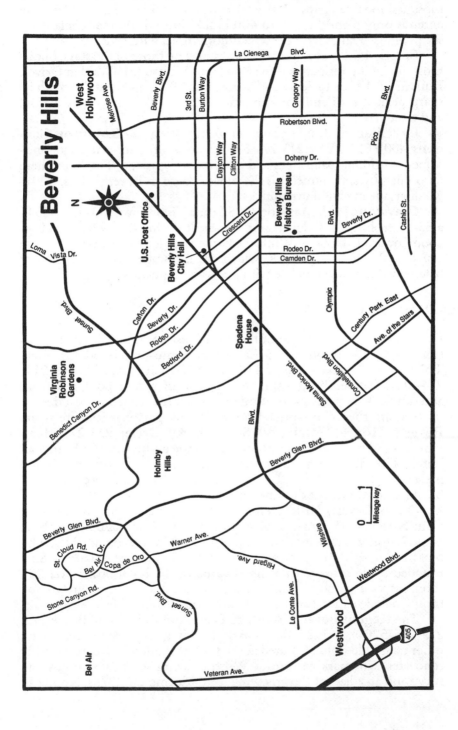

Drive, where would-be's walk with the wealthy, represents one of the most fashionable strips in the world of shopping. This gilded row extends only from the 200 to 400 block, but within that enclave are shops whose names have become synonymous with style.

Beverly Hill's most famous homes may be those of the stars, but its most intriguing residence is the **Spadena House** (516 Walden Drive). Built in 1921 as a movie set and office, this "Witch's House"—with its sharp peaked roof and cobweb ambience—evokes images of Hansel and Gretel.

By calling in advance you can tour the **Virginia Robinson Gardens** (1008 Elden Way; 213-276-5367; admission), a six-acre estate landscaped with king palm trees and a variety of gardens. The home here (also open by appointment) is the oldest house in Beverly Hills, a 1911 Mediterranean revival structure.

Greystone Park Mansion (905 Loma Vista Drive; 213-550-4654), a 55-room English Tudor manor, was built during the 1920s by oil tycoon Edward L. Doheny. While the house is closed to the public, visitors can tour the 16-acre grounds, which are landscaped in a succession of balustraded terraces complete with pools and fountains.

BEVERLY HILLS LODGING

Despite its standing as one of the wealthiest communities in the nation, Beverly Hills offers at least one moderate-priced lodging place. The **Beverly Terrace Motor Hotel** (469 North Doheny Drive; 213-274-8141) features 39 typical motel digs and includes a pool, restaurant and sun deck, as well as a location one block from Melrose Avenue.

Among the deluxe-priced hostelries my personal favorite is the **Beverly House Hotel** (140 South Lasky Drive; 213-271-2145), which is light on amenities but possesses the ambience of a European hotel. The 50 stylish guest rooms are furnished with hardwood pieces. Add a friendly staff, comfortable lobby and free continental breakfast to round out this fine small hotel.

One of Beverly Hills' premier addresses, the bright pink **Beverly Hills Hotel** (9641 Sunset Boulevard; 213-278-1487) was built way back in 1912. Today it remains a roosting place for Hollywood notables, who rent the hotel's 21 bungalows and haunt its Polo Lounge restaurant. Surrounded by 16 acres of palm-lined gardens, the hotel boasts over 200 rooms as well as shops, restaurants, pool, spa and tennis courts. Many rooms include patios, fireplaces and kitchens. Ultra-deluxe.

The **Regent Beverly Wilshire Hotel** (9500 Wilshire Boulevard; 213-275-5200), a 1928 Beaux-Arts building, represents the town's other grand old hotel. Located at the foot of Rodeo Drive, this freshly renovated landmark features a Wilshire wing with 146 rooms and suites and an adjacent Beverly wing, built during the 1970s. Rooms in the Wilshire wing are quite spacious, designed with flair and character. In the new wing each level is decorated in a different style—Mexican, Early California, etc. Ultra-deluxe.

Small and elegant, the all-suite **L'Ermitage** (9291 Burton Way; 213-278-3344) is tucked away on a quiet tree-lined street. Only the discreet sign reveals that it's a hotel. A rooftop garden terrace with a 360° view has a pool and spa filled with mineral water. Although L'Ermitage is ultra-deluxe, you're not dollared to death.

BEVERLY HILLS RESTAURANTS

Owned and frequented by celebrities, minimalist in decor, **Maple Drive** (345 North Maple Drive; 213-274-9800) has emerged as one of Beverly Hills' top trysts. Here you can dine on a number of gourmet tidbits while catching the flash and dance of Hollywood on parade. Ultra-deluxe.

Most Beverly Hills restaurants are places to be seen; **Kate Mantílini** (9101 Wilshire Boulevard; 213-278-3699) is a place to see. A kind of *Star Wars* diner, this 21st-century rendezvous is an artwork in steel and tile. A boxing mural covers an entire wall, and a sundial/skylight rises from floor to dome. For dinner there's rotisserie chicken, lamb shank and a half dozen steaks. Moderate to deluxe.

Opulence Chinese-style is the most appealing feature of **Mandarin** (430 North Camden Drive; 213-272-0267). Beautifully appointed with colored tile and carved wallhangings, this dining room offers Mongolian beef, smoked tea duck and spring crêpes. Moderate to deluxe.

Gourmet food, chic surroundings and beautiful people combine to make **Prego** (362 North Camden Drive; 213-277-7346) a popular rendezvous. This nouvelle Italian bistro serves pizza, pasta and several entrées. The kitchen is open to view, and the decor consists of modern artwork and track lights. Moderate.

Ranking among Los Angeles' finest restaurants, **La Scala** (410 North Cañon Drive; 213-275-0579) is an intimate and well-appointed dining room. Upholstered booths add to an elegant interior adorned with statues and oil paintings. The gourmets and celebrities frequenting this address also come for the excellent Italian cuisine. Ultra-deluxe.

BEVERLY HILLS SHOPPING

Without doubt, the capital of consumerism is Beverly Hills. At its heart lies the "golden triangle," an exclusive shopping district bounded by Wilshire Boulevard, Rexford Drive and Santa Monica Boulevard. The heart within the heart is, you guessed it, **Rodeo**

Drive. World-famous designer showcases like Gucci, Van Cleef and Cartier are part of the scenery. Some are soooo exclusive they open only by appointment.

The **Rodeo Collection** (421 North Rodeo Drive), a pink marble shopping complex, houses an array of designer boutiques.

The **Barakat** (429 North Rodeo Drive; 213-859-8408) collection of jewelry and art features amazing Old World antiquities, like 5th-century-B.C. Greek coins.

Eduard Nakhamkin Fine Art, Inc. (427 North Rodeo Drive; 213-550-1364) specializes in Russian emigré art.

Beverly Hills also supports several dozen art galleries, many located along Rodeo Drive. **Hanson Art Galleries** (323 North Rodeo Drive; 213-205-3922) spotlights contemporary figures such as Robert Rauschenberg and Peter Max. The breathtaking etchings by Rem-

---

STAR SEARCH

As in Hollywood, the favorite sport in Beverly Hills is stargazing. In fact, the best way to discover Hollywood is by driving through Beverly Hills.

*That Elizabethan cottage at 508 North Palm Drive was home to **Marilyn Monroe and Joe DiMaggio** in 1954 during their short and stormy marriage. The couple who lived on the next street had a happier and far more enduring marriage. If **George Burns and Gracie Allen's** place (720 North Maple Drive) looks familiar, that's because a model of the home was used for their 1950s television show.*

*Beverly Hills is nothing if not the story of marriages. The bond between **Elizabeth Taylor and Mike Todd** (1330 Schuyler Road) ended tragically in 1958 when Todd's private plane crashed over New Mexico. The couple was occupying this Mediterranean-style mansion when the movie producer died.*

***Lana Turner** and Johnny Stompanato's relationship didn't last long either. It seems that Lana's daughter, Cheryl Crane, stabbed him to death in their prim colonial house at 730 North Bedford Drive. Stompanato had threatened Turner's life during a heated argument.*

For over 60 years the winding side streets off Benedict Canyon Drive have housed a who's who of Hollywood celebrities. Today many of movieland's greatest talents still live in this wooded retreat.

*Roxbury Drive has several 1930s-era estates that celebrities once called home. **Marlene Dietrich** lived in the squarish, art deco mansion at number 822. **Jimmy Stewart** (918) set up residence in the brick Tudor house one block away, while **Lucille Ball** (1000) and **Jack Benny** (1002) lived next door to one another.*

*Newspaper baron William Randolph Hearst purchased the mansion at 1700 Lexington Road during the 1920s for his mistress, **Marion Davies**. Later in the decade **Greta Garbo** (1027 Chevy Chase Drive) moved into the neighborhood with a parrot, four cats and a chow chow.*

brandt are among the rare selections at **Galerie Michael** (430 North Rodeo Drive; 213-273-3377). A new wave of Japanese-American artists is represented at **Dyansen Gallery** (339 North Rodeo Drive; 213-275-0165). The more conservative **National Heritage Gallery of Fine Art** (315 North Rodeo Drive; 213-278-0530) features limited-edition bronzes by Harold Shelton and original paintings by Tom Perkinson.

A recent addition to this vaunted neighborhood, **Two Rodeo Drive**, is a $200-million cobblestone mall featuring about two dozen shops. Built along three levels, it's a brass-door-and-antique-street-lamp promenade reminiscent of a European boulevard.

"Little" Santa Monica Boulevard has less formal, less expensive shops, such as **Camp Beverly Hills** (9640 Little Santa Monica Boulevard; 213-274-8317), which stocks T-shirts, sweats and other Cali-

---

Pickfair (1143 Summit Drive), the estate of Douglas Fairbanks and Mary Pickford, is the most renowned of all Beverly Hills mansions. Hollywood's greatest stars, the couple lived here from 1920 until they were divorced in 1936, entertaining celebrities and royalty alike. After they parted, Mary Pickford stayed on in the mansion, dying at Pickfair in 1979. (Recently however, current owner Pia Zadora has drastically altered the place.)

Tower Road around the corner also saw its share of stars. **Juliet Prowse** *lived behind the mullioned windows at 1136;* **Arthur Rubinstein** *occupied 1139; and actor* **Spencer Tracy** *called 1158 Tower Road home.*

Greenacres, the estate of silent film comedian **Harold Lloyd** *(1740 Green Acres Place), has been reduced to a mere five acres. When Lloyd moved here in 1928 the grounds included 20 acres and were planted with 12 gardens. The house he occupied until his death in 1971 has 44 rooms, including 26 bathrooms.*

Rudolph Valentino *(1436 Bella Drive) chose the distant reaches of Benedict Canyon to escape his adoring fans. In 1925 he moved to Falcon Lair (named for his movie* The Hooded Falcon*), a magnificent mansion appointed with Renaissance art, Oriental carpets and medieval armor. Little did the young actor realize when he finally found his retreat that he would die from ulcers the next year.*

For years Hollywood's chief gossip factory was the **Beverly Hills Hotel** *(9641 Sunset Boulevard; 213-278-1487), a pink Mission revival building dating to 1912. During the 1930s the hotel's Polo Lounge attracted Darryl Zanuck, Will Rogers and other polo enthusiasts. Later its private bungalows became trysting places for celebrities. Clark Gable, Carole Lombard, Howard Hughes and Sophia Loren rented them. John Lennon and Yoko Ono holed up for a week here, Elizabeth Taylor and Richard Burton made love and war, and Marilyn Monroe reportedly entertained John and Robert Kennedy in a very private bungalow. Today the hotel's manicured grounds are tropically landscaped and well worth visiting, even when the stars are not out.*

fornia styles. **Banana Republic** (9669 Little Santa Monica Boulevard; 213-858-7900), an ever-popular emporium, sells fashionable safari clothing.

Some of the country's most famous department stores line Wilshire Boulevard between the 9600 and 9900 blocks. **Neiman-Marcus** (213-550-5900), **I. Magnin** (213-271-2131) and **Saks Fifth Avenue** (213-275-4211) are only part of this elite company. **Tiffany's** (210 North Rodeo Drive; 213-273-8880), in the stately Regent Beverly Wilshire Hotel, continues to awe and inspire.

BEVERLY HILLS NIGHTLIFE

An established Beverly Hills bar, the Old English-style **Rangoon Raquet Club** (9474 Little Santa Monica Boulevard; 213-274-8926) is very popular with the business and elite crowd.

Refined decor and sophisticated cabaret entertainment make **Romeo and Juliet** (435 North Beverly Drive; 213-273-2292) a popular Beverly Hills nightspot. Guest appearances by celebrities, as well as a lineup of regular jazz and blues performers, are the drawing cards.

Patrons of the Wilshire Theatre frequent the art deco **Christies Bar and Grill** (8442 Wilshire Boulevard; 213-655-8113) next door.

Another ritzy spot for celebrity voyeurs is **Jimmy's** (201 Moreno Drive; 213-879-2394), a lively art deco piano bar.

The **Polo Lounge** (9641 Sunset Boulevard; 213-276-2251) at the swank Beverly Hills Hotel has been a celebrity meeting place for decades.

The **Wilshire Theatre** (8440 Wilshire Boulevard; 213-410-1062), a 1929 movie house, has been restored and currently stages musicals and dramas.

Westside

Like Horace Greeley's proverbial pioneer, wealth in Los Angeles has gone west. With its elite country clubs and walled estates, the Westside has developed during the 20th century into the city's golden ghetto. Cultural diversity is defined here not so much by race and class as by whether one is already rich or simply striving to be. Business mavens from Bel Air whiz along in Maseratis, and coeds buzz by in battered Toyotas.

At UCLA in Westwood, more than 34,000 students are squeezed into one of the most valuable real estate districts in the nation. While this campus town is an odd mix of blocky apartment buildings and mundane office towers, Bel Air and Brentwood are exclusive colonies marked by manicured lawns and lofty mansions. Nearby Century

City, a former film studio, has been transformed into a futuristic city with plazas, greenswards and vaulting highrises.

WESTWOOD   To students everywhere, Westwood is the scholastic capital of Southern California. Home to UCLA, one of the largest universities in the country, the town was little more than ranch land in the early 20th century. Originally developed during the 1920s as a Mediterranean-style complex with shops and restaurants, Westwood boomed when UCLA opened in 1929. Now, with highrises continually springing up along Wilshire Boulevard, it's a major commercial center.

A sense of old Westwood pervades **Westwood Village** (centered around Westwood Boulevard), near the university. Here you can stroll past a succession of shops, many located in 1920s-era buildings of brick and wood. The Village's true identity, however, is revealed on Friday and Saturday nights, when major movies are previewed and the place becomes a world of bumper people, with traffic gridlocked and crowds milling everywhere.

Of Westwood's countless movie houses, the most inventive by far is **Mann's Village Theatre** (961 Broxton Avenue; 213-208-5576), with its lofty tower and Spanish moderne design. Built in 1931, the landmark features elevated pillars, ornamental scrollwork and a freestanding box office. The proximity of the 1937 **Mann's Bruin Theatre** (948 Broxton Avenue; 213-208-8998) across the street makes this the city's busiest crosswalk.

Just across Le Conte Avenue from this cinema center lies the **UCLA Campus**, an impressive 411-acre enclave. A true multiversity, UCLA contains 13 colleges and boasts 69 separate departments. The grounds are a labyrinth of grand staircases and brick walkways leading past 86 buildings, which constitute an architectural hodgepodge ranging from classic structures to blocky metal-and-glass highrises.

A walking tour of this tree-shaded campus begins at the **Visitor Center** (10945 Le Conte Avenue, #1417 Uberroth Building; 213-206-8147), where you can obtain information and sign up for guided tours. They can also tell you about the **Campus Express** (213-206-2908), a shuttle service around campus.

The geographic center of UCLA lies along the quadrangle at the top of **Janss Steps**. Anchoring the corners of the quad are the school's original buildings, magnificent Italian Romanesque structures dating to 1929.

Prettiest place on the entire campus is the **Franklin Murphy Sculpture Garden**, a five-acre park planted with jacaranda trees and adorned with works by Matisse, Rodin and many others. Brooding over the garden is the **Wight Art Gallery** (213-825-9345), which features classic and contemporary art.

The **Mildred Mathias Botanical Garden,** an enchanting spot in the southeastern corner of campus, displays over 400 tropical and subtropical plant species within its eight-acre domain. Visits to the **Hannah Carter Japanese Garden,** a traditional rock garden with teahouse and footbridges, can be arranged through the visitor's center.

WESTSIDE LODGING

Just one block from the UCLA campus, **Hilgard House Hotel** (927 Hilgard Avenue, Westwood; 213-208-3945) is a spiffy new brick building with 47 rooms at deluxe prices. Accommodations in this three-story structure are furnished with facsimile antiques; many have jacuzzis.

Directly across the street, but a big step uptown, stands the **Westwood Marquis Hotel and Garden** (930 Hilgard Avenue, Westwood; 213-208-8765), a 15-floor, all-suite hotel. This liveried-doorman establishment is beautifully appointed with fine furnishings and antique decorations. The many amenities include two pools and a complete health spa. Ultra-deluxe.

Del Capri Hotel (10587 Wilshire Boulevard, Westwood; 213-474-3511) is a bright, cozy complex complete with two tiers of rooms encircling a pool terrace. The tile baths include jacuzzi bathtubs; continental breakfast; deluxe.

CENTURY CITY

If Beverly Hills is the ultimate in residential communities, **Century City** *represents the final word in business centers. A former film studio converted into a futuristic city, this 180-acre highrise heaven is built of office towers and broad boulevards. The plazas and greenswards in this pre-planned metropolis are balanced by the* **ABC Entertainment Center** *(Avenue of the Stars), a megasized complex with shops, theaters and movie houses. The* **Century Plaza Hotel** *across the street is a twin-tower city in itself, a 1000-room hotel that vies with Century City's other metal-and-glass palaces for prominence and includes the top-rated California continental restaurant* **La Chaumière** *(213-277-2000).*

In addition to a business center, the ABC Entertainment Center makes Century City a top nightspot. The **Schubert Theatre** *(800-233-3123) can pack 1825 people into its cavernous facility for Broadway plays with top-bill casts.* **Harry's Bar and American Grill** *(213-277-2333), a replica of Harry's Bar in Florence, caters to the after-theater crowd. The New York-style* **Avenue Saloon** *(213-553-1855) features an open-air patio with views of the city lights.*

Los Angeles' most Eden-like address lies in a forested canyon surrounded by peach and apricot trees. A classic country inn, the **Hotel Bel Air** (701 Stone Canyon Road, Bel Air; 213-472-1211) is an exclusive 92-room complex and private haven for show business celebrities and European royalty. The 1920s Mission-style buildings are shaded by a luxuriant garden of palms and redwoods. A stream tumbles through the property, creating waterfalls and a pool with swans. Numbering among the nation's finest hotels, the Bel Air also provides an oval swimming pool and gourmet restaurant. Ultra-deluxe.

WESTSIDE RESTAURANTS

A campus hangout, **Stratton's Grill** (1037 Broxton Avenue, Westwood; 213-208-0488) is a turn-of-the-century saloon with a spectacular marble-and-hardwood bar. There are wood-slat booths along the walls for diners. Selections range from sandwiches to mesquite-grilled steak. Moderate.

Alice's Restaurant (1043 Westwood Boulevard, Westwood; 213-208-3171) has taken an antique building with marble floors and molded ceilings, then added neon signs and a brass rail bar. The effect is an odd mix of old and new. Fare includes grilled swordfish, seafood brochettes and chicken dijon. Moderate.

Farther south on Westwood Boulevard there is a string of ethnic restaurants worth trying. **La Bruschetta** (1621 Westwood Boulevard, Westwood; 213-477-1052) serves high Italian cuisine. Vibrant artwork decorates the place. Moderate to deluxe.

The flavor is Persian at **Shamshiry Restaurant** (1916 Westwood Boulevard, Westwood; 213-474-1410), a pleasant dining room with latticework booths and hanging plants. Moderate.

Enjoying a reputation for righteous Cajun food, **Patout's** (2260 Westwood Boulevard; 213-475-7100) is a chic cafe with a knack for Louisiana tradition. The ever-evolving menu might include crawfish pasta or Louisiana Bluepoint crab. There's an open-view kitchen. Moderate to deluxe.

All those two-wheelers suspended from the ceiling give the **Bicycle Shop Cafe** (12217 Wilshire Boulevard, West Los Angeles; 213-826-7831) its name. This casual bistro offers pasta, quiche and entrées like swordfish and scampi. Moderate.

Finding a restaurant with reasonable prices in Bel Air is a challenging feat, especially as you ascend the hills. At **Four Oaks Restaurant** (2181 North Beverly Glen Boulevard; 213-470-2265) you encounter a French dining room with deluxe prices. This comfortable and intimate spot is illuminated through skylights and features a brick patio for dining alfresco. Entrées include roasted lamb with sweet garlic and grilled medallion of veal with pesto crème.

The restaurant at the **Hotel Bel-Air** (701 Stone Canyon Road; 213-472-1211) is so low-key it doesn't even have a name. This is no glitzy, glamorous monument to gastronomy. At the end of a graceful arcade in the hotel's mission-style main building, its understated decor soothes diners who settle into comfortable Queen Anne chairs. A menu of topnotch continental/American food caters to the worldly, well-heeled patron looking for a traditional meal in a comfortable atmosphere. Ultra-deluxe.

WESTSIDE SHOPPING

Westwood houses a shopping district large enough to wear a hole in any shopper's shoes (and purse). **Westwood Village,** located along Westwood Boulevard adjacent to UCLA, is the Westside's premier shopping and entertainment district. Designed with the pedestrian in mind, "the village" is frequented by college crowds and fashionable Westside residents alike.

One of the most noteworthy shops, **Contempo Casuals** (1081 Westwood Boulevard; 213-208-8503), happens to be located in the oldest building in Westwood, a 1929 Mediterranean-style beauty. Ironically, this upbeat emporium specializes in ultracontemporary clothing for women.

Bookstores, of course, are a Westwood specialty. Among the finest is **Butler/Gabriel Books** (213-208-4424), a dual-location store with photography, architecture, art and cookbooks at 901 Westwood Boulevard, and fiction, cinema, travel and children's books in its 919 Westwood Boulevard store. If you can't find the title at either address, browse the 2000 to 2300 blocks of Westwood Boulevard, affection-ately known as "Booksellers Row."

Westside Pavilion (10800 West Pico Boulevard, West Los Ange-les), an urban mall designed by the architects of the 1984 Olympics, is a glass atrium affair with 150 shops. Among the independent shops is **Future Tronics** (213-470-7827), with every gadget from dancing Coke cans to radios shaped like parking meters. **Shaunzo's Hat City** (213-475-2085) designs its own line of headgear and claims to be the largest hat store in the country.

Commercial establishments in well-heeled Brentwood center around San Vicente Boulevard, a beautiful tree-lined street. **P. J. London** (11661 San Vicente Boulevard; 213-826-4649) is Brent-wood's ultimate resale shop, offering designer clothes handed down from wealthy Westside and Malibu residents. **Brentwood Country Mart** (26th Street and San Vicente Boulevard), a village-style shop-ping complex, features several dozen stores. Located in another small shopping center, **Martin Lawrence Galleries** (11701 Wilshire Boulevard; 213-479-5566) features limited editions and original works by major 20th-century artists.

Westwood Village bubbles with nighttime activity. Students and moviegoers crowd the sidewalks and spill into the streets, some heading for the clubs. Looking somewhat like a European cafe, **Bon Appétit** (1061 Broxton Avenue, Westwood; 213-208-3830) serves up jazz, blues and rhythm-and-blues in two nightly shows. Cover.

San Francisco Saloon and Grill (11501 West Pico Boulevard, West Los Angeles; 213-478-0152) is a small, cozy fern bar. Wood paneling, historic photos of San Francisco, and comfortable surroundings create a sense of intimacy.

The **UCLA Center for the Performing Arts** (James West Center, Westwood; 213-825-9261) holds performances on campus.

For escaping the college crowds, there's **Westwood Lounge** (930 Hilgard Avenue, Westwood; 213-208-8765), a restful piano bar in the gracious Westwood Marquis Hotel.

Igby's Comedy Cabaret (11637 Tennessee Place, West Los Angeles; 213-477-3553) headlines known and unknown comedians. Cover.

Hidden in a forested Bel Air canyon, **The Bar** (701 Stone Canyon Road; 213-472-1211) at the Bel Air Hotel is the perfect place for an intimate cocktail.

Pasadena Area

Tucked between the downtown district and the lofty San Gabriel Mountains lies the San Gabriel Valley. Extending east from the San Fernando Valley toward San Bernardino, this former orange-growing empire has developed into a suburban realm noted for its wealth, botanic gardens and smog.

Back in 1771, when 14 soldiers, two priests and several mule drivers founded a mission in San Gabriel, they laid claim to an outpost that controlled the entire countryside, including Los Angeles Pueblo. The priests became land barons as the region was divided into vineyards, cattle ranches and olive groves. In the mid-19th century American settlers further transformed the valley into an oasis of lemon and orange trees.

By the late-19th century Pasadena was supplanting San Gabriel as the cultural heart of the San Gabriel Valley. Boasting an ideal climate, it billed itself as a health lover's paradise and became a celebrated resort area. Its tree-trimmed boulevards were lined with Beaux-Arts, Mediterranean, Italian Renaissance and Victorian houses.

Today the original downtown district has been transformed into **Old Town**, a ten square block neighborhood of modern galleries and gourmet restaurants (bordered by Holly and Green streets, Pasadena Avenue and Arroyo Parkway).

Orienting visitors to the old and the new is the **Pasadena Convention and Visitors Bureau** (171 South Los Robles Avenue; 818-795-9311). They'll tell you that the best place to begin touring the town is **Pasadena City Hall** (100 North Garfield Avenue), a 1925 baroque building with a spectacular tile dome, courtyard and formal gardens.

Also stop at the **Pacific Asia Museum** (46 North Los Robles Avenue; 818-449-2742; admission), a Chinese palace-style building dedicated to Oriental art and culture. The museum showcases paintings, statuary, stoneware and porcelain.

Then drive out Colorado Boulevard, route of the New Year's Day Rose Parade, to the **Norton Simon Museum of Art** (411 West Colorado Boulevard; 818-449-6840; admission). Housed in this odd-looking edifice is one of the finest collections of European and Asian art in the country. Touring the Simon's several galleries is like striding through time and space. The works span 2500 years, traveling from

---

HUNTINGTON MUSEUMS AND GARDENS

*One of Southern California's most spectacular complexes and certainly the premier attraction in the San Gabriel Valley is the **Huntington Library, Art Collections and Botanical Gardens** (1151 Oxford Road, San Marino; 818-405-2273; admission).*

*The focal point of railroad tycoon Henry E. Huntington's 207-acre aesthetic preserve, the **Huntington Gallery**, was originally his home. Today the mansion is dedicated to 18th- and 19th-century English and French art and houses one of the finest collections of its kind in the country. Gainsborough's Blue Boy is here, as well as paintings by Turner and Van Dyck, tapestries, porcelains and furniture. Another gallery contains Renaissance paintings and French sculpture from the 18th century; the **Virginia Steele Scott Gallery of American Art**, housed in an enchanting building, traces American painting from 1730 to 1930.*

*Moving from oil to ink and from mansion to mansion, the **Huntington Library** contains one of the world's finest collections of rare British and American manuscripts and first editions.*

This describes only the buildings on the property! There are also the grounds, a heavenly labyrinth of gardens ranging from a verdant jungle setting to the austerely elegant Desert Garden. Rolling lawns are adorned with Italian statuary, and the Japanese garden features an arched bridge, koi pond and 16th-century teahouse.

ancient India and Southeast Asia to the world of contemporary art and including paintings by Rembrandt, Reubens, Raphael and Cézanne.

Another mansion with meaning is the imposing 1905 edifice hosting the **Pasadena Historical Society Museum** (470 West Walnut Street; 818-577-1660; admission). Besides the furnishings and keepsakes from Pasadena's early days, this neoclassical house showcases Finnish folk art and gardens, since it was once home to the Finnish consul.

Humbling all these estates is the **Gamble House** (4 Westmoreland Place; 818-793-3334; admission), jewel of Pasadena, a Craftsman-style bungalow designed in 1908. Heavily influenced by such Japanese innovations as overhanging roofs and pagoda flourishes, the wood shingle home is a warm blend of hand-rubbed teak and Tiffany glass.

Grandest of all the area's architectural achievements is the **Rose Bowl** (1001 Rose Bowl Drive; 818-577-3100). Built in 1902, this 104,700-seat stadium is the home for UCLA's football team and the site of the New Year's Day clash between the Big Ten and the Pacific Athletic Conference. The stadium is open to the public on weekdays.

Students with a more scientific bent are cracking the books at **Cal Tech** (California Institute of Technology, 1201 East California Boulevard; 818-356-6811), an internationally renowned science and engineering school whose faculty has won 21 Nobel Prizes and once included Albert Einstein. These hallowed halls, in case you were wondering, were modeled on a medieval cloister. There are campus tours daily.

While the big kids play with numbers, the little ones are fidgeting with hands-on exhibits—including fire-fighting equipment and a recording studio—at **Kidspace Museum** (390 South El Molino Avenue; 818-449-9144; admission).

El Molino Viejo (1120 Old Mill Road, San Marino; 818-449-5450), the Old Mill, represents a vital part of the area's Spanish tradition. Built in 1816 by Indians from San Gabriel Mission, it was Southern California's first water-powered grist mill. Only the millstones remain from the actual mill, but the building, an enchanting adobe beauty with red tile roof, is still intact.

Fourth in California's historic chain of missions, **Mission San Gabriel Archangel** (537 West Mission Drive, San Gabriel; 818-282-5191) is an oasis in an urban setting. Built in 1771, the church's buttressed walls and vaulted roof indicate Moorish influences and lend a fortress-like quality. But inside the sanctuary peace reigns: the grounds are covered in cactus gardens and grape arbors and are flanked by a cemetery.

The **Los Angeles State and County Arboretum** (301 North Baldwin Avenue, Arcadia; 818-446-8251; admission) may be the most photographed location in the world. Everything from Tarzan movies to Bing Crosby's *Road to Singapore* has been filmed in this 127-acre garden. With plants from every corner of the globe, it has portrayed Burma, Africa and Devil's Island.

The history of the surrounding region is captured in several historic structures still standing on the grounds. There are *wickiups* similar to those of the original Gabrieleño Indians. Representing the Spanish era is the Hugo Reid Adobe, an 1839 structure built with over 15,000 mud bricks. The Queen Anne Cottage is a castle-in-the-sky dream house, painted white with red stripes and topped by a turret. Also part of this complex is the 1890 Santa Anita Depot, filled with memorabilia from the great age of railroads.

In the trim little town of Claremont, the enchanting **Rancho Santa Ana Botanic Garden** (1500 North College Avenue; 714-625-8767) boasts the largest collection of native California plants in the world. Wandering its nature trails is like touring a miniature version of natural California.

NIXON SLEPT HERE

*There are hundreds, perhaps thousands of reasons to visit Los Angeles. But could any be as important as a **Richard Nixon pilgrimage**? Think about it, a sacred visit to the hometown of the only president who ever resigned from office.*

*Anyone who has ever heard a maudlin Nixon speech knows Whittier, where the 37th president was raised, schooled and elected to Congress. The **Whittier Chamber of Commerce** (8158 Painter Avenue; 213-698-9554), still proud of their native son, can provide information on Nixon points of interest.*

*Among the highlights are **East Whittier Elementary School** (Whittier Boulevard and Gunn Avenue), the Spanish-style campus of **Whittier College** (Painter Avenue and Philadelphia Street), where Nixon received his diploma in 1934, and the home at **14033 Honeysuckle Lane** where the young Congressman lived in 1946.*

*The Nixon family store was tragically converted into a gas station, but the **Pat Ryan Nixon House** (13513 Terrace Place), where the future First Lady lived when she met her husband, still stands.*

*Of course the true pilgrimage is to the **Richard Nixon Library** (18001 Yorba Linda Boulevard, Yorba Linda; 714-993-3393; admission). Here you'll find the 900-square-foot home (that "made up in love what it lacked in size") where Nixon was born "on the coldest day of one of the coldest winters in California history." Indeed.*

The library itself, with barely a book to be seen, is a marvelous succession of movies, interactive videos and touch-screen presentations that rewrite American history in a fashion that would make even a novelist blush.

PASADENA AREA LODGING

Over $100 million was poured into the revered **Ritz Carlton Huntington Hotel** (1401 South Oak Knoll Avenue, Pasadena; 818-568-3900), returning the 1907 grande dame to her turn-of-the-century glory. Situated on 20 manicured acres, this 383-room hotel combines modern amenities with the style and charm of another era. The Olympic-size swimming pool (reputed to be the first in California) has been restored, as have the hotel's Japanese and Horseshoe gardens and Georgian dining room. If you are seeking Old World elegance, this is the address. Ultra-deluxe.

PASADENA AREA RESTAURANTS

One of the San Gabriel Valley's best food bargains is the budget-priced **Restaurant Mérida** (20 East Colorado, Pasadena; 818-792-7371). Serving Yucatán-style dishes, this brick-walled eatery offers items like *birria de chivo* (goat in spicy sauce), as well as enchiladas and burritos. Patio courtyard.

East meets best at **Tra Fiori Ristorante** (9 North Raymond Avenue; 818-796-2233), where the chef is Japanese but the cuisine is Italian with a California/Oriental twist. Decorated with rotating contemporary art, this popular dining room serves everything from sashimi layered with wonton skins to duck in raspberry sauce. The service is equal to the cuisine. Deluxe.

At **Pappagallo** (42 South Pasadena Avenue; 818-578-0224) the taste runs to North Italian. With its dining atrium and open patio Pappagallo prepares duck lasagna and tortellini Sicilian amid an atmosphere of casual elegance. Moderate.

Tucked away in an art deco building on a side street, **Bistro 45** (45 South Mentor Avenue; 818-792-2535) is the newest gathering spot for Pasadena's "elegancia." The airy high-tech atmosphere, pastel walls and contemporary art match the handsomely presented California cuisine. The menu includes charbroiled free-range chicken with roasted peppers, grilled ahi in a basil sauce bièrge, and sautéed muscovy duck in raspberry sauce. Deluxe.

Foremost among Pasadena's California cuisine spots is **Parkway Grill** (510 South Arroyo Parkway; 818-795-1001), a brick-wall-and-bare-beam restaurant with track lights, stained glass and, *naturellement*, an open-view kitchen. The chefs prepare gourmet pizza, pasta dishes and entrées such as catfish in lime-soy sauce. Moderate to deluxe.

If you visit San Gabriel it will doubtless be to see the Spanish mission, so the most appropriate place to dine is nearby **Panchito's** (261 South Mission Drive; 818-289-9201), a Mexican restaurant down the street. Housed in a historic building that served as the town's original city hall, it offers an array of Mexican and gringo fare. Moderate.

East conquers West at **Chez Sateau** (850 South Baldwin Avenue, Arcadia; 818-446-8806), where a Japanese chef prepares French meals with special flair. The frosted-glass-and-private-booth dining room features poached salmon, sand dabs meunière and steak Diane. Moderate to deluxe.

PASADENA AREA SHOPPING

Shopping in the San Gabriel Valley centers around Pasadena, specifically the prestigious **South Lake Avenue**, where Bullocks and other department stores are joined by a host of small, sophisticated shops.

Among the high points are **The Chocolate Giraffe** (516 South Lake Avenue; 818-796-5437), a delightful children's boutique, and the elegant **Harold Grant of California** (238 South Lake Avenue; 818-405-8940), selling top-designer clothes for women.

Also stop by **The Colonnade** (350 South Lake Avenue; 818-796-8737), a small arcade that houses **Kokila's Boutique** (818-584-1157), where you'll find natural fiber fashions for women, and **Dirk Cable, Bookseller** (818-449-7001), specializing in rare books on California and the West. **Burlington Arcade** (380 South Lake Avenue), modeled after The Burlington in London, is another elegant gallery of specialty shops.

Just west of South Lake Avenue, visit **Haskett Court** (824 East California Boulevard), a charming group of English-style cottages. Here at the **Rose Tree Cottages**, you can browse for fine British imports or enjoy afternoon tea in a traditional setting. Reservations required for tea (818-793-3337).

Another major Pasadena shopping district lies along **Colorado Boulevard**. Here you'll find **Vroman's Bookstore** (695 East Colorado Boulevard; 818-449-5320), one of the area's oldest and finest booksellers.

Anchoring the entire street is **Plaza Pasadena** (between Marengo and Los Robles avenues), a megamall with over 100 stores. About 20 fine jewelers are represented across the street at **Pasadena Jewelry Mart** (440 East Colorado Boulevard; 818-449-9096).

Among the art galleries on Colorado Boulevard is **Lizardi/Harp** (290 West Colorado Boulevard; 818-792-8336), a contemporary studio representing both new and established artists.

Pasadena's current beautification and redevelopment program reaches its apogee in **Old Town** (bordered by Holly and Green streets, Pasadena Avenue and Arroyo Parkway). Particularly prevalent in this gentrified ghetto are antique stores and designer boutiques.

You'll also discover every kind of antique, collectible and curiosity at **Holly Street Bazaar** (16 East Holly Street; 818-449-6919), where more than a dozen dealers display their wares, and at the **Pasadena Antique Center** (480 South Fair Oaks Avenue; 818-449-7706), which houses more than 45 antique dealers.

Touted as the world's largest swap meet, the **Rose Bowl Flea Market** (1001 Rose Bowl Drive; 213-588-4411; admission) is a bargain hunter's heaven held on the second Sunday of each month.

Elsewhere in the San Gabriel Valley, there's **Santa Anita Fashion Park** (Baldwin Avenue and Huntington Drive, Arcadia), a colossal 150-store mall adjacent to Santa Anita Racetrack.

PASADENA AREA NIGHTLIFE

Like most everything else in the San Gabriel Valley, the entertainment scene centers around Pasadena.

Monahan's (110 South Lake Avenue, Pasadena; 818-449-4151), the quintessential Irish pub, is known for its friendly bartenders and Saint Patrick's Day extravaganzas. They also feature cabaret-style entertainment.

A woodsy decor and cozy fireplace set the stage at the **Sawmill** (340 South Lake Avenue, Pasadena; 818-796-8388), where Top-40 and country-and-western entertainers perform nightly.

SAN GABRIEL MOUNTAINS

With their sharp-faced cliffs and granite outcroppings, the San Gabriel Mountains form a natural barrier between the Los Angeles Basin and the Mojave Desert. They rise from the San Gabriel Valley to over 6000 feet in elevation. Embodied in the 691,000-acre Angeles National Forest, these dry, semibarren mountains are a mix of high chaparral, pine forest and rocky terrain.

*For an easygoing introduction to these heights, tour **Eaton Canyon Nature Center** (1750 North Altadena Drive, Pasadena; 818-398-5420). Set in the foothills, this 164-acre park mixes flora from both ocean and mountain regions.*

*Another of the region's botanic preserves, **Descanso Gardens** (1418 Descanso Drive, La Cañada; 818-952-4400; admission), stretches across 165 acres at the foot of the San Gabriels. This former estate has the largest camellia garden in the world, numbering 100,000 plants, as well as a rose garden and Japanese teahouse and garden.*

To fully explore the San Gabriel Mountains, follow the Angeles Crest Highway (Route 2) in its sinuous course upward from La Cañada. A side road from Route 2 leads to 5710-foot Mount Wilson, from which you can gaze across the entire expanse of Los Angeles to the Pacific.

The Ice House (24 North Mentor Avenue, Pasadena; 818-577-1894) presents new and established comedians nightly. Another section of the 1920s-era ice house, **Footsies**, features comedians and live music. Cover.

A cabaret-style dinner club, **Maldonados** (1202 East Green Street, Pasadena; 818-796-1126) entertains diners with Broadway musical medleys and light opera, sometimes by stage veterans. Reservations recommended for dinner, but you can see the show from the small bar.

At **Dodsworth** (2 West Colorado Boulevard, Pasadena; 818-578-1344), a New York-style restaurant and lounge, you'll find a tony crowd at the marble bar listening to live jazz.

San Fernando Valley

Sprawling across 177 square miles and containing a population of more than 1.3 million suburbanites, the San Fernando Valley is an inland version of Los Angeles. This mirror image across the mountains, known simply as "The Valley," is a smog-shrouded gridwork of tract homes and shopping malls, a kind of stucco version of the American Dream.

The portal to the land of the living, some say, is through the gates of death. In the San Fernando Valley that would be **Forest Lawn** (1712 South Glendale Avenue, Glendale; 818-241-4151), one of the most spectacular cemeteries in the world. Within the courtyards of this hillside retreat are replicas of Michelangelo's *David*, Ghiberti's *Baptism of Jesus*, and John Trumbull's painting *The Signing of the Declaration of Independence*. There are also re-creations of a 10th-century English church and another from 14th-century Scotland.

Far simpler in effect is the **Casa Adobe de San Rafael** (1330 Dorothy Drive, Glendale), a single-story, mud-brick home built in the 19th century and featuring lovely landscaped grounds.

Rising above it all, situated in the foothills overlooking Glendale, is the **Brand Library & Art Center** (1601 West Mountain Street; 818-548-2051). While neither the library nor the galleries are exceptional, both are set in **El Miradero**, a unique 1904 mansion modeled after the East Indian Pavilion of the 1893 Columbian World Exposition. With bulbous towers, crenelated archways and minarets, the building combines Spanish, Moorish and Indian motifs.

Local history is preserved at **Rancho de los Encinos State Historical Park** (16756 Moorpark Street, Encino; 818-784-4849), a five-acre facility studded with orange trees. The De La Ossa Adobe, built in 1850 and utilized as a resting place along El Camino Real, is a squat eight-room ranch house. Nearby stands the Garnier Building, a two-story limestone residence constructed in 1873 after the fashion of a French farmhouse.

Farther out in The Valley lies the town of Calabasas, which prides itself on a Wild West heritage but looks suspiciously like surrounding suburban towns. It does possess a few remnants from its romantic past, including the **Leonis Adobe** (23537 Calabasas Road; 818-712-0734), an 1844 mud-brick house expanded around 1879 into a stately two-story home with porches on both levels. Next door stands the **Plummer House**, an antique Victorian.

An ersatz but enchanting version of the Old West awaits at **Paramount Ranch** (2813 Cornell Road, Agoura; 818-597-9192), a 335-acre park that once served as the film location for Westerns. Today you

---

GRIFFITH PARK

Every great city boasts a great park. In San Francisco, it's Golden Gate Park, in New York, Central Park. In Los Angeles, **Griffith Park** *(entrances near Western Canyon Road, Vermont Avenue, Riverside Drive and Route 5) is the place. Set astride the Hollywood Hills, this 4000-acre facility offers a flatlands area complete with golf courses and picnic areas, plus a vast hillside section featuring meadows and forests.*

Along Crystal Springs Drive, traversing the eastern edge of the park, you'll pass the **Griffith Park & Southern Railroad** *(213-664-6788), a miniature train ride; nearby is a track offering* **pony rides** *(213-664-3266). The* **ranger station** *(213-665-5188) will provide maps and information while directing you across the street to the* **merry-go-round**, *a beautiful 1926-vintage carousel.*

Featuring real-life versions of the same animals, the **L.A. Zoo** *(5333 Zoo Drive; 213-666-4650; admission) is among the highlights of the park. Over 2000 animals inhabit this 113-acre facility, many in environments simulating their natural habitats.*

Travel Town *(5200 Zoo Drive; 213-662-9678; admission) is a transportation museum featuring a train yard full of cabooses, steam engines and passenger cars from the glory days of the railroad.*

For Hollywood's version of American history, there's the **Gene Autry Western Heritage Museum** *(4700 Zoo Drive; 213-667-2000; admission). The focus here is more on Westerns than the West. There are displays of saloons and stagecoaches, silver saddles and ivory-handled six-shooters, plus photos and film-clips of all your favorite stars, kids.*

Standing above the urban fray at the southern end of the park is the **Griffith Observatory and Planetarium** *(Observatory Drive; 213-664-1191), a copper-domed beauty featuring bas-reliefs and interior murals. The observatory includes the Planetarium Theatre and space-age Laserium (admission) complete with high-tech light shows. But a lot of people come simply for the view, which on clear days (in Los Angeles?) extends from the Hollywood Hills to the Pacific.*

can hike around the ranch. "Western Town" still stands, a collection of falsefront buildings housing a local bank, feed store and Wells Fargo office.

Orcutt Ranch Horticultural Center (23600 Roscoe Boulevard, West Hills; 818-883-6641), once a private estate, is now an outdoor museum in full bloom with rose gardens. citrus orchards and oak groves.

The **Tujunga Wash Mural** (Coldwater Canyon Boulevard between Burbank Boulevard and Oxnard Street, North Hollywood), one of Southern California's local wonders, is reputedly the world's longest mural. Extending for one-half mile, it portrays the history of California from prehistoric times to the present.

Among the finest of California's missions, **Mission San Fernando Rey de España** (15151 San Fernando Mission Boulevard, Mission Hills; 818-361-0186; admission) has been beautifully restored and reconstructed. Exploring the gardens and courtyards of this 1796 institution, visitors encounter the workshops of resident weavers, blacksmiths and carpenters, as well as an excellent collection of altar furnishings and religious oil paintings.

Nearby stands Los Angeles' second oldest house. Built before 1834 by mission Indians, the **Andrés Pico Adobe** (10940 Sepulveda Boulevard, Mission Hills; 818-365-7810) is a prime example of Spanish architecture. Just in case you thought Los Angeles County was entirely urban, there are 314 acres of oak forest and native chaparral at **Placerita Canyon State and County Park** (19152 Placerita Canyon Road, Newhall; 805-259-7721). A stream runs through the property, and there are hiking trails and a nature center.

Over at **William S. Hart Park** (24151 Newhall Avenue, Newhall; 805-259-0855) there's another 246-acre spread once owned by a great star of silent Westerns. While much of the property is wild, open to hikers and explorers, the most alluring parts are the buildings, including the old ranch house that was once Hart's office. The central feature is Hart's home, a 22-room Spanish hacienda filled with guns, cowboy paintings and collectibles from the early West.

California's haunting history of earthquakes is evident at **Vasquez Rocks County Park** (Escondido Road, northeast of Newhall off Route 14; 805-268-0840), where faulting action has compressed, folded and twisted giant slabs of sandstone. Tilted to 50° angles and rising 150 feet, these angular blocks create a setting that has been used for countless Westerns as well as science fiction films such as *Star Trek* (1979) and *Star Wars* (1977).

Shifting from the natural to the unnatural, **Six Flags Magic Mountain** (26101 Magic Mountain Parkway, Valencia; 818-367-5965; admission) is a colossal theme park spreading across 260 acres and featuring more than 100 rides. They include the Viper, a 188-

foot-high megacoaster, reputedly the highest looping roller coaster in the world. We're talking three vertical loops, plus a boomerang and corkscrew, all taken at 70 miles per hour. There are also gentler rides for small children (like the classic 1912 carousel), as well as a dolphin and sea lion show.

SAN FERNANDO VALLEY LODGING

The Safari Inn (1911 West Olive Avenue, Burbank; 818-845-8586) is that rarest of creatures, a motel with soul. In fact this 103-room facility also possesses a pool, jacuzzi, restaurant, lounge and an adjacent hotel. The location for several movies, it offers motel rooms at moderate prices and hotel accommodations, some with kitchens, in the deluxe range.

Universal City is big on highrise hotels. Among the most luxurious is the **Hilton Hotel** (555 Universal Terrace Parkway; 818-506-2500), an ultramodern 24-story steel-and-glass structure. Guest rooms are contemporary in decor and feature plate-glass views of the surrounding city. Among the amenities are a pool, jacuzzi and exercise room. Ultra-deluxe.

Cinderblock construction belies the charm of **Sportsman Lodge Hotel** (12825 Ventura Boulevard, Studio City; 818-769-4700). Hidden within this 200-room English country-style establishment are gardens with waterfalls and footbridges, as well as a pool stocked with trout. The interior courtyard contains a swimming pool. Deluxe.

Adding to the Valley's hospitality industry is the 15-story **Warner Center Hilton** (6360 Canoga Avenue, Woodland Hills; 818-595-1000). The updated art deco look extends from the lobby to the 327 soft pastel guest rooms and suites. The concierge level features a two-story lounge with sweeping mountain views. Suites offer wet bars; other amenities include a restaurant, gourmet dining room, nightclub and lobby bar. Deluxe to ultra-deluxe.

Set in a quiet North Hollywood residential neighborhood, **La Maida House and Bungalows** (11159 La Maida Street; 818-769-3857) is a gracious Old World villa built in the early 1920s. The house boasts extensive use of marble, oak and mahogany. Eleven airy rooms and suites are decorated in antiques, and many feature private patios. Pool. Deluxe to ultra-deluxe.

SAN FERNANDO VALLEY RESTAURANTS

The most striking feature at **Fresco Ristorante** (514 South Brand Boulevard, Glendale; 818-247-5541) is the interior. The whitewashed stucco, formed into a series of columns, creates a Mediterranean atmosphere. In addition to a dozen pasta dishes, this Italian kitchen features entrées like grilled swordfish with pine nuts. Moderate to deluxe.

For continental cuisine choose **Phoenicia** (343 North Central Avenue, Glendale; 818-956-7800), an intimate dining room with a reputation for fine dining. The interior features a contemporary pastel design, and the gourmet menu offers such enticements as rack of lamb and lobster tail with escargot sauce. Moderate to deluxe.

La Serre (12969 Ventura Boulevard, Studio City; 818-990-0500), which means The Greenhouse in French, impeccably serves quiet meals amid a profusion of beautifully tended plants. This is where executives from nearby studios come for power lunching in private white-latticed corners. The cuisine is superb. Chef Jean-Pierre Peiny's seasonal offerings include boneless rabbit with cinnamon and port, and pheasant with juniper berries. Ultra-deluxe.

The decor at **Teru Sushi** (11940 Ventura Boulevard, Studio City; 818-763-6201) is as inviting as the food, with hand-painted walls, a long dark wood sushi bar and a garden dining area with a koi pond. Besides sushi, they serve a selection of traditional dishes. Deluxe.

All the critics agree that the food at **Anajak Thai** (14704 Ventura Boulevard, Sherman Oaks; 818-501-4201) is outstanding. The menu features more than four dozen noodle, curry, beef and chicken dishes. Budget.

For French food and charming intimacy try **Mon Grenier** (18040 Ventura Boulevard, Encino; 818-344-8060). With a name that translates as "my attic," this whimsical dining room has a solid reputation for fine cuisine. Dinner only. Ultra-deluxe.

The **Sagebrush Cantina** (23527 Calabasas Road; 818-888-6062), out in the town of Calabasas, is a sprawling restaurant and bar with a sawdust-floor dining room and ample patio space. In addition to an assortment of Mexican dishes, they feature steak and ribs. Moderate.

A true conversation piece, the **94th Aero Squadron** (16320 Raymer Street, Van Nuys; 818-994-7437) is a wildly imaginative es-

---

SADDLE PEAK LODGE

*Way up in the Santa Monica Mountains, you'll uncover a rare find. **Saddle Peak Lodge** (419 Cold Canyon Road, Calabasas; 213-655-9770), a true country lodge, sits in an antique building constructed of logs lashed together with leather straps. Flintlocks and trophy heads adorn the walls, and leather-upholstered chairs surround a stone fireplace. Open for dinner and weekend brunch, the restaurant offers quail, buffalo burgers, game hen, rack of lamb and "kick ass chili"; deluxe.*

tablishment obliquely modeled after a World War I aviation head-quarters in France. The building resembles a provincial French farm-house, but it's surrounded by charred airplanes and other artifacts of war. The cuisine, that somehow seems irrelevant, is French and American. Moderate to deluxe.

SAN FERNANDO VALLEY SHOPPING

Out in "The Valley," shopping is such popular sport that the area has bred a new species—"mallies"—who inhabit the shopping malls from the moment the stores open until the second they close.

Shopping in Glendale centers around the **Glendale Galleria** (Central Avenue and Broadway), a mammoth 240-store complex anchored by such heavies as **The Broadway** (818-240-8411) and **Nordstrom** (818-502-9922).

Glendale's more personalized businesses still reside around Brand Boulevard (between California Avenue and Colorado Street). **Novotny's Antiques** (228 North Orange Street; 818-246-9800) has a grandma's attic worth of memorabilia, antiques and old records. If it happens to be the first Sunday of the month, add the **Glendale Civic Auditorium** (1401 North Verdugo Road; 818-548-2147) to your list of must-see addresses. That's when more than 100 antique dealers gather to sell their wares.

Stacked to the rafters with vintage Walt Disney mementos, **Nickelodeon** (13826 Ventura Boulevard, Sherman Oaks; 818-981-5325) is a surprising and welcome discovery.

The **Sherman Oaks Galleria** (15301 Ventura Boulevard, Sherman Oaks) is an atrium-style mall with a host of high-class shops and big department stores.

Strange as it may sound here in Shopperland, there are no department stores at **Town and Country Shopping Center** and **Plaza de Oro** (17200 Ventura Boulevard, Encino). These beautifully landscaped, multitiered plazas provide for more relaxed shopping and offer everything from clothing to chocolate.

Out in Calabasas, you'll discover a variety of small, one-of-a-kind shops. Among them is **Connie B's Exclusives** (23564 Calabasas Road; 818-703-0525), a small country craft gift shop.

Over at **Old Town Canoga Park's Antique Row** (Topanga Canyon Boulevard and Sherman Way, Canoga Park), you'll find a procession of thrift shops, discount centers and antique stores. **Ye Olde Curiosity Shoppe** (21602 Sherman Way; 818-347-6883), **Before My Time** (21529 Sherman Way; 818-884-5777), **Sadie's Corner Antiques** (21515 Sherman Way; 818-704-7600), and **The Antique Company** (21513 Sherman Way; 818-347-8778) are among the best and most unusual.

A life-size model horse stands at the entrance to **Nudie's Rodeo Tailors** (5015 Lankershim Boulevard, North Hollywood; 818-762-3105). Much more than a Western-wear outlet, this store was once a showcase for Nudie, the internationally renowned rodeo tailor. Even today the walls are filled with photos of celebrities like Roy Rogers and Gene Autry strutting about in Nudie's elaborate designs.

SAN FERNANDO VALLEY NIGHTLIFE

The giant 6000-seat **Greek Theatre** (2700 North Vermont Avenue; 213-410-1062), nestled in the rolling hills of Griffith Park, is patterned after a classical Greek amphitheater. The entertainment in this enchanting spot ranges from stellar jazz, classical, pop and rock music to dance and dramatic performances. Bring a sweater and picnic.

Jax Bar & Grill (339 North Brand Boulevard, Glendale; 818-500-1604), with its brass elephants and local clientele, is a supper club that headlines notable jazz musicians.

Chadney's (3000 West Olive Avenue, Burbank; 818-843-5333), popular with entertainment people from nearby NBC Studio, offers live jazz.

Named after Shirley Temple, **Dimple's** (3413 West Olive Avenue, Burbank; 818-842-2336) is a showcase for fledgling singers.

Telly's A Sporting Bar (333 Universal Terrace Parkway, Universal City; 818-980-1212) is named in honor of Sheraton Universal Hotel's in-house resident, Telly Savalas, who can often be seen controlling the television sports channels. The bar is decorated in sports memorabilia.

The Baked Potato (3787 Cahuenga West Boulevard, Studio City; 818-980-1615) serves up contemporary jazz every night. If you want to rub shoulders with L.A. music heavies, this is the place. Cover.

Representative of the gay scene in The Valley are three Studio City clubs: **Apache** (11608 Ventura Boulevard; 818-506-0404), the area's most popular disco; **Venture Inn** (11938 Ventura Boulevard; 818-769-5400), a stylish lounge; and **Queen Mary's** (12449 Ventura

---

CASTAIC LAKE

*Set at the foot of the Tehachapi Mountains, the 2300-acre manmade **Castaic Lake** (805-257-3610) is surrounded by rugged slopes. The countryside—covered with chemise, sage and chaparral—is stark but beautiful. Along the lake, which carves a V in the hills, are facilities for boating and waterskiing, and you can also swim here and fish for bass, trout and bluegill. The visitor center is located at 31849 North Lake Hughes Road in Castaic.*

Boulevard; 818-506-5619), a club with a camp floor show that features a parade of queens; cover.

The **L.A. Connection** (13442 Ventura Boulevard, Sherman Oaks; 818-784-1868) developed a unique comedy concept several years back. They show camp film classics with house comedians ad-libbing the dialogue. Cover.

The **L.A. Cabaret Comedy Club** (17271 Ventura Boulevard, Encino; 818-501-3737) also features stand-up comedy. Showcased on the lounge's two stages are top entertainers ranging from Milton Berle to Robin Williams. Cover.

The **Country Club** (18415 Sherman Way, Reseda; 818-881-5601), a massive 1000-seat nightclub, brings in headline entertainers. Cover.

For something more subdued, the lounge at **Calabasas Inn** (23500 Park Sorrento Drive, Calabasas; 818-888-8870) overlooks woods and waterfalls.

The Valley is a prime place for jazz. For live, nightly performances, try **The Money Tree** (10149 Riverside Drive; 818-769-8800): no cover, no minimum.

Norah's Place (5667 Lankershim Boulevard, North Hollywood; 818-980-6900) is an altogether different experience. This lively Bolivian supper club serves up tango music. Cover.

Several theaters in The Valley present contemporary plays starring familiar actors from television and cinema. The best among them is **Back Alley Theater** (15231 Burbank Boulevard, Van Nuys; 818-907-8711).

Sporting Life

JOGGING

Though driving seems almost an addiction in the city, many Angelenos still manage to exercise. Filling your lungs with smoggy air might not be the healthiest thing to do, but if you're interested in jogging anyway, join the troopers at **Exposition Park and Recreation Center** (3990 South Menlo Avenue, Los Angeles; 213-749-5884), **Elysian Park** (near the intersection of Routes 110 and 5; 213-485-5054), **San Vicente Boulevard** in the Brentwood area, **Lacy Park** (1485 Virginia Road, San Marino), the **arroyo** near the Rose Bowl in Pasadena or **Griffith Park** (4730 Crystal Springs Road, Los Angeles; 213-665-5188).

GOLF

In Los Angeles it's as easy to tee off at a golf course as it is to get teed off in a traffic jam. Among the more challenging or interesting courses are **Montebello Country Club** (901 Via San Clemente, Montebello; 213-721-2311), **Rancho Park Golf Course** (10460 West Pico Boulevard, Los Angeles; 213-838-7373), **Brookside Golf Course** (1133 North Rosemont Avenue, Pasadena; 818-796-0177) and **Harding Golf Course** and **Wilson Golf Course** (Griffith Park; 213-663-2555).

In the eastern end of the county try **Marshall Canyon Golf Course** (6100 North Stephens Ranch Road, La Verne; 714-593-6914), **Diamond Bar Golf Course** (22751 East Golden Springs Drive, Diamond Bar; 714-861-8282), **San Dimas Golf Course** (2100 Terrebonne Avenue, San Dimas; 818-966-8547), **Mountain Meadows Golf Course** (1875 Fairplex Drive, Pomona; 714-629-1166) or **Whittier Narrows Golf Course** (8640 East Rush Street, Rosemead; 818-280-8225).

In the San Fernando Valley consider **Knollwood Golf Course** (12040 Balboa Boulevard, Granada Hills; 818-363-8161) or **Sepulveda Golf Course** (16821 Burbank Boulevard, Encino; 818-995-1170).

TENNIS

Most public parks have at least one tennis court; the city's largest facility, **Griffith Park** (4730 Crystal Springs Road, Los Angeles; 213-662-7772 or 213-665-5188), has many. For information on other local parks, contact the nearest Los Angeles City and County Parks and Recreation Department office.

Tennis clubs dot the county; some, like the **Racquet Center** (10933 Ventura Boulevard, Studio City; 818-760-2303), are open to the public. For further information about clubs and tournaments, contact the **Southern California Tennis Association** (P.O. Box 240015, Los Angeles, CA 90024; 213-208-3838).

HORSEBACK RIDING

With its curving hills and flowering meadows, Griffith Park is a favorite spot among urban equestrians. Several places on the edge of the park provide facilities. Try **Sunset Ranch** (3400 North Beachwood Drive, Hollywood; 213-464-9612), **Griffith Park Livery Stables** (480 Riverside Drive, Burbank; 818-840-8401) or **Bar S Stables** (1850 Riverside Drive, Glendale; 818-242-8443).

HANG GLIDING

What better way to let yourself go than by coasting or floating on high? The adventurous can try hang gliding at **Windsports International** (16145 Victory Boulevard, Van Nuys; 818-988-0111).

BICYCLING

Bikeways in Los Angeles are almost as plentiful as freeways. Unlike the freeways, few of them are congested. Many run parallel to parks, rivers, aqueducts and lakes, offering a different view of this diverse area.

Over 14 miles of bike routes wind through Griffith Park. Two notable excursions skirt many of the park attractions: **Crystal Springs Loop**, which follows Crystal Springs Road and Zoo Drive along the park's eastern edge, passes the merry-go-round and Travel Town; **Mineral Wells Loop**, an arduous uphill climb, passes Harding Golf Course, then coasts downhill to Zoo Drive, taking in Travel Town and the zoo.

For a trip from the mountains to the sea, try the **San Gabriel River Bike Trail**. It begins in Azusa and extends 38 miles to the Pacific near Long Beach.

The **Kenneth Newell Bikeway** begins on Arroyo Boulevard in Pasadena, then dips down to Arroyo Seco and the famed Rose Bowl.

A strenuous but worthwhile excursion is a bike ride along **Mulholland Drive**. Not recommended during commuter hours, this route traverses the spine of the Santa Monica Mountains and offers fabulous views of the city and ocean.

For more information on bicycle routes contact the **Transportation Commission** (213-626-0370) for a brochure.

Transportation

BY CAR

Arriving in Los Angeles by car means entering a maze of freeways. For most Angelenos this is an everyday occurrence; they know where they're going and are accustomed to spending a lot of time getting there. For the visitor, the experience can be very intimidating. The best way to determine a path through this labyrinth is by learning the major highways to and from town.

BY AIR

Two airports bring visitors to the Los Angeles area: the very big, very busy Los Angeles International Airport and the less crowded Burbank-Glendale-Pasadena Airport.

Los Angeles International Airport, better known as LAX, is served by many domestic and foreign carriers. Currently (and this seems to change daily) the following airlines fly into LAX: Alaska Airlines, American Airlines, America West Airlines, Continental Airlines, Delta Air Lines, Hawaiian Airlines, Northwest Airlines, Pan American World Airways, Piedmont Airlines, Southwest Airlines, Trans World Airlines, United Airlines and USAir.

International carriers are: All Nippon Airways, Air Canada, Air France, Air New Zealand, British Airways, CAAC, China Airlines, Canadian Airlines International, Japan Airlines, KLM Royal Dutch Airlines, Lufthansa German Airlines, Mexicana Airlines, Philippine Airlines, Qantas Airways, Singapore Airlines and TACA International Airlines.

Flights to and from **Burbank–Glendale–Pasadena Airport** are currently provided by Alaska Airlines, American Airlines, America West Airlines, Continental Airlines, Delta Air Lines, Skywest Airlines, Stateswest Airlines, Trans World Airlines, United Airlines, United Express Airlines and USAir.

Taxis, limousines and buses line up to take passengers from LAX and Burbank. **SuperShuttle** (818-244-2700) travels between hotels, businesses and residences to both Burbank and Los Angeles airports.

BY BUS

Greyhound/Trailways Bus Lines has service to the Los Angeles area from all around the country. The main Los Angeles terminal is at 208 East 6th Street (213-620-1200). Other stations are found in Hollywood (1409 Vine Street; 213-466-6381), Pasadena (645 East Walnut Street; 818-792-5116), Glendale (6000 San Fernando Road; 818-244-7295) and North Hollywood (11239 Magnolia Boulevard; 818-761-5119).

BY TRAIN

Amtrak (Union Station, 800 North Alameda Street, Los Angeles; 800-872-7245) will carry you into Los Angeles via the "Coast Starlight" from the Northwest, the "San Diegan" from San Diego, the "Desert Wind" and "Southwest Chief" from Chicago, the "Eagle" from Chicago by way of Texas, and the "Sunset Limited" from New Orleans. There are also stations in Pasadena and Glendale.

CAR RENTALS

Having a car in Los Angeles is practically a must. Distances are great and public transportation leaves much to be desired.

Looking for a car at Los Angeles International Airport will bring you to **Avis Rent A Car** (213-646-5600), **Budget Rent A Car** (213-645-4500), **Hertz Rent A Car** (213-646-4861) or **National Car Rental** (213-670-4950).

Agencies providing free airport pick-up service include **Avon Rent A Car** (213-568-9990), **Century Car Rental** (213-673-0300), **Enterprise Rent A Car** (213-649-5400), **Snappy Car Rental** (213-937-2172) and **Thrifty Car Rental** (213-645-1880).

At the Burbank airport several companies rent autos: **Avis Rent A Car** (818-566-3001), **Dollar Rent A Car** (818-846-4471), **Hertz Rent A Car** (818-846-8220), **National Car Rental** (818-842-4847) and **USA Rent A Car** (818-843-3021).

PUBLIC TRANSPORTATION

If you arrive in Los Angeles without a car, believe it or not you can still get around. **Southern California Rapid Transit District** (213-626-4455), or RTD, has over 200 bus routes covering more than 2200 square miles. "Rapid" transit may not be quite accurate, but buses do get you where you want to go. Nine customer service centers are located throughout Los Angeles; call for the nearest location.

Before arriving in Los Angeles, write for a free **Rider's Kit** (RTD, Customer Service, 425 South Main Street, Los Angeles 90013). These have information on routes and fares. One brochure, "RTD Self-Guided Tours," covers the traditional sights.

For traveling around downtown Los Angeles or Westwood, the **DASH** (800-874-8883, within the L.A. area) shuttle service is available Monday through Saturday (except holidays). In the Fairfax area, try the **Fairfax Trolley** (213-778-9066).

THREE

Los Angeles Coast

L.A., according to a popular song, is a great big freeway. Actually this sprawling metropolis by the sea is a great big beach. From Long Beach north to Malibu is a 74-mile stretch of sand that attracts visitors in the tens of millions every year. Life here reflects the culture of the beach, a freewheeling, pleasure-seeking philosophy that combines hedonism with healthfulness.

Perfectly fitted to this philosophy is the weather and the coastal topography of Los Angeles. Together they provide an urban escape valve just minutes from downtown. The shoreline lies along the lip of the Los Angeles basin, a flat expanse interrupted by the sharp cliffs of the Palos Verdes Peninsula and the rocky heights of the Santa Monica Mountains. There are broad strands lapped by gentle waves and pocket beaches exploding with surf. Though most of the coast is built up, some sections remain raw and undeveloped.

Route 1, the Pacific Coast Highway, parallels the coast the entire length of Los Angeles County, tying its beach communities together.

Long Beach and San Pedro

Anchoring the southern end of Los Angeles County are Long Beach and San Pedro, industrial enclaves that form the port of Los Angeles, a world center for commerce and shipping. Embodying 50 miles of heavily developed waterfront, the port is a maze of inlets, islets and channels protected by a six-mile breakwater. It is a region of technological superlatives—the largest manmade harbor in the world, center of the seafood canning industry, the most productive port in the country. Despite all this hubbub, the waterfront supports 100 fish species and over 80 types of birds, including several endangered species.

You should find Long Beach a revealing place, a kind of social studies lesson in modern American life. Travel Ocean Boulevard as it parallels the sea and you'll pass from quaint homes to downtown sky-scrapers to fire-breathing smokestacks.

For a dynamic example of what I mean, visit the enclave of **Naples** near the south end of town. Conceived early in the century, modeled on Italy's fabled canal towns, it's a tiny community of three islands separated by canals and linked with walkways. You can wander along bayside paths past comfortable homes, contemporary condominiums and humble cottages. Fountains and miniature traffic circles, alleyways and boulevards, all form an incredible labyrinth along which you un-doubtedly will become lost.

Adding to the sense of old Italia is the **Gondola Getaway** (5437 East Ocean Boulevard, Long Beach; 213-433-9595), a romantic hour-long cruise through the canals of Naples.

The **Long Beach Museum of Art** (2300 East Ocean Boulevard, Long Beach; 213-439-2119) is a must. Dedicated to 20th-century art and noted for its video works, this avant-garde museum has ever-changing exhibitions ranging from German expressionism to con-temporary Southern California work.

For a touch of early Spanish culture, plan on visiting the region's old adobes. **Rancho Los Alamitos** (6400 Bixby Hill Road, Long Beach; 213-431-3541), built in 1806 with walls four feet thick, is Southern California's oldest remaining house. Among its gardens, brick walkways and majestic magnolias, you can tour old barns, a blacksmith shop and a feed shed.

Rancho Los Cerritos (4600 Virginia Road, Long Beach; 213-424-9423), a two-story Spanish colonial home, once served as head-quarters for a 28,000-acre ranch. Now the 19th-century adobe is filled with Victorian furniture and surrounded by gardens.

Chapter Two in the Long Beach civics lesson is the steel-and-glass downtown area, where highrise hotels vie for dominance. To tour this crowded commercial district, stroll **The Promenade**, a six-block brick walkway leading from 3rd Street to the waterfront. Midway along the landscaped thoroughfare sits the **Long Beach Area Con-vention & Visitors Council** (1 World Trade Center, #300; 213-436-9982), home to maps, brochures and other bits of information.

Long Beach Part III rises in the form of oil derricks and industrial complexes just across the water. To view the freighters, tankers and warships lining the city's piers, you can gaze out from the fringes of Shoreline Village.

Fittingly, the climax of a Long Beach tour comes at the very end. Just across the Los Angeles River, along Harbor Scenic Drive, lies one of the strangest sights I've ever encountered. An old-style ocean liner,

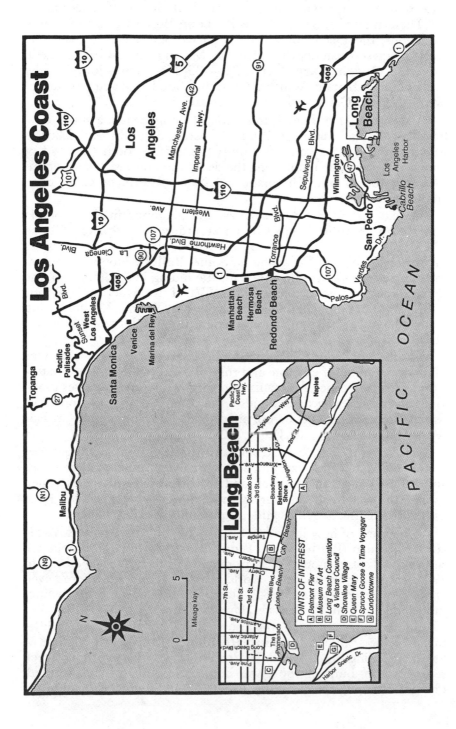

gleaming eerily in the harbor, appears to be parked on the ground. Next to it an overgrown geodesic dome swells up out of the earth.

These unearthly sights are really Long Beach's two top tourist attractions, the *Queen Mary* and the *Spruce Goose*, respectively the world's largest ocean liner and airplane. Making her maiden voyage in 1936, the **Queen Mary** (Pier J; 213-435-3511; admission) was the pride of Great Britain. Winston Churchill, the Duke and Duchess of Windsor, Greta Garbo and Fred Astaire sailed on her.

Today the *Queen Mary* is the pride of Long Beach, a 1000-foot-long "city at sea" transformed into a floating museum. An elaborate walking tour carries you down into the engine room (a world of pumps and propellers), out along the decks and up to each level of this multistage behemoth. The grand lady is a masterpiece of art deco architecture.

Unlike the elegant *Queen Mary*, the neighbor in the geodesic dome is an absurdity capped by an absurdity. The **Spruce Goose** (Pier J; 213-435-3511; admission), the largest plane ever built, resides in the world's biggest free-standing dome. Built by Howard Hughes, the bizarre billionaire who ended his life hiding in a hotel room, the *Spruce Goose* was intended to fly World War II troops across the Atlantic but was not completed until after the war. With a 320-foot wing span and a tail section eight stories high, it is the biggest white elephant in history.

Nearby San Pedro is home to the busiest sections of **Los Angeles Harbor**, a region of creosote and rust, marked by 28 miles of waterfront. This landscape of oil tanks and cargo containers services thousands of ships every year and houses the country's largest commercial fishing fleet. Tours of the harbor are provided by **Buccaneer Cruises** (Ports O' Call Village, San Pedro; 213-548-1085).

Head over to the **22nd Street Landing** (foot of 22nd Street, San Pedro) and watch the boats unload their hauls of tuna, mackerel, bass and halibut. You can buy crab and fish fresh from the nets. Then wander the waterfront and survey this frontier of steel and oil. Here awkward, unattractive ships glide as gracefully as figure skaters.

For a view of how it used to be, stop by the **Los Angeles Maritime Museum** (Berth 84, San Pedro; 213-548-7618). This dockside showplace displays models of ships ranging from fully rigged brigs to 19th-century steam sloops to World War II battleships. There's even an 18-foot re-creation of the ill-starred *Titanic* and the ocean liner model used to film *The Poseidon Adventure*.

Another piece in the port's historic puzzle is placed several miles inland at the **Phineas Banning Residence Museum** (401 East M Street, Wilmington; 213-548-7777; admission). This imposing Greek revival house, built in 1864, was home to the man who dreamed, dredged and developed Los Angeles harbor, and is now open for tours.

The **Cabrillo Marine Museum** (3720 Stephen M. White Drive, San Pedro; 213-548-7562) has several dozen aquariums with local fish and marine plants, along with displays of shells, coral and shorebirds. Nearby stretches 1200-foot **Cabrillo Fishing Pier**.

Of greater interest is **Point Fermin Park** (807 Paseo del Mar, San Pedro; 213-548-7756), a 37-acre blufftop facility resting above spectacular tidepools and a marine preserve. Also of note is the **Point Fermin Lighthouse**, a unique 19th-century clapboard house with a beacon set in a rooftop crow's nest. From the park plateau, like lighthouse keepers of old, you'll have open vistas of the cliff-fringed coastline and a perfect perch for sighting whales during their winter migration.

LONG BEACH AND SAN PEDRO RESTAURANTS

A cosmic center for burger lovers everywhere, **Hamburger Henry** (4700 East 2nd Street, Long Beach; 213-433-7070) is a classic diner decorated in neon and painted with murals of '50s-era convertibles. Each booth has a jukebox. We're talking vintage cuisine in a local hotspot that's open until the wee hours. There are hamburgers served with pineapple or peanut butter, caviar or ice cream. Moderate.

Southern cooking at the **Shenandoah Cafe** (4722 East 2nd Street, Long Beach; 213-434-3469) is becoming a tradition among savvy shore residents. The quilts and baskets decorating this understated establishment lend it a country air. Dinner is all she wrote here, but it's a special event occasioned with "riverwalk steak" (flank steak in mustard caper sauce), shrimp in beer batter and "granny's fried chicken." Moderate.

The Reef (880 Harbor Scenic Drive, Long Beach; 213-435-8013) is rambling, ramshackle and wonderful. Built of rough cedar, it sits along the waterfront on a dizzying series of levels. The cuisine includes such contemporary choices as blackened prime rib and beer batter shrimp, as well as traditional entrées. Deluxe.

HOTEL QUEEN MARY

*Where else but at the **Hotel Queen Mary** (Pier J, Long Beach; 213-435-6964) can you stay aboard a historic ocean liner and recapture the magic of British gentility before World War II? What other hotel offers guests a "sunning deck?" In the original staterooms of this grand old ship, you are surrounded by the art deco designs for which the Queen Mary is famous. Some guest rooms are small (this is a ship!) and dimly illuminated through portholes, but the decor is classic. There are also restaurants, lounges and shops on board. Deluxe to ultra-deluxe.*

Aboard the *Queen Mary* (Pier J, Long Beach; 213-435-3511) you will find everything from snack kiosks to coffee shops to first-class dining rooms. The **Promenade Cafe**, a lovely art deco room with wicker furnishings and period lamps, is a moderately priced coffee shop. For a true taste of regal life aboard the old ship, cast anchor at **Sir Winston's**. The continental cuisine in this elegant, wood-paneled dining emporium includes rack of lamb, beef medallions and broiled swordfish with caviar. Sunday brunch here is a grand affair. Deluxe to ultra-deluxe.

The Grand House and Cottages (809 South Grand Avenue, San Pedro; 213-548-1240) sits in a 50-year-old, warm and intimate Mediterranean home decorated with an ever-changing art exhibit. The continental-cum-California cuisine menu changes often and features such delicious delights as sweetbreads flambéed with cognac and tournedos topped with truffles and pâté. Moderate to deluxe.

LONG BEACH AND SAN PEDRO SHOPPING

The best street shopping in Long Beach is located near the Naples neighborhood along **East 2nd Street**. This 15-block strip between Livingston Drive and Bayshore Avenue is a gentrified row lined with art galleries, boutiques and import stores.

Shoreline Village (407 Shoreline Village Drive, Long Beach; 213-590-8427) is a typical Southern California waterfront mall. My favorite spot here is not a shop at all but the carousel, a vintage turn-of-the-century beauty awhirl with colorful animals.

A special fee gains shoppers access to the dozen-plus stores on board the **Queen Mary** (Pier J, Long Beach; 213-435-3511). Here you can buy souvenirs and articles from Great Britain. Perhaps the prettiest shopping arcade you'll ever enter, it's an art deco masterpiece.

Adjacent to the *Queen Mary* and *Spruce Goose*, **Londontowne Village** is a shopping plaza styled after a 19th-century British village and offering a variety of specialty shops.

Los Angeles Harbor's answer to the theme shopping mall craze is **Ports O' Call Village** (entrance at the foot of 6th Street, San Pedro; 213-831-0287), a mock 19th-century fishing village. Dozens of shops here are located right on the water.

LONG BEACH AND SAN PEDRO NIGHTLIFE

Panama Joe's (5100 East 2nd Street, Long Beach; 213-434-7417) cooks seven nights a week with an eclectic blend of music including jazz, rock and assorted others.

Any Long Beach nightspot would be hard pressed to match the elegance of the **Observation Bar** aboard the *Queen Mary* (Pier J,

Long Beach; 213-435-3511). Once the first-class bar for this grand old ship, it commands a 180° view across the bow and out to the Long Beach skyline. They feature live jazz and '30s and '40s music nightly. For softer sounds you can always adjourn aft to **Sir Winston's Piano Bar,** a cozy and elegant setting decorated with memorabilia of the World War II British leader.

Buccaneer/Mardi Gras Cruises (Ports O' Call Village, San Pedro; 213-548-1085) hosts sunset dining-and-dancing cruises around Los Angeles Harbor. Cover.

Landlubbers can enjoy a quiet drink on the waterfront at the spiffy oak bar or patio of **Ports O' Call Restaurant** (Ports O' Call Village, San Pedro; 213-833-3553).

LONG BEACH AND SAN PEDRO BEACHES AND PARKS

True to its name, **Long Beach City Beach** (213-594-0951) is broad and boundless, a silvery swath traveling much the length of the town. You'll find numerous facilities and good size crowds here. **Belmont Pier,** a 1300-foot-long, hammerhead-shaped walkway, bisects the beach and offers boat tours and fishing services. Located along Ocean Boulevard between 1st and 72nd places in Long Beach. Belmont Pier is at 39th Place.

Skirting unappealing Los Angeles Harbor, **Cabrillo Beach** (213-832-1179) is a two-part strand, covered with pewter-gray sand and bisected by a fishing pier. One half faces the shipping facility; the other looks out on the glorious Pacific.

Situated at the base of a cliff, **Royal Palms State Beach** (213-832-1179) is a boulder-strewn stretch that gains its name from a grove of elegant palm trees. Surfers and tidepoolers favor the spot. Even better, however, is a little gem of a beach to the south, Point Fermin Park's **Wilder Annex,** spectacularly built on a three-tiered cliff. The rocky beach offers promising tidepools and camera-eye views of Point Fermin. Both parks are located along Paseo del Mar in San Pedro, Royal Palms at Western Avenue and Wilder Annex near Meyler Street.

Palos Verdes Peninsula

Just a few miles west of San Pedro, along the **Palos Verdes Peninsula,** blue collar gives way to white collar, and the urban surrenders to the exotic. A region of exclusive neighborhoods and striking geologic contrasts, Palos Verdes possesses Los Angeles' prettiest seascapes. A series of 13 marine terraces, interrupted by sheer cliffs, descend to a rocky shoreline. For 15 miles the roadway rides high above the surf past tidepools, rocky points, a lighthouse and secluded coves.

The forces of nature seem to dominate as you proceed out along the peninsula from San Pedro. Follow 25th Street, then Palos Verdes Drive South, and encounter a tumbling region where terraced hills fall away to sharp coastal bluffs.

As you turn **Portuguese Bend**, the geology of this tumultuous area becomes startlingly evident when the road begins undulating through landslide zones. The earthquake faults that underlie the Los Angeles basin periodically fold and collapse the ground here. Of course the terrible power of nature has not dissuaded people from building. Along the ridgetops and curving hills below are colonies of stately homes.

Most lordly of all these structures is **The Wayfarer's Chapel** (5755 Palos Verdes Drive South, Rancho Palos Verdes; 213-377-1650), a simple but extraordinary center designed by the son of Frank Lloyd Wright. Nestled neatly into the surrounding landscape, the sun-lit chapel is built entirely of glass and commands broad views of the terrain and ocean.

The **Point Vicente Lighthouse** rises farther along the coast, casting an antique aura upon the area. While the beacon is not open to the public, the nearby **Point Vicente Interpretive Center** (31501

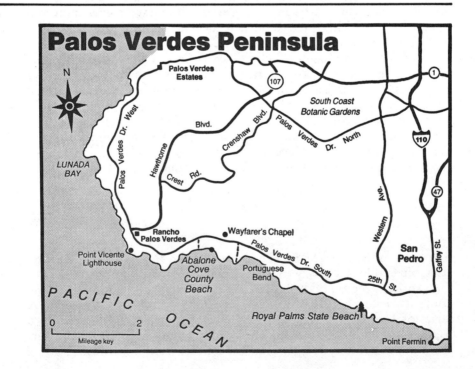

Palos Verdes Drive West, Rancho Palos Verdes; 213-377-5370; admission) offers a small regional museum.

For a vision of how truly beautiful this region is, turn off Palos Verdes Drive West in Palos Verdes Estates and follow Paseo Lunado until it meets the sea at Lunada Bay. This half-moon inlet, backdropped by the jagged face of a rocky cliff, looks out upon an unending expanse of ocean.

The setting is decidedly more demure at the **South Coast Botanic Gardens** (26300 South Crenshaw Boulevard, Palos Verdes; 213-544-6815; admission). This 87-acre garden is planted with exotic vegetation from Africa, New Zealand and other lands.

PALOS VERDES PENINSULA RESTAURANTS

The Admiral Risty (31250 Palos Verdes Drive West, Rancho Palos Verdes; 213-377-0050) is a nautical cliché, decorated outside with ropes and pilings and inside with brass fixtures. The place does have a full bar and a knockout view of the ocean. Play it safe and order fresh fish. The menu displays a typical surf-and-turf inventory. Dinner and Sunday brunch; moderate to deluxe.

For genuine elegance, make reservations at **La Rive Gauche** (320 Tejon Place, Palos Verdes Estates; 213-378-0267). With its upholstered chairs, brass wall sconces and vintage travel posters, this cozy dining room is unique to the peninsula. The menu is a study in classic French cooking. Moderate to deluxe.

PALOS VERDES PENINSULA BEACHES AND PARKS

A gray sand hideaway, **Abalone Cove County Beach** (213-832-1179) sits in a natural amphitheater guarded by rock formations and looks out on Catalina Island. There are tidepools to ponder and a marine ecological reserve. Located off Palos Verdes Drive South in Rancho Palos Verdes.

South Bay

The birthplace of California's beach culture lies in a string of towns on the southern skirt of Santa Monica Bay—Redondo Beach, Hermosa Beach and Manhattan Beach. It all began here in the South Bay with George Freeth, "the man who could walk on water." It seems that while growing up in Hawaii, Freeth resurrected the ancient Polynesian sport of surfing, which he then transplanted to California in 1907.

It wasn't until the 1950s that the surfing wave crested. That's when a group of local kids called The Beach Boys spent their days catching waves at Manhattan Beach and their nights recording classic surfing songs. The surrounding towns became synonymous with the sport, and a new culture was born, symbolized by blond-haired, blue-eyed surfers committed to sun, sand and the last wave.

Sightseeing spots are rather scarce in these beach towns. Each sports a municipal pier, however, with rows of knickknack shops, cafes and oceanview lounges.

In Redondo Beach, **Fisherman's Wharf** (Municipal Pier) is home to surfcasters and hungry seagulls. Walk out past the shops, salt breeze in your face, and you can gaze along the waterfront to open ocean.

Up in Hermosa Beach, the 1320-foot concrete **Municipal Pier** (foot of Pier Avenue) offers a sweeping view back along Hermosa Beach's low skyline.

Similarly, the **Manhattan Beach Pier** (foot of Manhattan Beach Boulevard) extends 900 feet from the beach and offers the generic bait store and take-out stand.

The other sightseeing diversion in these parts is the stroll. The stroll, that is, along the beach. **Esplanade** in Redondo Beach, and **The Strand** in Hermosa Beach and Manhattan Beach, are wide boulevards paralleling the waterfront.

SOUTH BAY LODGING

The **Portofino Inn** (260 Portofino Way, Redondo Beach; 213-379-8481) is a big, brassy hotel set on King Harbor. The 170 contemporary-style units look out either on the ocean or the adjoining marina. Swimming pool. Ultra-deluxe.

The best bargain on lodging in South Bay is found at **Sea Sprite Apartment Motel** (1016 Strand, Hermosa Beach; 213-376-6933). Located right on the beach, this complex offers clean and attractive oceanview rooms with kitchenettes at moderate-to-deluxe price. A swimming pool and sun deck overlook the beach. You can also rent deluxe suites or a turn-of-the-century, two-bedroom cottage (ultra-deluxe).

The **Sea View Inn** (3400 Highland Avenue, Manhattan Beach; 213-545-1504) is an eight-unit stucco hotel a block from the beach. There's a tiny swimming pool, plus two floors of cramped guest rooms. But it's close to the surf and lodging *is* rare in these parts, so. . .Moderate.

A mile inland, **Barnabey's Hotel** (3501 North Sepulveda Boulevard, Manhattan Beach; 213-545-8466) is a sprawling 128-room Edwardian-style hostelry. The stylish guest rooms have antique furnishings and vintage wallpaper. The dark-wood lobby is appointed with gilded clocks and crystal light fixtures. There's a restaurant, British pub, pool and jacuzzi. Deluxe.

SOUTH BAY RESTAURANTS

You'll find good Asian food in a very attractive setting at **Thai Thani** (1109 South Pacific Coast Highway, Redondo Beach; 213-316-1580). Selections include dozens of pork, beef, vegetable and seafood dishes. Unusual choices like spicy shrimp coconut soup and whole baby hen make this a dining adventure. Budget to moderate.

One wall of **Millie Riera's Seafood Grotto** (1700 Esplanade, Redondo Beach; 213-375-1483) is entirely filled with a plate-glass view of the ocean. True to its title, the grotto specializes in seafood, such as bouillabaisse, cracked crab and lobster newburg. Moderate to deluxe.

The capital of *in* dining around the South Bay is **Chez Melange** (1716 Pacific Coast Highway, Redondo Beach; 213-540-1222). As the name suggests and as current trends demand, the cuisine is eclectic. You'll find a hip crowd ordering everything from Cajun to Japanese. Deluxe.

Cafe Pierre (317 Manhattan Beach Boulevard, Manhattan Beach; 213-545-5252) is an excellent choice for budget-minded gourmets. This fashionable French bistro offers a feast of entrées including veal sweetbreads cognac, boneless saddle of lamb and scallops Provençal. Moderate.

SOUTH BAY NIGHTLIFE

The Comedy & Magic Club (1018 Hermosa Avenue, Hermosa Beach; 213-372-1193), upscale and appealing, features name acts nightly. Cover.

The Lighthouse Cafe (30 Pier Avenue, Hermosa Beach; 213-372-6911) spotlights reggae, rock and '60s-style surfing groups.

ST. ESTEPHE

Unassuming at first glance—with blond wood decor and oil paintings from the American Southwest—St. Estephe (2640 North Sepulveda Boulevard, Manhattan Beach; 213-545-1334) is in fact one of the region's finest, most innovative restaurants. Blending American Indian foods with Southwestern herbs and spices, all prepared in nouvelle style, the restaurant has created a series of unique dishes with lamb, veal, poultry and fish. Sauces are painted onto the plate, creating swirling, multihued designs reminiscent of New Mexico landscapes. Highly recommended by friends and critics alike. Ultra-deluxe.

Orville & Wilbur's Restaurant (401 Rosecrans Boulevard, Manhattan Beach; 213-545-6639) is a lush establishment with an upstairs oceanview bar. Live Top-40 or vintage rock nightly.

SOUTH BAY BEACHES AND PARKS

Surfers know **Redondo State Beach** (213-372-2166), and so should you. You'll find a long strip of white sand bordered by a hillside carpeted with ice plants. Bicyclists and joggers populate the area, too. Located along the Esplanade in Redondo Beach.

One of the great beaches of Southern California, **Hermosa City Beach** (213-372-2166) is a very, very wide (and very, very white) strand extending the entire length of Hermosa Beach. Along with two miles of pearly sand, it features a quarter-mile fishing pier and a local community known for its artistic creativity. Located at the foot of Pier Avenue in Hermosa Beach.

At **Manhattan State Beach** (213-372-2166) people come to surf, swim and check out the scene along The Strand. And no wonder. This sand corridor is as wide as a desert, fronted by an aquamarine ocean and backed by beautiful homes. Located at the foot of Manhattan Beach Boulevard.

Venice

Venice, California was the dream of one man, a tobacco magnate named Albert Kinney who envisioned a "Venice of America," a Renaissance town of gondoliers and single-lane bridges, connected by 16 miles of canals. In fact, the place became an early 20th-century Disneyland with gondola rides and amusement parks. The canals were lined with vaulted arches and rococo-style hotels.

When oil was discovered, it spelled the doom of Kinney's dream. Spills polluted the canals, and they were eventually filled in. But by the 1950s latter-day visionaries—artists and bohemians—rediscovered "Kinney's Folly" and transformed it into an avant-garde community.

Today Venice retains much of the old flavor. Palatial hotels have given way to beach cottages and funky wood houses, but the narrow streets and countless alleyways remain. More significant, the town is filled with galleries and covered by murals, making it one of the region's most important art centers.

In fact, the artists have seized control in Venice. City Hall has become the **Beyond Baroque Literary Arts Center** (681 Venice Boulevard; 213-822-3006), housing a library and bookstore devoted to small presses.

Next door, the Venice City Jail is home to **SPARK**, or the Social and Public Arts Resource Center (685 Venice Boulevard; 213-822-9560). The prison is an imposing 1923 art deco-style building with a cell block converted into an art gallery—you'll walk through an iron door to get to the exhibits.

To learn more about the community, stop by the **Venice Chamber of Commerce** (13470 Washington Boulevard; 213-827-2366) for maps, brochures and answers.

The commercial center of Venice rests at the intersection of Windward Avenue and Main Street. Windward was the central boulevard of Kinney's dream city, and the **Traffic Circle**, marked today by a small sculpture, was to be an equally grand lagoon. Continue along Windward Avenue to the **arcades**, a series of Italian-style colonnades that represent one of the few surviving elements of old Venice.

THE MURALS OF VENICE AND SANTA MONICA

Nowhere is the spirit of Venice and Santa Monica more evident than in the murals adorning their walls. Both seaside cities house major art colonies, and the numerous galleries and studios make them important centers for contemporary art. Over the years, as more and more artists made their homes here, they began decorating the twin towns with their art. The product of this creative energy lives along street corners and alleyways, on storefronts and roadways.

*Murals adorn nooks and crannies all over Venice. You'll find a cluster of them around Windward Avenue between Main Street and Ocean Front Walk. The interior of the **Post Office** (Main Street and Windward Avenue) is adorned with public art. There's a trompe l'oeil mural nearby that beautifully reflects the street (Windward Avenue) along which you are gazing. On the other side of the building, the old St. Mark's Hotel, **Venus Reconstituted** (Windward Avenue and Ocean Walk) brilliantly parodies Botticelli's Venus Rising From the Foam.*

*At last count Santa Monica boasted about two dozen outdoor murals, many along Lincoln Boulevard. **John Muir Woods** (Lincoln and Ocean Park boulevards) portrays a redwood forest; **Early Ocean Park and Venice Scenes** (two blocks west of Lincoln Boulevard along Kensington Road in Joslyn Park) captures the seaside at the turn of the century. Nearby Marine Park (Marine and Frederick streets) features **Birthday Party**, with a Noah's ark full of celebratory animals, and **Underwater Mural**, which pictures the world of the deep.*

*Ocean Park Boulevard is another locus of creativity. At its intersection with the 4th Street underpass you'll encounter **Whale Mural**, illustrating whales and underwater life common to California waters, and **Unbridled**, which pictures a herd of horses fleeing from the Santa Monica Pier carousel. One of the area's most famous murals awaits you at Ocean Park Boulevard and Main street, where **Early Ocean Park** vividly re-creates scenes from the past.*

The heart of modern-day Venice pulses along the **boardwalk**, a two-mile strip that follows Ocean Front Walk from Washington Street to Ozone Avenue. **Venice Pier** (Ocean Front Walk and Washington Street), an 1100-foot fishing pier, anchors one end.

Walking north, the real action begins around 18th Avenue, at **Muscle Beach**, where rope-armed heavies work out in the weight pen and flex their pecs before gawking onlookers.

The rest of the boardwalk is a grand open-air carnival that you should try to visit on the weekend. It is a world of artists and anarchists, derelicts and dreamers. Guitarists, jugglers, conga drummers and clowns perform for the crowds. Kids on roller skates and bicycles whiz past rickshaws and unicycles. Vendors dispense everything from corn dogs to cotton candy, T-shirts to wind-up toys.

VENICE LODGING

There's nothing quite like **The Venice Beach House** (15 30th Avenue; 213-823-1966). This charming bed and breakfast near the beach is an elegant and spacious California bungalow-style home built early in the century. The living room, with its beam ceiling and brick fireplace, is a masterwork. The nine guest rooms are beautifully appointed and furnished with antiques. Moderate to deluxe.

Also consider the **Marina Pacific Hotel** (1697 Pacific Avenue; 213-452-1111), located only 100 yards from the sand. The guest rooms are spacious and nicely furnished; very large one-bedroom suites, complete with kitchen and fireplace, are also available. Deluxe to ultra-deluxe.

VENICE RESTAURANTS

The best place for finger food and junk food in all Southern California might well be the **boardwalk** in Venice. Along Ocean Front Walk are vendor stands galore serving pizza, yogurt, hamburgers, falafels, corn dogs, etc., etc.

Regardless, there's really only one spot in Venice to consider for dining. It simply *is* Venice, an oceanfront cafe right on the boardwalk, **The Sidewalk Cafe** (1401 Ocean Front Walk; 213-399-5547). Skaters roll by, drummers beat rhythms in the distance, and the sun stands like a big orange wafer above the ocean. Food is really a second thought here, but you can get omelettes, hamburgers and pizza, or fish dishes with platters of wok-fried vegetables. Budget to moderate.

The landing ground for Venetians is a warehouse dining place called **The Rose Cafe** (220 Rose Avenue; 213-399-0711), which includes a full-scale deli, bakery counter and restaurant. The last serves moderately priced meals, with a changing menu that may include lemon linguine with flaked salmon and bay scallops salad. Wall murals highlight the vital culture of Venice.

For a gourmet, deluxe-to-ultra-deluxe restaurant, **West Beach Cafe** (60 North Venice Boulevard; 213-823-5396) is quite understated in decor. But the menu, which changes daily, demolishes any doubts about the standing of this trendy eating place. The restaurant serves fresh seafood dishes like salmon and swordfish with a host of delicious sauces.

72 Market Street (72 Market Street; 213-392-8720) could be the last word in modern art restaurants. The place is a warren of brick, mirrors, opaque glass and studio lights. It's adorned with striking art pieces and equipped with a sound system that seems to be vibrating from the inner ear. Moderne to the max, the restaurant serves Cajun-style catfish, chili, grilled Louisiana sausages and other regional dishes. Deluxe.

VENICE SHOPPING

To combine slumming with shopping, be sure to wander the **boardwalk** in Venice. Ocean Front Walk between Windward and Ozone avenues is lined with low-rent stalls selling beach hats, cheap jewelry, sunglasses and souvenirs. You'll also encounter **Small World Books and the Mystery Annex** (1407 Ocean Front Walk; 213-399-2360), a marvelous beachside shop with new and used books as well as magazines.

L.A. Louver (55 North Venice Boulevard and 77 Market Street; 213-822-4955) represents famed artists like David Hockney as well as up-and-comers.

VENICE NIGHTLIFE

The Townhouse (52 Windward Avenue; 213-392-4040), set in a '20s-era speakeasy, has live music and deejays spinning Top-40 platters. Cover.

Santa Monica

Originally developed as a beachside resort in 1875, the town of Santa Monica has also served as a major port and a location for early movies. Raymond Chandler immortalized the place as "Bay City" in his brilliant Philip Marlowe novels. Today it is a bastion of brown-shingle houses, flower-covered trellises and left-wing politics. Besides that, the city is *in*. Its clean air, pretty beaches and attractive homes have made it one of the most popular places to live in Los Angeles. The

Santa Monica Mountains extend to the very edge of the sea here. White sand beaches are framed by bald peaks, crystal waters and flourishing kelp beds that attract abundant sea life and make for excellent fishing and skindiving, while the mountains provide a getaway for campers and hikers.

Along Santa Monica's ocean promenade it's possible to walk for miles past fluffy sand, pastel-colored condominiums and refurbished woodframe houses. Roller skaters and bicyclists galore crowd the byways, and chess players congregate at the picnic tables.

Highlight of the beach promenade is the **Santa Monica Pier** (foot of Colorado Avenue). No doubt about it, the place is a scene. Acrobats work out on the playground below, surfers catch waves offshore and street musicians strum guitars. And I haven't even mentioned the official attractions. There's a turn-of-the-century carousel with hand-painted horses that was featured in that cinematic classic, *The Sting*. There are shooting galleries, video parlors, skee ball and bumper cars.

From here it's a jaunt up to the **Santa Monica Convention & Visitors' Bureau** information kiosk (1400 Ocean Avenue; 213-392-9631). They provide maps, brochures and answers.

The booth is located in **Palisades Park**, a pretty, palm-lined greensward that extends more than a mile atop the sandstone cliffs fronting Santa Monica beach. One of the park's stranger attractions is the **Camera Obscura** (located in the Senior Recreation Center, 1450 Ocean Avenue), a periscope of sorts through which you can view the pier, beach and surrounding streets.

For a glimpse into the city's past, take in the **Santa Monica Heritage Museum** (2612 Main Street; 213-392-8537). Heirlooms and antiques are housed in a grand 1894 American colonial revival home.

Angels' Attic (516 Colorado Avenue; 213-394-8331; admission) is more than a great name. Contained in this 1894 Victorian is a unique museum of antique playthings for children. Toy trains run along the ceiling, and doll houses in every shape, from Tudor home to crenelated castle, adorn the rooms.

The **Museum of Flying** (Santa Monica Airport, 2772 Donald Douglas Loop North; 213-392-8822; admission) is a miniature Smithsonian. Tracing the history of aviation in a single brightly painted hangar, the museum houses everything from a 1924 Douglas World Cruiser (built in Santa Monica, it was the first plane to circle the globe) to a Douglas A-4 Skyhawk flown by the Blue Angels.

At first glance, the **Self Realization Fellowship Lake Shrine** (17190 Sunset Boulevard; 213-454-4114) in nearby Pacific Palisades is an odd amalgam of pretty things—a Dutch windmill, a houseboat and a shrine topped with something resembling a giant artichoke. In fact, the windmill is a chapel welcoming all religions, the houseboat a

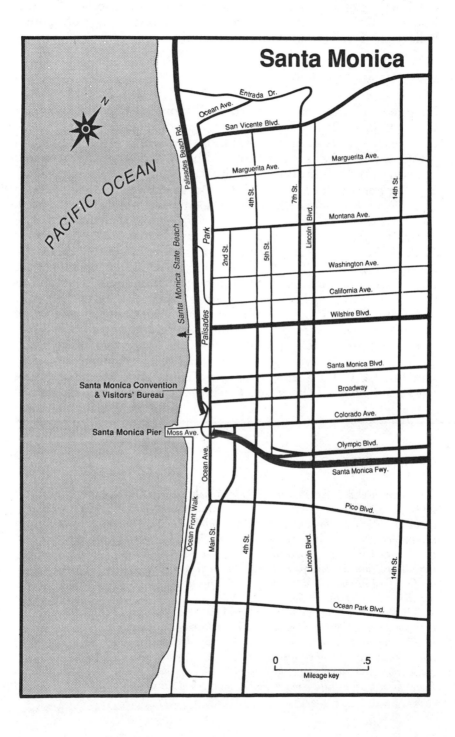

former stopping place of yogi Paramahansa Yogananda, and the over-sized artichoke a golden lotus archway near which some of Indian leader Mahatma Gandhi's ashes are enshrined. A strange but potent collection of icons in an evocative setting.

SANTA MONICA LODGING

Despite its location on a busy street, **Channel Road Inn** (219 West Channel Road; 213-459-1920) conveys a cozy sense of home. Colonial Revival in style, built in 1910, this sprawling 14-room bed and breakfast offers guests a living room, library, and dining room as well as a jacuzzi and hillside garden. Deluxe.

The **Pacific Shore Hotel** (1819 Ocean Avenue; 213-451-8711), a sprawling 168-room facility one block from the beach, boasts a pool, sauna, jacuzzi and sun deck. Guests are whisked to their art deco-style rooms in a glass elevator. Private balconies. Deluxe to ultra-deluxe.

The **Sovereign** (205 Washington Avenue; 213-395-9921) is the classic Southern California hostelry. Constructed during the 1920s, it's a grand, Mediterranean-style whitewashed building. The lobby is filled with antiques. Each guest room is furnished differently—some in art deco fashion, others with Oriental pieces or antiques. A good bargain—moderate for standard rooms and deluxe for the huge "superior" rooms with kitchens and terraces.

Now forget everything I've said. There's really only one place to stay. Just ask Cybil Shepherd, Diane Keaton, Bill Murray or Gene Hackman. They all check into the **Hotel Shangri-La** (1301 Ocean

---

LOEWS SANTA MONICA

The much-needed **Loews Santa Monica Beach Hotel** *(1700 Ocean Avenue; 213-458-6700) is the first hotel to be built in Santa Monica in 20 years (it opened in 1989) and the first L.A. luxury hotel with direct beach access. The peach, blue and seafoam green "contemporary Victorian" features a mock turn-of-the-century design. Its spectacular five-story glass atrium lobby and most of the 352 ultra-deluxe-priced rooms provide views of the famed Santa Monica Pier. Rooms are furnished in rattan and wicker and offer special amenities. Non-beachies love the oceanview indoor/outdoor pool.*

But it's **Riva***, the excellent beachview restaurant, that will put the place on the map. A menu featuring innovative northern Italian seafood is impeccably served in this dramatic black-and-white Mediterranean dining room. Polished mahogany chairs brush against white linen tablecloths set off by black candles. Entrées include garlic-lemon veal chops and grilled swordfish. The wine list features expected California favorites plus little-known Italian vintages. Deluxe to ultra-deluxe.*

Avenue; 213-394-2791). The place is private, stylish, nothing short of beautiful. A 1939 art deco building with a facade like the prow of a steamship, the 55-room hotel features art moderne furniture and appointments that are perfect expressions of the period. Every room has a kitchen, and many sport an ocean view. Deluxe.

SANTA MONICA RESTAURANTS

There's a sense of the Mediterranean at the sidewalk cafes lining Santa Monica's Ocean Avenue: palm trees, ocean views and a warm breeze blowing. Any of these bistros will do (since it's atmosphere we're seeking), so try **Ivy at the Shore** (1541 Ocean Avenue; 213-393-3113). It features a full bar, serves espresso and, if you want to get serious about it, has a menu with pizza, pasta, Cajun dishes and sandwiches. Deluxe to ultra-deluxe.

For Indian cuisine the best-known restaurant is **British Raaj Cuisine of India** (502 Santa Monica Boulevard; 213-393-9472). Trimly decorated with Asian chandeliers and carved wood screens, the place is small enough to convey intimacy. The menu includes *tandoori* chicken, lamb *tikka* (marinated in herbs and lemon) and Bombay *machli* (fresh fish with ginger in curry sauce). Moderate.

Zucky's (431 Wilshire Boulevard; 213-393-0551) is the place for late-night munchies. Open 24 hours on the weekend, this popular delicatessen has an endless assortment of hot platters, kosher sandwiches and delicious pastries. Budget to moderate.

Pioneer Boulangerie (2012 Main Street; 213-399-7771) is a sprawling establishment with a large dining room and full-fledged bakery. Out on the patio they serve cafeteria-style meals at budget to moderate prices. In the dining room there is an ample and traditional Basque country dinner. An incredible deal at a moderate price.

In the world of high chic, **Chinois on Main** (2709 Main Street; 213-392-9025) stands taller than most. Owned by famous restaurateur Wolfgang Puck, the fashionable dining room features track lights, a central skylight and a hand-painted curved bar. Once you drink in the glamorous surroundings, move on to the menu, which includes Shanghai lobster risotto, sizzling catfish and grilled Szechuan beef. Deluxe to ultra-deluxe.

The spot for breakfast in Santa Monica is **Rae's Restaurant** (2901 Pico Boulevard; 213-828-7937). With its formica counter and naugahyde booths, Rae's is a local institution, always packed. The place serves hearty American-style feasts for breakfast (including buttermilk biscuits and country-style gravy), sandwiches at lunch time and dinners of fried shrimp, pork chops, veal and fried chicken. Most important, dinner prices haven't changed since the place opened in 1958. Budget.

Many believe the dining experience at **Michael's** (1147 3rd Street; 213-451-0843) is the finest in all Los Angeles. Set in a restored stucco structure and decorated with original artwork by David Hockney and Jasper Johns, it is certainly one of the region's prettiest dining rooms. The menu is a nouvelle cuisine affair with original entrées like squab on duck liver and scallops on watercress purée, all prepared with true artistry. Deluxe to ultra-deluxe.

SANTA MONICA SHOPPING

Montana Avenue is Santa Monica's version of designer heaven, making it an interesting, if inflationary, strip to shop. **Artcessories** (1426 Montana Avenue; 213-395-8484) has a stunning assortment of hand-wrought jewelry and other decorative handcrafted pieces.

Browse Main Street and you'll realize that Montana Avenue is only a practice round in the gentrification of Santa Monica. Block after block of this thoroughfare has been made over in trendy fashion and filled with stylish shops.

Galleria Di Maio (2525 Main Street) is an art deco mall with several spiffy shops.

Main Street Gallery (208 Pier Avenue; 213-399-4161) specializes in Japanese folk art and antiques; the collection here is extraordinary. Even closer to museum status is the array of crystals and shell fossils at **Nature's Own** (2736 Main Street; 213-392-3807).

Venture out Wilshire Boulevard and you'll uncover several specialty locations. **I. M. Chait Gallery** (2409 Wilshire Boulevard; 213-828-8537) features a very exclusive selection of Oriental artworks. Next door at **Wounded Knee** (2413 Wilshire Boulevard; 213-394-0159) there is an assortment of Native American crafts including sand paintings and Kachina dolls.

In central Santa Monica sprawls **Santa Monica Place** (Broadway between 2nd and 4th streets; 213-394-5451), a mammoth triple-tiered complex with about 150 shops. This flashy atrium mall has everything from clothes to books to sporting goods to leather work, jewelry and shoes.

Step out from this glittery gathering place and you'll immediately encounter **Third Street Promenade** (between Broadway and Wilshire Boulevard), a three-block pedestrian mall lined with shops. Since the promenade is still in the process of redevelopment, the stores are a blend of traditional and contemporary. One in particular exemplifies Santa Monica's liberal politics. **Midnight Special Bookstore** (1350 Third Street Promenade; 213-393-2923) specializes in politics and social sciences, with windows displaying books on Latin America, world hunger or Africa.

Along this strip you'll also find **Muskrat Clothing** (1434 Third Street Promenade; 213-394-1713) which specializes in vintage items like aloha shirts, velour jackets and silk coats with maps of Japan embroidered on the backs. (Thought you'd never find one, eh?)

SANTA MONICA NIGHTLIFE

Merlin McFly (2702 Main Street; 213-392-8468) is a must. Magic is the password here: every evening magicians wander from table to table performing sleight-of-hand tricks. Matching the entertainment is the wildly baroque interior.

At My Place (1026 Wilshire Boulevard; 213-451-8596), a spacious dinner club with live acts nightly, offers an eclectic blend of jazz, rhythm-and-blues, pop music and comedy; cover. Reservations required.

Ye Olde King's Head (116 Santa Monica Boulevard; 213-451-1402) might be the most popular British pub this side of the Thames. From dart boards to trophy heads to draft beer, it's a classic English watering hole.

You can do almost anything (well, almost) at **Madame Wong's West** (2900 Wilshire Boulevard; 213-829-7361). This two-tier nightclub has live bands upstairs, a game room with billiard tables, and deejay dancing downstairs. Cover.

For blues try **Harvelle's** (1432 4th Street; 213-395-1676); if it's reggae you're after, then **Kingston 12** (814 Broadway; 213-451-4423) is the spot.

McCabe's Guitar Shop (3101 Pico Boulevard; 213-828-4497) is a folksy spot with live entertainment on weekends. The sounds are almost all acoustic and range from Scottish folk bands to jazz to blues to country. Cover.

For a raucous good time try **The Oar House** and **Buffalo Chips** (2941 Main Street; 213-396-4725). These adjoining bars are loud,

---

"THE HOUSE THAT JOKES BUILT"

*At **Will Rogers State Historic Park** (14253 Sunset Boulevard, Pacific Palisades; 213-454-8212; admission), you can tour the ranch and home of America's greatest cowboy philosopher. The comedian whose humorous wisdom plucked a chord in the American psyche lived here from 1928 until his tragic death in 1935.*

The 31-room house is large but basic and unassuming, true to Rogers' Oklahoma roots. Western knickknacks adorn the tables, and one room is dominated by a full-sized stuffed calf that Rogers utilized for roping practice. Well worth visiting, the "house that jokes built" is a simple expression of a vital personality.

brash places that draw hearty crowds. The music is recorded, and the decor is Early Insanity—sawdust floors, mannequins on the ceiling, alligator skins on the wall.

SANTA MONICA BEACHES AND PARKS

Santa Monica State Beach (213-394-8311) is part of the sandbox-gone-wild that stretches from Venice to Pacific Palisades—very white sand, blue water and broad beaches. Skaters, strollers and bicyclists pass along the promenade, sunbathers lie moribund in the sand and volleyball players perform acrobatic shots. At the center of all this stands the Santa Monica Pier with its amusement park atmosphere. Located at the foot of Colorado Avenue.

Will Rogers once owned the two miles of beachfront property that's now **Will Rogers State Beach** (213-451-2906). It's a wide, sandy strand looking up at the sharp cliffs that lend Pacific Palisades its name. Located along Route 1 at Sunset Boulevard in Pacific Palisades.

Santa Monica Mountains National Recreation Area (818-597-9192) highlights one of the few mountain ranges in the country running east to west. This federal preserve encompasses about 150,000 acres of the Santa Monica Range; in addition to high country, it includes a coastal stretch from Santa Monica to Point Mugu. Considered a "botanical island," the mountains support chaparral, coastal sage and oak forests; mountain lions, golden eagles and many of California's early animal species still survive here. Camping is permitted. Several access roads lead into the area.

Malibu

Lying along a narrow corridor between the Santa Monica Mountains and the sea is Malibu, that quintessential symbol of California, a rich, glamorous community known for its movie stars and surfers. During the 1930s such stars as Ronald Colman and John Gilbert found their paradise on the sands of Malibu. Like figures out of *The Great Gatsby*, they lived insouciant lives in movie-set houses. When the 1959 movie *Gidget* cast Sandra Dee and James Darren as Malibu beach bums, the seaside community was on its way to surfing immortality.

Today blond-mopped surfers still line the shore, and celebrities continue to congregate in beachfront bungalows. Matter of fact, the most popular sightseeing in Malibu consists of ogling the homes of the very rich. **Malibu Road**, which parallels the waterfront, is a prime strip.

One of Malibu's loveliest houses is open to the public. The **Adamson Home**, located at Malibu Lagoon State Beach (23200 Pacific Coast Highway; 213-456-8432; admission), is a stately Mediterranean-style structure adorned with ceramic tiles. With its bare-beam ceilings and inlaid floors, the house is a study in early 20th-century elegance. Outstanding as it is, the building is upstaged by the landscaped grounds, which border the beach and overlook a lagoon alive with waterfowl.

The town's most prestigious address is the **J. Paul Getty Museum** (17985 Pacific Coast Highway; 213-458-2003; advance reservation necessary), one of the wealthiest art museums in the world. Set on a hillside overlooking the sea, the building splendidly re-creates a 2000-year-old Roman villa. The colonnaded entranceway, which greets the visitor with a reflecting pool and fountains, is nothing short of magnificent. The galleries, equally as beautiful, focus on Greek and Roman antiquities, Renaissance and baroque art and French furniture. Some of the world's finest artwork can be found at this well-respected establishment.

A major seafront attraction is **Malibu Pier** (23000 Pacific Coast Highway), where you can walk out over the water, cast for fish or gaze back along the heavily developed coastline.

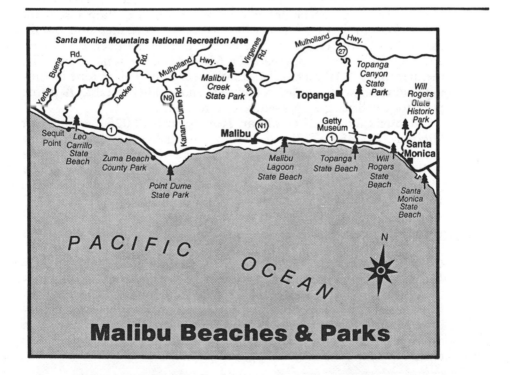

Malibu Beaches & Parks

MALIBU LODGING

Several motels lie along the coastal highway in Malibu, one of which I particularly recommend. At **Casa Malibu Motel** (22752 Pacific Coast Highway; 213-456-2219) you'll be in a 21-room facility that actually overhangs the sand. Located smack in the center of Malibu, the building features a central courtyard with an ocean view plus a balcony dripping with flowering plants. The rooms are attractive but casual; some have private balconies, kitchens and/or ocean views. Moderate to deluxe.

At last, Malibu has a slick beach motel. The **Malibu Beach Inn** (22878 Pacific Coast Highway; 213-456-6444) is posh and ultra-deluxe. Each of the 47 rooms offers spectacular ocean views from private balconies. Fireplaces and minibars round out the amenities.

MALIBU RESTAURANTS

Malibu's best-known eating spot sits at the foot of Malibu Pier. **Alice's Restaurant** (23000 Pacific Coast Highway; 213-456-6646) is a trim, glass-encased oceanview dining room. A gathering place for locals in the know and visitors on the make, it serves seafood, pasta and salads. A great place for carousing. Moderate to deluxe.

The quintessential Malibu dining experience is **Geoffrey's** (27400 Pacific Coast Highway; 213-457-1519), a clifftop restaurant overlooking the ocean. The marble bar and whitewashed stucco walls exude wealth and elegance. The entire hillside has been landscaped and beautifully terraced, creating a Mediterranean atmosphere. The menu features "Malibu fare," a variation on California cuisine including swordfish with onion, cucumber, and raddichio salsa. A prime place for celebrity gazing. Deluxe to ultra-deluxe.

Beaurivage Mediterranean Restaurant (26025 Pacific Coast Highway; 213-456-5733), another gourmet gathering place, is a cozy dining room. With exposed-beam ceiling and copper pots along the wall, it has the feel of a French country inn. But the food is strictly Mediterranean, with several pasta dishes, white fish in meunière sauce and daily specials like ragoût of wild boar. Deluxe.

MALIBU SHOPPING

Cheryl Wilson's Doll Works (22774 Pacific Coast Highway; 213-456-3940) is both unique and imaginative. Specializing in soft sculpture, the owner-artist creates lifelike (and sometimes life-size) dolls.

There's nothing very rustic about the pricey boutiques and galleries at **Malibu Country Mart** (3835 Cross Creek Road). But the two dozen stores here provide a sense of the Malibu lifestyle and give you a chance to shop (or window shop) for quality.

MALIBU BEACHES AND PARKS

You won't find much sand at **Topanga Canyon State Park** (213-827-3832), but you will discover forests of oak and fields of rye. This 9000-acre hideaway nestles in the mountains above Malibu. Along with 35 miles of hiking trails featuring fine views, there are meadows and a stream to explore. Located at 20825 Entrada Road, off Topanga Canyon Road.

Topanga State Beach (213-827-3832) is a narrow sand corridor extending for over a mile. The adjacent highway breaks the quietude, but the strand is still popular with surfers and those wanting to be close to Malibu services. Located along Route 1 near Topanga Canyon Road.

Once a movie set, **Malibu Creek State Park** (818-706-1310) is now a 6000-acre facility spreading through rugged, virgin country in the Santa Monica Mountains. Among its features are 15 miles of hiking trails, four-acre Century Lake and Malibu Creek, which is lined with willows and cottonwood. In spring the meadows explode with wildflowers; at other times of the year you'll encounter mule deer, bobcats and abundant bird life. Located off Mulholland Highway and Las Vírgenes Road above Malibu.

Malibu Lagoon State Beach not only boasts a pretty strip of sand but an estuary and wetlands as well. You can stroll the white beach past an unending succession of lavish oceanfront homes or study a different species entirely in the park's salt marsh. Here Malibu Creek

---

TOPANGA CANYON

*When you tire of Malibu's sand and surf, take a drive along one of the canyon roads that lead from Route 1 up into the Santa Monica Mountains. This chaparral country is filled with oak and sycamore forests and offers sweeping views back along the coast. Topanga Canyon Boulevard, perhaps the best known of these mountain roads, curves up to the rustic town of Topanga. Vestiges of its years as a fabled retreat for flower children can be found in the form of health food stores, New Age shops and vegetarian restaurants like **The Inn of the Seventh Ray** (128 Old Topanga Road; 213-455-1311). Many of the woodframe houses are handcrafted and the community still vibrates to a slower rhythm than coastal Malibu and cosmopolitan Los Angeles.*

*To reach the top of the world (while making a mountain loop of this uphill jaunt), continue on Old Topanga Canyon Road and turn left out on **Mulholland Highway**. With its panoramic views of the ocean, Los Angeles Basin and San Fernando Valley, Mulholland is justifiably famous. The road rides the ridgetop of the Santa Monica Mountains for almost 50 miles from Hollywood down to the Malibu shore.*

feeds into the ocean, creating a rich tidal area busy with marine life and shorebirds. Located along Route 1 at Cross Creek Road.

A long, narrow stretch, **Westward Beach Point Dume State Park** (213-457-9891) is really a southerly continuation of Zuma Beach, but it's away from the highway and bordered by lofty sandstone cliffs. There are tidepools here and trails leading up along the bluffs. For white sand serenity, this is a choice spot. The park entrance is adjacent to the southern entrance to Zuma Beach County Park, just off Route 1 about six miles west of Malibu.

The long, broad beach at **Zuma Beach County Park** (213-457-9891) is a study in territorial instincts. Los Angeles County's largest beach park, it is frequented by Latinos in one area, by "Vals" (young residents of the San Fernando Valley) in a second spot, and by families and students in another stretch. Not as pretty as other Malibu beaches, it offers more space and better facilities, making Zuma a popular spot. Located along Route 1 about six miles west of Malibu.

A white sand corridor extending more than a mile, **Leo Carrillo State Beach** (818-706-1310) was named for the television actor who played Pancho in "The Cisco Kid." The beach offers sea caves, tidepools and a natural tunnel. Nicer still is **Leo Carrillo Beach North**, a sandy swath located just beyond Sequit Point and backdropped by a sharp bluff. This entire area is a prime whale-watching site. You can camp here; and at the south end of this 1600-acre park you can bathe in the buff. Located on Route 1 about 14 miles west of Malibu. Access to Leo Carrillo Beach North is from a parking lot at 40000 Route 1.

Santa Catalina Island

"Twenty-six miles across the sea. . .Santa Catalina, the island of romance, romance." You know the song. Actually this Mediterranean hideaway is parked just 22 miles off the Los Angeles coastline. But for romance, the song portrays it perfectly. Along its 54 miles of shoreline Catalina offers sheer cliffs, pocket beaches, hidden coves and some of the finest skindiving anywhere.

To the interior, mountains rise sharply to over 2000 feet elevation. Island fox, black antelope, mountain goats and over 400 bison range the island, while its waters teem with marlin, swordfish and barracuda.

Avalon, the famous coastal resort enclave, is the only town on the island. The rest is given over to mountain wilderness and pristine shoreline.

The port of entry for the island, **Avalon** is set in a luxurious amphitheater of green mountains. The architecture is a blend of Mediterranean and Victorian homes as well as vernacular structures

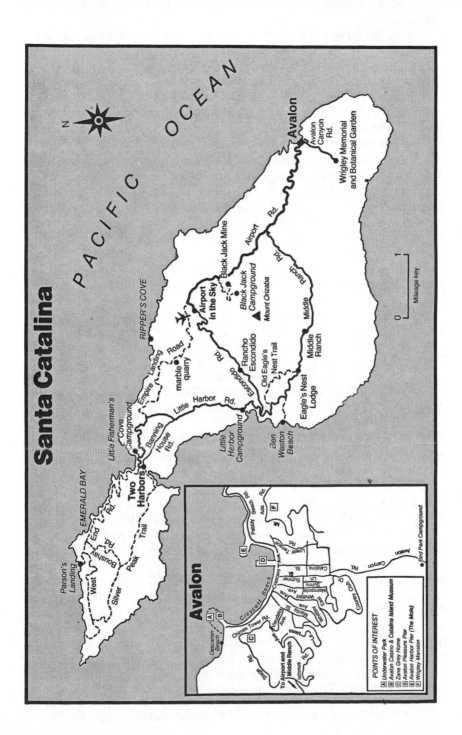

designed by creative locals who captured both the beautiful and whimsical.

From the ferry dock you can wander **Crescent Avenue**, Avalon's oceanfront boulevard. Stroll out along the **Avalon Pleasure Pier** (Crescent Avenue and Catalina Street) for a view of the entire town and its surrounding crescent of mountains. Along this wood plank promenade are food stands, the harbormaster's office and bait-and-tackle shops. The **Santa Catalina Island Chamber of Commerce and Visitors Bureau** (213-510-1520) has an information center here that will help orient you to Avalon and the island.

Among the pier kiosks are some offering glass-bottom boat tours out to a nearby cove, known as Catalina's "undersea gardens" and filled with colorful fish and marine plant life. **Santa Catalina Island Company** (Avalon Harbor Pier; 213-510-2000) features tours during the day and also at night when huge floodlights are used to attract sea life. During summer months they seek out the spectacular phosphorescent flying fish.

Farther along the waterfront, dominating the skyline, sits the **Avalon Casino** (end of Crescent Avenue). A massive circular building painted white and capped with a red-tile roof, it was built in 1929 after a Spanish moderne design. What can you say other than that the place is famous: it has appeared on countless postcards and travel posters. The ballroom has heard the big band sounds of Glenn Miller and Tommy Dorsey, and the entire complex is a study in art deco with fabulous murals and tile paintings. (For information on tours call 213-510-2000.) Downstairs is the **Catalina Island Museum** (213-510-2414) with a small collection of local artifacts and an excellent contour relief map of the island.

Another point of particular interest, located about two miles inland in Avalon Canyon, is the **Wrigley Memorial and Botanical Garden** (1400 Avalon Canyon Road; 213-510-2288; admission). The monument, an imposing 130-foot structure fashioned with glazed tiles and Georgia marble, features a spiral staircase in a solitary tower. The garden is a showplace for native island succulents and cactus.

The most exhilarating sightseeing excursion in Avalon lies in the hills around town. Head up Wrigley Terrace Road, one of the many terraces that rise above Avalon, and you will pass the **old Wrigley Mansion** (currently the Inn on Mt. Ada). This elegant estate with sweeping views was once the (ho hum) summer residence of the Wrigley family. Other scenic drives on the opposite side of town lie along Stage and Chimes Tower roads. Here you'll pass the **Zane Grey home** (199 Chimes Tower Road; 213-510-0966). The Western-novel writer's pueblo adobe is also now a hotel.

Both routes snake into the hills past rocky outcroppings and patches of cactus. The slopes are steep and unrelenting. Gaze around from this precarious perch and you'll see that Avalon rests in a green bowl surrounded by mountains.

When it comes time to venture farther afield, you'll find that traveling around Santa Catalina is more complicated than it first seems. No rental cars operate on the island, and visitors are not permitted to drive. You can hike or bicycle to most places on the island. **Brown's Bikes** (107 Pebbly Beach Road; 213-510-0986) rents bicycles, tandems and mountain bikes. In Avalon proper it's possible to rent golf carts from outfits like **Cartopia Cars** (615 Crescent Avenue; 213-510-2493) or **Catalina Auto Rental** (301 Crescent Avenue; 213-510-0111).

Santa Catalina Island Company (213-510-2000), which has a visitor information center at 420 Crescent Avenue, conducts coastal cruises and tours around the island, and drops off hikers and campers en route. To hike independently outside Avalon you will need a permit from the **Los Angeles County Department of Parks and Recreation** (213 Catalina Street; 213-510-0688).

Regardless of how you journey into Catalina's outback, there's only one way to get there, Airport Road. Offering magnificent views, it climbs past **Mt. Orizaba**, a flat-topped peak that represents the highest point on the island. A side road out to Black Jack Campground leads past **Black Jack Mine**, a silver mine closed since early in the century.

From Airport Road you can follow a figure eight course in your route around the island. Simply pick up Empire Landing Road, a curving, bumping track with side roads that lead down past an **old marble quarry** to **Ripper's Cove**. Characteristic of the many inlets dotting the island, the cove is framed by sharply rising hills.

Two Harbors, at the intersection of the figure eight's loops, is a half-mile-wide isthmus connecting the two sections of Catalina Island. A small fishing pier, several tourist facilities and a boat harbor make this modest enclave the only developed area outside Avalon.

Anchored off nearby **Emerald Bay** are several rock islets crowded with sea birds. En route back toward Avalon, Little Harbor Road (which, like most roads outside Avalon, is unpaved) climbs into the mountains, past ridges that drop along sheer rockfaces to the frothing surf below.

Take a detour up to **Rancho Escondido**, a working ranch that breeds champion Arabian horses. There's an arena where trainers work these exquisite animals through their paces and a fabulous saddle and trophy room.

Back at Little Harbor, Middle Ranch Road cuts through a mountain canyon past **Middle Ranch**, a small spread with livestock and oat fields. En route lies **Eagles' Nest Lodge**, a stagecoach stop dating to 1890.

SANTA CATALINA ISLAND LODGING

One fact about lodging in Catalina everyone seems to agree upon is that it is expensive. Particularly during summer months, hotels charge top rates for rooms. Rates jump seasonally more than on the mainland. If summer is the most expensive period, winter is the cheapest, with spring and fall somewhere in between. Weekend rates are also sometimes higher than weekday room tabs.

One of Santa Catalina's most popular hotels is the **Pavilion Lodge** (513 Crescent Avenue; 213-510-1788), a 72-room facility on Avalon's waterfront street. Designed around a central courtyard, it offers guests a lawn and patio for sunbathing. The rooms contain modern furniture and stall showers. Moderate in winter, otherwise deluxe to ultra-deluxe.

Plainly put, the **Hotel Vista Del Mar** (417 Crescent Avenue; 213-510-1452) is a true gem. Each of the 14 spacious Mediterranean rooms is decorated in soft pastels and features a wet bar, fireplace and full tiled bath. All open onto an open-air atrium courtyard lobby where guests can enjoy continental breakfasts and ocean views from comfortable wicker rockers. Deluxe to ultra-deluxe.

Catalina Canyon Hotel (888 Country Club Drive; 213-510-0325) is a chic, modern 80-room complex complete with pool, jacuzzi, sauna, weight room and restaurant. This Mediterranean-style hotel sits on a hillside in Avalon Canyon. The grounds are nicely landscaped with banana plants and palm trees. Each guest room is furnished in white oak and adorned with art prints. Moderate to deluxe.

The romantic **Hotel St. Lauren** (Metropole and Beacon streets; 213-510-2299) rises with a pink blush a block from the sand above Catalina's famed harbor. The contemporary-style hotel is a honeymoon paradise, with spacious rooms and jacuzzi tubs in minisuites.

THE INN ON MT. ADA

*Rare and incredible is the only way to describe **The Inn on Mt. Ada** (398 Wrigley Road; 213-510-2030). Perched on a hillside overlooking Avalon and its emerald shoreline, this stately hostelry resides in the old Wrigley mansion, a 7000-square-foot Georgian colonial home. A masterwork of french doors, elegant columns and curved ceilings, the grande dame is beautifully appointed with antiques and plush furnishings. The entire ground floor—with rattan sitting room, oceanfront veranda, formal dining room and spacious living room—is for the benefit of visitors. Amazingly, all this luxury serves just six guest rooms, guaranteeing personal service and an atmosphere of intimacy. Ultra-deluxe.*

Continental breakfast in the lobby can be brought back to your room or enjoyed on the sixth-floor view patio. Deluxe to ultra-deluxe.

Banning House Lodge (Two Harbors; 213-510-0303), the only hotel on the island located outside Avalon, is a turn-of-the-century hunting lodge. The living room boasts a brick fireplace and is adorned with a dozen trophy heads. Guest rooms come trimly decorated with throw rugs and rustic wood furniture. The lodge provides an excellent opportunity to experience the island's outback. Deluxe.

SANTA CATALINA ISLAND RESTAURANTS

It's hard to match the views from **The Busy Bee** (306-B Crescent Avenue; 213-510-1983), a local gathering place located right on the beach. At lunch you can dine on vegetable platters, tostadas and salads while gazing out at the harbor. Open year-round, the place also has dinners of lamb chops, swordfish and steak. Moderate.

Cafe Prego (603 Crescent Avenue; 213-510-1218), a small Italian bistro complete with oilcloth tables and stucco arches, comes highly recommended for its good food. The specialties are seafood dishes such as fresh swordfish, sea bass and halibut, plus plenty of pasta. Moderate to deluxe.

For a step upscale head to **Ristorante Villa Portofino** (111 Crescent Avenue; 213-510-0508), a romantic spot graced with a baby grand piano and candlelit tables. With art deco curves and colorful art prints, the place has an easy Mediterranean feel about it. The Italian cuisine includes scampi with garlic, scallions and brandy, cioppino chicken and New Zealand lamb chops. Moderate to deluxe.

SANTA CATALINA ISLAND SHOPPING

Within central Avalon are several minimalls, one of which, **Metropole Market Place** (Crescent and Sumner avenues), is a nicely designed modern complex.

SANTA CATALINA ISLAND NIGHTLIFE

Like other Catalina amenities, nightspots are concentrated in Avalon. The **Chi Chi Club** (107 Sumner Avenue; 213-510-2828) is one of the hottest dance clubs on the island, with deejay music and a lively crowd.

There's also dancing to deejay records at **Solomon's Landing** (101 Marilla Avenue; 213-510-1474). The bar here is outdoors and the motif decidedly Mexican.

Also check the schedule for **Avalon Casino** (end of Crescent Avenue; 213-510-2000). This fabulous vintage ballroom still hosts big bands and most of the island's major events.

SANTA CATALINA ISLAND BEACHES AND PARKS

About as relaxing as Coney Island, **Crescent Beach** stands in the center of the action. Avalon's main drag, Crescent Avenue, parallels the beach, and a pier divides it into two separate strips of sand. Facing Avalon Harbor, the strand is flanked on one side with a ferry dock and along the other by the famous Avalon Casino.

Happily, however, Santa Catalina's rugged back country offers several beautiful beaches. The mountains dominating the interior also provide some fine parks and campgrounds. For information contact the **Santa Catalina Island Conservancy** (206 Metropole Avenue; 213-510-1421).

Sporting Life

SPORTFISHING

Fish the waters around Los Angeles and you can try your hand at landing a barracuda, white croaker, halibut, calico bass or maybe even a relative of Jaws. For sportfishing outfits call, **Annie B Barge, Inc.** (Berth 79, San Pedro, 213-832-2274), **Queen's Wharf Sportfishing** (555 Pico Avenue, Long Beach; 213-432-8993), **Redondo Sportfishing** (233 North Harbor Drive, Redondo Beach; 213-372-2111) and **Marina del Rey Sportfishing** (13759 Fiji Way, Marina del Rey; 213-822-3625).

In Catalina contact the **Santa Catalina Island Chamber of Commerce and Visitors Bureau** (213-510-1520) for listings of private boat owners who outfit sportfishing expeditions.

---

26 MILES BENEATH THE SEA

Without doubt Santa Catalina Island offers some of the finest skindiving anywhere in the world. Perfectly positioned to attract fish from both the northern and southern Pacific, it teems with sea life. Large fish ascend from the deep waters surrounding the island, while small colorful species inhabit rich kelp forests along the coast. There are caves and caverns to explore as well as the wrecks of rusting ships.

Several outfits rent skindiving and scuba equipment and/or sponsor dive trips. In Avalon call Catalina Divers Supply (213-510-0330)or Argo Diving Service (213-510-2208). In Two Harbors, Catalina Safari Tours (213-510-2800) can fill your tanks but does not rent.

SKINDIVING

To explore Los Angeles' submerged depths, call **Pacific Sporting Goods** (11 39th Place, Long Beach, 213-434-1604), **Pacific Wilderness Ocean Sports** (1719 South Pacific Avenue, San Pedro, 213-833-2422), **Marina del Rey Divers** (2539 Lincoln Boulevard, Marina del Rey; 213-827-1131), **Dive n' Surf** (504 North Broadway, Redondo Beach; 213-372-8423), **Blue Cheer Ocean Water Sports** (1110 Wilshire Boulevard, Santa Monica; 213-828-4289) or **Malibu Divers** (21231 Pacific Coast Highway, Malibu; 213-456-2396).

WHALE WATCHING

During the annual whale migration the following outfits offer whale-watching trips: **Mickey's Belmont, Inc.** (Belmont Pier, Long Beach; 213-434-6781), **Spirit Adventures** (Berth 75, San Pedro; 213-831-1073) and **Billy V.** (Berth 79, San Pedro; 213-431-6837).

WINDSURFING AND SURFING

"Surfing is the only life," so grab a board from **Fun Bunns** (1144 Highland Avenue, Manhattan Beach; 213-545-3300), **Jeffers** (1338 Strand, Hermosa Beach; 213-372-9492), **Zuma Jay Surfboards** (22775 Pacific Coast Highway, Malibu; 213-456-8044) or **Catalina Adventure Tours** (the Mole, Avalon; 213-510-2888).

GOLF

For the golfers in the crowd, try **El Dorado Park Municipal Golf Course** (2400 Studebaker Road, Long Beach; 213-430-5411), **Skylink Golf Course** (4800 East Wardlow Road, Long Beach; 213-421-3388), **Recreation Park** (5000 Federation Drive, Long Beach; 213-494-5000), **Los Verdes Golf Course** (7000 West Los Verdes Drive, Rancho Palos Verdes; 213-377-7370), or **Penmar Golf Course** (1233 Rose Avenue, Venice; 213-396-6228). In Catalina call **Catalina Visitors Golf Club** (1 Country Club Drive, Avalon; 213-510-0530).

TENNIS

There are public tennis courts available in **El Dorado Park** (2800 Studebaker Road, Long Beach; 213-425-0553), **The Sport Center at King Harbor** (819 North Harbor Drive, Redondo Beach; 213-372-8868), **Marina Tennis World** (13199 Mindanao Way, Marina del Rey; 213-822-2255), and **Douglas Park** (26 Wilshire Boulevard, Santa Monica; 213-458-8311).

BICYCLING

Though Los Angeles might seem like one giant freeway, there are scores of bike trails and routes for scenic excursions. Foremost is the **South Bay Bike Trail**, with over 19 miles of coastal vistas. The trail, an easy ride, extends from King Harbor in Redondo Beach to the Santa Monica Pier.

Naples, a Venice-like neighborhood in Long Beach, provides a charming area for freeform bike rides. There are no designated paths, but you can cycle with ease past beautiful homes, parks and canals.

Of moderate difficulty is the **Palos Verdes Peninsula** coastline trail. Offering wonderful scenery, the 14-mile round trip ride goes from Malaga Cove Plaza in Palos Verdes Estates to the Wayfarers Chapel.

The **Santa Monica Loop** is an easy ride starting at Ocean Avenue and going up San Vicente Boulevard, past Palisades Park and the Santa Monica Pier. Most of the trail is on bike lanes and paths; ten miles round trip.

For maps, brochures and additional information on bike routes in Los Angeles contact the **Department of Transportation** (205 South Broadway; 213-485-3051).

Transportation

BY CAR

Route 1, which parallels the coast throughout Los Angeles County, undergoing several name changes during its course, is the main coastal route. **Route 101** shadows the coast farther inland, while **Route 405** provides access to the Los Angeles basin from San Diego and **Route 10** arrives from the east.

BY AIR

Two airports bring visitors to the Los Angeles coast area: the small Long Beach Airport and the very big, very busy Los Angeles International Airport (described in Chapter Two).

Presently, carriers into **Long Beach Airport** are American Airlines, Alaska Airlines, America West, Continental Airlines, Delta Airlines, Trans World Airlines, USAir and United Airlines.

The Airport in the Sky (213-510-0143), set at 1600-foot elevation in the mountains of Catalina, may be the prettiest landing strip anywhere. Allied Air Charter and National Air (also called Catalina Vegas Airlines; 619-292-7311) service the airport from the mainland.

Another means of transportation to Catalina is **Island Express** (213-491-5550), a helicopter service from Long Beach and San Pedro. (They also offer island tours.) Or try **Helitrans** (213-548-1314), a commuter jet helicopter service from Los Angeles International Airport, Long Beach Airport, San Pedro, and John Wayne Airport to Avalon.

BY BOAT

Several companies provide regular transportation to Catalina by boat. Contact **Catalina Express** (P.O. Box 1391, San Pedro; 213-519-1212), **Catalina Cruises** (P.O. Box 1948-B, San Pedro; 800-888-5939) or **Catalina Passenger Service** (400 Main Street, Newport Beach; 714-673-5245) for details.

BY BUS

Greyhound/Trailways Bus Lines has service to the Los Angeles area from all around the country. The Long Beach terminals are located at 6601 Atlantic Avenue (213-428-7777) and 464 West 3rd Street (213-432-1842); the Santa Monica terminal is at 1433 5th Street (213-394-5433).

CAR RENTALS

Having a car in Los Angeles is practically a must. Distances are great and public transportation leaves much to be desired.

At the Long Beach Airport you'll find **Avis Rent A Car** (213-988-3255), **Budget Rent A Car** (213-472-7299), **Dollar Rent A Car** (213-421-8841), **Hertz Rent A Car** (213-420-2322), **Sears Rent A Car** (213-425-4969) and **National Car Rental** (213-421-8877).

PUBLIC TRANSPORTATION

Long Beach Transit (1300 Gardenia Avenue; 213-591-2301) transports riders throughout the Long Beach area.

RTD Bus Line (425 South Main Street, Los Angeles; 213-273-0910) serves Los Angeles' Westside (for information on central Los Angeles call 213-626-4455); disabled riders can call a hotline for information, 800-621-7828.

The **Light Rail Blue Line** (213-972-6235), a modern commuter train, runs between downtown Los Angeles and Long Beach.

In Santa Monica, call the **Big Blue Bus** (Santa Monica Municipal Bus Lines, 1660 7th Street; 213-451-5444).

FOUR

Orange County

Places are known through their nicknames. More than official titles or proper names, sobriquets reveal the real identity of a region. "Orange Coast" can never describe the 42 miles of cobalt-blue ocean and whitewashed sand from Seal Beach to San Clemente. That moniker derives from the days when Orange County was row on row with orchards of plump citrus. Today prestigious homes and marinas sprout from the shoreline. The habitat of beachboys, yachtsmen and tennis buffs, it represents the "American Riviera."

The theme that ties both inland and coastal Orange County together and gives rise to these nicknames is money. Money and the trappings that attend it—glamor, celebrity, elegance, power. Orange County is a sun-blessed realm of beautiful people, where politics is right wing and real estate sells by the square foot.

Some half-dozen freeways crisscross the broad coastal plane where Spain's Gaspar de Portolá led the first overland expedition into present-day Orange County in 1769. Today, more than two million people live, work and play where during the mid-19th century a few hundred Mexican ranchers tended herds of livestock on a handful of extensive land grants.

Ever since Walt Disney founded his fantasy empire here in the 1950s, Orange County has exploded with population and profits. In Disney's wake came the crowds, and as they arrived they developed—housing projects and condominium complexes, minimalls and business centers. To the interior, towns now look alike and Orange County, once an empire of orange groves, has become a cookie-cutter civilization. Only in the distant mountain areas to the south and east does any wilderness remain.

Along the coast progress also levied a tremendous toll but has left intact some of the natural beauty, the deep canyons and curving hills, soft sand beaches and sharp escarpments. The towns, too, have retained their separate styles, each projecting its own identifying image.

It wasn't until the 1960s, amid the twanging strains of electric guitars, that Orange County earned its final nickname, "Surfer Heaven." As Huntington Beach and surrounding communities contributed to the nation's surfing craze, the rest of Orange County mushroomed with development. Within a few years Newport Center, the area's highrise district, was built. The entire region rapidly entered the modern age of multimillion-dollar development, adding a certain luster to Orange County's reputation and granting to its shoreline, for better or worse, an everlasting epithet—California's "Gold Coast."

Huntington Beach

In the mythology of surfing, Huntington Beach, the self-described "Surfing Capital of the World," rides with Oahu's North Shore and the great breaks of Australia. Since the 1920s boys with boards have been as much a part of the seascape as blue skies and billowing clouds. Today they paddle around what is left of storm-damaged **Huntington Pier** (end of Main Street), poised to catch the next wave that pounds the pilings. And at night Huntington's 500 fire rings blaze with light, making it one of Southern California's great party beaches.

Nearby **Bolsa Chica Ecological Reserve** (accessways are along Pacific Coast Highway across from the entrance to Bolsa Chica State Beach and at Warner Avenue) provides a natural counterpoint to all this activity. An important wetlands area dotted with islands and home to hundreds of bird and animal species, this 530-acre preserve features a mile-long loop trail.

HUNTINGTON BEACH RESTAURANTS

Step down to the foot of Huntington Pier and you'll discover **Maxwell's** (317 Pacific Coast Highway; 714-536-2555), a 1924-vintage building done entirely in art deco fashion. Specialty of the house is seafood: at dinner there are well over a dozen selections varying from fresh Hawaiian fish to Cajun-style shrimp, plus veal, steak and pasta entrées. A choice spot for an oceanfront meal; deluxe.

Tibbie's Music Hall (16360 Pacific Coast Highway; 714-840-5661) is decidedly not the place to go for a quiet dinner on the water. If you're looking for a full-fledged musical revue with dessert, this *is* the spot. The waiters and waitresses at this popular supper club become performers later in the evening, putting together a variety show that could range from an 1890s musical medley to a tribute to the Beach Boys. Corny but fun; deluxe.

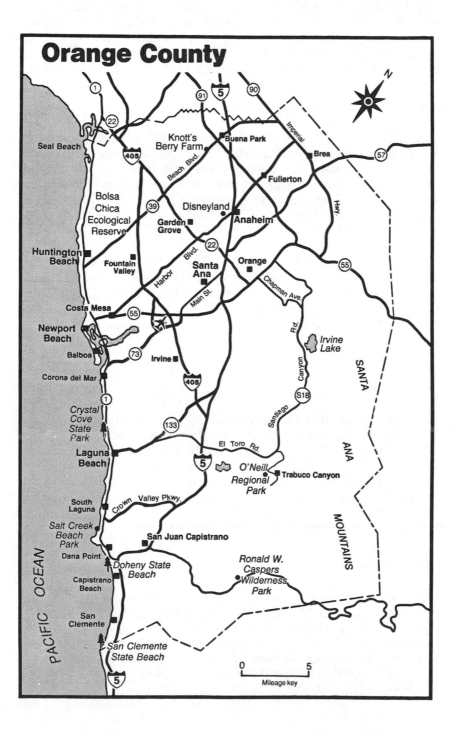

Orange County

Dating back to 1930, the **Glide'er Inn** (1400 Pacific Coast Highway, Seal Beach; 213-431-3022) is an unusual landmark indeed. The motif is aviation, as in model airplanes dangling from the ceiling and aeronautical pictures covering every inch of available wall space. The menu includes an extensive list of seafood selections as well as European dishes like wienerschnitzel. Moderate.

HUNTINGTON BEACH BEACHES AND PARKS

One of Southern California's broadest strands, **Huntington State Beach** (714-848-1566) extends for three miles along the Pacific Coast Highway. In addition to a desert of soft sand, it features tremendous surfing waves and a five-acre preserve for the protection of the endangered least tern. Unfortunately, these natural wonders are sandwiched between industrial plants and offshore oil derricks. Immediately to the north, **Huntington City Beach** (714-536-5281) runs for several miles more.

With six miles of fluffy sand, **Bolsa Chica State Beach** (714-848-1566) is another in this series of broad, beautiful beaches. Since the summer surf is gentler here than at Huntington Beach, Bolsa Chica is ideal for swimmers and families. Located along Pacific Coast Highway between Huntington Pier and Warner Avenue.

Newport Beach

The capital of Southern California's "Gold Coast," Newport Beach is a region of posh waterfront homes and fashionable yacht clubs. Established in 1863 as a "new port" between San Diego and San Pedro, the town took shape after the shallow mouth of the Santa Ana River was dredged to create a harbor, peninsulas and tiny islands. Early in this century Newport Beach became a major seaside recreation area, then

---

SEAL BEACH INN

With its wrought-iron balcony, ornate fence and garden ambience, the Seal Beach Inn and Gardens (212 5th Street, Seal Beach; 213-493-2416) has garnered a reputation for style and seclusion. Its 22 rooms, pricing from deluxe to ultra-deluxe, are furnished in hardwood antiques and appointed with period wallhangings. Guests breakfast in a cozy "tea room," then adjourn to the grounds, which are graced with wrought-iron furnishings and turn-of-the-century lampposts. In sum, a fine old inn.

during the past few decades blossomed into a fabulously wealthy community, populated by movie stars and other famous figures.

Today the town is a mélange of manmade islands and peninsulas surrounding a small bay. For help finding your bearings amid this labyrinth of waterways, contact the **Newport Harbor Area Chamber of Commerce** (1470 Jamboree Road; 714-644-8211) or the **Newport Beach Conference & Visitors Bureau** (366 San Miguel Drive, Suite 200; 714-644-1190).

After learning your way around, drop by the **Sherman Library and Gardens** (2647 East Coast Highway, Corona del Mar; 714-673-2261; admission). Devoted to the culture and recent history of the Pacific Southwest, this botanical garden is a kind of desert museum alive with cacti, succulents and other plant species.

Also consider the **Newport Harbor Art Museum** (850 San Clemente Drive; 714-759-1122; admission). Specializing in contemporary art, this facility possesses one of the finest collections of post-World War II California art anywhere.

One of the town's prettiest neighborhoods is **Balboa Island**, comprised of two manmade islets in the middle of Newport Bay. It can be reached by bridge along Marine Avenue or via a short ferry ride from Balboa Peninsula. Walk the pathways that circumnavigate both islands and you will pass clapboard cottages, Cape Cod homes and modern block-design houses that seem made entirely of glass.

Another landfill island, **Lido Isle**, sits just off Balboa Peninsula. Surrounded by Newport Bay, lined with sprawling homes and pocket beaches, it is another of Newport Beach's wealthy residential enclaves.

The central piece in this jigsaw puzzle of manmade plots is **Balboa Peninsula**, a long, narrow finger of land bounded by Newport Bay and the open ocean. Highlight of the peninsula is **Balboa Pavilion** (end of Main Street), a Victorian landmark that dates back to 1905. Marked by its well-known cupola, the bayfront building is an amusement park complete with carousel, ferris wheel, photograph booths, skee ball and video games.

This is also home to the **Balboa Island Ferry** (714-673-1070), a kind of floating landmark that has shuttled between Balboa Peninsula and Balboa Island since 1919. A simple, single-deck ferry that carries three cars and sports a pilot house the size of a phone booth, it crosses the narrow waterway every few minutes.

The beach scene in this seaside city extends for over five miles along the Pacific side of Balboa Peninsula and is centered around **Newport Pier** (Balboa Boulevard and McFadden Place) and **Balboa Pier** (Ocean Front Boulevard and Main Street). At Newport Pier the skiffs of the **Newport Dory Fishing Fleet** are beached every day while local fishermen sell their catch. This flotilla of small wooden boats has been here so long it has achieved historic landmark status.

The richness of Orange County's natural environment is evident when you venture through **Upper Newport Bay State Ecological Reserve** (Backbay Drive). Southern California's largest estuary, the bay is a vital stopping place for migrating birds on the Pacific flyway. Over 200 species can be seen here.

NEWPORT BEACH LODGING

The **Balboa Inn** (105 Main Street; 714-675-3412), next to the beach at Balboa Pier, is a Spanish-style hotel built in 1930. With its cream-colored walls and tile-roofed tower, this 34-room hostelry is vintage Southern California. The rooms, some of which have ocean views, are furnished in knotty pine, decorated with colorful prints and adorned with tile baths and brass fixtures. A Mediterranean atmosphere at a deluxe price.

    Portofino Beach Hotel (2306 West Ocean Front; 714-673-7030), a 15-room bed-and-breakfast inn, rests on the beach in an early 20th-century building. Richly appointed with brass beds, armoires and antique fixtures, each room is decorated with wallpaper and equipped with a private bath; many have jacuzzis and ocean views. Deluxe to ultra-deluxe.

    By way of full-facility destinations, Southern California-style, few places match the **Hyatt Newporter Resort** (1107 Jamboree Road; 714-644-1700). Situated on a hillside, it sprawls across 26 acres and sports three swimming pools, three jacuzzis, a nine-hole pitch-and-putt course and a tennis club. There are restaurants and lounges, a lavishly decorated lobby and a series of terraced patios. Ultra-deluxe.

    With ocean views and a shopping complex next door, the 20-story **Four Seasons Hotel** (690 Newport Center Drive; 714-759-0808) would seem to have the best of both worlds. The large, comfortable lobby, decorated in cool pastels, has marble and brass accents throughout. A garden pool, fitness center, massage service, restaurants and piano lounge round out the amenities. Ultra-deluxe.

NEWPORT BEACH RESTAURANTS

The **Cannery** (3010 Lafayette Avenue; 714-675-5777), a 1934 fish cannery, looks much as it did way back when. The conveyor belts and pulleys are still here, their gears exposed; and there are fire wagons, a fierce-looking boiler and more tin cans than you can imagine. All part of a waterfront seafood restaurant that also features dinner and weekend brunch cruises aboard a 54-foot boat. Deluxe to ultra-deluxe.

    Character is a quality in abundance at the **Bouzy Rouge Cafe** (3110 Newport Boulevard; 714-673-3440). This simple bistro doubles as a cultural center where dinner might be combined with French

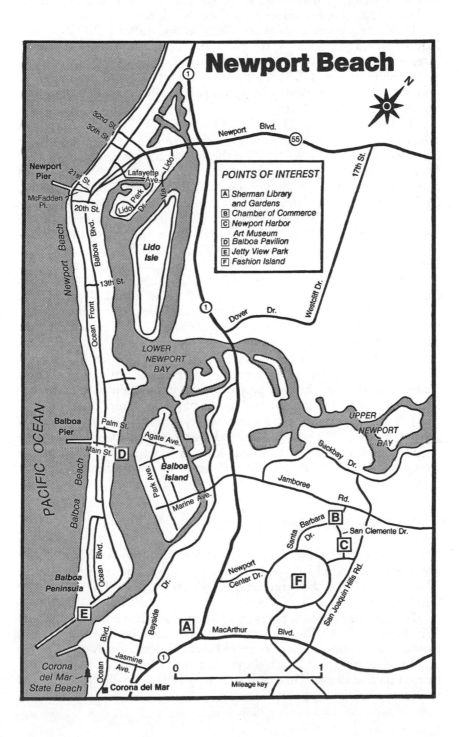

Newport Beach

POINTS OF INTEREST

- A Sherman Library and Gardens
- B Chamber of Commerce
- C Newport Harbor Art Museum
- D Balboa Pavilion
- E Jetty View Park
- F Fashion Island

Newport Blvd.

55

17th St.

Newport Pier

32nd St.
30th St.

21st St.

Lafayette Ave.

Lido

Via Lido

Lido Park Dr.

McFadden Pl.

20th St.

Balboa Blvd.

Lido Isle

13th St.

Ocean Front

Westcliff Dr.

1

Dover Dr.

LOWER NEWPORT BAY

Newport Beach

PACIFIC OCEAN

Balboa Pier

Palm St.

Main St. D

Agate Ave.

Balboa Island

Park Ave.

Marine Ave.

Balboa Beach

UPPER NEWPORT BAY

Backbay Dr.

Jamboree Rd.

Santa Barbara Dr.

B

San Clemente Dr.

C

F

Newport Center Dr.

San Joaquin Hills Rd.

Ocean Blvd.

Balboa Peninsula

E

Bayside Dr.

A

MacArthur Blvd.

Blvd.

Jasmine Ave.

Ocean

1

Corona del Mar State Beach

Corona del Mar

0   1

Mileage key

lessons, a string quartet or a Flamenco guitarist. The evening menu includes tapas, quiche and roast chicken. Moderate.

Don't worry, you won't miss **The Crab Cooker** (2200 Newport Boulevard; 714-673-0100): it's painted bright red, located at a busy intersection and has been a local institution since the 1950s. Actually, you don't *want* to miss The Crab Cooker. This informal eatery, where meals are served on paper plates, has fish, scallops, shrimp, crab and oysters at moderate prices.

21 Ocean Front (2100 West Ocean Front; 714-675-2566) is a gourmet seafood dining place known for fine cuisine. Located on the beach overlooking Newport Pier, the restaurant has an interior done (or rather, overdone) in a kind of shiny Victorian style with black trim and brass chandeliers. At dinner the chef prepares Hawaiian fish dishes, Maine lobster, rack of lamb and filet mignon. Deluxe to ultra-deluxe.

Who could imagine that at the end of Balboa Pier there would be a vintage 1940s-era diner complete with art deco curves and red plastic booths? **Ruby's Diner** (1 Balboa Pier; 714-675-7829) is a classic. Besides that, it provides 180° views of the ocean at budget prices.

The top Thai restaurant hereabouts is **Bangkok 3** (101 Palm Street; 714-673-6521), a sparkling dining room adorned with fabric paintings. The surroundings are ultramodern, but the cuisine is traditional, a tasteful mix of curry and ginger dishes. A fine restaurant with a friendly staff; moderate.

Amelia's (311 Marine Avenue; 714-673-6580), a family-run restaurant serving Italian meals and seafood, is a local institution over on Balboa Island. Here the chef prepares calamari stuffed with crab, Icelandic cod, veal piccata and a full round of pasta platters. Moderate.

For a multicourse feast, Moroccan-style, reserve a tent at **Marrakesh** (1100 West Coast Highway; 714-645-8384). Decorated in the fashion of North Africa, this well-known dining room conveys the sense and flavor of Morocco. Belly dancers Thursday through Sunday. Deluxe in price.

NEWPORT BEACH SHOPPING

The streets radiating out from **Balboa Pavilion** (end of Main Street) are lined with beachwear stores, sundries shops and souvenir stands. The scene is much the same around **Newport Pier** (Balboa Avenue and McFadden Place).

For more upscale shopping, cast anchor at **Lido Marina Village** (Via Oporto; 714-675-8662). This well-heeled complex features a host of shops lining a brick courtyard and adjacent boardwalk.

Another Newport Beach shopping enclave lies along Marine Avenue on Balboa Island. This consumer strip is door-to-door with beach wear and sundries shops.

After all is said and done, but hopefully before the money is all spent, the center for Newport Beach shopping is **Fashion Island** (Newport Center Drive; 714-721-2000). It is also the best place for beautiful-people watching. Every self-respecting department store is here. There's also an outdoor plaza filled with fashion outlets and an atrium displaying three floors of designer dreams.

NEWPORT BEACH NIGHTLIFE

For an evening on Newport Bay, climb aboard the *Pavilion Queen*, a double-deck boat that departs from the Balboa Pavilion on a **harbor cruise** (end of Main Street; 714-673-5245).

There's live jazz nightly at the **Studio Cafe** (100 Main Street; 714-675-7760), a waterfront watering hole near Balboa Pier.

Even if you don't care for '30s-era sounds, stop by **Bubbles Balboa Club** (111 Palm Street; 714-675-9093). This art deco club is trimly decorated with vintage accouterments and highpointed by a translucent "bubble column." The music fits the period motif, ranging from the Ink Spots to a 14-piece band; live nightly.

Rumpelstiltskin's (114 McFadden Place; 714-673-5025) has rock music and dancing seven nights a week during the summer. The rhythms range from hard rock to New Wave to jazz; cover.

The Cannery (3010 Lafayette Avenue; 714-675-5777) has entertainment nightly. Bands perform rock and Top-40 tunes Thursday through Sunday.

NEWPORT BEACH BEACHES AND PARKS

Located at the mouth of Newport Harbor, **Corona del Mar State Beach** (714-644-3047) offers an opportunity to watch sailboats tacking in and out of the bay. Throngs congregate because of its easy access, landscaped lawn and excellent facilities. Well protected for swimming. Located at Jasmine Avenue and Ocean Boulevard in Corona del Mar.

Set at the very end of the Balboa Peninsula, **Jetty View Park** is a perfectly placed triangle of sand. You can climb the rock jetty and watch the boats in Newport Harbor, or turn your back on these trifles and wander across the broad sand carpet that rolls down to the ocean. If you're daring enough, you can even challenge the waves at "The Wedge." Known to bodysurfers around the world, the area between the jetty and beach is one of the finest and most dangerous shore breaks anywhere, the "Mount Everest of bodysurfing."

Balboa Beach, a broad sandy strip, forms the ocean side of Balboa Peninsula and extends along its entire length. Similarly, **Newport Beach** reaches for several miles along the base of the peninsula. Both are outstanding beaches with large crowds and excellent pier facilities. They run parallel to Balboa Boulevard.

Laguna Beach

Next stop on this cavalcade of coastal cities is Laguna Beach. Framed by the San Joaquin Hills, the place is an intaglio of coves and bluffs, sand beaches and rock outcroppings. It conjures images of the Mediterranean with deep bays and greenery that runs to the sea's edge.

Little wonder that Laguna, with its wealthy residents and leisurely beach front, has become synonymous with the chic but informal style of Southern California. Its long tradition as an artist colony adds to this sense of beauty and bounty, aesthetics and aggrandizement.

Early in this century artists, attracted by the French Riviera setting, began congregating here. John Steinbeck wrote *Tortilla Flat* while living in Laguna, and film star Bette Davis made it her home during the 1940s. A freestyle community, Laguna developed into an artist colony filled with galleries and renowned for its cliff-rimmed beaches.

Laguna Beach's artistic heritage is evident in the many galleries and studios around town. The **Laguna Beach Chamber of Commerce** (357 Glenneyre Street; 714-494-1018), with its maps and brochures, can help you find your way about. The **Laguna Art Museum** (307 Cliff Drive; 714-494-6531; admission) has a wonderfully chosen collection of historic and contemporary California paintings.

PAGEANT OF THE MASTERS

*Highlighting the artistic tradition of Laguna Beach, the **Festival of Arts & Pageant of the Masters** (Irvine Bowl, 650 Laguna Canyon Road; 714-494-1145; admission) is staged every year during July and August. While the Festival of Arts and the nearby **Sawdust Festival** (935 Laguna Canyon Road; 714-494-3030) display the work of several dozen local artists and craftspeople, the Pageant of the Masters is the high point, an event you absolutely must not miss. It presents a series of tableaux vivants in which local residents, dressed to resemble figures from famous paintings, remain motionless against a frieze that re-creates the painting. Elaborate make-up and lighting techniques flatten the figures and create a sense of two-dimensionality.*

LAGUNA BEACH LODGING

One of the premier resting places in Laguna Beach is a sprawling 161-room establishment overhanging the sand. At the **Surf & Sand Hotel** (1555 South Coast Highway; 714-497-4477) nearly every room has a sea view and private balcony. Guests also enjoy two restaurants and an art deco lounge. Ultra-deluxe.

At the dreamlike **Casa Laguna Inn** (2510 South Coast Highway; 714-494-2996) the cottages and rooms are nestled in a garden setting complete with stone terraces and winding paths. Built in the 1930s, this Spanish-style complex features a courtyard, bell tower and a swimming pool overlooking the ocean. The rooms are small and furnished in antiques; many offer ocean views. Rooms price deluxe; suites and cottages with kitchens are ultra-deluxe.

It's not just the residential neighborhood that makes the **Carriage House** (1322 Catalina Street; 714-494-8945) unique. The colonial architecture of the "New Orleans-style" bed-and-breakfast inn also sets it apart. Within this historic landmark structure are six suites, renting at deluxe prices, each with a sitting room and separate bedroom.

Hotel San Maartéen (696 South Coast Highway; 714-494-1001), fashioned in the style of the French Caribbean, creates a luxurious atmosphere. The 54 guest rooms surround a lushly landscaped courtyard complete with swimming pool and patio restaurant. For a touch of the tropics right here in Laguna Beach, you can't go astray at this deluxe-priced hotel.

The **Ritz Carlton Laguna Niguel** (33533 Ritz Carlton Drive, Laguna Niguel; 714-240-2000), set on a cliff above the Pacific, is simply the finest resort hotel along the California coast. Built in the fashion of a Mediterranean villa, it dominates a broad sweep of coastline, a 393-room mansion replete with gourmet restaurants and dark wood lounges. The guest rooms, equal in luxury to the rest of the resort, are priced at the etherial end of the ultra-deluxe range.

Tucked into a secluded canyon is **Aliso Creek Inn** (31106 Coast Highway, South Laguna; 714-499-2271), an appealing 87-acre resort complete with swimming pools, restaurant and nine-hole golf course. Particularly attractive for families, every unit includes a sitting area, patio and kitchen. Studios and one-bedroom suites are deluxe; two-bedroom complexes are ultra-deluxe.

LAGUNA BEACH RESTAURANTS

The **Penguin Malt Shop** (981 South Coast Highway; 714-494-1353), a 1930s-era cafe with counter juke boxes and swivel stools, is a time capsule with a kitchen. Breakfast and lunch are all-American affairs ranging from ham and eggs to hamburgers and milk shakes. Budget.

Choose one place to symbolize the easy elegance of Laguna and it inevitably will be **Las Brisas** (361 Cliff Drive; 714-497-5434). A whitewashed Spanish building with arched windows, it rests on a cliff above the water. You can dine in a white-tablecloth room or out on the patio. The moderate-to-deluxe-priced menu consists of Mexican seafood dishes and other specialties from south of the border. Out on the patio there are sandwiches, salads and fajitas at moderate prices.

If any place in town can challenge Las Brisas in setting the style for Laguna Beach, it is **Ron's in Laguna** (1464 South Coast Highway; 714-497-4871). Rather than ocean vistas, here we are talking mirrored walls, upholstered booths and fireplaces, plus tuxedo-clad waiters. The continental cuisine includes duck, tournedos, veal marsala and fresh fish. Deluxe.

Five Feet Restaurant (328 Glenneyre Street; 714-497-4955) prepares "Chinese cuisine European style." The unique bill of fare includes blackened ahi, spring lamb in curry-cilantro sauce and goat cheese wontons. Applying the principles of California cuisine to Chinese cooking and adding a few French flourishes, Five Feet has gained an impressive reputation. Dinner only; deluxe.

The most remarkable aspect of the **Cottage Restaurant** (308 North Coast Highway; 714-494-3023) is the cottage itself, an early 20th-century California bungalow. Meal time in this historic house is a traditional American affair. You'll be served top sirloin, chargrilled lamb in Turkish spices, as well as daily fresh fish specials. Moderate.

Monique French Restaurant (31727 Coast Highway, South Laguna; 714-499-5359) is a little jewel set on a coastal bluff. Situated in a former home, it offers intimate dining indoors or outside on the patio. In addition to ocean views, you'll enjoy a menu that changes daily and might include scampi Provençal, filet of pork a l'orange and fresh seafood dishes. Deluxe.

LAGUNA BEACH SHOPPING

Given the town's long tradition as an artist colony, it's little wonder that Laguna Beach is crowded with galleries and studios. Add a few designer clothing shops plus antique stores and you have one of the most interesting shopping spots for miles around. The center of all this action lies along Coast Highway between Bluebird Canyon Drive and Laguna Canyon Road.

There are several art galleries clustered together that I found particularly interesting. Foremost is **Redfern Gallery** (1540 South Coast Highway; 714-497-3356); the others include **Vladimir Sokolov Studio Gallery** (1540 South Coast Highway; 714-494-3633) and **The Esther Wells Collection** (1390 South Coast Highway; 714-494-2497). All feature carefully chosen selections of contemporary California art.

Fine fashion is taken for granted at **Shebue** (540 South Coast Highway; 714-494-3148). This plush shop houses beautiful designer clothing for women. *Très chic* (and *très cher*).

Laguna Beach's other shopping strip is Forest Avenue, a three-block promenade wall-to-wall with specialty stores like **From Laguna** (241 Forest Avenue; 714-494-4300), specializing in upscale sportswear as well as jewelry by local designers.

There are also two rustic, raw wood malls, **Forest Avenue Mall** (332 Forest Avenue) and **Lumberyard Plaza** (384 Forest Avenue), which blend neatly into the background. The former features a pair of intriguing stores: **Kristalle Natural History Gallery** (714-494-7695) is noted for fine minerals and natural crystals, while **Aqua Classics** (714-494-0138) carries ceramics, paintings and sculpture, all with an aquatic theme.

LAGUNA BEACH NIGHTLIFE

Admirers of art deco are bound to fall in love with the **Towers Lounge** in the Surf & Sand Hotel (1555 South Coast Highway; 714-497-4477). This softly lit piano bar combines the ambience of the 1930s with wide-angle views of the ocean.

The White House (340 South Coast Highway; 714-494-8088) is a landmark 1918 building in downtown Laguna Beach. A long, narrow lounge with dark wood paneling and mirrored walls, it turns tradition upside down every night with live rock, reggae and Motown; cover.

One of Laguna Beach's hottest nightspots is also its most funky. **The Sandpiper Lounge** (1183 South Coast Highway; 714-494-4694) is a run-down club filled with dart boards and pinball machines. Often it is also filled with some of the finest sounds around.

CLIFFTOP PROMENADE

*One of Laguna's prettiest stretches of shoreline lies along the rocky bluffs in **Heisler Park** and below on the boulder-strewn sands of **Rock Pile Beach** and **Picnic Beach**. The park provides a promenade with grassy areas and shade trees. You can scan the coastline from Laguna Beach south for miles, then meander down to the shore where sedimentary formations shatter the wave patterns and create marvelous tidepools. Rock Pile and Picnic form adjacent coves, both worthy of exploration. Fishing is excellent here, as is swimming, and the surfing is recommended at Rock Pile. Heisler Park is located along Cliff Drive. Rock Pile Beach is at the end of Jasmine Street; Picnic Beach lies to the north at the end of Myrtle Street.*

Rock, reggae, oldies and other music is live nightly, sometimes performed by well-known groups. Cover.

Las Brisas (361 Cliff Drive; 714-497-5434), the sleek, clifftop restaurant overlooking the ocean, is a gathering place for the fast and fashionable.

Laguna Beach's gay scene centers around the **Boom Boom Room** (1401 South Coast Highway; 714-494-7588) at the Coast Inn. A three-tiered discotheque, it contains a dancefloor and two bars. Weekend cover.

The ultimate evening destinations are at the ultra-posh Ritz Carlton Laguna Niguel (Ritz Carlton Drive, Laguna Niguel; 714-240-2000). Here, along corridors of polished stone, is the **Club Grill and Bar**, a wood-paneled rendezvous decorated with 19th-century paintings of equestrian scenes. Also located in the Ritz Carlton is an elegant two-tiered, glass-walled lounge with sweeping ocean views called **The Bar**. The first offers a combo nightly and the latter features a solo pianist. Dinner jackets, gentlemen.

LAGUNA BEACH BEACHES AND PARKS

A truly outstanding facility, **Crystal Cove State Park** (714-494-3539) is a winding sand beach sometimes sectioned into a series of coves by high tides. The park stretches for over three miles along the coast and extends up into the hills. Grassy terraces grace the sea cliffs, and the offshore area is designated an underwater preserve. The perfect park when you're seeking solitude. Located along Coast Highway between Laguna Beach and Corona del Mar.

Main Beach (Broadway and Coast Highway) is located at the very center of Laguna Beach, with shopping streets radiating in several directions. A sinuous boardwalk winds along the waterfront, past basketball players, sunbathers, volleyball aficionados, little kids on swings and aging kids on roller skates. The Laguna Beach Marine Life Refuge lies just offshore, making this also a popular place for skindiving.

Set in a wide cove and bounded by low coastal bluffs, **Aliso Creek Beach Park** is popular with local folks. A sand scimitar with rocks guarding both ends, the beach is bisected by a fishing pier. To escape the crowds head over to the park's southern cove, a pretty beach with fluffy sand. Located in South Laguna along the 31300 block of Coast Highway.

Salt Creek Beach Park consists of two half-mile sections of beach divided by a lofty point. Each beach is a broad strip of white sand, backdropped by bluffs and looking out on Santa Catalina Island. Though both beaches are part of Salt Creek, the strand to the south is also known as **Laguna Niguel Beach Park**. Both lie off Route 1 in Laguna Niguel near the Ritz Carlton.

San Juan Capistrano Area

One of Orange County's most fabled spots is an unassuming mission town founded in 1776 by Father Junípero Serra. Seventh in the state's chain of 21 missions, it is considered "the jewel of the missions," a hauntingly beautiful site that conveys a sense of placidity and magic.

The centerpiece of the town, **Mission San Juan Capistrano** (Camino Capistrano and Ortega Highway; 714-493-1424; admission), represents the oldest building in California, the only remaining church used by Father Serra. This historic chapel, built in 1777, is decorated with Indian designs and baroque reredos.

There are also ponds and gardens here, as well as archaeological sites and the ruins of the original 1797 stone church, destroyed by an earthquake in 1812. The mission museum displays Native American crafts, early ecclesiastical artifacts and Spanish weaponry, while an Indian cemetery memorializes the enslaved people who built this magnificent structure.

Of course, the mission's claim to fame is not the church at all, but a 1939 ditty, "When the Swallows Come Back to Capistrano," a tune that describes the return of flocks of swallows every March 19. And return they do, though in ever-decreasing numbers and not always on March 19, only to depart in October for Argentina.

At the **O'Neill Museum** (31831 Los Ríos Street; 714-493-8444), housed in a tiny 1870s Victorian, there are walking-tour maps of the town's old adobes. Within a few blocks you'll discover about a dozen 19th-century structures.

DANA POINT

*Along the coast just below San Juan Capistrano, you'll encounter **Dana Point**. This ultramodern enclave, with its manmade port and 2500-boat marina, has a history dating back to the 1830s when Richard Henry Dana immortalized the place in* Two Years Before the Mast.

*Today you can trace Dana's course at the **Orange County Marine Institute** (24200 Dana Point Harbor Drive; 714-496-2274), which features a small sea life museum and a 121-foot replica of the brig* The Pilgrim, *which Dana sailed during the 1830s. The **Dana Point Lighthouse** (24532 Del Prado; 714-661-1001), a facsimile of an old beacon, also serves as a nautical museum.*

*Resting luxuriously on a bluff and overlooking these points of interest is the Cape Cod-style **Dana Point Resort** (25135 Park Lantern Avenue; 714-661-5000). Dana Point's premiere address, it offers spectacular ocean views from 350 guest rooms. The Victorian Cape Cod theme is played out in the individual rooms and lobby, softly decorated in mauves and grays. Ultra-deluxe.*

The **Capistrano Depot** (26701 Verdugo Street), a beautifully preserved 1895 structure, still functions as a station, for Amtrak's California coast line. Built of brick in a series of Spanish-style arches, the old depot houses railroad memorabilia and contains an antique pullman and brightly colored freight car.

The neighboring town of **San Clemente** gained a prominent place on the map when President Richard Nixon established the Western White House on a 25-acre site overlooking the ocean. **La Casa Pacifica**, a magnificent Spanish-style home, was famous not only during Nixon's presidency, but after his 1974 resignation when he retreated to San Clemente to lick his wounds. The Nixon house is located off Avenida del Presidente in a private enclave called Cypress Shore.

Another place of interest is **San Clemente Municipal Pier** (foot of Avenida del Mar; 714-361-8219), a popular fishing spot and centerpiece of the city beach. For information, contact the **San Clemente Chamber of Commerce** (1100 North El Camino Real; 714-492-1131).

SAN JUAN CAPISTRANO AREA LODGING

Capistrano Country Bay Inn (34862 Pacific Coast Highway, Capistrano Beach; 714-496-6656) is a 1930s-era Spanish-style establishment on the grounds of an old estate. All of the 28 guest rooms have fireplaces, tile floors, ceiling fans and vintage wallhangings. Moderate to deluxe; continental breakfast.

SAN JUAN CAPISTRANO AREA RESTAURANTS

One of San Juan Capistrano's many historic points, the 19th-century **El Adobe de Capistrano** (31891 Camino Capistrano; 714-493-1163) has been converted into a Mexican restaurant with a moderately priced menu.

Just up the street, the 1895 railroad station has been reincarnated as the **Capistrano Depot Restaurant** (26701 Verdugo Street; 714-496-8181). Brick archways lead from the old waiting room and station master's office to the freight and pullman cars, all neatly transformed into a restaurant and lounge. The dining room features regional Southwestern cuisine like blackened chicken, carnitas, and shrimp enchiladas. Moderate.

Who can match the combination of intimacy and French-Belgian cuisine at **L'Hirondelle** (31631 Camino Capistrano; 714-661-0425)? It's quite small, about two dozen tables and banquettes, and conveys a French country atmosphere. Meals begin with escargots and crab crêpes, then continue with roast duckling, rabbit in wine sauce, veal cordon bleu, sautéed sweetbreads and fresh fish specials. Moderate.

SAN JUAN CAPISTRANO AREA SHOPPING

Not surprisingly, the most common establishment in this two-century-old town is the antique store. Particularly noteworthy are **The Old Barn** (31792 Camino Capistrano; 714-493-9144), a warehouse-size store filled to the rafters with antiques, and **El Peón** (26832 Ortega Highway; 714-493-3133), a modern emporium crowded with such things as ironwood carvings, folk art, Southwestern jewelry, Peruvian wallhangings, Mexican tiles and other Latin American imports.

SAN JUAN CAPISTRANO AREA BEACHES AND PARKS

Quite simply, **Doheny State Beach** (714-496-6171) wrote the book on oceanside facilities. In addition to a broad swath of sandy beach there is a five-acre lawn complete with private picnic areas, beach rentals and food concessions. The grassy area offers plenty of shade trees. Surfers work the north end of the beach, and divers explore an underwater park just offshore. Camping permitted. Dana Point Harbor, with complete marina facilities, borders the beach. Located off Dana Point Harbor Drive in Dana Point.

Walk down the deeply eroded cliffs guarding **San Clemente State Beach** (off Avenida Calafia, San Clemente: 714-492-3156) and you'll discover a long narrow strip of sand that curves north from San Diego County up to San Clemente City Beach. There are camping areas and picnic plots on top of the bluff. Down below a railroad track parallels the beach and surfers paddle offshore.

Disneyland Area

Much of inland Orange County appears as a vast and bewildering plane of urbanization, an uninspiring amalgam of housing tracts and shopping centers. Anaheim might have remained like its seemingly identical neighbors, but for one overwhelming fact: within this thickly populated and frenetic city lies the virtual epicenter of visitor appeal—**Disneyland** (1313 South Harbor Boulevard; 714-999-4565; admission).

Almost everyone, no matter how reclusive, regardless of age, race, creed or religion, inevitably visits this colossal theme park. Cynics—who snicker at its fantasy formula, orderliness, ultracleanliness, cornball humor and conservative overtones—nevertheless often seem to be swept away by the pure joy of Walt Disney's fertile imagination.

If at all possible, plan your Disneyland visit to avoid the peak summer months. Huge crowds mean long waiting lines. In any case, it's a good idea to arrive as the park opens and to go directly down

Main Street (the park's entry corridor) to be among the first wave of visitors fanning out into the park's many theme lands.

The Magic Kingdom is divided into seven areas. *Main Street* portrays an all-American town at the turn of the century. *Adventureland* is a region of jungle rivers filled with hippos and crocodiles. In *Frontierland* you encounter blazing forts, Indians and Western saloons.

Wrought-iron balconies and Mardi Gras parades create a sense of the South at *New Orleans Square*, while in *Critter Country* you can listen to a jamboree performed by mechanical bears or venture down the harrowing "Splash Mountain" log ride. Sleeping Beauty's castle, Pinocchio's village and the white-knuckle "Matterhorn" ride are only some of the highlights of *Fantasyland*.

With ultramodern high-tech attractions, *Tomorrowland* draws the biggest crowds of all. A big hit is "Captain EO," a 3-D space adventure created by George Lucas, directed by Francis Coppola and starring Michael Jackson. The wizardry of George Lucas is also an ingredient in Disneyland's most sensational ride, "Star Tour."

California's second biggest tourist attraction, **Knott's Berry Farm** (8039 Beach Boulevard; 714-827-1776; admission), lies just five miles away in Buena Park. While some have alluded to it as a country cousin to Disneyland, this 150-acre theme park with more than 165 rides and attractions is both larger and some 15 years older than its sophisticated neighbor.

The original restaurant still serves up Mrs. Knott's chicken dinners, and the old *Ghost Town*, though rickety with age, looks much as it did in the beginning. Today, more than five million people visit "The Farm" each year.

Beyond the *Ghost Town* is *Fiesta Village*, a south-of-the-border entertainment center complete with California mission replicas, open markets, strolling mariachis and a wild ride called "Montezooma's Revenge," an upside-down-and-backwards thriller that reaches speeds of 55 miles per hour in less than five seconds.

Camp Snoopy is the official home of Charles Schulz's beloved "Peanuts" pals—Snoopy, Linus, Lucy and Charlie Brown. Life-size versions of the popular cartoon characters roam the six-acre area hugging guests and posing for pictures. Modeled after the Sierra Nevada mountains, Camp Snoopy features a lake, waterfalls, petting zoo, animal show and kiddie rides.

A fourth theme area, the *Roaring '20s*, has thrill rides, a penny arcade and an aquatic show, as well as the "Kingdom of the Dinosaurs," a boat ride where visitors encounter 21 animated dinosaurs amid what purports to be their natural habitat.

Knott's *Wild Water Wilderness* resembles a 1900s California river wilderness park highlighted by "Bigfoot Rapids," a wet and wild ride down California's longest manmade white water river.

Theme parks aren't the only visitor attractions in the inland reaches of Orange County. Their very existence, in fact, has spawned the growth of other travel destinations. The **Movieland Wax Museum** (7711 Beach Boulevard, Buena Park; 714-522-1154; admission), with its collection of more than 200 wax figures of movie and television stars, has grown up right in the shadow of Knott's Berry Farm.

Collectors and students of military history often visit the **Museum of World Wars** (7884 East La Palma Avenue, Buena Park; 714-952-1776; admission). The exhibit of uniforms, weapons, posters and flags here is reputedly the largest of its kind in the country.

Museums catering to broader interests include the **Anaheim Museum** (241 South Anaheim Boulevard; 714-778-3301), with exhibits depicting the city's meteoric growth from a 19th-century farm society.

Located on a prehistoric fossil field that may be as extensive as the famed La Brea Tar Pits, **Ralph B. Clark Regional Park** (8800 Rosecrans Avenue, Buena Park; 714-670-8045) permits visitors to dig through centuries-old fossil beds. This unique facility also offers an interpretive center with fossil displays and a working paleontology lab.

DISNEYLAND AREA LODGING

Surrounded by stately trees and parklike grounds, the **Danker House** (804 West Broadway, Anaheim; 714-991-4015) is a bed and breakfast set in a beautifully refurbished 1899 colonial revival home. Authentically decorated with turn-of-the-century furnishings, its most unusual feature is a pastel ceramic-tile fireplace, imported from Paris in 1900. The full gourmet breakfasts here are fit for a king. Located one mile from Disneyland. Moderate to deluxe.

CALIFORNIA SCENARIO

For a sense of Orange County's cultural life, head down Costa Mesa way. Here Japanese-American sculptor Isamu Noguchi has created California Scenario (South Coast Plaza Town Center, across Bristol Street from South Coast Plaza Shopping Center; 714-241-1700), a sculpture garden surrounded by office towers. An abstract expression of the Golden State, this stone-and-steel creation reflects the many faces of California.

The state's majestic redwoods are represented along Forest Walk. At the Energy Fountain, a stainless steel cone resembling the nose of a rocket symbolizes the Space-Age vitality of the state. The Desert Land section features an array of plants and cacti. The featured piece, Noguchi's tribute to the lima bean farmers who once worked this region, is a collection of 15 bronze-colored granite boulders, precisely cut and fit together to resemble a mound of the noble beans.

Most of Orange County's older homes have fallen before the developer's wrecking ball. One thankfully spared is the roomy 1910 Queen Anne now housing **Anaheim Country Inn** (856 South Walnut Street, Anaheim; 714-778-0150). It's a lovely home with Victorian furnishings, surrounded by porches and blessed with a tree-shaded, acre-sized lot. Eight rooms provide a variety of accommodations. Complete breakfasts; minutes from Disneyland; moderate.

Designed specifically for the needs of visitors bound for Disneyland (just three blocks away), **Days Inn** (1030 West Ball Road, Anaheim; 714-520-0101) offers "family suites" that can accommodate up to five adults, plus complimentary continental breakfast. It has a heated pool and spa as well as a large guest laundry. For honeymooners or other fun-seekers there are several suites with in-room spas and wet bars. Budget to deluxe, depending on the season.

Covering 60 acres and containing 1200 rooms, 16 restaurants and lounges, 61 shops and almost as many gimmicks as the Magic Kingdom itself, **Disneyland Hotel** (1150 West Cerritos Avenue, Anaheim; 714-778-6600) is a self-contained world. You can swim, play tennis, sun on a sandy "beach," watch a light show, shop, dine, dance—or even sleep here. And if that isn't enough, step out front to the monorail station and three minutes later you are at the real thing! Ultra-deluxe.

Two blocks from Disneyland stands the cavernous, 1577-room **Anaheim Hilton** (777 Convention Way, Anaheim; 714-750-4321), a glass-enclosed monolith. The airy atrium lobby, set off by brass railings and blue and mauve tones, holds three restaurants, two bars, a nightclub and assorted shops, along with a pond and fountain. The modern guest rooms are individually decorated and priced ultra-deluxe.

Like the little alpine lass who curtsies from her signboard perch above the entrance, the **Heidi Motel** (815 West Katella Avenue, Anaheim; 714-533-1979) is kind of cute. Rooms at this 30-unit court near Disneyland are small but well maintained and trimly furnished. Pool; budget.

Crisp, contemporary styling set **Best Western Park Place Inn** (1544 South Harbor Boulevard, Anaheim; 714-776-4800) apart from the hundreds of other hotels and motels encircling the perimeter of Disneyland. Accommodations are fresh and colorful. There's a pool, sauna and jacuzzi. Moderate to deluxe.

A bit off the mainstream but still only a few blocks from Knott's Berry Farm is **Fullerton "A" Inn** (2601 West Orangethorpe Avenue, Fullerton; 714-773-4900). This 43-room motel—with pool, sauna and exercise room—may be the best budget-priced lodging near Knott's.

Best of the old-time motels and "tourist courts" that line Beach Boulevard near Knott's Berry Farm is the **Silver Moon Motel** (212

South Beach Boulevard, Anaheim; 714-527-1102). The carefully maintained motel offers 44 rooms, some with kitchens. Located one mile from Knott's Berry Farm, five from Disneyland. Budget.

DISNEYLAND AREA RESTAURANTS

An exception to the many mediocre restaurants surrounding Disneyland, **Mr. Stox** (1105 East Katella Avenue, Anaheim; 714-634-2994) offers some of the area's best dining. It boasts a versatile menu of prime rib, rack of lamb, pasta and mesquite-broiled fresh seafood. Lunch and dinner; moderate to deluxe.

The top restaurant in these parts can be found at the Anaheim Marriott Hotel. **JW's** (700 West Convention Way, Anaheim; 714-750-0900) offers an outstanding continental cuisine menu. The candlelit ambience, attentive service and contemporary flourishes add to the experience. Ultra-deluxe.

A magical dining adventure is found at **The Hobbit** (2932 East Chapman Avenue, Orange; 714-997-1972), set in a gracious old 1930s hacienda. You'll be tempted with a parade of hot and cold hors d'oeuvres, soup, salad, fowl, beef and fish courses followed by sorbet and dessert. During "intermission" you can stroll in the art gallery and gardens. Ultra-deluxe; reserve weeks in advance.

Antonello Ristorante (3800 South Plaza Drive, Santa Ana; 714-751-7153), Orange County's best-decorated and most highly rated Italian eatery, is a re-creation of an actual Italian street setting. Quaint shutters and window flower boxes give the place a genuine Old Country feel. The nouvelle treatments of traditional Northern Italian dishes are outstanding. Deluxe to ultra-deluxe.

For curry lovers there's **Gandhi** (3820 South Plaza Drive, Santa Ana; 714-556-7273), an Indian restaurant with a decidedly British decor. Earth tones, wood panelling, English china, and heavy silver-plated tableware create a colonial atmosphere. The rich, exotic combination of herbs and spices that flavor the curried lamb, Muglai chicken, or tandoori treats make this award-winning restaurant a wise choice. Lunch and dinner; moderate to deluxe.

A high-tech Chinese restaurant? Lipstick reds and glossy blacks combine with lots of neon at **Chinatown Restaurant and Bar** (4139 Campus Drive, Irvine; 714-856-2211). The list of entrées includes 20 original house specialties such as gunpowder scallops and veal Marco Polo. Exciting and different. Budget to moderate.

Upscale, contemporary **Prego** (18420 Von Karman Avenue, Irvine; 714-553-1333) packs 'em in both for tasty, authentic Italian food and a breathtaking interior scheme accented by marble-top tables and a sizzling open-fire rotisserie. The aromas will quickly bring your attention to eating, a real pleasure at Prego. The big surprise is Prego's superb pizza. *Buon appetito!* Moderate.

DISNEYLAND AREA SHOPPING

Inland Orange County is a maze of suburban shopping centers large and small. Which is all right if you're really intent on buying but rather unappealing when you simply want to browse. For those charming little boutiques and artisan shops, stick to the beach area.

In spite of its discount-store facade, the **Crystal Factory** (8010 Beach Boulevard, Buena Park; 714-952-4135) is a treasure trove of crystal and glassware, with everything from stemware to handblown crystal lamps.

Fill a 16,000-square-foot building with 110 separate cubicles and you've got the **Old Chicago Antique Mall** (8960 Knott Avenue, Buena Park; 714-527-0275). Independent vendors sell wares ranging from fine old furniture to '50s memorabilia. One fellow displays more than 5000 model electric trains and some 4000 toys!

Hobby City (1238 South Beach Boulevard, Anaheim; 714-527-2323) looks like a miniature Knott's Berry Farm, anchored by a "perfect half-scale replica" of the White House and encircled by the wee tracks of the "Hobby City Choo Choo," a minitrain for kids. It also features an intriguing array of 24 specialized shops, each devoted entirely to the hobbyist and collector. Among them are stamp, coin, gem, antique and doll dealers.

Biggest and best of the Orange County malls is **South Coast Plaza Shopping Center** (3333 South Bristol Street, Costa Mesa; 714-241-1700). Some say this is the most distinguished retail address on the West Coast, loaded with showcase stores and sleek signature shops.

Orange County Market Place (Orange County Fairgrounds, 88 Fair Drive, Costa Mesa; 714-723-6616) is the area's biggest flea market, with some 1500 vendors displaying their wares every weekend.

A true "find" for bargain hunters is the **Cooper Building** (1928 South Grand Avenue, Santa Ana), a collection of about 20 shops proffering designer label fashions at 25 to 75 percent off. Although aimed at the ladies, there are some men's and children's outlets.

Considered the "antique capital of Southern California," **Orange Circle Antique Mall** (118 South Glassell Street, Orange; 714-538-8160) is the biggest and one of the best. Housed in a refurbished 1909 brick building are some 120 independently operated booths, each offering something different. Tiffany lamps, toy soldiers, barber poles, mahogany armoires...you name it.

DISNEYLAND AREA NIGHTLIFE

Sgt. Preston's Yukon Saloon (1150 West Cerritos, Anaheim; 714-778-6600) in the Disneyland Hotel is modeled on an old sourdough watering hole straight from Whitehorse or Dawson. It features an 1890s follies-type review plus dancing and other goings-on.

Bandstand (1721 South Manchester Avenue, Anaheim; 714-956-1410) is a nightclub where you can dance. Sundays, Tuesdays and Thursdays are big nights featuring live country-and-western bands. Otherwise it's deejays spinning Top-40 music. Cover.

While fading elsewhere, the fine art of dinner theater remains live and well received in Orange County. **Grand Dinner Theater** (Grand Hotel, No. 7 Freedman Way, Anaheim; 714-772-7777) offers Broadway plays and musicals with your meal.

It's a bit wacky and sometimes corny, but **Crackers** (710 East Katella Avenue, Anaheim; 714-978-1828) provides nonstop entertainment. You'll be regaled by singing bartenders, waitresses, magicians and jugglers. And, for better or worse, by your own peers. Audience participation is the thing here.

Peppers (12361 Chapman Avenue, Garden Grove; 714-740-1333) is a colorful Mexican-theme restaurant that owes most of its popularity to its dancefloor rather than its food. Young singles dig the scene as deejays spin Top-40 hits nightly; cover.

You can two-step to live country-and-western music at **Crazy Horse Steak House & Saloon** (1580 Brookhollow Drive, Santa Ana; 714-549-1512), Orange County's most popular and long-lived nightspot. Cover.

Owned by the Righteous Brothers, **The Hop** (18774 Brookhurst Street, Fountain Valley; 714-963-2366) is hot. Do your hopping here on a regulation high-school gym dancefloor (hoops included) to the nostalgic strains of '50s and '60s hits. Cover.

Orange County Performing Arts Center (600 Town Center Drive, Costa Mesa; 714-556-2787) is one of Southern California's great cultural assets, a 3000-seat theater that regularly features the New York City Ballet and Joffrey Ballet, plus a host of visiting dance, opera and musical companies.

Offering the best in classic and contemporary plays, **South Coast Repertory Theatre** (655 Town Center Drive, Costa Mesa; 714-957-4033) has established itself nationwide as a major theatrical presence.

IN DAYS OF OLDE

*It seems hokey at first: dining on a four-course meal in an imitation 11th-century castle while knights ride into battle. Actually, **Medieval Times** (7662 Beach Boulevard, Buena Park; 714-521-4740) is a brilliant concept, a re-creation of a medieval tournament, complete with flag tosses and javelin throws. It can get pretty wild when mounted knights—highly trained horsemen and stuntmen—perform dangerous jousting and sword-fighting routines.*

Pacific Amphitheatre (Orange County Fairgrounds, 100 Fair Drive, Costa Mesa; 714-634-1300) presents concerts by name performers in the largest outdoor concert setting on the West Coast. Closed during the winter.

Irvine Meadows Amphitheatre (8800 Irvine Center Drive, Irvine/Laguna Hills; 714-855-4515) features leading musical acts in a lovely outdoor amphitheater.

Sporting Life

SPORTFISHING AND WHALE WATCHING

Among the Orange County outfits offering sportfishing charters are **Davey's Locker** (400 Main Street, Balboa; 714-673-1434) and **Dana Wharf Sportfishing** (34675 Golden Lantern, Dana Point; 714-496-5794). For those more interested in gazing at California's big grays, these companies also sponsor whale-watching cruises during the migratory season.

SKINDIVING

The coastal waters abound in interesting kelp beds rich with sea life. To explore them, contact **Aquatic Center** (4537 West Coast Highway, Newport Beach; 714-650-5440), **Laguna Sea Sports** (925 North Coast Highway, Laguna Beach; 714-494-6965) or **Black Bart's Aquatics** (34145 Coast Highway, Dana Point; 714-496-5891).

SURFING AND WINDSURFING

Orange County is surfer heaven. So, grab a board from the **Fog House** (6908 West Coast Highway, Newport Beach; 714-642-5690), **Hobie Sports** (34195 Coast Highway, Dana Point; 714-496-1251) or **Steward Sports** (2102 South El Camino Real, San Clemente; 714-492-1085) and head for the waves.

SAILING

With elaborate marina complexes at Huntington Beach, Newport Beach and Dana Point, this is a great area for boating. Sailboats and powerboats are available for rent at **Davey's Locker** (400 Main Street, Balboa; 714-673-1434), **Balboa Boat Rentals** (Edgewater Avenue and Palm Street, Newport Beach; 714-673-1320) and **Embarcadero Marina** (Embarcadero Place, public launch ramp, Dana Point; 714-496-6177).

TENNIS

Try the **Hotel Tennis Club** (Marriott Hotel, 900 Newport Center Drive, Newport Beach; 714-640-2772), **Dana Hills Tennis Center** (24911 Calle de Tennis, Dana Point; 714-240-2104), **San Gorgonio Park** (Via San Gorgonio off Vaquero Avenida, San Clemente; 714-361-8264), **San Luis Rey Park** (Avenida San Luis Rey, San Clemente; 714-361-8264) or **Bonito Canyon Park** (El Camino Real and Calle Valle, San Clemente; 714-361-8264).

For courts around Anaheim and Buena Park try **Anaheim Tennis Center** (975 South State College Boulevard, Anaheim; 714-991-9090), **Disneyland's Tennisland** (1330 Walnut Street, Anaheim; 714-535-4851), or **Ralph B. Clark Regional Park** (8800 Rosecrans Avenue, Buena Park; 714-670-8045).

GOLF

The climate and terrain make for excellent golfing. Tee up at **Newport Beach Golf Course** (3100 Irvine Avenue, Newport Beach; 714-852-8681), **Aliso Creek Golf Course** (31106 Coast Highway, South Laguna; 714-499-1919), **The Links at Monarch Beach** (33080 Niguel Road, Laguna Niguel; 714-240-8247), **Shorecliffs Golf Course** (501 Avenida Vaquero, San Clemente; 714-492-1177) or **San Clemente Municipal Golf Course** (150 Avenue Magdalena, San Clemente; 714-492-3943).

ORANGE COUNTY'S OUTBACK

To explore the last vestiges of Orange County's open country, wander the area's eastern fringes. Here you'll discover two magnificent parks.

*Originally part of an 1841 Mexican land grant, the 1700-acre **O'Neill Regional Park** (714-858-9366) straddles Trabuco and Live Oak canyons in a delightfully undeveloped region of the Santa Ana Mountains. Topography varies from oak-lined canyon bottomlands to chaparral-covered hillsides. There's a surprising variety of wildlife: opossum, raccoons, coyotes, doves and roadrunners, as well as elusive but ever present mountain lions. Located in southeastern Orange County at 30892 Trabuco Canyon Road, 18 miles east of Route 405 via El Toro Road exit.*

*A real gem, **Ronald W. Caspers Wilderness Park** (714-728-0235) covers 7600 acres of rugged mountain and canyonland bordering Cleveland National Forest. Within this vast domain are more than 30 miles of marked trails for hiking and horseback riding. The key feature here is San Juan Hot Springs (714-728-0400), where nature's own hot mineral water is piped into a pool and 25 smaller hot tubs. Located at 35501 Ortega Highway (Route 74), San Juan Capistrano.*

The inland sections of Orange County feature numerous golf links. Among them are the **Dad Miller Golf Course** (430 North Gilbert Street, Anaheim; 714-774-8055) and **Anaheim Hills Golf Course** (6501 East Nohl Ranch Road, Anaheim; 714-637-7311).

BICYCLING

Route 1, the Pacific Coast Highway, offers cyclists an opportunity to explore the Orange County coastline. The problem, of course, is the traffic. Along **Bolsa Chica State Beach** in Huntington Beach, however, a special pathway runs the length of the beach. Other interesting areas to explore are Balboa Island and Balboa Peninsula in Newport Beach. Both offer quiet residential streets and are connected by a ferry that permits bicycles.

Transportation

BY CAR

Several major highways parallel the Orange County coast. **Route 1**, known in this area as the Pacific Coast Highway, ends its long journey down the California Coast in Capistrano Beach. A few miles farther inland, **Route 405** runs from Long Beach to Irvine, with feeder roads leading to the main coastal towns. Connecting Los Angeles and San Diego, **Route 5** follows an inland course through the heart of Orange County, then skirts the coast in San Clemente.

BY AIR

John Wayne International Airport, located in Irvine, is the main terminal in these parts. Major carriers presently serving it include Alaska Airlines, American Airlines, America West, Continental Airlines, Delta Airlines, Northwest Airlines, States West, Trans World Airlines, United Airlines and USAir.

BY BUS

Greyhound/Trailways Bus Lines serves inland Orange County as well as the coast. Most stops are flag stops; there are depots located in **San Clemente** (510 North Avenida de la Estrella; 714-492-1187), **Anaheim** (2080 South Harbor Boulevard; 714-635-5060) and other cities.

BY TRAIN

Amtrak's (800-872-7245) "San Diegan" travels between Los Angeles and San Diego, with Orange County stops at Fullerton, Anaheim Stadium, Santa Ana, San Juan Capistrano and San Clemente.

CAR RENTALS

Arriving at John Wayne International Airport, you'll find the following car rental agencies: **Avis Rent A Car** (714-852-8608), **Budget Rent A Car** (714-955-3700), **Dollar Rent A Car** (714-756-6100) and **Hertz Rent A Car** (714-756-8161).

PUBLIC TRANSPORTATION

Orange County Transit District (714-636-7433), or OCTD, carries passengers throughout Orange County, including most inland areas. Along the coast it stops in Seal Beach, Huntington Beach, Newport Beach, Corona del Mar, Laguna Beach, Dana Point, San Juan Capistrano and San Clemente.

In addition, the **Southern California Rapid Transit District** (213-626-4455), or RTD, serves the Disneyland/Knott's Berry Farm area.

FIVE

San Diego

San Diego County's 4261 square miles occupy a Connecticut-size **151** chunk of real estate that forms the southwestern corner of the continental United States. Geographically, it is as varied a parcel of landscape as any in the world. Surely this spot is one of the few places on the planet where, in a matter of hours, you can journey from bluff-lined beaches up and over craggy, pine-clad mountain peaks and down again to sun-scorched desert sands.

But it is the coast—some 76 sparkling miles stretching from the Mexican border to San Mateo Point near San Clemente—that always has held the fascination of residents and visitors alike.

One of its first European visitors, the doughty Franciscan missionary Junípero Serra, marched north from Mexico in 1769 with a company of other priests and soldiers and built Mission San Diego de Alcala. It was the first of a chain of 21 missions and the earliest site in California to be settled by Europeans.

Truth is, San Diego is no longer the sleepy, semitransparent little resort city it once was. Nowhere is the fact more evident than in the downtown district, where a building boom has brought new offices, condominiums and hotels as well as a spectacular business and entertainment complex at Horton Plaza.

But for all the city's manmade appeal, it is nature's handiwork and an ideal Mediterranean climate that most delights San Diego visitors. With bays and beaches bathed in sunshine 75 percent of the time, less than ten inches of rainfall per year and average temperatures that mirror a proverbial day in June, San Diego offers the casual outdoor lifestyle that fulfills vacation dreams. There's a beach for every taste, ranging from broad sweeps of white sand to slender scimitars beneath eroded sandstone bluffs.

Situated a smug 120 miles south of Los Angeles, San Diego is not so much a city as a collection of communities hiding in canyons and gathered on small shoulders of land that shrug down to the sea. As a result, it hardly seems big enough (just over 1.1 million) to rank as America's sixth largest city. Total county population is almost two and a half million, and nine of ten residents live within 30 miles of the coast.

It is safe to say that San Diego is not as eccentric and sophisticated as San Francisco, nor as glamorous and fast-paced as Los Angeles. But those who still perceive it as a laid-back mecca for beach bums—or as a lunch stop en route to Mexico—are in for a huge surprise.

North San Diego County

Stretching along the coast above San Diego are a string of towns with a host of personalities and populations. Residents here range from the county's wealthiest folks in Rancho Santa Fe to Marine privates at Oceanside's Camp Pendleton to yogis in retreat at Encinitas. This part of the county really shines, however, in its many sparkling beaches.

The best way to see North County's fine beaches is to cruise along Old Route 101. It changes names in each beach town along the way, but once you're on it you won't be easily sidetracked.

As you head into the county from the north, you'll soon arrive at **Carlsbad**, which has pushed to the front of the North County pack in terms of sprucing up its image and attracting visitors. Along with its redeveloped downtown area and oceanfront lodging, Carlsbad is a friendly, sunny beachfront town that sports cobblestone streets and quaint shops.

Encinitas is popularly known as the "Flower Capital of the World," and the hillsides east of the beach are a riot of colors. A quick call to the friendly folks at the local **Chamber of Commerce** (619-753-6041) will net you information concerning the area.

Spiritual seekers might want to make a stop at Paramahansa Yogananda's **Self Realization Fellowship Center** (216 K Street, Encinitas; 619-436-7220). The gold-domed towers of this monastic retreat were built by an Indian religious sect in the 1930s and are still used as a retreat. The views, overlooking the famous "Swami's" surfing beach, are spectacular.

Although **Del Mar** is inundated every summer by "beautiful people" who flock here for the horse racing, the town itself has retained a casual, small-town identity. Its trim, Tudor-style village center and luxurious oceanfront homes reflect the town's subtle efforts to "keep up with the Joneses" next door (i.e., La Jolla).

While seasonal, the **Del Mar Race Track** (Route 5 and Via de la Valle; 619-481-1207; admission) and companion **Fairgrounds** are the main attractions here. The track was financed back in the 1930s by such notables as Bing Crosby, Pat O'Brien and Jimmy Durante. The spot became a second home for these and many other top Hollywood stars.

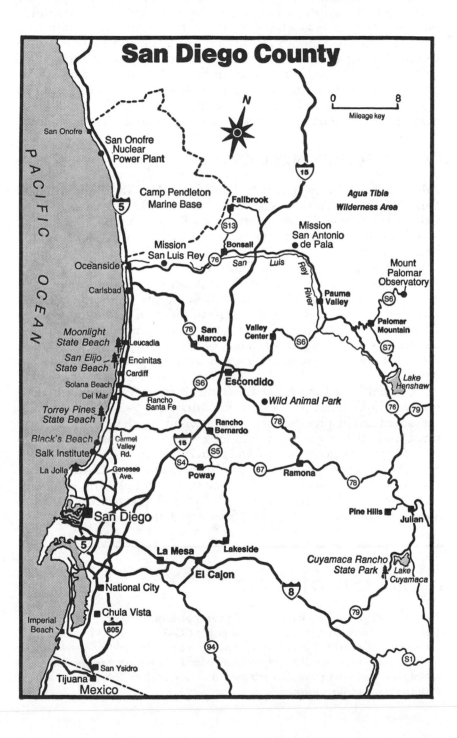

San Diego County

On the east side of Route 5 is **Rancho Santa Fe**. If La Jolla is a jewel, then this stylish enclave is the crown itself. Residing in hillside mansions and horse ranches parceled out from an old Spanish land grant are some of America's wealthiest folks. Rancho Santa Fe is like Beverly Hills gone country. The area became popular as a retreat for rich industrialists and movie stars in the 1920s when Douglas Fairbanks and Mary Pickford built their sprawling **Fairbanks Ranch**. To make a looping tour of this community, drive in on Via de la Valle, then return to Route 5 via Linea del Cielo and Lomas Santa Fe Drive.

NORTH SAN DIEGO COUNTY LODGING

Advertised as "a very special bed and breakfast," the **Pelican Cove Inn** (320 Walnut Avenue, Carlsbad; 619-434-5995) is a lovely Cape Cod-style house with eight guest rooms. Each features a fireplace and is well furnished with antique pieces. Located two blocks from the beach. Deluxe.

Sporting a fresh look, the fabled **La Costa Hotel & Spa** (Costa del Mar Road, Carlsbad; 619-438-9111) can justly claim to be one of the world's great "total" resorts. This luxurious 1000-acre complex boasts 482 rooms, plus villas and châteaus, its own movie theater, two 18-hole championship golf courses, 27 tennis courts (hard court, clay *and* grass), seven restaurants and one of the country's largest and most respected spa and fitness centers. Priced well up in the ultra-deluxe range.

Located on a lofty knoll above the Pacific, **Radisson Inn Encinitas** (85 Encinitas Boulevard, Encinitas; 619-942-7455) is one of the largest and best moderate-priced hotels in North County. Built on three levels, the 91-room complex looks like a condominium. Rooms include private balconies. Pool and jacuzzi.

A new spot with a great deal of history, **The Inn–L'Auberge at Del Mar** (1540 Camino del Mar, Del Mar; 619-259-1515) re-creates its 1920s to 1940s past, when Hollywood greats like Rudolph Valentino and Jimmy Durante frequented the place. The Tudor-

---

THE INN AT RANCHO SANTA FE

*For a truly elegant country inn consider **The Inn at Rancho Santa Fe** (Paseo Delicias and Linea del Cielo, Rancho Santa Fe; 619-756-1131). Widely known among the world's genteel, it is a secluded settlement of early California-style casitas on a wooded 20-acre site. Situated five miles inland, the inn offers individually decorated guest rooms as well as two- and three-bedroom cottages. Tennis courts, pool, croquet; deluxe to ultra-deluxe.*

Craftsman getaway has 123 guest rooms and suites, each with its own patio, and a rich lobby dominated by a replica of the original brick fireplace. Amenities include tennis courts, pool and a spa.

On a hill overlooking Del Mar's village center and coastline is the romantic little **Rock Haus Inn** (410 15th Street; 619-481-3764). One of the region's finest bed and breakfasts, it would be hard to top this sprawling Craftsman-style bungalow for location, charm or quality. Built in 1910 and located two blocks from the beach, it saw action during Prohibition as a speakeasy and gambling den. Today its ten rooms, four with private baths, are thematically decorated and reflect considerable taste and talent. Deluxe to ultra-deluxe.

NORTH SAN DIEGO COUNTY RESTAURANTS

A cozy Old World atmosphere is hard to find in Oceanside, so you'll appreciate the European flair and food at **Villa de Gallo** (1733 South Hill Street; 619-433-5811). A classic Italian menu makes this a worthwhile retreat. Moderate.

La Costa Hotel and Spa (Costa del Mar Road; Carlsbad; 619-438-9111) features eight restaurants, ranging from the stylish **Champagne Dining Room** to the wacky **Jose Wong**, which includes a mixed heritage of Mexican and Asian dishes. Of the eight, **The Spa Dining Room** offers the best and most interesting dishes. Low-calorie, low-cholesterol meals, designed to dovetail with La Costa's excellent spa programs, are superbly prepared and colorfully presented. Prices at the various restaurants range from moderate to ultra-deluxe.

Another popular dining spot is **Sakura Bana Sushi Bar** (1031 1st Street, Encinitas; 619-942-6414). The sushi here is heavenly, especially the sakura roll, crafted by Japanese masters from shrimp, crab, scallop, smelt egg and avocado. Budget to moderate.

Best of the beachfront dining spots in Cardiff is **Charlie's Grill and Bar** (2526 South Route 101; 619-942-1300), where the surf rolls right up to the glass. Here you can choose from an innovative selection of fresh seafood items or an all-American menu of ribs and steak. Charlie's has a smartly decorated contemporary setting with a full bar, but still creates an easy and informal atmosphere. Dinner and Sunday brunch only; moderate to deluxe.

Mille Fleurs (6009 Paseo Delicias, Rancho Santa Fe; 619-756-3085) tops everyone's list as San Diego's best French restaurant. The a la carte menu provides such entrées as rack of veal in garlic and rosemary and Norwegian salmon in pink grapefruit sauce. A sophisticated interior features fireside dining, Portuguese tiles and stunning trompe l'oeil paintings. Dinner only on weekends, lunch and dinner otherwise; ultra-deluxe.

The place is mobbed all summer long, but **The Fish Market** (640 Via de la Valle; 619-755-2277) remains one of my favorite Del Mar restaurants. I like the noise, nautical atmosphere, oyster bar, budget-to-moderate prices, on-the-run service and the dozen or so fresh fish items.

Scalini (3790 Via de la Valle, Del Mar; 619-259-9944), housed in a classy new contemporary-style building with arched windows over-looking a polo field, is strictly star quality. The place has been decorated in a mix of modern and antique furnishings. But the brightest star of all is the menu, featuring homemade pastas, exceptional mesquite-broiled veal chops and duck a l'orange. Deluxe to ultra-deluxe.

NORTH SAN DIEGO COUNTY SHOPPING

The best shopping in Oceanside is around the harbor at **Cape Cod Village**, a mock whaling port with a few interesting souvenir and beachwear shops.

Carlsbad has blossomed with a variety of trendy shops. You'll see many beach-and-surf-type shops as well as a variety of specialty gift shops like those tucked away in the arcade of **Old World Center** (Roosevelt Street and Grand Avenue; 619-434-4557).

Conveniently situated in Encinitas on the east side of Route 101 between I and E streets, **The Lumberyard** (619-943-8629) is an attractive woodframe shopping village on the former site of an old lumber mill.

Detouring, as every sophisticated shopper must, to Rancho Santa Fe, you'll find an assortment of chic shops and galleries along Paseo Delicias. My favorites are **Marilyn Mulloy Estate Jewelers** (6020 Paseo Delicias; 619-756-4010), with its stunning collection of old and new pieces, and **The Two Goats** (6012 Paseo Delicias; 619-756-1996), featuring designer fashions and exclusive gifts.

If little else, Solana Beach harbors an enclave of good antique stores. One of the best is the **Antique Warehouse** (212 South Cedros Avenue; 619-755-5156), with its collection of 101 small shops.

A seacoast village atmosphere prevails along Del Mar's half-mile-long strip of shops. Tudor-style **Stratford Square**, the focal point, houses a number of shops in what once was a grand turn-of-the-century resort hotel.

The stylized **Del Mar Plaza** (1555 Camino del Mar; 619-792-1555), a trilevel mall, is home to over 35 shops selling everything from sportswear to upscale Scandinavian fashions. **Flower Hill Mall** (2636 Via de la Valle, Del Mar; 619-481-7131), a rustic mall, has the usual fashion and specialty shops.

NORTH SAN DIEGO COUNTY NIGHTLIFE

There's a terrific ocean view from the upstairs bar at **Fisherman's Restaurant** (1 Oceanside Pier; 619-727-2314), located on the historic Oceanside Pier. For a nice harbor view, consider **Monterey Bay Canners** (1325 Harbor Drive North; 619-722-3474).

Located at the luxurious La Costa Hotel and Spa, **The Tournament of Champions Lounge** (2100 Costa del Mar Road, Carlsbad; 619-438-9111) features live nightly entertainment ranging from cabaret performers to big bands. La Costa's elegant **Lobby Lounge**, in the same building, is a classy piano bar.

You can watch deejays spinning platters and stand-up comedians working the crowd, plus hear live rock bands on weekends at the Spanish-style **Full Moon Nightclub** (485 1st Street, Encinitas; 619-436-7397). Cover for live shows.

Solana Beach's low-profile daytime image shifts gears at night with two of North County's hottest clubs. **Surfside Diego's** (635 South Route 101; 619-755-8247) is an opulent lounge, while the **Belly Up Tavern** (143 South Cedros Avenue; 619-481-9022) is a converted quonset hut that now houses a concert club and often draws big-name rock and blues stars. Cover.

NORTH SAN DIEGO COUNTY BEACHES AND PARKS

Over three miles of clean, rock-free sand make up the **Oceanside Beaches** (619-722-8000), stretching from Buena Vista Lagoon in the south to Oceanside Harbor in the north. Along the entire length the water is calm and shallow, ideal for swimming and bodysurfing. The nicest section of all is around Oceanside Pier, a 1900-foot-long fishing pier. Added to the attractions is **Buena Vista Lagoon**, a bird sanctuary and nature reserve. Located along The Strand in Oceanside; the pier is at the foot of 3rd Street.

A sand and rock beach bordered by bluffs, **Carlsbad State Beach** (619-729-8947) provides good rock and surf-fishing. It's even better at the adjoining Encinas Fishing Area, where Agua Hedionda Lagoon opens to the sea. **Carlsbad City Beach** connects to the north. Park entrance is at Tamarack Avenue, west of Carlsbad Boulevard.

The very popular **Moonlight State Beach** (619-729-8947) boasts a big sandy cove flanked by sandstone bluffs. Surf is relatively tame at the center, entertaining swimmers and bodysurfers. Surfers like the wave action to the south, particularly at the foot of D Street. Located in Encinitas near 4th Street and the end of B Street.

North County's most famous surfing beach, **Swami's Park** derives its name from an Indian guru who founded the nearby Self-Realization Fellowship Temple during the 1940s. A small, grassy picnic area gives way to stairs leading to a narrow, rocky beach favored almost exclusively by surfers for its spectacular waves. Located at 1298 Old Route 101 in Encinitas.

Although **San Elijo State Beach** is wide and sandy, low tide reveals a mantle of rocks just offshore, and there are reefs, too, making this one of North County's most popular surf-fishing and skin diving spots. Surfers brave big breakers at "Turtles" and "Pipes" reefs at the north end of the park. There is a campground (619-753-5091) atop the bluff overlooking the beach. Located off Old Route 101 north of Chesterfield Drive in Cardiff.

Cardiff State Beach (619-729-8947) begins where the cliffs of Solana Beach end and a network of tidepools begins. Popular with surfers because of the interesting pitches off its reef break, this wide, sandy beach is part of a two-mile swath of state beaches. Located off Old Route 101 in Cardiff directly west of San Elijo Lagoon.

Lined by cliffs and carpeted with sand, **Solana Beach Park** (619-755-1560) is a popular spot for water sports. There's a natural break in the cliffs where the beach widens and the surf eases up to allow comfortable swimming. Surfers gather for the big waves around Plaza Street. Located at the end of Plaza Street in Solana Beach.

La Jolla

Like a beautiful but slightly spoiled child, La Jolla is an enclave of wealth and stubborn independence that calls itself "The Village," although it is actually just another part of the extended San Diego family. Mediterranean-style mansions and small cottages shrouded by jasmine and hibiscus share million-dollar views of beaches, coves and wild, eroded sea cliffs. Swank shops and galleries, trendy restaurants and classy little hotels combine in a Riviera-like setting that rivals even Carmel for chicness.

A certain fascination centers around the origins of the name La Jolla. It means "jewel" in Spanish, but according to Indian legend it means "hole" or "caves." Both are fairly apt interpretations: this enclave perched on a bluff above the Pacific is indeed a jewel; and its dramatic coves and cliffs are pocked with sea caves.

To get the lay of the land, wind your way up **Mount Soledad** (east on Nautilus Street from La Jolla Boulevard), where the view extends across the city skyline and out over the ocean. That large white cross at the summit is a memorial to the war dead and the setting for sunrise services every Easter Sunday.

Ah, but exploring The Village is the reason you're here, so head back down Nautilus Street, go right on La Jolla Boulevard and continue until it leads into **Prospect Street**. This is La Jolla's hottest thoroughfare; where it intersects **Girard Avenue**, the town's traditional "main street," is the town epicenter. Here, in the heart of La Jolla, you are surrounded by the elite and elegant.

Although Girard Avenue features as wide a selection of shops as any place in San Diego, Prospect Street is much more interesting and stylish. By all means, walk Prospect's curving mile from the cottage shops and galleries on the north to the **Museum of Contemporary Art** (700 Prospect Street; 619-454-3541; admission) on the south. The museum, by the way, is a piece of art in itself. Its modern lines belie the fact it was designed as a private villa back in 1915, one of many striking contemporary structures in La Jolla by noted architect Irving Gill. The museum's highly regarded collection focuses on minimalist, California and pop art.

LA JOLLA LODGING

Tucked away on the north fringe of the village is **Andrea Villa Inn** (2402 Torrey Pines Road; 619-459-3311), a classy-looking 50-unit motel that packs more amenities than some resorts. There is a pool, spa, valet and concierge. The spacious rooms are beautifully decorated. Moderate to deluxe.

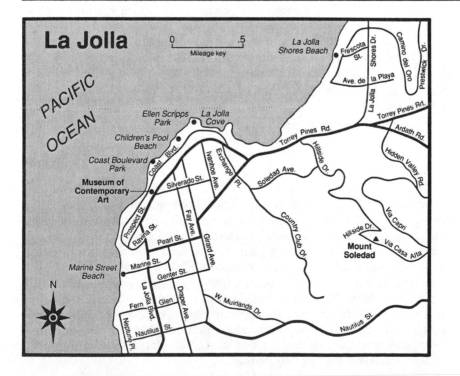

Small European-style hotels have always been popular in La Jolla, and the granddaddy of them all is the **Colonial Inn** (910 Prospect Street; 619-454-2181). Established in 1913, the 77-room establishment features lavishly redecorated rooms that beautifully blend antique and contemporary furnishings. Oceanfront rooms provide matchless views. Deluxe to ultra-deluxe.

More than just a hotel, **La Valencia** (1132 Prospect Street; 619-454-0771) is a La Jolla institution, one of the loveliest hotels in San Diego. Resplendent in pink stucco and Spanish tile, it is perched on a breezy promontory overlooking coves and sea cliffs. From the moment guests enter via a trellis-covered tile loggia into a lobby that could pass for King Juan Carlos' living room, they are enveloped in elegance. Rooms are rather small, however. Deluxe to ultra-deluxe.

The **Sheraton Grande Torrey Pines** (10950 North Torrey Pines; 619-558-1500), adorned with marble and polished wood, is an equally spectacular white-glove establishment. Here art deco visits the 21st century in a series of terraces that lead past plush dining rooms, multi-tiered fountains and a luxurious swimming pool. Ultra-deluxe.

The Bed and Breakfast Inn at La Jolla (7753 Draper Avenue; 619-456-2066) is so nearly perfect it deserves five stars. Listed as a historical site, it was designed as a private home in 1913 by Irving Gill. Faithfully restored as a 16-room inn, it's impeccably decorated and ideally situated a block from the ocean. Each room features period furnishings. Deluxe to ultra-deluxe.

La Jolla's only true beachfront hotel is **Sea Lodge** (8110 Camino del Oro; 619-459-8271). Designed and landscaped to resemble an old California hacienda, this 128-room retreat overlooks the Pacific on a mile-long beach. With its stuccoed arches, terra-cotta roofs and ceramic tilework, Sea Lodge offers a relaxing south-of-the-border setting. Deluxe to ultra-deluxe.

LA JOLLA RESTAURANTS

One of the village's great restaurants, **George's at the Cove** (1250 Prospect Street; 619-454-4244) based its climb to success on a knockout view of the water, a casual, contemporary environment, fine service and a trendsetting regional menu incorporating the freshest seafood, veal, poultry and pasta available. Deluxe to ultra-deluxe.

Manhattan (7766 Fay Avenue; 619-454-1182), which successfully replicates a New York City-style Italian restaurant (despite the palms and pink stucco), features Neapolitan waiters who sing as they toss your salad. The most popular dishes include zesty scampi *fra diavalo* over pasta, veal marsala, and rack of lamb. Wonderful Caesar salads and *cannoli* desserts. Moderate to deluxe.

Jose's Court Room (1037 Prospect Street; 619-454-7655), a noisy, down-to-earth Mexican pub, is the best place in town for quick, casual snacks. Budget to moderate.

John's Waffle Shop (7906 Girard Avenue; 619-454-7371) is a traditional La Jolla stopping place for old-fashioned, budget-priced, counter-style breakfasts or lunches.

One Italian dining room along La Jolla's "restaurant row" ranks among the city's best in that category. **Issimo** (5634 La Jolla Boulevard; 619-454-7004) is a tiny gourmet shop with a stone facade and devoted following. Sophisticated Northern Italian and French dishes are painstakingly prepared and beautifully presented. Favorites include canelloni, gnocchi Parisienne and *agnolotti*. Wall murals by internationally known Wing Howard create an artsy atmosphere. Moderate to deluxe in the cafe; ultra-deluxe in the restaurant.

LA JOLLA SHOPPING

La Jolla's boutiques, galleries and specialty shops offer style and substance. Shopping here focuses on Girard Avenue (from Torrey Pines Road to Prospect Street) and along Prospect Street.

Simic Galleries (7925 Girard Avenue; 619-454-0225) offers a fine selection of seascapes and master impressionist work. At nearby **Bennett Sculpture** (7916 Girard Avenue; 619-454-5257), the remarkable style of Bob and Tom Bennett's works—sleek, fluid, highly polished bronze—captivates collectors.

The **Landmark Gallery** (955 Prospect Street; 619-456-8078) features a variety of artists such as Erté, Frederick Hart, Chinese artist Jiange and popular contemporaries. **Hanson Art Galleries** (1227

SEASIDE SCHOLARS

*High above La Jolla's prettiest beaches rises the Scripps Institute of Oceanography, the oldest institution of its kind in the nation, home to the **Scripps Museum** (8602 La Jolla Shores Drive; 619-534-8665; admission). Here you'll find two dozen marine life tanks, a manmade tidepool and breathtaking exhibits of coastal underwater habitats.*

*Another research center, **The Salk Institute** (at the crest of North Torrey Pines Road just north of the University of California–San Diego campus) is renowned not only for its research but its architecture as well. The surrealistic concrete structure was designed by Louis Kahn in 1960 to be an environment that would stimulate original thinking. It is a stunning site, perched on the lip of a high canyon overlooking the Pacific. For information on tours call 619-453-4100.*

Prospect Street; 619-454-9799) features unique new graphic works and rare selections from 20th-century artists.

Housed in a landmark 1903 cottage covered with wisteria, **John Cole's Book Shop** (780 Prospect Street; 619-454-4766) provides a refuge from these slick, chic La Jolla shops. Its nooks and crannies are lined with books ranging from best sellers to rare editions.

Located some distance south of the village center, **Capriccio** (6919 La Jolla Boulevard; 619-459-4189) has been numbered by *Women's Wear Daily* among the top three fashion stores in America.

One of the oldest and most unusual shops in La Jolla guards the entrance to a sea cave and can actually be entered from land or sea. Dating to 1903, the **La Jolla Cave and Shell Shop** (1325 Coast Boulevard; 619-454-6080) displays every kind of shell imaginable along with a variety of nautical gifts and tourist baubles. From inside the shop, 141 steps lead down a tunnel to the main chamber of Sunny Jim Cave.

LA JOLLA NIGHTLIFE

The dark-paneled **Whaling Bar** (La Valencia Hotel, 1132 Prospect Street; 619-454-0771) attracts lots of La Jolla's big fish. A fine place to relax, listen to piano music, and nibble gourmet hors d'oeuvres.

Among the most romantic restaurants in town, **Top O' The Cove** (1216 Prospect Street; 619-454-7779) features an equally romantic piano bar.

A panoramic view of the ocean makes **Elarios** (Summer House Inn, 7955 La Jolla Shores Drive; 619-459-0541) the perfect place to enjoy a mix of local and national jazz acts nightly. Cover.

The Comedy Store (916 Pearl Street; 619-454-9176) spotlights nationally known comics. Cover plus minimum.

San Diego finally got its own **Hard Rock Cafe** (909 Prospect Street; 619-456-5456), where crowds line the streets nightly just to get in. The main attraction is the collection of rock-and-roll memorabilia; even the bar is modeled after Pete Townshend's guitar.

The La Jolla Chamber Music Society (619-459-3724) hosts summer and fall performances by such notables as the Vienna Boy's Choir and flautist James Galway. The prestigious **La Jolla Playhouse** (619-534-3960), located on the University of California campus, produces innovative dramas and musicals often starring famous actors.

LA JOLLA BEACHES AND PARKS

Torrey Pines State Beach (619-729-8947) is a long, wide, sandy stretch adjacent to Los Peñasquitos Lagoon and Torrey Pines State Reserve. It is popular for sunning, swimming, surf-fishing, volleyball and sunset barbecues. Nearby trails lead through the rich reserves.

Located just south of Carmel Valley Road in Del Mar. The beach is unpatrolled so exercise caution in and out of the surf.

With coastal bluffs above, narrow sand beach below and rich tidepools offshore, **Scripps Beach** is a great strand for beachcombers. Two underwater reserves are among the attractions. Located at the 8600 block of La Jolla Shores Drive.

The sand is wide and the swimming easy at **La Jolla Shores Beach**; so, naturally, it's covered with bodies whenever the sun appears. Just to the east is **Kellogg Park**, an ideal place for a picnic. Located off Camino del Oro near Frescota Street.

Ellen Scripps Park sits on a bluff overlooking La Jolla Cove and is the scenic focal point of La Jolla. The naturally formed cove is almost always free of breakers, has a small but sandy beach and is a popular spot for swimmers and divers. Located near Coast Boulevard and Girard Avenue.

Surely one of the most picturesque beaches in the county, **Windansea Beach** has been portrayed in movies and was immortalized in Tom Wolfe's 1968 nonfiction surfer classic, *The Pumphouse Gang*. Windansea is rated by experts as one of the best surfing locales on the West Coast. In the evenings, crowds line the sidewalk along the top of the cliffs to watch the sunset. Located at the end of Nautilus Street.

Mission Bay

Dredged from a shallow, mosquito-infested tidal bay, 4600-acre **Mission Bay Park** is the largest municipal aquatic park in the world. For San Diego's athletic set it is Mecca, a recreational paradise dotted with islands and lagoons and ringed by 27 miles of sandy beaches. Here, visitors join with residents to enjoy swimming, sailing, windsurfing, waterskiing, fishing, golf and tennis.

BLACK'S BEACH

*One of the world's most famous nude beaches, **Black's Beach** attracts bathers by the thousands, many in the buff. The sand is lovely and soft and the 300-foot cliffs rising up behind make for a spectacular setting. Hang-gliders soaring above add even more enchantment. Surfing here is excellent, although currents make swimming very dangerous. There's a parking lot at the Torrey Pines Glider Port on Torrey Pines Scenic Drive, but beware of the steep trails. Exercise caution, this beach is unpatrolled.*

Over on the East Shore you'll find landscaped picnic areas, a sandy beach for swimming and the park information center. De Anza Cove, in the northeast corner, has a sandy beach as well as an excellent private campground, **Campland On The Bay** (2211 Pacific Beach Drive; 619-274-6260). Mission Bay Park is located along Mission Boulevard between West Mission Bay Drive and East Mission Bay Drive.

More than just a playground, Mission Bay Park features a shopping complex, resort hotels, restaurants and the ever popular **Sea World** (Sea World Drive; 619-226-3901; admission). This 135-acre park-within-a-park has rapidly developed into the world's largest oceanarium, known for its killer whale shows and Penguin Encounter, an icy habitat for the largest colony of penguins north of Antarctica. Also be sure to take in the Forbidden Reef, home to dozens of bat rays and over 100 moray eels.

Down along the ocean front, **Mission Beach** is strung out along a narrow jetty of sand protecting Mission Bay from the sea. Mission Boulevard threads its way through this eclectic, wall-to-wall mix of shingled beach shanties, condominiums and luxury homes.

Thrill seekers crowd around the newly refurbished 1920 era "Giant Dipper" roller coaster at **Belmont Park** (Mission Boulevard and West Mission Bay Drive; 619-488-0668).

Pacific Beach, which picks up at the northern edge of the bay, is the liveliest of the city beaches, a frenetic area packed with high school and college students in designer shorts and Hawaiian shirts. Stop and see the 1920s-era **Crystal Pier** (end of Garnet Avenue).

MISSION BAY LODGING

Pacific Beach boasts the San Diego motel with the most character of all. **Crystal Pier Motel** (4500 Ocean Boulevard; 619-483-6983) is a throwback to the 1930s, when this quaint-looking assemblage of 19 cottages was built. Perched over the waves, this blue-and-white woodframe complex features little cottages with a kitchen and patio-over-the-sea. Deluxe in summer; moderate other times.

Only one Mission Bay resort stands out as unique—the **San Diego Princess** (1404 West Vacation Road; 619-274-4630). Over 40 acres of lush gardens, lagoons and white sand beach surround the villas and cottages of this 450-room resort. Among other extras, there's more than a mile of beach, a children's playground, eight tennis courts and five pools. Ultra-deluxe.

MISSION BAY RESTAURANTS

Don't punish yourself looking for a good breakfast in these parts—go straight to the Rack. The **Spice Rack** (4315 Mission Boulevard; 619-483-7666), that is. Locals know about it, so there is usually a crowd waiting for the fresh muffins or great herb-and-cheese omelettes. Wicker and garden greenery make for a relaxing atmosphere, and there is alfresco dining on the patio. Budget.

The most creative dining room in Pacific Beach is **Château Orleans** (926 Turquoise Street; 619-488-6744), one of the city's finest Cajun restaurants. Cajun, that is, with a delightfully different, delicate nouvelle twist. Tasty appetizers fresh from the bayous include Louisiana frogs' legs and Southern-fried 'gator bites. Entrées include pan-blackened prime rib and gorgeous tiger-tail scampi. Dinner only. Moderate to deluxe.

Hidden away in Ocean Beach is a cottage restaurant called **The Belgian Lion** (2265 Bacon Street; 619-223-2700). Nobody in San Diego provides lustier, tastier European provincial fare than the folks here, who prepare braised rabbit, crispy confit of duck and veal sweetbreads. But go easy when you order; the portions are meant to satisfy a Flemish farmer. Dinner only; moderate to deluxe.

MISSION BAY SHOPPING

Belmont Park (3190 Mission Boulevard; 619-488-0668) is a seaside shopping/entertainment center housing a host of shops and restaurants. Everything about **Art and Harmony** (3780 Mission Boulevard; 619-488-2352) is unique, especially the inventory, which includes beachwear, natural skin-care products and shells.

The **Promenade at Pacific Beach** (Mission Boulevard between Pacific Beach Drive and Reed Street; 619-272-5000), a modern, Mediterranean-style shopping complex, houses around 30 smartly decorated specialty shops.

MISSION BAY NIGHTLIFE

Pacific Beach has one of San Diego's trendiest nightlife districts, offering a wide range of entertainment options from jazz to rock, comedy to blues.

The undisputed king of beach area nightlife is **Club Diego's** (860 Garnet Avenue; 619-272-1241). Modeled after the high-tech video discos of New York and London, it features black-tile dancefloors and video screens monitoring the "beautiful people" who pack the place to capacity nightly. Above, **Diego's Loft** features local jazz groups on weekends. Cover.

Just next door, the **Improv Comedy Club** (832 Garnet Avenue; 619-483-4521), a 1930s-style cabaret, showcases many local and East Coast comedians. Cover.

Blind Melons (710 Garnet Avenue; 619-483-7844) on Crystal Pier is best described as a Chicago beach bar featuring live oldies bands Wednesday through Sunday. Cover.

Standing-room-only crowds are attracted to the **Old Pacific Beach Cafe** (4287 Mission Boulevard; 619-270-7522), where blues and reggae bands perform all week. Cover.

Texas Teahouse (4970 Voltaire Street; 619-222-6895) should be listed under "Dives" in the yellow pages. This musty, Ocean Beach hole-in-the-wall is the home on Thursday night of Tom "Cat" Courtney, a real-life legend who's strummed guitar with the likes of T-Bone Walker and Lightnin' Hopkins. More blues bands play on weekends. Cover.

San Diego Harbor

San Diego's beautiful harbor is a notable exception to the rule that big-city waterfronts lack appeal. Here, the city embraces its bay and presents its finest profile along the water.

The best way to see it all is via one of the vessels that make leisurely excursions around the 22-square-mile harbor, which is colorfully backdropped by commercial and naval vessels as well as the dramatic cityscape. My favorite harbor cruises are aboard the 151-foot schooner **Invader** (619-234-8687; admission).

All along the city side of the harbor from the Coast Guard Station opposite Lindbergh Field to Seaport Village is a lovely landscaped boardwalk called the **Embarcadero**. It offers parks and a thriving assortment of waterfront diversions.

The **Maritime Museum of San Diego** (1306 North Harbor Drive; 619-234-9153; admission) is composed of three vintage ships: most familiar is the 1863 *Star of India*, the nation's oldest iron-hulled merchant ship still afloat.

Nautical buffs or anyone concerned about American naval power will be interested in the huge **U.S. Navy** presence in San Diego harbor. San Diego hosts one of the world's largest fleets of fighting ships—from aircraft carriers to nuclear submarines. Naval vessels moored at the Broadway Pier hold open house on weekends.

Near the south end of the Embarcadero sits the popular shopping and entertainment complex known as **Seaport Village** (Pacific Highway and Harbor Drive). Designed to replicate an Early California seaport, it comprises 14 acres of bayfront parks and promenades, shops and galleries. On the south side is the 45-foot-high Mulkilto Lighthouse, official symbol of the village. Nearby is the Broadway Flying Horses Carousel, a hand-carved, turn-of-the-century model that originally whirled around Coney Island.

Looking much like a giant sailing ship, the new **San Diego Convention Center** (111 West Harbor Drive; 619-525-5115) overlooks San Diego Harbor. The controversial architectural design is at least worth a drive by (or you can take an hour-long walking tour).

Downtown San Diego

Billions of dollars invested in a stunning array of new buildings and in the restoration of many old ones have transformed San Diego during the last few decades. Within the compact city center there's Horton Plaza, an exciting experiment in avant-garde urban architecture, and the adjacent Gaslamp Quarter, which reveals how San Diego looked at the peak of its Victorian-era boom in the 1880s. Together they are a study in contrasts that provides one of the most fascinating architectural tours of any American city.

Horton Plaza (bounded by Broadway and G Street and 1st and 4th avenues) is totally unlike any other shopping center or urban redevelopment project. It has transcended its genre in a whimsical, multilevel, open-air, pastel-hued concoction of ramps, escalators, rambling paths, bridges, towers, piazzas, sculptures and greenery. Mimes, minstrels and fortune tellers meander about the six-block complex performing for patrons.

Horton Plaza was inspired by shopping districts in Athens, Barcelona and London. In all, its design includes 14 different styles, ranging from Renaissance to postmodern.

The **Gaslamp Quarter** is one of America's largest national historic districts, covering a 16-block strip along 4th, 5th and 6th avenues from Broadway to the waterfront. Architecturally, the Quarter reveals some of the finest Victorian-style commercial buildings constructed in San Diego during the 50 years between the Civil War and World War I. It was this area, along 5th Avenue, that became San Diego's first main street.

More than 100 grand old Victorian buildings have been restored to their original splendor, so history buffs and lovers of antique buildings should promptly don their walking shoes and begin exploring. One way to do this is to join a walking tour (see the "Transportation" section in this chapter). Or head out on your own, accompanied by a map available at the **William Heath Davis House** (410 Island Avenue; 619-233-5227; admission). This "salt box" family home, dating to about 1850, makes an excellent starting point. Framed on the East Coast, it was shipped to San Diego by boat around Cape Horn and represents the oldest structure in the Quarter.

Just across the street is the **Royal Pie Bakery** (554 4th Avenue). Almost unbelievably, a bakery has been on this site since 1875. Around the turn of the century the bakery found itself in the middle of a red-light district. It never stopped turning out cakes and pies, though a notorious bordello operated on the second floor.

Go back down Island Avenue to 5th Avenue and turn left. Not only was this block part of the notorious 19th-century Stingaree district, as hinted by the old 1887 hotel by the same name on your left, at

542 5th Avenue, but it was San Diego's Chinatown. **Wong's Nan-king Cafe** (467 5th Avenue) was built in 1913 and retains the atmosphere of the past.

The nearby **Timken Building** (5th Avenue and Market Street), notable for its fancy arched brick facade, was erected in 1894. Across the street is the **Backesto Building**, a beautifully restored late-19th century structure.

The tall, Romanesque revival **Keating Building** (5th Avenue and F Street) was one of the most prestigious office buildings in San Diego during the 1890s. Next door is the **Ingersoll-Tutton Building** (832 5th Avenue). When this 90-foot-long structure was built in 1894 for $20,000 it was considered the most expensive building on the block!

The block on the other side of 5th Avenue, from F up to E Street, represents the most architecturally significant row in the Gaslamp Quarter. From south to north, there's the **Marston Building** on the corner of F Street. Built in 1881, it was downtown San Diego's leading department store. Next is the 1887 **Hubbell Building**, originally a dry goods establishment. The **Nesmith-Greeley Building** next door is another example of the then-fashionable Romanesque revival style with its ornamental brick coursing. With twin towers and intricate baroque revival architecture, the 1888 **Louis Bank of Commerce** is probably the most beautiful building in the Quarter. It originally housed a ground-floor oyster bar that was a favorite haunt of Wyatt Earp.

Though it's situated a few blocks east of the Gaslamp Quarter, make a point to visit **Villa Montezuma** (1925 K Street; 619-239-2211; admission). This ornate, Queen Anne-style Victorian mansion, magnificently restored, was constructed by a group of culture-hungry San Diegans in 1887 as a gift to lure a world-famous troubadour here.

DOWNTOWN SAN DIEGO RESTAURANTS

A comfortable little bistro, **The French Side of the West** (2202 4th Avenue; 619-234-5540) has been heralded as one of the city's best values. The prix-fixe dinner is an intriguing four-course meal, while the changing menu may include filet mignon with roquefort and peppercorn or fresh sea bass with sorrel sauce. Dinner only, reservations strongly recommended; deluxe.

Everyone likes the warm, friendly atmosphere of a real family restaurant like **Hob Nob Hill** (2271 1st Avenue; 619-239-8176). Here's a place where the waitresses call you "hon" and remind you to finish your veggies. A gang of grandmas couldn't do a better job of serving the favorites like waffles, homemade breads and chicken and dumplings. Budget to moderate.

History, atmosphere and great cooking combine to make dining at **Ida Bailey's Restaurant** (311 Island Avenue; 619-544-6888) a memorable experience. Located in the Horton Grand Hotel, Ida's was once a brothel, operated back in the 1890s by a madam of the same name. The chef serves a varied menu highlighted by old-fashioned American fare, including Victorian pot roast, meat loaf, roasted chicken and leg of lamb. Moderate to deluxe.

Established in 1907 and now the Gaslamp Quarter's landmark restaurant, the **Golden Lion Tavern** (801 4th Avenue; 619-233-1131) occupies a building that's truly a work of art. Original penny-tile floors, handsome crown molding and a magnificent stained-glass dome add to the turn-of-the-century atmosphere. Among pasta and seafood items is a Golden Lion favorite and a dish invented here, the "screw-up": fettucine alfredo served with shrimp scampi. Budget to moderate in price.

You'd be remiss to visit San Diego without enjoying a fresh seafood feast at a spot overlooking the harbor. Why not go first class at **Anthony's Star of the Sea Room** (1360 North Harbor Drive; 619-232-7408)? This place wears more ribbons than a Navy admiral. Dramatically set over the water and elegantly decorated, Anthony's presents a remarkable menu including broad-bill swordfish and Flor-

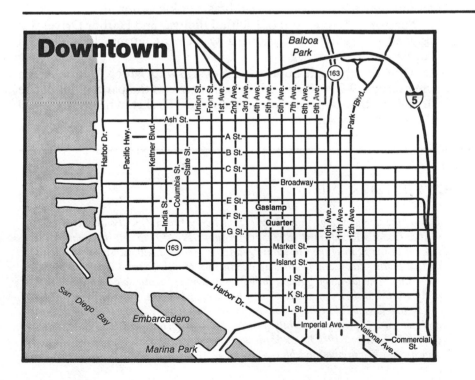

ida pompano. Reservations and coat and tie are essential. Deluxe to ultra-deluxe. If your budget can't handle the "Star," check out the other two Anthonys next door—the **Fish Grotto** (619-232-5103) and **Harborside** (619-232-6358). They're more moderately priced.

DOWNTOWN SAN DIEGO SHOPPING

No other shopping center in the county is quite like **Horton Plaza** (between Broadway and G Street, 1st and 4th avenues; 619-239-8180). More than 140 stores are situated here, including four department stores.

Worth a special visit is **Horton Plaza Farmers' Market** (619-696-7766), where 25,000 square feet of fresh produce and specialty food products are beautifully displayed.

The **Gaslamp Quarter** (along 5th Avenue) is a charming 16-square-block assemblage of shops, galleries and sidewalk cafes, where the streets are decked out in Victorian-era street lamps and window displays.

A favorite spot for antique lovers is the **Olde Cracker Factory** (448 West Market Street; 619-232-7961), which offers a 20-store selection in the restored 1913 Bishop Cracker Factory. Legend has it that a resident ghost named "Crunch" shuffles through mounds of broken crackers here searching for a small brass cookie cutter.

Seaport Village (foot of Pacific Highway and Harbor Drive) was designed to resemble a California waterfront setting. Its 65 varied shops dot a 14-acre village.

Thursday through Sunday, **Kobey's Swap Meet** (Sports Arena Boulevard; 619-226-0650; admission) converts the parking lot of the San Diego Sports Arena into a giant flea market where over 1000 sellers hawk new and used wares.

CROCE'S RESTAURANT

*Fans of the late pop singer Jim Croce ("Bad Leroy Brown") will surely enjoy a visit to **Croce's Restaurant** (802 5th Avenue; 619-233-4355). This bar and restaurant in the heart of the Gaslamp Quarter is managed enthusiastically by Jim's widow, Ingrid Croce, and features an eclectic mix of dishes served in a friendly cabaret setting. The far-ranging menu includes sandwiches, exotic salads, beef, chicken and fresh fish dishes, and the city's best blintzes. Moderate.*

*Croce fans will love the restaurant's bar, where family mementos line the walls and live jazz is performed nightly. Just next door, **Ingrid's Top Hat Cantina** (818 5th Avenue; 619-233-6945) is a snazzy New Orleans-style club featuring comedy and live rhythm-and-blues.*

DOWNTOWN SAN DIEGO NIGHTLIFE

THE BEST BARS An elegant Old World setting of marble, brass and leather makes **Grant Grill Lounge** (U.S. Grant Hotel, 326 Broadway; 619-232-3121) *the* place for the elite to meet. Pianists play a mix of contemporary tunes, popular standards and jazz.

Golden Lion Tavern (801 4th Avenue; 619-233-1131) is a Gaslamp Quarter landmark and a favored place to bend an elbow. Jazz on weekends.

Karl Strass Old Columbia Brewery (1157 Columbia Avenue; 619-234-2739) may well have the best beer in town, and it has been well greeted by San Diegans.

It's easy to spot the shocking pink, neon-lit facade of **Fat City** (2137 Pacific Highway; 619-232-0686). Art deco styling marks the exterior, but the bar features an authentic Victorian decor. Fat City is a favorite among friendly young singles and hosts a good jazz and light rock lineup Thursday through Sunday.

Plaza Bar (1055 2nd Avenue; 619-238-1818), at the distinctive Westgate Hotel, is a graceful period French lounge where prominent locals and visitors enjoy classy piano entertainment nightly.

Mr. A's (2550 5th Avenue; 619-239-1377) is the critics' choice for "best drinking with a view." The atmosphere at this piano bar is one of monied luxury, and gentlemen are expected to wear jackets.

Featuring views of San Diego Bay and one of the largest dancefloors in town, **Harbor House** (831 West Harbor Drive, Seaport Village; 619-232-1141) dishes up everything from Top-40 disco to bigband music nightly.

Part of San Diego's gay scene, **Club West Coast** (1845 Hancock Street; 619-295-3724) is a high-energy club featuring deejay disco dancing and special events.

THEATER The **Simon Edison Theatre Centre for the Performing Arts** (Balboa Park; 619-239-2255) presents classic and contemporary plays in three Balboa Park theatres. The **Gaslamp Quarter Theater Company** (619-234-9583) offers productions of classic and contemporary works.

In addition to performances of the noted San Diego Opera, the **San Diego Civic Theater** (202 C Street; 619-236-6510) presents a variety of entertainment ranging from pop artists to plays to dance performances.

The **San Diego Repertory Theatre** (79 Horton Plaza; 619-235-8025) performs dramas, comedies and musicals.

OPERA, SYMPHONY AND DANCE The **San Diego Opera** (202 C Street; 619-232-7636) presents such international stars as Luciano Pavarotti and Kiri Te Kanawa. The season runs January through May, with additional recitals in the fall.

Performing in the historic 1929 Spanish Renaissance-style Copley Symphony Hall (1245 7th Avenue), the **San Diego Symphony Orchestra** (619-699-4200) offers an array of guest conductors and artists. During the summer, the symphony presents outdoor performances at the Embarcadero Marina Park South (5th Street and Harbor Boulevard).

California Ballet (619-560-5676) presents a diverse repertoire of contemporary and traditional ballets.

Balboa Park

History is unclear as to whether it was intelligent foresight or unbridled optimism that prompted the establishment of **Balboa Park**. Certain that a fine neighborhood would flourish around it, city fa-

---

SAN DIEGO'S CLASSIC HOTELS

*My vote for the prettiest and most hospitable of San Diego's bed and breakfasts goes to the **Keating House Inn** (2331 2nd Avenue; 619-239-8585). This historically designated 1888 Victorian home offers eight comfy-cozy rooms with quality period furnishings. Outside, the beautifully restored Queen Anne has a gabled roof, octagonal window turret and conical peak. Moderate.*

*Looking much as it did when it was built in 1887, the majestic **Britt House** (406 Maple Street; 619-234-2926) stands three stories high and has space aplenty for ten rooms. This immaculate Victorian bed and breakfast, just steps from Balboa Park, is old lace and walnut and afternoon teas in the parlor. Just like staying at a rich aunt's. Deluxe.*

*No downtown hotel has a more colorful past than the **Horton Grand Hotel** (311 Island Avenue; 619-544-1886). This 132-room Victorian gem is actually two old hotels that were disassembled piece by piece, resurrected a few blocks away and linked by an atrium-lobby and courtyard. The 1880s theme is faithfully executed, from the hotel's antique-furnished rooms (each with a fireplace) to its period-costumed staff. Deluxe, with service and location well worth it.*

*Built in 1910, the **U.S. Grant Hotel** (326 Broadway; 619-232-3121) reigned as downtown San Diego's premier hotel for decades. Now, after an extensive refurbishing, it is once again a showcase, boasting 280 rooms and a restaurant. It is quite possibly the most elegant and certainly the most beautifully restored historic building in the city. There's a marble-floored lobby with cathedral-height ceilings and enormous crystal chandeliers. Rooms are richly furnished with mahogany poster beds and Queen Anne-style armoires. Ultra-deluxe.*

thers in 1868 set aside 1400 acres of rattlesnake-infested hillside above "New Town" as a public facility.

Today Balboa Park ranks among the largest and finest of America's city parks. Wide avenues and walkways curve through luxurious subtropical foliage leading to nine major museums, three art galleries, four theaters, picnic groves, the world's largest zoo, a golf course and countless other recreation facilities. Its verdant grounds teem with cyclists, joggers, skaters and weekend artists.

Begin your visit at the House of Hospitality at the southeast corner of Plaza de Panama. It contains the **Park Information Center** (619-239-0512), which has free pamphlets and maps on the park.

To the right, as you head east on the pedestrian-only section of El Prado, is the newly rebuilt Casa de Balboa. It houses the **San Diego Model Railroad Museum** (619-696-0199; admission), which features the largest collection of mini-gauge trains in the world. Here, too, is the **Museum of Photographic Arts** (619-239-5262; admission).

Sports fans will want to take in the **Hall of Champions and Hall of Fame** in Casa de Balboa. On display are exhibits featuring San Diego athletes from more than 40 sports.

Continuing east to the fountain, you'll see the **Reuben H. Fleet Space Theater and Science Center** (619-238-1168; admission) on your right. Among the park's finest attractions, it has one of the largest planetariums and most impressive multimedia theaters in the country.

Just across the courtyard is the **Natural History Museum** (619-232-3821; admission), with displays devoted mostly to the Southern California environment.

Going back along El Prado, take a moment to admire your reflection in the **Lily Pond**. With the old, latticed **Botanical Building** in the background, the scene is a favorite among photographers. The fern collection inside is equally striking.

Next is the **Timken Gallery** (619-239-5548), considered to have one of the West Coast's finest collections of European and early American paintings. The displays include works by Rembrandt and Cézanne, as well as an amazing collection of Russian icons.

Right next door on the plaza is the **San Diego Museum of Art** (619-232-7931; admission). The museum holds a permanent collection of Italian Renaissance, Dutch and Spanish baroque paintings and sculpture, a display of Asian art, a gallery of impressionist paintings and a contemporary American collection.

The grandest of all Balboa Park structures, built as the centerpiece for the 1915 Panama–California Exposition, is the 200-foot Spanish Renaissance **California Tower**. The **Museum of Man** (619-239-2001; admission), at the base of the tower, is a must for anthropology buffs and those interested in Native American cultures.

Another spot not to be missed is the **Aerospace Museum and Hall of Fame** (619-234-8291; admission), several blocks south of the plaza. It contains a replica of Charles Lindbergh's famous "Spirit of St. Louis," the original of which was built in San Diego. En route you'll pass the **Spreckels Organ Pavilion**. Those 4416 pipes make it the world's largest outdoor instrument of its kind.

Balboa Park's museums charge an admission fee but some can be visited free on the first Tuesday of the month.

Coronado

An isolated and exclusive community in San Diego Bay, Coronado is almost an island, connected to the mainland only by the graceful San Diego–Coronado Bay Bridge and by a long, narrow sandspit called the Silver Strand.

Once known as the "Nickel Snatcher," the Coronado ferry for years crossed the waters of San Diego Harbor between the Embarcadero and Coronado. All for five cents each way. That's history, of course, but the 1940s-vintage, double-deck *Silvergate* still plies the waters. The **San Diego Bay Ferry** (619-234-4111) leaves from the Bay Cafe on North Harbor Drive at the foot of Broadway.

The **Harbor Hopper** (619-229-8294) is a bay water taxi service that leaves from San Diego and docks at the Old Ferry Landing. From there the **Coronado Trolley Line** (619-437-1861), operating on the hour, will take you on a 20-minute sightseeing tour.

The tour includes the town's main attraction, the **Hotel del Coronado** (1500 Orange Avenue; 619-435-6611), a red-roofed, Victorian-style, wooden wonder and century-old National Historic Landmark.

THE SAN DIEGO ZOO

*The **San Diego Zoo** (Balboa Park, 619-234-3153; admission) needs no introduction. It quite simply is the world's top-rated zoo. The numbers alone are mind-boggling: 3200 animals, representing 500 species, spread out over 128 acres. Most of these wild animals live in surroundings as natural as man can make them. Rather than cages there are many moated enclosures where lions roam free on grassy islands, sun bears wander in an equatorial habitat, and exotic birds fly about in a tropical rain forest. All around is a manmade jungle overgrown with countless species of rare and exotic plants.*

*Best of the best is the zoo's state-of-the-art primate exhibit. And the zoo has a large collection of those cuddly koalas from Australia. You can pet one at the **Children's Zoo**.*

You can also cruise the quiet neighborhood streets that radiate off Orange Avenue between the bay and the ocean, enjoying the town's handsome blend of cottages and historic homes.

CORONADO LODGING

The best deal on a nice, moderately priced room in the heart of Coronado is at **El Cordova Hotel** (1351 Orange Avenue; 619-435-4131). Originally built as a private mansion in 1902, El Cordova's moderate size (40 rooms) and lovely Spanish-hacienda architecture make it a relaxing getaway spot.

Nothing can detract from the glamor of the **Hotel del Coronado** (1500 Orange Avenue; 619-522-8000). With its turrets, cupolas and gingerbread facade, it is one of the great hotels of California. This celebrated 100-year-old Victorian landmark boasts 691 rooms in addition to beautifully landscaped grounds. "Hotel Del" has two pools, a long stretch of beach, tennis courts, a first-class health club and a gallery of shops. Ultra-deluxe.

Across the street rises the **Glorietta Bay Inn** (1630 Glorietta Boulevard; 619-435-3101), a 1908 Edwardian mansion that's now an elegant 98-room hotel. Suites here reflect the grandeur of the inn's early days, but ordinary rooms are, in fact, rather ordinary. Deluxe.

CORONADO RESTAURANTS

Visitors are often lured into the Hotel del Coronado's **Crown-Coronet Room** (1500 Orange Avenue; 619-435-6611). Its grand Victorian architecture and enormous domed ceiling set a tone of elegance and style rarely matched along the Pacific Coast. The place is so magnificent the food seems unimportant. Most critics, in fact, assert that dinner in the hotel's **Prince of Wales Room** is better, but breakfast, lunch, dinner or Sunday brunch at the Crown Room will never disappoint; deluxe.

Locals looking to avoid the crowds at "Hotel Del" usually head for **Chez Loma** (1132 Loma Avenue; 619-435-0661). Located in a charming 1889 Victorian house, it serves lovely French meals. Dine inside or out. Moderate to deluxe.

Peohe's (1201 First Street; 619-437-4474) has been praised for its panoramic views of San Diego Bay and its tropical decor. Dinners consist of fresh fish items—lobster, shrimp and a featured daily catch. Lunch brings a tasty soup/salad/sandwich combo. Sunday brunch; moderate to deluxe.

Family dining is best at a family-run restaurant like **La Avenida** (1301 Orange Avenue; 619-435-6262). Housed in a rambling, attractive, Spanish-style building, La Avenida features Mexican entrées and their "famous steak sandwich." Budget to moderate.

CORONADO SHOPPING

Coronado's fancy Orange Avenue in the village center harbors six blocks of unusual shops and two minimalls, **Coronado Plaza** (1330 Orange Avenue; 619-435-4620) and one in the **El Cordova Hotel** (1351 Orange Avenue; 619-435-4131).

The **Old Ferry Landing** (619-435-8895) has been renovated to include a modern shopping area complete with boutiques, specialty shops and galleries.

The **Hotel del Coronado** (1500 Orange Avenue) is a city within a city and home to many intriguing specialty shops, such as the **British Importing Company** (619-435-6611), where you can locate your family's crest or coat of arms.

CORONADO NIGHTLIFE

You can stop for a cocktail in the Hotel del Coronado's **Ocean Terrace Lounge** (1500 Orange Avenue; 619-435-6611). Or try the Del's **Palm Court**, offering live piano music in a palm-studded lounge.

Mexican Village (120 Orange Avenue; 619-435-1822) is a Mexican-theme nightclub, but the piano music ranges from classic to contemporary from Sunday through Thursday; disco dancing on weekends.

CORONADO BEACHES AND PARKS

The widest beach in the county, **Coronado Shores Beach** is unfortunately backed by a row of towering condominiums. Still, crowds flock to this roomy expanse of clean, soft sand where gentle waves make for good swimming. Located off Ocean Boulevard.

That same wide sandy beach prevails to the north at **Coronado City Beach**. Here the city has a large, grassy picnic area known as Sunset Park where frisbees and the aroma of fried chicken fill the air. Located on Ocean Boulevard north of Avenue G.

A two-mile strip of fluffy white sand, **Silver Strand State Beach** (619-435-5184) fronts a narrow isthmus separating the Pacific Ocean and San Diego Bay. It was named for the tiny silver seashells found in abundance along the shore. Swimming here is good on both bay and ocean side. The park also is popular for surf-fishing, clamming and shell hunting. Located on Route 75 (Silver Strand Boulevard) between Imperial Beach and Coronado.

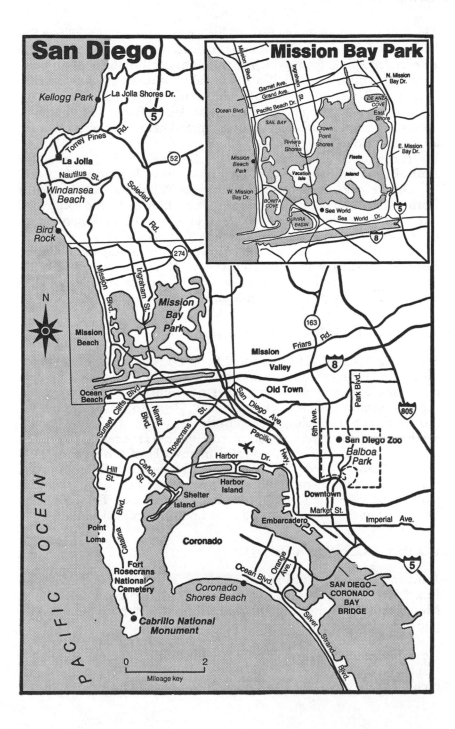

San Diego

Kellogg Park
La Jolla Shores Dr.
5
52
Torrey Pines Rd.
La Jolla
Nautilus St.
Windansea Beach
Soledad Rd.
Bird Rock
274
Ingraham St.
Mission Blvd.
N
Mission Bay Park
Mission Beach
Ocean Beach
Sunset Cliffs Blvd.
Nimitz Blvd.
Rosecrans St.
San Diego Ave.
Old Town
Mission Valley
Friars Rd.
163
8
Park Blvd.
6th Ave.
805
San Diego Zoo
Balboa Park
Pacific Hwy.
Harbor Dr.
Hill St.
Cañon St.
Catalina Blvd.
Shelter Island
Harbor Island
Downtown
Market St.
Embarcadero
Imperial Ave.
5
Point Loma
Coronado
Fort Rosecrans National Cemetery
Coronado Shores Beach
Ocean Blvd.
Orange Ave.
SAN DIEGO–CORONADO BAY BRIDGE
Cabrillo National Monument
Silver Strand Blvd.
PACIFIC OCEAN

0   2
Mileage key

Mission Bay Park

Mission Blvd.
Garnet Ave.
Grand Ave.
Ocean Blvd.
Pacific Beach Dr.
Ingraham St.
N. Mission Bay Dr.
DE ANZA COVE
East Shore
SAIL BAY
Riviera Shores
Crown Point Shores
E. Mission Bay Dr.
Mission Beach Park
Fiesta Island
Vacation Isle
W. Mission Bay Dr.
BONITA COVE
Sea World
Sea World Dr.
QUIVIRA BASIN
5
8

Point Loma Area

The Point Loma peninsula forms a high promontory that shelters San Diego Bay from the Pacific. It also provided Juan Rodríquez Cabrillo an excellent place from which to contemplate his 16th-century discovery of California. **Cabrillo National Monument** (1800 Cabrillo Memorial Drive; 619-557-5450; admission), featuring a statue of the navigator, stands facing his landing site at Ballast Point. The view here is outstanding. With the bay and city spread below, you can often see all the way from Mexico to the La Jolla mesa.

The visitor's center includes a small museum. The nearby **Old Point Loma Lighthouse** guided shipping from 1855 to 1891.

On the ocean side of the peninsula is **Whale Watch Lookout Point** where, during winter months, you can observe the southward migration of California gray whales. Close by is a superb network of tidepools where rangers lead daily tours (619-557-5450).

On the way out to Point Loma, you'll encounter the haunting **Fort Rosecrans National Cemetery**. Here, thousands of trim, white markers march down a grassy hillside in mute testimony to San Diego's fallen troops and deep military roots.

POINT LOMA AREA LODGING

A rare beachfront find in residential Point Loma is the **Ocean Manor Hotel** (1370 Sunset Cliffs Boulevard; 619-222-7901). This trim, white, two-story, 25-room apartment hotel sits right on the seaside cliffs. Rooms are neat and clean but very basic. Rates for bachelor and studio apartments, including kitchen facilities, are budget to moderate.

For a relaxing, offbeat alternative to the mammoth resorts on Shelter and Harbor Islands, try **Humphrey's Half Moon Inn** (2303 Shelter Island Drive; 619-224-3411). Surrounded by subtropical plants, this nautical-rustic 182-room complex overlooks the yacht harbor and gives the feeling of staying on an island. The rooms are tastefully but simply decorated. Spa and putting green. Deluxe.

POINT LOMA AREA RESTAURANTS

A marine view and whirling ceiling fans at **Humphrey's** (Half Moon Inn, 2303 Shelter Island Drive; 619-224-3411) suggest Casablanca. Mesquite-broiled fish specials and eastern-style "shore dinners" are popular at moderate to deluxe prices.

At Fisherman's Village in Point Loma you'll find the **Blue Crab Restaurant** (4922 North Harbor Drive; 619-224-3000). Appealing Cape Cod decor and terrific bay views set the mood for fresh seafood, including Maryland blue and soft-shell crabs. Moderate to deluxe.

San Diego's best soup-and-salad bar and a personal favorite for healthy budget dining is **Souplantation** (3960 West Point Loma Boulevard; 619-222-7404).

POINT LOMA AREA NIGHTLIFE

For the mellow crowd looking for cocktails and conversation while overlooking a picturesque marina, there's **Sunset Bar and Grill** (2051 Shelter Island Drive; 619-223-2572).

Aside from being a popular restaurant and lounge, **Tom Ham's Lighthouse** (2150 Harbor Island Drive; 619-291-9110) is a real lighthouse and the official Coast Guard-sanctioned beacon of Harbor Island. Live easy-listening and jazz.

POINT LOMA AREA BEACHES AND PARKS

The jagged cliffs and sandstone bluffs along Point Loma peninsula give **Sunset Cliffs Park** a spectacular setting. High-cresting waves make it popular with expert surfers, who favor the rocky beach at the foot of Ladera Avenue. Rich marine life attracts many divers. Located off Sunset Cliffs Boulevard south of Ocean Beach.

Where you toss down your towel at **Ocean Beach** will probably depend as much on your age as your interests. Surfers and sailors hang out around the pier; farther north, where the surf is milder and the beach wider, families and retired folks can be found sunbathing and strolling. Take Ocean Beach Freeway (Route 8) west until it ends; turn left onto Sunset Cliffs Boulevard, then right on Voltaire Street.

Old Town and Mission Valley

Back in 1769, Spanish explorer Gaspar de Portolá selected a hilltop site overlooking the bay for a mission that began the European settlement of California. Some of the buildings and relics of that early era survive and have been brought back to life at **Old Town San Diego State Historic Park** (park headquarters, 4002 Wallace Street; 619-237-6770). Lined with adobe restorations and brightened with colorful shops, the six blocks of Old Town provide a lively opportunity to stroll, shop and sightsee.

The park sponsors a free walking tour at 2 p.m. daily. Or you can easily do it on your own by picking up a map at the **Old Town Information Center** (2422 San Diego Avenue; 619-291-4903).Hop aboard the **Old Town Trolley** (4040 Twiggs Street; 619-298-8687; admission) for a delightful 90-minute narrative tour of Old Town and a variety of other highlights in San Diego and Coronado.

As it has for over a century, everything focuses on **Old Town Plaza** (sometimes called Washington Square). This was the social and recreational center of the town: political meetings, barbecues, shoot-outs and bullfights all happened here.

The 1827 **Casa de Estudillo** (Mason Street) is the finest of the plaza's original adobe buildings, a mansion in its time. **Casa de Bandini** (Mason and Calhoun streets) was built in 1829 and became a stagecoach station in the 1860s.

Casa de Altamirano (San Diego Avenue and Twiggs Street) was Old Town's first frame building and the site where the *San Diego Union* was first printed in 1868. It has been restored as a 19th-century printing office.

On the outskirts of Old Town lies **Heritage Park** (Juan and Harney streets). Seven historic 1880s-era houses and an old Jewish temple have been moved here and beautifully restored.

OLD TOWN AND MISSION VALLEY LODGING

For the romantic, **Heritage Park Bed & Breakfast Inn** (2470 Heritage Park Row; 619-295-7088), a storybook 1889 Queen Anne mansion with a striking turret, is an enchanting spot. Set on a grassy hillside, it provides a tranquil escape. Choose from nine distinctive chambers (five with private baths), each furnished with museum-quality antiques. Deluxe.

CALIFORNIA'S BIRTHPLACE

*The original San Diego mission and Spanish Presidio once stood high on a hill behind Old Town. This site of California's birthplace now houses **Serra Museum** (2727 Presidio Drive; 619-297-3258), a handsome Spanish colonial structure containing an excellent collection of Native American and Spanish artifacts from the state's pioneer days.*

*Within five years after Father Serra dedicated the first of California's 21 missions, the site had become too small for the growing numbers it served. So **Mission San Diego de Alcala** (10818 San Diego Mission Road; 619-281-8449; admission) was moved from Presidio Hill six miles east into Mission Valley. Surrounded now by shopping centers and suburban homes, the "Mother of Missions" retains its simple but striking white adobe facade topped by a graceful campanile. There's a museum containing mission records in Junípero Serra's handwriting and a lovely courtyard with olive trees.*

OLD TOWN AND MISSION VALLEY RESTAURANTS

Mexican food and atmosphere abound in Old Town, especially in the popular Bazaar del Mundo. Here two restaurants lure a steady stream of diners into festive, flowered courtyards. **Casa de Pico** (619-296-3267) is a favored place for nachos and margaritas. Entrées are served both outdoors and in the hacienda-style dining rooms.

Next door, in a magnificent 1829 hacienda, **Casa de Bandini** (619-297-8211), you'll find the cuisine a bit more refined. Seafood is good here. Mariachis often perform at both spots; budget to moderate.

Emil's (3928 Twiggs Street; 619-295-2343) is a European country restaurant, pure and simple. Veal picatta, wienerschnitzel and hearty specials such as Hungarian goulash are wonderfully prepared. Dinner only. Moderate; reservations recommended.

OLD TOWN AND MISSION VALLEY SHOPPING

Historic Old Town is blessed with several exciting bazaars and shopping squares. By far the grandest is the **Bazaar del Mundo** (Calhoun Street between Twigg and Juan streets; 619-296-3161), Old Town's version of the famous marketplaces of Spain and Mexico. Adobe casitas house a variety of international shops.

Walk down San Diego Avenue and take a gander at **Squibob Square** (2611 San Diego Avenue). The cactus-lined courtyard and bougainvillea-laced cottages lend an authentic feel of yesteryear to the souvenir shops.

A haven for art lovers is **Spanish Village Arts Center** (1770 Village Place, near the San Diego Zoo entrance; 619-233-9050). Its open-air studios are staffed by artists displaying original paintings, sculpture, ceramics, jewelry, and gems.

OLD TOWN AND MISSION VALLEY NIGHTLIFE

The **Old Town Mexican Cafe y Cantina** (2489 San Diego Avenue; 619-297-4330), a festive, friendly establishment, has a patio bar.

O'Hungry's (2547 San Diego Avenue; 619-298-0133) features folk singers and guitarists Tuesday through Sunday.

If you want to dance disco, **Confetti's** (5373 Mission Center Road; 619-291-8635) has a multilevel dancefloor and four bars, all packed nightly.

Inland San Diego County

Sightseeing San Diego County's rugged backcountry means wandering through a landscape filled with rambling hills, flowering meadows and rocky peaks. There are old missions and gold mines en route, as well as farms and ranches.

Beginning in the county's northwest corner, Route 76 will carry you to **Mission San Luis Rey** (619-757-3651). Known as the "King of the Missions," this beautifully restored complex was originally constructed in 1789 and represents the largest California mission.

Guajome Park (Route 76 about seven miles east of Route 5; 619-565-3600), a 569-acre playground, offers a variety of natural, historical and recreational opportunities. The park is centered around Guajome Adobe, considered one of the region's best examples of early Spanish architecture.

Farther inland lies **Mission San Antonio de Pala** (Pala; 619-742-3317). An *asistencia*, or branch of the larger mission, it has been conducting mass since it was built in 1816. The original chapel and bell tower have been faithfully restored, and the long, low walls of the church interior are still decorated with primitive Indian frescoes. Located on the Pala Indian Reservation, it is the only mission primarily serving Indians.

Rockhounds will be interested in **Gems of Pala** (35940 Magee Road, Pala; 619-742-1356), which has exhibits and retail displays of some of the world's finest tourmaline.

Head south to Escondido and you'll find **San Pasqual Battlefield State Historic Park** (15808 San Pasqual Valley Road, Escondido; 619-238-3380), where an interpretive center tells the story of a strange and little-known battle. It seems that during the Mexican War in 1846 about 100 U.S. Dragoons, including the famous scout Kit Carson, suffered an embarrassing defeat at the hands of California Mexicans.

On a more modern note, **Lawrence Welk Village** (8860 Lawrence Welk Drive, Escondido; 619-749-3000), an elaborate resort complex, contains a museum featuring the famous "one-ana-two" entertainer's memorabilia. High camp at its most bizarre.

From Escondido, a popular winegrowing region, you can drive northeast along scenic Route S6 to Pauma Valley and then pick up Route 76, which will carry you from a verdant region of citrus groves up into the pine-rimmed high country of Cleveland National Forest.

A spiraling road leads to that great silver dome in the sky, **Mount Palomar Observatory** (619-742-2119). With a clear shot heavenward from its 6100-foot-high perch, one of the world's largest reflecting telescopes scans the night skies for celestial secrets. You can glimpse the 200-inch Hale Telescope from the visitor's gallery, view a movie on how research is conducted, and look at photos in the museum.

Down the road in **Julian** you'll come upon the belle of Southern California mountain mining towns. During the 1890s, the local mines employed 2000 miners, who hauled up $15 million in gold ore. Today the region produces red apples rather than gold nuggets, and Julian, with its dusty aura of the Old West, has become a major tourist attraction.

Some of the falsefront stores along Main Street are 19th-century originals. Have a look, for instance, at the 1897 **Julian Hotel**, and don't miss the **Julian Drug Store**, an old-style soda fountain serving sparkling sarsaparilla. The white clapboard **Town Hall** still stands, and over at the Julian Museum (619-765-0227), the townsfolk have turned an old brewery into a charming hodgepodge of local collectibles.

The first hard rock mine in Julian and today a state historic site, **Washington Mine** (Geiger Road, an extension of C Street; 619-765-0174) is open daily. Although the tunnels have long since collapsed, the Julian Historical Society displays memorabilia depicting the mining era.

Operations closed in 1942, but the **Eagle and High Peak Mines** (end of C Street; 619-765-0036; admission) still offer tours of the tunnels and an opportunity to pan for gold. What seems certain to be a "tourist trap" actually pans out as an interesting and educational experience.

But remember, these days apples are actually the main business in Julian and dozens of orchards drape the hillsides below town. The countryside all around is quilted with pear and peach orchards as well, and there are Appaloosa ranches and roadside stands selling fruits and jams.

INLAND SAN DIEGO COUNTY LODGING

One of the county's leading resorts is **Rancho Bernardo Inn** (17550 Bernardo Oaks Drive, Rancho Bernardo; 619-487-1611). World-class

WILD ANIMAL PARK

*There's no finer wildlife sanctuary in the country than the San Diego Zoo's remarkable **Wild Animal Park** (15500 San Pasqual Valley Road, Escondido; 619-234-6541; admission). This 1800-acre spread, skillfully landscaped to resemble Asian and African habitats, houses over 2500 animals, many not found in zoos elsewhere. Many of the animals roam free while you view them from monorails and elevated walkways.*

golf and tennis aside, this handsome hacienda-style complex is a gracious country retreat. Rooms here, however, are rather ordinary considering the ultra-deluxe rates.

Overnighting in the Mount Palomar area is limited to camping, except for the **Lazy H Ranch** (Route 76, Pauma Valley; 619-742-3669). When the proprietor said the place "dates back to the '40s," I wondered which '40s—it has the look and feel of an early California homestead. But here you can adjourn to the Spanish-style patio, stroll among six acres of orchards or take a dip in the pool. Budget to moderate in price.

One of Southern California's oldest hostelries, the 1897 **Julian Hotel** (Main and B streets, Julian; 619-765-0201) is a Victorian charmer. Even though most of its 16 rooms share European-style baths, the place is often full, particularly on weekends, so reserve in advance. Two charming cottages as well as the standard guest rooms are done in period fashion with plenty of brass, lace, porcelain and mahogany. Moderate to ultra-deluxe.

Also consider **Pine Hills Lodge** (2960 La Posada Way, Pine Hills; 619-765-1100), a wonderfully rustic complex with a lodge and cabins that date back to 1912. Surrounded by pines and cedars, this cozy retreat features five European-style rooms (with shared bath) in the lodge and 12 equally countrified cabins. This miniresort features a restaurant, bar and dinner theater. Moderate to deluxe.

INLAND SAN DIEGO COUNTY RESTAURANTS

Aunt Emma's Restaurant (1495 East Valley Parkway, Escondido; 619-746-2131) is the hot ticket for tasty breakfasts. You can order bacon and eggs all day. Auntie also serves five kinds of waffles, 20 types of pancakes and complete dinners. Budget.

Whatever you do during your North County visit, don't pass up the chance to dine at **El Bizcocho** (17550 Bernardo Oaks Drive, Rancho Bernardo; 619-487-1611). Tucked away in the upscale Rancho Bernardo Inn, this award-winning restaurant rates among greater San Diego's best. The French haute cuisine includes a nice balance of beef, veal, fish and fowl dishes. Deluxe to ultra-deluxe.

The **Lazy H Ranch** (Route 76, Pauma Valley; 619-742-3669) serves up steaks, prime rib, chicken and fish dishes in a family-style dining room set in the leafy environs of a six-acre orchard. Moderate to deluxe.

The **Julian Grill** (2224 Main Street, Julian; 619-765-0173), situated in a 1920s-vintage house, is cozy and folksy, especially around the living room fireplace. The menu emphasizes such hearty mountain fare as steaks and prime rib, and sophisticated chef's specials like chicken Jerusalem. Moderate to deluxe.

At **Romano's Dodge House** (2718 B Street, Julian; 619-765-1003) you will feel like a Romano family guest. This intimate Italian restaurant, with its homespun ambience, dishes out delicious chicken cacciatore, veal parmigiana, lasagna, and authentic Sicilian pizza. At budget to moderate prices, Romano's is hard to beat.

At least a dozen places in Julian prepare the local specialty, apple pie. But buyer beware: some are definitely better than others. The pies at the **Julian Pie Company** (2225 Main Street; 619-765-2449), for instance, always have flaky crusts and just the right mix of apples, cinnamon and sugar.

For buffalo burgers and local gossip, the townsfolk all head over to **Kendall's Korner** (2603 B Street, Julian; 619-765-1560). This friendly cafe, with its all-American cuisine and Early American decor, serves up a standard-fare breakfast and lunch menu on weekdays; with special dinner plates, like steak and potatoes, on weekends at budget prices.

Among the region's swank restaurants, **Jorg's** (8235 University Avenue, La Mesa; 619-462-4800) represents one of the most noteworthy. The continental cuisine, prepared by a Swiss chef, is simply outstanding. The understated dining room, decorated in soft hues of rose and gray, is quite elegant (and inevitably crowded). Deluxe to ultra-deluxe.

INLAND SAN DIEGO COUNTY SHOPPING

Jewelry is a high art form at **The Collector** (912 South Live Oak Park Road, Fallbrook; 619-728-9121), where every piece is crafted by hand. The owners go right to the source for the best gems—Colombia for emeralds and Sri Lanka for rubies.

Megamalls are popping up all around San Diego these days, but few match Escondido's **North County Fair** (Via Rancho Parkway and Route 15; 619-489-2344). This 83-acre complex has a half-dozen department stores and a host of independent shops.

Collectibles are a way of life at **Family Affair** (13330 Paseo del Verano Norte, Rancho Bernardo; 619-485-5850). The plates, lithographs, figurines and ornaments assembled here from around the world are hand-numbered, limited-edition items.

Even if you're not in the market for nuts, dried fruit or candy, a visit to **Bates Nut Farm** (15954 Woods Valley Road, Valley Center; 619-749-3334) is mandatory. Name the nut and they have it.

Main Street in Julian is lined with dozens of antique, gift, clothing and curio shops. Among the more intriguing ones are the **Antique Boutique** (2626 Main Street; 619-765-0541), with an especially nice selection of furniture and collectibles; **Julian's Toy Chest** (2116 Main Street; 619-765-2262), featuring unusual educational toys as well as children's books; and **Quinn Knives** (2116 Main Street; 619-765-2230), where you can buy anything from a sword to a Swiss Army knife.

La Mesa Boulevard, the center of La Mesa's revitalized downtown, looks like an all-American hometown business district circa 1930. Old storefronts have been refurbished and filled with specialty shops, making it a great street to stroll and shop.

INLAND SAN DIEGO COUNTY NIGHTLIFE

J. P.'s Lounge (2001 South Highway 395, Fallbrook; 619-728-5881), a classy and contemporary watering hole at Pala Mesa Resort, is one of the region's top nightclubs. You can count on a sophisticated crowd and frequent live entertainment.

Escondido means "hidden" in Spanish, but young swingers from miles around know about the city's hottest club, **Time Machine** (302 North Midway; 619-743-1772). Rock bands, dance contests and good times are specialties of the house. Cover.

Built in 1912 as a training camp for Jack Dempsey, **Pine Hills Lodge** (2960 La Posada Way, Julian; 619-765-1100) uses the champ's old ring as a dinner theater stage. And it looks as though they've scored a knockout. A dedicated and talented local company performs light plays and musicals. Friday and Saturday only.

El Cajon's **Circle D Corral** (1013 Broadway; 619-444-7443) cooks up live country-and-western music six nights a week. Cover.

INLAND SAN DIEGO COUNTY PARKS

Thick forests of pine, fur and cedar combine with rambling mountain meadows at **Palomar Mountain State Park** (619-742-3462) to create a Sierra Nevada-like atmosphere. The average elevation here on the side of Mount Palomar is 5500 feet, so the evenings are cool and heavy snow is common in the winter. Camping is permitted. Located on Route S7 on top of Mount Palomar.

CUYAMACA RANCHO STATE PARK

Broad meadows, forests of pine and oak and numerous streams make the **Cuyamaca Rancho State Park** *one of Southern California's most beautiful areas. Encompassing 25,000 acres (including 13,000 acres of wilderness), the park provides a habitat for deer, coyote, fox, bobcat and mountain lion, as well as over 100 species of birds. Camping is permitted. Located on Route 79 about 15 miles south of Julian.*

Beautifully situated in a forest of pines and oaks, **William Heise Park** (619-565-3600) rests at 4200-foot elevation in the Laguna Mountains near Julian. The park is largely undeveloped and provides more than 900 acres of hiking and riding trails. It's also one of the few county parks where the snowfall is sufficient for winter recreation. Located off Route 79 about five miles from Julian.

Sporting Life

SPORTFISHING

The lure of sport and bottom fishing attracts thousands of enthusiasts to San Diego every year. Albacore and snapper are the close-in favorites, with marlin and tuna the prime objectives for longer charters. For deep-sea charters, see **Helgren's Sportsfishing** (315 Harbor Drive, Oceanside; 619-722-2133), **Seaforth Mission Bay Boat Rental** (1717 Quivara Road, Mission Bay; 619-224-3383), **Coronado Boat Rental** (1715 Strand Way, Coronado; 619-437-1514) or **H & M Sportfishing Landing** (2803 Emerson Street, Point Loma; 619-222-1144).

WHALE WATCHING

For whale-watching tours, contact **Helgren's Sportsfishing** (315 Harbor Drive, Oceanside; 619-722-2133), **Islandia Sportfishing** (1551 West Mission Bay Drive; 619-222-1164) or **H & M Sportfishing Landing** (2803 Emerson Street; Point Loma; 619-222-1144).

SKINDIVING

San Diego offers countless spots for skindiving. For diving rentals, sales, instruction and dive tips contact **Underwater Schools of America** (707 Oceanside Boulevard, Oceanside; 619-722-7826), **San Diego Diver's Supply** (7522 La Jolla Boulevard, La Jolla; 619-459-2691; and 4004 Sports Arena Boulevard, San Diego; 619-224-3439) or **Diving Locker** (1020 Grand Avenue, Pacific Beach; 619-272-1120).

SURFING AND WINDSURFING

Surf's up in the San Diego area. Oceanside is home to annual world-class boogie board and surfing competitions. Moonlight, Swami, La Jolla Shores, Windansea Beach, Tourmaline Surfing Park and Mission and Pacific beaches are well-known hangouts for surfers. Sailboarding is concentrated within Mission Bay.

BOATING AND SAILING

You can sail under the Coronado Bridge, skirt the gorgeous downtown skyline and even get a taste of open ocean in this Southern California sailing mecca. Several sailing companies operate out of Harbor Island West in San Diego, including **San Diego Sailing Club and School** (1880 Harbor Island Drive; 619-298-6623).

Other motor boat and sail rentals in the area can be found at **C. P. Sailing Sports** (2211 Pacific Beach Drive, Mission Bay; 619-276-4010) and **Coronado Boat Rental** (1715 Strand Way, Coronado; 619-437-1514). Yacht charters are available through **Hornblower Dining Yachts** (1715 Strand Way, Glorietta Bay Marina, Coronado; 619-435-2211).

GOLF

For the golfing set there's **Emerald Isle Golf Course** (660 El Camino Real, Oceanside; 619-721-4700), **Oceanside Golf Course** (825 Douglas Drive, Oceanside; 619-433-1360), **Rancho Carlsbad Golf Course** (5200 El Camino Real, Carlsbad; 619-438-1772), **Whispering Palms Golf Course** (4000 Cancha de Golf, Rancho Santa Fe; 619-756-2471), **Torrey Pines Municipal Golf Course** (11480 North Torrey Pines Road, La Jolla; 619-453-0380), **Mission Bay Golf Center** (2702 North Mission Bay Drive, Mission Bay; 619-273-1221), **River Valley Golf Course** (2440 Hotel Circle North, Mission Valley; 619-297-3391), **Coronado Golf Course** (2000 Visalia Row, Coronado; 619-435-3121) and **Balboa Park Municipal Golf Course** (Golf Course Drive, Balboa Park; 619-232-2470).

BALLOONING

*Hot-air ballooning is a romantic pursuit and one that has soared in popularity in the Del Mar area. A growing number of ballooning companies offer spectacular dawn and sunset flights, most concluding with a traditional champagne toast. Among the ballooning companies flying in the Del Mar Valley are **A Beautiful Morning** (619-481-6225) and **Del Mar Balloons** (619-259-3115).*

TENNIS

San Diego County has many private and public courts open to traveling tennis buffs.

North County suffers from a lack of public tennis courts; however, Del Mar has free courts located off 22nd Street between Camino
del Mar and Jimmy Durante Boulevard.

For information in other areas, call **La Jolla Recreation Center**
(615 Prospect Street, La Jolla; 619-454-2071), **Balboa Tennis Club**
(2221 Morley Field Drive, San Diego; 619-295-9278), **Peninsula
Tennis Club** (2525 Bacon Street, Ocean Beach; 619-226-3407),
Cabrillo Recreation Center (3051 Cañon Street, Point Loma; 619-
531-1534) and **Mission Valley YMCA** (5505 Friars Road, Mission
Valley; 619-298-3576).

In Coronado call the **Tennis Center Pro Shop** at 619-435-1616
for information on courts.

BICYCLING

Cycling has skyrocketed in popularity throughout San Diego County,
especially in coastal areas. Balboa Park and Mission Bay Park both
have excellent bike routes.

North County's Old Route 101 provides almost 40 miles of scin-
tillating cycling along the coast from Oceanside to La Jolla. Bike lanes
are designated along most of the route.

Transportation

BY CAR

Even though it is located in California's extreme southwest corner,
San Diego is the hub of an elaborate highway network. The city is
easily reached from north or south via **Route 5**; drivers from the east
are served by **Route 8**; and **Route 15** is the major inland freeway for
travelers arriving from the mountain west.

BY AIR

San Diego International Airport (Lindbergh Field) lies just three
miles northwest of downtown San Diego. The airport is served by
most major airlines, including Alaska Airlines, American Airlines,
America West Airlines, Continental Airlines, Delta Airlines, Northwest Airlines, Skywest Western Express, Southwest Airlines, States

West Airlines, Trans World Airlines, United Airlines and USAir and Wardair Canada.

Taxis, limousines and buses provide service from the airport. **San Diego Transit System** bus #2 (619-233-3004) carries passengers to downtown destinations. Or try the **Coast Shuttle** (619-231-1123) service to major points in the city as well as to Orange County and Los Angeles.

BY BUS

Greyhound Bus Lines (619-239-9171) services San Diego from around the country. The terminal is located in the downtown area at 120 West Broadway and 1st Avenue.

BY TRAIN

Chugging to a stop at historic Santa Fe Depot, at Kettner Boulevard and Broadway downtown, is a nice and convenient way to arrive in San Diego. **Amtrak** (800-872-7245) offers several coast-hugging roundtrips daily between Los Angeles and San Diego, with stops at Oceanside and Del Mar.

CAR RENTALS

Much like the rest of Southern California, San Diego is spread out over a wide area and is best seen by car. Car rental companies abound. Most major rental agencies have franchises at the airport. These include **Avis Rent A Car** (619-231-7171), **Budget Rent A Car** (619-297-3360), **Dollar Rent A Car** (619-234-3388), **Hertz Rent A Car** (619-231-7000) and **National Car Rental** (619-231-7103).

PUBLIC TRANSPORTATION

Several modern and efficient public transportation systems operate throughout San Diego. Information and schedules are available for all systems by calling **San Diego Transit** (619-233-3004).

North County Transit District (619-743-6283), or NCTD, covers the general area from Del Mar to Camp Pendleton and services most of the coastal communities north of San Diego.

Southwest Coaches (619-232-8505) runs from downtown San Diego to National City and Chula Vista and on to the Mexican border. In addition, Southwest runs from downtown San Diego to Coronado and along the Silver Strand to Imperial Beach.

The city's newest and most venturesome mode of public transportation is the **San Diego Trolley** (619-233-3004). Known as the "Tijuana Trolley," the system operates daily from the Santa Fe Depot to the Mexican border. It also serves the south bay communities of Imperial Beach, Chula Vista and National City and the new east line serves southeast San Diego to El Cajon.

WALKING TOURS

Several San Diego organizations and tour operators offer organized walks: **The Gaslamp Foundation** (410 Island Avenue; 619-233-5227) conducts walking tours of the restored downtown historic district while **Old Town Walking Tours** (3977 Twiggs Street; 619-296-1004) covers Old Town State Historical Park. Join **Coronado Touring** (1110 Isabella Avenue, Coronado; 619-435-5993) for a leisurely guided stroll through quaint Coronado.

SIX

The Desert

East of metropolitan Los Angeles lies a land of brilliant greens and **193** dusty browns, scorched flats and snow-thatched mountains. The Colorado or Low Desert, the hottest, driest expanse of its size in the country, covers a broad swath of California's southeastern quarter. Here winter, with daily highs in the 70s and 80s, attracts sun worshippers, while summer brings withering heat waves. It's a place where visitors can swim and ski in the same day. Little wonder that its entertainment capital, Palm Springs, has become a celebrity playground.

A little to the north, the desert changes shape. Here lies an endless realm guarded by the sharp teeth of the Sierra Nevada and the gaping maw of Death Valley. The Mojave (High) Desert reaches from Los Angeles County across an awesome stretch of territory to Arizona and Nevada. The sky in these parts is so immense as to swallow the land, and the landscape is so broad that mountains are like islands on its surface. The Mojave is a region of ancient lakebeds and crystalline sinks, ghost towns and deserted mines, a place that explorer Jedediah Smith once called "a country of starvation." Today, the towns of Barstow and Mojave have become oases in that country.

At the northern end of the Mojave, in a land the Indians knew as "Tomesha" or "ground on fire," lies Death Valley. Measuring 120 miles in length and varying in width from four to sixteen miles, it is among the hottest places on earth, second only to the Sahara Desert. During summer the *average* daily high temperature is 116°!

It was just a shade cooler down in the Low Desert when the Agua Caliente Indians first settled the region and discovered its hot mineral baths. Today much of this valuable Indian property is leased to tourist resorts. Located just 100 miles from Los Angeles, the Low Desert has become a major travel destination. Visitors arrive not only to soak in the sun and spas of Palm Springs, but also to tour the palm groves of Indio. The date-growing center of the country, this bland agricultural town is a date palm oasis, with gardens reaching from road's edge to the fringe of the mountains.

Farther south lies the Salton Sea, California's largest lake, a briny trough that sits astride the notorious San Andreas Fault. Nearby Anza-Borrego Desert State Park stretches across parts of three counties and encompasses a half-million acres of gemlike springs, rock promontories and sandstone chasms.

Joshua Tree National Monument, the area's other major park, lies astride the Low and High deserts, rising from the scorching Colorado Desert to the cooler climes and higher elevations of the Mojave. Its vast and unearthly landscape is dotted with spectacular cactus gardens and stands of Joshua trees.

Rising between Los Angeles and Palm Springs, creating a gateway to the Low Desert, is one of the state's fastest-growing regions, an area known as the Inland Empire. Bounded to the north by the San Bernardino Mountains, which embrace the popular resort areas of Lake Arrowhead and Big Bear Lake, it is bordered on the east by the San Jacinto Mountains. Here, too, lie the expanding cities of Riverside, Redlands and San Bernardino—Los Angeles suburbs that have blossomed with orange and lemon trees since the 19th century. The San Bernardino Mountains, with their pristine lakes, and the Inland Empire, with its trim orchards and burgeoning cities, make a fitting entranceway to the increasingly popular California desert.

San Bernardino Mountains

One of the highest ranges in California, the San Bernardino Mountains rise to over 11,000 feet elevation. Together with the San Gabriels to the west, they provide a pine-rimmed barrier between the Los Angeles Basin and the desert. A popular winter and water sports area, the mountains are encompassed within San Bernardino National Forest and offer a string of alpine lakes and lofty peaks.

A single highway, Route 18, "Rim of the World Drive," courses through the entire region. Beginning in Crestline, north of San Bernardino, it winds past several lakes, offering postcard vistas of the region. At **Silverwood Lake State Recreation Area** (619-389-2303) you'll find a 976-acre lake surrounded by 13 miles of hiking trails. Except for the recreation area and marina, Silverwood remains undeveloped, a great place to swim and fish. Almost 130 species of birds have been spotted here; coyotes, bobcats and ring-tailed cats range the forested slopes that encircle the lake.

The prettiest and most precious of the region's alpine gems is **Lake Arrowhead**, a socially exclusive enclave. Popular with Hollywood notables and Los Angeles business executives, the lake has pub-

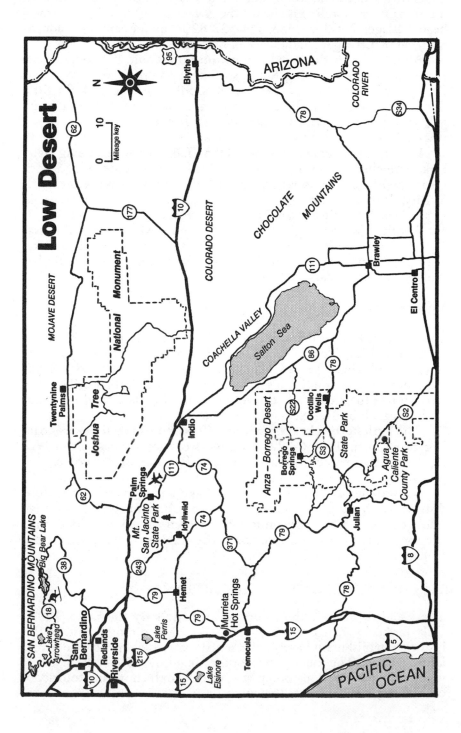

lic facilities along the south shore. The closest most people come to the remaining shoreline is aboard the *Arrowhead Queen* (Lake Arrowhead Village; 714-337-2553, 714-337-8204 in the summer; admission), a 60-passenger paddlewheeler that tours the lake.

About the only thing you'll encounter on Route 18 between Lake Arrowhead and Running Springs, except for panoramic views, is **Santa's Village** (714-337-2481; admission). A theme park for little ones, this mock North Pole outpost features a puppet theater, pony ride and other attractions. Open weekends year-round, seven days a week in summer months.

Larger, friendlier and less formal than Lake Arrowhead, **Big Bear Lake** stretches for seven miles at a 7000-foot altitude. Lined with resort facilities, it's a popular winter ski area and summer water sports facility. To tour the lake, you can climb aboard the *Big Bear Queen* (Big Bear Marina, Big Bear Lake; 714-866-3218; admission).

Another favored destination for children is **Moonridge Animal Park** (Moonridge Road two miles south of Route 18, Big Bear Lake; 714-585-3656), which contains bobcats, mountain lions, timber wolves and black bears.

SAN BERNARDINO MOUNTAINS LODGING

Saddleback Inn (300 South Route 173, Lake Arrowhead; 714-336-3571), just a few blocks from Lake Arrowhead, beautifully plays the role of mountain lodge. A vintage 1917 structure—complete with gables and stone chimney—it's a 34-unit bed and breakfast. The true attraction is the cluster of cottages featuring fireplaces and tile baths with jacuzzi tubs. Deluxe to ultra-deluxe.

The **Knickerbocker Mansion** (869 South Knickerbocker Road, Big Bear Lake; 714-866-8221), a three-story log cabin built in 1917, represents the perfect mountain retreat. Resting amid two acres of piney woods and bordering a national forest, the historic house is still within walking distance of Big Bear Lake and a major commercial district. With ten guest rooms, the mansion and an adjacent carriage house convey a feeling of comfortable rusticity. A double-sided stone fireplace and split-log staircase add to the architectural sophistication. Deluxe to ultra-deluxe.

SAN BERNARDINO MOUNTAINS RESTAURANTS

There's an air of the 19th century about **Lilly's By the Lake** (29020 Oak Terrace, Cedar Glen; 714-336-3619). The dining rooms of this historic establishment have showcases filled with old pantry items and lace-up boots. The menu, on the other hand, is quite contemporary, including a variety of seafood pastas, Greek lamb chops and tournedos of filet mignon. Moderate to deluxe.

Praised by critics far and wide as Big Bear Lake's finest restaurant, the **Iron Squirrel** (646 Pine Knot Avenue; 714-866-9121) is a class act indeed. It's quite a delight to find duckling in orange sauce and cherries jubilee at a restaurant deep in the mountains. Dinner and Sunday brunch only; deluxe.

Inland Empire

Extending south from the San Bernardino Mountains, California's Inland Empire encompasses the cities of San Bernardino, Redlands and Riverside. Once a cattle-ranching region and later a prime citrus-growing area, this interior belt is presently being developed at a mind-boggling rate.

Blessed with water from Big Bear Lake, the town of Redlands blossomed with oranges during the 1880s. By the turn of the century, wealthy Easterners seeking mild winters began building mansions amid the groves. Today the town numbers about 350 period homes, from tiny California-style bungalows to gaudy Victorian estates.

Among the most spectacular is **Kimberly Crest** (1325 Prospect Drive, Redlands; 714-792-2111), constructed in 1897. An overweening assemblage of turrets, gables, arches and fountains, this hilltop chateau is surrounded by five acres of Italian gardens. The grounds are open daily, and there are tours of the house every Thursday and Sunday from 1 to 4 p.m.

The **A. K. Smiley Public Library** (125 West Vine Street, Redlands; 714-798-7632) is a Moorish structure dramatized by carved sandstone friezes, stained-glass windows and elaborate woodwork. Behind this 1898 edifice stands the **Lincoln Memorial Shrine** (714-798-7632), a small but noteworthy museum devoted to Abraham Lincoln. Built in 1932 of polished limestone, the octagonal building displays marvelous WPA-type murals.

San Bernardino County Museum (2024 Orange Tree Lane, Redlands; 714-798-8570), one of the region's major historical facilities, has three floors of exhibits ranging from dinosaur displays to 19th-century dioramas. There's an anthropology hall with Indian artifacts and covered wagons, plus an excellent mineral collection.

Two cities, San Bernardino and Riverside, dominate the Inland Empire. While the former has few noteworthy attractions, the latter provides visitors with several opportunities. Riverside's chief landmark is 1337-foot **Mount Rubidoux**, a rocky prominence on the west side of town. Capped by a memorial cross and peace tower, the cactus-coated hill affords a full-circle vista of the Inland Valley.

Pride of the city is the **Riverside County Court House** (4050 Main Street), a Beaux-Arts beauty built in 1903. The community also boasts several museums. The **Riverside Art Museum** (3425 7th Street; 714-684-7111), set in a 1929 Mediterranean-style building designed by Julia Morgan, hosts changing exhibits and special events.

At the nearby **Riverside Municipal Museum** (3720 Orange Street; 714-782-5273), housed in the equally inviting 1912 Post Office building, cultural exhibits portray Native American crafts and trace the history of citrus growing in the region.

Riverside's most historic attraction was undergoing a $45-million facelift as this book went to press. The **Mission Inn** (3649 7th Street; 714-784-0300), one of California's most famous hotels, dates to the 1880s. A palace with room keys, the hotel sprawls across an entire city block and has entertained eight United States presidents.

If you tour the campus of the University of California–Riverside (west end of University Avenue), be sure to take in the **Botanic Gardens** (714-787-4650). Extending across 39 acres of rugged terrain, it contains cactus, rose and iris gardens as well as a fruit orchard.

INLAND EMPIRE LODGING AND RESTAURANTS

Redland's **Morey Mansion Bed & Breakfast Inn** (190 Terracina Boulevard; 714-793-7970), with its French mansard roof and onion dome, is nothing short of spectacular. An 1890s-era Victorian, the inn is garnished with Italianate balustrades, Gothic arched windows, beveled glass from Belgium and France and hand-carved oak. The six upstairs bedrooms are embellished with rare fixtures and antique furnishings. Deluxe.

HOT SPRINGS

A geologic hot spot, the Inland Empire contains some of California's finest spas. **Murrieta Hot Springs** *(39405 Murrieta Hot Springs Road, Murrieta; 714-698-1000; admission), a 47-acre resort, sits atop the Elsinore fault. The complex is beautifully landscaped with ponds, fountains and gardens. There are saunas, mud baths, mineral pools, jacuzzis and tennis courts as well as a complement of classes, lectures and exercise programs. Open to day visitors and overnight guests alike.*

Smaller and lacking the hotel facilities of Murrieta, **Glen Ivy Hot Springs** *(25000 Glen Ivy Road, Corona; 714-277-3529; admission) is also less formal than its health-conscious counterpart. Here at "Club Mud" you can down a platter of nachos while relaxing in a jacuzzi, sauna or mineral pool. The favorite spot, one for which Glen Ivy has gained its nickname, is the red clay mud bath. Guests plop down into this caramel-colored ooze, smear it across their everloving bodies, then bask in the sun until it hardens.*

The gorgeous Victorian **Edwards Mansion** (2064 Orange Tree Lane, Redlands; 714-793-2031) features numerous dining rooms paneled in dark wood and hung with ponderous chandeliers. Sunday champagne brunch only. Moderate to deluxe.

Idyllwild

Bordering the Inland Empire to the east are the San Jacinto Mountains, a spectacular chain of 10,000-foot peaks dividing the region from Palm Springs and the Low Desert. Routes 243 and 74 climb into this alpine environment from the north and west respectively.

At the center of the chain sits the mile-high town of **Idyllwild**. Tucked beneath bald granite peaks, this pine-tufted community is surrounded by the San Bernardino National Forest. Once inhabited by Cahuilla Indians, the area now is a major tourist destination. In addition to restaurants and shops, Idyllwild has a host of secluded cabins for rent. For information on trails and campgrounds throughout the region, stop by the **Idyllwild County Park Visitor Center** (54000 Route 243; 714-659-3850).

Extending from Idyllwild in the west to Palm Springs in the east, the magnificent **Mount San Jacinto State Park** (714-659-2607) encompasses a broad swath of the San Jacinto Mountains. It features mountain meadows and subalpine forests as well as granite peaks 10,000 feet high. Located on Route 243 in Idyllwild, the park can also be reached via the aerial tramway in Palm Springs.

IDYLLWILD LODGING

Strawberry Creek Inn (26370 Route 243; 714-659-3202) is a cozy, rambling old mountain home nestled among the pines and oaks of the San Jacinto Mountains, yet still within walking distance of Idyllwild's busy village center. Guests can choose an original room in the main house or one in the new wing. Full gourmet breakfast. Moderate to deluxe in price.

A place with a name like **Knotty Pine Cabins** (54340 Pine Crest Drive, Idyllwild; 714-659-2933) could easily devolve into a self-parody. But there they are, eight woodframe cabins nestled in a conifer grove. Nicely secluded yet only a stone's throw from town, the units feature fireplaces, and most offer a living room, bedroom and kitchen and price in the moderate range; there's one single-room, budget-priced cabin without kitchen.

You can also rent houses and cabins in Idyllwild through **Associated Idyllwild Rentals** (P.O. Box 43, Idyllwild, CA 92349).

IDYLLWILD RESTAURANTS

The local gathering place is **Jan's Red Kettle** (54220 North Circle Drive; 714-659-4063). Homey as a log cabin, it's a knotty-pine cafe with red-checkered curtains. Breakfast items fill about half the menu and include huevos rancheros and biscuits with gravy. Completing the offerings are soups, salads, hamburgers and sandwiches. No dinner; budget.

Among Idyllwild's finest restaurants is **Gastrognome** (54381 Ridgeview Drive; 714-659-5055), a pretty woodframe place with a stone fireplace and beam ceiling. The selections are diverse, the portions plentiful and the food delicious. Selections include beef tournedos, Australian lobster and calamari. Deluxe, with a moderate-priced cafe menu during the week. Dinner and Sunday brunch.

Palm Springs Area

Take a desert landscape thatched with palm trees, add a 10,000-foot mountain to shade it from the sun, then place an ancient mineral spring deep beneath the ground. What you have is a recipe for Palm Springs. It's a spot where the average daily winter temperature swings from an invigorating 55° to a toasty 85°.

Little wonder that the town represents the nation's desert showplace, one of the few western locales where winter brings the best weather. A fashionable health spa and celebrity playground, Palm Springs is the ultimate destination for sunning, swimming and slumming. Ever since 1930, when silent film stars Ralph Bellamy and Charlie Farrell began buying up desert land at $30 an acre, Hollywood has been vacationing in Palm Springs. Luminaries like Bob Hope, Frank Sinatra and Kirk Douglas continue to strengthen the spot's celebrity cachet.

Only 400 feet above sea level, the town nestles beneath mountains two miles high. Palm Springs is the golf capital of the world, sponsoring over 100 tournaments every year. In addition to dozens of golf courses, the region boasts hundreds of tennis courts and a swimming pool for every five residents. Together with the nearby towns of Rancho Mirage and Palm Desert, it has become an opulent desert enclave where manicured lawns are more common than cactus plants.

Many attractions here close or have limited hours during the hot summer months. It's advisable to call in advance.

To direct you through the area, there are two local agencies—the **Palm Springs Desert Resorts Convention and Visitors' Bureau** (69-930 Highway 111, #201, Rancho Mirage; 619-770-9000) and the

Palm Springs Chamber of Commerce (190 West Amado Road; 619-325-1577).

They'll inevitably point you toward the **Palm Springs Desert Museum** (101 Museum Drive; 619-325-7186; admission), one of California's great regional art centers. Contained in a dynamic contemporary structure with stone facade, the museum combines desert art, culture and natural history. Most appealing are the sculpture gardens—lovely, restful plots with splashing fountains and native palms.

If it's local history you're after, the **Village Green Heritage Center** (221 South Palm Canyon Drive; 619-323-8297; admission) will do quite nicely. Three antique buildings encapsulate the entire sweep of local history. In the **McCallum Adobe** you'll find tools, clothes and books from Palm Springs' early years. Constructed in 1884, the town's oldest building, it's also filled with photos of Hollywood stars, including one of Groucho Marx without his trademark moustache. Next door is **Cornelia White's House**, the 1893 home of a pioneer woman. Had Cornelia lived longer, she could have patronized **Ruddy's General Store**. A re-creation of a 1930s-era general store, this marvelous museum is literally lined with tins of Chase & Sanborn coffee and an entire wall of apothecary jars. Ruddy's contains 6000 original items, including penny gumball machines and, yes, Prince Albert in a can.

One of the most luxuriant labyrinths you will ever traverse is a place called **Moorten's Botanical Garden** (1701 South Palm Canyon Drive; 619-327-6555; admission). This living monument to the desert displays over 3000 varieties of cactus. It's an enchanted garden, inhabited by birds and lizards, dotted with petrified trees and filled with dinosaur fossils.

Now renowned as a retreat for millionaires and movie stars, Palm Springs for centuries was the private domain of the Agua Caliente Indians. Many tribal members still inhabit the **Indian Canyons** (four miles south of Palm Springs, off South Palm Canyon Road; 619-325-5673), a string of four lush mountain valleys that reach from desert bottomlands deep into the San Jacinto Mountains. For an admission

PALMS TO PINES TOUR

For an overwhelming view of the desert, head up Route 74 from Palm Desert on the **Palms to Pines Tour,** *which leads high into the Santa Rosa Mountains. As the tree-lined highway climbs to lofty heights, dramatic vistas of the Coachella Valley open to view. If you're ambitious, it's possible to connect with Routes 243, 10 and 111 on a 130-mile loop trip through the San Jacinto Mountains and back to Palm Springs.*

fee visitors can spend the day hiking, exploring and picnicking in these preserves, which contain mountain sheep, wild ponies, Indian rock art and thousands of palm trees.

You can soar into the San Jacinto Mountains on the **Palm Springs Aerial Tramway** (Tramway Road; 619-325-1391). Climbing at a teeth-clattering 50° angle to 8516 feet elevation, this mountain shuttle makes Mr. Toad's wild ride seem like a cakewalk. The reward for those white knuckles is a view of the Coachella Valley from Joshua Tree to the Salton Sea. On a clear day you might not see forever, but you will spot a mountain peak near Las Vegas, 175 miles away.

Back on the desert floor, **Cabot's Old Indian Pueblo** (67-616 East Desert View Avenue, Desert Hot Springs; 619-329-7610; admission), the home of a feisty desert pioneer, is a four-story adobe built in the fashion of the Hopi Indians. With 35 rooms, 150 windows and walls two feet thick, this mazelike building is carefully preserved and filled with pioneer relics and Indian artifacts.

South of Palm Springs lie **Rancho Mirage** and **Palm Desert**, two extraordinarily wealthy bedroom communities where a profusion of country clubs and landscaped estates create a kind of release from reality. They name streets after people like Bob Hope and Frank Sinatra and use water everywhere—for fountains, cascades, golf greens—in a spectacular display of excess.

Aptly named indeed is **The Living Desert** (47-900 Portola Avenue, Palm Desert; 619-346-5694; admission), a 1200-acre nature park that presents a raw and realistic picture of desert life. This grand outdoor zoo contains bighorn sheep, gazelles and Arabian oryx from the deserts of Africa. Bats, rattlesnakes and screech owls inhabit a special display that simulates the desert at night.

PALM SPRINGS AREA LODGING

There's nothing like acres of marble to give a place that 19th century-Europe look. **Hyatt Regency Suites—Palm Springs** (285 North Palm Canyon Drive, Palm Springs; 619-322-9000) has it in spades. All 194 suites in this ultra-deluxe six-story downtown hotel are done in the cooler desert colors of sunrise: rose pink, light blue and warm beige. The artistry of Pierre Cardin shows in touches such as sleek modular cabinets and small sculptures.

Travelers interested in rubbing elbows with show-biz types should consider the elegant little **Ingleside Inn** (200 West Ramon Road, Palm Springs; 619-325-0046). Garbo slept here, they say, and Sinatra, Schwarzenneger and Shields. And why not? The double rooms, villas and minisuites are cozy, charming and laden with unusual antiques. Extras include fireplaces, private steambaths and terraces, but everyone gets the same old-fashioned (i.e., attentive) service at this deluxe-priced inn.

Unlike many luxury resorts, **Villa Royale Inn** (1620 South Indian Trail, Palm Springs; 619-327-2314) displays its richness in an understated, personalized fashion. The sumptuous bed and breakfast inn was carefully furnished in European antiques. Many have kitchens, fireplaces and private patios. Covering more than three acres, the grounds are a series of interior courtyards framed by pillars, planted in bougainvillea and offering two pools and jacuzzis. Rooms with private baths are moderate to deluxe; studios and one- and two-bedroom accommodations are ultra-deluxe.

The hot mineral pools that the Agua Caliente Indians originally discovered are today part of the **Spa Hotel and Mineral Springs** (100 North Indian Avenue; 619-325-1461). On the grounds are two Roman-style tubs, an outsize swimming pool, a rooftop solarium, dry saunas and mineral baths, all free to guests. The entire hotel is lavishly decorated with pastel-hued carpets and contemporary oil paintings. Deluxe to ultra-deluxe.

The ultra-deluxe-priced private villas at **La Mancha Private Villas and Court Club** (444 Avenida Caballeros, Palm Springs; 619-323-1773) are the last word in romantic escapism. Spanish-Moroccan architecture, high arched windows and massive ceiling beams give the 50 accommodations an almost castlelike ambience. All the villas have private courtyards; many, private pools. Spa and in-room dining are among the amenities.

Out on the southern edge of Palm Springs, **Tiki Spa Hotel and Apartments** (1910 South Camino Real; 619-327-1349) is a 32-unit facility occupying almost two acres. Polynesian in style, it offers jacuzzis, saunas and a swimming pool. The accommodations vary from hotel rooms to apartment units with kitchens and private patios. Deluxe in winter, moderate the rest of the year.

Guests at any of the 240-plus accommodations at the **Ritz-Carlton Rancho Mirage** (68-900 Frank Sinatra Drive, Rancho Mirage; 619-321-8282) have only to open the french doors to their patio or balcony to enjoy a commanding view of the entire Palm Springs area. Located on a 650-foot-high plateau in the Santa Rosa Mountain foothills, this is a 24-acre hotel and tennis resort. Fine artwork, custom fabrics, antiques, crown moldings and luxury-level amenities are standard in the rooms; the suites are truly elegant. Ultra-deluxe.

The decor at **Marriott's Rancho Las Palmas Resort & Country Club** (41000 Bob Hope Drive, Rancho Mirage; 619-568-2727) is a little too heavy on the Spanish mission side for many tastes, but it suits the sprawling 248-acre property perfectly. A variety of spacious accommodations includes rooms, suites and haciendas clustered around quiet courtyards. All are done in rough-textured stucco and topped with the inevitable red-tiled roofs. Several pools, tennis courts, golf courses, restaurants and lounges are among the amenities at this ultra-deluxe-priced establishment.

Two Bunch Palms (67-425 Two Bunch Palms Trail, Desert Hot Springs; 619-329-8791) is an oasis unto itself, a world of hot mineral baths surrounded by ancient palm trees. This exclusive 28-acre retreat, with its guarded entrance, serves as a hideaway for Hollywood celebrities, who have been visiting since the 1930s. Legend has it that mobster Al Capone built the place back then, although a local sleuth now disputes the "Scarface" story. Today guests soak in two hot mineral pools, utilize a complete spa facility and wander a magnificent estate. Deluxe to ultra-deluxe.

La Quinta Golf and Tennis Resort (49499 Eisenhower Drive, La Quinta; 619-564-4111) is a flashback to the old days when movie stars and starlets slipped away from Hollywood for some private sun time in the desert. Tucked serenely in the eastern Coachella Valley, this 1926 Spanish-style resort has private casitas dotted around its luxurious grounds and offers 30 tennis courts and 36 holes of golf. All of which make it an ideal, and ever contemporary, getaway. Ultra-deluxe.

PALM SPRINGS AREA RESTAURANTS

Everybody's favorite lunch counter is **Louise's Pantry** (124 South Palm Canyon Drive, Palm Springs; 619-325-5124), a landmark cafe where locals are inevitably lined up outside the door. A plastic-and-formica eatery, it provides standard American fare like meat loaf or halibut at moderate prices.

A spacious hacienda with murals, fountains and inlaid tile, **Las Casuelas Terraza** (222 South Palm Canyon Drive, Palm Springs; 619-325-2794) is a classic Hispanic dining room. A step above other Mexican restaurants, the establishment serves such fare as *pollo asado* (marinated chicken) and *pescado greco* (fish filet in garlic and wine). Budget to moderate.

Perrina's (340 North Palm Canyon Drive, Palm Springs; 619-325-6544) features a dark, cozy sports bar and an excellent little restaurant. Photos of athletes are parked on the walls of this popular, unpretentious spot. The restaurant serves dinner only, with entrees such as chicken marsala and veal saltimbocca. Moderate to deluxe.

If you do nothing but admire the stained glass at **Lyon's English Grille** (233 East Palm Canyon Drive, Palm Springs; 619-327-1551), it will prove worth the price of admission. This grand British dining room displays a museum-quality collection of plates, Toby jugs and art pieces from Olde England. The bill of fare includes steak-and-kidney pie and braised lamb shank. Dinner only; moderate to deluxe.

For entertainment with your dinner, make reservations at **Moody's Supper Club** (123 North Palm Canyon Drive, Palm

Springs; 619-323-1806). You'll dine in an intimate lounge on a sumptuous variety of chicken, steak, fish and pasta dishes, while an ensemble performs songs from Broadway musicals. Deluxe to ultra-deluxe.

Caliente Restaurant (100 North Indian Avenue, Palm Springs; 619-325-1461) is easily one of the town's finest dining rooms. Painted brilliant colors and appointed in ultracontemporary fashion, this California cuisine restaurant serves excellent food such as grilled chicken in mustard sauce and grilled salmon. Moderate to deluxe.

Melvyn's (200 West Ramon Road, in the Ingleside Inn, Palm Springs; 619-325-0046) has as many awards on the wall as items on the menu. Among the toniest addresses in town, it's a classic continental restaurant complete with mirrors and upholstered armchairs. The inventory of entrées features Norwegian salmon hollandaise and chateaubriand. Deluxe to ultra-deluxe.

THE SALTON SEA

One of California's strangest formations lies deep in the southern section of the state, just 30 miles from the Mexican border. The Salton Sea, a vast inland waterway 36 miles long and 15 miles wide, may be the biggest engineering blunder in history.

Situated 234 feet below sea level, directly atop the San Andreas Fault, the area has been subject to natural flooding by the Colorado River for eons. In 1905 the irrigation system for the Imperial Valley went amok, the Colorado River overflowed its banks and a flood two years in duration inundated the land. The Salton Sea was born.

California's largest lake, this vast sea, ringed by palms and seeming to extend endlessly, resembles the ocean itself. Lying at the confluence of the Imperial and Coachella valleys, one of the lushest agricultural regions in the world, it possesses rare beauty. Along its northwest shore on Route 86, rows of date palms run to the water's edge and citrus orchards create a brilliant green landscape backdropped by chocolate-brown mountains.

*The best place to enjoy water sports and sandy beaches is at the **Salton Sea State Recreation Area** (619-393-3052) on Route 111. Long and narrow, this amazing park extends for 18 miles along the northeast shore. The Salton Sea supports 350 bird species, so birdwatchers also flock here in significant numbers.*

*Farther south lies the **Salton Sea National Wildlife Refuge** (entrances from Sinclair Road west of Calipatria and Vendel Road north of Westmorland; 619-348-5278). The southernmost refuge on the Pacific flyway, this preserve is a prime avian habitat. Some 371 bird species have been sighted here, including stilts, pintails, green-winged teal and the endangered Yuma clapper rail. The heightening of sea level has diminished the park's land area from 35,000 to 2000 acres, but you're still liable to see great blue herons wading along the shore and snow geese arriving for the winter.*

Le Vallauris (385 Tahquitz-McCallum Way, Palm Springs; 619-325-5059) is an enclave of country French cuisine and decor just off the main drag. A piano bar sets the tone in this converted private residence for rich dishes such as duck and foie gras and New Zealand venison. Plush armchairs and a garden of ivy and blooming cyclamen warm up this attractive two-room restaurant. Deluxe to ultra-deluxe.

In a town noted for celebrities, **Bono** (1700 North Indian Avenue; 619-322-6200), gained its reputation from its namesake owner, entertainer-turned-mayor Sonny Bono. The cuisine of Southern Italy is another logical step for such a warm climate. Meals may include homemade pastas, fresh seafood or steaks. Moderate to deluxe.

Tucked away in a shopping center, **Cattails** (68-369 Highway 111, Cathedral City; 619-324-8263) rewards its patrons with a romantic cave of a room done in natural shades. The deluxe-priced menu is slightly offbeat: beets stuffed with sour cream, linguine in cold lobster sauce, or chicken Rhineland, all beautifully presented.

Seafood provides a welcome change of pace in the landlocked desert. **Scoma's of San Francisco** (69-620 Highway 111, Rancho Mirage; 619-328-9000) specializes in shrimp, prawns, crab, scallops and fish like its namesake restaurant on Fisherman's Wharf. Every entrée is served with pasta in this peach-and-Celadon green restaurant, nicely lit from upturned seashell fixtures. Moderate to deluxe.

Cedar Creek Inn (73-445 El Paseo, Palm Desert; 619-340-1236) is a little old-fashioned, which might be the reason it's so popular with local residents. Plaid wallpaper and oak booths are a trademark here. The cuisine, accordingly, is American, with such entrées as fresh salmon and New York steak. Moderate to deluxe.

A minimalist setting in a regional shopping district is the easiest way to describe **Cuisto** (7311 El Paseo, Palm Desert; 619-340-1000). But that does not begin to communicate the otherworldly cuisine, a combination of French and California, presented at this critically acclaimed dining room. Ultra-deluxe.

For French and Continental dishes in a refurbished mansion, look no further than **Dolly Cunard's** (78045 Calle Cadiz, La Quinta; 619-564-4443). Romantic and highly recommended, this 1920s-era house is home to fine cuisine and friendly service. A warren of trimly decorated dining rooms, it also features a lounge, gazebo and garden. Ultra-deluxe.

PALM SPRINGS AREA SHOPPING

Swank Palm Canyon Drive, the Main Street of Palm Springs, contains the region's greatest concentration of shops, many of them signature stores. The center within the center is **Desert Fashion Plaza** (123 North Palm Canyon Drive; 619-320-8282), a stone-floor-and-splashing-fountain labyrinth that wends past jewelers, designer boutiques and department stores.

Adagio Galleries (193 South Palm Canyon Drive; 619-320-2230) down the street has a fine collection of Southwestern art, including oil paintings and Native American ceramics.

At **B. Lewin Galleries** (210 South Palm Canyon Drive; 619-322-2525) you'll find what is reputedly the world's largest collection of paintings by Mexican masters. Some of the works here are little short of magnificent.

Consumer central in Palm Desert is the **Palm Desert Town Center** (72-840 Route 111 at Highway 74; 619-346-2121), a mammoth mall offering several department stores and a host of small shops.

The region's more elegant stores line **El Paseo**, a multiblock extravaganza that runs through the heart of Palm Desert. Among the galleries lining this well-heeled boulevard are the **A. Albert Allen Fine Art Gallery** (73-200 El Paseo; 619-341-8655), with Indian rugs and Southwestern art as well as a more traditional collection of fine art. **Crock-R-Box** (73-425 El Paseo; 619-568-6688) features crafts fashioned from wood, metal and glass.

Also stop by **The Tortoise Shelf** (47-900 Portola Avenue, Palm Desert), the gift shop at the Living Desert Reserve (619-346-5694). They have an excellent collection of books, prints and jewelry, all relating to the desert.

PALM SPRINGS AREA NIGHTLIFE

The center of action in downtown Palm Springs is **Zelda's** (169 North Indian Avenue; 619-325-2375), a rocking disco with video screens, two dancefloors and eight bars. Contests and fashion shows punctuate sets of deejay music. Cover.

Over at the **Comedy Haven** (109 South Palm Canyon Drive; 619-320-7855) the menu includes stand-up comedy, improv and magic. There's also dancing to live Top-40 tunes in the lounge. Cover.

The place to view and be viewed in this celebrity-conscious town is **Melvyn's** (200 West Ramon Road; 619-325-0046). The lounge at this fashionable French restaurant features piano bar music and a small dancefloor.

The **Pompeii Nightclub** (67-399 Route 111; 619-328-5800) features a disco during the week, with a jazz duo added on weekends.

The **Cactus Corral** (67501 Route 111, Cathedral City; 619-321-8558) features live country music and will even teach you to dance Western-style. Cover.

State-of-the-art and ultra-fashionable, the **McCallum Theatre for the Performing Arts** (73-000 Fred Waring Drive, in the Bob Hope Cultural Center, Palm Desert; 619-340-2787) represents the desert showplace for symphonies, dramas and concerts. This 1176-seat theater is the cultural capital of the Palm Springs area.

Joshua Tree National Monument

One of America's great inland destinations, Joshua Tree National Monument is an awesome 850-square-mile sanctuary straddling California's High and Low deserts. Its northern region, of greater interest to visitors, rests at about 4000 feet elevation in the Mojave. To the south, where Joshua trees give way to scrub vegetation, lies the arid Colorado Desert.

The preserve's granite hills offer sport for rock climbers, while its miles of hiking trails attract day-hikers and wilderness enthusiasts alike. The desert life includes tarantulas, roadrunners, sidewinders, golden eagles and coyotes, but it is the desert plants that make the sanctuary truly special.

The main entrance to the Joshua Tree National Monument, off Route 62 in Twentynine Palms, leads to the **Oasis Visitors Center** (619-367-7511), a full-facility stop with a museum and ranger station. The best place to chart a course through the preserve, it rests in the Oasis of Mara, a grove of palms once used by Indians and prospectors. **Black Rock Canyon Visitors Center**, with a ranger station and small exhibit, lies approximately 30 miles farther west; and **Cottonwood Visitors Center** marks the southern gateway to the park.

As you proceed south and west into the heart of the park, weathered granite, smoothed by the elements, rises in fields of massive boulders. In the foreground, Joshua trees, their branches like arms raised heavenward, stand forth against a cobalt sky. Many of the rocks are carved and hollowed to create skulls, arches and whatever shapes the imagination can conjure.

The Joshua trees that complement this eerie landscape are giant yucca plants, members of the agave family, which grow to heights of almost 50 feet. They were named in the 1850s by Mormon pioneers, who saw in the stark, angular trees the figure of the prophet Joshua pointing them farther westward.

West of Jumbo Rocks Campground, **Geology Tour Road**, a dirt track, leads for nine miles past unusual rock sculptures, alluvial fans and desert washes. **Squaw Tank**, an ancient Indian campsite along the way, contains Indian bedrock mortars and a concrete dam built by ranchers early in the century. A pamphlet available from the information centers will also help locate petroglyphs, mine shafts and magnificent mountain vistas.

A paved route from the main roadway dead-ends at **Keys View**. The finest panorama in the park, it sweeps from 11,485-foot Mt. San

Gorgonio across the San Jacinto Mountains to the Salton Sea and takes in Palm Springs, the Colorado River Aqueduct and Indio.

Desert Queen Ranch, one of the few outposts of civilization in Joshua Tree, is accessible only by ranger-led tours. Built early in the century by William F. Keys—a former sheriff, prospector and Rough Rider—it's a ghost village complete with ranch house, school, corral and barn.

The unique transition zone between the Mojave and Colorado deserts becomes evident when you proceed toward the southern gateway to the park. As the elevation descends and temperatures rise, plant life becomes sparser. Yet here, too, the inherent beauty of the park is overwhelming. **Cholla Cactus Garden**, a forest of cactus that is a pure delight to walk through, is one of Joshua Tree's prettiest places.

JOSHUA TREE LODGING AND RESTAURANT

A desert traveler could not ask for more than a rustic, family inn in a palm oasis. Located in a natural setting within eyeshot of park headquarters, **29 Palms Inn** (73950 Inn Avenue, Twentynine Palms; 619-367-3505) has adobe cottages with fireplaces and country decor. This marvelous inn, encompassing 70 acres, was founded in 1928. Amenities include a pool, hot tub and lounge. There's also a homespun American restaurant with a friendly staff serving grilled halibut, steak and lobster. Moderate prices at both hotel and restaurant.

Anza-Borrego Desert State Park

The largest state facility in the United States, Anza-Borrego Desert State Park extends across a broad swath of the Colorado Desert, reaching almost to the Mexican frontier. Within its borders lie desert sinks, sculpted rocks and multicolored badlands. Bighorn sheep roam the mountains, and desert life abounds in the lowlands.

Created about 150 million years ago by an earthquake fault system, the region includes the Jacumba Mountains, a granite jumble filled with eerie rock formations. Named for Juan Bautista de Anza, the Spanish explorer who trekked through in 1774, and *borrego*, the desert sheep that inhabit its hillsides, Anza-Borrego was a vital route for 1850s-era stagecoaches and mail wagons.

Today Borrego Springs, the only sizable town in the entire preserve, contains an excellent **visitor center** (end of West Palm Canyon Drive; 619-767-5311) with nature trails, a cactus garden and a small museum.

Font's Point, one of the park's most popular vistas, will provide a close-up view of the Borrego Badlands. A truly spectacular spot, it overlooks rock formations painted brilliant colors and chiseled by wind and water. It lies off Route S22 about 12 miles east of Borrego Springs. The turnoff road, which runs for four more miles, is a rough, sandy track that lies at the bottom of a wash, so take care not to become mired in the sand.

The entire stretch of Route S22 from Borrego Springs east to the Salton Sea is nicknamed **Erosion Road**. Along its 30-mile length are countless sandstone hills, brilliant red in color and carved into myriad shapes.

South of Borrego Springs, Route S3 traverses Yaqui Pass. From the roadside (near the 2.0 mile sign), a quarter-mile trail leads to **Kenyon Overlook**, with views of Sunset Mountain and surrounding canyons.

Farther south in the park, Route S2 parallels the historic Southern Emigrant Trail. At **Box Canyon Monument** (nine miles south of Scissors Crossing), a path leads to a point overlooking the old trail. It was here in 1847 that the Mormon Battalion hewed a track wide enough for wagons. Ten years later the first transcontinental mail service passed through this region, and soon afterward the Butterfield Overland Stage Line began transporting passengers.

The **Vallecito Stage Station** (Route S2, 19 miles south of Scissors Crossing), built in 1852, served the Butterfield and other lines for years, and gold prospectors heading to California camped here. Today an adobe reconstruction of the building stands in Vallecito County Park.

For a dramatic idea of the terrain confronting these pioneers, continue to **Carrizo Badlands Overlook** (Route S2, 36 miles south of Scissors Crossing). In all directions from this windswept plateau, the

---

PEGLEG SMITH

No self-respecting badlands would be complete without at least one fable about lost treasure. In Anza-Borrego Desert, it's the lost gold mine of "Pegleg" Smith. Thomas Long "Pegleg" Smith, it seems, was a prospector with a talent for tall tales. The nickname, he claimed, resulted from an 1827 Indian battle from which he emerged missing one leg. A few years later Pegleg passed through California, discovering a small amount of gold, which in the alembic of his imagination was eventually transformed into an entire mine.

*Even a prospector needs a public relations man. Pegleg's publicity agent came along a century later when Harry Oliver, a Hollywood director, created the **Pegleg Monument** (Route S22 and Henderson Canyon Road, eight miles east of Borrego Springs). Drawing a circle on the ground, Oliver urged everyone hoping to discover Pegleg's lost gold mine to fill the area with rocks. Today the monument is a huge pile of stones to which you are obliged to contribute. Good luck!*

landscape is an inhospitable mix of mountain peaks and sandy washes. Heavy erosion has worked its magic here, creating stone sculptures and hills banded with color.

ANZA-BORREGO LODGING AND RESTAURANT

Anza-Borrego's premier hostelry is **La Casa del Zorro** (Borrego Springs and Yaqui Pass roads, Borrego Springs; 619-767-5323), a desert hideaway in a garden setting. Spread across several acres, the resort is a collection of Spanish-style buildings positioned around several swimming pools, jacuzzis and tennis courts. Guest rooms, all with private patios, vary from small motel rooms (deluxe) to lavish suites and casitas with fireplaces (ultra-deluxe). The dining room—with whitewashed walls, *vega* ceilings and candle sconces—is Southwestern in atmosphere. Among the entrées are scampi, Alaskan salmon and rack of lamb. Moderate to deluxe.

Mojave Desert

When Jedediah Smith, one of the West's great explorers, trekked through the Mojave Desert in 1826, he declared it "a country of starvation." Even today it seems desolate and unyielding. Winters are cold here, summers hot. Rainfall, which dwindles from six inches in the western Mojave to less than two inches around Death Valley, comes only during winter. But plants proliferate and the area is alive with reptiles and small mammals.

The land is equally rich in minerals. For four decades beginning in the 1870s, the Mojave was a major thoroughfare for 20-mule teams laden with borax and miners weighted down with gold, silver, zinc and tungsten.

One of the region's most impressive displays is **Red Rock Canyon State Park** (Route 14 about 20 miles north of Mojave; 805-942-0662), a photogenic badlands that resembles a miniature Grand Canyon. As you enter through the sheer-wall gorge that leads into the valley, the landscape opens into a succession of accordion-pleated cliffs. Eroded by water, the rockfaces are carved into minarets, spires and crenelated towers.

The "living ghost town" of **Randsburg**, as well as neighboring Johannesburg and Red Mountain, is rich in minerals and history. Together these frontier communities formed a mining district that boomed first from gold deposits, then tungsten and silver. Of course that was a century ago, but today Randsburg still retains an aura of the 1890s.

Communications central for this region is the **California Desert Information Center** (831 Barstow Road; 619-256-8313) in Barstow. This hilltop museum features displays reflecting the area's flora, fauna and history.

The nearby **Mojave River Valley Museum** (270 East Virginia Way, Barstow; 619-256-5452) has a more complete collection of artifacts and memorabilia. It contains discoveries from the Calico Early Man Site, specimens of desert minerals and gems and displays on Spanish exploration and the space industry.

Just a few miles from the drab streets of Barstow you'll discover folded and faulted mountains that are layer cakes of color. Drive out approximately 15 miles to **Rainbow Basin National Natural Landmark** and encounter a deep canyon surrounded by striped cliffs of sedimentary rock. Rich in fossil deposits, the hills were created over eons and contain the remains of mastodons, rhinos and camel-type creatures. Even more impressive is the bald beauty of the place. The three-mile road that loops through this rock preserve passes zebra-striped buttes, boulders formed into fists and tortuously twisted formations.

The commercial outlets are as numerous as the memories at **Calico Ghost Town San Bernardino Regional Park** (Ghost Town Road, ten miles northeast of Barstow; 619-254-2122; admission). It was 1881 when prospectors struck it rich and Calico boomed to life with over 20 saloons, a temperance society and its own Chinatown. Today, the town has been transformed into a kind of windblown theme park complete with narrow-gauge railroad rides, a hall of illusions and a hokey Western playhouse. Native charm endures despite it all.

Thousands of years before Calico Ghost Town was even conceived, hunters roamed the area around the **Calico Early Man Archaeological Site**. Back in those prehistoric times the landscape was lush with junipers, live oaks and pines. The climate was temperate and a large body of water, Lake Manix, attracted mammoths, sloths and

---

CALIFORNIA POPPIES

*For Angelenos, the Mojave Desert begins in Antelope Valley on the far side of the San Gabriel Mountains. Here urbanization has sprawled over the hills to create Lancaster, a nondescript town whose saving grace is the **Antelope Valley California Poppy Reserve** (15101 West Lancaster Road). From March until May, when California's state flower blooms, the slopes surrounding Lancaster are transformed into a wildflower wonderland. To determine whether the poppies are blooming and for general information on the Antelope Valley area, contact the **Lancaster Chamber of Commerce** (44335 Lowtree Avenue, Lancaster; 805-948-4518).*

saber-toothed cats. Today you can view the archaeological pits, see early stone tools and wander back in your mind to an age of ice when the desert was in bloom. To get there, take Route 15 for about 15 miles east from Barstow, get off at the Minneola exit and go north three miles. Closed Monday and Tuesday; for information contact the San Bernardino County Museum, 714-798-8570.

Death Valley National Monument

Simply stated, Death Valley is the most famous desert in the United States. Set between the lofty Black and Panamint ranges, it is a place renowned for exquisite but merciless terrain. A region of vast distances (the national monument is half again as large as Delaware) and plentiful plant life (over 900 plant species subsist here, 22 of them growing only in this area), Death Valley holds a magician's bag of surprises.

One of the most hauntingly beautiful places in the world, Death Valley received its ominous name in 1849 when a party of pioneers, intent on following a shortcut to the gold fields, crossed the wasteland, barely escaping with their lives. Later, prospectors stayed to work the territory, discovering rich borax deposits during the 1880s and providing the region with a home industry.

Testament to the diversity of the High Desert, Death Valley contains the lowest spot in the contiguous United States (Badwater, 282 feet below sea level), yet rests within 60 miles of the highest place (Mount Whitney, 14,495 feet above sea level).

A museum without air conditioning, Death Valley is a giant geology lab displaying salt beds, sand dunes and an 11,000-foot elevation climb. Its multitiered hills contain layers that are windows on the history of the earth. One level holds Indian arrowheads, another Ice Age fish, and beneath these deposits lies Precambrian rock.

Due to the extreme summer temperatures (average July highs of 116°!), travel to the valley is not recommended in summer months. The best time to see the park is from November through April. In late February and March (average highs of 73°, dropping to a cool 46° average at night) the desert comes alive with spring blossoms like Death Valley sage, rock *mimulus* and Panamint daisies.

Several roads lead into Death Valley: a good place to start would be the eastern section of Route 178, off Route 127. Touring Death Valley along this road, you'll travel west over two low-lying mountain passes before turning north onto the floor of the valley. Within a couple miles lie the ruins of **Ashford Mill**, built during World War I when gold mining enjoyed a comeback.

A nearby vista point overlooks **Shoreline Butte**, a curving hill marked by a succession of horizontal lines. Clearly visible to the naked eye, they represent the ancient shorelines of Lake Manly, which covered the valley to a depth of 600 feet and stretched for 90 miles. Formed perhaps 75,000 years ago when Pleistocene glaciers atop the Sierra Nevada began melting, the lake dried up about 10,000 years ago.

The main highway continues through the heart of the region to **Mormon Point**. From here northward Death Valley is one huge salt flat. As you traverse this expanse, notice how the Black Mountains to the east turn from dark colors to reddish hues as gray Precambrian rocks give way to younger volcanic and sedimentary deposits.

Then continue on to that place you've been reading about since third grade geography, **Badwater**, 282 feet below sea level, the lowest point in the United States. Legend has it the place got its name from a surveyor whose mule refused to drink here, inspiring him to scratch "bad water" on the map he was charting.

Take a stroll out onto the salt flats and you'll find that the crystals are joined into a white carpet that extends for miles. Despite the brackish environment the pool itself supports water snails and other invertebrates. Out on the flats you can gaze west at 11,049-foot **Telescope Peak** across the valley. Then be sure to glance back at the cliff to the west of the road. There high in the rocks above you a lone sign marks "Sea Level."

The water that carved **Natural Bridge** (off Route 178 about two miles along a bumpy dirt road and up a half-mile trail) cascaded from the mountains in torrents, punched a hole in the underlying rock and etched this 50-foot-high arch. Behind the bridge, you can still see the lip of this ancient waterfall.

Another dirt side road travels one mile to the **Devil's Golf Course**. Rather than a sand hazard, this flat expanse is one huge salt trap, complete with salt towers, pinnacles and brine pools. The three-to-five-foot-thick salt deposits were formed by a small lake that evaporated perhaps 2000 years ago.

Artist Drive, a nine-mile route through the Black Mountains, is one of Southern California's most magnificent roads. The hills all around are splashed with color—soft pastels, striking reds, creamy browns—and rise to sharp cliffs. En route at Artists Palette, the hills are colored so vividly they seem to pulsate. It's a spot admired by photographers from around the world, a place where the rainbow meets the badlands.

Mushroom Rock, the sculptor's answer to Artists Palette, rises on the right several hundred yards after you regain Route 178. A boulder of basalt lava, it was carved by windblown sand.

Up in **Golden Canyon**, erosion has chiseled chasms into the bright yellow walls of a narrow gorge. Climb the three-quarter-mile

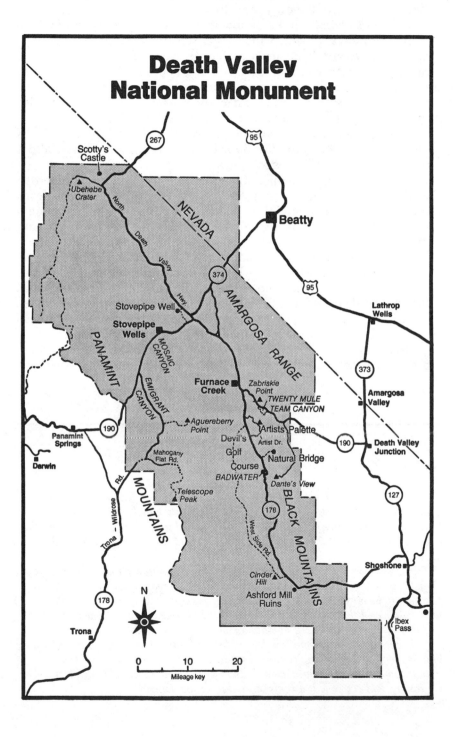

Death Valley National Monument

trail here and you arrive in a natural amphitheater, named for the iridescent quality of the canyon walls.

In this entire wasteland of wonders the only major center of civilization is **Furnace Creek**, where a gas station, campground, restaurants and two hotels create a welcome oasis. The **Death Valley National Monument Visitor Center** (619-786-2331) is a good resource for maps and information. It houses a museum re-creating the history of Native Americans and early prospectors. There are also mineral displays and an oversize relief map of the valley.

The nearby **Borax Museum** features the oldest house in Death Valley, a sturdy 1883 structure built by a borax miner. There's also a wonderful collection of stagecoaches.

A two-and-one-half-mile trail climbs from Golden Canyon to **Zabriskie Point**, but most folks follow Route 190, which leads southwest from Furnace Creek. In any case, everyone inevitably arrives at this place, as though it were a point of pilgrimage for paying homage to nature.

What else can a mortal do, confronted with beauty of this magnitude? In the east amber-hued hills roll like waves toward the horizon. To the west lies a badlands, burnished by blown sand to fierce reds and soft pastels. All around, the landscape resembles a sea gone mad, waves of sand breaking in every direction, with a stone tsunami, Manly Beacon, high above the combers, poised to crash into Death Valley.

Prosaic though it sounds, these mustard-colored hills are dry mud, lakebed sediments deposited two to twelve million years ago, then up-

---

A CASTLE IN THE DESERT

*At the northern tip of Death Valley, you'll find the strangest feature in the entire park—a castle in the desert. It's a place called **Scotty's Castle** (North Death Valley Highway; admission), though Scotty never owned it. In fact Scotty swindled the fellow who did own it, then became his lifelong friend. Sound preposterous? Perhaps.*

It seems that one Walter "Death Valley Scotty" Scott, a former trick rider in Buffalo Bill's Wild West Show, once convinced a Chicago millionaire, one Albert Johnson, to invest in a nonexistent gold mine. Johnson traveled west to see the mine, discovered that the dry desert clime helped his fragile health, forgave Scotty and decided during the 1920s to build a mansion in the sand.

The result was a two-million-dollar Moorish castle, a wonderfully ridiculous building with wrought-iron detailing, inlaid tile, carved-beam ceilings, expensive antiques and nothing for miles around. Scotty, the greatest storyteller in Death Valley history, told everyone it was his castle. Hence the name.

lifted to their present height. For a close-up view of those mud hills, follow the nearby dirt road through **Twenty Mule Team Canyon**.

Then to get above it all, venture on to **Dante's View**, a 5475-foot perch with a 360° vista. From this coign of vantage the salt flats and trapped pools of Death Valley are like a bleak watercolor. A steep half-mile trail (up the knoll north of the parking lot) leads to a point where, in a single glance, you can see Badwater and Mount Whitney, the lowest and highest points in the contiguous United States.

Backtracking to Furnace Creek, Route 190 proceeds north toward the upper end of Death Valley. The history of the region's most valuable mineral is revealed at the **Harmony Borax Works**. Surrounded by the ruins of Death Valley's first borax plant is an original 20-mule team rig.

Stovepipe Wells, Death Valley's other village, is even smaller than Furnace Creek. A motel, restaurant, store, gas station and campground comprise the entire town.

Six miles east of the village a graded road departs Route 190 and travels four miles past **sand dunes** before joining North Death Valley Highway, the road to Scotty's Castle. Alive with greenery, these undulating dunes support numerous plant species, including creosote bushes, mesquite and pickleweed.

Ubehebe Crater, toward the northern end of Death Valley, is another of the park's natural wonders. One-half mile in diameter and reaching a depth of 450 feet, this magnificent landmark was created by a single explosion of undetermined date. The volcanic force of the molten lava scattered debris over a six-square-mile area and blew the crater walls so clean that one side retains its original sedimentary colors.

DEATH VALLEY LODGING

Furnace Creek Ranch (619-786-2345) is a 124-unit resort sprawling across several acres and featuring three restaurants, a saloon and general store, and a swimming pool. Guest accommodations include duplex "cabins" (moderate), fully furnished but lacking extra amenities, and standard rooms (deluxe), which are plusher, more spacious and feature televisions and refrigerators.

The poshest place for many miles is **Furnace Creek Inn** (619-786-2345), a 70-room hotel set on a hillside overlooking Death Valley. This Spanish-Moorish-style building, built of stone and adobe, is surrounded by flowering gardens. Palm trees shade the grounds and a stream feeds three koi ponds. There are two restaurants, tennis courts, and a spring-fed swimming pool. Guest rooms are quite comfortably furnished and most have fireplaces. Ultra-deluxe, including breakfast and dinner.

Stove Pipe Wells Village (Stovepipe Wells; 619-786-2387) is an attractive 82-unit motel with a pool, restaurant, general store and gas station. If your heroes have always been cowboys, you'll sleep well here; some of the rooms are decorated Western-style with oxen yokes attached to the headboards. Moderate.

DEATH VALLEY RESTAURANTS

There are five restaurants in Furnace Creek, and all can be reached at 619-786-2345. The least expensive food in all Death Valley, except for dishes you cook around your campfire, is in the **Cafeteria** at Furnace Creek Ranch.

The **49er Coffee Shop** next door has omelettes, hot sandwiches, burgers and dinners such as pork chops or fried trout. With wood-plank walls and ranch atmosphere, it's a good place for a moderately priced meal.

The **Wrangler Steakhouse** serves filet mignon, barbecued chicken, broiled halibut, ribs and pork chops every evening. Cozy and informal, the "house" consists of an unassuming room decorated with Mexican rugs, plus a small dining patio. Moderate to deluxe.

The fine dining places are up at Furnace Creek Inn. At **L'Ottimos** you feast on shrimp scampi, veal scallopine and pasta primavera. Dinner only, deluxe.

Upstairs at the **Inn Dining Room**, candlelight and a beamed ceiling create a more formal atmosphere. Gentlemen are requested to wear jackets during dinner, and the menu is fixed price. The ultra-deluxe price tag allows you to choose from among nearly 40 entrées including sole Oscar and medallions of beef. Breakfast and lunch menus are standard.

In Stovepipe Wells you'll find a spacious **Dining Room** (619-786-2387) embellished with Indian rugs and paintings of the Old West. The cuisine matches the ambience, an all-American menu featuring fried chicken, rainbow trout, steak, veal picatta and cod. Moderate.

DEATH VALLEY NIGHTLIFE

The Furnace Creek Inn includes the **Oasis Lounge** (Furnace Creek; 619-786-2345) among its elegant facilities. Featuring live entertainment music nightly, it's a lovely spot to enjoy a quiet evening.

The **Badwater Saloon** (619-786-2387) in Stovepipe Wells also hosts a solo guitarist most nights. With Western-style decor and a dancefloor, it's a night owl's oasis.

The finest entertainment for many miles is at the **Amargosa Opera House** (Death Valley Junction; 619-852-4316). The amazing one-woman show here is the creation of Marta Becket, who performs dance pantomimes in a theater she personally decorated with colorful murals. Her performances run every Friday, Saturday and Monday from November to April and every Saturday in October and May. Locally renowned, she's extremely popular, so call for reservations.

Sporting Life
GOLF

Palm Springs golfers will think they have died and gone to heaven. This desert oasis is chockablock with courses open to the public, including **Palm Springs Municipal Golf Course** (1885 Golf Club Drive, Palm Springs; 619-328-1005), **Canyon South Golf Course** (1097 Murray Canyon Drive, Palm Springs; 619-327-2019), **Mesquite Country Club** (2700 East Mesquite Avenue, Palm Springs; 619-323-1502), **Desert Falls Country Club** (1111 Desert Falls Parkway, Palm Desert; 619-341-4020), **Oasis Country Club** (42-300 Casbah Way, Palm Desert; 619-345-2715), **Palm Desert Resort Country Club** (77-333 Country Club Drive, Palm Desert; 619-345-2791) and **De Anza–Palm Springs Country Club** (36-200 Date Palm Drive, Cathedral City; 619-328-1315).

TENNIS

In Palm Springs, public courts are located at **Demuth Park** (4365 Mesquite Avenue; 619-323-8272), **Palm Springs Tennis Center** (1300 East Baristo Road; 619-320-0020) and **Ruth Hardy Park** (Tamarisk Road and Avenida Caballeros). In Desert Hot Springs, try **Wardman Park** (66150 8th Street) or **Arroyo Park** (Arroyo Drive).

HORSEBACK RIDING

In Palm Springs, **Smoke Tree Stables** (2500 Toledo Avenue; 619-327-1372) offers guided rides through stunning desert terrain.

To rent horses around Victorville try **Mojave Narrows Riding Stables** (619-244-1644); in the Barstow area contact Dan McCue Ranch Stables (619-254-2184).

In Death Valley, **Furnace Creek Ranch** (619-786-2345) rents horses from October through May.

BALLOONING AND GLIDING

You can soar through the desert skies in a balloon manned by **American Balloon Charters** (Palm Springs; 619-568-6700), **Sunrise Balloons** (1-800-548-9912; in Palm Springs, Borrego Springs and Temecula) or **Balloon Adventure** (Lancaster; 818-888-0576).

Another way to sail through the air is in a glider: contact **Aronson's Air Service** (40th Street West, Rosamond; 805-256-2200) or **Crystal Soaring** (32810 165th North Street East, Llano; 805-944-3341).

BICYCLING

Cycling is popular throughout this area. There's mountain riding in the San Bernardino Mountains, desert cycling around Palm Springs, Joshua Tree and Anza-Borrego and recreational riding in the regional park areas.

Thirty-five miles of bike trails encircle Palm Springs. Popular riding spots include the luxurious residential neighborhoods, the Mesquite Country Club area, the Indian Canyons and around the local parks.

Death Valley may seem like the last place to ride a bicycle, but it's actually quite pleasant from October to April. The main road in the park is paved and there's little traffic.

Transportation

BY CAR

Route 10, the San Bernardino Freeway, travels east from Los Angeles through the heart of the Inland Empire and Low Desert. From San Diego, **Route 8** goes east along the southern fringes of the Low Desert near the Mexican border. In crossing the Mojave Desert, **Route 58** leads from Bakersfield to Barstow, the hub of the High Desert.

BY AIR

Two facilities, Ontario International Airport and Palm Springs Municipal Airport, serve the Low Desert region. Carriers flying into **Ontario International Airport** include Alaska Airlines, American Airlines, America West Airlines, Continental Airlines, Delta Air Lines, Skywest Airlines, Southwest Airlines, Trans World Airlines, United Airlines and USAir.

Carriers into **Palm Springs Municipal Airport** currently include Alaska Airlines, American Airlines, America West, Delta Air Lines, Skywest Airlines, Trans World Airlines, United Airlines and USAir.

BY BUS

Greyhound/Trailways Bus Lines offers service to San Bernardino (596 North G Street; 714-884-4796), Riverside (3911 University Avenue; 714-686-2345), Perris (637 South D Street; 714-657-7813), Palm Springs (311 North Indian Avenue; 619-325-2053) and Indio (45-524 Oasis Street; 619-347-3020).

BY TRAIN

Amtrak (800-872-7245) has two passenger trains to San Bernardino (1170 West Third Street; 714-884-1307), the "Desert Wind" and "Southwest Chief." Another train, the "Sunset," stops at the railroad platform on Jackson Street in Indio.

For service to Death Valley, the closest stops are Barstow and Las Vegas. The "Desert Wind" arrives in Barstow, and the "Southwest Chief" stops in Barstow and Las Vegas.

CAR RENTALS

Located at Ontario International Airport are the following rental agencies: **Avis Rent A Car** (714-983-3689), **Budget Rent A Car** (714-983-9691), **Dollar Rent A Car** (714-986-4541) and **Hertz Rent A Car** (714-986-2024).

Several agencies are located at the Palm Springs terminal: **Avis Rent A Car** (619-327-1353), **Budget Rent A Car** (619-327-1404), **Dollar Rent A Car** (619-325-7333), **Hertz Rent A Car** (619-778-5100) and **National Car Rental** (619-327-1438).

PUBLIC TRANSPORTATION

For local bus service in San Bernardino, Redlands and points in between call **OmniTrans** (714-825-8341). Riverside is served by the **Riverside Transit Agency** (714-682-1234).

In the Palm Springs area, **Sun Bus** (619-343-3451) carries passengers to destinations throughout the Coachella Valley. From Palm Springs, **Desert Stage Lines** (619-367-3581) provides transportation to Joshua Tree National Monument headquarters in Twentynine Palms.

From inland San Diego county, **Northeast Rural Bus System** (619-765-0145) takes passengers to Borrego Springs.

Central Coast

If the Central Coast were an oil painting, it would portray a surf-laced   **223**
shoreline near the bottom of the frame. Pearly beaches and bold
promontories would occupy the center, while forested peaks rose in
the background. Actually, a mural would be more appropriate to the
subject, since the coastline extends 350 miles from Ventura to Half
Moon Bay. The artist would paint several mountain ranges parallel to
the shore, then fill the area between with a patchwork of hills, headlands and farmland.

To call any single part of the painting the most alluring would be
to embark upon uncertain waters. For the entire coast is a region of
rare beauty. Stretching across Ventura, Santa Barbara, San Luis
Obispo, Monterey, Santa Cruz and San Mateo counties, it embraces
many of the West's finest beaches.

No fewer than 11 of California's 21 missions lie along this stretch.
Chosen by the Spanish in the 1780s for their fertile pastures, natural
harbors and placid surroundings, the mission sites are a historic testi-
monial to the varied richness of the landscape. The towns that grew
up around these missions are evocative of old Spanish traditions and
emblems of California's singular culture.

Ventura possesses beautiful beaches, and San Luis Obispo is set
amid velvet hills and rich agriculture areas. Unlike Spanish-style Santa
Barbara to the south and Monterey to the north, San Luis Obispo has
defined its own culture, a blend of hard-riding ranch hand and easygoing college student. Farther north civilization gives way to the
coastal quietude of untracked beaches and wind-honed sea cliffs, a
prelude to Big Sur. Incongruous amid these placid climes stands
California's own eighth wonder of the world, Hearst Castle, a symbol
of boundless artistry and unbridled egotism.

Beyond Big Sur lie Monterey and Carmel, fashionable residential
areas 125 miles south of San Francisco. These wealthy enclaves con-

trast sharply with bohemian, politically progressive Santa Cruz to their north.

The mountains paralleling this rich coastline look much the same as they did when the first European explorer, Juan Rodríguez Cabrillo, arrived on this coast in 1542. By the 1820s, Yankee merchant ships were plying Monterey waters, trading for hides and tallow. This early American presence, brilliantly described in Richard Henry Dana's classic *Two Years Before the Mast*, climaxed in 1846 during the Mexican War.

Monterey became the site of California's constitutional convention and, by the 1880s, a tourist mecca. Of course the old Spanish capital also developed into a major fishing and canning region during the early 20th century. It was then that John Steinbeck added to the already rich history of Monterey with his novels and stories.

Much of the landscape that became known as "Steinbeck Country" has changed drastically since the novelist's day, and the entire Central Coast is different from the era of the early missions. But the most important elements of the Central Coast—the foaming ocean, open sky and wooded heights—are still here, waiting for the traveler with a bold eye and robust imagination.

Ventura

Situated 60 miles northwest of Los Angeles and 30 miles to the southeast of Santa Barbara, the 18th-century mission town of Ventura has generally been overlooked by travelers. History has not been so remiss. Long known to the Chumash Indians, who inhabited a nearby village named Shisholop, the place was first discovered by Europeans in the 16th century. Father Junípero Serra founded a mission here in 1782, and the region soon became renowned for its fruit orchards.

Today the city preserves its heritage in a number of historic sites. Stop by the **Visitor and Convention Bureau** (89-C South California Street; 805-648-2075) for brochures and maps.

The highlight of a stroll through Ventura is **San Buenaventura Mission** (211 East Main Street; 805-643-4318; admission), a whitewash-and-red-tile church flanked by a flowering garden. The dark, deep chapel is lined with Stations of the Cross paintings and features a Romanesque altar adorned with statues and pilasters.

The **Ventura County Museum of History and Art** (100 East Main Street; 805-653-0323) traces the region's secular history with displays of Chumash Indian artifacts, cowboy spurs and saddles, oil industry photographs and simple agricultural tools.

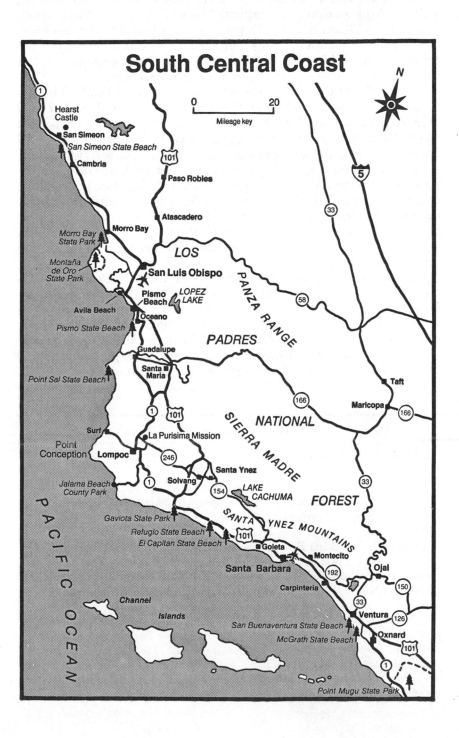

South Central Coast

N

0 — 20
Mileage key

① Hearst Castle
■ San Simeon
San Simeon State Beach
■ Cambria

⑤

US 101

■ Paso Robles

33

■ Atascadero

Morro Bay State Park
■ Morro Bay

LOS

Montaña de Oro State Park

San Luis Obispo

PANZA RANGE

58

Pismo Beach
LOPEZ LAKE

Avila Beach
■ Oceano

PADRES

Pismo State Beach

Guadalupe

Santa ■ Maria

Point Sal State Beach

■ Taft

166

Maricopa 166

① 101

Surf

NATIONAL

SIERRA MADRE

La Purisima Mission

Point Conception ■ Lompoc
246

Santa Ynez

33

Jalama Beach County Park

① Solvang
154

LAKE CACHUMA

FOREST

Gaviota State Park

SANTA YNEZ MOUNTAINS

Refugio State Beach
El Capitan State Beach
101

■ Goleta
■ Montecito

Santa Barbara
192

Ojai

150

Carpinteria

Channel

Islands

33

Ventura 126

San Buenaventura State Beach
McGrath State Beach
■ Oxnard

101

PACIFIC OCEAN

①

Point Mugu State Park

For a view of an archaeological dig that dates back 3500 years, visit the **Albinger Archaeological Museum** (113 East Main Street; 805-648-5823). At the dig site you'll see the foundation of an 18th-century mission church, an ancient earth oven and a remnant of the Spanish padres' elaborate aqueduct system. A small museum displays the arrowheads, crucifixes and pottery uncovered here.

Along the waterfront a **promenade** parallels the beach. This is a prime area for water sports, and countless surfers, with their blond hair and black wetsuits, will be waiting offshore, poised for the perfect wave. Along the far end of the esplanade, at the **Ventura Pier**, you'll encounter one more Southern California species, the surf fisherman.

Another local wonder is the **Ventura County Courthouse** (501 Poli Street), a sprawling neoclassical structure. The place is a mélange of Doric columns, bronze fixtures and Roman flourishes. But forget the marble entranceway and grand staircase. What makes it memorable is the row of friars' heads adorning the facade. Where else but in Southern California would a dozen baroque priests stare out at you from the hall of justice?

By contrast, the **Olivas Adobe** (4200 Olivas Park Drive; 805-644-4346 or 805-654-7831) is a spacious hacienda surrounded by flowering gardens. This two-story gem, with balconies running the full length of the upper floor, is a study in the Monterey-style architecture of 19th-century California. The rooms are furnished in period pieces, and there is a museum adjacent to the house, providing a window on the world of California's prosperous Spanish settlers.

THE CHANNEL ISLANDS

Gaze out from the Ventura or Santa Barbara shoreline and you will spy a fleet of islands moored offshore. At times fringed with mist, on other occasions standing a hand's reach away in the crystal air, they are the Channel Islands, a group of eight volcanic islands.

Situated in the Santa Barbara Channel from 11 to 40 miles off the coast, they are a place apart, a wild and storm-blown region of sharp cliffs, rocky coves and curving grasslands. Five of the islands—Anacapa, Santa Cruz, Santa Rosa, San Miguel and Santa Barbara—comprise Channel Islands National Park, while the surrounding waters are a marine sanctuary.

Nicknamed "America's Galapagos," the chain teems with every imaginable form of life. Like the Galapagos, this isolated archipelago has given rise to many unique life forms, including 40 endemic plant species and the island fox, which grows only to the size of a house cat.

The northern islands were created about 14 million years ago by volcanic activity. Archaeological discoveries indicate that they could be among the oldest sites of

VENTURA LODGING

For something spacious, plush and formal consider the **Bella Maggiore Inn** (67 South California Street; 805-652-0277). Set in downtown Ventura, this 32-room hostelry follows the tradition of an Italian inn. There are European appointments and antique chandeliers in the lobby and a Roman-style fountain in the courtyard. The accommodations are painted in soft hues and decorated with pastel prints. The furniture is a mixture of cane, washed pine and antiques. Moderate to deluxe.

Up the hill, overlooking Ventura and the ocean, sits **La Mer European Bed & Breakfast** (411 Poli Street; 805-643-3600). The flags decorating the facade of this 1890 house illustrate the inn's international theme. Each of the five guest rooms is decorated after the fashion of a European country—England, Austria, Norway, Germany and France. Deluxe.

VENTURA RESTAURANTS

For an elegant meal, consider the **Seafood and Beverage Co.** (211 East Santa Clara Street; 805-643-3264). Housed in a 1914-vintage home, this comfortable dining place features mesquite-broiled dishes. Moderate to deluxe.

Or try **Eric Ericsson's Fish Company** (1140 South Seaward Avenue; 805-643-4783), a small snuggery done in casual California style. Located near the beach, this understated restaurant is a good place for fresh fish. Moderate to deluxe.

---

human habitation in the Americas. When explorer Juan Cabrillo revealed them to the West in 1542 they were populated with thousands of Chumash Indians.

*Today, long since the Chumash were removed and the islands given over to hunters, ranchers and settlers, the Channel Islands are largely uninhabited. Several, however, are open to hikers and campers. At the mainland-based **Channel Islands National Park Visitor Center** (1901 Spinnaker Drive, Ventura; 805-644-8262), contemporary museum displays and an excellent 25-minute movie will familiarize you with the park.*

*Next door at **Island Packers** (1867 Spinnaker Drive, Ventura; 805-642-1393) you can arrange transportation to the islands. This outfit schedules regular day trips by boat to Anacapa, Santa Barbara, Santa Cruz, Santa Rosa and San Miguel islands. They can arrange camping trips on the first two islands or will book you into a room at the 19th-century Scorpion Ranch on Santa Cruz Island.*

The Nature Conservancy *(213 Stearns Wharf, Santa Barbara; 805-962-9111) also leads tours of Santa Cruz, the largest and most diverse of the islands. Just 24 miles long, Santa Cruz supports 600 species of plants, many unique to this area, and 130 types of land birds.*

VENTURA NIGHTLIFE

Bombay Bar & Grill (143 South California Street; 805-643-4404) offers live entertainment nightly with a musical medley that changes frequently. The South Seas-style bar features piano plunkers, while the room in back hosts live dance bands nightly. Cover on weekends.

Scene of scenes is the **Ventura Theatre** (26 South Chestnut Street; 805-648-1936), a refurbished movie house. With its intricate gold fixtures, stained-glass windows and ornamental molding, this 1928 structure has been redone in grand style and converted into a restaurant/concert hall. The club frequently draws top-name entertainers. Cover.

VENTURA BEACHES AND PARKS

Point Mugu State Park (805-987-3303) extends along four miles of beachfront and reaches back six miles into the Santa Monica Mountains. The park's beaches are wide and sandy, with rocky outcroppings and a spectacular sand dune. Over 70 miles of hiking trails lace this diverse park. Camping. Located on Route 1 about ten miles south of Oxnard.

Extending along two miles of ocean front, **McGrath State Beach** (805-654-4744) is bounded by dunes. A lake and wildlife area attract over 200 bird species, and the nearby Santa Clara River is home to tortoises, squirrels and other wildlife. Together the lake and preserve make it a great spot for camping or daytripping at the beach. Located at 2211 Harbor Boulevard in Oxnard.

In the world of urban parks, **San Buenaventura State Beach** (805-654-4611)—a two-mile-long swath bordered by dunes—ranks very high. Since the pier at one end of the park is a short stroll from the city center, the beach provides easy access to cultural attractions. The 1700-foot wharf is also renowned for fishing. Located along Harbor Boulevard southeast of the Ventura Pier in Ventura.

Ojai

To Chumash Indians the word "ojai" signified "the nest." And to the generations of mystics, health aficionados, artists and admirers who have settled here, the place is indeed a secluded abode. Geographically it resembles its Chumash namesake, nestling in a moon-shaped valley girded by the Topa and Sulphur Mountains.

A town of 7900 souls, Ojai is an artist colony crowded with galleries and studios. The site is also a haven for the health conscious, with spas and hot springs. To the metaphysically minded it is a center for several esoteric sects.

Ever since the 1870s, when author Charles Nordhoff publicized the place as a tourist spot, it has been popular with all sorts of visitors. Inland just 14 miles from Ventura, Ojai is a valley so extraordinary it was used as the setting for Shangri-La in the movie *Lost Horizon* (1937). Sun-bronzed mountains rise in all directions, fields of wild-flowers run to the verge of forested slopes and everywhere there is tranquility, making it clear why the region is a magnet for mystics.

Set atop a hill overlooking Ojai Valley is the **Krotona Institute of Theosophy** (Krotona Hill; 805-646-2653). This 118-acre forested estate is a center for "students of Theosophy and the ancient wisdom." Visitors can tour the library and enjoy the grounds, which are beautifully landscaped. Another sect, the **Krishnamurti Foundation**, has an equally secluded library (1130 McAndrew Road; 805-646-4948) in the hills on the other side of town.

Before venturing to these etherial spots, stop off at the **Ojai Valley Chamber of Commerce** (338 East Ojai Avenue; 805-646-8126), which has maps and brochures of the area.

To capture the spirit of Ojai, you should bicycle or drive the town's back roads and mountain lanes. **Grand Avenue loop** will carry you past orange orchards and horse ranches to the foot of the mountains. It leads along thick stone walls built by Chinese laborers during the 19th century. (Take Ojai Avenue, Route 150, east from town; turn left on Reeves Road, left again on McAndrew Road, left on Thatcher Road and left on Carne Road. This returns to Route 150, completing a ten-mile loop).

East End drive follows Route 150 east past palm trees and farm houses. Three miles from town, on a promontory with a stone bench inscribed "The Ojai Valley," is the overlook from which actor Ronald Colman gazed down on Shangri-La in *Lost Horizon*. With deep green orchards below and sharp gold mountains above, it truly evokes that fictional utopia.

OJAI LODGING

The premier mountain resort hereabouts is **Ojai Valley Inn** (Country Club Drive; 805-646-5511), a 200-acre retreat with tennis courts, pool and 18-hole golf course. Set on a ridge top with spectacular mountain vistas, the complex has been refurbished and modernized. Rooms are on a full European plan and rent in the ultra-deluxe category.

For bed-and-breakfast accommodations try **Ojai Manor Hotel** (210 East Matilija Street; 805-646-0961), set in a vintage 1874 school-house. The six-room facility has rentals with shared baths in the deluxe range. A typical guest room is small but attractively decorated with throw rugs and wrought-iron beds.

OJAI RESTAURANTS

Everyone's favorite Ojai restaurant is the **Ranch House** (South Lomita Avenue; 805-646-2360), an intimate dining terrace that rests in a tranquil garden surrounded by ferns, bamboo and rose bushes. Dinner includes Indonesian-style beef, Boston scrod and veal in cream sauce. Desserts come from the restaurant's bakery, as do the three varieties of bread served with each meal. A must for lunch, dinner or Sunday brunch; deluxe to ultra-deluxe.

For fine French dining **L'Auberge** (314 El Paseo Road; 805-646-2288), a venerable old house replete with brick fireplace and chandeliers, sets the tone. Here you can choose from a menu that includes scampi, poached sole and duckling in orange sauce. Dinner every night except Tuesday, lunch on weekends only; moderate to deluxe.

OJAI SHOPPING

The center of the shopping scene is **Arcade Plaza**, a promenade between Ojai Avenue and Matilija Street that extends from Montgomery Street to Signal Street. Within this tile-roofed warren and along surrounding blocks are crafts stores and galleries.

The Artist and the Outlaw Gallery (320 East Ojai Avenue; 805-646-0901) has an outstanding collection of contemporary work by local artists. There are batik-on-silk pieces, carved walking sticks, evocative oil paintings and impressive porcelain pieces.

Quite a collection it is at **The Antique Collection** (236 West Ojai Avenue; 805-646-6688): a number of dealers have combined their stock, filling an entire warehouse with room after room of heirlooms.

An important gathering place for the spiritual movement is the **Heart of Light Bookstore** (451 East Ojai Avenue; 805-646-3812),

---

WHEELER HOT SPRINGS

*A mecca for the health-conscious sits along Route 33 in the mountains surrounding Ojai. **Wheeler Hot Springs** Route 33, six miles from Ojai; 805-646-8131) draws on the area's natural mineral water. The private rooms here are pine-paneled affairs with skylights and hot and cold tubs. There are massage rooms, a spring-fed swimming pool and a lodge housing the fine **Restaurant at Wheeler Hot Springs**. Set creekside, the dining room features a stone fireplace and an ever-changing bill of fare that might include seafood stew, stuffed gulf shrimp and pan-fried oysters breaded with pine nuts. Dinner and weekend brunch only; moderate to deluxe.*

with its collection of mystical works, crystals and religious paraphernalia. But the bookstore of bookstores is a place called **Bart's Books** (302 West Matilija Street; 805-646-3755), which is almost entirely outdoors. Here browsers can soak up the sun, enjoy mountain breezes and wander through a maze of used books.

Outside town, in a hilltop estate flanked by gardens, is the **Beatrice Wood Studio** (8560 Route 150, Ojai), a place that you absolutely must visit. Beatrice Wood, a 95-year-old potter, has become over the years a regional institution. Her work is more like sculpture than pottery, with each piece portraying people or animals.

Santa Barbara Area

Tucked between a curving bay and the Santa Ynez Mountains lies one of the prettiest places in all California. It's little wonder that the Spanish who settled Santa Barbara, establishing a presidio in 1782 and a mission several years later, called it *la tierra adorada*, the beloved land.

The town was an important center of Spanish culture until the Americans seized California in the 19th century. These Anglo interlopers built a post-Victorian-style community. But a monstrous earthquake leveled the downtown area in 1925 and created a *tabla rasa* for architects and city planners.

Faced with rebuilding Santa Barbara, they returned the place to its historic roots, combining Spanish and mission architecture to create a Mediterranean metropolis. The result is modern day Santa Barbara, with its adobe walls, red-tile roofs, rounded archways and palm-lined boulevards.

Sightseeing Santa Barbara is as simple as it is rewarding. First stop at the **Santa Barbara Visitor's Center** (1 Santa Barbara Street; 805-965-3021). The materials here include more pamphlets, books and booklets than you ever want to see. The most important piece is a brochure entitled "Santa Barbara" that outlines a "Red Tile Tour" for walkers as well as a lengthier "Scenic Drive." Together they form two concentric circles along whose perimeter lie nearly all the city's points of interest.

RED TILE TOUR   This 14-block tour begins at the **Santa Barbara County Courthouse** (1100 Block of Anacapa Street; 805-962-6464), the city's grandest building. The interior of this Spanish-Moorish "palace" is a masterwork of beamed ceilings, arched corridors and palacio tile floors.

Another stop on the tour is the **Hill Carrillo Adobe** (11 East Carrillo Street), an 1826-vintage home built by a Massachusetts settler for his Spanish bride. Today the house is furnished with period pieces.

El Paseo (814 State Street), a labyrinthine shopping arcade comprised of several complexes, represents a unique mall. Incorporated into the architectural motif is **Casa de la Guerra,** a splendid house built in 1827 for the commander of the Santa Barbara presidio.

The **Santa Barbara Historical Museum** (136 East de la Guerra Street; 805-966-1601) certainly looks its part. Set in an adobe building with tile roof and wrought-iron window bars, the facility sits behind heavy wooden doors. Within are fine arts displays and sections depicting the Spanish, Mexican and early American periods of Santa Barbara history, including memorabilia from author Richard Henry Dana's visits.

Casa de Covarrubias (715 Santa Barbara Street), an L-shaped house, and the adjacent **Historic Fremont Adobe** (715 Santa Barbara Street), also evoke the early 19th century. The former structure, dating to 1817, is said to be the site of the last Mexican assembly in 1846; the latter became headquarters for Colonel John C. Fremont after Americans captured the town later that year.

El Presidio de Santa Barbara State Historic Park (123 East Cañon Perdido Street; 805-966-9719) features two original buildings from the town's 1782 presidio. El Cuartel, the guards' house, and La Cañedo Adobe both served as military residences. The most interesting feature of this outdoor museum, however, is the Santa Barbara Presidio Chapel, which re-creates an early Spanish church in its full array of colors.

SCENIC DRIVE   This drive around Santa Barbara, a 30-mile circle tour, incorporates several of the sites covered along the Red Tile Tour. To avoid repetition begin at the **Santa Barbara Museum of Art** (1130 State Street; 805-963-4364), with its collection of American paintings, Asian art and classical sculpture.

Then head up to **Mission Santa Barbara** (2201 Laguna Street; 805-682-4713; admission), which sits on a knoll overlooking the city. Founded in 1786 and restored in 1820, this twin-tower beauty follows an ancient Roman design. The interior courtyard is a colonnaded affair with a central fountain and graceful flower garden. There are also museum displays representing early mission life and a cemetery where 4000 Chumash Indians are buried in the shade of a Moreton Bay fig tree.

The **Santa Barbara Museum of Natural History** (2559 Puesta del Sol Road; 805-682-4711; admission) devotes successive rooms to marine, plant, vertebrate and insect life. Excellent for kids, it also features small exhibits of Indian tribes from throughout the United States.

Mission Canyon Road climbs into the hills for close-up views of the Santa Ynez Mountains and a tour of **Santa Barbara Botanical**

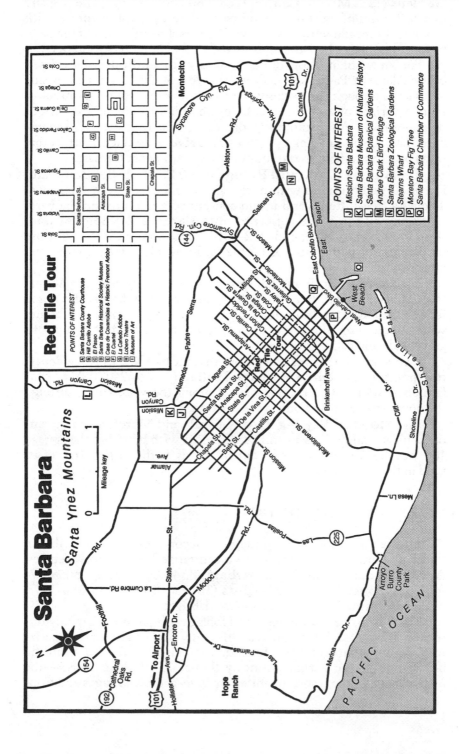

Santa Barbara

Santa Ynez Mountains

Red Tile Tour

POINTS OF INTEREST

A Santa Barbara County Courthouse
B Hill Carrillo Adobe
C El Paseo
D Santa Barbara Historical Society Museum
E Casa de Covarrubias & Historic Fremont Adobe
F El Cuartel
G La Cañeda Adobe
H Lobero Theatre
I Museum of Art

POINTS OF INTEREST

J Mission Santa Barbara
K Santa Barbara Museum of Natural History
L Santa Barbara Botanical Gardens
M Andree Clark Bird Refuge
N Santa Barbara Zoological Gardens
O Stearns Wharf
P Moreton Bay Fig Tree
Q Santa Barbara Chamber of Commerce

PACIFIC OCEAN

Gardens (1212 Mission Canyon Road; 805-682-4726). The five and one-half miles of trails here wind past a desert section carpeted with cactus and a meadow filled with wildflowers. Near the top of the park, beyond the ancient Indian trail, is a stand of cool, lofty redwood trees.

For views of million-dollar homes with million-dollar views, cruise Alameda Padre Serra. From this thoroughfare a series of side roads leads through the exclusive bedroom community of **Montecito**. Here a variety of architectural styles combine to create a luxurious neighborhood. After exploring the town's shady groves and manicured lawns, you can pick up **Channel Drive**, a spectacular street that skirts beaches and bluffs as it loops back toward Santa Barbara.

The **Andree Clark Bird Refuge** (1400 East Cabrillo Boulevard) is a placid lagoon filled with ducks, geese and other freshwater fowl. There's a tree-tufted island in the center and a trail around the park. Upstaging all this is the adjacent **Santa Barbara Zoological Gardens** (500 Niños Drive; 805-962-6310; admission) with its miniature train ride and population of monkeys, lions, elephants, giraffes and exotic birds.

For a taste of sea air and salt spray, walk out along **Stearns Wharf** (foot of State Street). Favored by local anglers, the wharf is also noted for the **Sea Center** (805-962-0885; admission), a marine museum with an aquarium, underwater photographs and a 37-foot replica of a gray whale and calf.

If you tire of walking, remember that Stearns Wharf is the departure point for the **Santa Barbara Trolley** (805-962-0209), an old-fashioned vehicle that carries visitors along the waterfront, through the downtown area and out to the mission.

The **Moreton Bay Fig Tree** (Chapala and Moreton streets), another local landmark, is a century-old giant with branches that spread 160 feet. This magnificent specimen stands as the largest tree of its kind in the United States.

SANTA BARBARA AREA LODGING

To provide an idea of the full range of accommodations available in the Santa Barbara area, there are two centralized reservation agencies. **Accommodations in Santa Barbara** (3344 State Street; 805-687-9191) and **Santa Barbara Hotspots** (36 State Street; 805-564-1637) can give information on prices and availability.

The **Miramar Hotel-Resort** (1555 South Jameson Lane, Montecito; 805-969-2203) is billed as "the only hotel right on the beach" in the Santa Barbara area. Indeed, there is 500 feet of beautiful beachfront. It also is right on noisy Route 101. Not to worry—the Miramar, a 15-acre resort inhabited by blue-roofed cottages and tropical foliage, is still the best bargain around. Where else will you find dining facilities, two swimming pools, tennis courts, health spa and shuffleboard at moderate to deluxe prices?

The Old Yacht Club Inn (431 Corona del Mar Drive; 805-962-1277) is two inns in one. The main facility is a 1912 California Craftsman-style house with five rooms (all with private baths), priced moderate to deluxe. The decorative motif throughout brings back cheery memories of grandmother's house. Next door, in a 1927-vintage stucco, are four rooms with private baths tabbed deluxe. The inn is just one block from East Beach and serves a full breakfast.

The **Upham Hotel** (1404 De la Vina Street; 805-962-0058), established in 1871, shares a sense of history with local country inns, but enjoys the lobby and restaurant amenities of a hotel. Victorian in style, the two-story clapboard structure is marked by sweeping verandas and a cupola. Around the landscaped grounds are cottages, lawn chairs and a gazebo. The deluxe price includes continental breakfast and evening wine. There is also a Carriage House with five Victorian-style rooms at ultra-deluxe rates.

Santa Barbara's two finest hotels dominate the town's two geographic locales, the ocean and the mountains. **The Four Seasons Biltmore Hotel** (1260 Channel Drive; 805-969-2261) is a grand old Spanish-style hotel set on spacious grounds beside the beach. It's the kind of place where guests play croquet or practice putting on manicured lawns. There are several dining rooms as well as tennis courts, swimming pools and whirlpools. Many of the guest rooms are located in multiplex cottages and are spotted around the magnificent grounds that have made the 1920s-era Biltmore one of California's most famous hotels. Ultra-deluxe.

A favorite hideaway among Hollywood stars, **El Encanto** (1900 Lasuen Road; 805-687-5000) sits back in the Santa Barbara hills. The hotel's 83 rooms are set in cottages and villas that dot this ten-acre retreat. The grounds are beautifully landscaped and feature a lily pond, tennis court and swimming pool. The ocean views are simply spectacular. Rooms are very spacious; all have an attached sitting room, and many have private patios. Most are done in French country style, highlighted by brass and etched-glass fixtures. Ultra-deluxe.

In the Santa Ynez foothills sits another retreat where the rich and powerful mix with the merely talented. **San Ysidro Ranch** (900 San Ysidro Lane, Montecito; 805-969-5046) sprawls across 550 acres, most of it wilderness. There are tennis courts, pool, riding stables, a nearby hot spring and a gourmet restaurant. Privacy is the password: all these features are shared by guests occupying just 44 units, dotted around the property in cottages and small multiplexes. The price tag is ultra-deluxe.

SANTA BARBARA AREA RESTAURANTS

For a scent of Santa Barbara salt air with your lunch or dinner, **Brophy Brothers Restaurant & Clam Bar** (119 Harbor Way; 805-966-4418) is the spot. Located out on the Breakwater, overlooking the mountains and open sea, it features a small dining room and patio. If you love seafood, it's heaven. Moderate.

Best of Santa Barbara's budget restaurants is **La Tolteca** (614 East Haley Street; 805-963-0847). This tortilla factory contains an informal, self-order eatery serving delicious Mexican food. Almost everything is fresh, making it *the* place for tacos, burritos and enchiladas.

Santa Barbara natives have been eating at **Joe's Cafe** (536 State Street; 805-966-4638) for 60 years. Crowds line the coal-black bar, pile into the booths and fill the tables. They come for a moderately priced, meat-and-potatoes menu that stars prime rib, pork chops, lamb, rainbow trout and steak. The walls are loaded with mementos, faded photographs and softball trophies, and the noise level is the same as the Indy 500.

Downey's (1305 State Street; 805-966-5006), a small, understated dining room, numbers among Santa Barbara's premier restaurants. The food is renowned: specializing in California cuisine, Downey's has a menu that changes daily. A typical evening's entrées might include salmon with forest mushrooms, sea bass with artichokes and duck with wild rice. Deluxe to ultra-deluxe. Very highly recommended.

The graphics on the wall tell a story about the cuisine at **The Palace Cafe** (8 East Cota Street; 805-966-3133). Portrayed are jazz musicians, catfish and scenes from New Orleans. The message is Cajun and Creole, and this informal bistro is very good at delivering it. Serving dinner only, the moderate-to-deluxe-priced restaurant prepares soft-shelled crab, blackened filet mignon, crawfish and jambalaya.

If you prefer your bistros French, there's an excellent place a few doors up called **Mousse Odile** (18 East Cota Street; 805-962-5393). Plaid tablecloths and folk art create an easy lunch ambience here. For dinner, out come the white and pink linens. Menu selections include couscous, mushrooms on pastry shell and veal in basil cream. Moderate to deluxe.

If your mother is Italian, you'll know what to expect at **Mom's Italian Village** (421 East Cota Street; 805-965-5588). If not, you'll still feel at home. Mom has been cooking at this friendly local institution for more than 50 years, preparing the North Italian dishes that fill the lunch and dinner menus. Moderate.

El Encanto (1900 Lasuen Road; 805-687-5000) resides in a hillside resort overlooking Santa Barbara. There's a luxurious dining room and a terrace for dining outdoors. The French and California cuisine is a gourmet experience. Changing daily according to harvest and catch, the menu could include steamed filet of salmon with dijon mustard crême or a breast of Muscovy duck in a *daube* with red wine (French stew).

The **Stonehouse Restaurant** (900 San Ysidro Lane, Montecito; 805-969-5046), located at the legendary San Ysidro Ranch, serves lunch, dinner and Sunday brunch with a decidedly southern European flavor. Delicate seafood dishes such as lobster risotto share an ornate menu with heartier fare such as duck, beef and various smoked meats. Deluxe.

SANTA BARBARA AREA SHOPPING

Since Santa Barbara's shops are clustered together, you can easily uncover the town's hottest items and best bargains by concentrating on a few key areas. The prime shopping center lies along State Street, particularly between the 600 and 1300 blocks.

Piccadilly Square (813 State Street) is a warehouse-type mall with boutiques and artisans' shops galore.

El Paseo (814 State Street; 805-963-8741), a renowned promenade, consists of a historic adobe house and surrounding buildings combined into a succession of stores. The art galleries, jewelry stores and designer dress stores number among the best.

La Arcada Court (1114 State Street; 805-966-6634) is another spiffy mall done in Spanish style. The shops here and nearby along the upper lengths of State Street are more chic and contemporary than elsewhere.

On the lower end of State Street, **Pacific Travellers Supply** (529 State Street; 805-963-4438) carries a complete stock of guidebooks. They also have luggage and travel paraphernalia.

Antiques in Santa Barbara are spelled Brinkerhoff Avenue. This block-long residential street conceals a half-dozen antique shops including **Sally's Alley and Cobweb Corners** (502 Brinkerhoff Avenue; 805-966-9454), **Redwood Inn Antiques** (124 West Cota Street; 805-965-2175) and **Carl Hightower Galerie** (528 Brinkerhoff Avenue; 805-965-5687).

For over 20 years Santa Barbara County artists and craftspeople have turned out for the **Arts & Crafts Show**. Every Sunday and holiday from 10 a.m. until dusk they line East Cabrillo Boulevard. The original artwork for sale includes paintings, graphics, sculptures and drawings. Among the crafts are macrame, stained glass, woodwork and jewelry.

SANTA BARBARA AREA NIGHTLIFE

The Palms (701 Linden Avenue, Carpinteria; 805-684-3811) features local rock and country-and-western bands every Thursday, Friday and Saturday night. There's a small dancefloor here for footloose revelers.

The State Street strip in downtown Santa Barbara offers several party places. Up at **Acapulco Restaurant** (1114 State Street; 805-963-3469) you can sip a margarita next to an antique wooden bar or out on the patio. No entertainment, but it's a pretty place to drink.

THE COAST BY TRAIN

America's railroads are associated more with interior valleys and broad plains than open ocean. But two trains, the "San Diegan" from San Diego to Los Angeles and the "Coast Starlight," which continues through California en route to Seattle, parallel the coast, passing areas inaccessible by automobile. With their dining cars, sleeping compartments and observation cars, they are a flash from the American past, part of Amtrak's (800-872-7245) 24,000 miles of track, final vestige of the nation's once-proud rail system.

In the course of its three-hour route, the "San Diegan" travels for an hour along the shore, taking in the sights from Del Mar to Dana Point. It rumbles past Los Peñasquitos Marsh Natural Preserve, a nesting place for migratory birds, then rims a series of lofty sea cliffs, which fall away to reveal narrow bands of sandy beach. Along the way lies one of the nation's major centers for cut flowers and ornamental plants. Eventually the "San Diegan" turns inland to the old mission town of San Juan Capistrano and cuts through the heart of Orange County.

Picking up the baton in Los Angeles, the "Coast Starlight" continues north and west to the Pacific, shuttling past stretches of open water populated with surfers and occasional fishermen. Here the tracks hone a fine line along sharp rockfaces. Farm houses flit by on one side, while looming offshore are oil rigs and the Channel Islands.

The mission towns of Ventura and Santa Barbara are stations on the itinerary. Then the train crosses high trestles and climbs above the shore toward Point Conception. This is California's geographic turning point, where the coast veers sharply right and the beaches, which earlier pointed south, turn to face the west.

Grand finale to the coast portion of the journey are the Nipomo Dunes— massive, wind-shaved sand hills that shadow the shore for over 20 miles. At Pismo Beach, known for the beds of Pismo clams within its sands, the "Coast Starlight" turns inland, trading the wide Pacific for California's broad, fertile Central Valley.

If you are ready to make this trip in deluxe style, Princess Railtours (800-835-8907) conducts five-star tours aboard the "California Sun Express." Sealed off from the rest of the "Coast Starlight," these plush dome cars offer stylish service and gourmet cuisine. En route, guests stay overnight at a hotel in Morro Bay and tour Hearst Castle.

If for no other reason than the view, **Harbor Restaurant** (210 Stearns Wharf; 805-963-3311) is a prime place for the evening. A plate-glass establishment, it sits out on a pier with the city skyline on one side and open ocean on the other. The bar upstairs features surf videos.

For sunset views, nothing quite compares to **El Encanto Lounge** (1900 Lasuen Road; 805-687-5000). Located in a posh hotel high in the Santa Barbara hills, it features a split-level terrace overlooking the city and ocean. In the early evening there's a piano bar, then later on a three-piece combo strikes up.

Also consider the **Lobero Theatre** (33 East Cañon Perdido Street; 805-963-0761), which presents a full schedule of dance, drama, concerts and lectures.

SANTA BARBARA AREA BEACHES AND PARKS

Carpinteria State Beach (805-684-2811) is a ribbon-shaped park extending for nearly a mile along the coast. Nicknamed "the world's safest beach," it provides exceptionally good swimming. Also favored by tidepoolers and snorkelers, the park encompasses a lagoon and breakwater reef. Located at the end of Palm Avenue in Carpinteria.

Everyone's favorite Santa Barbara beach, **East Beach** stretches more than a mile from Montecito to Stearns Wharf. In addition to a fluffy-sand corridor there are grassy areas, palm trees and a full-facility bathhouse (805-965-0509). Beyond Stearns Wharf the strand continues as **West Beach**.

Arroyo Burro County Park (805-687-3714), a six-acre facility, is a little gem. The sandy beach and surrounding hills are packed with locals on summer days. If you can arrive at an uncrowded time, you'll find beautiful scenery along this lengthy strand. Located at 2981 Cliff Drive in Santa Barbara.

Another of Southern California's sparkling beaches, **El Capitan State Beach** (805-968-1033) stretches along three miles of ocean front. The park is 168 acres and features a nature trail, tidepools and wonderful opportunities for hiking along the beach. Seals and sea lions often romp offshore, and in winter gray whales cruise by. Camping. Located in Goleta off Route 101 about 20 miles north of Santa Barbara.

Refugio State Beach (805-968-1033) is a 39-acre park with over a mile of ocean frontage. You can bask on a sandy beach, lie under palm trees on the greensward and hike or bicycle along the two-and-a-half-mile path that connects this park with El Capitan. There are also interesting tidepools. Located on Refugio Road in Goleta, off Route 101 about 23 miles north of Santa Barbara.

The mammoth **Gaviota State Park** (805-968-1033), a 2776-acre facility, stretches along both sides of Route 101. The beach rests in a

sandy cove guarded on either side by dramatic sedimentary rock formations. On the inland side a hiking trail leads up to **Gaviota Hot
Springs** and into Los Padres National Forest. Camping. The beach is
located off Route 101 about 33 miles north of Santa Barbara.

The remote **Jalama Beach County Park** (805-736-6316), a
broad sandy beach fringed by coastal bluffs and undulating hills, sits at
the far end of a country road. Jalama Creek cuts through the park,
creating a wetland frequented by the endangered California brown
pelican. A good area for beachcombing as well as rock-hounding for
chert, agate, travertine and fossils. Camping. From Lompoc take
Route 1 south for five miles; turn onto Jalama Road and follow it 15
miles to the end.

One of the most secluded and beautiful beaches along the entire
Central Coast is **Point Sal State Beach** (805-733-3713). Here a long
crescent strand curves out toward Point Sal, a bold headland with a
rock island offshore. The Casmalia Hills rise sharply from the ocean,
creating a natural amphitheater. Sea birds roost nearby, and the beach
is a habitat for harbor seals. From Route 1 three miles south of Guadalupe turn west on Brown Road, then pick up Point Sal Road. Together these roads, unpaved in places and impassable during wet
weather, twist for nine miles to a blufftop overlook. Steep paths lead to
the beach. No facilities.

Santa Ynez Valley

Thirty miles from Santa Barbara the mountains open onto the Santa
Ynez Valley. Here a string of sleepy towns creates a Western-style
counterpoint to California's chic coastline. **Santa Ynez** is a falsefront
town complete with a white-steeple church that dates to 1897. Downtown **Ballard** is one block long; the town was settled in 1880 and
features the **Ballard School** (2425 School Street), a little red school-
house that was constructed a few years later. Nearby **Los Olivos** is
home to **Mattei's Tavern** (Route 154; 805-688-4820). This former
stagecoach inn, constructed in 1886, is a fine old woodframe building
with a trellised porch.

The valley's other town, the most famous of all, does not resemble
any of the others. It doesn't really resemble anything in California.
Solvang is a town that looks like it was designed by Walt Disney. The
place is a Danish village complete with cobblestone walks, gaslights
and stained-glass windows. Steep-pitched roofs with high dormers
create an Old World atmosphere here. Stores and homes reveal the
tall, narrow architecture of Scandinavia, and windmills dominate the
view. What saves the place from being a theme park is that Solvang
actually is a Danish town. Emigrants from Denmark established a village and school here in 1911.

For visitors, wandering around town means catching a ride on a horse-drawn **Danish streetcar,** then popping into a **Scandinavian bakery** for hot pretzels or *aebleskiver*, a tasty Danish pastry.

To further confuse things, the centerpiece of Solvang in no way fits the architecture of the town. **Mission Santa Ines** (Mission Street) does, however, meet the building style of the rest of California. Founded in 1804, the mission church follows the long, narrow rectangular shape traditional in Spanish California. The altar is painted brilliant colors, and the colonnaded courtyard is ablaze with flowers. A small museum displays 18th-century bibles and song books, and one chapel contains a 17th-century statue of polychromed wood.

Northwest of Solvang, Route 1 approaches a similar facility, **La Purisima Mission** (2295 Purisima Road, Lompoc; 805-733-3713). The best-restored of all 21 California missions, this historic site has an eerie way of projecting you back to Spanish days. There's the mayordomo's abode with the table set and a pan on the oven, or the mission store, its barrels overflowing with corn and beans. The entire mission complex, from the sanctified church to the tallow vats where slaughtered cattle were rendered into soap, is re-created. Founded nearby in 1787, the mission was re-established at this site in 1813. Today you can tour the entire complex.

In spring and summer the hills around **Lompoc** dazzle with thousands of acres of flowers. The countryside is a rainbow of color throughout the season. Then in fall fields of poppies, nasturtiums and larkspurs bloom.

SANTA YNEZ VALLEY WINERIES

The Santa Ynez Valley is a prime winegrowing region with several dozen wineries scattered around the valley on picturesque back roads. The **Santa Ynez Valley Winery** *(343 North Refugio Road, Santa Ynez; 805-688-8381), housed in an old dairy building, is a 110-acre spread growing sauvignon blanc, chardonnay, gewürztraminer and other grapes.*

For a long country ride, travel out Zaca Station and Foxen Canyon roads in Los Olivos. A string of wineries begins with the most elegant. **Firestone Vineyard** *(5017 Zaca Station Road; 805-688-3940) is set in stone-trimmed buildings and features a courtyard with fountain and picnic tables. The largest winery in the valley, it offers several estate-grown varietal wines.*

Zaca Mesa Winery *(6905 Foxen Canyon Road; 805-688-3310) sits about nine miles from Route 101. Set in a modern woodframe building with an attractive tasting room, it's a beautiful winery with vineyards lining Foxen Canyon Road. Other wineries lie farther along the road and elsewhere throughout the valley.*

SANTA YNEZ VALLEY RESTAURANTS

A vestige of the Old West, **Cold Spring Tavern** (5995 Stagecoach Road off Route 154; 805-967-0066) is a former stagecoach stop dating back to the 19th century. The floors tilt, the bar is wood plank, and the walls are stained with a century of use; a cow head with antlers decorates the stone fireplace. Dinner in this roughhewn time capsule features marinated rabbit, Black Angus steak and swordfish. The evening special might be elk or buffalo. Make a point of stopping by. Deluxe-priced.

Another stagecoach-stop-turned-restaurant, **Mattei's Tavern** (Route 154, Los Olivos; 805-688-4820) is a mammoth old building that served as an inn back in the 1880s. Today it's a multiroom complex where you can dine in a rustically decorated room or out on the patio. They serve dinner only, a deluxe-priced meal featuring steaks, prime rib and fresh seafood dishes.

The Danish Inn (1547 Mission Drive, Solvang; 805-688-4813) is an appealing white-tablecloth dining room serving traditional Danish dishes such as stuffed cabbage leaves, steak with sautéed onions, smorgasbord and other specialties. Moderate to deluxe.

SANTA YNEZ VALLEY SHOPPING

Solvang is a choice spot to shop for imported products from northern Europe. Walk the cobbled streets and you'll encounter everything from cuckoo clocks to lace curtains. Many of the shops line **Copenhagen Drive**.

There are Danish handknit sweaters, music boxes, tiles and pewter items. The toy stores are designed to resemble doll houses, and shops throughout town feature the tile roofs and high gables of Scandinavian stores.

In the nearby town of **Los Olivos** several art galleries and antique shops will help round out your shopping spree.

ALISAL GUEST RANCH

*Tucked between the Santa Ynez and San Rafael mountains lies **Alisal Guest Ranch** (1054 Alisal Road, Solvang; 805-688-6411), a 10,000-acre working cattle ranch. Part of the ranch is an exclusive resort featuring 69 units, a golf course, swimming pool, spa, tennis courts and dining room. Guests ride horseback through the property and fish and sail on a mile-long lake. Square dances, hay rides and summer barbeque dinners add to the entertainment. Breakfast and dinner are included in the ultra-deluxe rate.*

SANTA YNEZ VALLEY NIGHTLIFE

Carousing at **Cold Spring Tavern** (5995 Stagecoach Road, off Route 154; 805-967-0066), a log cabin set high in the mountains outside Santa Barbara, is like being in an old Western movie. Every Friday through Sunday you can pull up a stool and listen to the rock, country-and-western and rhythm-and-blues bands that ride through.

AJ Spurs (350 Route 246, Buellton; 805-688-0889) hosts live bands every Thursday through Saturday night.

San Luis Obispo Area

San Luis Obispo, a pretty jewel of a town, lies 12 miles from the ocean in the center of an expansive agricultural region. Backdropped by the Santa Lucia Mountains, the town focuses around an old Spanish mission. Cowboys from outlying ranches and students from the nearby campus add to the cultural mix, creating a vital atmosphere that has energized San Luis Obispo's rapid growth.

For a sense of the region's roots, pick up information at the **San Luis Obispo Chamber of Commerce** (1039 Chorro Street; 805-543-1323). A self-guided tour of this historic town logically begins at **Mission San Luis de Tolosa** (Chorro and Monterey streets; 805-543-6850). Dating to 1772, the old Spanish outpost has been nicely reconstructed. There's a museum re-creating the Native American, Spanish and Mexican eras as well as a pretty church.

The **County Historical Museum** (696 Monterey Street; 805-543-0638) continues the historic overview with displays from the pre-Hispanic, Spanish and American periods. Across the street at the **San Luis Obispo Art Center** (1010 Broad Street; 805-543-8562) are exhibits of works by local artists.

St. Stephen's Episcopal Church (Nipomo and Pismo streets) is a narrow, lofty and strikingly attractive chapel. Built in 1867, it was one of California's first Episcopal churches. The **Dallidet Adobe** (Toro Street between Pismo and Pacific streets), constructed by a French vintner in 1853, is another local architectural landmark.

The **Ah Louis Store** (800 Palm Street) symbolizes the Chinese presence here. A sturdy brick building with wrought-iron shutters and balcony, it dates to 1874 and once served the 2000 Chinese coolies who worked on nearby railroad tunnels.

Those with young ones in tow can stop by the **San Luis Obispo Children's Museum** (1010 Nipomo Street; 805-544-5437; admission). In this imaginative environment kids can race to a fire engine, view themselves on television, visit a space shuttle and planetarium, learn the principles of photography and discover a Chumash Indian cave.

As Route 1 angles north and west from San Luis Obispo toward the ocean, the landscape is transfigured by a procession of nine volcanic peaks. Last in this geologic parade is a 576-foot plug dome called **Morro Rock**. The pride of Morro Bay, it stands like a little Gibraltar, connected to the mainland by a sand isthmus.

Years ago, before conservationists and common sense prevailed, Morro Rock was a quarry. Today it's a nesting area for peregrine falcons. In fact, this entire region serves as a bird sanctuary. Extending for miles out toward Morro Rock is a dramatic **sandspit**, a teeming region of sand dunes and sea life. From town there's a funky **sandspit shuttle** (699 Embarcadero; 805-772-8085) to boat you across to the dunes. For something more formal, **Tiger's Folly** (1205 Embarcadero; 805-772-2257) sponsors cruises of the harbor in an old-fashioned paddlewheeler.

Several miles southwest of San Luis Obispo lies Pismo Beach. An unattractive congeries of mobile homes and beach rental stands, this nondescript town has a single saving grace—its dunes. They are sand castles in the air, curving, rolling, ever-changing hills of sand. Wave after wave of them parallel the beach, like a crystalline continuation of the ocean.

In fact they comprise the most extensive coastal dunes in California. From Pismo Beach the sand hills run six miles south where they meet the 450-foot-high **Guadalupe dunes**, forming a unique habitat for wildflowers and shorebirds.

Stop by the **Pismo Beach Chamber of Commerce** (581 Dolliver Street, Pismo Beach; 805-773-2055) for brochures and maps of the San Luis Bay region. Of the three seaside communities lining this harbor—Pismo Beach, Shell Beach and Avila Beach—the prettiest of all is **Avila Beach**. Here you can comb a white-sand beach or walk out along three fishing piers. At the far end of town a dramatic headland curves out from the shoreline, creating a crescent-shaped harbor where sailboats bob at their moorings.

SAN LUIS OBISPO AREA LODGING

Why stop at just anyplace when you can spend the night dreaming in a historic building? The **Motel Inn** (2223 Monterey Street; 805-543-4000) is the world's first motel. It's a Spanish-style complex of stucco and red tile that dates back to 1925 when the architect, played with the idea of a "motor hotel," coined the term "motel." Budget.

For deluxe accommodations at reasonable rates, check in to **The Inn at Morro Bay** (19 Country Club Road, Morro Bay; 805-772-5651). Fashionable but casual, this waterfront complex has the amenities of a small resort: restaurant, lounge, swimming pool and an adjacent golf course. It sits on ten acres overlooking Morro Bay and contains 96 guest rooms. Moderate to deluxe.

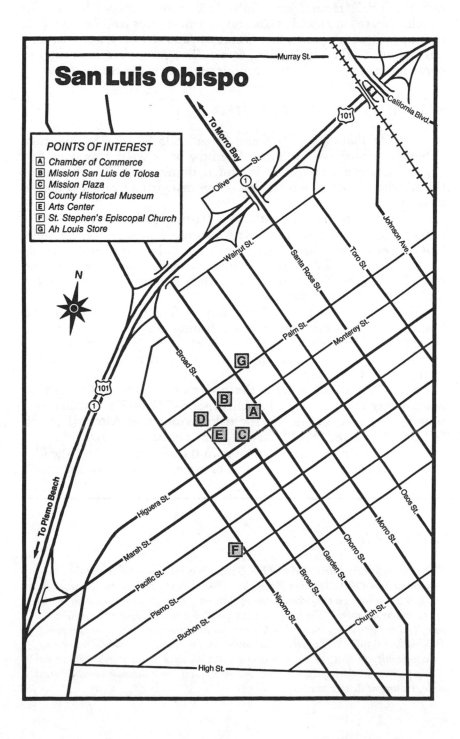

San Luis Obispo

POINTS OF INTEREST
- A Chamber of Commerce
- B Mission San Luis de Tolosa
- C Mission Plaza
- D County Historical Museum
- E Arts Center
- F St. Stephen's Episcopal Church
- G Ah Louis Store

N

To Morro Bay

To Pismo Beach

Murray St.

California Blvd.

101

Olive St.

Johnson Ave.

Walnut St.

Santa Rosa St.

Toro St.

Palm St.

Monterey St.

Broad St.

Higuera St.

Marsh St.

Pacific St.

Pismo St.

Buchon St.

Nipomo St.

Broad St.

Garden St.

Chorro St.

Morro St.

Osos St.

Church St.

High St.

Sycamore Mineral Springs Resort (1215 Avila Beach Drive; 805-595-7302) reposes on a hillside one mile inland from Avila Beach. Situated in a stand of oak and sycamore trees are 27 motel-style rooms, each with a private spa. There are also redwood hot tubs scattered about in the surrounding forest. The rooms are decorated in contemporary style and rent for moderate to deluxe prices.

SAN LUIS OBISPO AREA RESTAURANTS

At **Tortilla Flats** (1051 Nipomo Street; 805-544-7575) they have fashioned an attractive restaurant from the brick walls, bare ducts and exposed rafters of an old dairy. It's lunch, dinner and Sunday brunch at this Mexican eatery where the bar serves margaritas by the pitcherful; moderate.

Italy enters the picture with **Cafe Roma** (1819 Osos Street; 805-541-6800), a delightful restaurant decorated in country-inn style. Copper pots as well as portraits from the old country decorate the walls. Lunch and dinner include Italian sausage, steak *fiorentina* and several daily specials. Run by an Italian family, it serves excellent food; highly recommended; moderate.

You needn't cast far in Morro Bay to find a seafood restaurant. Sometimes they seem as frequent as fishing boats. One of the most venerable is **Dorn's Original Breakers Cafe** (801 Market Street; 805-772-4415), a bright, airy place with a postcard view of the waterfront. Moderate to deluxe.

Fine California cuisine is the order of the day at **The Inn at Morro Bay** (19 Country Club Drive; 805-772-5651). Situated in a waterfront resort, the dining room looks out over Morro Bay and features an enticing list of local and French entrées. Deluxe.

If you missed the swinging doors in the saloon you'll get the idea from the moose head trophies and branding irons. **F. McLintock's**

THE MADONNA INN

The most outlandish place in San Luis Obispo is a roadside confection called the **Madonna Inn** *(100 Madonna Road; 805-543-3000). Architecturally it's a cross between a castle and a gingerbread house; culturally it's somewhere between light opera and heavy metal. The lampposts are painted pink, the lounge looks like a cave, and the gift shop contains the biggest, gaudiest chandeliers you've ever seen. Personally, I wouldn't be caught dead staying in the place, but I would never miss an opportunity to visit. Where else does a waterfall serve as the men's room urinal? If you prove more daring than I, there are 109 rooms, each decorated in a different style, renting at deluxe prices.*

Saloon & Dining House (750 Mattie Road, Shell Beach; 805-773-1892) is the place where on Sunday you can get an 18-ounce steak for breakfast. Every evening, when the oak pit barbecue really gets going, there are a dozen kinds of steak as well as Cornish game hen and rainbow trout. So dust off that Stetson and prepare to chow down. Moderate to deluxe.

SAN LUIS OBISPO AREA SHOPPING

In this old Spanish town the best stores are located on the streets surrounding Mission Plaza. Stroll the two blocks along Monterey Street between Osos and Chorro streets, then browse the five-block stretch on Higuera Street from Osos Street to Nipomo Street.

The **Natural Selection** (1111 Morro Street; 805-541-6755) is a unique shop dedicated to nature and science. If you've been searching everywhere for that moon map, rain gauge or *Tyrannosaurus rex* T-shirt, look no further.

The **Network Mall** (778 Higuera Street) is a collection of crafts shops and small stores. Also consider **The Creamery** (Higuera and Nipomo streets; 805-543-1011), an old dairy plant converted into an ingenious arcade.

SAN LUIS OBISPO AREA NIGHTLIFE

The Rose and Crown (1000 Higuera Street; 805-541-1911) is an English pub complete with dart boards and 30 tap beers. The sound is an eclectic blend of live bands playing rock, jazz and rhythm-and-blues. From Thursday through Saturday it's a good place to dance and drink. Cover.

There's a posh piano bar at **The Inn at Morro Bay** (19 Country Club Drive, Morro Bay; 805-772-5651). Appointed with bentwood furniture and pastel paneling, it's a beautiful bar. The most striking feature of all is the view, which extends out across the water to Morro Rock.

SAN LUIS OBISPO AREA BEACHES AND PARKS

Saudi Arabia has nothing on **Guadalupe Dunes Beach** (805-343-2354). The sand dunes throughout this area are little short of spectacular, especially 450-foot Mussel Rock, the highest dune on the West Coast. These mountains of sand provide a habitat for California brown pelicans, California least terns and other endangered birds and plants. The Santa Maria River, which empties here, forms a pretty wetland area. From Route 1 in Guadalupe, follow Main Street west for five miles to the beach.

Pismo State Beach (805-489-2684), a magnificent strand, runs for six miles from Pismo Beach south to the Santa Maria River. Along its ocean front are some of the finest sand dunes in California, fluffy hills inhabited by shorebirds and tenacious plants. Also home to the pismo clam, it's a wonderful place to hike and explore. Camping. The park parallels Route 1 in Pismo Beach.

The 7000-acre **Montaña de Oro State Park** (805-528-0513), one of the finest parks on the entire Central Coast, stretches over a mile along the shore, past a sandspit, tidepools and sharp cliffs. There are remote coves for viewing seals, sea otters and migrating whales and for sunbathing on hidden beaches. Monarch butterflies roost in the eucalyptus-filled canyons, and a hiking trail leads to Valencia Peak, with views scanning almost 100 miles of coastline. Camping. Located on Pecho Valley Road about ten miles south of Morro Bay.

Situated amid one of the biggest marshlands along the California coast, 2435-acre **Morro Bay State Park** (805-528-0513) is like an outdoor museum. The tidal basin attracts over 250 species of sea, land and shore birds. There's a marina where you can rent boats to explore the salt marsh and nearby sandspit and a natural history museum with environmental displays. Camping. Located on Country Club Drive in Morro Bay.

Cambria

About 20 miles north of Morro Bay lies the seaside town of Cambria. Originally settled in the 1860s, Cambria later expanded into a major seaport and whaling center. As the railroad replaced coastal shipping, the town declined, only to be resurrected during the past few decades as an artist colony and tourist center.

It's a pretty place, with ridgetop homes, sandy beaches and rocky coves. But like many of California's small creative communities, Cambria has begun peering too long in the mirror. The architecture along Main Street has assumed a cutesy mock-Tudor look, and the place is taking on an air of unreality.

Still, there are many fine artists and several exceptional galleries here. It's also a choice place to shop and seek out gourmet food. There's even a **Cambria Chamber of Commerce** (767 Main Street; 805-927-3624).

To start your Cambria tour, head up to **Nit Wit Ridge** (Hillcrest Drive just above Cornwall Street). That hodgepodge house on the left, the one decorated with every type of bric-a-brac, is the home of Art Beal, a.k.a. Captain Nit Wit. He has been working on this folk-art estate, listed in the National Register of Historic Landmarks, since 1928.

Then take a ride along **Moonstone Beach Drive**, a lovely ocean-front corridor with vista points and tidepools.

CAMBRIA LODGING

The Olallieberry Inn (2476 Main Street; 805-927-3222), set in an 1870s-era Greek Revival house, contains six bedrooms, done in Early American style with period antiques. The sitting room is attractively furnished with wickerware, and each guest room enjoys a private bath. Moderate to deluxe.

If you would prefer to rusticate in a historic 1920s hotel, head up to **Cambria Pines Lodge** (2905 Burton Drive; 805-927-4200). Set amid a stand of Monterey pines, it's a rambling split-rail lodge with cottages dotted about the property. The main building offers a spacious lobby with stone fireplace plus a restaurant and lounge; other amenities include a swimming pool and jacuzzi. Cottages and rooms in the lodge are priced moderate to deluxe.

CAMBRIA RESTAURANTS

For fine California cuisine try **Ian's Restaurant** (2150 Center Street; 805-927-8649). The decor is contemporary, and the menu draws upon local fresh produce, herbs and seafood. Among the specialties are duck, rabbit, abalone and lamb. Serving dinner and Sunday brunch; deluxe.

THE HOUSE THAT HEARST BUILT

*Along the coast north of Cambria, rising from the mountains like a citadel, is the world-renowned **Hearst Castle** (Route 1, San Simeon; 805-927-2000; admission). Built by newspaper magnate William Randolph Hearst and designed by architect Julia Morgan, the Hearst San Simeon State Historical Monument includes a main house that sports 37 bedrooms, three guest houses and part of the old Hearst ranch, which once stretched 40 miles along the coast.*

An insatiable art collector, Hearst filled every building with priceless masterpieces. La Casa Grande, the main house, is fronted by two cathedral towers and filled with Renaissance art. To see it is overwhelming. There is no place for the eye to rest. The main sitting room is covered everywhere with tapestries, bas-relief works, 16th-century paintings and Roman columns. The walls are fashioned from 500-year-old choir pews, and the French fireplace dates back 400 years; there are hand-carved tables, silver candelabra and antique statuary.

Hearst Castle is so vast that four different two-hour tours are scheduled daily to various parts of the property. Since over one million people a year visit, the guided tours are often booked solid. I recommend that you reserve in advance and plan on taking Tour 1, which covers the ground floor of La Casa Grande, a guest house, the pools and the gardens. Reservations are made through MISTIX; in California call 800-444-7275; outside the state, 619-452-1950.

Ethnic and vegetarian food lovers will fare well at **Robin's** (4095 Burton Drive; 805-927-5007). Set in a 1930s Mexican-style house, it serves homemade lunches and dinners. Selections range from burritos to sweet-and-sour prawns to stir-fried tofu. It's an eclectic blend with the accent on Italian and Asian cuisine. Budget to moderate.

CAMBRIA SHOPPING

This important arts-and-crafts center offers numerous galleries, antique stores and specialty shops.

Among the foremost galleries is **Seekers Collection & Gallery** (4090 Burton Drive; 805-927-4352), a glass menagerie inhabited by crystal sculpture, stained-glass windows and handblown jewelry.

The Soldier Factory (789 Main Street; 805-927-3804) is a journey back to childhood. Part toy store and part museum, it serves as headquarters for thousands of hand-painted toy soldiers.

For a journey into another world, visit **Victoriana** (Arlington Street near Main Street; 805-927-3833), a diminutive store that sells miniatures of Victorian house furnishings.

CAMBRIA NIGHTLIFE

Camozzi's Saloon (2262 Main Street; 805-927-8941) is a century-old cowboy watering hole with longhorns over the bar, wagon wheels on the wall and a floor that leans worse than a midnight drunk. The place is famous. Besides that, it has a rock band every Friday and Saturday.

Big Sur

Extending south from the Monterey Peninsula for 90 miles and back-dropped by the steep Santa Lucia Mountains, Big Sur is one of the nation's most magnificent natural areas. Only 1500 residents live in this rugged region of bald crags and flower-choked canyons. None but the most adventurous occupy the nearby Ventana Wilderness, which represents the southernmost realm of the coastal redwoods.

Route 1, one of America's great stretches of roadway, courses through this stunning area. Each turnout en route provides a glimpse into a magic-lantern world. Here the glass pictures a beach crusted with rocks, there a wave-wracked cliff or pocket of tidepools. The canyons are narrow and precipitous, while the headlands are so close to the surf they seem like beached whales. Trees are broken and blasted before the wind. The houses, though millionaire affairs, appear inconsequential against the backdrop of ocean and stone.

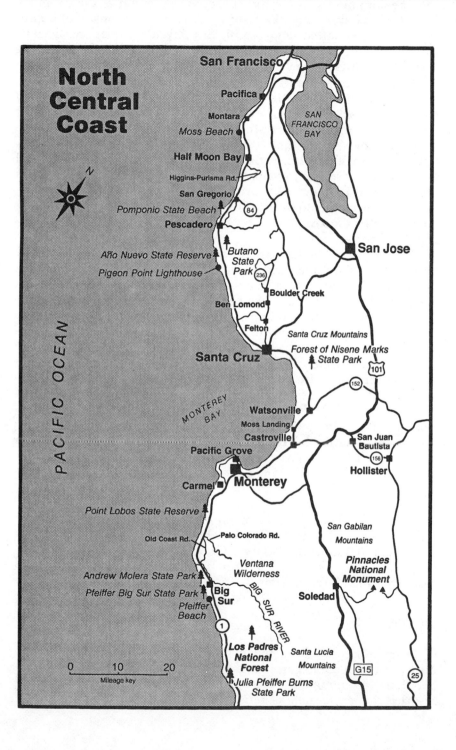

North Central Coast

San Francisco

Pacifica

Montara

Moss Beach

Half Moon Bay

Higgins-Purisma Rd.

San Gregorio

Pomponio State Beach

Pescadero

Año Nuevo State Reserve

Pigeon Point Lighthouse

Butano State Park

Boulder Creek

Ben Lomond

Felton

Santa Cruz

Santa Cruz Mountains

Forest of Nisene Marks State Park

Watsonville

Moss Landing

Castroville

Pacific Grove

Carmel

Monterey

Point Lobos State Reserve

Old Coast Rd.

Palo Colorado Rd.

Ventana Wilderness

Andrew Molera State Park

Pfeiffer Big Sur State Park

Big Sur

Pfeiffer Beach

Los Padres National Forest

Julia Pfeiffer Burns State Park

Santa Lucia Mountains

BIG SUR RIVER

San Juan Bautista

Hollister

San Gabilan Mountains

Pinnacles National Monument

Soledad

San Jose

SAN FRANCISCO BAY

PACIFIC OCEAN

MONTEREY BAY

0   10   20
Mileage key

The community of Big Sur stretches the length of the six-mile-long Big Sur River Valley. Lacking a town center, it consists of houses and a few stores dotted along the Big Sur River. The place received its name from early Spanish settlers, who called the wilderness south of Carmel *El País Grande del Sur*, "the big country to the south."

Later it became a rural retreat and artists' colony. Henry Miller lived here from 1947 until 1964, writing *Big Sur and the Oranges of Hieronymus Bosch*, *Plexus* and *Nexus* during his residence. There's not much to the **Henry Miller Memorial Library** (Route 1 about one mile south of Ventana Inn; 408-667-2574), but somehow the unassuming nature of the place befits its candid subject. Occupying a small woodframe house, the museum contains volumes from the novelist's library as well as his evocative artworks.

For information on the Big Sur area, you can write to the **Big Sur Chamber of Commerce** (Box 87, Big Sur, CA 93920; 408-667-2100) before you set out.

For an incredible side trip, follow **Old Coast Road** for about 11 miles up into the Santa Lucia Mountains. There are hawk's-eye vistas of the Pacific, the rolling Big Sur countryside and Pico Blanco, a 3709-foot lime-rich peak. Take heed, however: the road is curvy, unpaved, narrow, rutted and impassable in wet weather. But oh, those views! Old Coast Road begins at Andrew Molera State Park and rejoins Route 1 at Bixby Bridge.

If instead of detouring you stay on Route 1, it will pass a lengthy beach leading to **Point Sur Light Station**. Set on a volcanic headland, this solitary sentinel dates back to 1889. Then the road climbs along **Hurricane Point**, a promontory blessed with sweeping views and cursed by lashing winds.

Route 1 traverses **Bixby Creek Bridge**, which stretches from one cliff to another across an infernal chasm. Local legend cites it incorrectly as the world's longest concrete arch span. With fluted hills in the background and a fluffy beach below, it may, however, be the world's prettiest.

For an intriguing excursion into those hills, head about three miles up **Palo Colorado Road**, which intersects with Route 1 a couple of miles south of Garrapata Creek. Though paved, this country road is one lane. The corridor tunnels through an arcade of redwoods past log cabins and rustic homes.

BIG SUR LODGING

If you're seeking to fall completely beneath the spell of Big Sur, the only roosting place to consider is **Ventana** (Route 1; 408-667-2331). Set along 143 mountainside acres overlooking the Pacific, this fabled resort is the *ne plus ultra* of refined rusticity. Buildings are fashioned from raw wood, and most guest rooms are equipped with tile or marble fireplaces. With Japanese hot baths, saunas, two pools and a clothing-optional sun deck, the place exudes an air of languor. Ultra-deluxe.

Located within Pfeiffer Big Sur State Park is **Big Sur Lodge** (Route 1; 408-667-2171), a complex containing 61 cottages, a pool, saunas and restaurant. The cottages are simple frame houses with pine interiors; they rent upwards from the moderate range in winter and the deluxe range in summer.

BIG SUR RESTAURANTS

Perched on a cliff overlooking the Pacific, **Nepenthe** (Route 1, Big Sur; 408-667-2345) is without doubt Big Sur's most renowned restaurant. It's a gathering place for locals, tourists and everyone in between. Surprisingly, the menu is moderately priced. The entrées include fresh fish, broiled chicken, steak and other dishes. If you're not hungry, stop in for a drink—the place is a must.

Ventana Restaurant (Route 1; 408-667-2331), Big Sur's most elegant dining place, rests on a hillside overlooking the mountains and sea. Here you'll enjoy dinner in the wood-paneled dining room or lunch inside or alfresco along a sweeping veranda. You can start with oysters on the half shell or steamed artichoke, then proceed to such entrées as roast duckling, rack of lamb, scallops, or fresh fish grilled over oak. Deluxe to ultra-deluxe.

For a gourmet dinner at a moderate-to-deluxe price, **Glen Oaks Restaurant** (Route 1; 408-667-2623) is the prime location. Bentwood chairs, linen tablecloths and candlelight create an intimate atmosphere at this small establishment. The cuisine ranges from pasta to Chinese-style vegetables to mushroom stroganoff, steak and a host of seafood dishes.

BIG SUR SHOPPING

Set in a circular wooden structure resembling an oversized wine cask is one of Big Sur's best known art centers. The **Coast Gallery** (Route 1; 408-667-2301) is justifiably famous for its displays of arts and crafts by local artists. There are lithographs by novelist Henry Miller as well as paintings, sculptures, woodwork and blown glass by Northern California craftspeople.

BIG SUR NIGHTLIFE

In Big Sur the lights go out early. There is one place, **River Inn** (Route 1; 408-667-2700), that has a wood-paneled bar overlooking the Big Sur River and keeps a candle burning. During the week the bar is open until the wee hours; on weekends musicians range from Dixieland bands to string quartets. Or you can relax over a glass of California wine at **Ventana Restaurant** (Route 1; 408-667-2331).

BIG SUR BEACHES AND PARKS

Julia Pfeiffer Burns State Park (408-667-2315), an 1800-acre extravaganza, extends from the ocean to 1500 feet elevation. The central park area sits in a natural amphitheater backdropped by sharp hills. Paths lead to a spectacular vista point where a waterfall plunges into the ocean and to an isolated beach and underwater park. Camping. Located on Route 1 about 11 miles south of Pfeiffer Big Sur State Park.

Pfeiffer Beach, a sandy strand littered with boulders and bisected by a meandering stream, is one of Big Sur's many wonders. Just offshore loom rock formations into which the sea has carved tunnels and arches. Little wonder poet Robinson Jeffers chose this haunting spot as a setting for his primal poem "Give Your Heart to the Hawks." To get there follow Route 1 for about a mile south past the entrance to Pfeiffer Big Sur State Park. Turn right onto Sycamore Canyon Road, which leads downhill two miles to the beach.

One of California's southernmost redwood parks, **Pfeiffer Big Sur State Park** (408-667-2315) is an 821-acre facility complete with cottages, restaurant and a grocery. Nature still retains a toehold in these parts: the Big Sur River overflows with trout and salmon, Pfeiffer Falls tumbles through a fern-banked canyon, and the park serves as the major trailhead leading to Ventana Wilderness. Camping. Located along Route 1 in Big Sur.

An adventurer's hideaway, **Andrew Molera State Park** (408-667-2315) is a 4800-acre preserve rising from sea level to over 3000 feet and featuring three miles of beach and over 16 miles of hiking trails. The Big Sur River tumbles through the landscape, and the wildlife includes mule deer, bobcat, harbor seals, sea lions and gray whales. The only thing missing is a road: this is a hiker's oasis, its natural areas accessible only by heel and toe. Camping. The park is located along Route 1 about three miles north of Big Sur.

Garrapata State Beach (408-667-2315) is a broad swath of white sand favored by local people, some of whom use it as a nude beach. Easily accessible, it's nevertheless off the beaten tourist path, making an ideal rendezvous for picnicking and skinny dipping. It is situated along Route 1 about 12 miles south of Carmel. Watch for the parking lot just north of the Garrapata Creek bridge.

Carmel

The first law of real estate should be this: The best land is always occupied by the military, bohemians or the wealthy. Generally the military arrives first, on an exploratory mission or as an occupying force. It takes strategic ground, which happens to be the beaches, headlands and mountaintops. The bohemians select beautiful locales because they possess good taste. When the rich discover where the artists have settled, they start moving in.

Carmel is no exception. Here the military established an early beachhead when Spanish soldiers occupied a barracks in the 18th-century Catholic mission. Later the bohemians arrived in numbers. Poet George Sterling came in 1905, followed by Mary Austin, the novelist. Eventually such luminaries as Upton Sinclair, Lincoln Steffens and Sinclair Lewis, writers all, settled for varying periods. Jack London and Ambrose Bierce visited. Finally, photographers Ansel Adams and Edward Weston located here.

The figure most closely associated with this "seacoast of bohemia" was Robinson Jeffers, a poet who came seeking solitude in 1914. Quarrying rock from the shoreline, he built the Tor House and Hawk Tower, where he lived and wrote haunting epic poems about the coast.

Since the departure of the bohemians, Carmel has become a little too cute and much too crowded. Shopping malls have replaced artist garrets, and there are traffic jams where there was once solitude. Typifying the town is the **Tuck Box** (408-624-6365), a gingerbread-style building on Dolores Street between Ocean and 7th avenues (there are

---

CARMEL MISSION

*Even for the nonreligious, a visit to **Carmel Mission** (Rio Road just off Route 1; 408-624-3600) becomes a pilgrimage. Dating back to 1771, the place holds an Old World beauty that captivates and confounds. The courtyards are alive with flowers and birds. The adobe buildings surrounding have been dusted with time— their eaves hunchbacked, the tile roofs coated in moss.*

Established by Father Junípero Serra, this mission is one of California's most remarkable. The basilica is a vaulted-ceiling affair adorned with old oil paintings and wooden statues of Christ; its walls are lime plaster made from burnt seashells. The exterior is topped with a Moorish tower and four bells.

Junípero Serra lies buried in the sanctuary, his grave dramatically marked with a stone sarcophagus. There are also museum rooms demonstrating early California life—a kitchen with stone hearth and rudimentary tools, the state's first library (complete with water-stained bibles) and the cell where Father Serra died.

no street numbers in Carmel), or the fairy-tale-like **Hansel-and-Gretel cottages** on Torres Street between 5th and 6th avenues.

Nevertheless, there are many excellent art galleries, and some of the town's quaint characteristics have appeal. There are no traffic lights or parking meters and at night few street lights. Drive around the side streets and you will encounter an architectural mixture of log cabins, adobe structures, board-and-batten cottages and Spanish villas.

Carmel's most alluring feature is the one that early drew bohemians—the Pacific. At the foot of Ocean Avenue rests Carmel Beach, a snowy strand shadowed by cypress trees. From here, Scenic Road hugs the coast, winding above rocky outcroppings.

Robinson Jeffers' **Tor House** and **Hawk Tower** (26304 Ocean View Avenue near Stewart Way) seem drawn from another place and time, perhaps a Scottish headland in the 19th century. In fact, the poet modeled the house after an English-style home and built the three-story garret in the fashion of an Irish tower. Completed during the 1920s, the structures are granite and include porthole windows that Jeffers salvaged from a shipwreck. Tours of the house and tower are conducted on Friday and Saturday by reservation (information, 408-624-1813; admission).

CARMEL LODGING

Cantilevered above the hillsides of the scenic Carmel Valley, the 23 pale gray single-story buildings of the **Carmel Valley Ranch Resort** (1 Old Ranch Road, Carmel; 408-625-9500) look as though they've been there forever. In fact, the 1700-acre resort opened in 1987, offering 12 tennis courts, two swimming pools and an 18-hole, three-lake, Pete Dye-designed golf course. Spacious accommodations are handsomely appointed and offer palatial bathrooms and small private decks. Ultra-deluxe.

Highlands Inn (Route 1 about four miles south of Carmel; 408-624-3801) is one of those raw-wood-and-polished-stone places that evoke the muted elegance of the California coast. Ultramodern in execution, it features a stone lodge surrounded by wood shingle buildings. Guest rooms are done in blond woods and pastel tiles; most have fireplaces and patios. Parked on a hillside overlooking an awesome sweep of ocean, the inn is the ultimate in Carmel chic with room tabs spelled ultra-deluxe.

Judging from the stunning lobby, with its beautiful tilework and handsome arches, one expects grander accommodations than those found upstairs at **La Playa Hotel** (Camino Real and 8th Street, Carmel; 408-624-6476). But the rooms are mostly small, and seem smaller yet with handcarved furniture. Still, as the city's only full-service hotel, the Mediterranean-style La Playa has a lovely ambience, with beautifully landscaped grounds and views of the Pacific only four blocks away. Deluxe to ultra-deluxe.

Carmel's most closely kept secret is a hideaway resort set on 21 acres overlooking the ocean. Scattered about the tree-shaded grounds at **Mission Ranch** (26270 Dolores Street; 408-624-6436) are a dozen 1930s-era cottages with kitchens, a white clapboard farmhouse and several century-old structures. There are tennis courts, trim lawns and ancient cypress trees. A rare find indeed, with motel accommodations at moderate price, including breakfast; cottages and farmhouse rooms in the deluxe range.

The Pine Inn (Ocean Avenue between Lincoln and Monte Verde streets; 408-624-3851), Carmel's oldest hostelry, is a 49-room hotel that dates back to 1889. The lobby is a fashionable affair with red brocade settees, marble-top tables and a brick fireplace. Rooms start in the deluxe range, feature antique furnishings and are designed in Edwardian style.

Typical of many places frequented by wealthy golfers, the accommodations at **Quail Lodge** (8205 Valley Greens Drive, Carmel; 408-624-1581) are comfortable but not ostentatious. They are large, however, and stylishly decorated. Artwork, skylights and sliding doors lighten the interiors. Ultra-deluxe.

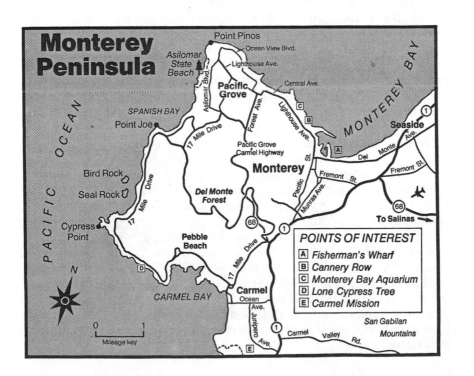

Monterey Peninsula

POINTS OF INTEREST
A Fisherman's Wharf
B Cannery Row
C Monterey Bay Aquarium
D Lone Cypress Tree
E Carmel Mission

The most unusual resting place in this corner of the world is the **Tassajara Zen Center** (contact the Zen Center, 300 Page Street, San Francisco, CA 94102; 415-863-3136.) Set deep in the Santa Lucia Mountains, Tassajara is a hot springs resort. With few phones or other distractions, it is ideal for people seeking serenity. Open from May until September, the hosts provide three vegetarian meals daily plus lodging in private rooms and cabins dotted about the grounds. Moderate.

CARMEL RESTAURANTS

In Carmel, the proper thing to do is drop by the **Tuck Box** (Dolores Street between Ocean and 7th avenues; 408-624-6365) for afternoon tea. The establishment sits in a dollhouse-like creation with a swirl roof and curved chimney. The prim and tiny dining room also serves breakfast and lunch. During the noon meal there are omelettes, sandwiches, shrimp salad and Welsh rarebit. Budget to moderate and sooo quaint!

Then there's **Hog's Breath Inn** (San Carlos between 5th and 6th avenues; 408-625-1044), a name so outrageous it begins to have appeal. Owned by actor Clint Eastwood, the restaurant features a courtyard with a flagstone dining patio. You can eat outdoors or inside next to a stone fireplace. A boar's head adorns one wall and the menu, as you may have guessed, runs heavy on meat. Moderate to deluxe.

Shabu Shabu (Mission Street between Ocean and 7th avenues; 408-625-2828), beautifully decorated with Japanese woodframe booths and floor cushions, features dishes like *yosenabe* and *shabu shabu*, prepared at your table. At lunch and dinner the menu also includes sukiyaki, sashimi, tempura and steak cooked on a hibachi. Adorned with pennants and paper lanterns, Shabu Shabu prices moderate to deluxe.

Moderately priced, casual, and contemporary. Who could ask for more than what they're offering at **Rio Grill** (Crossroads Shopping Center, Route 1 and Rio Road, Carmel; 408-625-5436)? The cuisine at this increasingly popular dining room is American grill with a Southwestern touch. Smoked chicken and artichokes and calf's liver with sweet potato pancake are among the entrées. Critically acclaimed.

If there's a nicer ocean view on the Monterey Peninsula than the one at **Pacific's Edge** (Highlands Inn, Route 1 about four miles south of Carmel, Carmel Highlands; 408-624-3801), I haven't discovered it. Ask for a seat near the plate-glass window, the better to watch the sun set on sea lions in the surf. Then be sure to order Monterey prawns, salmon or the many other delicacies from the ocean 200 feet below. The cooking is an elegant version of California cuisine. Deluxe to ultra-deluxe.

Of course the ultimate dining place is **The Covey** at Quail Lodge (8205 Valley Greens Drive; 408-624-1581), up in Carmel Valley. Set in one of the region's most prestigious hotels, The Covey is a continental restaurant with French emphasis. Richly decorated, it overlooks the lodge's lake and grounds. Deluxe to ultra-deluxe; dinner jackets and reservations, please.

CARMEL SHOPPING

In Carmel, shopping seems to be the raison d'être. If ever an entire town was dressed to look like a boutique, this is the one. Its shops are stylish and expensive.

The major shopping strip is along Ocean Avenue between Mission and Monte Verde streets, but the best stores generally are situated on the side streets. The **Doud Arcade** (Ocean Avenue between San Carlos and Dolores streets) is a mall featuring artisan shops. Here you'll find leather merchants, potters, jewelers, a metalsmith and woodworker.

Most of the artists who made Carmel famous have long since departed, but the city still maintains a wealth of art galleries. While many are not even worth browsing, others are outstanding. The **Car-**

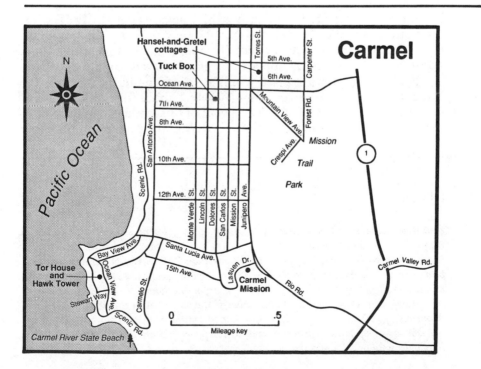

mel **Bay Company** (Lincoln Street and Ocean Avenue; 408-624-3868) features posters by contemporary artists, while the **Carmel Art Association Galleries** (Dolores Street between 5th and 6th avenues; 408-624-6176) offers paintings and sculptures by local figures.

Carmel is recognized as an international center for photographers. Two of the nation's most famous—Ansel Adams and Edward Weston—lived here. The **Weston Gallery** (6th Avenue between Dolores and Lincoln streets; 408-624-4453) displays prints by both men. At **Photography West Gallery** (Dolores Street between Ocean and 7th avenues; 408-625-1587) these photographers are represented, as well as Imogen Cunningham, Henri Cartier-Bresson and Brett Weston.

Carmel's prettiest shopping plaza is **The Barnyard** (Route 1 and Carmel Valley Road; 408-624-8886), an innovative mall housing dozens of shops. Set amid flowering gardens is a series of raw wood structures reminiscent of old farm buildings. Browse the boutiques and gift shops, then follow those brick pathways to the **Thunderbird Bookshop & Restaurant** (408-624-1803). With a marvelous collection of hardbacks and paperbacks, it is one of the finest bookstores along the Central Coast. Better still, they have an adjoining restaurant and a nearby book-and-toy store for children.

CARMEL NIGHTLIFE

For the warm conviviality of an English pub consider **Bully III** (Dolores Street and 8th Avenue; 408-625-1750). Another restaurant-cum-bar is **The Forge in the Forest** (Junipero Street and 5th Avenue; 408-624-2233), with its copper walls, hand-carved bar and open fire.

Possibly the prettiest place you'll ever indulge in the spirits is the **Sunset Lounge** at Highlands Inn (Route 1 about four miles south of Carmel; 408-624-3801). An entire wall of this leather-armchair-and-marble-table establishment is plate glass. And the picture on the other

POINT LOBOS

In a region packed with uncommonly beautiful scenery, Point Lobos State Reserve stands forth as something special. A 1225-acre peninsula and underwater preserve, it contains over 300 species of plants and more than 250 species of animals and birds. This is a perfect place to study sea otters, harbor seals and sea lions or to play amateur geologist amid multicolored sedimentary formations.

Along with Pebble Beach, Point Lobos is the only spot in the world where Monterey cypresses, those ghostly, wind-gnarled coastal trees, still survive. There are 80-foot-high kelp forests offshore as well as tidepools that are like miniature aquariums pulsing with color and sea life.

side of those panes is classic Carmel—rocky shoreline fringed with cypress trees and lashed by passionate waves. If that's not entertainment enough, there's a piano bar during the week and a three-piece combo on weekends.

CARMEL BEACHES AND PARKS

Carmel River State Beach (408-624-4909) would be more attractive were it not upstaged by Point Lobos, its remarkable neighbor to the south. Nevertheless, there's a sandy beach here as well as a view of the surrounding hills. The chief feature is the bird refuge along the river. To get there take the Rio Road exit off Route 1; the beach is at the end of Carmelo Road.

Set far inland amid the softly rolling San Gabilan Mountains are the sharp, dramatic volcanic peaks of **Pinnacles National Monument**. Sheer spires and solitary minarets vault 1200 feet from the canyon floor. Comprising the weathered remains of a 23-million-year-old volcano, these towering peaks challenge day hikers and technical rock climbers alike. There are caves to explore, plus 26 miles of trails leading into the core of the volcano. Wild boar, gray fox and bobcat roam the region, while golden eagles and peregrine falcons work the skies above. The best time to visit is spring, when the wildflowers bloom, or in autumn.

No road traverses the park. You must enter either on the east side, by following Route 25 south from Hollister; or on the west side along Route 146, about 13 miles east from Soledad. Camping is permitted on both sides. For information, call 408-389-4578.

Pacific Grove

Projecting out from the northern tip of Monterey Peninsula is the diminutive town of Pacific Grove. Covering just 1700 acres, it's a quiet community with an invitingly undeveloped waterfront.

Costanoan Indians once dove for abalone in these waters. By the 19th century, Pacific Grove had become a religious retreat. Methodist Episcopal ministers pitched a tent city and decreed that "bathing suits shall be provided with double crotches or with skirts of ample size to cover the buttocks." The town was dry until 1969. Given the fish canneries in Monterey and teetotalers in this nearby town, local folks called the area "Carmel-by-the-Sea, Monterey-by-the-Smell and Pacific Grove-by-God."

Today Pacific Grove is a sleepy residential area decorated with Victorian mansions, brown-shingle houses and clapboard ocean cottages. The waterfront drive goes past rocky beaches to **Point Pinos**

Lighthouse. When this beacon first flashed in 1856, it burned sperm oil. Little has changed except the introduction of electricity; this is the only early lighthouse along the entire California coast to be preserved in its original condition. There are weekend tours (408-648-3116).

Pacific Grove's major claim to fame lies in two areas several blocks inland: around George Washington Park on Melrose Street and in a grove at 1073 Lighthouse Avenue. This otherwise unassuming municipality is "Butterfly Town, U.S.A." Every November, brilliant orange-and-black **monarch butterflies** migrate here, remaining until March. Some arrive from several hundred miles away to breed amid the cypress and oak trees. At night they cling to one another, curtaining the branches in clusters that sometimes number over a thousand. Then, at first light, they come to life, fluttering around the groves in a frenzy of wings and color. Also of interest is the **Pacific Grove Museum of Natural History** (Central and Forest avenues; 408-648-3116), an excellent small museum.

Nearby **17 Mile Drive** (fee) leads to Pebble Beach, one of America's most lavish communities. This extraordinary region must not be missed: the road winds through pine groves down to a wind-combed beach where you'll see miles of rolling dunes tufted with sea vegetation.

Among the first spots you'll encounter is **Spanish Bay**, where Juan Gaspar de Portolá camped during his 1769 expedition up the California coast. (The picnic area here is a choice place to spread a feast.) At **Point Joe**, converging ocean currents create a wild frothing sea that has drawn several ships to their doom.

Seal Rock and **Bird Rock**, true to their nomenclature, are carpeted with sea lions, harbor and leopard seals, cormorants and gulls. Throughout this thriving 17 Mile Drive area are black-tail deer, pelicans, sooty shearwaters, sea otters and, during migration periods, California gray whales.

There are crescent beaches and granite headlands as well as vista points for scanning the coast. You'll also pass the **Lone Cypress**, the solitary tree on a rocky point that has become as symbolic of Northern California as the Golden Gate Bridge. Monterey cypresses such as this one grow nowhere else in the world except along Carmel Bay.

The **private homes** en route are mansions, exquisite affairs fashioned from marble and fine hardwoods. Some appear like stone fortresses, others seem made solely of glass. They range from American colonial to futuristic and were designed by such noted architects as Bernard Maybeck, Julia Morgan and Willis Polk.

This is also home to several of the world's most renowned **golf courses**—Pebble Beach, Spyglass Hill and Cypress Point. The AT&T Pro-Am Tournament at Pebble Beach takes place here each year. Even more than the designer homes and their celebrity residents, these courses have made Pebble Beach a place fabled for wealth and beauty.

PACIFIC GROVE LODGING

Gosby House Inn (643 Lighthouse Avenue; 408-375-1287), a century-old Victorian mansion, includes 22 refurbished rooms. Each is different and all have been decorated with special attention to detail. In any one you are liable to discover an antique armoire, brass lighting fixtures, stained glass, a Tiffany lamp or a clawfoot bathtub. All this warmth is deluxe-priced for a room with shared bath or ultra-deluxe with a private facility.

Green Gables Inn (104 5th Street; 408-375-2095), one of the region's most impressive bed and breakfasts, is an 1888 Queen Anne Victorian. Adorned with step-gables, stained glass and bay windows, it rests in a storybook setting overlooking Monterey Bay. Five bedrooms upstairs and a suite below have been fastidiously decorated with lavish antiques. Most bedrooms share a pair of bathrooms and rent at

---

PEBBLE BEACH

*Pebble Beach is one of those places people think of almost as a state of mind. This 8400-acre beachfront enclave was acquired around the turn of the century by the Pebble Beach Company (formerly Del Monte Properties) and converted into a habitat for trees, greenswards, fauna and wealthy golfers. King of the hill is **The Lodge at Pebble Beach** (on 17 Mile Drive, Pebble Beach; 408-624-3811), an oceanfront resort comprising a number of low-rise buildings and bungalows, as well as a swimming pool and a veritable village of expensive boutiques. Fireplaces and ocean views not withstanding, it is not the 160 accommodations that draw people here, but the camaraderie of golf, tennis, horseback riding and socializing in Old World style. Ultra-deluxe.*

*The Lodge at Pebble Beach also has a French continental restaurant, **Club XIX**, which overlooks the 18th green and Point Lobos. Added to this spectacular view are such entrées as châteaubriand, scallops and rack of lamb. Deluxe to ultra-deluxe.*

*The latest addition to the golfing kingdom is **The Inn and Links at Spanish Bay** (on 17 Mile Drive, Pebble Beach; 408-624-3811). Fronted by Pebble Beach's spectacular golf course, the sprawling, two-story 270-room inn offers spacious rooms with lovely views. Two restaurants, a spa, swimming pool, eight tennis courts and membership privileges at the nearby Beach and Tennis Club make this a resort in its own right, and one less formal than The Lodge. Ultra-deluxe.*

*The Inn's formal dining room, **The Bay Club**, boasts a 270° view of the Pacific and surrounding golf links. Featuring Northern Italian cuisine, this Mediterranean-style restaurant offers such tempting entrées as veal chop with sun-dried tomato and sage butter and rack of lamb with mustard, bread crumbs and basil. Ultra-deluxe.*

deluxe prices. Five ultra-deluxe suites in a building adjacent to the main house have fireplaces and private baths.

Just down the street, **Roserox Country Inn** (557 Ocean View Boulevard; 408-373-7673) commands an even finer view. This turn-of-the-century house has a vista sweeping 180° along the ocean. Within its eight guest rooms and four baths are specially selected antiques such as English brass beds and clawfoot tubs. Each room follows a different decorative motif; all feature ocean views, share baths and rent in the deluxe and ultra-deluxe categories. Complete breakfast included.

PACIFIC GROVE RESTAURANTS

The Old Bath House Restaurant (620 Ocean View Boulevard; 408-375-5195), a luxurious building decorated in etched glass, sports an attractive dining room and a Victorian-style bar. The continental/California cuisine includes duckling, lamb, lobster, steak and seafood dishes. Open for dinner only; deluxe to ultra-deluxe.

PACIFIC GROVE SHOPPING

The main area for window browsing in Pacific Grove can be found along Lighthouse Avenue. Just above this busy thoroughfare, on 17th Street, artisans have renovated a row of small beach cottages. In each is a creatively named shop. There's **Reincarnation Antique Clothing** (214 17th Street; 408-649-0689), selling vintage clothing and jewelry, and **Past and Presents** (226 17th Street; 408-373-7157), which features European and Asian collectibles and antiques.

PACIFIC GROVE BEACHES AND PARKS

Asilomar State Beach (408-372-8016) features over 100 acres of snowy white sand dunes, tidepools and beach. It's a perfect place for daytripping or collecting driftwood. Since northern and southern currents run together here, the waters are teeming with marine life. Located along Sunset Drive in Pacific Grove.

Monterey

Over three million visitors tour the Monterey area every year. Little wonder. Its rocky coast fringed with cypress forests, its hills dotted with palatial homes—the area is unusually beautiful.

History in Monterey is a precious commodity that in most cases has been carefully preserved. Old adobe houses and Spanish-style buildings are so commonplace that some have been converted into shops and restaurants. Others are museums or points of interest that can be seen on a walking tour along the **Path of History**. This "Path," carrying through the center of Monterey, measures over two miles if walked in its entirety.

The best place to begin is the **Custom House** at #1 Custom House Plaza across from Fisherman's Wharf. California's earliest public building, the structure dates back to 1827. It was here in 1846 that Commodore Sloat raised the American flag, claiming California for the United States. Today the stone and adobe building houses displays from an 1830s-era cargo ship.

Pacific House (10 Custom House Plaza), an 1847 adobe with a luxurious courtyard, was used over the years to house everything from a tavern to a courtroom. The exhibits inside trace California's history from Native American days to the heyday of the canning industry in the 1930s. Today, the building houses **California Heritage Guides** (408-373-6454), which provides maps, brochures and guided tours. For more information about the area, you can contact the **Monterey Peninsula Chamber of Commerce** (380 Alvarado Street; 408-649-1770).

Just behind Pacific House sits **Casa del Oro** (Olivier and Scott streets), a tiny white adobe that served as Monterey's general store during the 1850s. Today it houses the Boston Store (408-649-3364), a shop selling early American items.

California's First Theater (Scott and Pacific streets; 408-375-4916) certainly qualifies as a living museum. It's a landmark building that is still used to stage theatrical performances.

Casa Soberanes (336 Pacific Street), a Monterey-style house with red-tile roof and second-story balcony, was completed around 1830. Hourly tours. **Casa Serrano** (412 Pacific Street), built in 1843, contains wrought-iron decorations over its narrow windows. Weekend tours only; 408-372-2608.

Nearby spreads **Friendly Plaza**, a tree-shaded park that serves as a focus for several important places. The **Monterey Peninsula Museum of Art** (559 Pacific Street; 408-372-7591) features works by local artists as well as special exhibits. Pierce Street, running along the upper edge of the plaza, contains a string of historic 19th-century homes. **Colton Hall** is an imposing stone structure with white pillars and classical portico. Site of California's 1849 constitutional convention, it displays memorabilia from that critical event. The squat **Old Jail** next door, fashioned from granite, with wrought-iron bars across the windows, dates back to the same era. **Casa Gutierrez** (across the street) was built by a cavalryman with 15 children. That was back in 1841; today the old adobe is a restaurant.

Allen Knight Maritime Museum (550 Calle Principal) houses model ships and old nautical photographs. The nearby **Larkin House**

(Calle Principal and Jefferson Street), designed in 1835, is an elegant example of Monterey-style architecture. Combining New England and Spanish principles, it's a two-story adobe house with ground floor veranda and second-story balcony. Today the antique home is a house-museum filled with period pieces that provide a glimpse into early American life on the West Coast.

The **Cooper-Molera Adobe** (Polk and Munras streets) is a sprawling affair that includes a 19th-century museum as well as a "historic garden" filled with herbs and vegetables of the Spanish era.

Stevenson House (530 Houston Street), a grand two-story edifice with shuttered windows and landscaped yard, was Scottish novelist Robert Louis Stevenson's residence for several months in 1879. In addition to its period furniture and early California decor, the house features numerous items from Stevenson's life. (For guided tour information, contact Monterey State Historic Park, 408-649-7118; they also provide hourly guided tours of Casa Soberanes, Larkin House and Cooper-Molera Adobe; admission.)

Several other places of historical note are located elsewhere in Monterey. The **Royal Presidio Chapel** (550 Church Street; 408-373-2628), a mission church founded by Father Junípero Serra in 1770, is an old adobe structure with a towering belfry and a narrow chapel hung with dusty oil paintings.

The **Presidio of Monterey** (Pacific and Artillery streets; 408-647-5414), established as a fort by the Spanish in 1792, currently serves as a foreign language institute for the military. The small U.S. Army Museum here has displays of old dress uniforms and cavalry saddles, as well as swords, cannonballs and other implements of destruction. This is also the site of an ancient Costanoan Indian village and burial ground.

While Monterey's fishing fleet works at **Municipal Wharf #2** (foot of Figueroa Street), the waterfront's prime sightseeing attraction, **Fisherman's Wharf**, is more like an outdoor mall, a macadam corridor lined on either side with shops. A few fish markets still sell live crabs, lobsters and squid, but the pier is primarily filled with concession stands and seafood restaurants.

Cannery Row, made famous by John Steinbeck's feisty novels *Cannery Row* and *Sweet Thursday*, has also been transformed into a neighborhood of nightclubs, restaurants and antique shops. As Steinbeck remarked upon returning to the old sardine canning center, "They fish for tourists now."

At the far end of the Row, Steinbeck aficionados will still find a few literary settings. La Ida Cafe has given way to **Kalisa's Restaurant** (851 Cannery Row) but retains the same tumbledown appearance; Wing Chong Market is now **Alicia's Antiques** (835 Cannery Row), and the building that housed **Doc Rickett's Marine Lab**

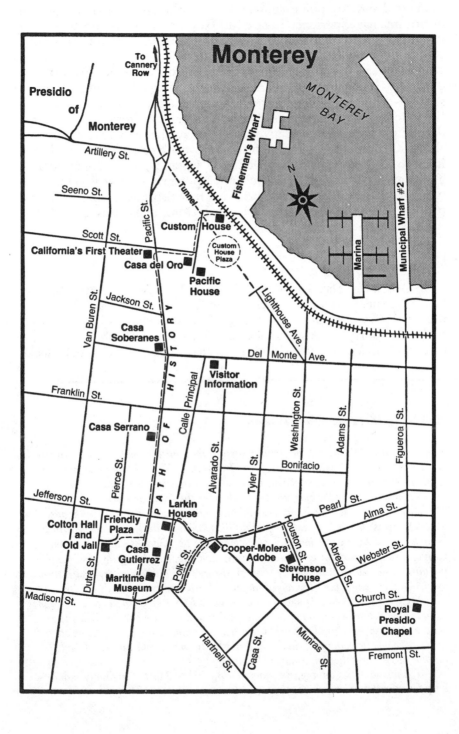

stands at 800 Cannery Row. Elsewhere, old warehouses have been converted into shopping centers, new buildings have risen and the entire area has experienced a face lift. Brightest tooth in the new smile is the **Edgewater Packing Company** (640 Wave Street; 408-649-189

An attraction not to be missed is the **Monterey Bay Aquarium** (Cannery Row and David Avenue; 408-649-6466; admission), a state-of-the-art museum that re-creates the natural habitat of local sea life. Monterey Bay is one of the world's biggest submarine canyons, deeper than the Grand Canyon. At the aquarium you'll encounter about 100 display tanks representing the wealth of underwater life that inhabits this mineral-rich valley. For instance, the Monterey Bay Tank, a 90-foot-long glass enclosure, portrays the local submarine world complete with sharks, brilliant reef fish and creosote-oozing pilings. The many displays and exhibitions make this one of the world's great aquariums.

MONTEREY LODGING

The **Monterey Bay Inn** (242 Cannery Row, Monterey; 408-373-6242) is a special find. Occupying a bayfront corner, it has 47 accommodations in a modest-looking four-story C-shaped building that shelters a courtyard. A sophisticated color scheme of subtle green and rose, well-made furniture, and extra space provided by small decks

---

THE OLD SPANISH MISSION TOWN

*Time permitting, there's one overland excursion that must be added to your itinerary—a visit to the **Mission at San Juan Bautista**. While this graceful mission town, located 90 miles south of San Francisco, is easily reached from Route 101, the most inspiring route is over country roads from the Monterey Peninsula.*

Anyone who has read Frank Norris' muckraking novel about the railroads, The Octopus, will recognize this placid village with its thick, cool adobe church. Founded in 1797, the mission was completed in 1812. Today it numbers among California's most enchanting locales. With its colonnade and sagging crossbeams, the mission has about it the musty scent of history. The old monastery and church consist of a low-slung building roofed in Spanish tile and topped with a belfry.

*My favorite spot in this most favored town is **Mission Cemetery**, a small plot bounded by a stone fence and overlooking valley and mountains. It's difficult to believe that over 4300 Indians are buried here in unmarked graves. Just below the cemetery, symbolic perhaps of change and mortality, are the old Spanish Road (El Camino Real) and the San Andreas Fault.*

*The mission rests on a grassy square facing **Plaza Hall**. Originally a dormitory for unwed Indian women, this structure was rebuilt in 1868 and used as a*

make this worth the ultra-deluxe price tag. Be sure to check out the rooftop hot tub, which commands heavenly views of the city as well as the bay.

For good cheer and homespun atmosphere, the **Old Monterey Inn** (500 Martin Street; 408-375-8284) provides the final word. The ten-room bed and breakfast rests on a quiet street not far from downtown Monterey. Among the trimly appointed rooms are several with tile fireplaces, wicker furnishings and delicate wallhangings. There are spacious dining and drawing rooms downstairs, and the landscaped grounds are studded with oak and redwood. Full breakfast; ultra-deluxe.

Merritt House (386 Pacific Street; 408-646-9686), a 25-room inn, rests in a vintage 1830 adobe home along Monterey's "Path of History." Accommodations in the old house and the adjoining modern quarters are furnished with hardwood period pieces and feature vaulted ceilings, fireplaces and balconies. Continental breakfast; deluxe to ultra-deluxe.

Oceanfront on Cannery Row stands the **Spindrift Inn** (652 Cannery Row; 408-646-8900), an ultramodern 41-room hotel. Painted in pastel hues and decorated with tile floors and contemporary art, it is the final word in chic surroundings. The lobby is fashionably laid out with sculptures and a rooftop solarium overlooks the waterfront. Guest rooms carry out the award-winning architectural motif with bay windows, marble fireplaces and built-in armoires. *La carte, monsieur?* Ultra-deluxe.

---

meeting place and private residence. Peek inside its shuttered windows or tour the building and encounter a child's room cluttered with old dolls, a sitting room dominated by a baby grand piano and other rooms containing period furniture.

*Behind the hall sits a **blacksmith shop**, filled now with wagon wheels, oxen yokes and the "San Juan Eagle," a hook-and-ladder wagon drawn by a ten-man fire fighting crew back in 1869. Nearby **Plaza Stable** houses an impressive collection of buggies and carriages.*

*The **Plaza Hotel** (admission) lines another side of the square. Consisting of several adobe structures, the earliest built in 1814, the place once served as a stagecoach stop. Today its myriad rooms contain historic exhibits and 1860s-era furnishings. Similarly, the **Castro-Breen Adobe** next door is decorated with Spanish-style pieces. Owned by a Mexican general and later by Donner Party survivors, it is a window on California frontier life. Nearby are **San Juan Jail**, an oversized blockhouse constructed in 1870, and the **settler's cabin**, a rough log cabin built by East Coast pioneers in the 1830s or 1840s.*

All are part of the state historic park (information, 408-623-4881) that comprises San Juan Bautista. Like the plaza, Third Street is lined with 19th-century stores and houses. Here amid porticoed haciendas and crumbling adobe are antique stores, a bakery, cobbler and other shops.

Since overnight facilities fill rapidly around Monterey, particularly on weekends and during the summer, it's wise to reserve in advance. Two agencies—**Resort To Me** (408-624-5070 and **Carmel's Tourist Information Center** (408-624-1711) might prove useful in securing that elusive room.

MONTEREY RESTAURANTS

One place that should top your itinerary is **Sancho Panza** (590 Calle Principal; 408-375-0095), a Mexican restaurant housed in a historic adobe that dates from 1841. It's a small, crowded place that lends an authentic feel for early Spanish life in California. The menu features standard Mexican dishes and is budget to moderate in price.

My favorite Monterey dining place is the **Clock Garden Restaurant** (565 Abrego Street; 408-375-6100), which features a host of seafood dishes as well as spare ribs with honey and soy sauce and chicken with a peach glaze. Prices are budget to moderate if you arrive by 6 p.m. for the early bird specials; otherwise the tab runs a little more. I haven't even mentioned the decor yet. It's Early Hodgepodge: here a sculpture fashioned of wine bottles, there a collection of antique clocks, each set to a different time.

Visiting Monterey, you'll inevitably end up in a seafood restaurant along Cannery Row. Among the best is **Steinbeck's Lobster Grotto** (720 Cannery Row; 408-373-1884) with it's wraparound view of the Pacific. The menu is a surf-and-turf offering with a few fresh catches every day. Moderately tabbed; arrive before 6 p.m. and you can enjoy a budget-priced early bird meal; lunch during the summer, dinner year-round.

Small and personalized with an understated elegance is the most fitting way to describe **Fresh Cream** (Heritage Harbor, Pacific and Scott streets; 408-375-9798). Its pastel walls are decorated with French prints and leaded glass. Only dinner is served at this gourmet retreat; on a given night you might choose from beef tournedos in Madeira sauce, duckling in black currant sauce or salmon in puff pastry. And the desserts should be outlawed. Four stars. Ultra-deluxe.

MONTEREY SHOPPING

In Monterey, there are stores throughout the downtown area and malls galore over on **Cannery Row**. Every year another shopping complex seems to rise along the Row. Already the area features cheese and wine stores, clothiers, antique shops, a fudge factory and a gourmet supply store. There's also a collector's comic book store, the inevitable T-shirt shop, knickknack stores and galleries selling artworks that are like Muzak on canvas.

MONTEREY NIGHTLIFE

The classiest spot around is **The Club** (321-D Alvarado Street; 408-646-9244). Entertainment here changes nightly—rock videos, a disc jockey spinning platters or a band playing Top-40. Once a week The Club spotlights nationally known entertainers. Cover.

 Doc Rickett's Lab (95 Prescott Avenue; 408-649-4241) has dancing to Top-40 rock bands. If you'd prefer a snug corner overlooking the ocean, consider **Mark Thomas Outrigger** (700 Cannery Row; 408-372-8543). This watering hole enjoys a plate-glass window on the world and offers dancing to live bands on weekends.

 In the realm of the performing arts, the **Monterey County Symphony** (408-624-8511) performs a wide-ranging series of concerts. The **Chamber Music Society** (408-625-2212) also features an excellent series of performances and often spotlights guest ensembles such as the Juilliard String Quartet.

Santa Cruz

In the seaside town of Santa Cruz, you'll encounter a former retirement community that has been transformed into a dynamic campus town. When the University of California opened here in the 1960s, it created a new role for this ever-changing place. Originally founded as a Spanish mission in 1791, Santa Cruz became a lumber port and manufacturing center when Americans moved in around 1849. Then in the late 19th century it developed into a tourist resort filled with elaborate Victorian houses.

 Today Santa Cruz is a playground. It enjoys spectacular white sand beaches, entertaining nightlife and an old-style boardwalk amusement park. The city faces south, providing the best weather along the Central Coast. Arts and crafts flourish here, and vintage houses adorn the area.

 The Santa Cruz shoreline is a honeycomb of tiny coves, sea arches and pocket beaches. From **Lighthouse Point** on a clear day, the entire 40-mile curve of Monterey Bay silhouettes the skyline. Even in foggy weather, sea lions cavort on the rocks offshore, while surfers ride the challenging "Steamer Lane" breaks. Testament to their talent is the tiny **Surfing Museum** (West Cliff Drive and Lighthouse Point; 408-429-3429), situated in the lighthouse. Here vintage photos and antique boards re-create the history of the Hawaiian sport.

 Nearby **Santa Cruz Municipal Wharf** is a half-mile-long pier lined with bait shops, restaurants and fishing charters. It's a perfect place to promenade, soak up sun and seek local color.

Several places that merit short visits include **The Octagon** (118 Cooper Street; 408-425-2540), dating back over a century and housing the Santa Cruz County Historical Museum within its eight brick walls; **Santa Cruz Mission** (126 High Street; 408-426-5686), a reduced-scale replica of the 1791 structure (temporarily closed due to the earthquake); and the **Art Museum of Santa Cruz County** (for the time being sharing space in The Octagon; 408-429-1964), featuring permanent and rotating exhibits of traditional and contemporary art.

The **Santa Cruz County Conference and Visitors Council** (701 Front Street; 408-425-1234) is a helpful information center; among the brochures available here is one describing **architectural tours** of the city. Santa Cruz's rich history has left a legacy of noteworthy buildings and elegant homes, including many Victorians. Most of these points of interest can be divided into four walking tours, each about 20 minutes long.

No ivory tower ever enjoyed a view like the one from the **University of California–Santa Cruz** campus (408-459-0111). Set on a hillside overlooking Monterey Bay, with redwood forest and range land all around, the 2000-acre campus possesses incredible beauty. The university itself is divided into eight colleges, insular and self-defined, each marked by a different architectural style. Of particular interest is the arboretum with its Mediterranean garden and outstanding collection of Australian and South African plants.

SANTA CRUZ LODGING

It's big, brash and blocky, but the **Dream Inn** (175 West Cliff Drive; 408-426-4330) is also right on the beach. With pool, jacuzzi, oceanfront restaurants and lounge, this multitiered establishment extends from a hilltop perch down to a sandy strand. Guest rooms are trimly done with fabric walls and contemporary furnishings; each sports a private balcony and ocean view. Deluxe to ultra-deluxe in summer; less during the rest of the year.

For country-inn-style accommodations consider **Cliff Crest Bed & Breakfast Inn** (407 Cliff Street; 408-427-2609), a five-bedroom establishment in a historic 1887 Victorian home. Among the features are an outdoor belvedere, a yard landscaped by the designer of San Francisco's Golden Gate Park and a solarium illuminated through stained-glass windows. The guest rooms feature patterned wallpaper, antique beds and tile baths with clawfoot tubs. Moderate to deluxe.

Another member of this elite club, **Château Victorian** (118 1st Street; 408-458-9458), sits in a vintage home just one block from the boardwalk. The entire house has been done by masterful decorators and is chockablock with antiques. There are two sundecks and a luxu-

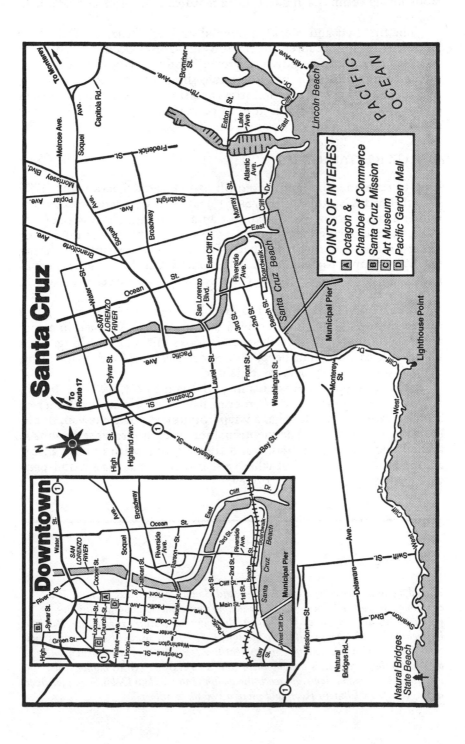

rious sitting room. Each guest room features a fireplace and tile bath. Deluxe.

The first bed-and-breakfast opened in Santa Cruz, the **Babbling Brook Inn** (1025 Laurel Street; 408-427-2437) occupies a historic creekside setting in a redwood grove. Twelve accommodations are divided among the main house and two shingled two-story outbuildings. Eyelet or floral print comforters and small freestanding fireplaces create a warm country look in most of the rooms; some have private decks overlooking the creek or garden. Deluxe.

SANTA CRUZ RESTAURANTS

True to its name, the multitiered **Shadowbrook Restaurant** (1750 Wharf Road, Capitola; 408-475-1511) sits in a wooded spot through which a creek flows. Food is almost an afterthought at this elaborate affair; upon entering the grounds you descend either via a funicular or along a sinuous, fern-draped path. Inside lies a labyrinth of dining levels and rooms, each luxuriously decorated. Cuisine includes rack of lamb, salmon filet and scallops corsica. Dinner and weekend brunch; moderate to deluxe.

Ideal Fish Company (106 Beach Street; 408-423-5271) is a tourist trap with tradition. It's been one since 1917. Wedged in a corner between the beach and the pier, it looks out on everything, from boardwalk to bounding deep. The specialty is seafood—sand dabs, oysters and salmon. Moderate to deluxe.

Cozy **Casablanca Restaurant** (101 Main Street; 408-426-9063), with its overhead fans and Moroccan flair, is excellent for dinner or Sunday brunch. The place has a wraparound view of the ocean, not to mention a tony decor. The menu includes such gourmet selections as grilled duck, seafood linguine and filet mignon with brandy. Prices are moderate to deluxe, but where else can you sit along a wood-paneled bar gazing at a photo of Bogey?

MOSS LANDING

Tucked along the coast between Monterey and Santa Cruz, Moss Landing is a charming, if weather-beaten, fishing harbor. With its one-lane bridge, bright-painted boats and unpainted fish market, the town has a warm personality. Particularly enchanting is nearby **Elkhorn Slough***, a 1240-acre world of salt marshes and tidal flats. Within this delicate environment live some 100 species of waterfowl, about 50 other bird species (among them golden eagles), as well as harbor seals, muskrats, oysters and clams. To reach the visitor center, follow Dolan Road for three miles, go left on Elkhorn Road and proceed two more miles.*

Covering the rest of the Far Eastern spectrum is **India Joze** (1001 Center Street, Santa Cruz; 408-427-3554), which serves creative meals at moderate prices. At breakfast there's *masala dolsa*, an Indian *urad dahl* crepe filled with spiced new potatoes. At lunch try the dragon calamari (calamari with fresh mint, cilantro glaze, bamboo shoots and black Asian mushrooms). The dinner menu offers snapper *Me Saltsa* (Greek feta cheese, wine and fresh herb glaze). Located in the Santa Cruz Art Center, India Joze is decorated with artworks by local artisans, illuminated through skylights, and surrounded by pink pastel walls.

SANTA CRUZ SHOPPING

Before the 1989 earthquake the central shopping district in Santa Cruz was along Pacific Garden Mall, a six-block strip of Pacific Avenue converted to a promenade. The section was neatly landscaped with flowering shrubs and potted trees and its sidewalks, widened for window browsers, overflowed with people.

Today many merchants are housed in temporary units while they wait for buildings destroyed in the earthquake to be reconstructed. You can stop by **Folk Arts** (710 C Cedar Street; 408-425-1955), which displays an irresistible array of tapestries, jewelry, sculpture, and pottery. **Artisans Cooperative** (710 C Cedar Street; 408-423-8183) deals in fine handcrafts and gift items by local artists. They feature outstanding pottery, woodwork, glassware, and wall rugs. Before the earthquake **Bookshop Santa Cruz** (Cedar Street, Pavilion G; 408-423-0900) was the finest among this college town's many wonderful bookstores.

Also visit the **Santa Cruz Art Center** (1001 Center Street; 408-425-5041). Here is more merchandise fashioned by area craftspeople. There are galleries, gift stores, plus arts and crafts shops. Also, many artisans' studios are located at the center, making it a gathering place for artists as well as a clearinghouse for their wares.

Another short jog from Pacific Avenue places you in **Galleria Santa Cruz** (Front and Cooper streets; 408-425-5711), one of the town's most modern malls. There are three tiers of shops comprising this stucco-and-brick enclave.

SANTA CRUZ NIGHTLIFE

South of Santa Cruz, several of the restaurant lounges lining Capitola's waterfront provide nightly entertainment. Over at **Edgewater Seafood Grill** (215 Esplanade; 408-475-6215) the deejay cranks up the victrola and let's fly with rock-and-roll dance music. Weekend cover. A few doors down at **Zelda's** (203 Esplanade; 408-475-4900) there's live music nightly, ranging from salsa to rock.

For mellow piano bar music, try **Shadowbrook Restaurant** (1750 Wharf Road, Capitola; 408-475-1511). Its soft lighting and luxurious surroundings create a sense of well-being, like brandy and a blazing fire.

For nightly dancing head out to **Bitchin'** (3660 Soquel Drive; 408-476-3939) in nearby Soquel. Cover Thursday through Saturday.

The Crow's Nest (2218 East Cliff Drive, Santa Cruz; 408-476-4560) offers eclectic entertainment. On a given night they will be headlining a jazz, country-and-western or soft rock band. Ocean view; cover.

SANTA CRUZ BEACHES AND PARKS

Over three miles of beach and sand dunes create one of the area's prettiest parks, **Sunset State Beach** (408-724-1266). There are bluffs and meadows behind the beach as well as stands of Monterey pine and cypress. This 324-acre park is a popular spot for fishing and clamming. Camping. Located 16 miles south of Santa Cruz.

Forest of Nisene Marks State Park (408-335-4598) is a semi-wilderness expanse, several miles inland, encompassing nearly 10,000 acres. Within its domain are redwood groves, meandering streams, rolling countryside and dense forest. About 30 miles of hiking trails wind through the preserve (including a two-mile trail that leads to the epicenter of the 1989 earthquake). Along them you can explore fossil beds, deserted logger cabins, old trestles and railroad beds. To get there from Route 1 take the Seacliff Beach exit in Aptos.

A very popular park (almost too popular during summer), **Seacliff State Beach** (408-688-3222) provides the safest swimming along this section of coast. There are roving lifeguards on duty and a protective headland nearby. The beach also sports a pier favored by anglers. Located off Route 1 in Aptos.

SANTA CRUZ BEACH BOARDWALK

Santa Cruz Beach Boardwalk (400 Beach Street; 408-423-5590), dating to 1907, is Northern California's answer to Coney Island. You'll find shooting galleries and candy stalls, coin-operated fortune tellers and do-it-yourself photo machines. Then there are the ultimate entertainments: a slow-circling ferris wheel with chairs suspended high above the beach; the antique merry-go-round, a whirl of mirrors and flashing color; a funicular whose brightly painted cars reflect the sun; rides with names that instantaneously evoke childhood memories—tilt-a-whirl, haunted castle, bumper cars; and that soaring symbol of amusement parks everywhere, the roller coaster.

New Brighton State Beach (408-475-4850), a sandy crescent adjoining Seacliff Beach, enjoys a wide vista of Monterey Bay. Headlands protect the beach for swimmers; beachcombers frequently find fossils in the cliffs here. Within its mere 94 acres, the park contains hiking trails and a forested bluff. Camping. Located off Route 1 in Capitola.

Just south of Santa Cruz Harbor lies **Twin Lakes State Beach** (408-688-3241). This odd-shaped strand, smaller than other Santa Cruz beaches, is also less crowded. A very pretty spot, the park encompasses 110 acres, with a lagoon behind the beach and a jetty flanking one side. Located along East Cliff Drive, south of Santa Cruz Harbor.

Seabright State Beach (408-688-3241), an important link in Santa Cruz's chain of beaches, extends from near the boardwalk to the jetty at Santa Cruz Harbor. It's long, wide and backdropped by bluffs. The views are magnificent, and the crowds will be lighter than along the boardwalk. Access to the beach is along East Cliff Drive at the foot of Mott and Cypress avenues, or at the end of Atlantic Avenue.

Of the major beaches extending along the Santa Cruz waterfront, **Santa Cruz Beach** is the most popular, most crowded and most famous. All for a very simple reason— the Santa Cruz Boardwalk, with its amusement park and restaurants, runs the length of the sand, and the Santa Cruz Municipal Pier anchors one end of the beach. Located along Beach Street.

Northernmost of the Santa Cruz beaches, **Natural Bridges State Beach** (408-423-4609) features a small park and a half-moon-shaped beach. All but one of the beach's namesake sea arches have collapsed, leading local wags to dub the spot "Fallen Arches." This is also an excellent spot to watch monarch butterflies during their annual winter migration. Located off Route 1 near the northern edge of Santa Cruz.

North of Santa Cruz

North along the coast from Santa Cruz, Route 1 streams past bold headlands and magnificent seascapes. There are excellent beaches to explore and marvelous vista points along the way.

About two miles north of Santa Cruz along Route 1 you'll discover **Wilder Ranch State Park** (408-426-0505). This 5000-acre spread has been designated a "cultural preserve" because of the Ohlone Indian shell mounds and historic houses dotting the property. In addition to an 1839 adobe, the complex features a Greek revival farmhouse dating to the 1850s and an 1890s-era Queen Anne Victorian. You can also tour the outlying barns and workshops as well as a nearby cove reputedly used by smugglers.

Farther north rises **Pigeon Point Lighthouse**, a 115-foot senti-nel that's one of the tallest lighthouses on the West Coast. The point gained a nasty reputation during the 19th century when one ship after another smashed on the rocks. The lighthouse went up in 1871 and originally contained a 1000-piece lens.

Pescadero represents a timeworn town hidden a short way from Route 1. It's a woodframe hamlet of front-porch rocking chairs and white steeple churches. The name translates as "fisherman," but the Portuguese and Italian residents are farmers, planting artichokes, brus-sel sprouts and lettuce in the patchwork fields surrounding the town.

Also a short distance from the highway, you'll encounter **San Gregorio**, another weather-beaten little town. Once a resort area, it today reveals a quaint collection of sagging roofs and unpainted barns. Be sure to drop by **Peterson and Alsford General Merchandise**, a classic general store that's been around almost a century.

Half Moon Bay is what happens when the farm meets the sea. It's a hybrid town, half landlubber and half old salt. They are as likely to sell artichokes here as fresh fish. The town was named for its crescent beach but thinks of itself as the pumpkin capital of the world. At times the furrowed fields seem a geometric continuation of ocean waves, as if the sea lapped across the land and became frozen there.

On the southern outskirts of Half Moon Bay, watch for **Higgins Purisima Road**, a country lane that curves for eight miles into the Santa Cruz Mountains, returning to Route 1. This scenic loop passes old farmhouses and sloping pastures, redwood-forested hills and mountain meadows. Immediately upon entering this bumpy road, you'll spy a stately old New England-style house set in a plowed field. That will be the **James Johnston House**, a saltbox structure with sloping roof and white clapboard facade. Dating back to 1853 and built by an original '49er, it is the oldest house along this section of coastline.

AÑO NUEVO STATE RESERVE

*Awesome in its beauty, abundant in wildlife, **Año Nuevo State Reserve** is one of the most spectacular parks on the California coast. It consists of a peninsula heaped with sand dunes. A miniature island lies just offshore. Seals and sea lions inhabit the area; eagles and albatrosses fly above. But most spectacular of all the denizens are the elephant seals, those lovably grotesque two-ton creatures who come here be-tween December and March to breed. During breeding season the bulls stage bloody battles and collect large harems, creating a spectacle that draws crowds every year. Visitors are allowed near the breeding areas only as part of docent-led tours that must be booked in advance (415-879-0852). Located off Route 1 about 22 miles north of Santa Cruz.*

This placid landscape soon gives way to some of California's most unpredictable countryside. As the road rises above a swirling coastline, you'll be entering a geologic hotspot. The San Andreas fault, villain of the 1906 San Francisco earthquake, heads back into shore near Pacifica. As the road cuts will reveal, the sedimentary rock along this area has been twisted and warped into bizarre shapes. At **Devil's Slide**, several miles south of Pacifica, unstable hillsides periodically collapse into the sea. Outstanding ocean vistas are revealed at every hairpin turn as rocky cliffs, pocket beaches and erupting surf open to view.

NORTH OF SANTA CRUZ LODGING

Among lodgings on this stretch of coastline, **San Benito House** (356 Main Street, Half Moon Bay; 415-726-3425) is a personal favorite. Set in a turn-of-the-century building, it's a 12-room bed and breakfast inn with adjoining bar and restaurant. One room I saw featured a brass light fixture, framed drawings and wood furniture. Add a sauna and you have a bargain at the price. Moderate.

For a touch of the truly magnificent, plant yourself a few blocks inland at **Mill Rose Inn** (615 Mill Street, Half Moon Bay; 415-726-9794). This turn-of-the-century home has been decorated by a master of interior design. There are hand-painted wallpapers and European antiques throughout. The grounds resemble an English garden and include a kiosk with hot tub. Each of the six guest rooms is brilliantly appointed; even the least expensive displays an antique armoire and marble-top dresser. Ultra-deluxe.

NORTH OF SANTA CRUZ RESTAURANTS

In the restaurant-scarce stretch between Santa Cruz and Half Moon Bay lies **Duarte's Tavern** (202 Stage Road, Pescadero; 415-879-0464), a restaurant and tavern that has earned a reputation all along the coast. The dishes are moderately priced and delicious. There's a menu filled with meat and fish entrées, omelettes and sandwiches. Be adventurous and try the artichoke soup and olallieberry pie.

For contemporary California cuisine in a country-inn setting, there's **San Benito House** (356 Main Street, Half Moon Bay; 415-726-3425). This gourmet restaurant incorporates fresh seafood and produce from the surrounding ocean and farm country; as a result, the prix-fixe dinner menu changes twice a week. On a typical night you might choose rack of veal or mesquite-grilled halibut. Sunday brunch is also served; deluxe.

Set in a Cape Cod-style building overlooking the water, **The Shore Bird** (390 Capistrano Road, Princeton-by-the-Sea; 415-728-5541) is an expansive seafood restaurant featuring a dining room, seafood cafe, cocktail lounge, garden patio and more. Lunch, dinner and Sunday brunch. Moderate to deluxe.

For dinner overlooking the ocean, there's nothing quite like **Moss Beach Distillery** (Beach Way and Ocean Boulevard, Moss Beach; 415-728-5595). The place dates back to Prohibition days, when this area was notorious for supplying booze to thirsty San Francisco. Today it's a quiet plate-glass restaurant with an adjoining bar and splendid sea views. The moderate-to-deluxe menu includes gulf shrimp, Australian lobster tail and rack of lamb.

NORTH OF SANTA CRUZ BEACHES AND PARKS

One of the most secluded strands around, **Greyhound Rock** is a beauty. There are startling cliffs in the background and a gigantic boulder in the foreground; the area is a favorite among those who love to fish. Located along Route 1 about 19 miles north of Santa Cruz.

Several miles from the coast, **Butano State Park** (415-879-0173) provides a welcome counterpoint to the beach parks. About 2200 acres, it features a deep redwood forest, including stands of virgin timber. Located off Route 1 about 27 miles north of Santa Cruz.

NUDE BEACHES

Those who really want to strip off the shackles of civilization can find plenty of company (or privacy, as the case may be) on one of California's famed nude beaches. The stretch of coast between Santa Cruz and San Francisco features several places where naturists and naturalists alike can bare it all.

*One of the state's most popular spots, compact **Bonny Doon Beach** is protected on either flank by rugged cliffs. There are dunes at the south end, caves to the north, plus bevies of barebottomed bathers in between. Located off Route 1 about ten miles north of Santa Cruz. Watch for the parking lot near the junction with Bonny Doon Road; follow the path across the railroad tracks and down to the beach.*

*Reputedly the first beach of its type in California, the nude beach just north of **San Gregorio State Beach** (415-879-0832) is among the nicest in the state, featuring a narrow sand corridor shielded by high bluffs. Entrance is several hundred yards north of San Gregorio entrance, on Route 1 about 11 miles south of Half Moon Bay.*

*A lovely half-mile-long sand swath backdropped by a rocky bluff, **Montara State Beach** is popular with nude sunbathers, who congregate near the north end of the beach. Located along Route 1 seven miles south of Pacifica.*

*Tucked discreetly in a beautiful spot beneath steep cliffs, **Gray Whale Cove** (415-728-5336) is a popular white sand nude beach. Located along Route 1 five miles south of Pacifica. Watch for the parking lot on the east side of the highway.*

The small, sandy **Bean Hollow State Beach** (415-879-0832) is bounded by rocks, so sunbathers go elsewhere while tidepool watchers drop by. Particularly interesting is nearby **Pebble Beach**, a coarse-grain strand studded with jasper, serpentine, agates and carnelians. Located along Route 1 about 17 miles south of Half Moon Bay; Pebble Beach is about a mile north of Bean Hollow.

Backed by sand dunes and saltwater ponds, the lovely **Pescadero State Beach** (415-879-0832) also features a wide expanse of sand. There are tidepools to the south and a wildlife preserve across the highway. Located on Route 1 about 15 miles south of Half Moon Bay.

Pomponio State Beach (408-688-3241) has a white-sand swath crossed periodically by a creek. There are headlands on either side of the beach. Located on Route 1 about 13 miles south of Half Moon Bay.

The wide sand strip at **San Gregorio State Beach** (415-879-0832) is framed by sedimentary cliffs and cut by a small creek. Located along Route 1 about 11 miles south of Half Moon Bay.

Boasting the best facilities among the beaches in the area, **James V. Fitzgerald Marine Reserve** (415-728-3584) also has a sandy beach and excellent tidepools. It's a great place to while away the hours watching crabs, sea urchins and anemones. Located off Route 1 in Moss Beach about eight miles south of Pacifica.

Sporting Life

FISHING

Albacore, rock cod, salmon, barracuda and marlin are just some of the fish that ply the waters off the Central Coast. If you're interested in a fishing cruise or charter, contact one of the following companies: **Captain Don's** (Stearns Wharf, Santa Barbara; 805-969-5217), **Virg's Fish'n** (1215 Embarcadero, Morro Bay; or across from Hearst Castle, San Simeon; 805-772-1222), **Paradise Sportfishing** (Avila Beach; 805-595-7200), **Monterey Sport Fishing** (96 Old Fisherman's Wharf #1, Monterey; 408-372-2203), **Shamrock Charters** (Santa Cruz Yacht Harbor, Santa Cruz; 408-476-2648) or **Captain John's Fishing Trips** (111 Pillar Point Harbor, Princeton-by-the-Sea; 415-726-2913).

WHALE WATCHING

To see the whales during their annual migration from December to April, head for whale-watching lookouts at the coast around Cypress

Point in Point Lobos State Reserve, Point Pinos in Pacific Grove, Davenport or Pillar Point in Half Moon Bay.

If you'd prefer a close look at these migrating mammals and other marine life, catch a cruise with **Cisco's Sportfishing** (Captain Jack's Landing, 4151 South Victoria Avenue, Oxnard; 805-985-8511), **Sea Landing Aquatic Center** (The Breakwater, Santa Barbara; 805-963-3564), **Virg's Fish'n** (1215 Embarcadero, Morro Bay; 805-772-1222), **Paradise Sportfishing** (Avila Beach; 805-595-7200), **Randy's Fishing Trips** (66 Fisherman's Wharf, Monterey; 408-372-7440) or **Shamrock Charters** (Santa Cruz Yacht Harbor, Santa Cruz; 408-476-2648).

SKINDIVING

For those more interested in exploring the deep, there are several outfits in the Central Coast area sponsoring dive boats; some also offer skindiving rentals and lessons. In the Oxnard–Ventura area try **Ventura Dive and Sport** (1559 Spinnaker Drive #108, Ventura; 805-656-0167).

In Santa Barbara call **Divers Den** (22 Anacapa Street, Santa Barbara; 805-963-8917). **Sea Wink** (750 Price Street, Pismo Beach; 805-773-4794) serves the San Luis Obispo area. Farther north, try **Aquarius Dive Shop** (2240 Del Monte Avenue, Monterey; 408-375-1933) or **Adventure Sports** (303 Potrero Street, Santa Cruz; 408-458-3648).

SURFING AND WINDSURFING

Hang ten or catch the wind with board rentals from the following enterprises: **Pipe Line Surf Shop** (1124 South Seaward Avenue, Ventura; 805-652-1418; surfing only), **Sundance Windsurfing** (2036 Cliff Drive, Santa Barbara; 805-966-4400), **Good Clean Fun** (136 Ocean Front, Cayucos; 805-995-1993) or **Wavelengths Surf Shop** (998 Embarcadero, Morro Bay; 805-772-3904; surfing only).

Catching a wave when the surf's up near Lighthouse Point north of Santa Cruz is a surfer's dream. Known as "Steamer's Lane," this stretch of coastline hosts many international surfing championships. Surfboards and wet suits (the water is always cold) are available at **Freeline Design** (861 41st Avenue, Santa Cruz; 408-476-2950) or at **O'Neill's Surf Shop** (1149 41st Avenue, Capitola; 408-475-4151). Or catch the wind on a windsurfing board. Rentals are available at **Santa Cruz Ski Shop** (124 River Street, Santa Cruz; 408-426-6760).

SEA KAYAKING

Whether you are young or old, experienced or a novice, the Central Coast awaits discovery by sea kayak. Explore Monterey Bay, Elkhorn Slough or other coastal waters with **Monterey Bay Kayaks** (693 Del Monte Avenue, Monterey; 408-373-5357).

BALLOONING AND HANG GLIDING

If your preference is to soar through the air, hang-gliding lessons at Marina Beach are the way to fly. Call **Western Hanggliders** (Reservation Road and Route 1, Marina; 408-384-2622) for more information. Or, for a hot air balloon ride, try **Balloons By the Sea** (71 Myrtle Court, Salinas; 408-424-0111).

TIDEPOOLS

It's a climactic scene in that Hollywood classic, Chinatown. Jack Nicholson, portraying a 1930s-era private eye, is about to accuse John Huston of murdering his own partner. But Huston, a deceitful and powerful businessman playing the innocent, waxes sentimental about the dead friend. His partner, Hollis Mulwrey, had been water commissioner, a great man who early in the century brought water to the Los Angeles basin, transforming a dusty town into a metropolis. Yet Hollis was a simple man, sensitive to nature, and loved the sea.

"Hollis was always fascinated by tidepools," Huston intones. "Do you know what he used to say? 'That's where life begins—sloughs, tidepools.' " As Huston knows, tidepools are also where life ends: he murdered Mulwrey by drowning him in one.

Poor Hollis' fascination with tidepools is shared by everyone. These rocky pockets, exposed to view at low tide, are microcosms of the world. Delicately poised between land and sea, they are a frontier dividing two wildly varied environments.

Near the sand you'll discover barnacles and limpets. A little further in are mussels, which grow in clumps, forming their own biological communities. Lying within deeper waters are starfish, crabs, octopus and chitons, those oval-shaped mollusks that date back to before the age of dinosaurs.

When you go searching for these prehistoric creatures remember, even out here in the wild, there are a few rules of the road. Collecting plants and animals, including dead ones, is strongly discouraged and in some places entirely illegal. Follow the old adage and look but don't touch. If you do turn over a rock or move a shell, replace it in the original position; it may be someone's home. Also watch out for big waves and, unlike the erstwhile water commissioner, exercise caution, it can be dangerous out there.

GOLF

Golf enthusiasts will enjoy the weather as well as the courses along the Central Coast. Try **River Ridge** (2401 West Vineyard Avenue, Oxnard; 805-983-4653), **Santa Barbara Community Course** (Las Positas Road and McCaw Avenue, Santa Barbara; 805-687-7087), **Twin Lakes Golf Course** (6034 Hollister Avenue, Goleta; 805-964-1414), **Ojai Valley Inn and Country Club** (Ojai Valley Inn, Country Club Drive, Ojai; 805-646-5511), **Pismo State Beach Golf Course** (Le Sage Drive, Grover City; 805-481-5215), **Laguna Lake Golf Course** (11175 Los Osos Valley Road, San Luis Obispo; 805-549-7309) and **San Luis Bay Golf Course** (Avila Beach Road, Avila Beach; 805-595-2307).

For golfers, visiting the Monterey Peninsula is tantamount to arriving in heaven. Several courses rank among the top in the nation. Most renowned is **Pebble Beach Golf Course** (17 Mile Drive, Pebble Beach; 408-624-3811). Or you might want to tee off at **Spyglass Hill Golf Course** (Stevenson Road, Pebble Beach; 408-624-3811), **Old Del Monte Golf Course** (1300 Sylvan Road, Monterey; 408-624-3811) or **Pacific Grove Municipal Links** (77 Asilomar Boulevard, Pacific Grove; 408-375-3456).

TENNIS

Courts are available at the following sites: **Moranda Park** (200 Moranda Parkway, Port Hueneme; 805-986-6584), **Santa Barbara Municipal Courts** (contact the Santa Barbara Recreation Department; 805-963-0611) and **Cuesta College** (Route 1, San Luis Obispo; 805-544-5356).

HORSEBACK RIDING

A variety of riding opportunities are available on the Central Coast. Call **Circle Bar B Stables** (1800 Refugio Road, Goleta; 805-968-3901) or **The Livery Stable** (1207 Silverspur Place, Oceano; 805-489-8100). There are escorted tours along 20 miles of trails at the **Pebble Beach Equestrian Center** (Portola Road, Pebble Beach; 408-624-2756). With its four-mile white sand beach and surrounding farm country, Half Moon Bay is also a choice region for riding. **Friendly Acres Ranch** (2150 Route 1, Half Moon Bay; 415-726-8550) rents horses and has pony rides for kids.

Transportation

BY CAR

As it proceeds north from the Los Angeles area, coastal highway **Route 1** weaves in and out from **Route 101**. Generally Route 1 hugs the coast, while 101 follows an inland course.

BY AIR

Santa Barbara, San Luis Obispo and Monterey have small airports serving the Central Coast. Several airlines stop at the **Santa Barbara Municipal Airport,** including American Airlines, United Airlines, Delta Airlines and Sky West Airlines. The **Santa Barbara Airbus** (805-964-7759) meets all scheduled arrivals and transports folks to surrounding towns.

San Luis Obispo Municipal Airport is serviced by West Air, Wings West and Sky West Airlines. Ground transportation is provided by **Yellow Cab** (805-543-1234).

Currently, United Express and American Eagle Airlines fly regular schedules to the **Monterey Peninsula Airport.**

BY BUS

Greyhound/Trailways Bus Lines has service all along the Central Coast from Los Angeles or San Francisco. Terminals are located in Ventura (805-653-0164), Santa Barbara (805-965-3971), Pismo Beach (805-773-2144), San Luis Obispo (805-543-2123), Monterey (408-373-4735) and Santa Cruz (408-423-1800).

CAR RENTALS

At the airport in Santa Barbara try **Avis Rent A Car** (805-964-4848), **Budget Rent A Car** (805-964-6791), **Hertz Rent A Car** (805-967-0411) or **National Car Rental** (805-967-1202).

In San Luis Obispo, car rental agencies at the airport include **Avis Rent A Car** (805-544-0630), **Budget Rent A Car** (805-541-2722), **Hertz Rent A Car** (805-543-8843) and **Thrifty Car Rental** (805-544-3777).

If flying directly into Monterey, you can rent a car at the airport from **American Auto Rental** (408-649-0200), **Avis Rent A Car** (408-373-3327), **Budget Rent A Car** (408-373-1899), **Dollar Rent A Car** (408-373-6121), **Hertz Rent A Car** (408-373-3318) or **National Car Rental** (408-373-4181).

San Francisco

It is a city poised at the end of the continent, civilization's last fling   **287**
before the land plunges into the Pacific. Perhaps this is why visitors
demand something memorable from San Francisco. People expect the
city to resonate along a personal wavelength, speak to them, fulfill
some ineffable desire at the center of the soul.

There is a terrible beauty at the edge of America: the dream begins here, or ends. The Golden Gate Bridge, that arching portal to
infinite horizons, has also been a suicide gangplank for hundreds of
ill-starred dreamers. Throughout American history, those who
crossed the country in search of destiny ultimately found it here or
turned back to the continent and their own past.

Yet San Francisco is only a city, a steel-and-glass metropolis
mounted on a series of hills. With a population of about 725,000, it
covers 47 square miles at the tip of a peninsula bounded by the Pacific
Ocean and San Francisco Bay. A gateway to Asia, San Francisco supports a multicultural population with large concentrations of Chinese, Hispanics, blacks, Italians, Filipinos and Japanese. Adding to the
cosmopolitan atmosphere is a gay population constituting perhaps 15
percent of the city's residents.

The myth of San Francisco originates not only from its geography,
but its history as well. If, as early Christians believed, the world was
created in 4004 B.C., then the history of San Francisco began on
January 28, 1848. That day a hired hand named James Marshall discovered gold in California.

For adventurers, California gold was the quintessence of the
American dream. Along with the call of Manifest Destiny, the discovery impelled 100,000 people to cross an implacable land and create a
civilization on the fringes of a continent.

San Francisco became the capital of that civilization. The peaceful
hamlet was transmogrified into a hellbent city, a place to make the

(Text continued on page 290.)

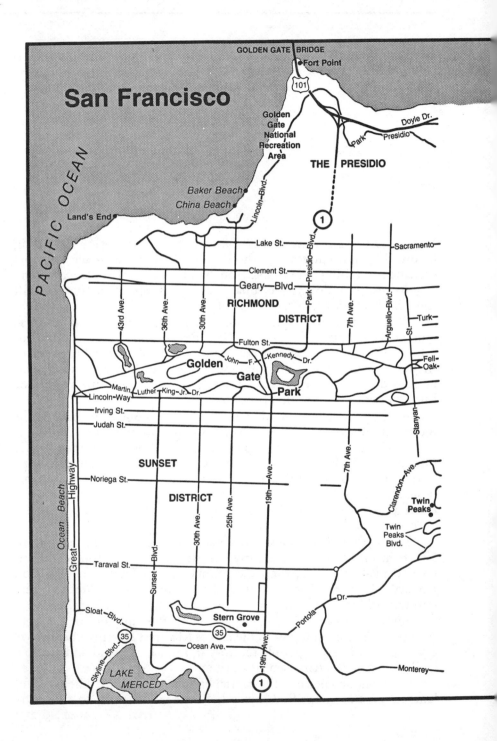

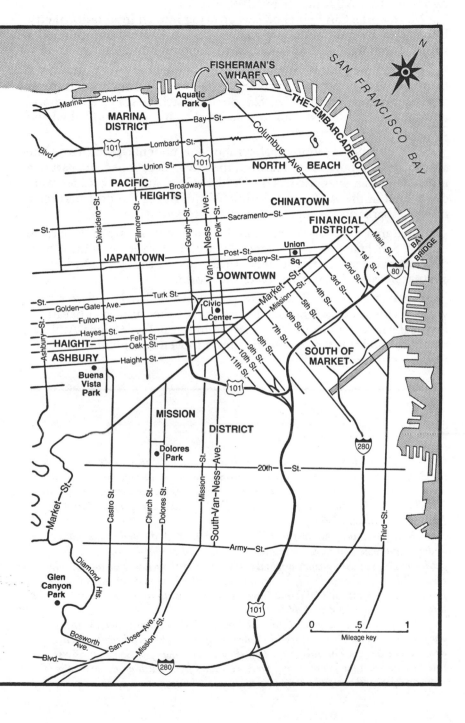

Wild West look tame. Its population exploded from 900 to 25,000 in two years; by 1890 it numbered 300,000.

Meanwhile, San Francisco was growing into an international city. Because of its multicultural population, San Francisco developed a strong liberal tradition, an openness to the unusual and unexpected.

But the unexpected can have dire consequences—one such event nearly leveled the city on April 18, 1906. Dream turned to nightmare as a horrendous earthquake, 8.3 on the Richter scale, rocked and buckled the land. Firestorms tore across the city, 452 people died and 250,000 were left homeless.

The city whose municipal symbol is a phoenix rising from the ashes quickly rebuilt. City Hall and the Civic Center became part of a resurrected San Francisco. The Golden Gate and Bay bridges were completed in the 1930s, and during World War II the port became a major embarkation point for men and materiel.

It entered the post–World War II era at the vanguard of American society. San Francisco's hallmark is cultural innovation. This city at continent's edge boasts a society at the edge of thought. During the 1950s it became the beat capital of the world.

But not even the Beats were prepared for San Francisco's next wave of cultural immigrants. This mecca for the misplaced became a mystical gathering place for myriads of hippies. The Haight-Ashbury neighborhood was the staging area for a movement intent on revolutionizing American consciousness.

CABLE CARS

Cable cars, those clanging symbols of San Francisco, are the way to see this city of perpendicular hills. The system covers a ten-mile section of downtown San Francisco. A major embarkation point near Union Square is the turnaround station at Powell and Market streets. From here the brightly painted cars climb toward Nob Hill and Fisherman's Wharf.

The cable car was invented in 1873 by Andrew Hallidie and works via an underground cable that travels continuously at a speed of nine-and-a-half miles per hour. Three of the system's original twelve lines still operate year-round. The Powell–Mason and Powell–Hyde cars travel from the downtown district to Fisherman's Wharf; the California Street line runs east to west and passes through Chinatown and Nob Hill.

Built partially of wood and furnished with old-style running boards, these open-air vehicles are slow and stylish. Edging up the city's steep heights, then descending toboggan-run hills to the bay, they provide many of San Francisco's finest views. Half the joy of riding, however, comes from watching the operators of these antique machines, who treat passengers to a clanging street symphony.

By the 1970s San Francisco was also becoming home to a vital and creative minority, gay men and women. The city's gay population had increased steadily for decades; then, suddenly, San Francisco's open society and freewheeling lifestyle brought a great influx of gays. They won increasing social and political power throughout the 1980s.

In October 1989 San Francisco once again demonstrated its unsettling ability to rebound from terrible tragedy. A 7.1 level earthquake rolled through Northern California, leaving 67 dead, and causing more than $10 billion in damage, but failed to daunt the local spirit.

A multicultural society from its early days, San Francisco remains a city at the edge, open to experiment and experience. Rudyard Kipling once called the place "a mad city—inhabited for the most part by perfectly insane people." William Saroyan saw it as "a city that invites the heart to come to life . . . an experiment in living." The two thoughts do not contradict: San Francisco is madly beautiful, a marvelous and zany place. Its contribution to the world is its lifestyle.

Union Square

Visit any city in the world and the sightseeing tour will begin in a vital but nebulous area called "downtown." San Francisco is no different. Here, the center of downtown is spelled **Union Square** (Geary and Stockton streets), a tree-dotted plot in the heart of the city's hotel and shopping district.

Stroll over to **Maiden Lane**, headiest of the city's high-heeled shopping areas. Of particular interest among the galleries and boutiques lining this pedestrian-only thoroughfare is the building at **140 Maiden Lane**. Designed by Frank Lloyd Wright in 1948, its circular interior stairway and other unique elements foreshadow the motifs he later used for the famous Guggenheim Museum.

UNION SQUARE LODGING

It's a one-class-fits-all establishment. Of course, at the 17-story **Campton Place Hotel** (340 Stockton Street; 415-781-5555), the class is definitely first: 126 luxurious rooms and suites are outfitted with sinfully comfortable beds, Henredon armoires, writing desks, limited edition art and marble baths. Innumerable services are available around the clock. Located half a block from Union Square, this is the place to stay when you can afford to pay ultra-deluxe prices.

European elegance at low cost: that's what the **Beresford Hotel** (635 Sutter Street; 415-673-9900) has offered its clientele for years. You'll sense a touch of class immediately upon treading the lobby's red carpet and settling into a plump armchair. Upstairs the rooms are outstanding—original paintings, comfortable furnishings and a marble-top vanity in the bathroom. All this just two blocks from Union Square. Moderate.

The little **Hotel Carlton** (1075 Sutter Street; 415-673-0242) possesses many splendors of more expensive hostelries. There's room service, a lovely cafe hung with chandeliers, and a rich lobby with marble floors and brass wall sconces. The rooms have been decorated with great care. Although located about a half-mile from Union Square, the Carlton is highly recommended. Deluxe.

The brilliant polished wood facade of the **Savoy Hotel** (580 Geary Street; 415-441-2700) provides only a hint of its luxurious interior. The lobby is the first word in elegance with beveled glass, brass fixtures and dark woods. The spacious rooms sport French-country motifs and feature attractive wood furniture. One very noteworthy hotel. Deluxe.

Following the lead of European hotels is **The Raphael Hotel** (386 Geary Street; 415-986-2000), a 151-room affair set at the heart of the theater district. The small lobby is adorned with high-back chairs and wooden antiques. The true elegance lies upstairs in the warm and spacious private rooms, decorated with an aesthetic eye. The wise will pay a few dollars more for a "deluxe room" that includes a sitting room complete with game table. Deluxe.

Built early in the century, the 131-plus-room **Hotel Union Square** (114 Powell Street; 415-397-3000) was recently refurbished. Mystery writer Dashiell Hammett and playwright Lillian Hellman, who reputedly frequented the place, might recognize it even today. The lobby still possesses an art deco ambience with its mosaic murals. The rooms have been exquisitely decorated in quiet hues and floral prints. Deluxe.

A sparkling, well-run, family-owned hotel in one of the best shopping blocks in San Francisco is always worth checking out—or checking into. The 114-room **Cartwright Hotel** (524 Sutter Street; 415-421-2865) offers eight floors of accommodations individually decorated in personally selected antiques. The family's attention to detail shows in touches such as plump reading pillows. A good bargain at moderate rates.

For intimacy and charm, you can't do much better than **The Inn at Union Square** (440 Post Street; 415-397-3510). Corridors are fashionably lined with mirrors and brass wall sconces, and most rooms are equipped with a brass lion-head door knocker. The entire inn numbers only 30 rooms, each plush and cozy with quilted bedspreads and antique Georgian furnishings. There is a small lobby with a fireplace on each floor. One of the city's finest bed and breakfasts. Deluxe to ultra-deluxe.

The **York Hotel** (940 Sutter Street; 415-885-6800) is a sumptuous seven-story establishment built in 1922 and nicely renovated. The
spacious rooms are done in pastel hues and include such features as
hand-designed bedding and watercolors by local artists. Since one of
the city's top cabarets is here, the York is a prime gathering place at
night and caters to a mixed crowd. Deluxe.

Once inside the 21-story **Pan Pacific San Francisco** (500 Post
Street; 415-771-8600), some guests simply cannot believe there are
330 rooms and suites here; the ambience is more like that of an intimate small hotel. Rooms have fine furnishings, custom cabinetry and
distinctive arched windows. Despite their size, they feel cozy, almost
too much so. Oversized marble baths and attentive valet service are
extra indulgences at this ultra-deluxe-priced hotel one block west of
Union Square.

Elegance reigns at the **White Swan Inn** (845 Bush Street; 415-
775-1755). A five-story, English-style 1908 building with curved bay
windows, the White Swan is a fashionable bed and breakfast with a
living room, library, solarium and small courtyard. Each beautifully
appointed guest room contains a fireplace, refrigerator and wet bar.
Ultra-deluxe.

Personalized service and beautiful surroundings are taken for
granted at the **Four Seasons Clift Hotel** (495 Geary Street; 415-775-
4700). This grand old building, dating to 1916 and rising 17 stories
above the city, has over 300 rooms. The lobby is a study in marble,
redwood paneling and crystal chandeliers, and the guest accommodations are furnished with select hardwood pieces and finely decorated.
Ultra-deluxe.

Accommodations at the 25-story **Hotel Nikko** (222 Mason
Street; 415-394-1111) exude *shibui*, a Japanese word expressing elegant
simplicity. Smooth-edged contemporary furnishings in pearl gray are
offset by soft pinks and mauve in carpeting and upholstery. Deluxe to
ultra-deluxe rates include access to business services and fitness facilities, including a glass-enclosed rooftop swimming pool.

There's an emphasis on style and service at **Stouffer's Stanford
Court Hotel** (905 California Street; 415-989-3500), whose hallmark
is the *porte cochère*, illuminated through a leaded-glass dome. The 402
guest rooms combine antiques and modern pieces to create a singular
effect. There are several shops and lounges, plus an excellent staff. Five
stars. Ultra-deluxe.

UNION SQUARE RESTAURANTS

Campton Place Restaurant (340 Stockton Street in the Campton
Place Hotel; 415-781-5555) transforms the freshest all-American ingredients into haute cuisine, all in a blush-pink room where chande-

liers are reflected in silver, crystal and Wedgwood china. Breakfast is worth a special trip for items like scrambled eggs with smoked trout and caviar. At lunch and dinner, seafood, pasta and lamb share the menu with entrées such as grilled quail and fricassée of rabbit. Ultra-deluxe.

Dashiell Hammett fans always track down **John's Grill** (63 Ellis Street; 415-986-3274), the restaurant that detective Sam Spade popped into during a tense scene in *The Maltese Falcon*. Today the wood-paneled walls, adorned with memorabilia and old photos, still breathe of bygone eras. Waiters dress formally and the menu features broiler and seafood dishes. Moderate.

In a neighborhood that loves deli food, **David's** (474 Geary Street; 415-771-1600) is a classic lox-and-bagel establishment. Just pull up a counter stool or tuck yourself into a booth. The sandwich menu has pastrami and tongue; entrées include Hungarian goulash and beans with kosher franks. There is also a tantalizing selection of bakery goodies. Budget to moderate.

The spot in San Francisco for Sunday brunch is **Lehr's Greenhouse** (740 Sutter Street; 415-474-6478). First, there's the decor—ferns, spider plants and other botanical wonders hang everywhere. The tables are laden with lox, caviar, fresh fruit, crêpes, roast chicken and on and on. This tropical wonderland has a dinner menu with dry-aged prime rib and fish dishes. Moderate to deluxe.

WALKING TOURS

San Francisco is a city made for walkers. Appropriately, it offers a number of walking tours that explore various neighborhoods and historical spots.

Chinese Heritage Walks, conducted by the Chinese Culture Center (750 Kearny Street; 415-986-1822; fee), reveals the true Chinatown. They also offer a Culinary Walk that visits markets and herb shops, then stops for lunch in a dim sum restaurant. Or you can sign up for a culinary/historical tour with Wok Wiz Chinatown Tours (415-355-9657).

The Dashiell Hammett Walking Tour (707-939-1214; fee) is a three-mile search for the old haunts of the mystery writer and his fictional sleuth, Sam Spade. Hammett lived in the bay city from 1921 to 1930 and used it as the setting for numerous short stories and novels, including The Maltese Falcon.

Precita Eyes Muralists (348 Precita Avenue; 415-285-2287) offer tours of the Mission District murals.

City Guides (415-557-4266 or 415-557-4257) offers free tours of Pacific Heights Victorians, Historic Market Street, North Beach, Nob Hill, Coit Tower and other points of interest.

Sushi Man (731 Bush Street; 415-981-1313) is a matchbox sushi bar with matchless style. The tiny wooden bar is decorated with fresh flowers and serene silk screens. Owner Ryo Yoshioka has earned a deserved reputation for his sushi creations, including *sake* (smoked salmon) and *mirugai* (clam). Dinner only; moderate.

Donatello (501 Post Street; 415-441-7182) has written the final word on fine Italian cuisine. An intimate restaurant with two small dining areas and a marble bar, it specializes in regional dishes from northern Italy. The changing menu features entrées like salmon in black olive sauce. The real allure is the fixed-price dinner—four courses, each served with a different Italian wine. Ultra-deluxe.

It is the rare restaurateur who can please both Los Angeles and San Francisco, but that's exactly what Wolfgang Puck has done in bringing his talents north to **Postrio** (545 Post Street; 415-776-7825). Puck's innovative food pairings, such as Chinese duck with mango sauce and salmon with warm spinach, compete for attention with a stunning dining room. Deluxe to ultra-deluxe. Reserve far in advance.

Chef Barbara Tropp has created a unique blend of Asian and California foods at **China Moon Cafe** (639 Post Street; 415-775-4789). Few of the dishes could be found elsewhere: spring rolls with chile sauce, fresh water chestnuts and a stir fry incorporating lamb, red peppers and snap peas in hoisin sauce draped over a crisp brown-noodle pancake. Moderate to deluxe.

Fleur de Lys (777 Sutter Street; 415-673-7779) is an updated San Francisco classic, where the elegant rooms (tented in red floral silk-screened canvas) promise equally top-notch service. At ultra-deluxe prices, you not only dine well here (scallop and sea urchin mousseline, loin of venison, *foie gras*), but you are coddled throughout a two- to three-hour gustatory experience.

Another small and romantic dining room, **Masa's** (648 Bush Street; 415-989-7154) is my favorite San Francisco restaurant. Elite yet understated, the decor is a mix of brass sconces, upholstered chairs and dark trim. From Masa's famous kitchen come contemporary French entrées like sweetbreads in crayfish sauce, lobster with shrimp quenelles or breast of muscovy duck. But inventorying the menu can never do justice to this splendid place. You have to experience it yourself. Ultra-deluxe.

UNION SQUARE SHOPPING

Union Square quite simply is *the* center for shopping in San Francisco. First of all, this grass-and-hedgerow park is surrounded by department stores: **I. Magnin** (415-362-2100) and **Macy's** (415-397-3333) along one border, **Sak's Fifth Avenue** (415-986-4300) guarding another. **Neiman-Marcus** (415-362-3900), the Texas-bred emporium, claims one corner; an elite men's clothing shop named **Bullock & Jones** (415-392-4243) is also situated in this well-heeled neighborhood.

Nearby **Gumps** (250 Post Street; 415-982-1616) features fine imported decorations for the home. If you get bored looking through the antiques, china pieces and Oriental art, you can always adjourn to the Jade or Crystal room or the gourmet shop.

The streets all around host a further array of stores. You'll encounter jewelers, dress designers, tailor shops and more.

Spiffy designer boutique **Jeanne-Marc** (262 Sutter Street; 415-362-1121) sells five different "seasons" of sportswear. Among the offerings are women's suits and frocks, plus an array of gorgeous cotton clothes.

Braunstein/Quay Gallery (250 Sutter Street; 415-392-5532) is an outstanding place to view the work of local and international artists.

Tillman Place Bookshop (8 Tillman Place; 415-392-4668) is a postage-stamp-size store tucked into an alleyway. Within, however, you'll find a tasteful collection of coffee-table books, paperback classics, travel guides and color prints, all contained in a Victorian setting.

For toys, there's no place like **FAO Schwartz** (48 Stockton Street; 415-394-8700). A branch of New York's famous Fifth Avenue emporium, it includes three huge floors dripping with spectacular kites, monstrous stuffed animals and designer doll dresses.

The **Galleria** (50 Post Street; 415-956-2846) is a glass-domed promenade lined with fashionable shops. A center for well-heeled business crowds, the mall showcases designer fashions and elegant gifts.

When looking for maps and travel guides, it's hard to top **Thomas Brothers Maps** (550 Jackson Street; 415-981-7520), which has gained renown for its excellent city maps.

Most of these shops are located along the eastern flank of Union Square. There are also countless stores on the other side. The **500 and 600 blocks of Sutter Street**, for instance, contain a covey of art galleries.

Harold's Hometown News (599 Post Street; 415-441-2665) sells daily newspapers from all over the world.

A nine-story vertical mall, **San Francisco Centre** (5th and Market streets; 415-495-5656) sports six stacked spiral escalators that ascend through an oval-shaped, marble-and-granite atrium toward the retractable skylight. The mall includes nearly 90 upscale shops selling everything from men's and women's sportswear to jewelry and unique gifts. It's all crowned by a five-floor **Nordstrom's** (415-243-8500), the high-quality fashion department store.

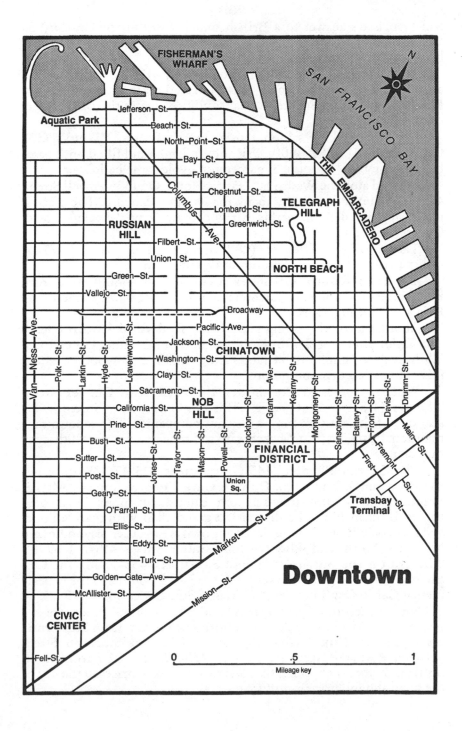

Downtown

UNION SQUARE NIGHTLIFE

San Francisco's answer to a British pub is **Edinburgh Castle** (950 Geary Street; 415-885-4074), a cavernous bar complete with dart board and convivial crowd.

At **S. Holmes, Esq.** (480 Sutter Street; 415-398-8900), you'll encounter a pub for the upper crust. Located on the top floor of the Holiday Inn–Union Square, it beautifully re-creates the Baker Street detective's digs.

For key-plunking saloon music, there's **Lefty O'Doul's** (333 Geary Street; 415-982-8900). Friendly, informal and filled with baseball memorabilia, the place is named for an old-time ballplayer.

Located atop the Westin St. Francis Hotel, **Oz** (335 Powell Street; 415-774-0116) is favored by many for its disco dancing. The place is nicely appointed with marble bar and draws a well-heeled crowd. Cover; dress code.

The **Warfield Theater** (982 Market Street; 415-775-7722) brings in top national rock groups to its nightclub.

The **Plush Room** (940 Sutter Street; 415-885-6800) in the York Hotel caters to an upscale clientele and draws big name cabaret acts. It's a lovely setting. Cover.

Another favored relaxing place is the **Redwood Room** (Geary and Taylor streets; 415-775-4700) in the Four Seasons Clift Hotel. With art deco lamps, marble tables and burnished redwood paneling, it is nothing less than sumptuous.

When it comes to live theater, the **American Conservatory Theater** (415-673-6440), or ACT, is the biggest show in town. It's also one of the nation's largest resident companies. The repertoire is traditional, ranging from Shakespeare to French comedy to 20th-century drama.

The **Curran Theatre** (445 Geary Street; 415-474-3800) brings Broadway musicals to town. **Golden Gate Theatre** (6th and Market streets; 415-474-3800) attracts major theater shows and national companies. Built in 1922, the theater is a grand affair with marble floors and rococo ceilings. Among the downtown area's other playhouses are **Marine's Memorial Theatre** (609 Sutter Street; 415-771-6900), **Theatre on the Square** (450 Post Street; 415-433-9500), the **Orpheum Theatre** (1192 Market Street; 415-474-3800) and the experimental **Cable Car Theatre** (430 Mason Street; 415-861-6895).

Since tickets to major theatrical and other cultural events are expensive, consider buying day-of-performance tickets from **San Francisco Ticket Box Office Service** (STBS) on Stockton Street between Post and Geary streets (415-433-7827). Open from noon until just before show time, they sell tickets at half-price on the day of the show and full price for future events.

Many local radio stations sponsor event hotlines in the Bay Area. There's the **KKSF Bayline** (415-982-4636) with information on theater, comedy, live music and other activities in the city. Check the **KJAZ Jazz Line** (415-769-4818) for local jazz events and **KFOG's Entertainment Line** (415-536-4386) for music events and happenings at clubs throughout the area. It's also advisable to consult the "Datebook," commonly called the "pink section," in the Sunday *San Francisco Examiner & Chronicle* for current shows and performers.

Civic Center

Southwest of the downtown district rises the Civic Center, architectural pride of the city, where politics meets the arts. The prettiest pathway through this municipal meeting ground begins in **United Nations Plaza** at Fulton and Market streets. With the dome of City Hall before you, walk up Fulton through a corridor of marble and granite.

That imposing building on your right, not the first one but the second, is **San Francisco Public Library** (Larkin and McAllister streets; 415-558-3191). Culturally inclined residents ascend its interior marble staircase en route to the "San Francisco Room." This mini-museum houses fascinating photographs, memoirs and other relics of bygone days. Guided tours of the Civic Center (415-558-3981) also begin here.

With its bird-whitened statues and gray-columned buildings, the Civic Center is the domain of powerbrokers and political leaders; ironically, its grassy plots and park benches have at times made it the haunt of the city's homeless population. As you pass the reflecting pool and formal gardens, then ascend the steps of **City Hall** (Polk and Grove streets), you'll see how both halves live.

Modeled after the national capitol, this granite and marble edifice sports a dome that was based on St. Peter's Cathedral in Rome and is higher than the one in Washington. The rotunda is a dizzying sandstone and marble affair encrusted with statuary and encircled by a wrought-iron balcony.

As you step out the back of City Hall on to Van Ness Avenue, you'll be standing face to facade with the center of San Francisco culture. To the right rises the Veterans' Building, home to the **San Francisco Museum of Modern Art** (Van Ness Avenue and McAllister Street, 415-863-8800; admission). In addition to a superb collection that includes Picasso, Matisse, Klée and Pollock, the museum has premiered such visual extravaganzas as Judy Chicago's *Dinner Party* exhibit.

Centerstage is the **War Memorial Opera House** (Van Ness Avenue and Grove Street), home to one of the world's finest opera companies and performance space for the country's oldest ballet company. To the left, that ultramodern glass-and-granite building is the **Louise M. Davies Symphony Hall** (Van Ness Avenue and Grove Street), home of the San Francisco Symphony. You can tour this glamorous building and its cultural cousins next door (415-552-8338; admission).

CIVIC CENTER LODGING

For fans of the opera (or the symphony or the ballet), the **Inn at the Opera** (333 Fulton Street; 415-863-8400) is heaven on earth. Located virtually within earshot of the major performing arts houses, it plays the ham with concierge services (especially helpful for last-minute tickets) and little touches (such as sheet-music drawer liners) in the 30 rooms and 18 suites. Rooms have tasteful furnishings, along with wet bars and mini-fridges. Ultra-deluxe.

A two-story motor court flanking a pool courtyard, spacious rooms and suites with a soft tropical motif, a Caribbean-style restaurant . . . can this be the heart of San Francisco? It is, and it's the **Phoenix Inn** (601 Eddy Street; 415-776-1380), just a block from Civic Center. Concierge services, in-room screenings of locally filmed movies and the patronage of music-business mavens may make the Phoenix the hippest inn in town. Moderate.

CIVIC CENTER RESTAURANTS

This area spotlights several outstanding dining rooms. One of the best in my opinion is **Hayes Street Grill** (320 Hayes Street; 415-863-5545), a chic establishment situated within strolling distance of the opera and symphony. Specializing in mesquite-grilled entrées, it features fresh fish dishes, dry-aged steak and chicken breast. Excellent food at moderate to deluxe prices.

Stars (150 Redwood Alley; 415-861-7827) earned its stripes from day one with the stylish cuisine of Jeremiah Tower, a highly celebrated chef in the California cuisine constellation. Seafood (particularly tuna and salmon), warm salads and French-inspired veal entrées shine especially bright here. Deluxe to ultra-deluxe.

Leave it to that same Jeremiah Tower to transform a former carburetor shop into an airy, tropical restaurant that set new speed records for success. **690** (Van Ness Avenue at Turk Street; 415-255-6900) traffics in hip cuisine: a "lamburger" on lentils and couscous, for instance, or a Hong Kong noodle salad with Thai basil. Moderate to deluxe.

At **Monsoon** (601 Van Ness Avenue; 415-441-3232) the decor includes red-lacquered columns and a multi-hued dragon along the ceiling. The cuisine at this increasingly popular restaurant is a multi-cultural mix of Asian foods. Dinner only; deluxe.

CIVIC CENTER SHOPPING

Opera buffs enjoy the **San Francisco Opera Shop** (199 Grove Street; 415-565-6414), with its good selection of literature, photographs, videos and tapes.

The **Vorpal Gallery** (393 Grove Street; 415-397-9200), one of the city's finest galleries, features works by contemporaries like Jesse Allen and Ken Matsumoto, and such 20th-century masters as Pablo Picasso and M. C. Escher.

The **San Francisco Women Artists Gallery** (370 Hayes Street; 415-552-7392) features artworks by Bay Area women.

Just a few blocks away lies **Opera Plaza** (Van Ness and Golden Gate avenues), an atrium mall with shops, restaurants and a movie theater collected around a courtyard and fountain. A pretty place to sit and enjoy the day, for booklovers who happen into the excellent bookstore here it is also **A Clean Well-Lighted Place For Books** (601 Van Ness Avenue; 415-441-6670).

CIVIC CENTER NIGHTLIFE

San Francisco takes nothing quite so seriously as its opera. The **San Francisco Opera** (War Memorial Opera House, Van Ness Avenue and Grove Street; 415-864-3330) is world class in stature. Marilyn Horne, Wieslaw Ochman, Pilar Lorengrar and other greats perform regularly. As a result, tickets are very difficult to obtain. The international season begins in mid-September and runs for 13 weeks. There is also a spring and summer **Pocket Opera** (333 Kearny Street, Suite 703; 415-346-2780) with many performances in English.

The **San Francisco Symphony** (Davies Hall, Van Ness Avenue and Grove Street; 415-431-5400) stands nearly as tall on the world

---

ROSALIE'S REDUX

*With high ceilings, raspberry-colored walls and soaring aluminum palm trees, the decor at **Rosalie's Redux** (1415 Van Ness Avenue; 415-923-1415) could serve as the backdrop for a surrealistic film about desert life. The food is American cuisine with continental touches such as grilled chicken with lemon-tarragon sauce, loin of lamb with a cabernet sauce and crab ravioli in lobster sauce. This spot, about a mile north of Civic Center, also includes a long list of small courses that make it an ideal place to play with your food, which is consistently good. Moderate to deluxe.*

stage. The season extends from September until May, with a series of special concerts during the summer. Herbert Blomstedt conducts and guest soloists have included Pinchas Zuckerman and Jean-Pierre Rampal.

The **San Francisco Ballet** (War Memorial Opera House, Van Ness Avenue and Grove Street; 415-621-3838), performing for more than a half-century, is the nation's oldest permanent ballet and one of the finest. Featuring *The Nutcracker* during Christmas, the company's official season runs from February until May. In addition to original works, they perform classic ballets.

Kimball's (300 Grove Street; 415-861-5555) features jazz combos on weekends. Cover.

Over at the **Great American Music Hall** (859 O'Farrell Street; 415-885-0750), a vintage 1907 building has been splendidly converted to a nightclub featuring a variety of top entertainers.

Financial District

East of the Union Square area stands the "Wall Street of the West," **Montgomery Street**, locus of the Financial District. The center of Pacific commerce and trade, this is the roosting place for San Francisco's skyscrapers. Here you'll encounter windswept canyons of glass and steel.

Behind the granite and marble along Montgomery are more banks than one could imagine. **A. P. Giannini Plaza**, between Pine and California streets, a combination mall and office building, memorializes the brilliant Italian banker who developed an upstart savings company into one of the world's largest financial institutions, the Bank of America.

Another bank at 420 Montgomery hosts the **Wells Fargo History Museum**. In addition to glistening gold specimens and postal artifacts, there are photos recapturing the raffish days of the Old West and a reconditioned nine-passenger stagecoach.

That bizarrely shaped edifice between Clay and Washington streets is none other than the **Transamerica Building**. Designed like a pyramid that's been put through a wringer, it is the most striking feature along San Francisco's skyline. Known to local residents as the "Pyramid," it's a 48-story structure that rises 853 feet above the city pavement. Since its opening in 1972, visitors have been elevatoring up to the 27th floor where an unfortunately small window area offers a picture-frame view of San Francisco.

The 700 block of Montgomery contains a cluster of buildings dating back to 1850. These are part of the **Jackson Square** area, a misnomered enclave extending from Washington to Pacific streets and from Columbus Avenue to Sansome Street. There is no "square" here, but you will find an official historic district sprinkled with brickface buildings and interior courtyards. During the 1850s, this represented the black heart of the Barbary Coast.

FINANCIAL DISTRICT LODGING

Especially convenient for business travelers, the exquisite **Mandarin Oriental Hotel** (222 Sansome Street; 415-885-0999) is located in the heart of the Financial District. The 160 rooms and suites are located on the 38th through 48th floors of a commercial building and afford sweeping views (sometimes from small balconies) of the cityscape. Handsomely appointed interiors, accented with hand-picked furniture and marble baths. Ultra-deluxe.

FINANCIAL DISTRICT RESTAURANTS

Sam's Grill (374 Bush Street; 415-421-0594), established in 1867, is a classic San Francisco businessperson's restaurant. The menu, which changes daily, features fresh fish, steaks and chops. There are diner car booths, waiters in bow ties and tuxedos, a friendly bar and white walls adorned with hunting scenes. Moderate to deluxe.

Tadich Grill (240 California Street; 415-391-2373) means woodpaneled walls, tile floor, art deco light fixtures and white-linen-covered tables. The history of the place—beginning in that gilded year, 1849—is so rich it consumes the first page of the menu. The specialty is seafood (sole, salmon, swordfish), but charcoal-broiled steak, chops and chicken are also available. Moderate.

London Wine Bar (415 Sansome Street; 415-788-4811), established in 1974, claims to be "America's first wine bar." Fittingly, there is an impressive list of California and imported wines. To quench the appetite, they serve lunch and evening hors d'oeuvres such as prawns, pâtés and artichokes stuffed with turkey. Moderate.

At **Yank Sing** (427 Battery Street; 415-362-1640), you'll discover designer dim sum in a restaurant that has elevated the tea house idea to a culinary art. Yank Sing provides a serene setting with white linen, fresh flowers and cane-back chairs. The restaurant offers delights like stuffed snow crab claws and rabbit-shaped shrimp dumplings. Lunch only; moderate.

Chic and popular is the best way to describe **MacArthur Park** (607 Front Street; 415-398-5700). Particularly favored by the pin-stripe crowd, this brick-wall dining room serves dishes prepared in an oakwood smoker and on a mesquite grill. There are baby back ribs, live Maine lobster, duck and dry-aged steak. The decor is casual but self-conscious: padded park benches, track lights and a marble bar with an impressive wine rack. Moderate to deluxe.

Located in a landmark 1907 building, **Ernie's** (847 Montgomery Street; 415-397-5969) has been practically synonymous with dining out in San Francisco for some 65 years. A facelift in late 1988 transformed the restaurant's trademark red interior into a vision of soft creamy silk wall coverings. The updated menu incorporates old favorites (including an award-winning wine list) with fresh offerings such as grilled swordfish with citrus-cilantro butter. Now serving lunch as well as dinner. Ultra-deluxe.

San Francisco's modern version of upscale camp is **Fog City Diner** (1300 Battery Street; 415-982-2000). Check out the exterior with its art deco curves, neon lights and checkerboard tile. Then step into a wood-and-brass paneled restaurant that has the feel of a club car on the Orient Express. Featuring California cuisine, the menu changes seasonally—on the day I was there they were offering garlic custard with mushrooms, quesadilla with hazelnuts and grilled rabbit. Book well in advance; moderate.

Have lunch during the week at **Square One** (190 Pacific Street; 415-788-1110) and you'll mix with business people. In the evening the crowd is more varied. The changing menu features international cuisine, with an emphasis on Mediterranean dishes like fusilli with pancetta and chicken in Moroccan marinade. Deluxe.

FINANCIAL DISTRICT NIGHTLIFE

A favorite bar is the **Carnelian Room** (555 California Street; 415-433-7500) atop the Bank of America. Perched on the 52nd floor, this luxurious lounge has incredible views, sweeping from the bay out across the boundless deep. Dress code.

The **Punch Line** (444 Battery Street; 415-397-7573) books a wide variety of comedy acts from around the country.

Embarcadero

East of the Financial District, where the city's skyscrapers meet the bay, is the Embarcadero. Back in Gold Rush days, before the pernicious advent of landfill, the entire area sat beneath fathoms of water and went by the name of Yerba Buena Cove. Matter of fact, the hundreds of tall-masted ships abandoned here by crews deserting for the gold fields eventually became part of the landfill.

Fittingly enough, the first place encountered is **Embarcadero Center**, a skein of five skyscrapers rising sharp and slender along Sacramento Street to the foot of Market Street. This $645-million complex features a three-tiered pedestrian mall that links the buildings together in a labyrinth of shops, restaurants, fountains and gardens.

Just across the road, where Market Street encounters the Embarcadero, rises San Francisco's answer to the Statue of Liberty. Or what *was* the city's answer at the turn of the century, when the clock tower of the **Ferry Building** was as well-known a landmark as the Golden Gate Bridge is today. Built in 1896, the old landmark is making a comeback: today sleek, jet-powered ferries stream into refashioned slips.

You might want to walk the ramp that leads up to the **World Trade Center** (Embarcadero at the foot of Market Street). It's lined with Covarrubias'' murals preserved from the 1939 Golden Gate International Exposition.

Across from Pier 23, **Levi Plaza** (1155 Battery Street) features a grassy park ideal for picnicking; just beyond Pier 35 there's a waterfront park with a wonderful vantage for spying on the ships that sail the bay.

EMBARCADERO SHOPPING

Shoppers along the Embarcadero head for either of two places— Embarcadero Center or Pier 39. Preferable by far is **Embarcadero Center** (Sacramento Street near the foot of Market Street), a vaulting glass-and-concrete "town" inhabited by stores and restaurants. This multifaceted mall consists of the lower three levels of four adjoining skyscrapers. The place possesses positively everything—bookstores,

---

BAY CRUISES

Some of the Bay Area's choicest sights lie out on the bay itself. A ferry trip can acquaint visitors with local treasures like the East Bay, Marin County and the wondrous bridges that connect them all.

*Pier 41 is the departure point for the **Red and White Fleet** (415-546-2810), which sponsors bay cruises, Alcatraz tours and ferry service to Angel Island, Sausalito, the Wine Country and Marine World–Africa USA.*

*The trip to **Alcatraz** is highlighted with a National Park Service tour of the infamous prison. Originally a fort and later a military prison, Alcatraz gained renown as "The Rock" when it became a maximum security prison in 1934. Al Capone, "Machine Gun" Kelly and Robert "Birdman of Alcatraz" Stroud were among its notorious inmates. On the tour, you'll enter the bowels of the prison, walk the dank corridors and experience the cagelike cells in which America's most desperate criminals were kept.*

*A cruise to **Angel Island** (415-435-1915) is a different adventure entirely. This star-shaped island is covered with forest and rolling hills where deer roam free. The largest island in San Francisco Bay, it is a lacework of hiking and biking trails and flowering meadows.*

bakeries, jewelry stores, gift bazaars, a "general store," plus dozens of restaurants, cocktail lounges and espresso bars.

With its wooden boardwalks and clapboard buildings, **Pier 39** (Embarcadero and Beach Street; 415-981-7437) is one of the most popular tourist spots in the country. It features gift stores that range from cutesy card shops to places selling posters and contemporary art. There are restaurants and stores galore, plus an amusement arcade and a colony of several hundred sea lions who have taken up residence on nearby docks. Kids often enjoy the carnival atmosphere here. On a given day there might be jugglers, clowns or other entertainers performing free for the public.

EMBARCADERO NIGHTLIFE

The best evening spot is **The Holding Company** (2 Embarcadero Center; 415-986-0797).

Over at the Hyatt Regency, there's a revolving rooftop bar, **The Equinox** (5 Embarcadero Center; 415-788-1234). A glass-encased elevator whisks you to this aerie.

Pier 23 (Embarcadero and Pier 23; 415-362-5125) is a funky roadhouse. The sounds are jazz, and the vibrations are those of San Francisco before the age of skyscrapers and condominiums. They also feature reggae, salsa and blues music.

Chinatown

It's the largest Chinatown outside Asia, a spot that older Chinese know as *dai fao*, Big City. San Francisco's Chinatown also ranks as the city's most densely populated neighborhood. Home to 40,000 of the city's 150,000 Chinese, this enclave has been an Asian stronghold since the 1850s. Originally a ghetto where Chinese people were segregated from San Francisco society, the neighborhood today opens its arms to burgeoning numbers of immigrants from a host of Asian nations.

On the surface, this pulsing, noisy, chaotically colorful 70-square-block stretch projects the aura of a tourist's dream—gold and crimson pagodas, stores brimming with exquisite silks and multicolored dragons, more restaurants per square foot than could be imagined, roast ducks strung up in shop windows next door to Buddhist temples and fortune cookie factories.

But Chinatown is far more than a tourist mecca. This crowded neighborhood is peopled with families, powerful political groups, small merchants, poor working immigrants and rising entrepreneurs molding a more prosperous future. Although the "city within a city" that Chinatown once symbolized now encompasses only a quarter of San Francisco's Chinese people, it's still a center of Chinese history, culture, arts and traditions that have lived for thousands of years.

In appropriately dramatic fashion, you enter Chinatown through an arching gateway bedecked with dragons. Stone lions guard either side of this portal at Grant Avenue and Bush Street.

To stroll the eight-block length of Chinatown's **Grant Avenue** is to walk along San Francisco's oldest street. Today it's a modern thoroughfare lined with Chinese arts and crafts shops, restaurants and Asian markets. It's also one of the most crowded streets you'll ever squeeze your way through. Immortalized in a song from the musical *Flower Drum Song*, Grant Avenue, San Francisco, California, U.S.A., is a commotion, clatter, a mix of cultures.

At the corner of California Street rises the lovely brick structure of **Old St. Mary's Church**. Dating to 1854, this splendid cathedral was originally built of stone quarried in China.

Next you'll encounter **Nam Kue School** (755 Sacramento Street). With iron, mullioned doors and pagoda-like facade, it's an architectural beauty.

As you walk along Grant Avenue, with its swirling roof lines and flashing signs, peek down Commercial Way. Here you'll happen upon a hole-in-the-wall museum that will open wide your perspective on Chinatown. The **Chinese Historical Society of America** (650 Commercial Way; 415-391-1188) displays a magnificent collection of photographs and artifacts re-creating the Chinese experience in San Francisco from the days of pig-tailed "coolies" to the recent advent of ethnic consciousness.

After you've immersed yourself in Chinese history, head down to **Portsmouth Square** (Kearny and Washington streets) for a lesson in the history of all San Francisco. Formerly the city's central plaza, it was here in 1846 that Yankees first raised the Stars and Stripes. Today this gracious park is a gathering place for old Chinese men playing mah jongg and practicing tai chi. From the center of the plaza, a walkway arches directly into the **Chinese Culture Center** (750 Kearny Street; 415-986-1822), with its displays of Asian art.

CABLE CAR MUSEUM

*Just uphill from Chinatown stands the **Cable Car Museum** (1201 Mason Street; 415-474-1887), a brick goliath that houses the city's cable cars. The museum here provides a great opportunity to see how these wood-and-steel masterpieces operate. The system's powerhouse is here, along with the 14-foot diameter sheaves that neatly wind the cable. The museum also has on display three antique cable cars.*

Now that you've experienced the traditional tour, you might want to explore the hidden heart of Chinatown. First take a stroll along **Stockton Street**, which runs parallel to and one block above Grant Avenue. It is here, not along touristy Grant Avenue, that the Chinese shop.

The street vibrates with the crazy commotion of Chinatown. Open stalls tumbling with vegetables cover the sidewalk, and crates of fresh fish are stacked along the curb. In store windows hang ducks, and on the counters are displayed pigs' heads and snapping turtles.

The local community's artwork is displayed in a fantastic **mural** that covers a half block between Pacific and Jackson streets.

To further explore the interior life of Chinatown, turn down Sacramento Street from Stockton Street, then take a quick left into Hang Ah Street. This is the first in a series of narrow corridors leading for three blocks from Sacramento Street to Jackson Street.

A universe unto themselves, these **alleyways of Chinatown** are where the secret business of the community goes on, as it has for over a century. Each door is a barrier beyond which you can hear the rattle of mah jongg tiles and the sounds of women bent to their tasks in laundries and sewing factories.

The next alley, **Spofford Lane**, is a corridor of painted doorways and brick facades humming with the strains of Chinese melodies. It ends at Washington Street where you can zigzag over to **Ross Alley**. This is the home of the **Golden Gate Fortune Cookie Factory** (56 Ross Alley), a small family establishment where you can watch your fortune being made.

The last segment in this intriguing tour will take you back to **Waverly Place**, a two-block stretch leading from Washington Street to Sacramento Street. At first glance, the wrought-iron balconies draped along either side of Waverly evoke images of New Orleans. But not even the French Quarter can boast the beauty contained in those Chinese cornices and pagoda swirl roof lines.

Prize jewel in this architectural crown is **Tin Hou Temple** (125 Waverly Place). Here Buddhists and Taoists worship in a tiny temple overhung with fiery red lanterns. There are statues portraying battlefields and country landscapes; incense smolders from several altars.

CHINATOWN RESTAURANTS

For luxurious dining in the heart of Chinatown, no place matches the **Empress of China** (838 Grant Avenue; 415-434-1345). Set on the top floor of the China Trade Center, it is a culinary temple. Dining rooms are adorned with carved antiques. The menu includes a royal variety of chicken, duck, pork and beef dishes, as well as unique selections like hundred blossom lamb, prepared with sweet and sour ginger. Deluxe.

Of course, the ultimate Chinatown experience is to dine dim sum style, selecting finger-size dishes from trundle carts laden with steaming delicacies. My favorite dim sum restaurant is tucked away in an alley above Grant Avenue. Personalized but unpretentious, **Hang Ah Tea House** (1 Hang Ah Street; 415-982-5686) is a rare find. Enter the foyer, and step down to the semi-subterranean dining room with its private rooms and mismatched decor. Hang Ah serves a full Mandarin cuisine as well as dim sum portions.

CHINATOWN SHOPPING

Grant Avenue is the neighborhood's shopping center, but local Chinese favor Stockton Street. My advice is to browse both as well as the side streets between. Some of the city's best bargains are right here in Chinatown.

While there is a lot of gimcrackery sold in Chinatown, many specialty shops provide a sense of the richness of Chinese arts and crafts. Slip into one of the district's silk stores to admire the kimonos, or drop by a tea shop and sample one of the hundreds of varieties of teas.

Best place to begin is a charming shop across the street from the Grant Avenue gateway to Chinatown. A store of "a million little things"—bangles and boxes, amber and amethyst—**Filia** (517 Bush Street; 415-391-5224) features beads and jewelry.

A mandatory stop is at **Canton Bazaar** (616 Grant Avenue; 415-362-5750). This four-story emporium is a browser's warehouse. Six-foot-high wooden statues and laughing Buddhas surround the entrance. From the ceramic pieces to the gold and jade jewelry to clothing and antiques, the shelves are laden with exceptionally tasteful goods.

At the **Far East Flea Market** (729 Grant Avenue; 415-989-8588) you'll find everything from clothing to bird cages.

At the New China Trade Center, the multilayered **Chong Imports** (838 Grant Avenue; 415-982-1434) offers bright kites, lacy cutouts and China teapots at bargain prices.

For books and periodicals for adults and children, be sure to peek into **New China Bookstore** (642 Pacific Avenue; 415-956-0752). Owner Jimmy Lee goes out of his way to answer questions. His shop—a general store with its shelves of knickknacks and tea boxes—is a bilingual, bicultural center. And a magical place as well.

If you're ready for more of the real Chinatown, head up to **Stockton Street**. The outdoor stalls and family markets offer items that are part of everyday life in China. Particularly recommended is the **Ying Company** (1120 Stockton Street; 415-982-2188), which sells woks, chopsticks and other Asian kitchenware.

North Beach

It's a region of contrasts, a neighborhood in transition. North Beach combines the sex scene of neon-lit Broadway with the brooding intellect and Beat heritage of Grant Avenue and Columbus Street. Traditionally an Italian stronghold, North Beach still retains its fabulous pasta palaces and bocci ball courts, but it's now making way for a growing influx of Chinese residents.

Introductions to places should be made gradually, so the visitor comes slowly but certainly to know and love the area. In touring North Beach, that is no longer possible, because the logical spot to begin is on Broadway, at night when the neon arabesque of the boulevard is in full glare.

Broadway, you see, is San Francisco's answer to Times Square, a tawdry avenue that traffics in sex. Lined bumper to bumper with strip joints, transsexual revues, peekaramas and X-, Y-, Z-rated theaters, it's a present-day Barbary Coast.

All this sexual teasing climaxes at Broadway and Columbus Avenue. Nested on the corner is **The Condor**, the former roosting place of Carol Doda, San Francisco's own silicon angel. According to the bronze plaque that the local historic commission (undoubtedly in one of its wilder moments) placed on the building, The Condor is "the birthplace of the world's first topless and bottomless entertainment."

Now that you've dispensed with North Beach's sex scene, your love affair with the neighborhood can begin. Start at **City Lights Bookstore** (261 Columbus Avenue; 415-362-8193). Established in 1953 by poet Lawrence Ferlinghetti, City Lights is the old hangout of the beat poets. Back in the heady days of the '50s, Allen Ginsberg, Jack Kerouac, Gary Snyder and Neal Cassady haunted its book-lined rooms and creaking staircase. Today the place remains a vital cultural scene and gathering point, where you can browse, carouse or even plop into a chair and read awhile. **Vesuvio's** bar next door (255 Columbus Avenue; 415-362-3370) was another hallowed Beatnik retreat.

Named for the semaphore station located on its height during the 1850s, **Telegraph Hill**, at the end of Lombard Street, was a bohemian haunt during the 1920s and 1930s. Money moved the artists out; today, this hillside real estate is among the most desirable, and most expensive, in the city.

Poking through the top of Telegraph Hill is the 210-foot-high **Coit Tower** (admission for elevator to observation platform). Built in 1934, this fluted structure was named for Lillie Hitchcock Coit, a bizarre character who chased fire engines and became a fire company mascot during the 1850s. Lillie's love for firemen gave rise to stories that the phallic tower was modeled after a fire hose nozzle. Architectural critics scoff at the notion. Some of the nation's most outstanding

WPA murals, depicting the lives of California laborers, decorate the tower interior. Upstaging these marvelous artworks is the view from the summit. All San Francisco spreads before you.

A few blocks west of Coit Tower you'll find **Washington Square** (Filbert and Stockton streets), the heart of North Beach. This is the gathering place for San Francisco's "Little Italy."

St. Peter & Paul Catholic Church (Filbert and Stockton streets) anchors one side of the square, its twin steeples dominating the North Beach skyline. The facade is unforgettable, an ornate affair upon which eagles rest in the company of angels. The interior is a wilderness of vaulting arches hung with lamps and decorated in gilt bas-relief. Tourists proclaim its beauty. For my taste, the place is overdone; it drips with architectural jewelry.

North Beach Museum, housed inside Eureka Federal Savings (1435 Stockton; 415-391-6210), presents a history in black-and-white. Here are sepia photos of Sicilian fishermen, pictures of the terrible quake and other images of the people who make this neighborhood such an intriguing place to visit.

NORTH BEACH LODGING

Millefiori Inn (444 Columbus Avenue; 415-433-9111) is a subdued bed-and-breakfast hotel that will cause you quickly to forget the garish side of North Beach. To be safe though, ask for a quiet room in back. You'll be ushered into one of the hotel's 15 small, cozy rooms. From the porcelain chandeliers to the oak night tables, they have all been decorated with loving care. Deluxe, and highly recommended.

THE GREENWICH AND FILBERT STEPS

Right next to Coit Tower, one of San Francisco's most popular attractions, you can discover some of the city's hidden crannies. After exiting the tower, turn right, cross the street and make your way down the brick-lined staircase. Though in the middle of San Francisco, you have just entered a countrified environment. Ferns and ivy riot on either side of the Greenwich Steps, while vines and conifers climb overhead.

At the bottom of the steps, turn right, walk a short distance along Montgomery Street, then head left down the Filbert Steps. The art deco apartment house on the corner (1360 Montgomery Street) was featured in one of Humphrey Bogart's great but unheralded movies, Dark Passage. Festooned with flowers and sprinkled with baby's tears, the steps carry you into a fantasy realm inhabited by stray cats and framed with clapboard houses.

NORTH BEACH RESTAURANTS

If San Franciscans were to choose their favorite Italian restaurant, **Little Joe's and Baby Joe's** (523 Broadway; 415-982-7639) might very well win. Not only is the food outstanding, it's prepared before your eyes by some of the city's great showmen. With a snap of the wrist, they flip sizzling veal, steak, lamb or calamari skyward, then nonchalantly catch it on the way down. Very crowded; moderate.

The best pizza in town is served at **Tommaso's Neapolitan Restaurant** (1042 Kearny Street; 415-398-9696), where the chefs use an oak-fired oven. Entering the place is like stepping down into a grotto. The walls are lined with booths and covered by murals; it's dark, steamy and filled with inviting smells. Filmmaker Francis Ford Coppola drops by occasionally, as should every pizza and pasta lover. Priced moderate.

Dining is elevated to the level of high adventure at **Caffe Sport** (574 Green Street; 415-981-1251). The decor is a baroque nightmare—tacky candelabra and antiques circa 1972. Besides that, it's hot, steamy, unbelievably crowded and the waiters are rude. What more can I say, except that you'll love the place. Known for its pasta, this is also *the* spot for Italian-style seafood. Deluxe. Reservations required.

Why anyone would want to dine in a place frequented by writers is beyond me, but if the spirit moves you and your stomach agrees, head over to the **Washington Square Bar & Grill** (1707 Powell Street; 415-982-8123). This literary gathering spot is often elbow-to-elbow with such questionable characters as local novelists and newspaper reporters, who come here to gossip and drink at the brass-rail bar. The focus in this excellent restaurant is on pasta, veal and seafood dishes. Moderate to deluxe.

The **Shadows Restaurant** (1349 Montgomery Street; 415-982-5536) is a high-heeled French restaurant perched atop Telegraph Hill. The bay views are well worth the price of admission, and the continental dinners are outstanding. Entrée choices include grilled *médaillons* of lobster tail and prawns with fresh papaya. They specialize

---

THE CAFES OF NORTH BEACH

The heart of North Beach beats in its cafes. Gathering places for local Italians, the neighborhood's coffee houses are also literary scenes. Foremost among these people-watching posts is **Caffe Trieste** *(601 Vallejo Street; 415-392-6739), the old beatnik rendezvous. Other prime locations include* **Caffe Roma** *(414 Columbus Avenue; 415-391-8584),* **Caffe Puccini** *(411 Columbus Avenue; 415-989-7033) and the* **Bohemian Cigar Store** *(566 Columbus Avenue; 415-362-0536).*

in low-fat, low-cholesterol items. The stunning decor is highlighted by antiqued chairs and pink tablecloths. Dinner only; deluxe. Open weekends only; reservations required.

The *New Yorker* once called **Hunan Restaurant** (924 Sansome Street; 415-956-7727)"the best Chinese restaurant in the world." Those are pretty big words, hard to substantiate this side of Peking. But it's certainly one of the best San Francisco has to offer. Understand now, we're talking cuisine, not ambience. The atmosphere at Hunan is characterized by noise and crowds; there's a bar and contemporary-style dining room adorned with color photographs. The food is hot, spicy, and delicious. From the dining room you can watch masterful chefs working the woks, preparing pungent sauces, and serving up Kung pao chicken, bean curd with meat sauce, Hunan scallops, and a host of other delectables. Well worth the moderate price of admission.

NORTH BEACH SHOPPING

Shopping in North Beach is a grand escapade. As you browse the storefronts here, do like the Sicilians and keep an eye out for Italian treasures, like hand-painted ceramics and colorful wallhangings.

The array of postcards at **Quantity Postcards** (1441 Grant Avenue; 415-986-8866) is staggering—Mao cards, 3-D cards, movie star cards and talking postcards that squeak when you squeeze them.

Biordi Art Imports (412 Columbus Avenue; 415-392-8096), specializing in kitchen goods, is loaded with Italian imports like hand-painted pitchers from Florence and folk art from Palermo.

At **Postermat** (401 Columbus Avenue; 415-421-5536) you'll find movie posters, art prints and novelty cards. Of particular interest at this San Francisco institution is the outstanding collection of posters from the old Fillmore and Avalon ballrooms.

No North Beach shopping spree would be complete without a visit to **A. Cavalli & Co.** (1441 Stockton Street; 415-421-4219). Operating since 1880, this family business offers Italian cookbooks, records and tapes, Puccini opera prints and magazines from Rome.

NORTH BEACH NIGHTLIFE

Spec's Museum Cafe (12 Saroyan Place; 415-421-4112) is one of North Beach's fabled bohemian haunts. There's nary a bald spot on the walls of this literary hangout; they're covered with all manner of mementos from bumpersnickers to a "whale's penis bone."

Built the year after the earthquake, the **San Francisco Brewing Company** (155 Columbus Avenue; 415-434-3344) is a mahogany-paneled beauty with glass lamps and punkah wallah fans. Legend tells that boxer Jack Dempsey once worked here as a bouncer. Today it's one of a growing number of pubs in the Bay Area that brews their own beer on the premises.

The Stone (412 Broadway; 415-391-547-1954) showcases hot groups, mixing rock with occasional blues and jazz.

Finocchio's (506 Broadway; 415-982-9388) presents a succession of screamingly outrageous female impersonators. The costuming is colorful and the acts very bitchy. Cover.

Club Fugazi (678 Green Street; 415-421-4222) features an outlandish musical revue, *Beach Blanket Babylon*, that has been running for years. The scores and choreography are good, but the costumes are great. The hats—elaborate, multilayered confections—make Carmen Miranda's adornments look like Easter bonnets. Cover.

Fisherman's Wharf

Places have a way of becoming parodies of themselves—particularly if they possess a personal resonance and beauty or have some unique feature to lend the landscape. People, it seems, have an unquenchable need to change them.

Such is the fate of Fisherman's Wharf. Back in the 19th century, a proud fishing fleet berthed in these waters, and the shoreline was a quiltwork of brick factories, metal canning sheds and woodframe warehouses. Genoese fishermen with rope-muscled arms set out in triangular-sailed *feluccas* that were a joke to the west wind. They had captured the waterfront from the Chinese and would be supplanted in turn by Sicilians. They caught sand dabs, sea bass, king salmon and Dungeness crab.

Today the woodplanked waterfront named for their occupation is hardly a place for fishermen. It has become "Tourist's Wharf," a bizarre assemblage of shopping malls and penny arcades that make Disneyland look like the real world. But salt still stirs the air here, and fog fingers through the bay. There are sights to visit along "the Wharf." It's a matter of recapturing the past while avoiding the plastic-coated present. To do that you need to follow a basic law of the sea—hug the shoreline.

Pier 45 is a working wharf, bleached with guano and frequented by fishing boats. From here it's a short jog to the docks on Jefferson Street, between Jones and Taylor streets. The remnants of San Francisco's fishing fleet lies gunnel to gunnel here. The *Nicky-D*, *Saint Teresa*, *Santa Anna*, *Hai Tai Loc* and an admiralty of others cast off every morning around 4 a.m. to return in late afternoon. With their brightly painted hulls, Christmas tree rigging and roughhewn crews, they carry the odor and clamor of the sea.

For a breather, it's not far to the Hyde Street Pier. Docked along the length of this wharf are the **Historic Ships** (415-556-6435; admission). Part of the San Francisco Maritime National Historical Park, they include a wood-hulled, three-masted schooner, *C. A. Thayer*, that once toted lumber along the California coast. You can also board the *Eureka*, an 1890 ferryboat. To walk this pier is to stride back to San Francisco's waterfront at the turn of the century. Salt-bitten lifeboats, corroded anchors and old coal engines are scattered hither-thither. There's also a three-masted merchant ship built in Scotland in 1866, the *Balclutha*. This 301-foot, steel-hulled craft sailed around Cape Horn 17 times in her youth. Today the old ship's cargo consists of a below-deck maritime museum and a hold full of memories.

It's enough to make a sailor of you. Especially after you've visited the nearby **National Maritime Museum** (Beach and Polk streets; 415-556-2904), an art deco building designed to resemble a ship. Onboard the museum there's a weird collection of parts from old ships plus models and a magnificent photo collection.

All these nautical showpieces are anchored in **Aquatic Park**, which sports a lovely lawn that rolls down to one of the bay's few sandy beaches. A melange of sounds and spectacles, the park has a bocci ball court where you'll encounter old Italian men exchanging stories.

FISHERMAN'S WHARF LODGING

Sheraton at Fisherman's Wharf (2500 Mason Street; 415-362-5500) is a sprawling 526-room facility, with spacious accommodations tastefully furnished in Sheraton fashion and offering nightly turndown service. The hotel has other alluring features such as a brick-paved entranceway, liveried doormen and a swimming pool. Ultra-deluxe.

The shortage of good hotels around Fisherman's Wharf was remedied when **Hyatt at Fisherman's Wharf** (555 North Point Street; 415-563-1234), a 313-room luxury retreat, and the **Tuscan Inn** (425 North Point Street; 415-561-1100), an Italian-style boutique hotel, opened within a block of each other. Faced in brick and illuminated through skylights, the Hyatt comes complete with pool, spa, and fitness center. Smaller in scale, the Tuscan is richly decorated and more intimate. Both are ultra-deluxe in price.

FISHERMAN'S WHARF RESTAURANTS

Would you believe a hidden restaurant in tourist-mobbed Fisherman's Wharf? **Scoma's** (Pier 47 near the foot of Jones Street; 415-771-4383) is the place. Seafood is the password to this chummy restaurant.

There's *calamone alla anna*, squid prepared "in a totally different manner," lobster tail and Dungeness crab. Moderate to deluxe.

For spicy food from the subcontinent, everyone's choice is **Gaylord India Restaurant** (900 North Point Street; 415-771-8822). From a corner roost in Ghirardelli Square, it enjoys a startling view of San Francisco Bay. It also hosts an extensive menu that varies from tandoori chicken and spiced lamb to meatless entrées such as eggplant baked in a clay oven. Decor features unusual artwork and Asian statuary. Moderate to deluxe.

El Tapatio (475 Francisco Street; 415-981-3018) evokes old Mexico. The high-ceilinged interior has been decorated with sombreros, serapes and Spanish murals. The menu features everything from enchiladas to flautas, and there's a cantina upstairs. Moderate.

FISHERMAN'S WHARF SHOPPING

For locally crafted goods, be sure to watch for the **street vendor stalls** along Beach Street between Hyde and Larkin and on side streets throughout the area. You'll find jewelry, leather belts, kites and anything else the local imagination can conjure.

Before savvy shoppers buy anything in the city, they go to **Cost Plus Imports** (2552 Taylor Street; 415-928-6200) and see if it's there. If so, it's cheaper. An enormous complex, Cost Plus sprawls across several blocks of Fisherman's Wharf. The main building has temple rubbings from Thailand, amber jewelry from Egypt, brassware, gourmet foods, etc. Other brickfront buildings contain the wine shop and nursery.

Another popular spot among San Franciscans is the old brick canning factory on Jefferson and Leavenworth streets. Thanks to innovative architects, **The Cannery** (415-771-3112) has been transformed into a trilevel mall dotted with interesting shops, many selling handcrafted originals.

Chocoholics will be delighted to discover the home of Ghirardelli chocolate, **Ghirardelli Square** (900 North Point Street; 415-

---

THE EAGLE FLIES AGAIN

*The **Eagle Cafe** (Pier 39; 415-433-3689), a famous old-timer, is so much a part of San Francisco that plans to tear the place down a few years ago occasioned a public outcry. Instead, the old woodframe building was moved—lock, stock and memories—to the second floor of the fashionable Pier 39 shopping mall. Today it looks like an ostrich at a beauty pageant. The walls are covered with faded black-and-white photographs, baseball caps and other memorabilia. All-American cuisine; breakfast and lunch only; budget.*

775-5500), now converted into yet another shopping complex. This early 20th-century factory is another example of old industrial architecture being turned to contemporary uses. Around the factory's antique chocolate-making machines are designer outlets, import stores and boutiques.

FISHERMAN'S WHARF NIGHTLIFE

The bar at the **Eagle Cafe** (Pier 39; 415-433-3689) remains old and crusty, filled with waterfront characters. Old photos and baseball caps adorn the walls, and in the air hang memories 50 years old.

Buena Vista Cafe (2765 Hyde Street; 415-474-5044) is popular with local folks and tourists alike. There's a fine old bar and friendly atmosphere, and the place claims to have introduced Irish coffee to America.

Union Street

People go to Union Street, on the city's northern flank, for two reasons—shopping and singles bars. But since many of the district's trendy shops are housed in magnificent Victorians, sightseeing can become a case of shopping in architectural wonders.

Foremost is the **Octagon House** (2645 Gough Street; 415-441-7512), built in 1861. This eight-sided heirloom capped with a turret is open to the public on the second and fourth Thursdays and second Sunday of each month.

The structure at 1980 Union Street gained a mark on the map when an eccentric father built this Siamese twin of a house for his two daughters. It seems they were newlyweds needing dowries, who soon found themselves cozily ensconced in these **Wedding Houses**.

Actually, a grander example of the Victorian-in-a-mirror can be seen in the imposing pair of houses across the street at **1923-1929 Union Street**.

Vendanta House (2963 Webster Street) is another structural curiosity, built to celebrate the Hindu religion. It's a sprawling three-story house, maroon and grey, capped with several towers. One tower sports battlements, another a bulbous dome and yet another a cluster of cupolas.

The **Casebolt House** (2727 Pierce Street) is the last link in this chain of architectural jewels. With two magnificent palm trees guarding the entranceway and a flanking retinue of willows, it presents an imposing sight. Dating from 1865, the ornate white Italianate edifice is just as grand today.

UNION STREET LODGING

In this turn-of-the-century neighborhood, my personal favorite is **The Bed and Breakfast Inn** (4 Charlton Court; 415-921-9784), located on a quiet cul de sac. The highly personalized hotel is set in two ivy-covered Victorians with a smiling bay window. Accommodations range from moderate-priced pension rooms with shared bath to deluxe rooms. There is also a cozy library, an English dining room and garden for continental breakfast. It's very popular; book several months ahead.

Antiques, marble fireplaces and rich fabrics give the 14 accommodations at the **Sherman House** (2160 Green Street; 415-563-3600) the feeling of 19th-century opulence. Which is as it should be, since this charming Victorian and carriage house were built in 1876 by a devoted opera buff who installed a three-story recital hall for visiting performers. Every room has something extra—a private garden, a view deck. This luxurious hotel has 24-hour room service from the private dining room. Ultra-deluxe.

At **Edward II Inn** (3155 Scott Street; 415-921-9776) the proprietors have recaptured the original British bed-and-breakfast concept. The 30-room inn lets guests enjoy bed-and-breakfast luxury at boarding house cost (doubles with shared or private bath are moderately priced). The room I saw was English in decor and included such features as a quilted bedspread and a dresser with beveled mirror. Highly recommended; ask for a quiet room in back.

UNION STREET RESTAURANTS

With its brass rails and mirrored walls, **Prego** (2000 Union Street; 415-563-3305) is high tech to the max. The Milanesque interior features a brick oven in which many of the Italian dishes are prepared. There's grilled lamb, veal chops and pizza-with-everything. Highly recommended; moderate.

THE MANSION

*If a short spell in a bed-and-breakfast museum intrigues you, consider **The Mansion Hotel** (2220 Sacramento Street; 415-929-9444), just east of Pacific Heights. Set in a Queen Anne Victorian, this monument to palatial living is chockablock with antique furniture, Bufano statuary and brilliant wall murals. The first floor features a grand, crystal-chandeliered foyer. Individual bedrooms are each dedicated to a historic figure and decorated with a mural depicting that individual's life. Ultra-deluxe.*

Doidge's (2217 Union Street; 415-921-2149) is everybody's favorite breakfast spot. I've always thought the place slightly overrated, but I seem to be a minority of one. Its best feature is that it serves breakfast until the middle of the afternoon. Moderate.

Tiny **Bonta** (2223 Union Street; 415-929-0407) is an intimate, white-walled trattoria with an authentic Italian flair. Moderately priced housemade pastas, fresh fish and grilled meats are the mainstays, but some first courses (especially the rice ones) are definitely in order.

The history of the **Balboa Cafe** (3199 Fillmore Street; 415-921-3944) is almost as rich as its brass, oak and stained-glass interior. In operation since 1914, it specializes in California cuisine. The menu includes fresh fish, rabbit and fettucine with smoked salmon. A splendid restaurant at a moderate price.

Over on Chestnut Street you'll find **Judy's Restaurant** (2268 Chestnut Street; 415-922-4588). As the local crowds here attest, it's an excellent dining choice. Judy's is intimate and decorated with wicker lamps and linen-covered tables. On the balcony level you can enjoy sandwiches or omelettes for lunch, breakfast or Sunday brunch. No dinner served; moderate.

One of San Francisco's finest seafood restaurants is **Scott's** (2400 Lombard Street; 415-563-8988). With an oak-paneled bar, white tablecloths and softly lit interior, it provides an inviting atmosphere. The food is simply outstanding. You can sample cracked crab, cioppino or poached salmon. Moderate.

For a quick, no-jet-lag trip back to Paris, go no farther than **Rodin** (1779 Lombard Street; 415-563-8566). Framed black-and-white photographs of the French sculptor's works create a gallery-like setting for equally artistic presentations such as a nouvelle oysters Rockefeller or tender duck rolled with wild rice. Ultra-deluxe.

Fashionable, French, intimate, and imaginative—**La Folie** (2316 Polk Street; 415-776-5577) combines all the ingredients required of a small San Francisco restaurant. Those heavy French sauces of yore have been replaced with salsas and vegetable purées. The menu includes specialties like cream of tomatillo soup and roast salmon with cucumber and yogurt sauce. Dinner only; deluxe to ultra-deluxe.

UNION STREET SHOPPING

No doubt about it, Union Street is a budget-busting boulevard, with its designer fashions and rare imports. But as the saying goes, it doesn't cost to look.

One place where you can look, or more properly gaze, is **Enchanted Crystal** (1771 Union Street; 415-885-1335). Aglitter with art glass pieces by about 50 artists, this glass palace is also known for its world-class collection of quartz pieces. The extravagant window displays are magical.

H. P. Corwith, Ltd. (1833 Union Street; 415-567-7252) traffics in plastic pie slices, blueprints of ice cream cones and stuffed people. *The* place for pop art.

Specializing in jewelry, **Anne** (1931 Union Street; 415-921-6818) numbers among Union Street's more colorful stores.

Yankee Doodle Dandy (1974 Union Street; 415-346-3337) sells antique quilts and handmade items from rural America.

Masquerade (2237 Union Street; 415-567-5677) is a vintage men's clothing store. Among the precious finds are Hawaiian shirts, jackets, gabardine vests and hand-painted ties from the '40s.

For rare pieces and exquisite decorative items, consider **Silkroute** (3119 Fillmore Street; 415-563-4936). You'll find carpets from India, ceremonial masks from Africa and handcrafts from Afghanistan.

UNION STREET NIGHTLIFE

In an area known for its singles bars, the most popular, crowded and famous of all is **Perry's** (1944 Union Street; 415-922-9022). It's a meat market for the over-30 set. Cover.

The only place that's sometimes more crowded is **Pierce Street Annex** (3138 Fillmore Street; 415-567-1400). A throbbing, dimly lit nightspot, it is pick-up central. On weekends you have to elbow your way in for a drink; during the week you're liable to have the bar to yourself. Loud, hot and fast. Cover.

While in the neighborhood, check out the nearby scene at **Balboa Cafe** (3199 Fillmore Street; 415-921-3944) and the **Golden Gate Grill** (3200 Fillmore Street; 415-931-4600). Together with Pierce Street Annex, they form what is commonly referred to as The Triangle.

For an archetypal San Francisco fern bar, try **The Royal Oak** (2201 Polk Street; 415-928-2303).

Pacific Heights

San Francisco's most prestigious neighborhood resides on a hill looking down upon the bay. In addition to Rolls-Royces and Mercedes Benzes, Pacific Heights contains some of the city's most outstanding architecture. Stroll the wide streets and you'll encounter straitlaced Tudor homes, baroque confections and elaborate Victorians.

Best place to begin touring this palatial ridgetop is the corner of Franklin and California streets. That twin-turreted structure on the corner is a **Queen Anne-style Victorian**, built for a 19th-century figure who made his fortune in gold and lumber. Its poorer neighbors up the hill are **Italianate-style Victorians**, characterized by slanting edge bay windows; both date to the 1870s.

The **Haas–Lilienthal House** (2007 Franklin Street; 415-441-3004), perhaps the grandest of all San Francisco's Victorians, is a gingerbread fantasy constructed in 1886 and adorned with gables, bas-relief figures and a bold tower. It's open to the public Wednesday and Sunday afternoons (admission).

Nearby is **Grenlee Terrace** (1925 Jackson Street). With its white stucco facade and red tile roof, this sophisticated apartment house follows a mission revival motif and dates from 1913. The nearby **Whittier Mansion** (2090 Jackson Street; 415-567-1848; admission), a red sandstone structure built in 1896, is open for public viewing Wednesday, Saturday, and Sunday afternoon. With an interior paneled in mahogany, cherry birch and other fine woods and featuring a collection of California oil paintings, it's well worth a wistful visit.

Down on Broadway, you'll find a stern three-story edifice with lions on either side of the entranceway, the **Hamlin School** (2120 Broadway), a baroque revival mansion constructed in 1901. James Flood, the man who commissioned the building, also built the white marble **Renaissance-style palazzo** at 2222 Broadway.

Continue to **Lafayette Park** (Washington and Laguna streets), a beautiful tree-dotted park with a rolling lawn. Across the street rises the **Spreckels Mansion** (2080 Washington Street), an ornate edifice with a white limestone surface.

THE SACRAMENTO STREET SCENE

A true neighborhood shopping area, Sacramento Street combines galleries, boutiques and antique stores with shops serving the immediate needs of local folks.

Between Lyon and Spruce streets, from the 3200 to 3600 blocks, you'll find a bevy of boutiques and trendy shops. **Santa Fe** *(3571 Sacramento Street; 415-346-0180), as stylish as it is pricey, has artwork from the Southwest, Native American jewelry and rugs, and Mexican silverwork and antiques. At* **Vignette** *(3625 Sacramento Street; 415-567-0174) there are fine-crafted goods for the home.*

Several restaurants have also joined the parade of stores along Sacramento Street. Included in the gourmet lineup is **Le Castel** *(3235 Sacramento Street; 415-921-7115), one of the city's finest French restaurants. Open only for dinner, this deluxe-to-ultra-deluxe-priced establishment serves beef médaillons, scallops and poached salmon, as well as esoteric dishes like stuffed squab and calf's brain.*

Nob Hill

Perhaps the most famous of all the knolls casting their ever-loving shadows on San Francisco is a prominence called Nob Hill. You can take any of the city's three cable car lines to Nob Hill's **Powell–California Street stop**, the only spot in San Francisco where they all intersect.

Nob Hill is a monument to San Francisco's crusty rich—those old powerbrokers who trace their heritage back to the Big Four. It seems that in the 19th century, Misters Crocker, Huntington, Hopkins and Stanford—the tycoons who built the transcontinental railroad—chose Nob Hill as the place to honor themselves. They all built estates on top of the 338-foot rise, each more ostentatious than the other. It became, as Robert Louis Stevenson described it, "the Hill of palaces."

THE BIG FOUR

San Francisco's best-known hotels could be called the Big Four (mimicking the Big Four railroad barons of the 19th century). It's a short list of hotels that have become synonymous with first-rate accommodations. To stay at these addresses is to brush with history while enjoying the service and amenities of ultra-deluxe-priced hotels.

Facing Union Square since before the 1906 earthquake, the **Westin St. Francis** *(335 Powell Street; 415-397-7000) has become a landmark, attracting celebrities, presidents and chiefs of state from around the world. In 1972, a 32-story tower doubled the number of accommodations to 1202.*

Equally popular with conventioneers, the **Fairmont Hotel** *(Mason and California streets; 415-772-5000) also has a tower addition, a 24-story shaft of gold and white accessible via outdoor elevator. Better known for its service and myriad restaurants and lounges than for its room decor, the Fairmont offers simply appointed accommodations in a wide range of configurations.*

Recent renovations at the 19-story **Mark Hopkins Inter-Continental** *(One Nob Hill; 415-392-3434) have given many of its 392 guest rooms and suites the look of a modern cruise liner. Alternating color schemes of silver gray or khaki with gold, standard rooms have quilted chintz bedspreads, thick carpeting, Regency-style writing desks and imaginative window treatments that make the most of the dazzling views.*

The decor and service at the **Huntington Hotel** *(1075 California Street; 415-474-5400) attract a devoted following among travelers familiar with the European tradition of small luxe hotels. With 140 rooms and suites, the Huntington can offer individual attention matched by few of its competitors. Fine antiques and tasteful works of art make some guests feel they're actually staying at an elegant weekend home in the English countryside. That is, except for the sweeping bay and city views visible through extra-large windows.*

Until 1906: the fire that followed the great earthquake burned Nob Hill's mansions to the ground.

All that remains from the robber baron age is the **Pacific Union Club** (1000 California Street), a blocky brownstone built in 1855 for a silver king named James Flood. The **Fairmont Hotel** (950 Mason Street) across the street is a partial survivor. Built just prior to 1906, the shell of this grand building endured; the interior was refurbished in time for the hotel to open on the first anniversary of the earthquake. Today the hotel lobby, with its marble columns and gilt bas-relief, evokes memories of the Big Four.

Nearby **Grace Cathedral** (1051 Taylor Street) marks San Francisco's attempt at Gothic architecture. Consecrated in 1964 and constructed of concrete, it's not exactly Notre Dame. But this mammoth, vaulting church does have its charm. Foremost are the doors atop the cathedral steps; they represent Lorenzo Ghiberti's "Doors of Paradise," cast in bronze from the artist's original work in Florence. Tiers of stained-glass windows picture such latter-day luminaries as labor leader John L. Lewis and astronaut John Glenn. The cathedral is filled with objects as dear as they are sacred, including a 15th-century carved oak altar piece and an organ boasting 7000 pipes.

NOB HILL NIGHTLIFE

Without doubt the city's finest bar pianist is a facile-fingered gentleman named Peter Mintun. He works the ivory nightly at fashionable **Mason's** (Fairmont Hotel, 950 Mason Street; 415-722-5000) on Nob Hill. The sounds will be Porter and Gershwin, the crowd elegant and the drinks expensive.

If San Francisco tourists were asked to name the best bar with a view, 101 out of every 100 would list **The Top of the Mark** (California and Mason streets; 415-392-3434). With good reason: from its roosting place in Nob Hill's Mark Hopkins Inter-Continental, this venerable lounge enjoys extraordinary vistas of the bay and beyond.

Japantown

Center of culture for San Francisco's burgeoning Japanese population is Japantown, a self-contained area bounded by Geary and Post, Laguna and Fillmore streets. This town-within-a-city consists of two sections: the old part, where residential housing is located, and a newer commercial area. The latter, **Japan Center**, is a five-acre monstrosity. Built in 1968, it exemplifies the freeway architecture of the era. There are, nonetheless, fascinating shops and outstanding restaurants located in this Asian mall.

You'll also encounter special features like the **Peace Pagoda**, a five-tiered structure designed by world renowned architect Yoshiro Taniguchi as an expression of friendship and goodwill between the people of Japan and America.

During the April Cherry Blossom Festival, August Street Fair, Autumn Bon Dances and the Aki Matsuri festival in September, Japantown turns out in splendid costumes for musical celebrations. All year round you can enjoy **Nihonmachi Mall** (on Buchanan Street) with its *torii* gate, cobblestone pathway and lovely Ruth Asawa origami fountains.

After a full day sightseeing, you can luxuriate at **Kabuki Hot Spring** (1750 Geary Boulevard; 415-922-6000). This Japanese-style bathhouse features saunas, steam cabinets, hot tubs and cold tubs.

JAPANTOWN LODGING

Among the best of the city's Asian-style hotels is the **Miyako** (1625 Post Street; 415-922-3200). Pass through the sliding glass doors and you'll enter an Oriental milieu. The private rooms are adorned with Japanese prints; behind the colorful *shoji* screens are balconies overlooking a garden. Be sure to ask for a sunken Japanese tub. Some rooms are entirely Japanese in furnishing with *tatami* mats, futons and built-in saunas. Ultra-deluxe.

The Hotel Majestic (1500 Sutter Street; 415-441-1100) is a five-story structure that dates from 1902, when it opened as one of the city's first grand hotels. The current 59-room establishment features a restaurant and attractive lobby. Some rooms are strikingly appointed with canopied beds and European antiques. Deluxe.

JAPANTOWN RESTAURANTS

The Japan Center Building houses several Japanese restaurants including a *shokuji dokoro*, or traditional bistro called **Misono** (1737 Post Street; 415-922-2728). Here the atmosphere is mannered and reserved with waitresses preparing dinner at your table. Japanese tradition at its finest. Deluxe.

Tired of humdrum sushi bars? Then nearby **Isobune** (1737 Post Street; 415-563-1030) is the place for you. Here those raw fish finger foods scud past on wooden boats along a miniature canal. You simply sit at the counter and pluck off your favorite cargo from the numerous sushi selections as the boat goes by. Moderate.

Recommended by local residents and gourmets alike, **Sanppo Restaurant** (1702 Post Street; 415-346-3486) serves excellent food at budget prices. In addition to outstanding sushi, they offer *chanko nabe* (a fish, chicken and vegetable dish) and tempura dishes. The interior is unsophisticated cafe-style, but the cuisine is worthy of a plush establishment. Three stars over Japantown.

JAPANTOWN SHOPPING

In this Asian neighborhood, most shopping is done in Japan Center. Here **Shige Nishiguchi** (1730 Geary Boulevard; 415-346-5567) specializes in antique kimonos and dolls.

Nearby **Asakichi** (1730 Geary Boulevard; 415-921-2147) features antique furniture as well as Asian arts and crafts. Take special note of those heavy wood antique chests called *tansu*.

Kinokuniya Bookstore (1581 Webster Street; 415-567-7625) is a warehouse of a store, chockablock with volumes on Japanese language and culture. The same building houses **Kinokuniya Stationery and Gift**, which stocks Japanese postcards, calendars and writing supplies.

One of Japan Center's most captivating stores is **Mashiko** (1581 Webster Street; 415-346-0748), a museum-cum-shop displaying Japanese folk art. Among the exhibits, you might find an 18th-century tobacco set or a hand-painted papier-mâché pillow.

RUSSIAN HILL

Among the city's better-kept secrets is a tumbling residential area called Russian Hill, roughly bordered by Green and Bay streets and Van Ness Avenue and Taylor Street. According to legend, the neighborhood's vaulting slopes were once the site of a cemetery for Russian seal hunters. The Russians have long since departed, leaving the district to local folks and a few canny travelers.

*There's a single block amid Russian Hill's checkerboard streets that stands out in the public imagination. Located along **Lombard Street** between Hyde and Leavenworth, it has earned the sobriquet of "The Crookedest Street in the World." (The nearby block, where Filbert Street plummets from Hyde to Leavenworth, is the steepest in the city.)*

Visitors come from around the world to stand astride Lombard's crest and take in the postcard views that stretch in several directions. Then they begin the dizzying descent down the beautifully landscaped street. The brick-paved road winds around hedgerows and banks of hydrangea bushes.

*But Russian Hill offers even more etherial realms. If heaven possessed country paths, they'd be modeled on **Macondray Lane**. It waits off Jones between Green and Union streets. For a solitary block, its cobblestone path leads through a garden, then opens onto a wooden staircase overlooking the bay. You enter a tunnel of greenery, walled on one side with shingle houses and on the other with an ivy-embowered hillside. It's a realm of flower pots and fluttering birds, one of San Francisco's secret and magical walks.*

For gifts at reasonable prices, step over from the Japan Center to **Nichi Bei Bussan** (1715 Buchanan Mall; 415-346-2117). Here is a collection of Asian wares ranging from standard kimonos to batik wallhangings.

JAPANTOWN NIGHTLIFE

An important member of the city's group of small theaters is the **Asian American Theatre Company** (403 Arguello Boulevard; 415-751-2600), which while no longer located in Japantown, still represents the community.

The **Old Fillmore** (1807 Geary Street; 415-567-2060), owned by rock impresario Bill Graham, brings in top groups from around the country. (Still closed due to earthquake damage.)

Haight-Ashbury

Places that are part of the cultural mythology have usually gained their prominence centuries before. For Haight-Ashbury that is simply not the case. This neighborhood of quiet streets and Victorian houses blazed across the public consciousness within the past few decades, leaving a vapor trail that may never vanish.

For an entire generation, 1967 was the "Summer of Love," a heady season when psychedelic drugs were food for thought and acid rock was king. By that summer, San Francisco had become a mecca for young people seeking religious truth and righteous dope. Haight-Ashbury's streets were thronged with a new breed—clad in motley and carrying bells, feathers, beads and cymbals.

While many will always remember those days, Haight-Ashbury seems to have almost forgotten. As it was before the first hippie floated along its streets, Haight-Ashbury is an upper-middle-class neighborhood resplendent with tree-lined avenues and backyard gardens. Tucked between two of San Francisco's prettiest parks—Golden Gate and Buena Vista—it also sports some of the city's loveliest Victorians. There are Queen Anne styles marked by solitary turrets and boldly painted facades. On **Ashbury Heights**, the hillside overlooking Haight Street, are houses drawn from a gingerbread cakeboard.

Today the Haight is an area in transition. The gay population has increased, and the neighborhood is being gentrified. On **Haight Street**, between Masonic and Stanyan streets, the sidewalks are door-to-door with mod shops, gay bars, antique clothing stores and art galleries.

Before strolling this refurbished street, be sure to explore **Buena Vista Park** (Haight and Lyon streets). Dense with conifers and eucalyptus trees, the park's angling hills offer splendid views of San Francisco from ocean to bay.

HAIGHT-ASHBURY LODGING

One of San Francisco's most reasonable bed and breakfast hotels can be found right along Haight Street, center of the fabled Summer of Love. **The Red Victorian Inn** (1665 Haight Street; 415-864-1978) evokes a sense of that era. Owner Sami Sunchild promotes an individualistic atmosphere in her 14-room hotel. Each chamber is decorated according to a different theme. The Japanese Tea Garden Room and the Rainbow Room reflect the style of the 1960s. All rooms are nicely appointed with handsome wood tables and chairs, chandeliers, and lacy curtains. Moderate.

HAIGHT-ASHBURY RESTAURANT

The **Ironwood Cafe** (901 Cole Street; 415-664-0224) is a spiffy little restaurant filled to the beams with upscale diners. Wood is the word in decor: oak chairs, pine booths, hardwood floor. The changing menu of American and continental dishes includes such entrées as pasta with mussels and pernod and chicken with plum sauce. Definitely recommended; moderate.

HAIGHT-ASHBURY SHOPPING

Among the finer shops in the area, **Spellbound** (1670 Haight Street; 415-863-4930) features classical clothing from the 1890s and 1920s— from formal attire to whimsical chiffons.

    The Soft Touch (1580 Haight Street; 415-863-3279), operated by a Bay Area collective of artists, displays original sculpture, jewelry and clothing.

    Off The Wall (1669 Haight Street; 415-863-8170) has an appealing collection of contemporary poster art.

    You'll find some fascinating holograms at **Holos Gallery** (1792 Haight Street; 415-668-4656).

    Then you can **Play With It, Ltd.** (1682 Haight Street; 415-621-8787) at the ultimate toy store. The place is bursting with playthings like aerodynamic kites and elaborate bathtub toys.

    Nearby **Distractions** (1692 Haight Street; 415-621-7355) offers beautiful gay and mixed greeting cards and magazines, plus sunglasses and posters.

HAIGHT-ASHBURY NIGHTLIFE

Nightbreak (1821 Haight Street; 415-221-9008) is small, local and alive with sound and color. Live and canned music; cover.

Hottest of all the city's dancehalls is the cavernous **I-Beam** (1748 Haight Street; 415-668-6006), with bands wailing into the wee hours. Cover.

The Other Cafe (100 Carl Street; 415-296-8437) draws many talented comic performers.

Golden Gate Park

With its folded hills and sloping meadows, its lakes, forests and museums, Golden Gate is everyone's favorite park. It extends from the Haight-Ashbury neighborhood across nearly half the width of San Francisco, all the way to the ocean.

Two roads span the length of the park. Each begins near Stanyan Street on the east side of Golden Gate Park and runs about four miles westward to the Pacific. The best way to see this area is to travel out along John F. Kennedy Drive and back by Martin Luther King, Jr. Drive, detouring down the side roads that lead into the heart of the park.

The first stop along John F. Kennedy Drive lies immediately after the entrance. That red-tile building overgrown in ivy is **McLaren Lodge** (415-666-7200), park headquarters and home base for maps, brochures, pamphlets and information. (McLaren Lodge is closed on weekends, but maps are available at the kiosk near the carousel.)

The startling glass palace nearby is the **Conservatory**. Built in 1879 and Victorian in style, it houses a plant kingdom ruled by stately palm trees and peopled with fingertip flowers, pendent ferns and courtly orchids.

You'll find the kingdom's colonies spread throughout the park, but one of particular import is **Rhododendron Dell**, just down the street. A lacework of trails threads through this 20-acre garden; if you're visiting in early spring, when the rose-hued bushes are blooming, the dell is a concert of colors.

Just beyond this garden beats the cultural heart of Golden Gate Park. Located around a tree-studded concourse are San Francisco's top museums. The **M. H. De Young Memorial Museum** (415-750-3659; admission) houses an impressive collection that traces the course of American art from colonial times to the mid-20th century. The pièce de résistance of this entire complex is the **Asian Art Museum** (415-668-8921; admission) adjacent to the De Young. Featuring major pieces from China, Tibet, Japan and throughout the continent, this superlative facility was the first museum in the country devoted exclusively to Asian art. Some of the exhibits date back 6000 years.

It takes a facility like the **California Academy of Sciences** (415-750-7145; admission) to even compete with a place like the De Young Museum. Here you'll find a planetarium and a "roundabout" aquarium in which you stand at the center of a circular glass tank while creatures of the deep swim around you. A tremendous place for kids, this natural history museum also features numerous "hands-on" displays and a "Life Through Time" exhibit that carries viewers on a three million year evolutionary journey.

When museum fatigue sets in, it's time for the **Japanese Tea Garden** (admission). Here you can rest your heavy eyes on carp-filled ponds and handwrought gateways. There are arch footbridges, cherry trees, bonsai gardens and, of course, a tea house where Japanese women serve jasmine tea and cookies.

All these cultural gathering places cluster around a **Music Concourse** where concerts regularly are staged. The concourse is also a departure point for horse-and-buggy rides (for information call 415-761-8272). With turn-of-the-century carriages and drivers attired in formal livery, they provide a marvelous way to see the park.

Otherwise, by car or foot, you can get back on John F. Kennedy Drive and resume your self-guided tour by continuing to **Stow Lake**. This is a donut-shaped body of water with an island as the hole in the middle. From the island's crest you can gaze across San Francisco from bay to ocean. Or, if an uphill is not in your day's itinerary, there's a footpath around the island perimeter that passes an ornate Chinese pagoda.

Spreckels Lake is home to ducks, sea gulls and model sailboats; nearby is the **Buffalo Paddock**, where American bison still roam, though within the confines of a barbed wire fence.

Immediately beyond is the **Chain of Lakes**, a string of three reservoirs stretching the width of the park. Framed by eucalyptus trees, they offer hiking paths around each shoreline. As you circumnavigate these baby lakes, you'll notice they are freckled with miniature islands.

Where the road meets the Pacific you'll come upon the **Dutch Windmill**, a regal structure with wooden struts and scalelike shingles

---

L'AVENUE

L'Avenue (3854 Geary Boulevard; 415-386-1555) harkens back to the days when the Richmond District, just north of Golden Gate Park, boasted a number of small chef-owned European restaurants. The bistro has gained a steady following for its Mediterranean, Provençal and American cuisine. The menu changes seasonally at this attractive restaurant, where huge framed artwork and an open bar provide a soupçon of French ambience. Dinner only; deluxe.

built in 1903. The Dutchman's cousin, **Murphy Windmill**, an orphan with broken arms, lives several hundred yards down the coast.

From here at continent's edge, it's a four-mile trip back through the park along Martin Luther King, Jr. Drive. After picking it up at Murphy Windmill, you'll find that this softly curving road passes lakes and forests, meadows and playgrounds. More important, it borders **Strybing Arboretum** (415-661-0668), a place specially made for garden lovers. Strybing is a world within itself, a 70-acre flower quilt stitched together by pathways. Over 5000 species peacefully coexist here—dwarf conifers and sprawling magnolias, as well as plants from Asia, the Andes, Australia and the Americas.

Gay Neighborhoods

San Francisco's gay neighborhoods center around Polk Street and Castro Street. With a population that today numbers perhaps 100,000, the community has become a powerful social and political force. In 1977, Supervisor Harvey Milk became the nation's first outfront gay elected to a major municipal post. Since then, despite the AIDS epidemic, San Francisco has retained a gay supervisor and the gay community has remained an integral part of the city's life.

GAY NEIGHBORHOODS LODGING

For an establishment located in the center of the action, consider the **Inn on Castro** (321 Castro Street; 415-861-0321), a seven-room bed and breakfast housed in an old Victorian. A class establishment all the way, this comfortable inn adds subtle touches like fresh flowers and nightly turndown service. Moderate to deluxe.

TWIN PEAKS AREA

*The view of views in San Francisco is from **Twin Peaks** (Twin Peaks Boulevard), a pair of windy summits rising almost 1000 feet above the city. From here atop these bald knobs the eye traces a circle around the entire bay, the Golden Gate Bridge becomes a mere corridor that opens onto a mountain range called Marin, and the bay is a pond inhabited by sailboats.*

*A wooded retreat rests nearby atop **Mount Davidson**. From the corner of Myra Way and Sherwood Court a trail climbs sharply to the summit of San Francisco's highest peak. Here stands a 103-foot cross, the site of Easter sunrise services. On any day, you can peer through the eucalyptus forest out over the Pacific.*

Several blocks from Castro Street is **The Willows Bed and Breakfast Inn** (710 14th Street; 415-431-4770), a beautiful 11-room facility which attracts both gay and straight guests. The trademark of this cozy hostelry is the willow-branch furniture designed expressly for the Inn. Shared baths. Moderate.

GAY NEIGHBORHOODS RESTAURANTS

Dollar for dollar, the best dining spot along Polk Street is **Swan Oyster Depot** (1517 Polk Street; 415-673-1101). It's a short-order place serving fresh crabs, lobster, shrimp and oysters. Lunch only; moderate.

Potted palms and caneback chairs create an inviting ambience at **Luisa's** (544 Castro Street; 415-621-8515). The cuisine is Italian with the accent on dishes like sautéed calamari and chicken parmigiana. Luisa also features calzone-style pizza and homemade bread. Moderate.

GAY NEIGHBORHOODS SHOPPING

Polk Street has a wonderfully cluttered antique store called **J. Goldsmith Antiques** (1924 Polk Street; 415-771-4055). There is a marvelous collection of miniatures here, as well as old bottles, toys and jewelry.

Banana Republic (2253 Polk Street; 415-474-9711) features the best selection of safari outfits this side of Nairobi, along with outstanding cotton clothes.

At the **Tibet Shop** (1807 Polk Street; 415-982-0326) are *sili* bangles, Buddha figurines and "incredible monastic incense," along with clothing made in Nepal and Afghanistan.

Kyriakos of Hydra (1609 Polk Street; 415-441-1768) has a tasteful assortment of garments imported from the Aegean and Mediterranean areas.

Headlines (1217 Polk Street, 549 and 557 Castro Street and 838 Market Street; 415-956-4872) is a chain of stores, each featuring clothing, novelty buttons, outrageous greeting cards, jewelry and teddy bears.

For beads and turquoise and silver jewelry, try **The Bead Store** (417 Castro Street; 415-861-7332).

Speaking of generic names, how about **Brand X Antiques** (570 Castro Street; 415-626-8908)? They feature an assortment of antiques, decorative artwork and estate jewelry.

Then there's **Image Leather** (2199 Market Street; 415-621-7551) for black leather and **Wild Wild West** (2193 Market Street; 415-626-1700) for cowboy boots and Western wear.

Unique Custom Framers (4129 18th Street; 415-431-2333) has one of the finest collections of art prints anywhere in the city, including several by Erté.

One of the best-stocked women's bookstores in the West is **Old Wives' Tales Women's Visions and Books** (1009 Valencia Street; 415-821-4675).

GAY NEIGHBORHOODS NIGHTLIFE

One example of San Francisco's wide-open tradition is the presence of almost 200 gay bars—everything from rock clubs to piano bars to stylish cabarets. Some are strictly gay, while others have a mixed clientele.

The **Polk Gulch Saloon** (1100 Polk Street; 415-771-2022) starts early and parties late. With its raw-wood interior the place has an open air about it. Nicest of all the neighborhood bars, however, is **Kimo's** (1351 Polk Street; 415-885-4535).

For live entertainment, check out **The Q. T.** (1312 Polk Street; 415-885-1114). Open seven nights a week, it has live music Wednesday through Saturday, featuring local bands as well as hot sounds from out of town.

Among the nicest of Castro Street's many bars is **Twin Peaks Tavern** (401 Castro Street; 415-864-9470), with its overhead fans and mirrored bar. Other major bars include the disco-blasting **Castro Station** (456 Castro Street; 415-626-7220) and the brass-rail **Phoenix** (482 Castro Street; 415-552-6827).

The finest drinking place in the entire Castro sits upstairs at **Cafe San Marcos** (2367 Market Street; 415-861-3846). It's a glass-and-mirror affair with high-tech furnishings and track lighting.

South of Market, you'll find **The Stud** (399 9th Street; 415-863-6623), everybody's favorite gay bar. Everybody in this case includes aging hippies, multihued punks, curious straights and even a gay or two, all packed elbow to armpit into this pulsing club. Cover on weekends.

Among the city's numerous lesbian bars is **Amelia's** (647 Valencia Street; 415-552-7788), featuring a jukebox and small dancefloor downstairs and a full-bore dancehall upstairs, complete with deejays, mirrored walls and flashing lights. Over in the Castro, **Francine's** (4149 18th Street; 415-552-4858) is a neighborhood bar whose patrons come to drink and shoot pool.

Mission District

Depending on your personal taste or maybe just your mood, you'll come away from the Mission District thinking it either a poem or a ghetto. In truth, it's both. "The Mission," San Francisco's own Spanish barrio, is the vibrant home of the city's Mexican, Colombian,

Guatemalan, Nicaraguan and Salvadoran populations. It's a neighborhood where brilliant murals vie with graffiti-scrawled walls and where
children compete with old folks for a seat on the bus or park bench.

The *corazón* of the Mission is **24th Street** with its outdoor markets and indoor murals. And **Mission Street** is its nerve center. By day
it's a collection of shoe stores, hair salons and pawn shops. At night,
particularly on weekends, the area is transformed into a cruising strip.

On **Dolores Street,** you'll find one of San Francisco's prettiest
boulevards. Bordered on either side by bay window homes, the street's
proudest feature is the grassy median planted with stately palm trees.
Better still, this marvelous promenade opens onto **Dolores Park**
(Dolores and 20th streets), a rectangle of rolling hills dotted with
magnolia and pepper trees.

Farther downhill, at Dolores and 16th streets, stands the historic
building that gave the neighborhood its name. Crown jewel of the
city, **Mission San Francisco de Asis** (415-621-8203; admission), or
Mission Dolores, completed in 1791, was one of the 21 Spanish missions built along the California coast by Franciscans. Its thick adobe
walls (and perhaps a few prayers) helped the church survive the earthquake and fire; today it is the city's oldest building. There's a minimuseum behind the chapel and a massive 20th-century basilica next
door, but the most intriguing feature on the mission grounds is the
cemetery. Studded with yew trees and tombstones, it is the last resting
place of several famous (and infamous) San Francisco figures.

MISSION DISTRICT RESTAURANTS

Definitely among the best Latin-style restaurants in San Francisco is
El Tazumal (3522 20th Street; 415-550-0935). Specializing in
Salvadoran dishes, they feature adventurous entrées like *lengua en salsa*
(beef tongue in red wine sauce) and *chuletas de puerco entomadas* (pork
chops with tomato sauce). Moderate.

It's Christmas every day at **La Rondalla** (901 Valencia Street;
415-647-7474). Where else will you encounter religious scenes and
Christmas lights in July? The menu is also unique: those pots on the
stove are liable to contain *albóndigas* (meatball soup), *birria de chivo*
(barbequed goat meat) or more standard Mexican fare. Budget to
moderate.

Clever decor and excellent value belie the drab look outside at
Garibaldi Cafe (1600 17th Street, 415-552-3325), which lies about
half a mile east of the Mission District. A short standard menu of fish,
chicken and a few meats is overshadowed by straight-from-the-pur-
veyor daily specials such as tuna wrapped in grape leaves and salmon
with raspberry-brandy sauce (risky, but successful). Moderate.

Nearby, the cheery and modest **S. Asimakopoulos Cafe** (288 Connecticut Street; 415-552-8789) is a prime example of San Francisco neighborhood dining. The menu is solidly, but not overbearingly, Greek. There is moussaka, yes, but also a mild lemon chicken, for instance. Tremendous value at moderate prices.

MISSION DISTRICT NIGHTLIFE

César's Latin Palace (3140 Mission Street; 415-648-6611) features live music with a salsa beat. The ballroom is as big as a warehouse, with enough tables and dance space to fit a Latin American army. It's hot. Cover Friday and Saturday.

Many of the city's important experimental theater groups are located in or near the Mission District. Among them are the **Eureka Theatre** (2730 16th Street; 415-558-9898), **Theatre Artaud** (450 Florida Street; 415-621-7797) and the **Julian Theatre** (100 Dolores Street; 415-626-8986).

This area also is home to many outstanding dance companies. Featuring modern and experimental dance, they include the **Margaret Jenkins Dance Company** (3153 17th Street; 415-863-1173), **Oberlin Dance Company** (3153 17th Street; 415-863-6606) and **Della Davidson and the Moving Company** (223 Mississippi Street; 415-861-5797).

South of Market

The South of Market neighborhood has been a warren of factories, warehouses and wholesale outlets for years. Today it is undergoing a redevelopment program aimed at rejuvenating the entire area. Centerpiece of this gentrification project is the **Moscone Center** (Howard Street between 3rd and 4th streets). With restaurants, hotels, apartments and stores encircling it like satellites, this 11-acre center is the dominant feature in San Francisco's fastest-changing district.

With trendy restaurants, hip nightclubs and proliferating fashion and design centers, the South of Market district is rapidly becoming San Francisco's answer to New York's artsy Soho section. In fact, everyone calls it SOMA.

This burgeoning neighborhood has spawned numerous galleries and museums. Among the more prominent, **The Ansel Adams Center** (250 4th Street; 415-495-7000; admission) features five galleries of fine art photography. Four of them have changing exhibits that range from 19th century to contemporary. The fifth and most popular gallery is devoted exclusively to the works of Ansel Adams.

SOUTH OF MARKET LODGING

Set in a 1900s-era sailor's hotel near the waterfront, the **Griffon** (155 Steuart Street; 415-495-2100) is a freshly refurbished hotel with 62 rooms. Exposed brick, wood trim and indirect lighting create an intimate and contemporary atmosphere. Deluxe.

SOUTH OF MARKET RESTAURANTS

The **Cadillac Bar** (1 Holland Court; 415-543-8226) is a raucous Mexican eatery that may be the noisiest place you've ever entered. The bar is a massive wood structure adorned with sombreros. Cooking is by mesquite grill (what else?). The menu is far from standard south-of-the-border fare—prawns with *aguacate* sauce, chicken stuffed with jalapeños and bacon. Warehouse chic. Moderate.

Or try **Max's Diner** (311 3rd Street; 415-546-6297), the '80s version of a classic old diner. The music is vintage, the menu is meat and potatoes and the bar is jammed with nostalgic people. Moderate.

It's not every day you can enjoy a dry martini while seated at a curved pink leatherette bar right out of the '50s and then be treated to a postmodern nouvelle American dinner, but that's the case at **Julie's Supper Club** (1123 Folsom Street; 415-861-4084). Despite the loud music, insist on a table in the front room, to enjoy the passing array of trendy South-of-Market clubgoers. Stick with the imaginative salads for starters, followed by outstanding chicken, lamb or fish dishes. Moderate.

More than just cuisine is notable at **Undici** (374 11th Street; 415-431-3337). This southern Italian restaurant, with its lamb shank dishes and Sicilian seafood, also sports a sophisticated decor. The antiqued walls are painted with grapevines and set off by a loft ceiling, creating an al fresco atmosphere. Moderate.

SOUTH OF MARKET SHOPPING

Headquarters for discount shopping in San Francisco is the South of Market area—outlets sell everything from leotards to wedding dresses. The best time to visit is early Saturday morning, before the vanloads of out-of-town shoppers begin arriving. The very nature of off-price boutiques means limited hours and often limited lifespans; always try to call in advance to check hours of operation. Concentrated in the blocks bounded by Market and Townsend, 2nd and 9th streets are a variety of concerns:

Rainbeau Bodywear (300 Fourth Street; 415-777-9786) has two levels plush with leotards, tights, socks and other dancewear at prices well below those at major department stores.

An outlet for designs by localite Jessica McClintock, **Gunne Sax** (35 Stanford Street; 415-495-3326) stocks dresses suitable for a high-school prom and other frothy concoctions.

Brand-name apparel for the whole family, as well as some jewelry, is discounted as much as 40 to 70 percent at **Six Sixty Center** (660 Third Street; 415-227-0464). For bargains in outerwear, try the **Coat/Fur Factory Outlet** (1350 Folsom Street; 415-864-5050), which promises rainwear, woolens, sweaters, furs and leathers by names such as London Fog, Misty Harbor and Bill Blass. Discounts are in the 20 to 60 percent range.

The highly regarded auction house **Butterfield & Butterfield** (220 San Bruno Avenue; 415-861-7500) has regular sales that are open to the public.

Walking or driving around will net additional possibilities, from seconds outlets for ceramics to temporary warehouse displays of baskets and wicker furniture. **George Smith Ltd.** (3350 Sacramento Street, in Elements; 415-431-5326) is one of the few places where the public can buy ceramic accessories at wholesale prices.

Also in SOMA is the **California Flower Terminal** (6th and Brannan streets), where dozens of florists offer excellent prices.

Slightly farther afield is one of the best outlets in town. The **Esprit Outlet** (16th and Illinois streets; 415-957-2500) is a gigantic emporium where most shoppers push grocery carts around to select pants, dresses, blouses, suits and shoes.

SOUTH OF MARKET NIGHTLIFE

The fanciest club in this hip area is **Club DV8** (55 Natoma Street; 415-957-1730), with several levels decorated in an eclectic mix ranging from Greco-Roman columns to Keith Haring murals. The music (live and canned) is cutting edge; the crowd is mostly in the 20s-to-30s range with an inclination toward European fashions. Cover.

Club NV (715 Harrison Street; 415-495-6868) is the last word in trendy elegance. In addition to a spacious dancefloor, they occasionally feature live entertainment. But generally the music is deejay-style. Cover.

1015 Folsom (1015 Folsom Street; 415-626-2899) offers up contemporary dance music on weekends. Cover.

The Oasis (278 11th Street; 415-621-8119) is a club that headlines bands on Wednesday and Friday and deejay music during the rest of the week. Restaurant and swimming pool. Swimming pool? Cover.

The **DNA Lounge** (375 11th Street; 415-626-1409) has lasted much longer than most trendy clubs. The scene is high-decibel with a mixed crowd clearly born to dance. And dance they do, on all sides of an oval bar in the middle of a bare-wood floor. At a quieter upstairs bar you can watch the goings-on. Cover.

It's a slightly older than usual SOMA crowd that patronizes **Slim's** (330 11th Street; 415-621-3330), possibly because entertainer Boz Scaggs is an owner. Whatever, it's the place where you're most likely to run across a jam session with traveling high-profile musicians. The music may be local bands or legends like Etta James or Bay Area-bred talents such as Huey Lewis. Cover.

TownSend (177 Townsend Street; 415-974-6020), opened in 1989 in a veritable cavern, that, despite its size, is SRO on weekends. The inevitable doorman picks couples to let in ahead of others from the line outside. Attitude is everything here; those who don't know how to dance to rap music might not fit in. Cover.

The **San Francisco Mime Troupe** (855 Treat Avenue; 415-285-1717) has performed musical political satires in the city's parks for a quarter of a century. **Pickle Family Circus** (400 Missouri Street; 415-826-0747), a delightful collection of acrobats, jugglers and other performers, also tours the area.

Golden Gate National Recreation Area

One of San Francisco's most spectacular regions belongs to us all. The Golden Gate National Recreation Area, a 31,000-acre metropolitan park, draws about 25 million visitors annually.

A place of natural beauty and historic importance, this magnificent park stretches north from San Francisco throughout much of the Bay Area. In the city itself, the Golden Gate National Recreation Area forms a narrow band around the waterfront. It follows the shoreline of the bay from Aquatic Park to Fort Mason to the Golden Gate Bridge. On the ocean side it encompasses Land's End, an exotic and untouched preserve, as well as the city's finest beaches.

You can start at the **Golden Gate Promenade**, a three-and-a-half-mile walk across a swath of heaven that extends from Aquatic Park to the shadows of the Golden Gate Bridge. Just start in the park and make the short jaunt to the **Municipal Pier**. As you follow its curving length a 360° view unfolds—from the Golden Gate to the Bay Bridge to downtown San Francisco.

From the pier it's uphill and downstairs to **Fort Mason Center** (Marina Boulevard and Buchanan Street; 415-441-5705), a complex of old wharves and tile-roofed warehouses that was once a major military embarkation point. Fort Mason today is the cultural heart of avant-garde San Francisco, home to over 50 nonprofit organizations including dance, theater, crafts and music groups, as well as environmental organizations such as Greenpeace.

Permanently docked at one end of Fort Mason is the **S.S. Jeremiah O'Brien** (415-441-3101; admission), the only one of 2751 World War II Liberty Ships to remain in original condition. Visitors are welcome to walk the decks of the old tub, explore the sailors' quarters and descend into the depths of the engine room.

Continue on the shoreline to the **Marina**, along Marina Boulevard. (The remainder of the tour can be completed by car, though walking is definitely the aesthete's and athlete's way.) Some of this sailor-city's spiffiest yachts are docked along the esplanade.

Nearby **Marina Green**, a stretch of park paralleling the bay, is a haven for bicyclists, joggers, jugglers, sunbathers and the kite-fliers who fill the blue with a rainbow of soaring colors.

The **Palace of Fine Arts**, a domed edifice built of arches and shadows, resides along Marina Boulevard. Adorned with molded urns and bas-relief figures, this Beaux-Arts beauty represents the only surviving structure from the 1915 Panama–Pacific International Exposition. Happily, it borders on a sun-shivered pond peopled by mallards and swans. One of the city's loveliest spots for sitting and sunning.

Or, if education is on your mind, note that the Palace houses the **Exploratorium** (Marina Boulevard and Lyon Street; 415-561-0360; admission). This "hands-on" museum, with imaginative exhibits demonstrating the principles of optics, sound, animal behavior, etc., was once deemed "the best science museum in the world" by *Scientific American*.

THE PRESIDIO

A key stop on your itinerary could very well be an Army base. Of course, this is not just any military installation. It happens to be the Presidio, 1500 acres of undulating hills sprinkled with acacia, madrone, pine and redwood trees. Now a National Historic Landmark, it was established by the Spanish in 1776 and taken over by the United States in 1846. The area has the feel of a country retreat. Hiking trails snake through the property, and there are expansive bay views that would gladden the eye of any sentry.

*Best way to explore the Presidio is by stopping first at the **Presidio Army Museum** (Funston Avenue near Lincoln Boulevard; 415-561-4115), an imposing structure faced with pillars and protected by a collection of antique cannons. The displays inside consist primarily of military uniforms and weapons. (Maps of the reservation are available from the Presidio Community Relations Office, Building 37, Graham Avenue; 415-561-3870).*

*The nearby **Officers' Club** (Moraga Avenue), a tile-roofed, Spanish-style structure, includes part of the original 1776 Presidio, one of the first buildings ever constructed in San Francisco. The **National Cemetery** (Lincoln Boulevard) is San Francisco's salute to the nation's war dead.*

Modeled on Fort Sumter and completed around the time Confederate forces opened fire on that hapless garrison, **Fort Point** (end of Marine Drive; 415-556-1693) represents the only brick fort west of the Mississippi. With its collection of cannons and Civil War-era exhibits, it's of interest to history buffs.

From Fort Point, a footpath leads up to the observation area astride the **Golden Gate Bridge**; if driving, take Lincoln Boulevard to the vista point. You've arrived at one of the world's most beautiful spans, a medley of splayed cable and steel struts. It's one of the longest suspension bridges anywhere—6450 feet of suspended concrete and steel, with twin towers the height of 65-story buildings and cables that support 200 million pounds. It is San Francisco's emblem, an engineering wonder that has come to symbolize an entire metropolis. If you're game, you can walk across, venturing along a dizzying sidewalk out to one of the most magnificent views you'll ever experience.

The Golden Gate Promenade ends at the bridge, but Lincoln Boulevard continues along the cliffs that mark the ocean side of San Francisco. There are **vista points** overlooking the Pacific and affording startling views back toward the bridge. After about a mile you'll reach **Baker Beach** (off Lincoln Boulevard on Gibson Road), a wide corridor of white sand ideal for picnicking and sunbathing.

Lincoln Boulevard transforms into El Camino del Mar, which winds through Sea Cliff, one of San Francisco's most affluent neighborhoods. Here, too, is **China Beach** (off 25th Avenue at the end of

---

*The remainder of our Presidio tour is of a more natural bent. There's **El Polin Spring** (end of MacArthur Avenue) where, as the brass plaque proclaims, "the early Spanish garrison attained its water supply." History has rarely been made in a more beautiful spot. The spring is set in a lovely park surrounded by hills upon which eucalyptus trees battle with conifers for strategic ground. The battle lines are drawn at **Lover's Lane**. On one side, standing sentinel straight, are the eucalyptus. Mustered along the other front, clad in darker uniforms, are the conifer trees. Look around. You are standing in an awesome spot, one of the last forests in San Francisco.*

***Mountain Lake Park** (Lake Street between 8th and Funston avenues), stationed along the Presidio's southern flank, is another idyllic locale of grassy meadows and wooded walkways. The duck-filled lake is skirted with tule reeds and overhung with willows.*

*The base's prettiest walk is actually in civilian territory along the **Presidio Wall** bordering Lyon Street and starting at the Lombard Street Gate. As you walk up Lyon, you'll see the city's chic Union Street district to your left. To the right, beyond the Presidio's stone enclosure, are the tumbling hills and towering trees of the old garrison.*

Sea Cliff Avenue). More secluded than Baker, this pocket beach is backdropped by a rocky bluff atop which stand the luxurious plate-window homes of Sea Cliff.

Continuing on El Camino del Mar as it sweeps above the ocean, you'll come upon San Francisco's prettiest museum. With its colonnaded courtyard and arching entranceway, the **Palace of the Legion of Honor** (34th Avenue and Clement Street, in Lincoln Park; 415-750-3659; admission) is modeled after a gallery in Paris. Appropriately, it specializes in European art and culture, from the Middle Ages to the 20th century.

Then head back out to Geary, which becomes Point Lobos Avenue, turn right on El Camino del Mar and follow it to the end. This is **Land's End**, a thumblike appendage of real estate that San Francisco seems to have stolen from the sea. Hike the trails that honeycomb the hillsides hereabout and you'll enter a wild, tumbling region where winds twist cypress trees into the contours of the earth.

Continuing down Point Lobos Avenue, at the corner where the road turns to parallel the Pacific, rest the ruins of the **Sutro Baths**. Sprawling across three oceanfront acres, these baths built by San Francisco philanthropist Adolf Sutro could have washed the entire city. There were actually six baths, Olympian in size, as well as three restaurants and 500 dressing rooms—all contained beneath a stained-glass dome.

Towering above them was the Cliff House, a Gothic castle that survived the earthquake only to be consumed by fire the next year. Following numerous reincarnations, the **Cliff House** (1090 Point Lobos Avenue) today is a rather bland structure housing several restaurants and tourist shops. Most important among its features are the National Park Service information office (415-556-8642) and the view. From this crow's nest you can gaze out over a sweeping expanse of ocean. Just offshore the **Seal Rocks** lie anchored. Those barking

---

GREENS

San Francisco's most popular vegetarian restaurant, incongruously situated in an old waterfront warehouse, has the aura of an airplane hangar. But the outstanding **Greens at Fort Mason** *(Fort Mason, Building A; 415-771-6222) has been deftly furnished with burlwood tables, and there's a view of the Golden Gate. Lunch features items such as vegetable brochettes fired over mesquite charcoal. The changing dinner menu might include fugasse with red onions, Tunisian salad and eggplant soup. A la carte items are moderately priced; prix-fixe dinners are ultra-deluxe. Reservations recommended.*

beasts sunning themselves on the rock islands might look like giant sea slugs, but they are sea lions, San Francisco's wild mascots.

Below the Cliff House, extending to the very end of vision, is the Great Highway. The salt-and-pepper beach beside it is **Ocean Beach**, a slender ribbon of sand that decorates three miles of San Francisco's western perimeter. Remember, this is San Francisco—land of fog, mist and west winds—beachwear here more often consists of sweaters than swimsuits. Nevertheless, to walk this strand is to trek the border of eternity. The Indians called San Francisco's ocean the "sundown sea." If you'll take the time some late afternoon, you'll see that the fiery orb still settles nightly just offshore.

Fort Funston (Skyline Boulevard, at the far end of Ocean Beach) is the prettiest stretch to stroll. The fort itself is little more than a sequence of rusting gun emplacements, but there is a half-mile nature trail here that winds along cliffs overlooking the sea. It's a windblown region of dune grass and breathtaking views. Hang gliders dust the cliffs.

Across the highway lies **Lake Merced** (Skyline and Lake Merced boulevards), a U-shaped reservoir that was once salt water. If you decide to pass up the hang gliding at Fort Funston, you might rent a rowboat or sailboat at the clubhouse here and try a less nerve-jangling sport.

Heading back along the Great Highway, you'll encounter the **San Francisco Zoo** (Sloat Boulevard at 45th Avenue; 415-753-7061; admission). With over 100 endangered species, plus an excellent gorilla habitat and Primate Discovery Center, it's a great place to visit.

GOLDEN GATE RECREATION AREA NIGHTLIFE

Where San Francisco meets the Pacific, there's a bar called **Phineas T. Barnacle** (1090 Point Lobos Avenue; 415-386-7630). Set in the Cliff House, it's heavily touristed and rather pricey, but the views are unmatched. Seal Rocks stand sentinel offshore, with barking denizens who can be heard even over the din of drinkers.

The **Magic Theatre** (Fort Mason, Building D; 415-441-8822) has premiered several plays by Pulitzer Prize-winning dramatist Sam Shepard, who was playwright-in-residence here for several years.

Sporting Life

FISHING

If you hanker to spend a day deep-sea fishing for rock cod, bass, or salmon, check out **Muni Sportfishing** (Fisherman's Wharf; 415-871-1691), **New Easy Rider Sport Fishing Center** (561 Prentiss Street; 415-285-2000), **Miss Farallones** (Taylor Street at Jefferson Street; 415-352-5708) or **Quite A Lady** (Fisherman's Wharf; 415-821-3838).

SAILING

Some of the world's most challenging sailing can be found on San Francisco Bay. To charter boats and captains, contact **A Day on the Bay** (San Francisco Marina; 415-922-0227) or **Pacific Marine Yacht Charters** (San Francisco Marina; 415-388-3400).

KITE FLYING

San Francisco has been called the "city of kites." Ocean breezes, mild weather and lots of open space create perfect conditions for kite flying. Popular kite-flying spots include the Marina Green, Golden Gate Park's Polo Field, Lake Merced and Fort Funston.

Local kite stores sell exotic designs ranging from traditional box kites to tandems, octagons, hexagons and silk dragons. Try **The Kite Shop** (Ghirardelli Square, 900 North Point Street; 415-673-4559) or **Kitemakers of San Francisco** (Pier 39; 415-956-3181) for your flyer.

GOLF

For the earthbound, golf can be a heavenly sport in San Francisco. Several courses are worth checking out, including **Glen Eagles International Golf Club** (2100 Sunnydale Avenue; 415-587-2425), **Golden Gate Park Golf Course** (47th Avenue and Fulton Street; 415-751-8987), a short but tricky nine-hole course and **Harding Park Golf Course** (Harding Park Road; 415-664-4690), considered to be one of the finest public courses in the country.

JOGGING

In a city of steep hills, where walking provides more than enough exercise, jogging is nevertheless a favorite pastime. There are actually places to run where the terrain is fairly level and the scenery spectacular. Most popular are the Golden Gate Bridge, the Presidio Highlands, Glen Canyon Park Trail, Ocean Beach, Golden Gate Park and Angel Island.

Parcourses, combining aerobic exercises with short jogs, are located at Justin Herman Park (the foot of Market Street near the Ferry Building; half course only), Marina Green (along Marina Boulevard near the foot of Fillmore Street), Mountain Lake Park (Lake Street between 8th and Funston avenues) and the Polo Field in Golden Gate Park.

BICYCLING

San Francisco is not a city designed for cyclers. Some of the hills are almost too steep to walk, and downtown traffic can be grueling. There are places, however, that are easy to ride and beautiful as well.

Golden Gate Park, the Golden Gate Promenade and Lake Merced all have excellent bike routes.

Among the city's most dramatic rides is the bicyclists' sidewalk on the Golden Gate Bridge. Or, if you're less adventurous, the Sunset Bikeway begins at Lake Merced Boulevard, then carries through a residential area and past views of the ocean to the Polo Field in Golden Gate Park.

SEA BIRDS

Somehow the mud flats of San Francisco Bay are the last place to go sightseeing, particularly at high tide, after the flood has stirred the ooze. But it is at such times that birdwatchers gather to view flocks of as many as 60,000 birds.

The California shore is one of the richest bird habitats anywhere in North America. Over 500 species are found across the state, many along the coast and its offshore islands.

Coastal species fall into three general categories—near-shore birds like loons, grebes, cormorants and scoters, that inhabit the shallow waters of bays and beaches; offshore birds, such as shearwaters, which feed several miles off the coast; and pelagic or open-ocean species like albatross and Arctic terns, that fly miles from land and live for up to 20 or 30 years.

Joining the shore birds along California's beaches are ducks, geese and other waterfowl. While waterfowl dive for fish and feed on submerged vegetation, near-shore birds use their sharp, pointed beaks to ferret out intertidal animals. Both groups flee the scene each year, flying north in the spring to Canada and Alaska or south during autumn to Mexico and Central America, following the Pacific flyway, that great migratory route spanning the western United States.

Another intriguing species is the peregrine falcon. A kind of streamlined hawk, they are among the fastest birds alive, capable of diving at 200 miles an hour to prey on ducks, coots and terns. While peregrine falcons nest on rock ledges, ospreys build large nests which can often be seen high in shoreline trees. Also known as fish hawks, these are handsome birds with brown head crowns and six-foot wingspans.

Among the most beautiful birds are the egrets and herons. Tall, slender, elegant birds, they live from January until July in Bolinas and other coastal towns, engaging in elaborate courtship rituals. Together with more common species like sea gulls, sandpipers and pelicans, they tend to turn travelers into birdwatchers and make inconvenient times, like the edge of dawn, and unusual places like swamps, among the most intriguing possibilities California has to offer.

Transportation

BY CAR

The major highways leading into San Francisco are **Route 1**, the picturesque coastal road, **Route 101**, California's main north–south thoroughfare, and **Route 80**, the transcontinental highway that crosses the country.

BY AIR

San Francisco International Airport, better known as SFO, sits 15 miles south of downtown San Francisco off Routes 101 and 280. A major destination from all points of the globe, the airport is always bustling.

Most domestic airlines fly into SFO, including Alaska Airlines, American Airlines, Continental Airlines, Delta Airlines, Eastern Airlines, Hawaiian Airlines, Pan American World Airways, Piedmont Airlines, Southwest Airlines, Trans World Airlines, United Airlines and USAir.

International carriers are also prominent: Air Canada, British Airways, Air China, China Airlines, Canadian Airlines International, Japan Airlines, Lufthansa German Airlines, Mexicana Airlines, Philippine Airlines, Qantas Airways, Singapore Airlines and TACA International Airlines have regular flights into San Francisco's airport.

To travel from the airport to downtown San Francisco, there's a **San Francisco Airporter** (415-673-2433) bus service that runs every 20 minutes. Or you can catch a **San Mateo County Transit**, or Sam-Trans, bus (800-660-4287) to the Transbay Terminal (425 Mission Street) or transfer in Daly City to **BART** (415-788-2278) transfer points. Taxi and limousine service are also available, or try **Lorrie's Airport Service** (415-334-9000) or **Super Shuttle** (415-558-8500), which provide economical door-to-door service.

BY BUS

Greyhound Bus Lines (415-558-6789) services San Francisco from around the country. The terminal is located at 7th and Market streets; there is also service to the Transbay Terminal (415-495-1569).

BY TRAIN

Amtrak (800-872-7245) offers daily train service to the Bay Area via the "Coast Starlight," "California Zephyr" and "San Joaquin." These trains arrive and depart the Oakland train station, with connecting bus service to San Francisco's Transbay Terminal.

CAR RENTALS

If you decide to rent a car, most major rental agencies have franchises at the airport. These include **Avis Rent A Car** (415-877-6780), **Budget Rent A Car** (415-877-4477), **Dollar Rent A Car** (415-952-6200), **Hertz Rent A Car** (415-877-1600) and **National Car Rental** (415-877-4745).

PUBLIC TRANSPORTATION

San Francisco is a city where public transit works. For information on how to get anywhere in the city, call **San Francisco Muni** (415-673-6864).

For complete information on the Muni system, obtain a copy of the "Ride the Muni" map from the Visitors Center (900 Market Street; 415-391-2000), at the information desk at City Hall or at local bookstores.

The **Bay Area Rapid Transit System** (415-788-2278), or BART, operates streamlined cars that zip beneath city streets.

Bay Area

Geologists demythologize even the most romantic places. San Fran- **347**
cisco Bay, they state, is a drowned river valley. Glaciers melting 10,000
years ago created it by raising sea levels and causing the ocean to flood
a canyon that earlier had been carved by the Sacramento and San
Joaquin rivers.

Mountains surround the entire area. The Santa Cruz Mountains
rise to the west and south; on the other side are the East Bay Hills and
Diablo Range; to the north looms Mt. Tamalpais. At the mouth of the
bay is the Golden Gate, a rocky conduit through which California's
major drainage system empties into the Pacific.

Then the geographers take over, explaining that San Francisco Bay
covers 900 square miles. It extends 50 miles south from the Golden
Gate to San Jose and ranges east for 30 miles through San Pablo and
Suisun bays to the Delta.

Along the west side of the bay sits the Peninsula. Containing
wealthy suburban towns, it reaches to Palo Alto, home of Stanford
University. Santa Clara Valley, better known as Silicon Valley, capital
of the computer industry, sprawls along the South Bay. San Jose, with a
population greater than San Francisco, dominates the area.

The East Bay, directly across the water from San Francisco, features Oakland, one of the world's largest container shipping ports, and
the dynamic campus town of Berkeley, home to the radical political
movements of the 1960s and now moving closer to the liberal center.
To the north lies Marin County, often lampooned by the media as a
realm of hot tubs and peacock feather massages, a posh enclave highlighted by the town of Sausalito, with its aura of the Mediterranean.

Rather than visualizing the Bay Area as scientists, it's time to look
at the region through the eyes of the traveler. To ease the visitor's
entry, this chapter is divided into six sections. Proceeding counter-
clockwise from San Francisco, they are the Peninsula, the Santa Cruz

Mountains, South Bay, East Bay and Marin, followed by a northeastern tangent out into the Delta, a dreamy maze of waterways linked by drawbridges.

The Peninsula

Jutting south from San Francisco, the Peninsula is a spit of land with the Pacific to the west, San Francisco Bay to the east and the Santa Cruz Mountains running down it like a spine. It's a suburban enclave filled with wealthy bedroom communities. Along the Peninsula's winding roads stand spectacular mansions and secluded estates.

Small rural Woodside is one of these elite communities. Situated near Route 280, Woodside boasts fabulous homes tucked away in forested heights. Most splendid of all is **Filoli** (Cañada Road; 415-364-2880; admission), a sumptuous 43-room mansion designed in 1916 by Willis Polk. The floors are inlaid with exquisite designs, murals decorate the ballroom, and the marble work is impeccable. The gardens surrounding the house, equally beautiful, once required the maintenance of 18 gardeners. Tour reservations are required.

Also of interest is the old **Woodside Store** (Kings Mountain and Tripp roads, Woodside; 415-851-7615), a bare-wood structure that dates back to 1854. A general store in the days when this region was a lumbering center, the establishment is now a three-room museum containing old tools and other artifacts.

Heading south, you will ultimately arrive in Palo Alto, home to one of America's prettiest college campuses. Named for a "tall tree" that served as an early landmark, this wealthy community is still noted for its beautiful arbors. The centerpiece of the town, however, is **Stanford University**, an 8200-acre campus created by railroad baron Leland Stanford during the 1880s.

A magnificent arcade of trees lines the entrance along Palm Drive. You'll also pass the **Stanford University Museum of Art** (Museum Way and Lomita Drive; 415-723-4177). Among the pieces in this diverse collection are an Egyptian mummy and the golden spike that marked completion of the transcontinental railroad. (At present the museum is still closed because of damage from the 1989 earthquake.)

The center of campus, the **Quadrangle**, lies at the end of Palm Drive. Built of sandstone and capped with red tile, it's an elegant Spanish-style courtyard.

Fittingly, the **Memorial Church** anchors the far edge of the plaza. That tile mosaic facade portraying the Sermon on the Mount was fashioned in Venice. Inside, behind the altar, hangs *The Last Supper*, re-created from the Sistine Chapel original. (Also closed because of earthquake damage.)

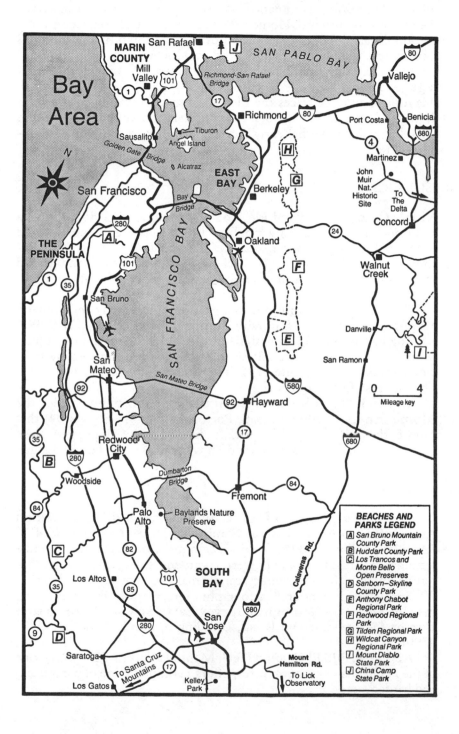

Bay Area

MARIN COUNTY

San Rafael

SAN PABLO BAY

J

Mill Valley

101

1

Richmond-San Rafael Bridge

17

Vallejo

80

Richmond

80

Port Costa

Benicia

680

4

Martinez

Sausalito

Tiburon

Angel Island

Golden Gate Bridge

Alcatraz

H

EAST BAY

John Muir Nat. Historic Site

To The Delta

San Francisco

Berkeley

G

Concord

Bay Bridge

280

A

101

Oakland

24

Walnut Creek

THE PENINSULA

F

1

35

San Bruno

Danville

I

E

San Ramon

San Mateo

92

San Mateo Bridge

92

Hayward

580

0   4

Mileage key

35

Redwood City

17

680

B

280

Woodside

Dumbarton Bridge

84

Palo Alto

Baylands Nature Preserve

Fremont

84

SAN FRANCISCO BAY

Calaveras Rd.

C

82

SOUTH BAY

Los Altos

35

85

101

9

D

280

San Jose

680

Saratoga

To Santa Cruz Mountains

17

Kelley Park

Mount Hamilton Rd.

To Lick Observatory

Los Gatos

BEACHES AND PARKS LEGEND

A San Bruno Mountain County Park
B Huddart County Park
C Los Trancos and Monte Bello Open Preserves
D Sanborn–Skyline County Park
E Anthony Chabot Regional Park
F Redwood Regional Park
G Tilden Regional Park
H Wildcat Canyon Regional Park
I Mount Diablo State Park
J China Camp State Park

Just west of the Quad rises **Hoover Tower** (415-723-2053; admission), a 285-foot landmark from the top of which you can survey the campus and beyond. Home to the Hoover Institution, a conservative think tank, the tower also houses the memorabilia of Stanford's most famous graduate, President Herbert Hoover.

Ingenuity is the password to the **Museum of American Heritage** (275 Alma Street, Palo Alto; 415-321-1004). Truly an original, this little showplace traces the history of mechanical invention with displays of cameras, calculators, cash registers and kitchenware. There are velocipedes and other early bicycles as well as an 1890s-era "stocking knitter."

PENINSULA RESTAURANTS

Nina's Cafe (2991 Woodside Road, Woodside; 415-851-4565), a country-style place set in a clapboard house, prepares meals you'd expect to find in a stone mansion. The changing dinner menu includes entrées like veal shank, blackened New York steak and grilled swordfish, while lunch involves crêpes and fresh fish. Moderate to deluxe.

To dine in style while visiting Stanford, I heartily recommend **MacArthur Park** (27 University Avenue, Palo Alto; 415-321-9990). Resting in a 1918 building designed by noted Bay Area architect Julia Morgan, the lovely restaurant specializes in food prepared by oakwood smoker or mesquite grill. There's pheasant breast, baby back ribs and fresh fish. Moderate.

Way up in the hills above Palo Alto, there's a roadhouse called the **Alpine Inn** (3915 Alpine Road, Portola Valley; 415-854-4004) that dates back to the 1850s. It's a simple, homey and very popular place serving hamburgers, sandwiches and a few hot platters for lunch. Budget.

PENINSULA SHOPPING

The loveliest spot to shop in all California may well be the **Allied Arts Guild** (75 Arbor Road at Cambridge Drive, Menlo Park; 415-325-3259), adjacent to the Stanford campus. Contained in a parklike setting amid fruit trees and flowering gardens, this artists' colony features numerous crafts—ceramics, candle making, weaving, woodwork.

For detailed maps and cartographic information, it's hard to top the **United States Geological Survey Earth Science Information Center** (345 Middlefield Road, Building 3, Menlo Park; 415-329-4390).

Kepler's (1010 El Camino Real, Menlo Park; 415-324-4321), one of the Peninsula's best bookstores, offers a complete line of paperbacks and hardcovers.

Don't miss **Phileas Fogg's** (87 Stanford Shopping Center, Palo Alto; 415-327-1754), a travel bookstore with an excellent selection of guides and maps.

In downtown Palo Alto, plan to stroll University Avenue from Alma Street to Webster Street, then return along Hamilton Avenue. This area is door-to-door with boutiques and galleries.

PENINSULA NIGHTLIFE

Molloy's (1655 Old Mission Road, Colma; 415-755-9545), a few miles from San Francisco, is a 100-year-old bar crowded with memories and memorabilia. There's live banjo music every Thursday and Friday.

Big name entertainers show up regularly at the **Circle Star Theatre** (1717 Industrial Road, San Carlos; 415-366-7100), an auditorium featuring a rotating stage; cover.

The Edge (260 California Avenue, Palo Alto; 415-324-1402) offers modern deejay rock, dancing, video and special events; cover.

Check the "Once Around the Quad" section of the *Stanford Daily* and other university publications for information about programs on the Stanford campus. You can also call 415-723-0336 for a tape-recorded calendar of events.

PENINSULA PARKS

The 2500-acre **San Bruno Mountain State and County Park** (415-992-6770) is one of San Francisco's last wild places, harboring six endangered plant species and three endangered butterflies. It provides one of the Bay Area's most spectacular views, a 360° panorama from atop 1314-foot San Bruno Mountain. Located in Brisbane a few miles south of San Francisco. From Bayshore Boulevard, take Guadalupe Canyon Parkway to the park entrance.

BAYLANDS NATURE PRESERVE

*Palo Alto may be known for its academic heights, but it also possesses mucky lowlands along the shores of San Francisco Bay. **City of Palo Alto Baylands Nature Preserve** (2775 Embarcadero Road; 415-329-2506) is a land of pickleweed and cord grass, home to the endangered clapper rail and red-bellied harvest marsh mouse.*

There's a nature center here, as well as a boardwalk that leads through the marsh to the edge of the bay. Most important, the preserve is a birdwatcher's paradise. A major stop along the Pacific flyway, these marshlands are visited by over one million birds each year.

Situated on the bay side of the Santa Cruz Mountains, the densely forested **Huddart County Park** (415-851-0326) provides a touch of the wild within whistling distance of San Francisco. Twenty-five miles of hiking trails crisscross the landscape, and the park is a habitat for blacktail deer, raccoons and coyotes. Located at 1100 Kings Mountain Road in Woodside.

Together, the adjoining **Los Trancos** and **Monte Bello Open Space Preserves** (415-949-5500) cover almost 30,000 acres of rolling countryside. They're located in the hills above Palo Alto and provide sweeping views from San Francisco to Mount Diablo. Most visitors are drawn here by the San Andreas Fault, which bisects Los Trancos and can be explored along a hiking trail. From Route 280 in Palo Alto, take Page Mill Road seven miles southwest.

Santa Cruz Mountains

Serving as southwestern boundary and urban escape valve for the Bay Area are the Santa Cruz Mountains, a 3000-foot-high spur of the Coast Range. Blanketed with redwood and Douglas fir, the heights are explored along Route 35 and Route 9. These rustic highways climb along a ridgetop, revealing vistas of both the ocean and San Francisco Bay before the forest closes in and the roadways tunnel through dense, tall timber.

Big Basin Redwoods State Park (Route 236; 408-338-6132) is a spectacular preserve studded with 2000-year-old redwood stands. Descending from a 2300-foot elevation all the way to the ocean, the park offers 20,000 acres and features 80 miles of hiking trails, campgrounds, and a host of facilities.

Three mountain towns—Boulder Creek, Ben Lomond and Felton—are central to the area's travel facilities. They house numerous antique stores and crafts shops. One of the marvelous features in Felton is its **covered bridge** (at the edge of town on Covered Bridge Road). A wood-plank span with sagging shingle roof, the structure dates from 1892. Appropriately, it's set in a secluded spot along the San Lorenzo River.

Over at **Roaring Camp & Big Trees Narrow Gauge Railroad** (Graham Hill Road, Felton; 408-335-4484), a vintage steam engine whistles through redwood stands en route to Bear Mountain. Passengers are invited to picnic on the mountain, hike the area, then return on a later train. Or you can climb aboard the **Santa Cruz, Big Trees and Pacific Railway** (408-335-4400), with full-size cars, for a scenic eight-mile journey to the Santa Cruz boardwalk.

SANTA CRUZ MOUNTAINS LODGING

The **Tyrolean Inn** (9600 Route 9, Ben Lomond; 408-336-5188) offers duplex cottages, small but intimate, with oil paintings hanging on wood-paneled walls and wall-to-wall carpeting. Or you can rent a private cottage. Preferable to the duplexes, this unit is warm and bright, done entirely in knotty pine and furnished with a four-poster bed. Moderate.

    Merrybrook Lodge (Big Basin Highway, Boulder Creek; 408-338-6813), set in a redwood grove, has pretty cottages right on a creek. They are one-bedroom structures, with living room, kitchen and porch. The floors are hardwood, the walls knotty pine, and as a final touch, there's a brick fireplace. Moderate.

SANTA CRUZ MOUNTAINS RESTAURANTS

The rustic little restaurant at the **Tyrolean Inn** (9600 Route 9, Ben Lomond; 408-336-5188) serves specialty sandwiches for lunch. During the dinner hour, they stoke the fires and prepare an array of German dishes like sauerbraten and wienerschnitzel. Moderate.

    Around since 1904, **Scopazzi's Inn** (Big Basin Highway, Boulder Creek; 408-338-6441) can still be trusted for a good meal. The place is perfectly fitted to its mountain environment, with wood-paneled walls, a lofty, exposed-beam ceiling and a tile fireplace. The numerous dinners include roast beef, filet of sole and specials, while the lunch menu features sandwiches, salads and several platters such as veal cutlet. Moderate.

SANTA CRUZ MOUNTAINS PARKS

A redwood preserve covered with hiking trails, the 327-acre **San Mateo County Memorial Park** (415-363-4021) has a creekside swimming hole, campsites, a minimuseum and a redwood tree dating back 1500 years. It's a good place to avoid crowds. It's also a gateway to 5973-acre **Pescadero Creek County Park**, with a network of hiking trails and hike-in campsites. Located at 9500 Pescadero Road about five miles from La Honda.

    With dense stands of redwood, Douglas fir and oak, **Portola State Park** (415-948-9098) is a great place for exploration. There are 21 miles of hiking trails, including one leading to the "shell tree," a fire-scarred redwood whose crown still blooms tall and green. Add creeks filled with trout, campgrounds and an undergrowth thick with huckleberry to the attributes of this lovely park. From Route 35, take Alpine Road west to Portola State Park Road.

    A hiker's paradise, **Castle Rock State Park** (408-867-2952) is a 3600-acre semiwilderness area with no entry roads. For those who hike in, the rewards are several: a network of trails; redwood forests; a waterfall; and the sandstone boulder that crowns this retreat at 3214 feet. Camping. Located on Skyline Boulevard three miles south of the intersection with Route 9.

An 1800-acre park on the San Lorenzo River, **Henry Cowell Redwoods State Park** (408-438-2396) features a short nature trail through a redwood forest, where one goliath measures 285 feet. With 15 miles of hiking trails and numerous facilities, it's a favorite among picnickers. Camping. Located off Route 9 just south of Felton.

The South Bay

Located about 50 miles south of San Francisco, the San Jose area is a sprawling collection of cities and towns laid out like Los Angeles. It's one of California's wealthiest and fastest-growing sections, home to the state's vital electronics industry.

When the Spanish arrived here in 1777, they built Mission Santa Clara de Asis and established the pueblo of San Jose with 66 residents. After the Americans took over California in the next century, the South Bay blossomed with fruit farms. The area remained a peaceful farming community until the 1950s, when the electronics boom sounded and the South Bay moved to center stage of the infant computer industry.

Between 1940 and 1980, the population of Santa Clara County increased over 400 percent. Today a staggering percentage of the nation's electronic components originate from this region, now known as Silicon Valley.

For sightseeing information on the region, your best resource is the **Tour and Travel Information Center** (333 West San Carlos Street, San Jose; 408-295-9600).

Kelley Park (Keyes and Senter roads; 408-277-4193) contains more than 150 wooded acres with recreation facilities, including a petting zoo (admission) and puppet shows. Next to this playland sits the Japanese Friendship Garden, a serene setting with koi pond and a tea house.

The park's highlight is the **San Jose Historical Museum** (1600 Center Road; 408-287-2290; admission), an outdoor showplace featuring several antique buildings in a plaza setting. Inside the old Pacific Hotel, you'll find displays tracing San Jose's history from the Indians through the trappers, miners and farmers. The nearby soda fountain, still operating, is definitely the highpoint of any visit.

Downtown, a billion-dollar renovation is bringing a metamorphosis to this formerly rundown area. Center stage stands the 435,000-square-foot **San Jose Convention Center** (West San Carlos Street between Almaden Boulevard and Market Street; 408-277-3601).

Critical raves met this unique soft-peach-colored structure—with its enormous vaulted entranceway highlighted by a porcelain-tile facade, its multilevel glass-enclosed arcade and concourse, and its black-and-white marble terrazzo promenade—upon its completion in 1989.

High-class hotels, restaurants, shops and financial centers are also sprouting in the area, where people can now zip along via a modern light-rail system. Landscaping has not been forgotten amid all this glass and concrete. The city has planted 600 sycamore trees to shade the new downtown transit mall and has spiffed up **Plaza Park**, a green oasis with palms and acres of grass along Market Street across from the convention center.

The nearby **Children's Discovery Museum** (180 Woz Way; 408-298-5437; admission) presents an amazing re-creation of urban life. Kids can climb on real fire trucks and ambulances, operate traffic lights along simulated roadways, or help run the city's water department.

For larger kids and adults there's the **Technology Center of Silicon Valley** (145 West San Carlos Street; 415-279-7150; admission). Here you'll discover a collection of interactive exhibits in which you can drive a space rover through a Martian landscape, view a tower of 500 telephone books representing the amount of information in a single DNA molecule and explore the cutting edge of technology.

Certainly San Jose's most unusual and exotic site is the **Rosicrucian Egyptian Museum** (Park and Naglee avenues; 408-287-2807; admission). The landscaping and buildings throughout this elaborate complex (which includes a planetarium and science museum) re-create ancient Egypt. There are sphinxes, tile murals of charioteers and temples decorated with hieroglyphs. The museum entranceway is lined by stone statues of rams, reproducing an ancient avenue in Thebes.

In nearby Santa Clara, **Marriott's Great America** (Great America Parkway; 408-988-1800; admission) is a 100-acre theme park that

---

THE STRANGE CASE OF THE MYSTERY HOUSE

*You might call it a study in the meaningless lives of the idle rich. The **Winchester Mystery House** (525 South Winchester Boulevard, San Jose; 408-247-2101; admission), a Victorian monstrosity numbering 160 rooms and covering six acres, is still unfinished. It was built by Sarah Winchester, heiress to the Winchester rifle fortune, who kept adding on rooms for 38 years in the belief that she would live as long as the house continued to grow. Either the carpenters took a day off or Sarah's seeress miscalculated—she died in 1922. Her legacy is an architectural riddle complete with stairways leading nowhere and closets that open onto walls. The interior design is sometimes beautiful, however, and ghost stories galore surround the house and its unbalanced owner.*

mimics New England during the Revolutionary War, New Orleans in the 1850s and the Klondike gold rush. There are also theatrical revues, a flight simulator and white-knuckle rides with menacing names like "Demon" and "The Edge." Closed in winter.

The South Bay's other features are farther afield and far more placid. **Los Gatos**, a wealthy and luxurious town in the foothills of the Santa Cruz Mountains, provides peaceful country lanes and carpenter Gothic-style homes. **Saratoga** also contains sumptuous hillside homes.

None, however, match the grandeur of **Villa Montalvo** (15400 Montalvo Road, Saratoga; 408-741-3421). This Mediterranean-style mansion and surrounding estate was home to a former mayor of San Francisco. Today the 19-room house serves as a cultural center featuring artistic exhibits and events; the luxurious grounds have been converted to an arboretum laced with nature trails.

Hakone Gardens (21000 Big Basin Way, Saratoga; 408-867-3438), smaller and more modest, is a lovely Japanese-style retreat with wisteria arbors, dwarf pines, a waterfall and koi pond. A perfect place to meditate, this enchanting garden also contains a small house built without nails.

The drive to the **Lick Observatory** (Mount Hamilton Road; 408-274-5061), atop 4209-foot Mount Hamilton, will carry you even farther from the smoggy center of San Jose. One of the world's largest telescopes, a giant eye 120 inches in diameter, stares heavenward from this lofty perch.

SOUTH BAY LODGING

Combining easy suburban living with a rustic setting is the **Inn At Saratoga** (20645 4th Street; 408-867-5020), a contemporary, European-style 46-room hotel. Located in downtown Saratoga, the inn is backdropped by a creek and wooded park. Each guest room looks out on a forest of maple, pine and eucalyptus. Guest rooms are decorated with soft pastels and California artwork. Ultra-deluxe.

The **Fairmont Hotel San Jose** (170 South Market Street; 408-998-1900), a stunning 20-story structure of pink granite, is a 544-room hotel featuring four restaurants, an outdoor pool on the fourth floor and a sensational marble-clad lobby. Accommodations are large, handsomely appointed and decorated in understated pastels. For a summertime splurge, book a fourth-floor lanai suite with its own patio and palm trees fronting the pool. Ultra-deluxe.

SOUTH BAY RESTAURANTS

In downtown San Jose's business world, **Eulipia Restaurant and Bar** (374 South 1st Street; 408-280-6161) is invitingly informal. With its local crowd and light, airy, bistrolike atmosphere, the place is a prime choice for mesquite-grilled fish and chicken, as well as pasta dishes; moderate to deluxe.

Paolo's Restaurant (520 East Santa Clara Street, San Jose; 408-294-2558) is a lavishly decorated dining room with a sophisticated Italian cuisine. The menu, which changes monthly, features more than a dozen pasta dishes as well as entrées like roast breast of pigeon and poached prawns. Lunch and dinner; deluxe.

You'll have to travel many leagues to find a seafood restaurant as good as **Steamer's Fish Again and Pasta Too!** (50 University Avenue, Los Gatos; 408-395-2722). This spiffy cafe serves scallops, prawns and calamari, plus a host of seafood pasta dishes. Attractively paneled in hardwood, the popular, crowded establishment features an oyster bar, dining area and fashionable saloon. Moderate to deluxe.

SOUTH BAY SHOPPING

The **Pavilion Shops** (150 South 1st Street; 408-286-2076), a peach-and-aqua Mediterranean-style shopping mall that's part of the refurbished San Jose downtown area, offers 45 specialty shops and ten restaurants, along with occasional musical and theatrical events in the summer.

Saratoga features an upscale shopping strip in the center of town along Saratoga Avenue. There are antique stores and galleries galore, as well as malls.

Los Gatos is quite simply a window browser's dream. Along Santa Cruz Avenue from Saratoga–Los Gatos Road to Main Street are block on block of posh establishments. There are stores specializing in antique interiors, teddy bears, gourmet food and high fashion. **Old Town**, a misnomered mall at 50 University Avenue, is an attractive hacienda-style building with a string of shops.

SOUTH BAY NIGHTLIFE

The **Saddlerack** (1310 Auzerais Avenue; 408-286-3393) is San Jose's answer to Gilley's in Texas. A country-style saloon with enough room to herd cattle, the place has four dancefloors and two house bands. They also bring in top name rock and country-and-western entertainers once a week.

Mountain Charley's Saloon (15 North Santa Cruz Avenue, Los Gatos; 408-395-8880) is a down-home drinking hole with a magnificent old wooden bar and live rock music ranging from 1950s-style to contemporary. Cover.

The focus for San Jose high culture is the **Center for the Performing Arts** (255 Almaden Boulevard at San Carlos Street, San Jose; 408-288-7469). The **San Jose Symphony** (408-288-2828) performs here regularly, as does the **San Jose Civic Light Opera**

(408-971-1212), and the center presents many other special events. Also consider the **San Jose Repertory Company** (Montgomery Theatre, West San Carlos and Market streets, San Jose; 408-294-7572).

In local comedy circles, there's one club that always has **The Last Laugh** (29 North San Pedro Street and 150 South 1st Street, San Jose; 408-287-5233). It draws professional joke mongers from across the country. Cover.

SOUTH BAY PARKS

Rising from the foothills of the Santa Cruz Mountains to 3000 feet and spreading over 2800 acres, **Sanborn–Skyline County Park** (408-867-9959) is an outstanding facility covered with Douglas fir and redwoods. Along the ten miles of hiking trails, there are extraordinary views of the Santa Clara Valley. Camping. Located off Route 9 about four miles west of Saratoga, the park is at 16055 Sanborn Road.

The East Bay

The great earthquake that hit San Francisco in 1906 sparked a migration to the East—but only a few miles east, across the bay to the quiet rural reaches of Oakland and Berkeley. Then in the 1930s, when thousands of people were commuting back into the city each day, the two areas were linked via the Bay Bridge, an engineering marvel that spanned four and a half miles of water and brought still more transbay migration.

East Bay communities bloomed, particularly the town of Berkeley with its flagship University of California campus, respected as one of the nation's top centers of learning. But the East Bay and the university were to become known for more than academic accomplishment.

History in the 1960s was written in red and black. Berkeley became a rallying point, first for the Free Speech Movement in 1964, and later for the anti-Vietnam War mobilization. In 1967, the Black Panther Party was founded in Oakland. The East Bay was a staging ground for political demonstrations and riots that continued into the early 1970s.

Today, Berkeley politics have mellowed and moved from the radical fringes to the liberal center. Oakland, while experiencing more than its share of urban problems, has also expanded its port at the expense of San Francisco's shrinking waterfront and has refurbished part of its downtown area. To tour this city of 372,000 people, pick up maps and brochures from the **Oakland Convention and Visitors Bureau** (1000 Broadway #200; 415-839-9000).

Prettiest place in all Oakland is **Lake Merritt**, an unassuming body of water that happens to be the world's biggest saltwater tidal lake located within a city. You can join the legions of joggers and bicyclists continually circling the lake's three-mile perimeter. Or rent a sailboat or canoe at the Sailboat House (568 Bellevue Avenue; 415-444-3807) or stroll the park's botanical gardens. For kids, there are duck feeding areas and a "Children's Fairyland" (415-452-2259; admission) complete with a train and puppet shows. Also part of this lakeside complex is the **Camron-Stanford House** (1418 Lakeside Drive; 415-836-1976; admission), an 1876 Victorian.

Just a few blocks from Lake Merritt sits the **Oakland Museum** (1000 Oak Street; 415-273-3401), a beautifully landscaped, triple-tiered facility. With its Babylonian hanging gardens, courtyards and lily ponds, the place has won international acclaim. The theme of exhibits here is California—its history, art and environment.

Chinatown in Oakland is a miniature neighborhood compared to San Francisco's crowded enclave, but it's an active and stimulating area to stroll. Most of the markets and restaurants lie along 8th and 9th streets between Harrison and Franklin streets.

Another area that will be of increasing interest is **Victorian Row** on 9th Street between Broadway and Washington Street. All around this cluster of old Victorian houses, downtown blocks are being refurbished and developed. Hotels, restaurants, shops and offices are moving to this formerly rundown section of town and promise to turn it into an upscale commercial district.

From Oakland, Telegraph Avenue beelines into Berkeley. One of the nation's finest schools, the **University of California–Berkeley** is home to 32,000 students. Founded in 1868, it covers over 1200 acres and is easy to tour with a map available at the **Student Union** (Telegraph Avenue and Bancroft Way; 415-642-4636).

ON THE TRAIL OF JACK LONDON

Jack London Square (foot of Broadway) is everyone's favorite Oakland sightseeing spot. Today it harbors overpriced restaurants and heavily touristed bars, but the place packs a lot of history. Richard Henry Dana visited the area in 1835 while gathering material for Two Years Before the Mast.

Jack London, who grew up in Oakland, was in turn a sailor and oyster pirate along this hard-bitten waterfront. You can conjure visions of the fabled adventure writer while visiting the **Jack London Cabin***. It's a classic log cabin, little more than a dozen feet across, where London lived in 1897 during the Klondike gold rush. Back then it rested along the north fork of Henderson Creek up in the Yukon. Today it sits next to* **Heinolds' First and Last Chance** *(56 Jack London Square; 415-839-6761), a funky woodframe saloon that London haunted as a young man and where you can still sample spirits.*

From here you can stroll across **Sproul Plaza**, site of countless 1960s-era rallies and demonstrations. Sproul Hall, the administration building, was the scene of a massive sit-in during the 1964 Free Speech Movement.

Centerpiece of the campus is **Sather Tower** (usually called the Campanile), a 307-foot spire modeled after St. Mark's campanile in Venice. A 48-bell carillon tolls from this lofty perch, and an elevator (admission) brings visitors to the top for extraordinary views. Just west of the campanile sits **South Hall**, the oldest and prettiest building on campus, and **Bancroft Library**, which houses the world's finest western Americana collection.

Among its many features, the university also offers several important museums. The **University Art Museum** (2626 Bancroft Way; 415-642-0808; admission), with its skylights and spiraling ramps, features a permanent collection of Western and Asian artwork, as well as a sculpture garden.

En route to the next museum, located in the hills above campus, visit the **Botanical Garden** (Centennial Drive; 415-642-3343). One of the finest in the world, it contains over 11,000 species arranged in environments including African, South American, Himalayan and Australasian.

Continue uphill to the **Lawrence Hall of Science** (Centennial Drive; 415-642-5132; admission). Intended for the eight-to-eighty set, this marvelous place is a hands-on museum with a wizard's lab where you perform experiments and play computer games. Kids can handle animals in the biology lab, and the planetarium features a series of stellar shows.

For a tour of the **Berkeley hills**, follow Centennial Drive up to Grizzly Peak Boulevard and continue north; Euclid Avenue will lead you back down to central Berkeley. All through these magnificent hills are splendid houses of brick and brown shingle; others re-create Spanish styles with red-tile roofs and whitewashed facades. The views spread across the bay to San Francisco and out beyond the Golden Gate.

EAST BAY LODGING

The white cupola and peaked roofs of the **Claremont Resort Hotel** (Ashby and Domingo avenues, Oakland; 415-843-3000) have served as a distinctive East Bay landmark for decades. First-rate tennis courts, a par course, landscaped grounds, a good restaurant, an Olympic-size swimming pool and extensive spa facilities make the Claremont the best resort between San Francisco and Lake Tahoe. Typical high-ceilinged accommodations are large and luxurious with residential-style furnishings. Ultra-deluxe.

A 1927 art deco beauty, the **Lake Merritt Hotel** (1800 Madison Street, Oakland; 415-832-2300) has been completely refurbished and brought up to 1990s' standards. Overlooking Lake Merritt, this 51-room hotel has stylish rooms and suites at deluxe prices.

One of the coziest spots in the Bay Area is **Gramma's Bed & Breakfast Inn** (2740 Telegraph Avenue, Berkeley; 415-549-2145), set in a 1905 Tudor-style house. Public areas include several ornately designed sitting rooms as well as a spacious yard and deck. The 11 guest rooms in the main house and those in three adjacent buildings are creatively appointed with items such as hand-carved headboards and antique wardrobes. Deluxe.

EAST BAY RESTAURANTS

In Oakland's Chinatown, the excellent **Hunan Restaurant** (366 8th Street; 415-444-1155) serves Mandarin-style cuisine with special flair. Among the dozens of dishes are smoked tea duck, five spices tripe and shredded pork with noodles. Recommended; budget to moderate.

In high-rent Jack London Square, **Il Pescatore** (57 Jack London Square, Oakland; 415-465-2188) stands out as a reasonably priced place with a view of the marina and estuary. The decorative motif is nautical and the menu follows the theme, specializing in such seafood entrées as scampi, prawns and salmon. There are also numerous Italian-style dishes. Moderate.

With its handpainted bar and contemporary artwork, **Cafe Pastoral** (2160 University Avenue, Berkeley; 415-540-7514) is the latest word in modern dining. The menu, which changes as frequently as fashions, reflects the surroundings. The appetizer offerings might include sautéed salt cod cake, warm lamb salad, and carrot and parsnip soup. Settling into a banquette or bentwood chair at dinner you could enjoy a linguine dish with rock shrimp, braised duck leg, or mahimahi in a black bean sauce. Deluxe.

The finest hamburgers in the Bay Area are served at **Fatapple's Restaurant and Bakery** (1346 Martin Luther King Jr. Way, Berkeley; 415-526-2260), and the place is inevitably crowded. Decorated with photos of Jack London, it's a comfortable cafe that also offers lasagna, soup and outrageously delicious pies. Budget.

EAST BAY SHOPPING

College Avenue is one of the area's chic shopping sections. From Broadway in North Oakland all the way to Russell Street in Berkeley, this thoroughfare hosts every type of specialty store imaginable.

North Berkeley, along Shattuck Avenue north of University Avenue, has been nicknamed the **gourmet ghetto** for its specialty food shops. Here you can fill your picnic basket with goods from the wine shop, Japanese delicatessen and cheese store. And don't miss **Black Oak Books** (1491 Shattuck Avenue; 415-486-0698), an exceptionally fine bookstore and important literary gathering place.

A shopping district of another sort lies along Berkeley's Telegraph Avenue between Dwight Way and Bancroft Way. While this campus area is being steadily remodeled, it still retains the charm and native funk of Berkeley circa 1968. **Street vendors** line either side of this open-air marketplace, selling clothes, metalwork, leather goods and jewelry.

Telegraph also supports enough bookstores to keep even a college town busy. Two of them, practically next door to one another, are among the best in the country. **Moe's Books** (2476 Telegraph Avenue; 415-849-2087), operated by a cigar-chomping bibliophile named Moe Moskowitz, contains four floors of new and used titles. **Cody's Books** (2454 Telegraph Avenue; 415-845-7852), with its beautiful design and smart layout, features new volumes ranging from recondite titles to best sellers.

EAST BAY NIGHTLIFE

Evening activities here revolve around places of high culture and high spirits. From September to December, the **Oakland Ballet** (415-465-

---

REVOLUTION IN THE KITCHEN

During the late 1970s Berkeley softened its image as a center of revolt and assumed the role of gourmet capital. Turbulence these days is as likely to occur in the Cuisinart as on the campus.

Several exemplary restaurants were born of this movement. Developing a cooking style termed "California cuisine," they serve select dishes to small groups. All ingredients, from spice to shellfish, are fresh; the focus is on locally produced foods in season. Menus change daily and sometimes include dishes invented that afternoon to be tested on an adventurous clientele.

*The vanguard of this culinary revolution is **Chez Panisse** (1517 Shattuck Avenue; 415-548-5525). Set in a modest woodframe building, it hardly looks the part of a world-famous restaurant. But owner Alice Waters has long been the guiding light in gourmet kitchens. Dinner is served downstairs in her two-tiered establishment and features a fixed menu nightly. A typical evening will include salmon and cucumber salad with caviar, velouté of chicken, grilled pigeon breasts, baked apples, garden salad and melon sherbet, all for a mere $55 prix fixe. Reservations are de rigueur. The cafe upstairs, which takes no dinner reservations (but*

6400), a nationally acclaimed company, presents dazzling premieres and classic ballets. The ballet is at home in the **Paramount Theatre** (2025 Broadway, Oakland; 415-465-6400), a restored art deco building that's a showcase of structural flourishes and decorative details.

The **Berkeley Repertory Theatre** (2025 Addison Street; 415-845-4700) is one of the more visible examples of Berkeley's rich dramatic tradition. Also check with **Cal Performances** (101 Zellerbach Hall, University of California, Berkeley; 415-642-9988) for a current listing of campus cultural events such as jazz concerts, chamber music and modern dance recitals. **Pacific Film Archive** (2625 Durant Avenue; 415-642-1124) is an extraordinary showcase for early and artistic movies.

As for spirits, there's **Heinold's First and Last Chance** (56 Jack London Square, Oakland; 415-839-6761), a roisterous little bar once frequented by Jack London. Blues enthusiasts head for **Eli's Mile High Club** (3629 Martin Luther King, Jr. Way, Oakland; 415-655-6661), one of the Bay Area's finest blues club. Cover.

On the Berkeley waterfront, **Skates on the Bay** (100 Seawall Drive, Berkeley; 415-549-1900) provides otherworldly views of the bay and San Francisco skyline.

Shattuck Avenue Spats (1974 Shattuck Avenue, Berkeley; 415-841-7225) is a popular campus-area bar, crowded with turn-of-the-century memorabilia and endowed with an ample drink list.

---

does take them at lunch), requires an endless wait. Patience is rewarded, however, with moderately priced meals in a serene setting. The cafe often serves calzone with goat cheese, oysters on the half shell, sorrel soup, plus daily specials such as sautéed sole, fettucine with sweetbreads and grilled steak with rosemary butter.

*Another well-known Berkeley restaurant is the **Santa Fe Bar & Grill** (1310 University Avenue; 415-841-4740), set in a turn-of-the-century train station. Evening meals include smoked Petaluma duck, pork loin and mesquite-grilled chicken, plus special entrées like grilled game hen in green peppercorn sauce, bluefin tuna smothered in ginger-cilantro butter and snapper with salsa. Moderate to deluxe.*

*Berkeley exported the revolution to Oakland's **Bay Wolf Restaurant** (3853 Piedmont Avenue; 415-655-6004), a gourmet restaurant in a woodframe house. There are two dining rooms, one decorated with modern art pieces, the other displaying ceramic platters. Run by a friendly staff, the place has the feel of home. Lunch and dinner menus vary daily and price in the deluxe range. If they're not serving sautéed duck breast or swordfish with braised leeks, the chefs may be preparing roast veal leg, salmon in pastry or cured ham with artichoke purée. In any case, the food is outstanding, the service impeccable and the ambience soft as candlelight.*

EAST BAY PARKS

Spreading across 7000 acres in the Oakland Hills are the adjoining **Anthony Chabot Regional Park** and **Redwood Regional Park** (415-531-9300). Foremost among their features are Lake Chabot, a haven for anglers, campers and boaters, and the redwoods in Redwood Park. Chabot Park alternates between grass-covered hills and dense stands of eucalyptus, live oak and madrone; the forests of Redwood Park are home to deer, raccoons and bobcats. Both parks are located off Route 580 and can be entered from Skyline Boulevard or Redwood Road in Oakland or San Leandro.

Another pair of adjacent gems, **Tilden Regional Park** and **Wildcat Canyon Regional Park** (415-531-9300) lie in the hills above Berkeley. Tilden, by far the more diverse and popular, is a magnificent park. Stretching over 4500 acres, it features swimming in Lake Anza, an extensive botanic garden and a rolling landscape that varies from volcanic rock to grassy meadows. A wonderland for kids, it also offers an antique merry-go-round with beautiful carved animals and a miniature steam train. Wildcat Canyon Park, with its meandering creek and forested arroyos, is a rustic counterpoint to Tilden's crowded acres. Tilden lies off Wildcat Canyon Road in Berkeley; Wildcat Canyon is reached from McBryde Avenue in Richmond.

Mount Diablo State Park (415-837-2525), covering 20,000 acres, is home to the Bay Area's loftiest peak. Mount Diablo rises 3849 feet above sea level. From its summit, you can gaze east to the Sierra Nevada and west to the Pacific. The mountain landscape ranges from shady cottonwood canyons to hillsides carpeted with wildflowers. Golden eagles soar here, and you can spot blacktail deer and an occasional mountain lion. Camping. Located five miles east of Danville off Route 680, the park is reached via Mount Diablo Scenic Boulevard or North Gate Road out of Walnut Creek.

Marin

The rest of the Bay Area calls it "mahvelous Marin," with a sharp cynicism and perhaps a touch of envy. New wealth, boatloads of BMWs and a reputation for narcissism have also led the media to portray this chic county as an enclave that worships hot tubs and perfect bodies. Certainly there's a bit of truth to all this. But Marin also offers outdoor splendors (the coastal section of Marin is covered in Chapter Eleven) that include rolling hills and pasturelands dotted with cattle and horses, small, dense redwood forests and splendidly quiet country roads where nearby San Francisco seems light years away.

One Marin highpoint is the quaint if crowded town of Sausalito, a paradise for shoppers and those seeking breathtaking bay views. You can best tour Sausalito along Bridgeway, a sinuous road paralleling the waterfront. I won't even begin to describe the views of Belvedere, Angel Island and Alcatraz along this esplanade. Suffice it to say that the Sausalito waterfront offers the single element missing from every vista in San Francisco—a full-frame view of the city itself.

Galleries, boutiques and antique stores line Bridgeway and creep uphill along side streets. **Plaza Vina del Mar** (Bridgeway and El Portal), with its elephant statues and dramatic fountain, is a grassy oasis in the midst of the commerce. Several strides seaward lies **Gabrielson Park**, where you can settle on a bench or plot of grass at water's edge.

Then continue along the piers past chic yachts and rows of millionaires' motorboats. To get an idea of the inland pond where the rich sail these toys, check out the U.S. Army Corps of Engineers' **Bay Model** (2100 Bridgeway; 415-332-3870). Built to scale and housed in a three-acre warehouse, this hydraulic model of San Francisco Bay is used to simulate currents and tidal flows. You can watch an entire day's tidal cycle in 14 minutes.

Imagine a cluster of seven buildings, all devoted to children. Add more than 100 hands-on exhibits. Throw in a music studio, a miniature model of the Golden Gate Bridge and a multi-media theater. What you have is a wonderfully original place called the **Bay Area Discovery Museum** (557 East Fort Baker; 415-332-7674; admission).

Over in Tiburon, I heartily recommend the quarter-mile self-guided tour through the **Richardson Bay Wildlife Sanctuary** (376 Greenwood Beach Road; 415-388-2524; admission). It will provide an inkling of what Marin was like before the invention of cars and condominiums. Several hundred bird species inhabit this preserve; during winter months harbor seals rest along the shore. Also contained on the property is **Lyford House**, a magnificent Victorian.

FRANK LLOYD WRIGHT'S MARIN

*From the freeway it's a striking sight, that sprawling, buff-colored complex gracefully spanning three hills. You'd probably never guess it's a government building. The **Marin County Civic Center** (Civic Center Drive, San Rafael; 415-499-7407), constructed of concrete and steel, nevertheless evokes the rolling brown hills and blue-domed sky of Northern California. Perhaps that's because it was designed by Frank Lloyd Wright, whose passion was blending a building to the surrounding landscape. A self-guided tour will reveal interior corridors brilliantly illuminated by skylights and landscaped with trees and shrubs.*

MARIN LODGING

One of the top resting places in this area is the **Sausalito Hotel** (16 El Portal, Sausalito; 415-332-4155), a 15-room bed and breakfast near the waterfront. Accommodations range from moderate to deluxe for a small room with shared bath to ultra-deluxe for the Marquis of Queensbury room, which contains furniture once owned by Ulysses S. Grant. All the rooms are beautifully decorated with antiques: claw-foot tubs, brass lamps, mahogany wardrobes.

The **Casa Madrona Hotel** (801 Bridgeway, Sausalito; 415-332-0502) features a modern complex of rooms attached to a 19th-century landmark house overlooking San Francisco Bay. Rooms have a personal feel and individual decoration, with views ranging from garden to harbor. There are also five private cottages and a houseboat available at this 35-room bed and breakfast. Deluxe to ultra-deluxe.

MARIN RESTAURANTS

Sausalito sports many seafood restaurants, most overpriced and not very good. So it's best to steer a course for **Seven Seas** (682 Bridgeway; 415-332-1304). They serve scallops, salmon steaks and other seafood as well as meat platters and breakfast items. Moderate.

If you long for a sea vista and an eyeful of San Francisco skyline, try **Horizons** (558 Bridgeway, Sausalito; 415-331-3232). Housed in the turn-of-the-century San Francisco Yacht Club, this spiffy seafood restaurant has a wall of windows and a menu including shellfish and other aquatic fare, plus chicken, pasta, and steak dishes. Moderate to deluxe.

If the tide doesn't carry you, current trends may very well deliver you to the door at **Guaymas** (5 Main Street; 415-435-6300) in Tiburon. This upscale-Mexican restaurant bakes fresh tortillas and tamales daily. Pork, steak, and shrimp dishes are prepared on a mesquite grill; or try the duck with pumpkin seed sauce or the red snapper sautéed with jalapeños and onions. Located next door to the ferry dock, Guayamas rounds out the bill of fare with a bay view. Deluxe.

When chef Bradley Ogden departed San Francisco's Campton Place Hotel to open his own restaurant in Marin county, the suspense was thicker than a filet of organically grown beef. But the **Lark Creek Inn** (234 Magnolia Avenue, Larkspur; 415-924-7766) was an immediate hit, as much for its hearty food as for its woodsy, romantic setting. Quail, fish, poultry and meats are prepared on an oak-fired rotisserie, quite fitting for the country ambience at this deluxe-priced eatery.

Possibly the prettiest restaurant in Marin County, **Il Fornaio** (232 Corte Madera Town Center, Corte Madera; 415-927-4400) has red-and-white tile floors and walls painted the ochre of a Mediterranean sunset. Specialties are clay-pot cuisine (Coho salmon is a winner), terrific meal-sized salads and a long list of pastas, including offbeat versions such as *bigoli* done Venetian style with sausage, onion and red wine. Moderate to deluxe.

MARIN SHOPPING

Sausalito sports few bargains, but it does host an assortment of elegant shops. **California Visions** (21 Princess Street; 415-332-0770) displays a variety of natural crystal pieces and handcrafted jewelry. The nearby **High As A Kite** shop (34 Princess Street; 415-332-8944) is fun to walk through, even if you are afraid of heights.

Several shops in the minimall at 660 Bridgeway are also worth a browse. Glass menagerie lovers will peek into the **Crystal Dolphin** (415-332-4050). And style-savvy women will check out **Kolonaki** (415-332-8076) with its designer line of cotton resort wear.

Of the several art shops lining Sausalito's streets, **Shelby Galleries** (673 Bridgeway; 415-332-4991) displays the most interesting collection of quality art.

The most crowded downtown facility, **Village Fair** (777 Bridgeway; 415-332-1902) boasts over 30 stores—leather shops, clothing stores and crafts galleries.

You could spend all day—and very pleasantly—at **The Village at Corte Madera** (1554 Redwood Highway; 415-924-8557), the best place for one-stop shopping in Marin County. A low-rise, open-air complex anchored by major department stores, it has dozens of chain outlets and quality one-of-a-kind shops.

MARIN NIGHTLIFE

The window simply reads "Bar"; the address is 757 Bridgeway in Sausalito; and the place is famous. Famous for its name, the **no name** (415-332-1392), and because it's a favored hangout among young swingers and old salts alike. With an antique bar, piano and open-air patio, it's a congenial spot to bend an elbow. Live jazz every night.

Sweetwater (153 Throckmorton Avenue, Mill Valley; 415-388-2820) jams every night. Featuring blues and rock sounds, the club often headlines big-name groups. Cover.

MARIN BEACHES AND PARKS

Located along San Pablo Bay, 1500-acre **China Camp State Park** (415-456-0766) is heavily wooded and adorned with several midget islands just offshore. It has a special allure, partly because of the old Chinese fishing village, dating to the 1860s. This ghost community of tumbledown houses was home to thousands of Asians who were uprooted by the 1906 San Francisco earthquake and fire. Now it's a peaceful park inhabited by shore birds, anglers and daytrippers. Situated along North San Pedro Road about five miles east of San Rafael.

The Delta

California's two major rivers, the Sacramento and San Joaquin, flow together around the city of Sacramento, creating the state's fertile delta region. It's a timeless, dreamy land of drawbridges, meandering waterways and murky mists. Sam Goldwyn once claimed that the California Delta "looks more like the Mississippi than the real thing" and chose it as the movie location for *Huckleberry Finn*.

The heart of this bayou country lies about 70 miles northeast of San Francisco. Route 160, which travels through the center of the region, can be reached from Route 12 to the north, or Route 4 to the south (both lead off Route 80). The second course allows you to see a greater stretch of the Delta along Route 160. It will also carry you near two waterfront towns—Port Costa and Benicia—that should not be missed.

Port Costa enjoyed its heyday early in the century when the town served as a major grain-shipping port. Today it's a lazy community at the end of a country lane. A few sagging stores have been converted to artists' quarters and antique shops, and one of the warehouses has become a cavernous restaurant. Otherwise, the wrinkled hills all around seem like time warps in which this church-steeple village rests suspended. Farmland and forest enclose Port Costa, so finding your way becomes half the enjoyment of exploring the town: well-marked side roads lead to it from Route 4.

A few miles farther along this highway sits the **John Muir National Historic Site** (4202 Alhambra Avenue, Martinez; 415-228-8860; admission). This grand 17-room Victorian was home to the renowned naturalist for almost a quarter-century until his death in 1914. Within, each room has been restored as it originally appeared. Muir's "scribble den," or study, remains littered with manuscripts, and the family quarters are opulently furnished.

Across the Carquinez Strait from Port Costa looms **Benicia**, a community whose early dreams proved to be delusions of grandeur. The folks who founded the town foresaw it as the state capital, a title it held for a single year, 1853. The founding mothers and fathers also pictured Benicia as a magnificent port. Today the nearby waterfront is home to a mothball fleet, rusting at permanent anchor.

All of which makes it a great place to visit. The **Benicia Capitol** (West 1st and G streets; 707-745-3385; admission) still stands, an imposing brick building marked by twin pillars. True to antiquity, every desk in the Senate chamber is illuminated by candle, and the Assembly chamber has a spittoon as a centerpiece. There are walking tour booklets here (or at the Benicia Chamber of Commerce, 601 1st Street; 707-745-2120) that will lead you past the other historic sites that make Benicia the little town that couldn't.

Visitors following Route 80 can stop at **Marine World–Africa USA** (Marine World Parkway, Vallejo; 707-643-6722; admission), particularly when they have children to entertain. This 160-acre theme park features an aquarium with killer whales, a 55-acre lake and many exhibits and shows. Special care has been taken so that children can interact closely with the animals.

On Route 160, you can travel north along the Sacramento River all the way to the state capital. Back in the 1850s, steamboats sidewheeled upriver from San Francisco to the Gold Country outside Sacramento. Residents still tell of the pirates who stretched chains across the river to snag steamboats laden with gold. The area is renowned among anglers, waterskiers and other aquatic enthusiasts.

The Delta is an endless expanse of orchards and flatlands, levees and dikes. A thousand miles of waterways meander through this mazework. There are channels bearing names like Hog Slough and Whiskey Slough.

The high point of any Delta trip is a visit to **Locke** (population 75; elevation 13 feet), a creaky community of clapboard houses and falsefront stores. This intriguing town, located on Route 160, is the only rural community in the entire country built and occupied by Chinese. Many contemporary residents trace their ancestry back to the Asian immigrants who mined California gold fields and helped build the transcontinental railroad, then moved on to construct the Delta's intricate levee system.

During its heyday in the early 1900s, Locke was a wide-open river town. Chinese and Westerners alike frequented its gambling parlors, speakeasies and opium dens. These raffish denizens have long since disappeared, but little else has changed.

HOME PORT FOR CASTAWAYS

*Where else but at **East Brother Light Station** (117 Park Place, Point Richmond; 415-233-2385) can you find a bed-and-breakfast inn located in a lighthouse on an island? The old beacon was built in 1873 and operated for almost a century. Today the two-story house and light station feature four bedrooms furnished with period pieces. Guests travel out to this one-acre hideaway by motorboat and enjoy a five-course dinner as well as breakfast the next morning. Ultra-deluxe; Thursday through Sunday only; reserve far in advance.*

Today Locke is like an outdoor museum, an example of what America's small towns would be like if time were measured not in terms of human progress, but in the eternal effects of the elements. You can still stroll along wooden sidewalks, which now slope like the pathways in an amusement park funhouse. Elderly Asians sit in the doorways reading Chinese newspapers. Along the edge of town are the trim orchards and communal gardens that residents have tended for generations.

DELTA LODGING

A wonderful resting place, the **Union Hotel** (401 1st Street, Benicia; 707-746-0100) presents itself as a place where you can "sleep in the 19th century." The building is a white clapboard structure, three stories tall, with pretty green shutters. Each of its 12 rooms has been decorated in period fashion. One features a canopy bed, another a Chinese Chippendale armoire. To remind you it's really the 20th century, every room has a private bath with jacuzzi. Deluxe.

The finest way to experience the Delta is by staying aboard a houseboat. These vessels are quite simple to operate with 45 minutes of instruction and require no captain's license. Among the many companies renting houseboats are **Delta Country Houseboats** (Walnut Grove; 916-776-1741) and **Herman & Helen's Marina** (Eight Mile Road, Stockton; 209-951-4634).

DELTA RESTAURANTS

For an upscale adventure, try the dining room at the **Union Hotel** (401 1st Street, Benicia; 707-746-0100). The menu at this stained-glass establishment features dishes like duck, quail, pizzeta and fresh fish. Moderate to deluxe.

For local color, nothing compares to **Giusti's** (Old Thornton Road, Walnut Grove; 916-776-1808), an outstanding seafood and prime rib restaurant priced moderately. Dating to 1896, it's a place where the walls are decorated with autographed photos and the ceiling is covered with 800 baseball caps. At lunch they serve steaks and burgers, for dinner fish and veal dishes.

The Delta's most bizarre restaurant is **Al's Place** (Main Street, Locke; 916-776-1800). The bar out front has hunting trophies protruding from the walls, and the ceiling is plastered with dollar bills (it'll cost you a buck to find out how they got there). The moderately priced dinner consists of steak and steak. At lunch, every table is set with big jars of peanut butter and jelly. The idea is to swab the peanut butter on bread, add a dollop of jelly and enjoy it with your steak. Sorry you asked?

DELTA NIGHTLIFE

By car or boat you can cruise to several spots around the Delta, including the **Grand Island Inn** (Route 160, Ryde; 916-776-1318). This rambling, multistoried affair features a plush bar and an intimate dining room; open weekends only.

DELTA PARKS

Located along the Sacramento River, **Brannan Island State Recreation Area** (916-777-6671) sits amid sloughs and levees, a region of willows and cottonwoods. There's a beach for swimmers, picnic tables for daytrippers and a maze of waterways for anglers. Camping. Located on Route 160 about four miles south of Rio Vista.

Sporting Life

FISHING

Deep sea expeditions for salmon, rock cod and bass draw countless anglers to the Bay Area. For charters, contact **Berkeley Marina Sport Center** (225 University Avenue, Berkeley; 415-849-2727), **Caruso's Sportfishing Center** (foot of Harbor Drive, Sausalito; 415-332-1015), **Loch Lomond Live Bait House** (Loch Lomond Marina, San Rafael; 415-456-0321) or the folks at **Crockett Sport Fishing** (Port Street, Crockett; 415-787-1047).

Fishing the Delta is another favored sport: try **Delta Fish Finders** (169 West Brannan Island Road, Isleton; 916-777-6411) or call **Outrigger Marina** (Sherman Island Road, Three-Mile Slough; 916-777-6480) for information on charter companies.

BOATING

San Francisco Bay offers some of the greatest sailing in the world. If you yearn for salty breezes and ocean vistas, contact **Dave Garrett Sailing School** (455 Seaport Court, Redwood City; 415-367-0850), **D'Anna Yacht Center** (11 Embarcadero West, Suite 100, Oakland; 415-451-7000) or **Cass' Rental Marina** (1702 Bridgeway, Sausalito; 415-332-6789).

GOLF

Duffers and professionals alike tee off at **Crystal Springs Golf Course** (6650 Golf Course Drive, Burlingame; 415-342-0603), **San Jose Municipal Golf Course** (1560 Oakland Road, San Jose; 408-441-4653), **Lake Chabot Golf Course** (Golf Links Road, Oakland; 415-351-5812), **Tilden Park Golf Course** (Grizzly Peak Boulevard and Shasta Road, Berkeley; 415-848-7373) or **Peacock Gap Golf and Country Club** (333 Biscayne Drive, San Rafael; 415-453-4940).

JOGGING

Keeping in shape while sightseeing is one of the Bay Area's favorite pastimes. On the Peninsula, there are paths through the Stanford campus and trails along Crystal Springs Reservoir. The South Bay offers Kelley Park in San Jose. Oakland's Lake Merritt provides a three-mile jaunt around a saltwater inlet. In Sausalito, Bridgeway hugs the waterfront; nearby Tiburon features the Marin County Trail along Richardson Bay.

TENNIS

The Bay Area is the third most active region in the nation for tennis. Cities all around the Bay have public courts, many lighted for night play. For information in Palo Alto, call 415-329-2361; South Bay, 408-277-5556; Oakland, 415-444-5663; Berkeley, 415-644-6530; and Sausalito, 415-289-4125.

BICYCLING

With its Mediterranean climate and gentle terrain, the Bay Area is a perfect place to travel by bicycle.

Cycling is a great way to explore the sights of the Peninsula. There's a beautiful 15-mile loop through Portola Valley with an interesting side trip to the quaint town of Woodside. For a journey through a eucalyptus grove, try the four-mile loop in Coyote Point Park. To ride through academia, check out the numerous paths at Stanford University in Palo Alto.

If you take your bicycle on a sightseeing tour of the South Bay, Kelley Park in San Jose is a great place to begin. Another jaunt travels between two stunning garden parks—Villa Montalvo and Hakone Gardens. More challenging is the steep 24-mile climb up Mount Hamilton Road to the Lick Observatory.

The East Bay offers diverse routes for two-wheeling sightseers. In Oakland, there's a bike path around Lake Merritt, the city's saltwater lake. Tunnel Road and Skyline Boulevard climb the East Bay hills to several regional parks. Out at Point Pinole Regional Shoreline, a path takes cyclists through grassy meadows to the shores of San Pablo Bay.

In Marin, the Sausalito Bikeway carries along the shoreline past marshes and houseboats. Another bikeway in Tiburon offers spectacular views of Sausalito and San Francisco.

For a truly enjoyable bike ride past mud flats, ponds, sloughs, rickety towns, country lanes and levees, take your bicycle to the Delta. The roads are flat, lightly traveled and offer a chance to experience Huck Finn's Mississippi right here in Northern California.

For even more extraordinary bicycle tours, contact **Backroads Bicycle Touring Company** (415-527-1555). This group offers various tours through California, designed for beginning, intermediate and advanced peddlers.

Transportation

BY CAR

The Bay Area is a sprawling region threaded with major highways. Along the Peninsula, **Routes 101, 280** and **82** travel north and south. All three lead to the South Bay; from here, **Route 17/880** travels up along the East Bay.

From San Francisco, **Route 101** streams north to Marin and **Route 80** cuts through the East Bay and connects with other roads leading into the Delta.

BY AIR

Three major airports service the Bay Area: **San Francisco International Airport** (see Chapter Eight for arrival information), San Jose International Airport and Oakland International Airport.

Airlines flying into **San Jose International Airport** include Alaska Airlines, American Airlines, America West Airlines, Continental Airlines, Delta Air Lines, USAir, Trans World Airlines and United Airlines.

Several bus companies provide ground transportation from the San Jose airport. Check with **Greyhound Bus Lines** (408-297-8890) and the **Airport Connection/Airport Limousine** (408-730-5555) for schedules and destinations. **Santa Clara County Transit** (408-287-4210) provides frequent service to downtown San Jose.

Oakland International Airport is serviced by Alaska Airlines, American Airlines, America West Airlines, Continental Airlines, Southwest Airlines and United Airlines.

Ground transportation to and from the Oakland airport is provided by The Bay Area Bus Service (415-444-4200) and Alameda–Contra Costa Transit (415-839-2882), or AC Transit. For a quick trip to various East Bay points, climb aboard the Oakland Air-Bart, which connects the airport with the Bay Area Rapid Transit (415-465-2278), or BART, system.

BY BUS

Greyhound Bus Lines (415-834-3070) offers extensive bus service to the Bay Area from around the country. Peerless Stages (415-444-2901) carries passengers from Oakland to San Jose and south.

BY TRAIN

Amtrak (800-872-7245) has several trains coming into the Bay Area daily. Two cover California routes: the "Coast Starlight" runs from Los Angeles to Seattle with stops in San Jose and Oakland, and the "San Joaquin" covers the San Joaquin Valley, stopping in Oakland. From Chicago, the "San Francisco Zephyr" carries passengers across the western United States to Oakland.

CAR RENTALS

To pick up a car at the San Jose airport, call Avis Rent A Car (408-993-2224), Budget Rent A Car (408-286-7859), Dollar Rent A Car (408-280-1111), Hertz Rent A Car (408-437-5700) or National Car Rental (408-295-1344).

At the Oakland airport, check with Avis Rent A Car (415-562-9000), Budget Rent A Car (415-875-6850), Dollar Rent A Car (415-638-2750), Hertz Rent A Car (415-568-1177) or National Car Rental (415-632-2225).

PUBLIC TRANSPORTATION

On the Peninsula, San Mateo County Transit (800-660-4287), or SamTrans, carries passengers from San Francisco as far south as Palo Alto.

The South Bay is traversed by Santa Clara County Transit buses (408-287-4210), with service extending from Palo Alto through San Jose.

A network of bus routes crisscrosses the East Bay. Call **Alameda–Contra Costa County Transit** (415-839-2882), or AC Transit, for schedules. **Peerless Stages** serves the South Bay (408-298-8990) and the East Bay (415-444-2901).

Marin County is serviced by **Golden Gate Transit** (415-453-2100) buses from points in San Francisco to Sausalito, San Rafael and beyond.

Daily commuter trains run the length of the Peninsula from San Francisco to San Jose. Call **CalTrain** (415-557-8661) for information.

Bay Area Rapid Transit (415-465-2278), or BART, runs from Fremont north to Richmond, stopping in Oakland and Berkeley, and from Daly City through San Francisco to the East Bay.

TEN

Wine Country

Just one hour from the streets of San Francisco lies an agricultural area that can match for beauty farmlands anywhere in the country. It's a region of tree-tufted mountains and luxurious valleys. Tilled fields create quiltlike patterns across the landscape, and country roads wind into its hills.

Despite the grandeur of the place, its visual appeal is only a secondary feature. The lure of the land is its temptation to all the senses, particularly taste and smell. The plants stippling those picturesque fields are grapes, and the product is wine, fine vintages that rival even those of France.

Winemaking in California dates back to the 18th century when Spanish padres planted vineyards at the missions. Today winemaking has become a multibillion dollar business, with millions of people touring California's vineyards each year.

The natural elements for this success story have always been present, though only recently did the social factors begin to coalesce. Geography and climate play vital roles in winemaking and combine north of San Francisco to create ideal growing conditions. Here several valleys—Napa, Sonoma and the Russian River—are protected by mountains from the cold winds and rain along the Pacific coast. They enjoy hot (very hot!) summers and cool, moist winters, ensuring good harvests.

In Napa Valley, sun, low hills and fog drifting up from San Francisco Bay produce one of the world's finest winegrowing regions. The area has become so well-known and fashionable that it is not only drawing fog from San Francisco. Celebrities and millionaires are moving here even faster than new wineries. Gourmet restaurants and country inns have multiplied, and tourists are causing weekend traffic jams in this once rustic realm. Even the health spa at Calistoga has gained such importance that France's Perrier took over the mineral-water bottling. It's a far cry from a century ago when a penniless writer named Robert Louis Stevenson explored the isolated farming community.

Sonoma Valley's history traces back further than that of Napa, but lately the "valley of the moon" has been hard pressed to keep pace with its starstruck neighbor. Resting between the Sonoma and the Mayacamas mountains, it was once inhabited by Coastal Miwok, Pomo, Wappo and Patwin Indians. The advent of the Spanish mission changed their lifestyle unalterably and led eventually to the American conquest of California.

Today Sonoma Valley is planted with an extraordinary variety of grapes. So too is its neighbor to the north, the Russian River region. Moving in a southerly course from Mendocino County, the Russian River passes Alexander Valley, Dry Creek Valley and other regions that have greatly contributed to California's wine renaissance.

Then, where it turns west toward the sea, it has engendered a different sort of rebirth, a gay renaissance. Since the 1970s, the area around Guerneville, long popular for its excellent canoeing and fishing, has become Northern California's top gay resort. Country inns, restaurants and nightclubs catering to gays from San Francisco and around the country have mushroomed along the riverbanks and in the region's deep redwood forests.

Napa Valley

California's premier winegrowing region is a long, narrow valley, laid out like a checkerboard and stretching 35 miles. Here grape arbors alternate with wild grasses, and rich bottomland gives way to forested slopes. If natural beauty were a question for the palate, Napa Valley would be the rarest of vintages. It is a landscape of windmills and wooden barns, clapboard cottages and stone wineries.

To avoid crowds try to visit during the week and plan to explore not only the main highway, but also the Silverado Trail. An ideal itinerary will carry you up the valley on Route 29, then back down along the parallel roadway. In its initial stretch, Route 29 is a divided freeway that streams through the town of Napa. At the roadside **information booth** (4076 Byway East; 707-253-2929) there are maps and brochures available.

An unusual option for touring the wine country is to climb aboard the **Napa Valley Wine Train** (1275 McKistry Street, Napa; 707-253-2111). Service was restored on the old line between the city of Napa and the vineyards slightly north of St. Helena in 1989. Travelers may choose either the luncheon or the dinner trip, each of which takes three hours and smoothly chugs past some of the most scenic

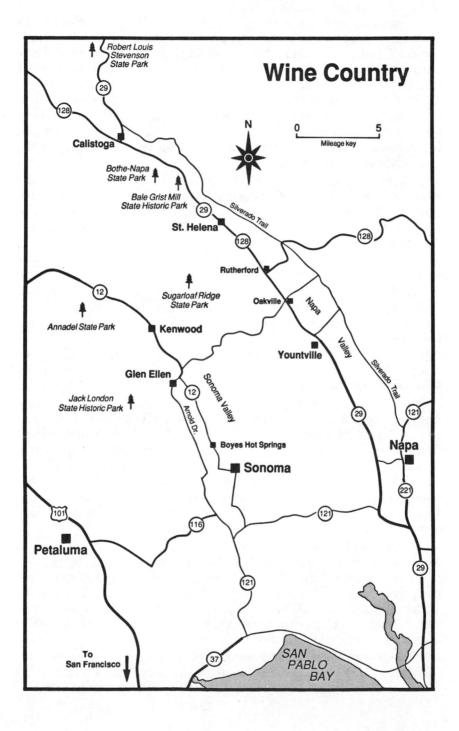

Wine Country

Robert Louis
Stevenson
State Park

29

128

Calistoga

Bothe-Napa
State Park

Bale Grist Mill
State Historic Park

29

St. Helena

128

Silverado Trail

128

Rutherford

Sugarloaf Ridge
State Park

12

Oakville

Napa

Annadel State Park

Kenwood

Yountville

Valley

Glen Ellen

12

Silverado Trail

Sonoma Valley

Jack London
State Historic Park

121

Arnold Dr.

Boyes Hot Springs

29

Sonoma

Napa

101

221

Petaluma

116

121

121

29

N

0   5
Mileage key

To
San Francisco

37

SAN
PABLO
BAY

parts of the valley. Two lounge cars have been beautifully restored; the dining car is straight out of a romance novel.

If you choose to do it on your own, you'll find one of the area's most interesting wineries right in Napa. Located on the site of the former Christian Brothers' Mont LaSalle winery, the **Hess Collection** (4410 Redwood Road; 707-255-1144) is where fine wine meets fine art. The self-guided tour is unique: it is the only winery in the valley that includes two floors displaying some 130 museum-quality artworks by contemporary European and American artists. The Hess Collection also refers to the cabernets and chardonnays that are just being released and are available for sampling (at a small fee) in the ground-floor tasting room.

North of Napa, several major wineries lie clustered around the rural town of Yountville. **Domaine Chandon** (1 California Drive; 707-944-2280), owned by France's fabled champagne producer, Moët & Chandon, sits on a knoll west of town. Producing some of California's foremost sparkling wines, this winery provides a close look into the production and bottling of the bubbly. The regularly scheduled tours are free, but there's a charge to taste.

Back on Route 29, you'll continue through the tiny towns of Oakville and Rutherford, passing a patchwork of planted fields. Among the prettiest wineries is **Inglenook Vineyards** (1991 St. Helena Highway, Rutherford; 707-967-3358), with its ivy-draped buildings. Constructed in the 1880s, adorned with cupolas and arched doors, this stone-walled winery specializes in cabernet sauvignon, sauvignon blanc and chardonnay.

In a valley virtually spilling over with wineries, how does a new one get noticed? In the case of **St. Supery Vineyards & Winery** (8440 Route 29, Rutherford; 707-963-4507), it's by constructing a first-rate gallery with numerous exhibits on Napa Valley winemaking. Three-dimensional displays include a replica of an actual grapevine growing out of deep soil and topographical maps that show why the valley is good for grapes. An outdoor tasting room (again, nominal fee) and a restored Victorian add spice to the guided or self-guided winery tour.

Capital of the Wine Country is the charming falsefront town of St. Helena. In the Victorian-style downtown area, the brick-and-stone **IOOF Building** (1352 Main Street) looms several stories above the pavement, as it has for a century. The cynosure of St. Helena is the **Ritchie Block** (1331 Main Street), a stone structure with brick-and-wood facade. Featuring more frills and swirls than a wedding cake, it is a study in ornate architecture.

The town's **Silverado Museum** (1490 Library Lane, St. Helena; 707-963-3757) houses a collection of artifacts from Robert Louis Stevenson's sojourn in the Napa Valley in 1880. Stevenson was en route to Hawaii and the South Seas, seeking a salubrious environment in which to escape his lifelong illnesses. Among the memorabilia at the museum are manuscripts, letters, photographs and first editions, as well as personal effects left behind by the globe-girdling Victorian.

At **Beringer Vineyards** (2000 Main Street, St. Helena; 707-963-7115) the vintage product is the Rhine House, a century-old Tudor-style mansion. With its mansard roof and stone inlay, it is a masterwork of spires, turrets and gables. Among the winery's other features are 1000-foot-long tunnels cut into the neighboring hillside by 19th-century Chinese laborers. To taste you must take the tour, which takes in several interesting parts of the operation, including the tunnels.

North of St. Helena, **Bale Grist Mill State Historic Park** (Route 29; 707-942-4575) has restored an 1846 water-wheel mill. Sitting beside a tumbling stream, it creates a classic scene. The old mill is now fully functioning, and there are demonstration grindings, a minimuseum, as well as self-guided tours.

Set atop a knoll near the head of Napa Valley, the Greek monastery-style winery at **Sterling Vineyards** (1111 Dunaweal Lane, Calistoga; 707-942-5151) is reached via an aerial tramway (fee). The gondolas carry visitors to a multitiered building that commands sentinel views of the surrounding valley. A self-guided tour leads through various winemaking facilities to an elegant tasting room. It also takes in the spectacular stained-glass windows and 18th-century church bells that add an exotic element to this unusual winery.

Back on terra firma, you'll arrive in the town of **Calistoga**. Founded in 1859, this well-known health spa owes its origin and name to Sam Brannan. Determined to create a California version of New York's famous Saratoga spa, he named the region Calistoga. Today this quaint 19th-century town is home to numerous spas and health resorts.

After imbibing at vineyards throughout the valley, visitors arrive in Calistoga to luxuriate in the region's mineral waters. Sign up for the works and you will be submerged in a mud bath, led into a whirlpool bath, then a steam room, wrapped head to toe in a blanket and finally given a massage. By the end of the treatment, your body will be completely loose and your mind will reside somewhere in the ozone. If you're game, contact **Nance's Hot Springs** (1614 Lincoln Avenue; 707-942-6211), **Le Spa Français** (1880 Lincoln Avenue; 707-942-4636) or one of the other resorts in town.

More evidence of Calistoga's infernal geology issues forth from **Old Faithful Geyser** (1299 Tubbs Lane; 707-942-6463; admission), a hokey but interesting tourist attraction. A subterranean stream heated to 350° blows skyward every two-and-a-half hours, reaching 60 feet high.

Other Calistoga points of interest are the **Sharpsteen Museum** and adjacent **Sam Brannan Cottage** (1311 Washington Street; 707-

942-5911). Dedicated to the town's original settlers, the museum displays tools from a blacksmith's shop and early California kitchen. There are also a few beautiful Chinese artifacts to mark the 19th-century Asian presence in Napa Valley. Sam Brannan's cottage is furnished in period fashion with hand-embroidered furniture and a glorious old piano. Highlight of the entire display, however, is an elaborate diorama portraying Brannan's health resort in miniature. Representing Calistoga circa 1865, it contains everything from railway station to racetrack, hotel to distillery.

As mentioned earlier, there's an alternate route through the valley, an old stagecoach road called the Silverado Trail. Fully paved, it parallels Route 29 on the east and links with it via a succession of cross-valley roads. In addition to providing glimpses of Napa Valley as it was 30 years ago, it's an excellent place to search out small wineries. All along this rural stretch are family-owned vineyards, set on the valley floor or tucked into nearby hills.

After arriving in Calistoga, the Silverado Trail trades the warm, level terrain of the valley for the cool, rugged landscape of the mountains. It climbs and winds through thick coniferous forests and past bald rockfaces. In touring Napa, you've undoubtedly noticed the stately mountain that stands sentinel at the north end of the valley. **Mount St. Helena**, named by 19th-century Russian explorers for their empress, rises 4343 feet, dominating the skyline.

ALL IN THE FAMILY

Small wineries, where the operation is family run and tours are personalized, create the Napa Valley's most memorable experiences. Usually the winemaker or a member of the family will show you around, providing a glimpse into their lives as well as their livelihoods. Here are just a few choice samples; these and other small operations usually require advanced reservations for tours.

Mayacamas Vineyards (1155 Lokoya Road, Napa; 707-224-4030), located deep in the mountains west of Napa Valley, sits astride an extinct volcano. The blocks of vineyard appear hewn from surrounding rock walls. Indeed, the fields of chardonnay and cabernet sauvignon rest on terraces along the mountainside. Like the encircling hills, the winery is made of stone, built in 1889. Tours by appointment; the vineyards lie about ten miles off Route 29 along winding mountain roads.

Another side road leads from Route 29 to Tudal Winery (1015 Big Tree Road, St. Helena; 707-963-3947). Touted as one of the world's smallest wineries, this family affair can be toured in about ten minutes, after which the owner may regale you for hours with tales of the Wine Country. Tours and tasting by appointment.

Perched on the side of this mountain, along Highway 29 about eight miles north of Calistoga, is **Robert Louis Stevenson State Park** (707-942-4575). The Scottish writer and his wife honeymooned in these parts, camping in the hills and enjoying the recuperative air. Here Stevenson wrote sections of "The Silverado Squatters" and studied settings later used in *Treasure Island*.

NAPA VALLEY LODGING

For a dash of history in your evening glass of port, consider the **Magnolia Hotel** (6529 Yount Street, Yountville; 707-944-2056), built in 1873 and now a fashionable bed and breakfast. There are seven rooms in the old ivy-covered structure and others in two adjacent buildings, each room crowded with antiques. Quilts and rag dolls adorn the beds, while chandeliers and brass lamps illuminate the historic setting. There's also a swimming pool and jacuzzi. Deluxe to ultra-deluxe, with full breakfast.

The **Vintage Inn Napa Valley** (6541 Washington Street, Yountville; 707-944-1112) is ideally located for exploring the Wine Country. Bold landscaping, including trickling fountains, surrounds two-story villas comprising 80 accommodations. Fireplaces, louvered windows, small patios or decks, contemporary furnishings and low-key decor make these some of the most pleasant rooms in the valley. Pool, tennis courts. Ultra-deluxe.

Perched on a hillside studded with olive trees, **Auberge du Soleil Resort** (180 Rutherford Hill Road, Rutherford; 707-963-1211) is a curious blend of adobe-style buildings named after French winegrowing regions and decorated in a breezy California/Southwest style. Bare Mexican tile floors, louvered doors, fireplaces and small decks are a refreshing change from the cluttered feel of older hotels in the valley. A dozen low-rise villas stagger down the hill, each containing four to eight accommodations. Pool. Ultra-deluxe.

Located in the center of town, the **Hotel St. Helena** (1309 Main Street, St. Helena; 707-963-4388) is a traditional falsefront building dating to 1881. The 18 rooms, some with shared bath, include such decorative flourishes as brass beds, antique armoires and marble-top vanities. Guests share an indoor reading room and sitting room with fireplace, plus other facilities like the hotel's wine bar and ground-floor shops. Moderate to deluxe.

Located at the end of a tree-shaded country road, **Meadowood Resort** (900 Meadowood Lane, St. Helena; 707-963-3646) comprises 70 ultra-deluxe-priced accommodations, a nine-hole golf course, two croquet courses, a pool and tennis courts. Guests may choose to stay in cozy, weathered gray cabins or in the newer Croquet

Lodge; either way, they'll have comfortable furnishings and serene views of the grounds.

Several Calistoga spas also provide overnight accommodations. **Indian Springs Hotel Resort** (1712 Lincoln Avenue; 707-942-4913) offers housekeeping cottages at deluxe cost. These are refurbished duplexes with complete kitchens. Guests are welcome to use the spa's 90° mineral pool for free. Indian Springs also features mud baths, steam baths and massages.

Built in 1917, the **Mount View Hotel** (1457 Lincoln Avenue, Calistoga; 707-942-6877) has the aura and feel of a classic small-town hotel. It's a 30-room affair with dining room and lounge downstairs and art deco flourishes throughout. Rooms upstairs are plainly furnished but are nicely decorated with patterned wallpaper or wall-hangings. There's also a pool and jacuzzi on the premises. Moderate to ultra-deluxe.

Several agencies offer reservation services, very convenient during peak tourist periods. If interested, contact **Bed & Breakfast Exchange** (1458 Lincoln Avenue, Calistoga; 707-942-5900).

NAPA VALLEY RESTAURANTS

The only thing generic about **The Diner** (6476 Washington Street, Yountville; 707-944-2626) is its name. This unassuming eatery, popular with local residents, prepares a mix of Mexican and American dishes at budget prices.

Domaine Chandon (California Drive, Yountville; 707-944-2892) features a widely acclaimed restaurant at its winery. A multitiered affair with curved ceiling and colorful banners, it serves award-winning French cuisine. Lunch includes such delicacies as salmon with champagne, while dinner features entrées like duck in cabernet sauce or lamb with rosemary. Deluxe.

Set in an old building, **The French Laundry** (6640 Washington Street, Yountville; 707-944-2380) is a family-owned venture featuring country French cuisine. The food is excellent, the wine list extensive, the price deluxe. The prix-fixe menu changes nightly.

At **Mama Nina's** (6772 Washington Street, Yountville; 707-944-2112) you'll encounter a moderate-priced Italian restaurant whose specialty is homemade pasta. The setting is quite attractive, and there's an outdoor deck for those warm Napa evenings.

Mustards Grill (7399 St. Helena Highway, Yountville; 707-944-2424) is an ultramodern brass-rail restaurant complete with track lighting and contemporary wallhangings. But the important features are the woodburning grill and oven, where the chefs prepare rabbit, smoked pork loin, baby back ribs and fresh grilled fish. Moderate.

A gourmet hideaway in a curving stucco structure, **Auberge du Soleil** (180 Rutherford Hill Road, Rutherford; 707-963-1211) boasts a circular lounge capped by a skylight-cum-cupola and a dining area with exposed beams and open fireplace. The seasonal menu features such entrées as stuffed squab, duckling with marinated pears, T-bone veal and milk-fed sweetbreads. There are enough wines to fill the Napa Valley. This culinary extravaganza prices in the ultra-deluxe range.

Tra Vigne (1050 Charter Oak Avenue, St. Helena; 707-963-4444) can claim the most dramatic interior in the Wine Country. Soaring ceilings, unusual lighting, an open kitchen and festive displays of peppers and garlic make the setting as exciting as the deluxe-priced menu. The theme here is Tuscan: chewy breads, bold pizzas, hearty salads, lots of veal, chicken and grilled seafood dishes, and a first-rate wine list.

NAPA VALLEY SHOPPING

Almost by definition, shopping malls are unattractive. **Vintage 1870** (6525 Washington Street, Yountville) is a rare exception to a modern rule. Housed in the historic Groezinger Winery, a massive brick building smothered in ivy, it contains several dozen fashionable stores, including clothing boutiques and arts and crafts shops. In an adjacent building, the **Groezinger Wine Company** (707-944-2331) features a wine bar. Also of interest is the **Keith Rosenthal Photography Theatre and Gallery** (707-944-2525), with slide shows of the Napa Valley.

Oakville Grocery (Route 29, Oakville; 707-944-8802) is a prime place to stock up for a picnic. This falsefront country store sells wines and cheeses, fresh fruits and baked goods, as well as a host of gourmet items.

Main Street, St. Helena is a falsefront boulevard lined with a stationery shop, newspaper office and grocer. Of interest to visitors are the boutiques, bookstore, jewelers and wine shop.

BOTHE–NAPA VALLEY PARK

*Rising from the valley floor to about 2000 feet elevation, the outstanding **Bothe–Napa Valley State Park** (707-942-4575) is fully developed along one side, wild and rugged on the other. Ten miles of hiking trails lead along steep hillsides to redwood groves. There are coyotes, bobcats, deer and fox. The park's developed area features spacious picnic groves, campgrounds and a swimming pool. Located on Route 29 about five miles north of St. Helena.*

The **Napa Valley Olive Oil Co.** (835 McCorkle Avenue, St. Helena; 707-963-4173) is more than a gourmet shopping spot: it's a sightseeing adventure as well. Housed in a former oil manufacturing plant, it contains the original press and crusher. Today this tiny factory sells delicious cheeses and salami, as well as pasta and condiments.

Outside town, **Hurd Beeswax Candles** (3020 North St. Helena Highway, St. Helena; 707-963-7211) elevates candlemaking to the level of art. The waxworks resemble statues in a myriad of intricate shapes.

Up the road at **Vintner Village** (3111 North St. Helena Highway, St. Helena; 707-963-4082; admission) you'll encounter a winetasting center where over a dozen wineries are represented.

Up in Calistoga, shops of general interest are mixed with those catering to local concerns. Along Lincoln Avenue, near the barber shop and town cobbler, are antique stores, clothing shops and a bookstore. The historic **Calistoga Depot** (1458 Lincoln Avenue, Calistoga) has been converted to a mall. Within this former railway station are assorted stores, including **Calistoga Wine Stop** (707-942-5556), which is housed in an antique railroad car.

NAPA VALLEY NIGHTLIFE

During summer months, several wineries sponsor concerts and other special events. Otherwise, the scene centers around the hotel and restaurant bars.

The **California Cafe** (6795 Washington Street, Yountville; 707-944-2330) serves up piano music nightly. The **Mount View Hotel** (1457 Lincoln Avenue, Calistoga; 707-942-6877) has an elegant art deco bar. Adorned with black and silver wallpaper, old art prints and antique wall sconces, it's strikingly attractive.

Sonoma Valley

Touring the wineries of Sonoma provides a perfect excuse not only for tasting California's fine varietals, but also to explore the state's beautiful interior. Cutting a long, luxurious swath between the ocean and the distant Sierra, this piedmont country divides its terrain between vineyards, ranches and dense forest.

The logical place to begin a tour of the valley is in Sonoma, a Spanish-style town of 7300 people. And the spot to begin this tour-within-a-tour is the **Plaza** (bounded by 1st Street East, 1st Street West, Spain and Napa streets). The center of Sonoma for 150 years, this shady park is an excellent picnic place. The largest plaza in the state, it contains a playground, open-air theater, duck pond and rose garden. At the **Sonoma Valley Chamber of Commerce** (645 Broadway; 707-996-1033) there are maps and brochures of the area.

Spanish adobes, stone buildings and falsefront stores surround the historic square. Mission San Francisco Solano, or **Sonoma Mission** (1st Street West and East Spain Street), stands at one corner. Founded in 1823, this was the last and most northerly of the 21 California missions. With its stark white facade, the low-slung adobe houses a small museum. The chapel has also been painted brilliant colors and adorned with carved wood statues.

The **Sonoma Barracks** (1st Street East and East Spain Street), across the street, were built with Indian labor during the 1830s to house the troops of Mexico's General Mariano Guadalupe Vallejo, who controlled Sonoma at the time. A two-story adobe with sweeping balconies, it also houses a museum devoted to early California history.

Next door, the 1852 **Toscano Hotel** (20 East Spain Street) is furnished in 19th-century fashion with woodburning stoves, brocade armchairs and two gambling tables with poker games in progress.

The only remains of General Vallejo's 1840 house, **La Casa Grande** (East Spain Street between 1st Street East and 1st Street West) is the servant's house with its sagging adobe facade. Together with the mission and other antique buildings encircling the plaza, it is part of **Sonoma State Historic Park** (707-938-1519); all these noteworthy places can be toured for a single admission price.

Just north of the plaza stands the **Depot Park Museum** (270 1st Street West; 707-938-9765), housing a hodgepodge collection of paintings and 19th-century artifacts. About one-half mile from the town square, you'll find another antique structure. **Lachryma Montis** (end of 3rd Street West; 707-938-1519) was the home General Vallejo built in 1852. It's well worth touring. Every room is appointed in 19th-century style, as though Vallejo were expected to arrive any moment. The old pendulum clock still swings, and the dinner table is set.

While Vallejo was settling into his American-style home, Count Agoston Haraszthy, a Hungarian aristocrat, moved to Sonoma and founded **Buena Vista Winery** (18000 Old Winery Road; 707-938-1266) in 1857. Today the actual winemaking occurs elsewhere, but you can taste sample vintages in the old stone winery and take a self-guided tour around the grounds.

Kids who tire of all this dusty history can be bribed with a visit to **Train Town** (20264 Broadway; 707-938-3912; admission). Miniature steam engines chug around a ten-acre park, passing over trestles and through a tunnel and arriving at a scale-model Western town.

One of Spain's premier winemaking families began winning awards with their very first vintages from **Gloria Ferrer Champagne Caves** (23555 Highway 121, Sonoma; 707-996-7256). Typical of their native country, the Ferrers carved caves out of the hillside for storing premium sparkling wines. These are available for purchase or for tasting (at a nominal fee) either indoors or on a wide patio with lovely views of the surrounding countryside.

Sam Sebastiani, of the famous Sonoma family of vintners, opened his own winery, **Viansa** (25200 Arnold Drive, Schellville; 707-935-4700), in the heart of the prolific Carneros region. A multilevel stucco compound mounted on a hill at the south end of the Sonoma Valley, this Tuscan-style winery offers tours (by reservation) and tastings of premium wines.

Route 12, the Sonoma Highway, travels north through Sonoma Valley, past miles of vineyard and forest. Numerous small wineries dot this rustic area, including **Kenwood Vineyards** (9592 Sonoma Highway, Kenwood; 707-833-5891), founded in 1906.

The strikingly beautiful **Château St. Jean Winery** (8555 Sonoma Highway, Kenwood; 707-833-4134) sits beside a colonnaded mansion built during the 1920s. The winery has won several awards for its chardonnays and Johannesburg rieslings. You can taste these and other varietals while taking a self-guided tour of the grounds.

SONOMA VALLEY LODGING

The **Sonoma Mission Inn and Spa** (18140 Sonoma Highway 12, Boyes Hot Springs; 707-938-9000) lives up to its name, in all three senses of the word. The pale pink stucco facade on this gracious mission-revival-style hotel harks back to the days when the native Indians enjoyed the natural mineral waters of this area. The 170 ac-

---

JACK LONDON COUNTRY

If the Napa Valley is Stevenson country, Sonoma Valley belongs to Jack London, the writer, world adventurer and self-described "sailor on horseback." Calling this area "the valley of the moon," London and his wife, Charmian, acquired a 1400-acre ranch and began construction of his dream home, Wolf House, which mysteriously burned as it neared completion. Three years later in 1916, after producing 51 books and becoming America's first millionaire author, he committed suicide at age 40.

Today at Jack London State Historic Park (2400 London Ranch Road, Glen Ellen; 707-938-5216; admission) you can wander the old estate. The house of Happy Walls, occupied by Charmian after her husband's death, is a museum containing first editions and original manuscripts. London's study is adorned with the original artwork for his stories, and many keepsakes from his world adventures are here. The cottage where London lived and wrote from 1911 until his death still stands. The author's grave is simply marked by a stone boulder.

commodations are appointed in earthy tones, with wooden shutters and ceiling fans adding a touch of the plantation. A full-service spa, tennis courts and two swimming pools add up to the best retreat in the Wine Country. Ultra-deluxe.

The **Sonoma Hotel** (110 West Spain Street, Sonoma; 707-996-2996), which dates to around 1872, is a 17-room facility decorated entirely with antiques. The lobby contains a stone fireplace, and the adjoining lounge features a hand-carved bar. The rooms (moderate-priced with shared bath, deluxe-priced with private bath) offer such flourishes as marble top dressers and beveled mirrors.

Now that the 50 acres of surrounding vineyards have matured, the **Vintners Inn** (4350 Barnes Road, Santa Rosa; 707-575-7350) blends in with the landscape. Huge deluxe accommodations are decorated in European country style, with antiques and homemade quilts. Little piazzas and lots of open landscaping between two-story townhouses create a luxurious ambience.

SONOMA VALLEY RESTAURANTS

The Grille (Sonoma Mission Inn and Spa, 18140 Sonoma Highway 12, Boyes Hot Springs; 707-938-9000), a handsome Southwestern-inspired dining room, is the best restaurant in the county. Startlingly innovative but not pretentious, the menu features a dozen entrées such as grilled fish, leg of veal and lamb dishes, virtually all from local sources. The Grille also offers items low in calories, cholesterol and sodium. Deluxe.

The **Sonoma Cheese Factory** (2 West Spain Street; Sonoma; 707-996-1931) is *the* spot to stop on the way to a picnic. In addition to a grand assortment of cheeses, it sells wines, sandwiches and gourmet items. There's also a small patio for diners.

For fine French dining, **Les Arcades** (133 East Napa Street, Sonoma; 707-938-3723), an intimate dining room in a dollhouselike setting, is exceptional. Seating only a few dozen people, it is situated in a small building and decorated with stained glass, murals and a bar fashioned from Hawaiian hardwood. The ever-evolving menu includes coq au vin, veal and rabbit dishes and elegant entrées like chicken with truffles and cognac. Dinner only; deluxe.

If you prefer Mexican cuisine, try **La Casa** (121 East Spain Street, Sonoma; 707-996-3406). Located just off the plaza, this colorful restaurant offers a full menu from south of the border at budget-to-moderate prices.

London Lodge (13740 Arnold Drive, Glen Ellen; 707-996-3100) sits just down the road from Jack London's estate. The dining room is a plate-glass facility overlooking forest and stream. In addition to views, there are ample lunch and dinner menus at moderate prices. Entrées include roast duck, chicken paprika and Hungarian goulash.

Long overlooked by visitors, **Oreste's Golden Bear Lodge** (1717 Adobe Canyon Road, Kenwood; 707-833-2327) is being re · discovered. The setting is unequalled. Sequestered alongside a winding country road, it offers seating outside by the creek or inside the modest dining room. An all-Italian menu blends classic pastas and veal dishes with more adventuresome offerings such as Sonoma sausage with grilled polenta. Moderate to deluxe.

SONOMA VALLEY SHOPPING

The best shops in Sonoma surround the plaza. Here you'll encounter gourmet stores, boutiques, a designer lingerie company, antique stores and a brass shop. Many of these establishments are housed in historic Spanish adobes.

Robin's Nest Samples 'n' Seconds (140 East Napa Street; 707-996-4169) specializes in discount cookware and kitchen accessories. Around the corner, the **Arts Guild of Sonoma** (460 First Street East; 707-996-3115) boasts the best selection of local crafts such as pottery, ceramics, jewelry and weavings, beautifully arranged and reasonably priced.

Two stores slightly west of the square are worth a short stroll. **Cat & the Fiddle** (135 West Napa Street; 707-996-5651) features a wide range of antiques, gifts and collectibles. And the **Sonoma Country Store** (165 West Napa Street; 707-996-0900) is out-and-out adorable, with a comely collection of glassware, ceramics, decorative items and paper goods perfectly suited to the small-town ambience of the valley.

On the way to Jack London State Park, be sure to stop at **Jack London Bookstore** (14300 Arnold Drive, Glen Ellen; 707-996-2888), which contains numerous first editions of the author's works.

SONOMA VALLEY NIGHTLIFE

As in the Napa area, Sonoma Valley nightlife revolves around hotel bars and summer events at the wineries. There's a particularly good lounge at the antique **Sonoma Hotel** (110 West Spain Street, Sonoma; 707-996-2996) on the town plaza.

London Lodge (13740 Arnold Drive, Glen Ellen; 707-996-3100) has a pretty, brick-faced barroom that draws a mixture of locals and visitors.

Located on the upper floor of the historic Sebastiani Theater, the **Cabaret Sauvignon** (478 1st Street East, Sonoma; 707-996-3600) is the town's premier night spot. The multilevel room has pink walls and a blue ceiling studded with cloud patterns. Rock bands perform, along with the occasional stand-up comic and, on some Sunday afternoons, big-band groups. Cover.

SONOMA VALLEY PARKS

Two different ecological systems and 25 miles of hiking trails lie within the 2800-acre **Sugarloaf Ridge State Park** (707-833-5712). There are chaparral-coated ridges with views of San Francisco and the Sierra Nevada, plus forests of maple, laurel, madrone and alder. Sonoma Creek tumbles through the park and features fishing for steelhead and trout. There are 50 campsites. The park is located at 2605 Adobe Canyon Road in Kenwood.

A volcanic mountain flanks one end of the 5000-acre **Annadel State Park** (707-539-3911), which has 35 miles of trails through meadow and forest. A lake provides fishing for black bass and bluegill, and blacktailed deer and coyotes roam the region. Located off Route 12 about five miles east of Santa Rosa.

Russian River

With its headwaters in Mendocino County, the Russian River rambles south through north central California to Healdsburg. Here it turns west toward the sea, as the surrounding landscape changes from rolling ranchland to dense redwood forest.

The southern reaches of the Russian River, around Guerneville where the river begins its headlong rush to the Pacific, has enjoyed a rebirth as a **gay resort** area. Today, it is San Francisco's answer to Fire Island.

Still popular with families as well, this stretch of river offers good fishing and excellent canoeing. As the river rumbles downslope, it provides miles of scenic runs past overhanging forests. Black bass, steelhead, bluegills and silver salmon swim these waters, and there are

---

PIPER SONOMA CELLARS

Though the miles don't number many, the ultramodern Piper Sonoma Cellars (11447 Old Redwood Highway, Healdsburg; 707-433-8843) is a world apart from the small, family-run wineries along the Russian River. Born of an international marriage between Sonoma Vineyards and France's Piper-Heidsieck, it produces sparkling wines after the French tradition. There are tours (by appointment) of this elegant complex, followed by a tasting at the winery's cafe (fee).

numerous beaches for swimming and sunbathing. The **Visitors Information Center** (14034 Armstrong Woods Road, Guerneville; 707-869-9009) provides brochures and maps on facilities and water sports.

The heart of the winegrowing region lies farther upriver around Healdsburg, a country town centered on a plaza and dating back to 1852. From here, wineries lead south toward Santa Rosa and north to Cloverdale. Route 101 cuts through the middle of this vine-rich country, but the secret to touring the Russian River resides along country lanes paralleling the highway. At the **Healdsburg Chamber of Commerce** (217 Healdsburg Avenue; 707-433-6935) you can pick up maps, brochures and other information on the region.

To the south of Healdsburg, around the tiny towns of Forestville and Windsor, are numerous family wineries. Without doubt, one of the prettiest vineyard settings in all California belongs to **Iron Horse Vineyards** (9786 Ross Station Road, Sebastopol; 707-887-1507). The driveway snaking into this hidden spot is bordered with flowers and palm trees. The winery buildings, painted barn-red, follow the classic architecture of American farms. Laid out around them in graceful checkerboard patterns are fields of pinot noir and chardonnay grapes. Appointments necessary.

In addition to wineries, there are countless orchards around Sebastopol, California's premier apple-producing area. Many farms allow visitors to wander the orchards and **pick produce**. For details, contact the **Sebastopol Chamber of Commerce** (265 South Main Street; 707-823-3032) and ask for a Sonoma County farm trails map. It will lead you to farms producing apples, pears, berries, cherries, peaches and vegetables.

Dry Creek Valley, a luxurious landscape of vineyards and forest, stretches to the west of Healdsburg. One small winery warrants special attention. **Dry Creek Vineyard** (3770 Lambert Bridge Road, Healdsburg; 707-433-1000) sits in an ivy-covered building surrounded by shade trees. Tours are by appointment only, but there's a tasting every day. Among the excellent wines produced are chenin blancs, fumés, cabernets, chardonnays, merlots and zinfandels.

East of Healdsburg lies the Alexander Valley, a region whose wines are gaining an increasingly fine reputation. Because of its warm climate, the valley is sometimes compared with the Bordeaux area of France. Its vintages, however, have a quality all their own.

A lavish facility built along the lines of a Bordeaux château, **Jordan Vineyard & Winery** (1474 Alexander Valley Road, Healdsburg; 707-433-6955) is a family operation with the Jordans residing on the premises. A tour of the estate is a rare experience, providing a glimpse into a winery whose elegance matches its excellence. No tasting is permitted; tours are by appointment.

A long dirt road leads to an unpainted barn at **Johnson's Alexander Valley Winery** (8333 Route 128, Healdsburg; 707-433-2319). The slap-dash ambience, however, ends at the front door. Within this nondescript tasting room sits a pipe organ used for the winery's occasional concerts. There is also a wealth of modern equipment around the place, which produces fine pinot noirs and cabernets. Founded by three brothers, the little winery offers tasting anytime and tours by appointment.

RUSSIAN RIVER LODGING

Southside Resort (13811 Route 116, Guerneville; 707-869-2690), located on the Russian River, has facilities for campers or others looking for a cozy cottage. The cottages are attractive woodframe structures tucked beneath shade trees. They are comfortably furnished and include kitchens and stall showers; many have wood stoves. Primarily renting to families and couples. Moderate to deluxe. Facilities available year-round; campground open May through October.

CALIFORNIA WINE

The Greeks had it all wrong. They fervently believed that the gods drank nectar. Anyone who has explored the vineyards of California knows that wine, not sweet ambrosia, is the drink of the gods. It's also obvious that deciding on the finest wine is as simple as determining the true religion. There are an endless number to choose from, and the only answer is to decide for yourself.

This is not to say that a tour of the Wine Country is a pilgrimage, though it can have a lifetime effect on the drinking habits of mere mortals. At the very least, it will be a robust adventure, one that couples sightseeing with a taste of California's heavenly drink.

The best season to visit the vineyards is during the harvest in late September and early October. The scent of freshly fermenting wine fills the air, and the vineyards are colored brilliant red and gold. Winter is the rainy season and a fallow period. It's also less crowded than the rest of the year and allows opportunities for more relaxed and personalized tours, particularly at small wineries. The growing season begins in March when buds appear on previously bare, gnarled vines. By early summer, the buds are miniature grape clusters that ripen during the torrid months of midsummer.

Once the berries are picked in autumn, the activity shifts from the vineyard to the winery. The berries are crushed; white wines are then filtered or clarified and fermented in temperature-controlled tanks. Red wines are fermented, together with their skins and seeds, at higher temperatures (70° to 90°). Later the wines are racked, or stored, in wooden barrels to add flavor and then bottled. Requiring two or three years to reach their potential, reds mature more slowly than whites.

Resting on 18 waterfront acres, **Fifes** (16467 River Road, Guerneville; 707-869-0656) is the Russian River's biggest gay resort. In addition to a restaurant and bar, Fifes offers such outdoor facilities as a beach, pool and volleyball courts. Accommodations are as varied as the sports activities. There are campsites at budget prices, tiny, nicely decorated individual cabins and larger units, some with living room, fireplace and kitchen. Moderate to ultra-deluxe.

Numerous country inns dot the Healdsburg area, including the **Haydon House** (321 Haydon Street; 707-433-5228), a lovely eight-bedroom bed and breakfast set in a vintage 1912 house. Each room is beautifully appointed with antique furniture and artistic wallhangings. The tree-shaded lawn and luxurious front porch are a perfect expression of Main Street, America. Rooms in the main building are moderate; carriage house accommodations are deluxe. Like many local bed and breakfasts, it belongs to the **Wine Country Inns of Sonoma County** (707-433-4667), a referral service that can help you with hotel reservations.

Built around the turn of the century as a private summer retreat, the **Madrona Manor Country Inn** (1001 Westside Road, Healdsburg; 707-433-4231) is a charming example of Gothic Victorian architecture, complete with a balconied porch, turrets and gables. The best rooms are in the main house; they are spacious (two upstairs sport private verandas) and furnished in serious antiques, including chaises longues and armoires. Twenty-one accommodations in the deluxe-to-ultra-deluxe-price range include several outbuildings on an eight-acre site, including a carriage house. Pool, full breakfast.

"BAHL GORMS"

Beyond the Napa and Sonoma valleys, Route 101 streams north past Ukiah and several more wineries. A more interesting course lies along Route 128, which leads northwest from Cloverdale through piedmont country. En route, the two-lane road meanders like an old river, bending back upon itself to reveal sloping meadows and tree-tufted glades. It's a beautiful country drive through rolling ranchland.

*As the road curls down into Anderson Valley, it passes **Boonville**, a farming community of 1000 folks. Back in the 1880s, this town invented a kind of local language, "boontling," known only to residents. With a vocabulary of over 1000 words, it neatly reflected Anderson Valley life. A photograph became a "Charlie Walker" after the Mendocino fellow who took portraits. Because of his handlebar whiskers, "Tom Bacon" lent his name to the moustache. Vestiges of the old ling remain: restaurants, for instance, still boast of their "bahl gorms," or good food.*

RUSSIAN RIVER RESTAURANTS

Truffles (234 South Main Street, Sebastopol; 707-823-8448) tempts the palate with several deluxe-priced dishes that blend California ingredients with Oriental concepts, such as a first course of oysters wrapped in spinach. Entrées include crispy quail with black rice as well as pasta, fish, rabbit and chicken dishes. Moderate to deluxe.

The restaurant at **Fifes** (16467 River Road, Guerneville; 707-869-0656) is an intimate dining room with stone fireplace, pine walls and exposed-rafter ceiling. There's also a sundeck for warm-weather dining. Moderate in price, it features a sophisticated California-cuisine menu that changes seasonally.

In Healdsburg's plaza you'll find the **Plaza Grill** (109-A Plaza Street; 707-431-8305), a cozy dining room. Lunch at this modern restaurant features fresh fish, salads and sandwiches, while dinner brings veal, lamb, beef and chicken dishes. All are mesquite-grilled; moderate to deluxe.

One of the most beloved restaurants in Sonoma County, **John Ash & Co.** (4350 Barnes Road in the Vintners Inn, Santa Rosa; 707-575-7350) resides in an elegant adobe-style building, decorated with local artworks that blend in nicely with vineyards visible through enormous windows. John Ash, known for his devotion to local fish, fowl and produce, prepared with a confident flair, has created a widely varied menu. Deluxe.

RUSSIAN RIVER NIGHTLIFE

As in most of the Wine Country, night owls will discover that evening entertainment, such as it is, centers around the lounges in local hotels and restaurants.

Numerous gay nightspots cluster around Guerneville. **The Woods** (16881 Armstrong Woods Road; 707-869-0111) hosts a multifaceted extravaganza. There's a bar with pool table in one room, dancefloor in another area and a terrace for warm-weather drinking. They also feature live entertainment during summer months, sometimes drawing top-name talent. Cover.

Fifes (16467 River Road, Guerneville; 707-869-0656) has a beautiful bar area that spreads through several pine-paneled rooms and extends out to a poolside deck. Country-western dancing on weekends.

RUSSIAN RIVER PARKS

Lying side by side, **Armstrong Redwoods State Reserve** and **Austin Creek State Recreation Area** (707-869-2015) are a study in contrasts. Armstrong features a deep, cool forest of redwood trees measuring over 300 feet high and dating back 1400 years. Rare redwood orchids blossom here in spring, and there is a 1200-seat amphitheater for summer concerts. Austin Creek offers sunny meadows, oak forests, campsites, a lake for fishing and 20 miles of trails. Located at 17000 Armstrong Woods Road in Guerneville.

Sporting Life

CANOEING

The Russian River is *the* place to explore in a canoe. The scenery, ranging from rolling ranchland to dense redwood groves, is stunning. Several outfits offer everything from one-day excursions to five-day expeditions. Contact **W. C. "Bob" Trowbridge Canoe Trips** (20 Healdsburg Avenue, Healdsburg; 707-433-7247), **California Rivers** (10070 Old Redwood Highway, Windsor; 707-838-7787) or **Rubicon Whitewater Adventures** (Forestville; 707-887-2452).

GOLF

The Wine Country's excellent weather makes golf a popular pastime. In the Napa Valley, tee off at **Chimney Rock Golf Course** (5320 Silverado Trail, Napa; 707-255-3363), **Napa City Municipal Golf Course** (2295 Streblow Drive, Napa; 707-255-4333) or **Mount St. Helena Golf Course** (Napa County Fairgrounds, Calistoga; 707-942-9966). In the Sonoma Valley, you'll find greens at **Sonoma National Golf Club** (17700 Arnold Drive, Sonoma; 707-996-0300), **Oakmont Golf Club** (7025 Oakmont Drive, Santa Rosa; 707-539-0415) or **Sebastopol Golf Course** (2881 Scott's Right of Way, Sebastopol; 707-823-9852). Around the Russian River, try **Northwood Golf Course** (19400 Route 116, Monte Rio; 707-865-1116).

HORSEBACK RIDING

The hills and valleys of the Wine Country provide wonderful opportunities for equestrians. In Napa, saddle up at the **Wild Horse Valley Ranch** (Wild Horse Valley Road, Napa; 707-224-0727). Around Sonoma, there's **Cloverleaf Ranch** (3890 Old Redwood Highway, Santa Rosa; 707-545-5906) or **Sonoma Cattle Company** (P.O. Box 877, Glen Ellen, CA 95442; 707-996-8566).

BALLOONING AND GLIDING

All puns aside, no sport in the Wine Country has taken off like hot-air ballooning. Every morning, colorful balloons dot the sky, providing riders with a billowing crow's nest from which to view the sweeping countryside. For a ride straight from the pages of *Around the World in 80 Days*, call **Napa's Great Balloon Escape** (Napa; 707-253-0860) or **Once in a Lifetime Balloon Company** (1458 Lincoln Avenue, Calistoga; 707-942-6541) in the Napa Valley. In the Sonoma area, try **Airborn of Sonoma County** (Santa Rosa; 707-528-8133).

If you'd prefer to soar silently in a glider, contact **Calistoga Soaring Center** (1546 Lincoln Avenue, Calistoga; 707-942-5000).

BICYCLING

One of the nicest ways to explore the Wine Country is to bicycle the back roads, pedaling between wineries, historic sites and health spas. The Silverado Trail through Napa Valley is the best road to travel. It's less crowded than Route 29, the main thoroughfare, and is fairly level.

Several steep mountain roads lead from Napa Valley across to Sonoma Valley. Then, in Sonoma, a bike path on the western edge of the city passes numerous sightseeing spots. Up in Russian River country, River Road, between Windsor and Guerneville, meanders past rolling hills and rural scenery but carries a moderate amount of traffic.

Transportation

BY CAR

The quick, painless and impersonal way to the Napa Valley is along **Route 37** and then **Route 29**, the main road through Napa Valley. For a more scenic drive, turn off Route 37 onto **Route 121**, a curving country road that connects with Route 29 and with Sonoma Valley's **Route 12**.

Route 101 runs like a spine through the Russian River region. Another road, **Route 116**, leaves this freeway and heads to the gay resort area around Guerneville.

BY BUS

Greyhound Bus Lines has frequent service to both the Napa (707-226-1856) and Sonoma (Cloverdale; 707-894-2099) areas. It also stops in Healdsburg, Geyserville and points farther north.

PUBLIC TRANSPORTATION

There is no public transportation system in the Napa Valley. In Sonoma, **Sonoma County Transit** (707-576-7433) covers the area pretty thoroughly.

North Coast

When visitors to San Francisco seek a rural retreat, paradise is never far **399** away. It sits just across the Golden Gate Bridge along a coastline stretching almost 400 miles to the Oregon border. Scenically, the North Coast compares in beauty with any spot on earth.

There are the folded hills and curving beaches of Point Reyes, Sonoma's craggy coast and old Russian fort, plus Mendocino with its vintage towns and spuming shoreline. To the far north lies Redwood Country, silent domain of the world's tallest living things.

Along the entire seaboard are fewer than a dozen towns with populations over 600 people. Civilization appears in the form of fishing villages and logging towns. Much of the coast is also preserved in public playgrounds. Strung like pearls along the Pacific are a series of federal parks—the Golden Gate National Recreation Area, Point Reyes National Seashore and Redwood National Park.

The North Coast has become home to the country inn as well. All along the Pacific shoreline, bed and breakfasts serve travelers seeking informal and relaxing accommodations.

The great lure for travelers is still the environment. This coastal shelf, tucked between the Coast Range and the Pacific, has mountains and rivers, forests and ocean. It's a place where you can fish for salmon, go crabbing and scan the sea for migrating whales. Or simply ease back and enjoy scenery that never stops.

Marin Coast

In Marin County, just north of San Francisco, stretch bold headlands, broad beaches and lofty redwoods. The area also includes part of the Golden Gate National Recreation Area and Point Reyes National Seashore, outdoor preserves rarely equaled for breadth and beauty. A bit farther north, tiny seaside towns dot the coastline and offer respite with their small inns and relaxed pace.

An exploration of the northern coast begins immediately upon crossing the Golden Gate Bridge on Route 101. There's a **vista point** at the far end of the bridge affording marvelous views back toward San Francisco and out upon the bay.

Once across the bridge, take the first exit, Alexander Avenue, and pick up Conzelman Road, which leads past a series of increasingly spectacular views of San Francisco. Ahead the road will fall away to reveal a tumbling peninsula, furrowed with hills and marked at its distant tip by a lighthouse. That is **Point Bonita**, a salient far outside the Golden Gate.

Nature writes in big letters around these parts. You're in the **Marin Headlands** section of the Golden Gate National Recreation Area, an otherworldly realm of spuming surf, knife-edge cliffs and chaparral-coated hillsides. From Point Bonita the road leads down to Bunker Road; a left turn here will carry you to the ranger station (415-331-1540), with maps and information about the area.

Walk along **Rodeo Beach**, a sandy corridor separating the Pacific from a tule-fringed lagoon awhirr with waterfowl. Miles of hiking trails lace up into the hills. At the far end of the beach you can trek along the cliffs and watch the sea batter the continent.

At the nearby **California Marine Mammal Center** (415-331-7325) are seals, sea lions and other marine mammals who have been found injured or orphaned in the ocean and brought here to recuperate.

Just a few miles away you can pick up Route 1, one of the most beautiful roads in America. With its wooded sanctuaries and ocean vistas, this coastal highway is for many people synonymous with California.

Nearby Panoramic Highway leads to **Muir Woods** (415-388-2595), a 550-acre park inhabited by *Sequoia sempervirens*, the coast redwood, a forest giant that can live for millennia. In Muir Woods they reach 240 feet, while farther up the coast they top 350 feet (with roots that go no deeper than six feet!).

Facts can't convey the feelings inspired by these trees. You have to move among them, walk through Muir's Cathedral Grove where redwoods form a lofty arcade above the narrow trail. It's a forest primeval, casting the deepest, most restful shade imaginable.

Next stop is **Mt. Tamalpais**, a 2571-foot peak. Mt. Tam, as it is affectionately known, represents one of the Bay Area's most prominent landmarks. Rising dramatically between the Pacific and the bay, the site was sacred to Indians. Even today some people see in the sloping silhouette of the mountain the sleeping figure of an Indian maiden. So tread lightly up the short trail that leads to the summit. You'll be rewarded with a full circle view that sweeps across the bay, along San Francisco's skyline and out across the Pacific.

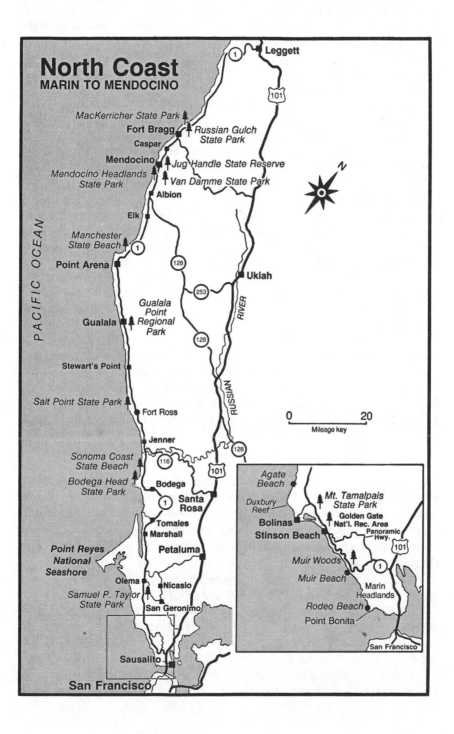

North Coast
MARIN TO MENDOCINO

Leggett

MacKerricher State Park
Fort Bragg
Russian Gulch State Park
Caspar
Mendocino
Jug Handle State Reserve
Mendocino Headlands State Park
Van Damme State Park
Albion
Elk
Manchester State Beach
Point Arena

PACIFIC OCEAN

Ukiah

Gualala Point Regional Park
Gualala

Stewart's Point

Salt Point State Park
Fort Ross

RUSSIAN RIVER

Jenner

Sonoma Coast State Beach
Bodega Head State Park
Bodega
Santa Rosa
Tomales
Marshall
Petaluma

Point Reyes National Seashore
Olema
Nicasio
Samuel P. Taylor State Park
San Geronimo

Sausalito

San Francisco

0   20
Mileage key

Agate Beach
Duxbury Reef
Bolinas
Stinson Beach
Mt. Tamalpais State Park
Golden Gate Nat'l. Rec. Area
Panoramic Hwy.
Muir Woods
Muir Beach
Marin Headlands
Rodeo Beach
Point Bonita
San Francisco

Back on Route 1 you'll encounter **Muir Beach**, a crescent-shaped cove with a sandy beach. Though swimming is not permitted, this is a good spot for picnicking. About a mile up the road, follow the "vista point" sign to **Muir Beach Overlook**. Here you can walk out along a narrow ridge for a view extending from Bolinas to the coastline south of San Francisco.

You have entered a realm that might well be called the Land of a Thousand Views. Until the road descends to the flat expanse of Stinson Beach, it follows a tortuous route poised on the edge of oblivion. Below, precipitous cliffs dive to the sea, while above the road, rock walls edge upward toward Mt. Tamalpais. (At press time Route 1 was still closed between Muir Beach and Stinson Beach because of the 1989 earthquake. For information on current road conditions call CalTrans at 415-923-4444.)

Stinson Beach, that broad sandy hook at the bottom of the mountain, is one of Northern California's finest strands. A few miles north on Bolinas Lagoon lies **Audubon Canyon Ranch** (415-868-9244), a mecca for birdwatchers. Open only on weekends and holidays from March to July, the ranch includes four canyons, one of which is famed as a rookery for egrets and herons. From the hiking trails here you can see up to 90 bird species as well as gray fox, deer and bobcats.

Continue north on Route 1 through Olema Valley, a peaceful region of horse ranches fringed by forest. Peaceful, that is, until you realize that the **San Andreas Fault**, the global suture that shook San Francisco back in 1906, cuts through the valley. Matter of fact, the highway you are traveling parallels the fault line. During the great quake, houses collapsed, trees were uprooted and fences decided to mark new boundaries.

POINT REYES NATIONAL SEASHORE   One of the finest seaside parks in the world, **Point Reyes National Seashore** is a realm of sand dunes and endless beaches, Scottish moors and grassy hillsides, salt marshes and pine forests. Bobcats, mountain lions, fox and elk inhabit its wrinkled terrain, while harbor seals and gray whales cruise its ragged shoreline. It supports dairies and cattle ranches.

The first stage in exploring this multifeatured preserve involves a stop at the **Bear Valley Visitor Center** (415-663-1092). Here you can obtain maps, information and camping permits. A short hike from the center will lead you to a **Miwok Indian Village**, where the round-domed shelters of the area's early inhabitants have been re-created.

Like the information center, most points of interest lie along Sir Francis Drake Boulevard. It will carry you past the tiny town of Inverness, with its country inns and ridgetop houses, then out along Tomales Bay.

Deeper in the park, a side road twists up to **Mount Vision Overlook**, where vista points sweep the peninsula. At **Johnson's Oyster Farm** (415-669-1149), along another side road, workers harvest the rich beds of an estuary. Raw oysters are for sale here, and you are also welcome to visit the farm.

Chimney Rock, a sea stack islet, stands at one end of Point Reyes' hammerhead peninsula. On your way you'll pass an **overlook** that's ideal for watching sea lions; then from Chimney Rock, if the day is clear, you'll see all the way to San Francisco.

At the other tip is **Point Reyes Lighthouse** (415-669-1534), an 1870s–era beacon located at the foggiest point on the entire Pacific coast. The treacherous waters offshore have witnessed numerous shipwrecks, the first occurring way back in 1595. The original lighthouse,

---

BOLINAS

*Pay close attention. You'll have to if you want to find one quaint town that hides off Route 1. That would be **Bolinas**, subject of a book called* The Town That Saved Itself, *a place I prefer to call "The Town That Loves Itself." To get there as you travel north on Route 1, watch for the crossroad at the foot of Bolinas Lagoon; go left, then quickly left again and follow the road along the other side of the lagoon; take another left at the end of the road.*

There probably won't be any signs to direct you. It seems that local residents subscribe to the philosophy that since Bolinas is beautiful and they got there first, they should keep everyone else out. They tear down road signs and discourage visitors.

*The place they are attempting to hide is a delightful little town that rises from an S-shaped beach to form a lofty mesa. There are country roads along the bluff and a beautiful strand, **Bolinas Lagoon Beach**, that curves around the town's perimeter. Houses here display a wild architectural array of domes, glass boxes, curved-roof creations and huts.*

*Abutting on the Point Reyes National Seashore, Bolinas is also a gateway to the natural world. Follow Mesa Road for several miles outside town and you'll encounter the **Point Reyes Bird Observatory**, where a research station studies a bird population of over 350 species.*

*On the way back to town take a right on Overlook Drive, then a right on Elm Road; follow it to the parking lot at road's end. Hiking trails lead down a sharp 160-foot cliff to **Duxbury Reef**, a mile-long shale reef. Tidepool-watching is great sport here at low tide: starfish, periwinkles, limpets and a host of other clinging creatures inhabit the marine preserve. Just north of this rocky preserve is **Agate Beach**, an ideal spot to find agates, driftwood and glass balls (no collecting permitted).*

constructed to prevent these calamities, incorporated over 1000 pieces of crystal in its intricate lens. A modern beacon eventually replaced it, but the old lighthouse is still open to the public.

Back in Olema, Route 1 continues north along Tomales Bay, a lovely fjord-shaped inlet. Salt marshes stretch along one side of the road; on the other are rumpled hills tufted with grass. The waterfront village of **Marshall** consists of fishing boats moored offshore and woodframe houses anchored firmly onshore. Then the road turns inland to **Tomales**, another falsefront town with clapboard church and country homes. It continues past paint-peeled barns and open pastureland before turning seaward at Bodega Bay.

MARIN COAST LODGING

At **The Pelican Inn** (Route 1, Muir Beach; 415-383-6000) guests consider the coastal fog part of the ambience, a final element in the Old English atmosphere at this seven-chamber bed and breakfast. The Tudor-style inn re-creates 16th-century England. There's a pub complete with dart board and a dining room serving such country fare as meat pies. One bedroom contains a canopied bed and a wooden chest that looks to have barely survived its Atlantic crossing. Highly recommended; reserve well in advance; deluxe.

As country living goes, it's darn near impossible to find a place as pretty and restful as Point Reyes. Not surprisingly, country inns have sprung up to cater to imaginative travelers. Seven have formed an information service, **The Inns of Point Reyes** (415-663-1420). You can also contact **Coastal Lodging of West Marin** (415-663-1351), a telephone service providing information on cottages, guest homes and inns in the Point Reyes area.

Foremost among this bed-and-breakfast confederacy is **Blackthorne Inn** (266 Vallejo Avenue, Inverness Park; 415-663-8621), an architectural extravaganza set in a forest of oak and Douglas fir. The four-level house features a maze of skylights, bay windows and french doors, capped by an octagonal tower. On the top deck, both a hot and cold tub are available to guests. There are five personalized bedrooms, two with private baths. Deluxe to ultra-deluxe.

Another favorite bed and breakfast lies along the flagstone path at **Ten Inverness Way** (10 Inverness Way, Inverness; 415-669-1648). The place is filled with pleasant surprises, like fruit trees in the yard, a player piano and a warm living room with stone fireplace. The four bedrooms are small but cozy and imaginatively decorated with hand-fashioned quilts. Deluxe.

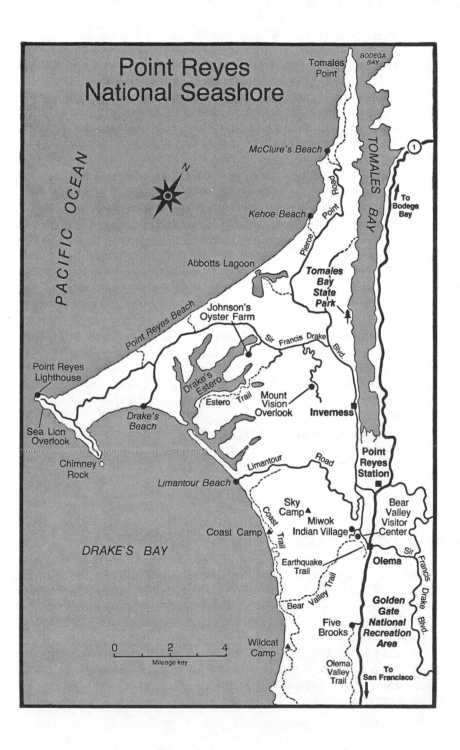

Point Reyes National Seashore

BODEGA BAY

Tomales Point

PACIFIC OCEAN

McClure's Beach

TOMALES BAY

①

To Bodega Bay

Kehoe Beach

Pierce Point Road

Abbotts Lagoon

Tomales Bay State Park

Point Reyes Beach

Johnson's Oyster Farm

Sir Francis Drake Blvd.

Point Reyes Lighthouse

Drake's Estero

Estero Trail

Mount Vision Overlook

Inverness

Sea Lion Overlook

Drake's Beach

Chimney Rock

Point Reyes Station

Limantour Road

Limantour Beach

DRAKE'S BAY

Sky Camp

Miwok Indian Village

Bear Valley Visitor Center

Coast Camp

Coast Trail

Earthquake Trail

Olema

Sir Francis Drake Blvd.

Bear Valley Trail

Golden Gate National Recreation Area

Five Brooks

Wildcat Camp

Olema Valley Trail

To San Francisco

0   2   4
Mileage key

MARIN COAST RESTAURANTS

My favorite Stinson Beach eatery is the **Sand Dollar Restaurant** (3458 Route 1; 415-868-0434), where you can dine indoors or on the patio. This local gathering point serves hamburgers and sandwiches at lunch and fresh fish and meat dishes at dinner. Moderate.

Inverness Inn Restaurant (Sir Francis Drake Boulevard and Inverness Way, Inverness; 415-669-1109) has a wide array of dishes. The lunch menu features sandwiches and omelettes. At dinner there are oysters from local beds, chicken and prawn dishes, lamb chops, pastas and fresh fish; moderate.

Highly recommended by locals, the **Station House Cafe** (Main Street, Point Reyes Station; 415-663-1515) has wood paneling and a down-home feel. But it's the food that draws folks from the surrounding countryside. The menu includes fresh oysters, chicken, steak and fish dishes, plus daily chef's specials such as salmon with a dill-smoked salmon sauce. Moderate.

MARIN COAST SHOPPING

Stinson Beach Books (Route 1, Stinson Beach; 415-868-0700) may be located in a small town, but it handles a large variety of books, from travel to best sellers to how-to handbooks.

Gallery Route One (11431 Route 1, Point Reyes Station; 415-663-1347) spotlights paintings, sculptures, photography and by contemporary artists.

Shaker Shops West (5 Inverness Way, Inverness; 415-669-7256) is a marvelous store specializing in reproductions of Shaker arts and crafts, including furniture, rag rugs and beautifully handcrafted boxes. Touring the store is like visiting a minimuseum dedicated to this rare American community.

MARIN COAST NIGHTLIFE

When the sun goes down in Bolinas, you are left with several options. Sleep, read, curl up with a loved one or head for **Smiley's Schooner Saloon** (41 Wharf Road; 415-868-1311). You'll find local folks parka-to-parka along the lavish wood-paneled bar or shooting pool. Occasional live music.

Local folks in Point Reyes Station ease up to a similar wooden bar at **Western Saloon** (Route 1; 415-663-1661). On every other Friday or Saturday, when the place features dancing 'til the wee hours, the biggest crowds arrive.

MARIN COAST BEACHES AND PARKS

A broad sandy swath, **Rodeo Beach** (415-331-1540) is magnificent not only for the surrounding hillsides and nearby cliffs, but also for the quiescent lagoon at its back. A favorite among San Franciscans, it boasts a miniature island offshore. Located along Bunker Road in the Marin Headlands section of the Golden Gate National Recreation Area.

Spectacularly situated between Mt. Tamalpais and the ocean, the 6400-acre **Mt. Tamalpais State Park** offers everything from mountaintop views to a rocky coastline. Thirty miles of hiking trails wind past stands of cypress, Douglas fir and Monterey pine. The countryside draws nature lovers and sightseers alike. Camping is permitted.

One of Northern California's finest beaches, the broad, sandy corridor of **Stinson Beach Park** (415-556-0734) curves for three miles. Backdropped by rolling hills, Stinson also borders beautiful Bolinas Lagoon. Besides being a sunbather's haven, it's a great place for beachcombers and birdwatchers. Stroll up to the north end of the beach to escape the crowds on weekends. Located along Route 1.

Situated several miles inland, **Samuel P. Taylor State Park** (415-488-9897) provides an opportunity to experience the coastal interior. The place is heavily wooded and offers 2600 acres to roam. In addition to the campgrounds, there are hiking trails and swimming holes. Located on Sir Francis Drake Highway, east of Route 1 and five miles from Olema.

POINT REYES BEACHES AND PARKS   The white-sand **Limantour Beach** is actually a spit, a narrow peninsula pressed between

---

DRAKE'S BEACH

*Edged by cliffs, the crescent-shaped **Drake's Beach** looks out upon the tip of Point Reyes. Since it's well protected by Drake's Bay, this is a good swimming spot. It also provides interesting hikes along the base of the cliffs to the inlet at Drake's Estero.*

As you gaze up at those cliffs, you might wonder whether they truly resemble the White Cliffs of Dover. In that question resides a story told by one school of historians and vehemently denied by others. It seems that in 1579 the English explorer Sir Francis Drake anchored somewhere along the Northern California coast. But where? Some claim he cast anchor right here in Drake's Bay, others say Bolinas Lagoon, even San Francisco Bay. A brass plate, purportedly left by Drake, was discovered near San Francisco Bay in 1936 but later was deemed a counterfeit.

Located off Sir Francis Drake Boulevard 15 miles from the headquarters of Point Reyes National Seashore.

Drake's Bay and an estuary. It's an exotic area of sand dunes and sea breezes. Ideal for exploring, the region shelters over 350 bird species. Once in Point Reyes National Seashore, follow Limantour Road to the end.

The delightful **Tomales Bay State Park** (415-669-1140), which abuts Point Reyes National Seashore, provides a warm, sunny alternative to Point Reyes' frequent fog. The water, too, is warmer here, making it a great place for swimming, as well as fishing and boating. Rimming the park are several sandy coves, and hiking trails lead to other secluded beaches. Located on Pierce Point Road in Point Reyes National Seashore.

Of the many beautiful beaches hereabouts, **McClure's Beach** is by far my favorite. It is a white-sand beach protected by granite cliffs standing like bookends on either flank. Tidepool watching, as well as birdwatching and driftwood gathering, are popular sports here. Located at the end of Pierce Point Road. A steep trail leads a half-mile down to the beach.

It will become wonderfully evident why **Point Reyes Beach** (also referred to as North Beach and South Beach) is nicknamed "Ten Mile Beach" when you cast eyes on this endless sand swath. It's a great place for whale watching, beachcombing, fishing and enjoying the wild beauty of Point Reyes. At its northern end lies **Kehoe Beach**, covered with wildflowers in spring and boasting a seasonal lagoon. Located off Sir Francis Drake Boulevard about 14 miles from park headquarters.

Sonoma Coast

Route 1 twists along the Sonoma County coast past cliffside vista points, rugged shorelines and antique towns dating back to the mid-19th century. State beaches cover nearly the entire length of coastline, which remains largely undeveloped and inhabited primarily by anglers and shorebirds.

Placid range land extends inward, while along the shoreline surf boils against angular cliffs. Far below are pocket beaches and coves; offshore rise dozens of tiny rock islands, or sea stacks. Rip currents, sneaker waves and the coldest waters this side of the Arctic make swimming inadvisable. But the landscape is wide open for exploration, enchanting and exotic.

First point along the way is the fishing village of **Bodega Bay**. The town might look vaguely familiar, for it was the setting of Alfred Hitchcock's eerie film *The Birds*. It's questionable whether any cast members remain among the current population of snowy egrets, brown pelicans and blue herons.

A bit farther north, the Russian River surges into the Pacific. In 1812, the Russians for whom the river is named built **Fort Ross**, a wooden fortress overlooking the sea, at a point north of this watery meeting ground. The old Russian stronghold, 13 miles north of Jenner, is today a state historic park (707-847-3286; admission). Touring the reconstructed fort, you'll encounter a museum, an old Russian Orthodox chapel and a stockade built of hand-tooled redwood. Together they provide an insight into an unusual chapter in California history.

From Jenner north through Fort Ross and beyond, Route 1 winds high above the coast. Every curve exposes another awesome view of adze-like cliffs slicing into the sea. Driving this corkscrew route can jangle the nerves, but the vistas are soothing to the soul. You'll pass sunbleached wooden buildings in the old town of Stewart Point. Then the road courses through **Sea Ranch**, a development bitterly opposed by environmentalists, that nevertheless displays imaginative contemporary-design houses set against a stark sea.

WHALE WATCHING

It is the world's longest mammal migration: 6000 miles along the Pacific coast from the Bering Sea to Baja California, then back again. The creatures making the journey measure 50 feet and weigh 40 tons. During the entire course of their incredible voyage they neither eat nor sleep.

Every year from mid-December through early February, the California gray whale cruises southward along the California coast. Traveling in "pods" numbering three to five, these magnificent creatures hug the shoreline en route to their breeding grounds.

Since the whales use local coves and promontories to navigate, they are easy to spot from land. Just watch for the rolling hump, the slapping tail or a lofty spout of spurning water. Sometimes these huge creatures will breach, leaping 30 feet above the surface, then crashing back with a thunderous splash.

California gray whales live to 40 or 50 years and have a world population numbering about 17,000. Their only enemies are killer whales and humans. They mate during the southern migration one year, then give birth at the end of the following year's migration. The calves, born in the warm, shallow waters of Baja, weigh a ton and measure about 16 feet. By the time they are weaned seven months later, the young are already 26 feet long.

*Blue whales, humpback whales, dolphins and porpoises also sometimes visit the coast. Gray whales can be seen again from March through mid-May, though farther from shore, during their return migration north. Several outfits sponsor whale-watching cruises: these include **Oceanic Society Expeditions** (San Francisco; 415-474-3385), **New Sea Angler & Jaws** (Box 1148, Bodega Bay; 707-875-3495) and **King Salmon Charters** (3458 Utah Street, Eureka; 707-442-3474).*

Just north of Point Arena a side road from Route 1 leads out to **Point Arena Lighthouse** (707-882-2777; admission). The original lighthouse, built in 1870, was destroyed in the 1906 San Francisco earthquake, which struck Point Arena even more fiercely than the bay city. The present beacon, rebuilt shortly afterward, rises 115 feet from a narrow peninsula. The lighthouse is open for tours. The views, by definition, are outstanding.

SONOMA COAST LODGING

A prime Jenner resting spot is **Murphy's Jenner by the Sea** (Route 1, Jenner; 707-865-2377), a bed and breakfast overlooking the river. Several buildings comprise Murphy's spread: you can rent a room, a suite, even a house. Prices start in the moderate range. Less expensive accommodations may feature a quilted bed and a deck overlooking the river, while higher-priced suites might add a living room with a wood stove and antique rocker.

Accessible via a scenic country lane, **Timberhill Ranch** (35755 Hauser Bridge Road, Cazadero; 707-847-3258) is as serene and simple a resort as you'll find anywhere in California. Ten handmade cedar cabins dot the forested hillside property, each with cozy quilts, fireplaces and decks where you can enjoy breakfast . . . or share it with the resident ducks. Tennis courts, a pool and a jacuzzi with a view may be enough to keep guests ranch-bound for days. Ultra-deluxe prices include breakfast and dinner, the last a multicourse gourmet affair in the main lodge.

Several lodges along the California coast reflect in their architecture the raw energy and naked beauty of the surrounding sea. Such a one is **Timber Cove Inn** (21780 North Route 1, 15 miles north of Jenner; 707-847-3231), a labyrinth of unfinished woods and bald rocks. The heavy timber lobby is dominated by a walk-in stone fireplace and sits astride a Japanese pond. The 50 guest rooms are stark but afford marvelous views of the mountains and open sea. Many have decks, fireplaces and hot tubs. Deluxe to ultra-deluxe.

SONOMA COAST RESTAURANTS

In Jenner the best bet for an economical meal is **Bridgehaven Restaurant** (Route 1, Jenner; 707-865-2095), a comfortable place with plate-glass views of the Russian River. The many breakfast selections, hamburgers and club sandwiches are the budget-minded diner's wisest choice. Lunch entrées like lasagna and such dinner dishes as oysters or pork chops are moderately tabbed.

For the best meal hereabouts head for **River's End Restaurant** (Route 1, Jenner; 707-865-2484). Situated at that momentous crossroad of the Russian River and Pacific Ocean (and commanding a view of both), this outstanding little place is a restaurant with imagination. The dinner menu ranges from *médaillons* of venison to coconut-fried shrimp. Deluxe in quality and price.

Salt Point Lodge (23255 Route 1; 707-847-3234), 17 miles north of Jenner, features a small, moderate-priced restaurant. The menu relies heavily on seafood—halibut, oysters, scallops—but also includes chicken and steak dishes.

SONOMA COAST BEACHES AND PARKS

The pocket beaches at **Bodega Head State Park** (707-875-2640) are dramatically backdropped by granite cliffs. A good place to picnic and explore, this is also a favored whale-watching site. Located off Route 1 in Bodega Bay along Bay Flat Road.

The magnificent **Sonoma Coast State Beach** (information at Salmon Creek Beach, 707-865-2391) extends for 13 miles between Bodega Head and the Russian River. It consists of a number of beaches separated by steep headlands; all are within easy hiking distance of Route 1. The beaches range from sweeping strands to pocket coves and abound with waterfowl and shorebirds, clams and abalone. Pick your favorite—hiking, tidepooling, birdwatching, camping, picnicking, fishing—and you'll find it waiting along this rugged and hauntingly beautiful coastline. Located along Route 1 between Bodega Bay and Jenner.

Extending from the ocean to over 1000 feet elevation, the 6000-acre **Salt Point State Park** (707-847-3221) includes coastline, forests and open rangeland. Along the shore are weird honeycomb formations called tafoni, caused by sea erosion of coastal sandstone. There's also a pygmy forest, where fully mature redwoods reach only a few feet in height. Blacktail deer, wild pig and bobcat roam the area. Camping. Located on Route 1 about 18 miles north of Jenner.

Mendocino Coast

In Mendocino County, the highway passes through tiny seaside villages. Elk, Albion and Little River gaze down on the ocean from rocky heights. The coastline is an intaglio of river valleys, pocket beaches and narrow coves. Forested ridges, soft and green in appearance, fall away into dizzying cliffs.

The houses hereabouts resemble Maine saltboxes and Cape Cod cottages. In the town of **Mendocino**, which sits on a headland above the sea, you'll discover New England incarnate. Settled in 1852, the town was built largely by Yankees who decorated their village with wooden towers, Victorian homes and a Gothic revival Presbyterian church. The town, originally a vital lumber port, has become an artists' colony. With a shoreline honeycombed by beaches and a villagescape capped with a white church steeple, Mendocino is a mighty pretty corner of the continent.

The best way to experience this antique town is by stopping at the **Kelley House Museum** (45007 Albion Street; 707-937-5791; admission). Set in a vintage home built in 1861, the museum serves as a historical society and unofficial chamber of commerce.

Among Mendocino's other intriguing locales are the **Chinese Temple** (Albion Street), a 19th-century religious shrine, and the **Masonic Hall** (Ukiah Street), an 1865 structure adorned with a cupola. Also be sure to visit the **Ford House** (Main Street; 707-937-5397), an 1854 home with a small museum and visitor center.

North of town, on the way to Fort Bragg, stop at **Jug Handle State Reserve** (along Route 1 about one mile north of Caspar; 707-937-5804). Here you can climb an ecological stairway, a series of marine terraces that feature the coast, dune and ridge environments forming this area's diverse ecosystem.

Near the center of Fort Bragg you can board the **Skunk train** for a half- or full-day ride aboard a steam engine or a diesel-powered railroad. Dating back to 1885, the Skunk was originally a logging train; today it also carries passengers along a 40-mile route through mountains and redwoods to the inland town of Willits. For information, contact California Western Railroad (707-964-6371) in Fort Bragg.

MENDOCINO COAST LODGING

The **Old Milano Hotel** (38300 Route 1, Gualala; 707-884-3256), dating from 1905, is one of those very special places that people return to year after year. The two-story shiplap house, a registered historic place, rises between a delicately tended garden and the sea. Each of the

---

MENDOCINO COAST BOTANICAL GARDENS

*For a thoroughly delightful stroll to the sea, meander through the **Mendocino Coast Botanical Gardens** (18220 North Route 1, Fort Bragg; 707-964-4352; admission). This coastal preserve, with two miles of luxuriant pathways, is "a garden for all seasons" with something always in bloom—colorful heathers and rhododendrons as well as ivy, ferns and drawf conifers. Trails follow a coastal bluff with vistas up and down the rugged shoreline.*

six bedrooms upstairs has been furnished and decorated with lovely antiques: oil paintings, brass lamps and plump armchairs. Deluxe to ultra-deluxe.

Among the more renowned of this area's country inns is **Harbor House** (5600 South Route 1, Elk; 707-877-3203). Set on a rise overlooking the ocean, the house is built entirely of redwood. The living room alone, with its unique fireplace and exposed-beam ceiling, is an architectural feat. Of the ten bedrooms and cottages, several have Potter stoves or fireplaces and antique appointments. Ultra-deluxe; breakfast and dinner included.

Heritage House (5200 South Route 1, Little River; 707-937-5885) was constructed in 1877 and reflects the New England architecture popular then in Northern California. Baby Face Nelson is reputed to have hidden in the old farmhouse that today serves as the inn's reception and dining area. Most guests are housed in nearby cottages that overlook a rocky cove. Deluxe to ultra-deluxe, including breakfast and dinner.

The New England-style farmhouse that has become **Glendeven** (Route 1, Little River; 707-937-0083) dates back to 1867. The theme is country living, with a meadow out back and a comfortable sitting room warmed by a brick fireplace. In the rooms you're apt to find a bed with wooden headboard and an antique wardrobe. As charming and intimate as a country inn can be. Moderate to deluxe; light breakfast.

Set in a falsefront 1878 building, the **Mendocino Hotel** (45080 Main Street, Mendocino; 707-937-0511) has 51 quarters with shared bath at moderate cost (deluxe in summer). It's a wonderful place, larger than other nearby country inns, with a wood-paneled lobby, full dining room and living quarters adorned with antiques. Rooms in the garden cottages out back range upward from deluxe price (ultra-deluxe in summer).

The queen of Mendocino is the **MacCallum House** (45020 Albion Street; 707-937-0289), a gingerbread Victorian built in 1882. The place is a treasure trove of antique furnishings, knickknacks and other memorabilia. Many of the rooms are individually decorated with rocking chairs, quilts and wood stoves. Positively everything—the carriage house, barn, gazebo, even the water tower—has been converted into a guest room. Moderate to deluxe; continental breakfast.

Also consider **Mendocino Village Inn** (44860 Main Street, Mendocino; 707-937-0246), a vintage 1882 house that has two attic rooms, one with a sea view, in the moderate price range. A white shingle-and-clapboard building with mansard roof, the place offers spacious accommodations with private baths at moderate to deluxe prices. In a land of pricey hotels, this represents a rare discovery (full breakfast included).

MENDOCINO COAST RESTAURANTS

Okay, so **St. Orres** (36601 Route 1, Gualala; 707-884-3303) is yet another California cuisine restaurant. But it's the only one you'll see that looks as though it should be in Russia, not along the California coast. With its dizzying spires, this elegant structure evokes images of Moscow and old St. Petersburg. Serving dinner only, the kitchen provides an evolving menu of fresh game and fish dishes. Ultra-deluxe.

The **Albion River Inn** (3790 North Route 1, Albion; 707-937-4044), set high on a hillside above the Albion River and the ocean, is a plate-glass dining spot serving California cuisine. The pasta, seafood, vegetables and herbs are all fresh. Dinner only; moderate.

I'm told that the **Little River Restaurant** (7750 North Route 1, Little River; 707-937-4945) is an absolute must. It's only open Friday through Monday for dinner, and has but a half-dozen tables. The California cuisine includes roast duck with apricot-vermouth sauce and rack of lamb smeared with apple brandy and garlic. Moderate to deluxe.

In Mendocino, moderate prices went out when the flood of tourists came in. Over at **The Sea Gull** (Lansing and Ukiah streets; 707-937-2100) you can still order solid meals at reasonable prices. The menu is a standard blend of fresh seafood, meat and poultry dishes. With a knotty-pine interior and nautical decor, The Sea Gull is inviting.

For French and California cuisine, **955 Ukiah** (955 Ukiah Street, Mendocino; 707-937-1955) is an address worth noting. Candles, fresh flowers and impressionist prints set the tone at this moderate-priced restaurant. Serving dinner only, it prepares brandied prawns, red snapper in filo pastry, roast duck and calamari.

MENDOCINO COAST SHOPPING

Mendocino is a shopper's paradise. Prices are quite dear, but the window browsing is unparalleled among the creative shops housed in the town's old Victorians and Cape Cod cottages.

CAFE BEAUJOLAIS

*Mendocino's best-known dining room is well deserving of its renown. **Cafe Beaujolais** (961 Ukiah Street; 707-937-5614), situated in a small antique house on the edge of town, serves designer dishes. Breakfast and lunch alone are culinary occasions, with the afternoon menu including Mendocino fish stew and cold poached salmon. Dinner is less predictable given the ever-changing menu. Perhaps they'll be serving sautéed trout with Szechuan peppercorns or steamed salmon with chervil beurre blanc sauce. Excellent cuisine; ultra-deluxe.*

Particularly noteworthy among the galleries are **Gallery Fair** (Kasten and Ukiah streets; 707-937-5121) and **Highlight Gallery** (45052 Main Street; 707-937-3132), with their displays of handmade furniture, contemporary art, jewelry and woodwork, and the **Mendocino Art Center** (45200 Little Lake Street; 707-937-5818), which has numerous craft studios as well as an art gallery.

MENDOCINO COAST NIGHTLIFE

The **Top of the Gull** (Lansing and Ukiah streets, Mendocino; 707-937-2100), upstairs in the Sea Gull Restaurant, has various ensembles performing Friday and Saturday nights.

Or enjoy a quiet drink at the **Mendocino Hotel** (45080 Main Street, Mendocino; 707-937-0511) in the Victorian-style lounge or enclosed garden patio.

There's music seven nights a week at the **Caspar Inn** (Caspar Road, Caspar; 707-964-5565). This down-home barroom spotlights local and outside bands. Hit it on the right night and the joint will be rocking.

MENDOCINO COAST BEACHES AND PARKS

Located where the Gualala River meets the ocean, **Gualala Point Regional Park** (707-785-2377) is a charming place that has everything from sandy beach to campgrounds to redwood groves. Located along Route 1 due south of Gualala.

Wild, windswept **Manchester State Beach** (707-937-5804) extends for miles along the Mendocino coast. Piled deep with driftwood, it's excellent for beachcombing, camping and hiking. Located along Route 1 about eight miles north of Point Arena.

Extending from the beach to an interior forest, the 2069-acre **Van Damme State Park** (707-937-5804) has a "pygmy forest" where pine trees reach heights of only six inches to eight feet, a "fern canyon" and a "cabbage patch" filled with that fetid critter with elephant ear leaves—skunk cabbage. This park is also laced with hiking trails and offers excellent beachcombing opportunities. Camping. Located on Route 1 about 30 miles north of Point Arena.

Mendocino Headlands and **Big River Beach State Parks** form the seaside border of the town of Mendocino. And quite a border it is. The white-sand beaches are only part of the natural splendor. There are also wave tunnels, tidepools, sea arches, lagoons and 360° vistas that sweep from the surf-trimmed shore to the prim villagescape of Mendocino.

Set in a narrow valley with a well-protected beach, **Russian Gulch State Park** (707-937-5804) offers marvelous views from the craggy headlands, as well as coastal pines, a waterfall and a blowhole that rarely blows. Rainbow and steelhead trout inhabit the creek, while hawks and ravens circle the forest. Camping is permitted. Located along Route 1 just north of Mendocino.

Another outstanding spot, **MacKerricher State Park** (707-937-5804) features a crescent of sandy beach, dunes, headlands, a lake, forest and wetlands. Harbor seals inhabit the rocks offshore, and over 90 bird species frequent the area. Camping. Located along Route 1 about three miles north of Fort Bragg.

Redwood Country

California's vaunted **Redwood Country** is the habitat of *Sequoia sempervirens*, the coastal redwood, a tree whose ancestors date to the age of dinosaurs and that happens to be the world's tallest living thing. These "ambassadors from another time," as John Steinbeck called them, inhabit a 30-mile-wide coastal fog belt stretching 450 miles from the Monterey area north to Oregon. Redwoods live five to eight centuries, though some have survived over two millennia, while reaching heights over 350 feet and diameters greater than 20 feet.

There is a sense of solitude here uncaptured anywhere else. The trees form a cathedral overhead, casting a deep shade across the forest floor. Solitary sun shafts, almost palpable, cut through the grove; along the roof of the forest, pieces of light jump across the treetops, poised to fall like rain. Ferns and a few small animals are all that survive here. The silence and stillness are either transcendent or terrifying. It's like being at sea in a small boat.

The Redwood Highway, Route 101, leads north to the tallest and densest stands of *Sequoia sempervirens*. At **Richardson Grove State Park** the road barrels through the very center of a magnificent grove.

North of Garberville, follow the **Avenue of the Giants**, a 33-mile alternative route that parallels Route 101. This two-lane road winds along the South Fork of the Eel River, tunneling through thick redwood groves. Much of the road is encompassed by **Humboldt Redwoods State Park**, a 50,000-acre preserve with some of the finest forest land found anywhere. Park headquarters contains a visitor center (707-946-2311).

Farther along is **Founder's Grove**, where a nature trail loops through a redwood stand. Nearby **Rockefeller Forest** has another short loop trail leading to a 362-foot goliath, the tallest tree in the area.

After meandering through this imposing landscape, Route 101 reaches Eureka, whose 25,000 inhabitants make it the largest town on the Northern California coast. Founded in 1850, the town's first industry was mining. Today fishing and lumbering have replaced more romantic occupations, but much of the region's history is captured in points of interest. Stop at the **Chamber of Commerce** (2112 Broad-

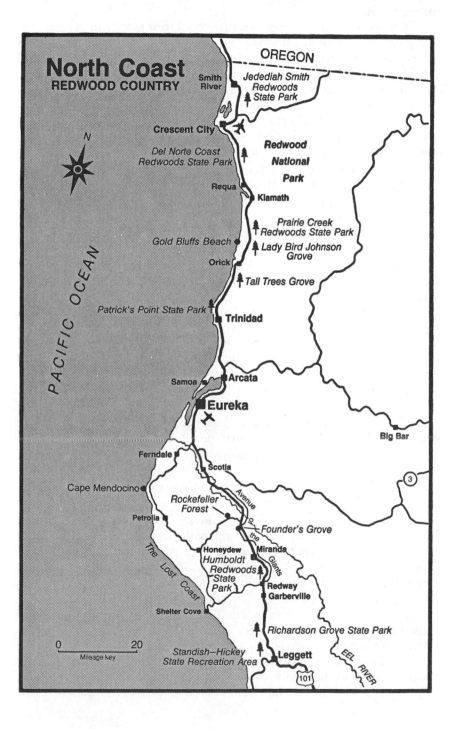

North Coast
REDWOOD COUNTRY

OREGON

Smith River

Jedediah Smith Redwoods State Park

N

Crescent City

Del Norte Coast Redwoods State Park

Redwood National Park

Requa

Klamath

Prairie Creek Redwoods State Park

Gold Bluffs Beach

Lady Bird Johnson Grove

Orick

PACIFIC OCEAN

Tall Trees Grove

Patrick's Point State Park

Trinidad

Samoa

Arcata

Eureka

Big Bar

Ferndale

Scotia

3

Cape Mendocino

Rockefeller Forest

Avenue

Petrolia

Founder's Grove

of

the

Honeydew

Miranda

Humboldt Redwoods State Park

Giants

The Lost Coast

Redway

Garberville

Shelter Cove

Richardson Grove State Park

0   20
Mileage key

Standish–Hickey State Recreation Area

Leggett

EEL RIVER

101

way; 707-442-3738) on the way into town for maps, brochures and information.

Make certain to ask for the architectural tour map. Eureka has over 100 glorious **Victorian homes** ranging from understated designs to the outlandish **Carson Mansion** (2nd and M streets), a multilayered confection that makes other Gothic architecture seem tame.

Of a more subdued nature are the **covered bridges** on the southern outskirts of town. To reach them from Route 101, take Elk River Road two miles to Berta Road or three miles to Zanes Road (there is a wooden span covering both). You'll enter a picture of red barns and green pasture framed by cool, lofty forest.

Fort Humboldt (3431 Fort Avenue; 707-445-6567) is also stationed at this end of town. Built in the early 1850s to help settlers war against indigenous tribes of Yurok, Hoopa and Mattole Indians, it has been partially restored. In addition to re-creating army life (experienced here by a hard-drinking young officer named Ulysses S. Grant), the historic park displays early logging traditions.

Then head to **Old Town**, Eureka's answer to the nation's gentrification craze. This neighborhood was formerly the local bowery; the term "skid row" reputedly originated right here. It derived from the bums residing beside the nearby "skid trails," along which redwood logs were transported to the waterfront. Now the ghetto is gilded: old Victorians, woodframe warehouses, brick buildings and clapboard houses have been rebuilt and painted striking colors. Stylish shops have sprung up, and restaurants have opened.

At the foot of C Street in Old Town, where the bowery meets the bay, the **Humboldt Bay Harbor Cruise** (707-445-1910) departs. For several well-invested dollars, you'll sail past an egret rookery, pelican roosts and the town's flashy new marina.

If you're a landlubber, however, and prefer a shoreside tour of Eureka, you can always take a horse-and-buggy ride. The **Old Town Carriage Company** (707-442-7264) has turn-of-the-century reproduction carriages pulled by massive horses.

Last, but in my heart first, is **Clarke Museum** (240 E Street; 707-443-1947), with its outstanding collection of California Indian artifacts. Here are ornate baskets, feather regalia and a dugout redwood canoe. It provides a unique insight into this splendid Humboldt Bay region before the age of gold pans and axe handles.

Just ten miles from Eureka you'll find **Ferndale**, a Victorian-style hamlet set in the Eel River valley. Like a town under glass, a living museum, this quaint community is so perfectly refurbished it seems unreal. Main Street and nearby thoroughfares are lined with Gothic revival, Queen Anne, Eastlake and Italianate-style Victorians, brightly painted and blooming with pride. The best way to see the town is by stopping first at the **Ferndale Museum** (515 Shaw Avenue; 707-786-

4466; admission). Here is an ever-changing collection of antiques and memorabilia from the region, plus an old blacksmith shop. There are also maps available for self-guided walking tours of this historic community. It's an architectural wonder that shouldn't be missed.

Heading north from Eureka, you'll find two towns worth noting. **Arcata**, home of Humboldt State University, is a student town with an outstanding collection of old Victorians. For a self-guided architectural tour, obtain a map at the **Chamber of Commerce** (1062 G Street; 707-822-3619).

Trinidad, one of the area's oldest towns, perches above a small port. Sea stacks and sailboats lie anchored offshore, watched over by a miniature lighthouse. For a tour of the pocket beaches and rocky shores lining this beautiful waterfront, take a three-mile trip south from town along Scenic Drive.

THE LOST COAST

*After following the coast all the way from Southern California, Route 1 abruptly relinquishes its seaside perch and turns inward at a point near Leggett. The reason is the mysterious **Lost Coast of California**.*

Along this coast, where no highway could possibly run, the King Range vaults out of the sea, rising over 4000 feet in less than three miles. It is a wilderness inhabited by black bears and bald eagles, with an abandoned lighthouse and a solitary beach piled with ancient Indian shell mounds. From the beach, seals, sea lions, dolphins and whales can be seen. One of the wettest areas along the Pacific Coast, the King Range receives about 100 inches of rain annually. But it's a fascinating area for hiking and exploring.

To reach this region, from Route 101 near Redway take Briceland-Thorne Road, which turns into Shelter Cove Road as its winds through the King Range.

Shelter Cove *is a tiny bay neatly folded between sea cliffs and headlands. A point of embarkation for people exploring the Lost Coast, it has a few stores, restaurants and hotels. To the north rest the general-store town of **Honeydew**, where a colony of hippies is bound to be sitting on the stoop swapping tales, and the forest hamlet of **Petrolia**. Nestled in a river valley and marked by a white-steeple church, the town is a scene straight from a Norman Rockwell painting.*

Next, along Mattole Road, you'll ascend a succession of plateaus to a ranch-land of unpainted barns and broad shade trees, then nose down to the coastline and parallel the waves for perhaps five miles. Here the setting is Scottish. Hillsides are grazed by herds of sheep and covered with tenacious grasses that shake in the sea wind. The gray sand beach is covered with driftwood. Along the horizon peaks rise in jagged motions, seemingly thrust upward by the lash or the surf.

*It's not far to **Cape Mendocino**, most westerly point in the contiguous United States. Here you'll have broad views of the ocean, including the menacing shoals where countless ships have been slapped to timber.*

REDWOOD COUNTRY LODGING

One of Northern California's finest old lodges is the imposing, Tudor-style **Benbow Inn** (445 Lake Benbow Drive, Garberville; 707-923-2124). Located astride a shimmering lake, this regal retreat is bounded by lawns, gardens and umbrella-tabled patios. The lobby, paneled in carved wood and adorned by ornamental molding, is a sumptuous sitting area with a grand fireplace. Guest quarters offer such flourishes as quilted beds with wooden headboards, hand-painted doors and marble-topped nightstands. Deluxe.

Miranda Gardens Resort (Avenue of the Giants, Miranda; 707-943-3011) is a good choice among the many motels along redwood-lined Avenue of the Giants. The 16 accommodations include rooms with kitchens and fully equipped cabins at moderate to deluxe cost. The place features a heated swimming pool, shuffleboard, playground and market. The facilities are tucked into a redwood grove, and the rooms are paneled entirely in redwood.

In Eureka, a town chockablock with precious Victorians, one of the most precious of all is **The Gingerbread Mansion** (400 Berding Street; 707-786-4000). Turrets and gables, an intimate garden, interesting antiques and delicious homemade delectables are among the features; but what you'll find particularly special about this bed and breakfast inn are the bathrooms. One has mirrored ceilings and walls; another, his-and-hers clawfoot tubs set near a Franklin stove. Nine distinct accommodations are comfortably cozy. Deluxe to ultra-deluxe.

Mark and Christi Carter added the 20-room **Hotel Carter** (301 L Street, Eureka; 707-444-8062) to their lodging empire a few years ago. Its pale pine furniture and peach-colored walls offer a refreshing counterpoint to the Carter House across the street. Accommodations are quite spacious; some have fireplaces and whirlpool baths. Complimentary continental breakfast is served in the ground floor dining room, where colorful dhurrie rugs and crystal candle holders add an elegant touch. Deluxe to ultra-deluxe.

For traditional and stylish lodging, also consider **Eureka Inn** (7th and F streets, Eureka; 707-442-6441). Set in an imposing 1922 Tudor-gabled building that's registered as a National Historic Landmark, it provides excellent accommodations. The 105 guest rooms are well-appointed, and there's a wood-beamed lobby with a large fireplace. Amenities include a jacuzzi, sauna and gourmet restaurant. Deluxe.

For an extra dash of history in your nightly brew, there is the **Shaw House** (703 Main Street; 707-786-9958) in nearby Ferndale. It's the oldest home in a town that's an island in time. A carpenter Gothic creation, it was modeled on Hawthorne's *House of the Seven Gables*. A library, two parlors, dining room and balcony are available to guests, and the home is furnished throughout with precious antiques. Moderate.

You will be hard pressed anywhere along the coast to find a view more alluring than that of **Trinidad Bed & Breakfast** (Edwards and Trinity streets, Trinidad; 707-677-0840). This New England-style shingle house looks across Trinidad Bay, past fishing boats and sea rocks, seals and sandy beaches, to tree-covered headlands. There are four country-style guest rooms, plus a fireplace and dining room for guests to share. Deluxe.

REDWOOD COUNTRY RESTAURANTS

My favorite dining place in these parts is the **Benbow Inn** (445 Lake Benbow Drive, Garberville; 707-923-2124). This Tudor lodge serves meals in a glorious wood-paneled dining room that will make you feel as though you're feasting at the estate of a British baron. The bill of fare includes rack of lamb, duck sausage and filet mignon. Deluxe.

In the southern redwoods region you'll be hard pressed to find a better moderate-priced restaurant than **Woodrose Cafe** (911 Redwood Drive, Garberville; 707-923-3191). 'Tain't much on looks—just a counter, a few tables and a small patio out back. But the kitchen folk cook up some potent concoctions. That's why the place draws locals in droves. Breakfast includes buckwheat pancakes and spinach and feta cheese omelettes. At lunch they make homemade soups and tofu burgers; no dinner.

Eureka's historic Old Town section supports several good restaurants. For Asian fare there's **Samurai Restaurant** (621 5th Street; 707-442-6802), a simple dining room appointed with bamboo screens. It's dinner only, folks, with a standard Japanese menu, plus a "Shogun's Feast" that features marinated shrimp and beef. Moderate.

For a seafood dinner in a historic setting, consider **Lazio's** (327 2nd Street; 707-442-3766). This sprawling restaurant has been a Eureka institution for years. Priced in the moderate category, it features shrimp, stuffed halibut, broiled salmon, plus steak and chicken.

SAMOA COOKHOUSE

*For a dining experience lumberjack-style, there's **Samoa Cookhouse** (Samoa Road, Samoa; 707-442-1659) just outside Eureka. A local lumber company has opened its chow house to the public for three meals daily. Just join the crowd piling into this unassuming eatery, sit down at a school-cafeteria-style table and dig in. You'll be served redwood-size portions of soup, salad, meat, potatoes, vegetables and dessert—you can even request seconds. Ask for water and they'll plunk down a pitcher; order coffee and someone will bring a pot. It's noisy, crowded, hectic and great fun. Moderate prices, with reduced rates for children.*

The **Seascape Restaurant** (Trinidad Pier, Trinidad; 707-677-3762) is small and unassuming. But the walls of plate glass gaze out upon a rocky headland, expansive bay and the town's tiny fishing fleet. The dishes, many drawn from surrounding waters, include halibut, rock cod and salmon, as well as filet mignon. Moderate.

REDWOOD COUNTRY SHOPPING

Eureka's Old Town section has been beautifully restored. Window browse down 2nd and 3rd streets from C Street to H Street and you're bound to find several inviting establishments. Of particular interest are **Imperiale Place** (320 2nd Street), a multilevel mall, and **Humboldt Cultural Center** (422 1st Street; 707-442-2611), an art gallery housed in an 1870s mercantile store.

Ferndale has attracted a number of artisans, many of whom display their wares in the 19th- and early 20th-century stores lining Main Street. There are shops selling wood stoves, stained glass and kinetic sculptures; others deal in boots and saddles, dolls and "nostalgic gifts."

REDWOOD COUNTRY NIGHTLIFE

The **Benbow Inn** (445 Lake Benbow Drive, Garberville; 707-923-2124) features a fine old lounge with an ornate fireplace and a pianist on weekends.

The Ritz Club (240 F Street, Eureka; 707-445-5850) is an art deco jewel with etched-glass adornments. Here you can relax over a tall cool one while admiring the architecture. Comedy and live bands on weekends.

There's rock, blues and reggae live at **Jambalaya** (915 H Street, Arcata; 707-822-4766). This college town bar has a dancefloor and down-home crowd. The bands are local and the scene is loose. Cover.

REDWOOD COUNTRY BEACHES AND PARKS

Near the southern edge of Redwood Country, the 1000-acre **Standish-Hickey State Recreation Area** (707-925-6482) park primarily consists of second-growth trees. The South Fork of the Eel River courses through the area, providing swimming holes and fishing spots. Camping is permitted. Located along Route 101 two miles north of Leggett.

The first of the virgin redwood parks, **Richardson Grove State Park** (707-247-3318) is a 1000-acre facility featuring a grove of goliaths. There is also swimming, camping and trout fishing. Located on Route 101 about 18 miles north of Leggett.

One of the state's great parks, **Humboldt Redwoods State Park** (707-946-2311) lies within a 20-million-year-old forest. Today

100 miles of hiking trails lead through redwood groves and along the South Fork of the Eel River. Within the park's 30-mile length there are also ample opportunities for swimming, biking and camping. Located along the Avenue of the Giants between Garberville and Eureka.

The 632-acre **Patrick's Point State Park** (707-677-3570) is particularly known for Agate Beach, a long crescent backdropped by wooded headlands. Here it's possible to gather not only driftwood but semiprecious agate, jasper and black jade. There are tidepools to explore, sea lions and seals offshore, campgrounds and several miles of hiking trails. Located off Route 101 about 25 miles north of Eureka.

The splendid **Humboldt Lagoon State Park** (707-488-5435) is a 1036-acre facility that can be reached from two places. The main entrance leads to a sandy beach tucked between rocky outcroppings and heaped with driftwood. Behind the beach an old lagoon has slowly transformed into a salt marsh. The northern entrance leads to the campground and a sandy beach backed by a beautiful lagoon. Located off Route 101 about 31 miles north of Eureka; the campground is just north of the main entrance.

REDWOOD NATIONAL PARK

*Park of parks, fitting finale to a tour of California's North Coast, **Redwood National Park** is a necklace strung for over 40 miles along the coast. Among its gems are secluded beaches, elk herds and the world's tallest tree.*

*First link in the chain is the **information center** at Orick (707-488-3461). In addition to information, there is a shuttle service (fare) here for the trailhead to **Tall Trees Grove**. A one-and-a-third-mile hike leads to a redwood stand boasting the loftiest of all California's redwoods, including the tallest tree in the world, a 367-foot giant. **Lady Bird Johnson Grove**, located off Bald Hill Road on a one-mile trail, represents another magnificent cluster of ancient trees.*

*Redwood National Park encompasses three state parks—Prairie Creek, Del Norte and Jedediah Smith. Just before the main entrance to the first you'll pass **Elk Prairie**, where herds of Roosevelt elk graze across open meadows. Immediately past the entrance, Cal Barrel Road, another short detour, courses through dense redwood forest.*

*The Del Norte section of the park reveals more startling sea views en route to Crescent City, where the main **park headquarters** is located (1111 2nd Street; 707-464-6101). There is travel information aplenty here and at the **Chamber of Commerce** building across the street (1001 Front Street; 707-464-3174).*

*Route 101 north to Route 199 leads to the park's Jedediah Smith section with its mountain vistas and thick redwood groves. The Smith River, rich in salmon and steelhead, threads through the region. For further details on this remote area check with the **Hiouchi Information Center** (707-458-3134) on Route 199, four miles east of Route 101.*

Sporting Life

FISHING

All along the coast, charter boats depart daily to fish for salmon, Pacific snapper or whatever else is running. If you hanker to try your luck, contact **Bodega Bay Sportfishing** (1500 Bay Flat Road, Bodega Bay; 707-875-3344), **Noyo Fishing Center** (32450 North Harbor Drive, Fort Bragg; 707-964-7609) or **King Salmon Charters** (3458 Utah Street, Eureka; 707-442-3474).

HORSEBACK AND LLAMA RIDING

There are few prettier places to ride than Point Reyes National Seashore, where you can canter through rolling ranch country and out along sharp sea cliffs. **Five Brooks Stables** (8001 Route 1, Olema; 415-663-1570) conducts mounted tours of this extraordinary area.

For a unique pack trip on the back of a llama, contact **Mama's Llamas** (P.O. Box 655, El Dorado, CA 95623; 916-622-2566), which

---

CALIFORNIA SEA LIFE

The poet William Butler Yeats wrote of "the mackerel-crowded seas," oceans filled with a single species. Along California's lengthy coastline, in the shallow waters alone, over 250 kinds of fish thrive. Most are small, exotically colored creatures, which in an entire lifetime barely venture from their birthplace. Others, like the king salmon and steelhead trout, live off the Northern California coast until summer and fall, then run upstream for miles to spawn in freshwater.

Grunion actually climb onto land to lay their eggs. These small silvery fish come ashore between March and August after particularly high tides. The females anchor themselves in the sand and lay as many as 3000 eggs, which are hatched by surf action.

Among California's other well-known species are halibut, surf perch and rockfish, found along the entire coast, and gamefish like barracuda, yellowtail and bonito, which inhabit the kelp beds of Southern California.

*Methods for catching these different species are about as numerous as the fish themselves. There's surf casting, rock fishing, trolling, poke-pole fishing in tidepools, and deep-sea fishing from party boats. Fishing licenses are required of everyone over 16 years old, except people fishing from public piers. Regulations and information can be obtained from the **Department of Fish and Game** (3211 S Street, Sacramento, CA 95816; 916-739-3380). The rest is a question of equipment, skill, and whether the fish are biting.*

conducts tours of Point Reyes and other areas, or **Lost Coast Llama Caravans** (77321 Usal Road, Whitethorn, CA 95489), which explores the Lost Coast region.

BICYCLING

Point Reyes National Seashore features miles of bicycling, particularly along Bear Valley Trail. Other popular areas farther north include the towns of Mendocino and Ferndale, where level terrain and beautiful landscape combine to create a cyclist's paradise.

Transportation

BY AIR AND CAR

When traveling by car you can choose between coastal **Route 1** or inland **Route 101**. For those flying, **United Express** (800-241-6522) services the North Coast area. Departing from San Francisco, they stop in Eureka/Arcata and also serve Crescent City.

PUBLIC TRANSPORTATION

Greyhound Bus Lines (707-442-0370) travels the entire stretch of Route 101 between San Francisco and Oregon, including the main route through Redwood Country.

Golden Gate Transit (415-332-6600) has bus service between San Francisco and Sausalito, then beyond to Point Reyes National Seashore. It also covers Route 101 from San Francisco to Santa Rosa. From Santa Rosa you can pick up coastal connections on **Mendocino Transit Authority** (707-884-3723), which travels Route 1 from Jenner to Point Arena.

Also, Greyhound runs a bus along Route 128 between Cloverdale and Fort Bragg. **Mendocino Stage** (707-964-0167), a local line, serves Gualala, Point Arena, Mendocino and Fort Bragg and travels inland to Ukiah.

Gold Country

Rivers born high in the Sierra Nevada—bearing names like Stanislaus   **427**
and Tuolumne—become white-water currents that slice through the
mountains, carving canyons and dumping rich minerals along the riverbanks. Among these precious metals, one altered the course of California history. It also gave its name to the foothill region that lies
between the heights and the lowlands—the Gold Country.

Sacramento rests at the heart of California's Central Valley, the
richest farming area in the world. Wheat, cotton, rice, pears, onions,
tomatoes and countless other fruits and vegetables grow throughout
this agricultural belt. Sacramento's current business is politics; this city
of 369,000 is the state capital. Originally, however, its business was
gold.

No yellow metal was ever found along Sacramento streets; nor
were the rivers outside town worth dipping a gold pan into. Sacramento made its fortune supplying the gold fields, providing men and
materials for the nearby strikes.

The man who founded the town was also directly responsible for
the original discovery of gold. John Sutter created Sacramento in 1839
when he built a fort to protect the huge land grant that the Spanish
government bestowed upon him. Then an event occurred that should
have secured his power and fortune, but that instead destroyed him.
Gold was discovered on John Sutter's land in January, 1848.

By the next year, a hunger for the precious ore brought over
40,000 miners to the region; three years later there were 100,000.
Sutter's workers quit in search of gold, farm land fell fallow and he
went bankrupt.

His town, however, boomed. In 1854, Sacramento became the
capital. By 1856 it boasted California's first railroad, and in 1860 the
city was a center for the Pony Express. The transcontinental railroad
was conceived in Sacramento, and by the turn of the century, this river
town was adorned with the beautiful Victorian homes it still displays.

The precious metal that built Sacramento was found throughout the Gold Country east of the capital. There a rich vein of quartz and gold, the Mother Lode, still parallels the Sierra Nevada range for several hundred miles.

Sacramento

The state capital doesn't get a lot of respect from California's other metropolitan areas, which often brand it as a big cow town, culturally in the back woods. But the area has come into its own of late. Sacramento is not just the site of state government; it's the gateway to the Gold Country and the center of the richest agricultural area in the world. Those who tour the town will discover it has several faces.

Old Sacramento, a 28-acre national historic landmark with more than 100 restored and re-created buildings, provides a perfect introduction to the Gold Country. Lined with wooden sidewalks and heavy-masonry storefronts, its streets date to Sacramento's gilded era. The neighborhood can easily be seen in the course of a short walking tour. For complete details, begin by stopping by at the **Old Town Information Center** (917 Front Street;916-443-7815).

Begin in the **B. F. Hastings Building**: also behind the iron doors of this 1852 structure is a museum commemorating the western headquarters of the Pony Express.

It's just one block to the **California State Railroad Museum** (2nd and I streets; 916-445-4209; admission). The highpoint of any visit to Old Sacramento, this showplace challenges all the senses. The sights, sounds and smells of the railroads are here in a series of evocative displays. Trains hoot and steam engines hiss as you wander past antique locomotives and narrow gauge passenger trains. On summer weekends, you can take a six-mile train ride on a historic locomotive from the museum's Central Pacific Depot.

A walking tour will also carry you past the **Eagle Theatre** (Front and J streets; 916-446-6761), an 1849 playhouse where Gold Rush-era plays and dramas are still presented, and the **Globe** (foot of K Street), a replica of a brig that sailed around Cape Horn in 1849. The **Old Sacramento Schoolhouse** (Front and L streets), with its bolted desks and wood stoves, evokes the days when stern taskmasters wielded cane rods.

From Old Sacramento, follow Capitol Mall, a tree-lined boulevard, to the **State Capitol Building** (9th Street between L and N streets; 916-324-0333). Set in a gracefully landscaped park, adorned with statuary and lofty pillars, it's an impressive sight. The Roman Corinthian structure is capped with a golden dome and dominated by a grand rotunda. Many of its rooms have been renovated and opened

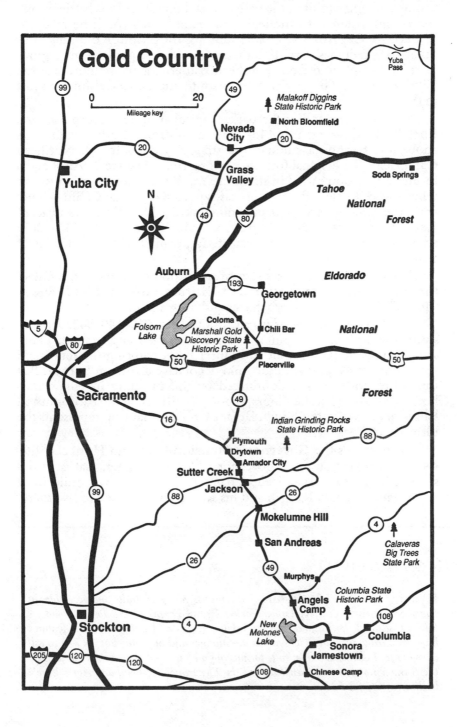

Gold Country

99

0   20
Mileage key

49

Yuba Pass

Malakoff Diggins
State Historic Park

North Bloomfield

Nevada City

20

20

Grass Valley

Soda Springs

Yuba City

N

Tahoe

National

Forest

49

80

Auburn

Eldorado

193

Georgetown

Coloma

Folsom Lake

Marshall Gold
Discovery State
Historic Park

Chili Bar

National

50

50

Placerville

5

80

Sacramento

Forest

49

16

Indian Grinding Rocks
State Historic Park

88

Plymouth
Drytown
Amador City

Sutter Creek

99

88

Jackson

26

Mokelumne Hill

26

San Andreas

4

Calaveras
Big Trees
State Park

26

49

Murphys

Columbia State
Historic Park

Stockton

Angels Camp

108

Columbia

4

New Melones Lake

Sonora

205

120

120

Jamestown

108

Chinese Camp

to the public. Wander up to the third floor when the legislature is in session and you can sit in the gallery watching the solons battle it out.

Having listened to the legislators ramble on, you'll be ready to adjourn to **Capitol Park**. Surrounding the Capitol Building, this urban oasis includes a trout pond, cactus and rose gardens and a grove of trees transplanted from Southern battlefields to memorialize the Civil War dead. There's also a Vietnam memorial to Californians lost in that war.

From the east end of the park, Capitol Avenue leads to **Sutter's Fort** (2701 L Street; 916-445-4209; admission). Built in 1839, the adobe fort became a cultural and strategic center for all Northern California. The original fortress has long since dissolved to dust and a re-created version raised in its stead. You'll see a cooper shop where wheels were fashioned, museum cases portraying early California life and a room hung with traps and animal skins. Then from the adjacent **California State Indian Museum** (2618 K Street; 916-445-4209; admission), you'll gather an idea of California before the advent of Sutter.

The capital city features several other points of interest. Contact the **Sacramento Convention and Visitors Bureau** (1421 K Street; 916-449-6711) for maps, brochures and information.

The **Crocker Art Museum** (216 O Street; 916-449-5423; admission) provides a grand example of form overwhelming content. There are drawings by Rembrandt and Dürer here, paintings by renowned American artists, plus sculpture and decorative arts from Europe. But the entire collection is dominated by the building in which it is housed. With its parquet floors, repoussé ceilings, grand ballroom and hand-carved walls, the Edwin Bryant Crocker mansion represents the ultimate artwork.

Then there's the **Governor's Mansion** (16th and H streets; 916-445-4209) that houses no governors. Not any longer, that is. It did serve as home to 13 state leaders from 1877, when it was built, until 1966, when Ronald Reagan and his wife Nancy refused to live there.

DOWN ON THE FARM

*For a taste of country life in the city, you can pick your own fruits and vegetables at one of Sacramento's outlying farms. **Pocket Brand Farms** (7938 Pocket Road; 916-391-8689), for instance, has pumpkins, gourds and Indian corn and features hayrides during autumn. The seasons are summer and autumn, but it's best to call ahead to find out what's ripe; costs for picking are minimal. For a list of farms in the Sacramento area and elsewhere, call the Department of Food and Agriculture's hotline (800-952-5272).*

The old mansion, a Victorian Gothic structure that looks like a wood-frame wedding cake, became a museum. Within its 15 rooms are antiques and artifacts from an earlier, wilder period in California history.

SACRAMENTO LODGING

A relatively new addition to the Sacramento lodging scene, the **Sterling Hotel** (1300 H Street; 916-448-1300) doesn't have to be as pretty as it is to succeed. A typical room has a four-poster bed, armoire, Henredon furniture, fine art, an elegant chandelier and a jacuzzi in the marble-tiled bathroom. When this 1894 mansion was remodeled, 12 accommodations were arranged on the three upper floors and the cellar was converted into a restaurant. Deluxe to ultra-deluxe.

For inexpensive accommodations near the downtown area, it's hard to compete with the **Mansion View Lodge** (711 16th Street; 916-443-6631). The 41 budget rooms are done in naugahyde and simulated wood, but nicely done. There is wall-to-wall carpeting, television and a telephone in every unit.

Located just a few blocks from Sutter's Fort, the **Bear Flag Inn** (2814 I Street; 916-448-5417) is a five-bedroom bed and breakfast. Personalized in every aspect, the hostelry is a cream-shingle bungalow with forest green trim. The rooms are tastefully decorated with patterned wallpaper and antique furnishings. Moderate to deluxe.

SACRAMENTO RESTAURANTS

Situated in Old Sacramento, **Fulton's Prime Rib** (900 2nd Street; 916-444-9641) conveys a sense of the 19th century. The setting is an 1860s building with brick-and-wood-paneled interior, and the waitresses are dressed in the fashion of the period. True to the name, the menu specializes in beef dishes, but it also includes such seafood selections as halibut and snapper. Dinner only on weekends; moderate in price.

Sacramento's capital restaurant is **The Firehouse** (1112 2nd Street; 916-442-4772), a plush Victorian-style dining room set in an 1850s-era fire station. The cuisine at this jacket-and-tie establishment is continental, as in châteaubriand, steak Diane and rack of lamb. During summer months you can dine outdoors in a brick courtyard. Deluxe to ultra-deluxe.

Or climb aboard the **Delta King** (foot of K Street; 916-444-5464), a five-decked riverboat that serves as a floating restaurant, hotel and cultural curiosity. Deluxe.

SACRAMENTO SHOPPING

There are two important sections for shoppers in the capital city. First is Old Sacramento, where 19th-century buildings have been renovated and converted into shops and malls. Within the course of a few short blocks are knickknack stores, antique shops and clothiers. The **Railroad Museum Gift Shop** (I Street between Front and 2nd streets) has a wealth of railway memorabilia. **Artists' Collaborative** (2nd Street between J and K streets; 916-444-3764) is an excellent place to pick up locally wrought items including woodwork, stained glass and ceramics.

The other shopping district lies along **K Street**, a 14-block pedestrian walkway. Extending from Old Sacramento past the Capitol Building to 14th Street, this street-cum-shopping mall is attractively landscaped and lined with major department stores, small shops and fashionable restaurants.

SACRAMENTO NIGHTLIFE

After sundown in the state capital, there are two places to look for entertainment. Old Sacramento has several saloons and dancehalls. Better yet, head for the downtown area, where you'll find an array of nightclubs and watering holes.

Without doubt the weirdest spot in Old Sacramento is **Fanny Ann's Saloon** (1023 2nd Street; 916-441-0505), a multitiered bar and restaurant. The staircase rises past an endless series of rooms, each decorated in high-tack fashion with old boots, wagon wheels, dangling bicycles and striped barber poles.

Located downtown, **Harry's Bar & Grill** (4th and L streets; 916-448-8223) is not only a spiffy place to bend an elbow, it also features live music, from jazz to rock to bluegrass.

Southern Gold Country

Touring California's Gold Country means traveling Route 49. This appropriately numbered highway heads north and south through the heart of the diggings. From Mariposa to Sierra City, it streams almost 300 miles past an endless succession of old mining camps. Many of these are ramshackle ghost towns; others have become historic centers in fashionably rebuilt communities.

At the southern end of the Mother Lode, a likely place to start is the town of **Mariposa**. The mine here was discovered in 1849 by the famous scout Kit Carson and became part of the 45,000-acre tract owned by his colleague, Colonel John C. Fremont. The **Mariposa**

Museum (5119 Jessie Street; 209-878-3015) displays a collection of artifacts from that era ranging from children's boots to mining tools. Along Bullion Street, on a hill overlooking town, the **old jail** and **St. Joseph's Catholic Church** still stand. Most impressive of these period structures is the **Mariposa County Courthouse**. The state's oldest court of law and still in use, it was built back in 1854 with wooden pegs and square-cut nails.

The region between Mariposa and Jamestown represents the least developed section of the Gold Country. It's a perfect place to capture a pure sense of the past. Particularly picturesque is the stretch from Mariposa to Coulterville, where Route 49 weaves wildly through the Merced River valley and provides grand vistas of the surrounding mountains.

Nestling beneath forested slopes, **Coulterville** is an architectural hodgepodge that includes several historic buildings. The **Northern Mariposa County History Center** (209-878-3015) sits astride a sturdy stone-and-iron structure that once housed Wells Fargo.

In **Chinese Camp**, another falsefront town with a gilded past, are ruins of the Wells Fargo building, a 19th-century store, plus an old church and cemetery. Once home to 5000 Chinese miners, this placid area was the scene of a violent war between two Chinese fraternal groups.

North of Chinese Camp, Route 49 leads to **Jamestown**. More commercially developed than mining centers to the south, this town has been ambitiously gentrified. *High Noon* and *Butch Cassidy and the Sundance Kid* were filmed here.

HORNITOS

North of Mariposa, there's a memorable side trip to the ghost town of **Hornitos**. *A Mexican-style village centered around a plaza, Hornitos was a hideout for the notorious bandito Joaquin Murieta. According to legend, this Robin Hood figure, a semimythical hero to the Spanish miners, used a secret tunnel in the fandango hall to escape the law.*

The Anglos in this rowdy mining town also claimed a famous citizen. Domingo Ghirardelli, the San Francisco chocolate manufacturer, built one of his earliest stores here in 1859. Several walls still remain, as do many of the town's old buildings. There's also an old jail, measuring little more than the size of a cell but possessing granite walls two feet thick.

The community contains something more than ruins of brick and stone. Because of its removal in time and space, Hornitos reflects the old days more fully than surrounding towns. There are windmills and range fences, grazing cows and crowing roosters and an old stone-and-wood church gazing down on the scene.

During summer months, **Rail Town State Historic Park** (5th Avenue and Reservoir Street, Jamestown; 209-984-3953), the old Sierra Railroad, is open. There's a roundhouse museum with blacksmith shop, turntables and historic locomotives. You can also ride several miles to nearby mining towns aboard a 19th-century steam locomotive.

Sonora marks the center of the southern Gold Rush region. The seat of Tuolumne County and one of the largest towns in the Mother Lode, it has been preeminent almost since its founding in 1848. Settled by Mexicans, Sonora gained an early reputation both for its lawlessness and commercial potential.

Much of the history is written in the town's architecture. The best way to explore is with a walking tour brochure available from the **Tuolumne County Museum and Historical Society** (158 West Bradford Avenue; 209-532-1317). With about 20 points of interest, the tour will carry you through the historic and geographic heart of the old "Queen of the Southern Mines."

Of the countless gold towns strung along Route 49, one that all travelers should visit is Columbia. Much of the old mining center has been preserved as **Columbia State Historic Park** (209-532-4301). Here is a window on 19th-century life in the Sierra foothills. The refurbished buildings and rare artifacts create a picture that will help make sense of the random ruins found elsewhere in the Mother Lode.

Wandering the several streets that comprise this time-capsule town, you'll pass the old newspaper office, miners' boarding house, livery stable and schoolhouse. Indeed, the four dozen buildings in this outdoor museum present a perfect reconstruction of an imperfect era.

SOUTHERN GOLD COUNTRY LODGING

The **Jamestown Hotel** (Main Street, Jamestown; 209-984-3902) is one of the best-restored hostelries in the Gold Country. An attractive two-story brick building with a balconied falsefront, it blends modern comforts such as a deck and solarium with old-fashioned Victorian decor, including floral wallpaper, brass beds, patchwork quilts and wicker settees. Complimentary continental breakfast. Moderate.

Set in a sprawling Spanish-style structure, the **Sonora Inn** (160 South Washington Street, Sonora; 209-532-7468) has 63 guest rooms. This is a full-service hotel complete with restaurant, lounge and swimming pool. The modern hotel is unimaginatively decorated— you'll encounter simulated-wood desks and naugahyde chairs. The rooms, moderately priced, are small and tidy and equipped with lovely tile showers.

Staying at the **City Hotel** (Main Street, Columbia; 209-532-1479) is almost a civic responsibility. Situated in Columbia State Historic Park, this charming nine-room establishment, dating from 1856, has been nicely restored and furnished with period pieces. There's a dining room and saloon downstairs. The guest rooms feature refinished pine floors, patterned wallpaper and wall sconces; some have patios. Moderate.

SOUTHERN GOLD COUNTRY RESTAURANTS

For gourmet dining in a Gold Rush-era atmosphere, try the **City Hotel** (Main Street, Columbia; 209-532-1479). The dining room is appointed with brass chandeliers, high-back chairs and gold-framed oil paintings. Dinner is an extravaganza featuring grilled duck breast with a black fig and apple raisin sauce, veal loin chop with an herbed crust and swordfish filets. Moderate to deluxe; highly recommended.

Good Heavens, A Restaurant (49 North Washington Street, Sonora; 209-532-3663) serves quiche dishes and salads during lunch hour. There are also open-face sandwiches like turkey and cranberry, ham and pineapple, and entrées like tarragon shrimp pasta. This homemade restaurant is a diner's dream (and budget-priced besides!). Lunch and Sunday brunch only.

SOUTHERN GOLD COUNTRY SHOPPING

Jamestown has almost as many antique stores as saloons. Dotted along falsefront Main Street are shops selling pieces that date back almost as far as the stores themselves.

Up in **Sonora**, you'll encounter a full-blown shopping scene. This is the commercial center for the Southern Gold Country. Washington Street is lined with stores along its entire length. In addition to local shops, you'll find clothiers, art galleries, bookshops and antique stores.

SOUTHERN GOLD COUNTRY NIGHTLIFE

Jamestown is one place that remembers its rowdy past. Main Street in this 19th-century community is still decorated with a string of drinking spots. For casual imbibing in an easy setting, the hotel bars, like **National Hotel** (Main Street; 209-984-3446), are best. Some folks prefer a lively crowd and head for a backslapping bar like **Lulu's Saloon** (18201 Main Street; 209-984-3678).

The scene is more upscale over at the spiffy **Sonora Inn** (160 South Washington Street, Sonora; 209-532-7468). Top-40 bands and jazz ensembles work out in the lounge some weekends; other nights the place is silent but for the clink of glasses.

In Columbia, the **Columbia Actors Repertory** (209-532-4644) performs at the Fallon House Theatre. **The Claypipers** (209-

245-4604) take center stage at the Piper Playhouse in Drytown. Out in Volcano, the **Volcano Pioneers Community Theatre Group** (209-223-4663) headlines the Cobblestone Theatre.

Central Gold Country

About nine miles north of Sonora, a side road leads from Route 49 to the reconstructed **Mark Twain Cabin**, where the fledgling writer lived for five months during the 1860s. It was Twain's Gold Country story, "The Celebrated Jumping Frog of Calaveras County," that first propelled him to fame.

The annual jumping frog contest takes place every May up in **Angels Camp**, an old mining town which Twain once visited. The community boasts several antique buildings and a museum, but its chief notoriety is literary; it hosted not only the creator of Huckleberry Finn, but also Bret Harte, who probably used the mining center as a model in his story "The Luck of Roaring Camp."

Moaning Cavern (209-736-2708; admission) and **Mercer Caverns** (209-728-2101; admission), located several miles east of Route 49 on Route 4, are extraordinary limestone formations descending hundreds of feet underground. Guided tours lead into these subterranean cathedrals where rock formations are twisted into bizarre figures.

Nearby **Murphys** is an attractive little town, established by two enterprising Irishmen in 1848. Among the historic buildings fronting its tree-lined streets is **Murphys Hotel** (457 Main Street; 209-728-3454). Built in 1856, it has housed an impressive assemblage of guests, among them Bret Harte, Jacob Astor, Jr. , Count Von Rothschild and Ulysses S. Grant.

Many of the 19th-century luminaries signing the Murphys Hotel guest book were en route to the "Big Trees," which had been recently discovered and were fast becoming a world famous tourist destination. Today **Calaveras Big Trees State Park** (209-795-2334) preserves these "Monarchs of the Forest." Located along Route 4 about 25 miles east of Angels Camp, the park rests at 4000 to 5000 feet elevation and contains 40 miles of hiking trails.

Within it are two groves of giant sequoias, the largest living things on earth. Closely related to coastal redwoods, these trees trace their ancestry back to the age of dinosaurs. One tree in the park stands 320 feet high; another measures 27 feet in diameter.

The spirit of '49 remains alive and well on Route 49 as it continues north from Angels Camp. There are buildings of note in **San Andreas**, and the argonaut community of **Mokelumne Hill** contains a Main Street lined with old-time structures.

If you haven't tired yet of walking tours, pick up a map of **Jackson** at the **Amador County Chamber of Commerce** (30 South Route 49; 209-223-0350). In addition to a balconied Main Street, this county seat features the **Amador County Museum** (225 Church Street; 209-223-6386). One of the region's best museums, it features geologic showcases and honors the Chinese with displays of abacuses, Chinese drums and coolie hats.

The town next door, **Sutter Creek**, also warrants a walking tour. Within a few blocks along Main and Spanish streets are dozens of buildings and homes rich with history.

Volcano is another well-preserved mining center. Located on Sutter Creek Road about 12 miles east of the town of Sutter Creek, Volcano was a booming town of 5000 back in the days of the argonauts. In addition to a Masonic hall, express office and three-story hotel, the community sports another relic—"Old Abe." According to local folks, this cannon was used during the Civil War to warn off Confederate sympathizers who sought to divert the town's gold to the rebel cause.

There are other motives for visiting this mountainside retreat. **Limestone caves**, where secret orders of Masons once held meetings, are open for exploration; they lie just outside town along Pine Grove–Volcano Road.

On the same road two miles from Volcano is **Indian Grinding Rocks State Historic Park** (209-296-7488). Here along a limestone outcropping the Miwok Indians gathered to collect acorns and grind seeds, berries and nuts. Using the limestone bedrock as a natural mortar, they eventually ground over a thousand cavities in the rock. These unusual mortar holes, together with several hundred petroglyphs, can be toured along a self-guided trail. You'll also pass a recon-

---

WHERE IT ALL BEGAN

Marshall Gold Discovery State Historic Park (916-622-3470; admission), located north of Placerville, is the spot where modern California history began. Here on January 24, 1848, James Marshall found shining metal in a sawmill owned by John Sutter. "Boys," Marshall exclaimed, "I believe I have found a gold mine." The history of California and the West was changed forever. Within the park, a self-guiding trail leads past a reconstruction of Sutter's mill and to the discovery site on the banks of the American River.

There's also a museum with display cases portraying the days of '49, a saddle shop smelling of oil and leather and a miner's cabin complete with long johns and animal pelts hanging from the rafters. In all, this 265-acre park features two dozen points of interest, each evoking a unique aspect of California's glittery past.

structed Miwok village including ceremonial roundhouses, bark houses, granaries and a Native American playing field.

North from Sutter Creek, Route 49 bisects **Amador City**. The focus of a quartz mining operation, this pretty community still contains many of its original brick and woodframe buildings.

From nearby Plymouth, take a side trip up Shenandoah Road (county road E16) to the **Shenandoah Valley winegrowing region**. Vineyards have prospered here since Gold Rush days, and at present almost two dozen wineries dot the area. Many are clustered along a ten-mile stretch of Shenandoah Road.

Foremost is **Sobon Estate** (14430 Shenandoah Road, Plymouth; 209-245-4455), which specializes in zinfandel. You can enjoy the tasting room and take a guided tour through the original rock-walled cellar. While this winery is open daily, others have limited schedules and often require reservations. So it's wise to pick up a free winetasting brochure from the **El Dorado County Chamber of Commerce** (542 Main Street, Placerville; 916-621-5885).

If visiting between September and December during the apple harvest, also ask for information about **Apple Hill**. Located on a mountain ridge east of Placerville, this area is crowded with orchards where for a modest fee you can pick your own apples.

Placerville, one of the largest towns in the Mother Lode, has been heavily developed and lacks the charm of neighboring villages. There are a few historic places remaining, however, such as the **Gold Bug Mine** (on Bedford Avenue, one mile from downtown), where you can step between the timbers and explore a narrow stone tunnel that leads deep into the earth.

CENTRAL GOLD COUNTRY LODGING

At the 1850s-era **Murphys Hotel** (457 Main Street, Murphys; 209-728-3454) all nine rooms are still maintained much as they were back when. There are oak wardrobes, antique dressers and patterned wallpaper. All the rooms share baths; moderate.

In a nice switch from the usual "store-bought" furnishings of most bed-and-breakfast inns, **The Heirloom** (214 Shakeley Lane, Ione; 209-274-4468) is filled with the lifelong possessions of the two innkeepers. The accommodations in this scaled-down antebellum house are so different from one another that it's hard to believe they share the same premises. Antique beds, country-style quilts and fresh flowers decorate the four main-house rooms. Exquisite breakfasts are included in the moderate rates.

The most commodious lodging around is at **Sutter Creek Inn** (75 Main Street, Sutter Creek; 209-267-5606). Innkeeper Jane Way has been running this 19-room facility since 1966 and doing so with special flair. Among her trademarks are four rooms with swinging beds, a complete country-style breakfast and a spacious lawn with shade trees and hammocks for lounging guests. There's an 1859 redwood home plus cottages dotting the grounds. Moderate to deluxe.

The **Mine House Inn** (Route 49, Amador City; 209-267-5900) represents the region's most intriguing hostelry, located in the former office building of an old mining company. To protect all the gold it once held, the place was built of brick with walls 13 inches thick. You might even find yourself checking into the "Vault Room" with its ceiling-high iron vault. An inn since 1955, the Mine House is creatively furnished with period pieces. Moderate; swimming pool.

CENTRAL GOLD COUNTRY RESTAURANTS

Murphys Hotel (457 Main Street, Murphys; 209-728-3454) features an informal dining room. Though there are antiques dotted about, the restaurant lacks the charm of the hotel. But the moderately priced menu features a full breakfast, lunch sandwiches and an array of dinnertime spreads, including prime rib and fried chicken.

Set in a vintage 1884 building, the **Sutter Creek Palace** (76 Main Street, Sutter Creek; 209-267-9852) served as a saloon back in the 19th century. Today this fashionable restaurant boasts three dining rooms, a polished bar and a decor highlighted with stained-glass pieces. The moderately priced cuisine includes shrimp scampi, chicken piccata, filet mignon and lobster tails.

Zachary Jacques (1821 Pleasant Valley Road, Placerville; 916-626-8045), a semiformal French restaurant, is trimly appointed with paintings and decorative china plates. A fireplace and pink-tablecloth ambience add to the appeal. Among the evening entrées you can choose from filet mignon, beef Wellington and scallops. Deluxe.

CENTRAL GOLD COUNTRY SHOPPING

There are several arts and crafts shops in Angels Camp, Murphys, Jackson and Volcano. Then, proceeding north, you'll encounter a pair of towns with antique buildings that have been remodeled into charming stores. Foremost is Sutter Creek. Along the 19th-century Main Street are shops like **The Doll House** (40-B Main Street; 209-267-5887), with nifty miniatures. **Labelle's Antiques** (64 Main Street; 209-267-0631) boasts six rooms of antiques. Within a couple of blocks there are also a dozen antique shops.

Amador City has been renovated in like fashion. Route 49 barrels through the center of this aged town, past handicrafts shops, art galleries and those places that seem more plentiful than restaurants—antique stores.

Placerville serves as a regional shopping area for the Central Gold Country, with stores of all sizes.

CENTRAL GOLD COUNTRY NIGHTLIFE

Up at the old **Murphys Hotel** (457 Main Street, Murphys; 209-728-3454) there's a saloon. The crowd here is drawn not only by the nightlife but also because of the fame of this hostelry. Live entertainment on summer weekends.

There's a Western-style saloon in the historic **National Hotel** (2 Water Street, Jackson; 209-223-0500). The place is complete with bright red wallpaper, gilded mirrors and glittery chandeliers.

PJ's (5641 Mother Lode Drive, El Dorado; 916-626-0336), just outside Placerville, hosts country-and-western bands every weekend.

The **Coloma Club** (Route 49, Coloma; 916-626-6390), just north of town, features country-and-western bands on weekends. It's a down-home bar complete with pool table and dancefloor. The **Coloma Crescent Players** (916-626-5282) are featured at the Coloma Theatre in Coloma.

Northern Gold Country

The northern stretches of California's Gold country are dominated by three towns—Auburn, Grass Valley and Nevada City.

Unlike many of the smaller towns to the south, **Auburn** has outgrown its rural charm. The only section of note is "Old Town," built in the 19th century along the American River. There's an interesting walking tour through this brick-and-woodframe neighborhood, which you should take after obtaining a map from the **Auburn Area Chamber of Commerce** (601 Lincoln Way; 916-885-5616). Among the sights are a trim three-story firehouse capped with a bell tower, a miniature Chinatown and a maze of falsefront streets.

The mines to the north along Route 49 were a far cry from the simple mining claims with which the Gold Rush started. Prominent during the latter half of the 19th century, these corporate operations were heavily industrialized. **Grass Valley**, for instance, has 367 miles of tunnels running beneath its streets. The town's **North Star Mining Museum** (end of Mill Street on Allison Ranch Road; 916-273-4255) displays the sophisticated machinery that replaced the gold pan and rocker.

At nearby **Empire Mine State Historic Park** (10791 East Empire Street, Grass Valley; 916-273-8522; admission) you can view the engineering office and machine shops of the richest hardrock gold mine in California. Peer into the black entranceway of a shaft that leads more than a mile down and wander through the many buildings comprising this multimillion dollar venture. With its tailing piles and eroded hillsides, the surrounding area presents a graphic illustration of how mining destroyed the landscape.

Despite the scars, Grass Valley still reveals several pretty sections. Along Mill and Main streets, the gaslamps, awnings, balconies and brick facades remain from the gold era. A replica of the **Lola Montez House** stands at 248 Mill Street, containing the Nevada County Chamber of Commerce (916-273-4667), where you can obtain brochures and walking maps. After rising in Europe as a dancer and the mistress of King Ludwig of Bavaria, Lola Montez settled in Grass Valley in 1852.

Nevada City was once the third largest city in California. Still grand by local standards, it nevertheless has a country village charm. There are gaslights, turreted Victorians and balconied stores along Broad Street. A walking map of the town, available from the **Nevada City Chamber of Commerce** (132 Main Street; 916-265-2692), will guide you through the historic heart of town. Be sure to see the art deco **Courthouse** on Church Street and **City Hall** at 317 Broad Street.

NORTHERN GOLD COUNTRY LODGING

In a region of venerated hostelries, the **National Hotel** (211 Broad Street, Nevada City; 916-265-4551) is perhaps the most renowned. It claims, in fact, to be the oldest continuously operating hotel west of the Rockies. With its ornate bar, sumptuous dining room and Victorian decor, the place has served travelers since the 1850s. Budget rooms

---

MALAKOFF DIGGINS STATE HISTORIC PARK

*For an adventurous side trip from Nevada City, head to **Malakoff Diggins State Historic Park** (916-265-2740), a fully developed spot hidden away in a remote and beautiful area. You reach it via North Bloomfield–Graniteville Road, a 17-mile journey that will carry you over the Yuba River. The last half of the road is unpaved, and parts of it are quite steep and sinuous. But the scenery is startling and the seclusion splendid. There's a reservoir for swimming and plenty of hiking opportunities.*

The park includes the rustic town of North Bloomfield, built during the 1860s as a hydraulic mining center. There's a livery stable filled with wagons, plus a whitewashed church and old general store, all neatly preserved. The immediate area has been heavily eroded by hydraulic mining, but the rest of the region is wild and untouched, wide open for exploration.

(without baths) are plain but comfortable; moderate accommodations feature loveseats and canopy beds.

NORTHERN GOLD COUNTRY RESTAURANTS

Several good restaurants cluster near the "Old Town" section of Auburn. Among them is **Shanghai Restaurant** (289 Washington Street; 916-823-2613), a budget-priced Chinese eatery, with a traditional Cantonese menu, that has been around since 1912.

At **Friar Tuck's** (111 North Pine Street, Nevada City; 916-265-9093) you can dine in a cozy back room or in a livelier dining area next to the wine bar. Private booths and a guitarist add warmth to one of the region's most popular restaurants. Fresh fish is a specialty here; you can also order teriyaki steak or pasta primavera. Dinner only; moderate.

For that special occasion, try **Peter Selaya's California Restaurant** (320 Broad Street, Nevada City; 916-265-5697). Open only for dinner, it features delicacies like scallops Rockefeller and beef Wellington. The decor is lace-and-brass Victorian and the mood very inviting. Downstairs in the "diggin's" you'll discover an entirely different ambience—a mine shaft with brick walls and wooden beams. Deluxe.

NORTHERN GOLD COUNTRY SHOPPING

Auburn contains expansive shopping sections and serves as a regional center for folks throughout the Mother Lode. Window browsing Auburn's "Old Town" section is tantamount to a historic adventure. Most of the 19th-century buildings have been converted to shops.

Grass Valley and **Nevada City** constitute the other shopping destinations in the northern Mother Lode area. The better of the two is Nevada City, where early stores have received a face-lift. The best places to browse are along Broad, Commercial and North Pine streets.

NORTHERN GOLD COUNTRY NIGHTLIFE

Nevada City has two varied nightspots within a few doors of one another. **McGee's** (315 Broad Street; 916-265-3205) is a posh brick-walled drinking emporium with overhead fans and stained-glass decoration that's good for a quiet cocktail. **Cirino's** (309 Broad Street; 916-265-2246) is neither so formal nor as neatly decorated.

NORTHERN GOLD COUNTRY PARKS

Covering 42,000 acres, **Auburn State Recreation Area** (916-885-4527) follows the American River basin and includes Lake Clementine, a small reservoir. There are opportunities to hike, swim, fish and camp. The ranger station is located along Route 49 about one mile south of Auburn.

One of California's most popular parks, the mammoth, full facility **Folsom Lake State Recreation Area** (916-988-0205) completely encircles Folsom Lake's 75-mile shoreline. Visitors come to boat, waterski, ride horseback, picnic, swim, fish and camp. There are also 65 miles of hiking trails around the lake. Located along Folsom–Auburn Road between Auburn and Folsom; park headquarters is 16 miles south of Auburn.

Rising from 4000 feet elevation to 7447-foot Eureka Peak, **Plumas–Eureka State Park** (916-836-2380) contains waterfalls, creeks and two small lakes and is home to great blue herons, deer and beaver. Foremost among its features is Johnsville, a beautifully preserved woodframe community dating from the 1870s. It's a popular ski region, and camping is permitted from May 15 to October 15. Located on County Road A14 about five miles west of Greagle.

Sporting Life

FISHING

Pick almost any lake or river in the Gold Country, bait a hook and you're bound to come up with trout for dinner. In Sacramento, contact **Sacramento Sport Fishing Guides** (1531 Wyant Way; 916-487-3392). For lake trolling in the Gold Country, call **Fishing Guide Bob Leslie** (418 Calaveras Way, Sonora; 209-532-4453).

WHITE-WATER RAFTING

If your favorite carnival ride is the roller coaster, you're ready for the adrenalin-pumping thrill of white-water river rafting. At one time it was strictly a sport for daredevils, but more and more vacationing adventurers are taking to the rapids.

Whether you're looking for a true test of nerve, or prefer excitement in smaller doses, many California rivers provide an enjoyable whitewater experience. You're liable to wind up in the drink at least once, especially if you choose one of the more challenging runs. But getting wet is part of the intoxicating rush created by a fast-moving stretch of river. There's also the serenity of paddling past untracked forests and bald mountains.

*In the Sacramento area, check out **American River Recreation** (11257 South Bridge Street, Rancho Cordova; 916-635-4516). In the Gold Country, contact **Chili Bar Outdoor Center** (P.O. Box 554, Coloma, CA 95613; 916-622-6104), **A.B.L.E. Rafting Company** (Coloma; 916-626-6208) or **Zephyr River Expeditions** (Columbia; 209-532-6249).*

HORSEBACK RIDING

Cantering through the parks of Sacramento or packing in to the Gold Country, nothing brings you closer to the Old West than horseback riding. In the Sacramento area, contact **Shadow Glen Riding Stables** (4854 Main Street, Orangeville; 916-989-1826). In the Gold Country, try **Camanche North Shore Resort** (Ione; 209-763-5295).

BALLOONING AND GLIDING

A hot air balloon may not get you there sooner, but it will carry you higher while offering spectacular views of Sacramento's rich farm country. Just contact **Balloons of Woodland** (1233 East Beamer Street, Suite E1, Woodland; 916-666-6424).

GOLD PROSPECTING

If sifting dirt along cold mountain streams sounds like fun, try your luck panning for gold. You may not strike it rich, but then again, who knows? Several outfits provide equipment and lessons: **Gold Prospecting Expeditions** (18170 Main Street, Jamestown; 209-984-4653), **Roaring Camp Mining Co.** (Pine Grove; 209-296-4100) and **Gold Country Prospecting** (3119 Turner Street, Placerville; 916-622-2484).

BICYCLING

Exploring the Gold Country by bicycle can be an exciting experience, but if possible cyclists should scout routes in advance. The mountain roads are steep and arduous, and the high altitude makes pedaling even more strenuous.

Transportation

BY CAR

From San Francisco, **Route 80** travels northeast directly to Sacramento, then bisects the Gold Country, which can be toured south to north along **Route 49**.

BY AIR

Several major airlines fly into **Sacramento Metropolitan Airport**.
These include American Airlines, United Airlines, Delta Air Lines,
Continental Airlines, America West Airlines and USAir.

BY TRAIN

Train aficionados can climb aboard **Amtrak** (800-872-7245) for excursions to and from Sacramento.

BY BUS

Greyhound Bus Lines provides service to Sacramento (916-444-
6800) from around the country.

CAR RENTALS

If you fly into Sacramento, the following agencies rent cars at the
airport: **Avis Rent A Car** (916-922-5601), **Budget Rent A Car**
(916-922-7315), **Hertz Rent A Car** (916-927-3882), **Dollar Rent A
Car** (916-924-1100) and **National Car Rental** (916-927-3644).

PUBLIC TRANSPORTATION

To get around Sacramento by bus, call **Sacramento Regional Transit** (916-321-2877).

THIRTEEN

Sierra Nevada

If it was gold that brought grandeur to California history, an even more spectacular grandeur envelopes the mountains that forged the gold. The snow-rimmed Sierra Nevada is the largest single mountain range in the country. It's a solitary block of earth, tilted and uplifted, 430 miles long and 80 miles wide.

A mere child in the long count of geologic history, the Sierra rose from the earth's surface a few million years back and did not reach its present form until 750,000 years ago. During the Pleistocene epoch, glaciers spread across the land, grinding and cutting at the mountains. They carved river valleys and deep canyons and sculpted bald domes, fluted cliffs and stone towers. The glaciers left a landscape dominated by ragged peaks where lakes number in the hundreds and canyons plunge 5000 feet. There are cliffs sheer as glass that compete with the sky for dominance. It is, as an early pioneer described it, a "land of fire and ice."

Today the prime visitor spot for the Sierra is Lake Tahoe, an alpine resort that goes year-round. Tahoe enjoys 300 sunny days annually but also manages to receive 18 feet of snow. Skiers challenge its slopes at Squaw Valley, Alpine Meadows, Powder Bowl and a dozen other runs. In summer, anglers, boaters and waterskiers take over, transforming Lake Tahoe into a warm-weather playground.

To the south lies Yosemite Park, a kind of national heritage etched in stone, a land where glaciers, sequoias and alpine meadows are ringed by stately mountains. Yosemite is the capital of the Sierra, representing in its angled cliffs and tumbling rivers a unique land of gold and granite.

On the southern flank of this massive range lie Kings Canyon and Sequoia national parks. Within eyeshot of the brine pools and scrub growth of Death Valley, they contain more than 1000 glacial lakes and boast rich stands of giant sequoia trees, the largest living things on earth.

Unlike its western face, which slopes gently down into California's verdant Central Valley, the eastern wall of the southern Sierra Nevada falls away in a furious succession of granite cliffs to the alkali floor of the Owens Valley.

Folded between three mountain ranges, with 14,000-foot peaks on either side, the long, slender Owens Valley was at the turn of the century a prime ranch and farm region planted in corn, wheat and alfalfa.

Then in 1905 agents from water-hungry Los Angeles began buying up land and riparian rights. Over the next few decades, as Los Angeles systematically drained the basin, trees withered, ranchers sold out and farms went unwatered. Today most of the ranches are gone, but bristlecone pines, the oldest living things on earth, still occupy the nearby White Mountains, as they have for 4000 years.

The nearby Mammoth Lakes region, with its alpine forests and steep slopes, is a favorite ski area. Here volcanoes and earthquakes have wracked the region, leaving a legacy of lakes.

Lake Tahoe Area

As soon as a traveler spots **Lake Tahoe** from one of the nearby curving mountain roads, it becomes evident why the region's rivers run fast and pure. This lake, situated 6225 feet above sea level, contains water so clear that objects 200 feet below the surface are visible. With depths reaching an incredible 1645 feet, it is the biggest alpine lake of such purity in all North America. Named for an Indian word meaning "big water" or "water in high place," Tahoe is 22 miles long and measures 72 miles around. The entire lake is framed by 10,000-foot mountain peaks, a translucent gem set in a granite ring.

Washoe Indians once inhabited the lakeshore regions and enjoyed uninterrupted predominance until 1844, when Captain John Fremont and Kit Carson, searching a mountain pass into California, "discovered" the lake. By the 1870s, with the advent of the railroad, Tahoe emerged as a popular resort area.

But before the trains came, travel in the High Sierra could be a treacherous undertaking. During the terrible winter of 1846–47, a party of stalwart pioneers, unable to cross the mountains because of drifting snow, camped for the winter. Many perished from exposure and hunger, others went insane and some resorted to cannibalism. Today the Emigrant Trail Museum (off Route 80, two miles west of Truckee, 916-587-3841; admission) at **Donner Memorial State Park** commemorates their passing. There is also a monument with a base that stands 22 feet high—the depth of the snow that winter. Today the accommodations are more commodious. There are camp-

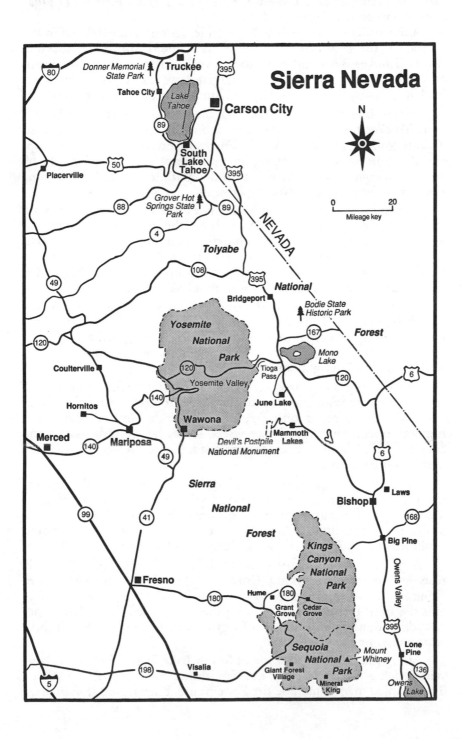

Sierra Nevada

N

0   20
Mileage key

grounds, picnic areas, a museum, hiking trails and a resident population of porcupines, beaver and deer.

A few miles east on Route 80, astride a mountain pass high in the Sierra, sits the 19th-century town of **Truckee**. Bounded by forested slopes, Truckee is a woodframe town overlooking an old railroad yard and depot. The main street, Commercial Row, is lined with falsefront buildings, many from the town's old lumbering and railroad days.

To tour one of the most famous of the area's ski resorts, head south from Truckee toward Lake Tahoe on Route 89 and follow the signs to **Squaw Valley**. The 1960 Winter Olympics put this vale on the map, and ski bums have been making the pilgrimage ever since. Ringed by 8200-foot-high mountains and sprinkled with lodges and condominiums, it's a favored jet set landing ground.

The highway from Squaw Valley rises to meet the region's main attraction, breathtaking Lake Tahoe. Today the tourist scene along this alpine jewel centers around the North Shore and the South Shore. The former includes a series of small towns, each featuring resort facilities, restaurants and various attractions. The latter highlights South Lake Tahoe, the region's most populous town.

On either shore, crossing the border between California and Nevada is like passing from one country to another. The reason is simple—gambling. It's legal in Nevada and not in California. Within a few steps of the border rise the casinos of Incline Village and Stateline, with their brilliant lights and promise of easy wealth.

The lake region is a magical place. To see Tahoe fully, you should circle the entire lake, along roads that cut through dense conifer forests and pass dramatic outcroppings of granite. Intermittently the highway opens onto broad lake vistas, swept by westerly winds and adorned with the sails of careening sloops. Along the way are magnificent private mansions.

The best known of these is **Vikingsholm** (916-525-7277; admission), a 38-room granite castle situated a few miles west of South Lake Tahoe. Open for tours during the summer, this unusual structure was designed on the lines of a ninth-century Norse fortress. Anchored offshore, on tiny **Fanette Island**, sits a stone tea house.

As if this extraordinary stonework were not enough, the castle rests beside three-mile-long **Emerald Bay**. From the vista point along Route 89, this spectacular cove, guarded by lofty conifers, presents the most picturesque site along the entire lake. At the near end, cascading along granite steps, is **Eagle Falls**, to which you can hike from a vista point.

Along the western outskirts of South Lake Tahoe, between Baldwin Beach and Pope Beach, are the **Tallac Historic Site Estates**. These fabled manses include the Pope house, built in 1884; Valhalla, a

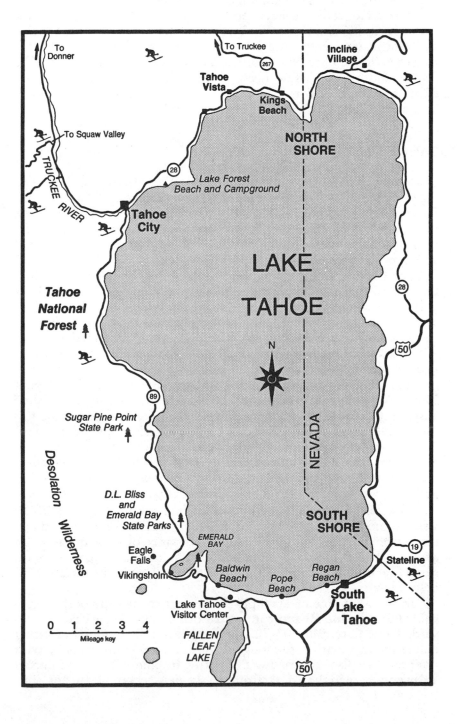

To Donner

To Truckee

Incline Village

267

Tahoe Vista

Kings Beach

To Squaw Valley

NORTH SHORE

TRUCKEE RIVER

28

Lake Forest Beach and Campground

Tahoe City

LAKE TAHOE

Tahoe National Forest

28

N

50

89

Sugar Pine Point State Park

Desolation Wilderness

NEVADA

D.L. Bliss and Emerald Bay State Parks

SOUTH SHORE

19

EMERALD BAY

Eagle Falls

Stateline

Vikingsholm

Baldwin Beach

Pope Beach

Regan Beach

South Lake Tahoe

Lake Tahoe Visitor Center

0 1 2 3 4
Mileage key

FALLEN LEAF LAKE

50

brown-shingle beauty; and the McGonagle estate, a prestigious house designed ironically in the fashion of a log cabin.

The estate trail lies between the **Lake Tahoe Visitor Center** (916-573-2600) and Camp Richardson, along Route 89. Other helpful information centers are located at the Chamber of Commerce offices in Tahoe City (950 North Lake Boulevard, Suite 3; 916-583-2371), South Lake Tahoe (3066 Lake Tahoe Boulevard; 916-541-5255) and the U.S. Forest Service (870 Emerald Bay Road, Suite 1, South Lake Tahoe, CA 96150; 916-573-2600).

LAKE TAHOE AREA LODGING

In a chic and flashy area like Lake Tahoe, it's a pleasure to discover a place such as the **Truckee Hotel** (Bridge Street and Commercial Row, Truckee; 916-587-4444). Built in 1863 and nicely renovated, this four-story falsefront building sprawls across an entire block. The rooms, which possess an Old West charm, are cluttered with antiques and crowded with character. Moderate to deluxe.

For lakeside facilities on the North Shore, try **Beesley's Cottages** (6674 North Lake Boulevard, Tahoe Vista; 916-546-2448), a collection of pine-frame houses fronting a private sand beach. Set in a grove of lodgepole pines, this homey establishment has individual rooms as well as private cottages. These are neatly furnished, spacious affairs with full kitchen and living room. Rooms are moderate, cottages moderate to deluxe.

You could get lost in the enormous, sparkling suites at beachfront **Tahoe Vista Inn & Marina** (7220 North Lake Boulevard, Tahoe Vista; 916-546-4819). Each of the seven accommodations in this multilevel, wood-shingled inn offers sweeping lake views (many overhang the water), bedrooms, living room, stone fireplace, jacuzzi, several bathrooms, full gourmet kitchen and private lanai. Sun pours through wall-sized windows into rooms lightened even more by soft grays and off-white modern decor. Ultra-deluxe, and worth it.

Mayfield House (236 Grove Street, Tahoe City; 916-583-1001), a five-room bed and breakfast set in a 1930s-era house, is located one block from the lake and within walking distance of shopping areas. In addition to cozy guest accommodations, there is a living room with stone fireplace. The rooms all share baths and rent in the moderate to deluxe range.

Mountain lodge meets high-class resort at the redwood, many-gabled **Sunnyside Restaurant and Lodge** (1850 West Lake Boulevard, Tahoe City; 916-583-7200). Nestled in pine woods and sitting before its own marina, the lodge features a cozy country lobby with river rock fireplace adorned with hunting trophies. Ducks and decoys are everywhere in the 23 lakefront or lakeview accommodations, simply furnished in wicker and wood and featuring individual touches like an old sea chest or armoire. Many have fireplaces and wet bars; restaurant; deluxe to ultra-deluxe.

The **Resort at Squaw Creek** (1000 Squaw Creek Road, Olympic Valley; 916-583-6300) lures guests with an extravagant 405-room hotel that is showcased by a stream and waterfall which plunge 250 feet through the property. Situated a half-mile from Squaw Valley's vaunted ski slopes, the resort is a summer destination as well as winter hideaway. For warm weather enthusiasts there are eight tennis courts, an 18-hole golf course, bike paths, miles of horseback riding and hiking trails in the surrounding mountains and an aquatic center with three pools and a water slide. Ultra-deluxe.

Camp Richardson Resort (Route 89, South Lake Tahoe; 916-541-1801), a multifaceted facility with a lodge, cabins and motel units, sits along a pretty beach on the western outskirts of South Lake Tahoe. The lodge is a classic mountain retreat with a comfortable lobby and hanging trophy heads. The rooms are neatly if unimaginatively furnished. The comfortable and rustic-looking woodframe cabins include complete kitchen facilities. Moderate to deluxe.

The best lodging bargain in hectic South Lake Tahoe is **Sail In Motel Apartments** (861 Lakeview Avenue; 916-544-8615). Not only is the place away from the busy section of town, it's also located

---

THE HIGH SIERRA

There are few better ways to experience High Sierra country than by following the mountain roads leading from Lake Tahoe to Yosemite. Route 89 heads out from South Lake Tahoe and intersects with Route 395, which in turn links with Route 120, the back road into Yosemite.

Along the way are views of bald-domed mountains, lofty and elegant, back-dropped by even taller ranges. The road courses just below the ridge of the world, where jagged peaks dominate the sky, with valleys spread below. There are alpine meadows wild with flowers and aspen trees palsied in the wind.

Several miles south of Bridgeport and 13 miles east along a pothole-studded dirt road, Bodie State Historic Park (619-647-6445) rests like a kind of woodframe time capsule. One of the West's finest ghost towns, this 1880 boom center, once home to 10,000 people, is now an outdoor museum complete with the houses, taverns and churches of a bygone era.

In the mountains high above Yosemite, Route 395 arrives at Mono Lake, one of California's strangest spots. Located along the western edge of the Great Basin, it's a saline-alkaline body of water, the remnant of a prehistoric inland sea. The lake seems eerie and forbidding, an alien place with weird stalagmite-like formations that resemble a moonscape.

right on a beach. The rooms are few, which might be why the owners have taken such care in furnishing them. Moderate.

Tahoe travelers who just have to be where the action is will find refined charm amid the chaos along Route 50 at the stone-and-shingle **Inn by the Lake** (3300 Lake Tahoe Boulevard, South Lake Tahoe; 916-542-0330). The 100 accommodations, set back from the highway on landscaped grounds, feature blond woods and lush pastel bedspreads and wallhangings. Many view the lake across the street; suites offer full kitchens. Pool and sauna; deluxe to ultra-deluxe.

Another recommended spot is **Hansen's Resort** (1360 Ski Run Boulevard; 916-544-3361), located on the road to Heavenly Valley ski area. A collection of cabins tucked beneath arching pines, this facility is splendidly situated close to the center of South Lake Tahoe. For a quiet but convenient retreat, the place is ideal. There are individual cabins, four-plex cabin and motel units, all pine-paneled and well-furnished. Moderate.

LAKE TAHOE AREA RESTAURANTS

China Chef Restaurant (10115 Commercial Row; 916-587-1831) seems like an anomaly in the rugged mountain community of Truckee. Actually, the Chinese worked this Old West town during the 19th century, building the railroad. But they never had anything like this: a moderately priced restaurant that serves standard Szechuan fare plus live Maine lobsters, crab and jumbo shrimp.

Col. Clair's (6873 North Lake Boulevard, Tahoe Vista; 916-546-7358) is the ideal spot for that special meal. It's chic but comfortable and specializes in traditional Cajun and Creole dishes. The interior is paneled in knotty pine, with such decorative touches as stained glass and hooded lamps. Moderate to deluxe.

Dark woods, white linens, a stone fireplace and windows brimming with plants create romance at **Captain Jon's** (7220 North Lake Boulevard, Tahoe Vista; 916-546-4819). The European menu changes daily and favors fresh fish entrées such as Australian lobster tail, scallops shiitake and salmon en croûte. There's also a waterside lounge. Extensive wine list; deluxe to ultra-deluxe.

French-country dining to the max, **Le Petit Pier** (7252 North Lake Boulevard, Tahoe Vista; 916-546-4464) greets guests with blue awnings outside and a partially glass-enclosed, candlelit dining room highlighted by red curtains, white linens and walls covered with culinary awards. A horde of black-tie waiters serve entrées such as pheasant souvaroff, châteaubriand grille and filet sauté au poivre vert. Ultra-deluxe.

Bacchi's Inn (2905 Lake Forest Road, Tahoe City; 916-583-3324) has been owned and operated by the same family for three generations. Famed for its minestrone soup, this Italian eatery serves family-style meals at moderate prices. The dining room, open for dinner only, is decorated with traditional red-checkered tablecloths and lantern candles.

Tahoe House (Route 89, Tahoe City; 916-583-1377), a dinner-only establishment, is owned by a Swiss family. The decor is Swiss country, the cuisine a mix of Swiss, German, French and Italian. Specialties include veal dishes, homemade pasta and lavish desserts with Swiss chocolate. Moderate to deluxe.

It's the only sushi spot on the North Shore, but that's just the beginning at **Emma Murphy's and the Avalanche Sushi Bar** (425 North Lake Boulevard, Tahoe City; 916-583-6939). Add a steak and seafood restaurant with Japanese entrées, plus a lounge featuring large-screen video and live rock music. This outrageous combo sits in a 1920s dark wood structure (one of the oldest in town) that adds to the good-time cowboy feeling of the place. Moderate.

Rosie's Cafe (571 North Lake Boulevard, Tahoe City; 916-583-8504) is a laid-back California eating spot. Just across the street from the lake, the place is bizarrely decorated with old sleds and wall mirrors. The imaginative cuisine includes eggs "benecado" (with guacamole and hollandaise sauce) for breakfast, sandwiches and tostadas at lunch and pasta, roast duckling and chicken scaloppine at dinner. Tasty and popular; moderate.

Wolfdale's (640 North Lake Boulevard, Tahoe City; 916-583-5700) touts itself as a "gourmet seafood restaurant." It's a well-known and critically acclaimed restaurant serving dinner only. Featuring delicacies like fresh swordfish and quail, it's well worth a taste test. Deluxe.

With a wrap-around glass dining room, the chalet-style **Christy Hill** (115 Grove Street, Tahoe City; 916-583-8551) commands great lake views that complement its modern, minimalist decor. This California-cuisine eating spot is highly regarded by guests and locals. Fresh food in light sauces are Christy Hill's hallmark, with entrées such as Hawaiian ono in mango, ginger and lime sauce. Deluxe.

A lovely little Tahoe cottage houses **Evan's American Gourmet Cafe** (536 Emerald Bay Road, South Lake Tahoe; 916-542-1990), where the menu ranges from continental to Oriental to American regional. Soft lighting, large original watercolors and mauve and blue decor set off an appealing room of only 11 tables. The far-ranging menu includes entrées such as beef filet with green peppercorns and brandy, plus killer homemade desserts. Moderate to deluxe.

The Dory's Oar (1041 Fremont Avenue, South Lake Tahoe; 916-541-6603) is a unique and fashionable establishment. The place sits in a red Cape Cod-style cottage with green shutters. In keeping with the architecture, the bill of fare includes eastern clams and oysters, plus live Maine lobsters. Moderate to deluxe.

LAKE TAHOE AREA NIGHTLIFE

For a get-down, stomping good time, the place to head is Truckee. This Old West town has as many saloons as any self-respectin' frontier outpost. Lining the falsefront main drag are places like **Bar of America** (Commercial Row at Bridge Street; 916-587-3110) and **O. B.'s Pub & Restaurant** (10046 Commercial Row; 916-587-4164). Some wail through the weekend with live rock.

There are waterfront lounges and other nightspots around Lake Tahoe, particularly along the North Shore and in South Lake Tahoe. The real action, though, lies across the line in Nevada. Here legalized gambling has resulted in miles of neon casinos.

On the North Shore, the scene centers around Incline Village. Down along the South Shore everyone gravitates over to Stateline, Nevada. Here a string of casinos lines a Vegas-like strip. Good luck!

LAKE TAHOE AREA BEACHES AND PARKS

A tiny eight-acre plot, **Kings Beach State Recreation Area** (916-546-7248) is one of the few public beaches near Nevada on the North Shore. It's got a small sandy beach plus a few amenities. Located in Kings Beach along Route 28 about 12 miles northeast of Tahoe City.

Lake Forest Beach and Campground (916-583-5544) features a stretch of sand bordered by aspen trees and an inland campground with 20 sites. Located off Route 28 along Lake Forest Road about two miles east of Tahoe City.

One of Tahoe's most precious jewels, the magnificent **Sugar Pine Point State Park** (916-525-7982) extends along almost two miles of lakefront and nearly four miles inland. Within the park are Jeffrey and sugar pines, as well as Sierra junipers that naturalist John Muir claimed

---

GROVER HOT SPRINGS

Set in a mountain meadow and backdropped by 10,000-foot peaks, the 519-acre **Grover Hot Springs State Park** *(916-694-2248) is a lovely sight. The Toiyabe National Forest completely surrounds it; hiking trails lead from the park to lakes and other points throughout the forest. There is fishing for rainbow and cutthroat trout, as well as two campgrounds.*

The central attractions, however, are the springs. Water bubbles up from underground at 148° and is cooled to an inviting 101° to 104° for the park's hot bath. Together with a swimming pool, the spa is situated in a meadow. If you long for an outdoor hot tub in an alpine setting, this is the ticket. The park is located off Route 89, about four miles from Markleeville.

were the largest he had ever encountered. Camping is permitted. The lakefront is dotted with sandy beaches, and the park possesses several historic structures, including an old mansion that's now a museum. Located on Route 89 about ten miles south of Tahoe City.

The adjoining **D. L. Bliss State Park** (916-525-7277) and **Emerald Bay State Park** (916-525-7277) curve along six miles of lakefront and contain some of the area's most picturesque sites. The forest that dominates both parks includes ponderosa pine, incense cedar and quaking aspen. The parks are located along Route 89; D. L. Bliss is 17 miles south of Tahoe City, Emerald Bay 22 miles south.

Situated a few miles west of South Lake Tahoe on Route 89, **South Shore Beaches** (916-573-2600) include several of the region's loveliest strands. The stretch from Baldwin Beach, near Emerald Bay, to the edge of South Lake Tahoe, is a golden swath of sand that includes Kiva and Pope beaches. Edged by trees, backdropped by mountains, it's an idyllic site overlooking the entire lake.

Yosemite National Park

It is a national institution, one of America's foremost playgrounds, a spectacular park climbing across the Sierra Nevada from 2000 feet elevation to a dizzying 13,000 feet—Yosemite. Within its 760,917-acre domain is a valley whose sheer granite cliffs have been carved by the cold blade of a glacier. It's a region of bald domes, sunshot waterfalls and stately sequoias. At the lower elevations are broad mountain meadows browsed by deer. During spring and summer the place riots with wildflowers; in winter it's cloaked in snow.

Center of this natural wonderland is **Yosemite Valley**, a canyon whose flat meadow floor is surrounded by vertical precipices. It seems that glacial action tore away softer sections of granite, leaving the more durable rocks like El Capitan and Half Dome.

For thousands of years, the Ahwahneechee and other Indians inhabited the valley. After its "discovery" by whites in the 19th century, the region became a curiosity point for tourists. To protect the place, President Lincoln in 1864 declared Yosemite Valley and the Mariposa Grove to be public parks. Several years later, naturalist John Muir campaigned to have Yosemite declared a national park. In 1890 his efforts succeeded. About 90 percent of the park has been given wilderness status.

What Muir saved cannot be adequately described in words; it must be experienced. Above the valley bed, vertical cliffs extend on either side to the limit of sight. In the far distance rises **Clouds Rest**, at 9926 feet the highest mountain visible from the valley. In front of that stands **Half Dome**, a monstrous rock that appears to have been cleft in two by the hand of God, leaving a sheer wall 2000 feet straight up. There is **Mirror Lake**, a mountain jewel named for the peaks reflected in its gleaming waters, and **Royal Arches**, granite shells formed into great arcs by time and glaciation.

Before them looms **Sentinel Rock**, last remnant of a mammoth block of granite. It's named for its resemblance to a watchtower, while **Leaning Tower** gains its name from the rock's disconcerting tilt.

There are the **Cathedral Spires**, granite shafts rising about 2000 feet above the floor; **Three Brothers**, imposing forms honoring the three sons of Yosemite's greatest Indian chief; and **Yosemite Falls**, among the world's tallest waterfalls, tumbling 2425 feet in two dramatic cascades.

King of kings among these grand geologic formations is **El Capitan**. It might well be the largest exposed monolith on earth, for this hard granite giant measures twice the size of the Rock of Gibraltar. Rock climbers, antlike in proportion, inch along its unyielding walls. Its sheer cliff rises 3000 feet from the valley floor.

Yosemite Valley is generally a beehive of activity. The busiest spot of all is **Yosemite Village**, a cluster of buildings and shops along the northern wall of the valley. The visitor center (209-372-0299) keystones the complex. In addition to an information desk, the center hosts a photographic display of the valley and a regionally oriented bookstore.

Next door sits an **Indian Cultural Museum** with exhibits and a mock village illustrating the cultures of the Miwok and Paiute Indians who once inhabited the area.

To avoid the enormous crowds and traffic jams that pack the park in summer and on holidays and weekends, it's best to visit during the week or in the off-season. Also consider walking, bicycling or using the free shuttle service around the valley.

Something else to remember: Yosemite Valley covers seven square miles, and everyone seems intent on crowding into its confines. For good reason—the valley is an extraordinary sight and must not be missed. But there are 1200 square miles of Yosemite National Park, many of them hardly touched by visitors.

Plan to visit the High Sierra country above the valley by following Route 120, Tioga Road, in its eastward climb toward the top of the mountain range. This road is closed during snowy months, but in periods of warm weather it leads past splendid alpine regions with meadows, lakes and stark peaks.

At about 7000 feet, it passes a virgin stand of red fir, then continues up to **White Wolf**, which has a lodge, campground, restaurant and stable. Past this enclave a spectacular view of the **Clark Range** is revealed.

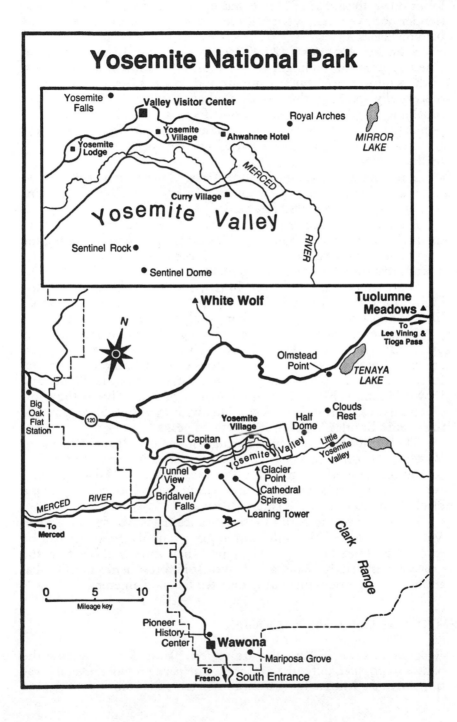

Yosemite National Park

Yosemite Falls

Valley Visitor Center

Yosemite Village

Royal Arches

Ahwahnee Hotel

MIRROR LAKE

Yosemite Lodge

MERCED

Curry Village

Yosemite Valley

RIVER

Sentinel Rock

Sentinel Dome

White Wolf

Tuolumne Meadows

To Lee Vining & Tioga Pass

N

Olmstead Point

TENAYA LAKE

Big Oak Flat Station

120

Clouds Rest

Yosemite Village

Half Dome

El Capitan

Yosemite Valley

Little Yosemite Valley

Tunnel View

Glacier Point

MERCED RIVER

Bridalveil Falls

Cathedral Spires

Leaning Tower

Clark Range

To Merced

0   5   10
Mileage key

Pioneer History Center

Wawona

Mariposa Grove

To Fresno

South Entrance

Olmstead Point has a short trail leading to a granite dome that looks down toward Half Dome and up to **Tenaya Lake**. This long, slender body of water, set at 8149 feet, is shadowed on either side by bald rockfaces.

Soon **Mt. Conness**, 12,590 feet in elevation, comes into view. Then appears the highlight of the journey, **Tuolumne Meadows**, with its information center, campground, lodge, store and restaurant. Statistically speaking, this wonderland constitutes the Sierra's largest subalpine meadow. Located at 8600 feet, its sun-glinted fields are populated with smooth granite boulders and cut by a meandering stream. In summer, mountain wildflowers carpet the hillsides with brilliant colors.

Then the road rises into **Tioga Pass**. Constructed at 9941 feet, this roadway marks the highest automobile pass in California. Yosemite Valley is now over 5000 feet below.

Another interesting trip from the valley carries along Route 41 to the park's southwestern boundary. Shortly after leaving the valley, the road passes **Bridalveil Falls**, where a short path leads to a 620-foot cascade that tumbles along a sharp rockface.

Soon afterward, just before burrowing into the mountain, the highway arrives at **Tunnel View**. From here, Yosemite Valley looks like God's playpen, bounded by sharp walls and domed in azure sky.

For an even finer view, follow the long side road that corkscrews up to 7214-foot-high **Glacier Point**. The vital fact here is that you are *above* Yosemite Valley, looking into the chasm and outward along its granite profile. Across the valley a two-tiered cascade, Upper and Lower Yosemite Falls, tumbles thousands of feet. This is the most spectacular of all Yosemite viewpoints, with the High Sierra stretching along a limitless series of snowcapped peaks.

The main road continues through miles of tall, cool forest to Wawona, a small settlement in the park's southwest corner. Here, just past an old covered bridge, is the **Pioneer Yosemite History Center**. There are log cabins and houses dating to the 19th century, plus a blacksmith shop and Wells Fargo Office.

Beyond, near the park's south entrance, rises **Mariposa Grove**. Most impressive of Yosemite's three giant sequoia groves, it can be reached by tram or along a two-and-a-half mile trail. Within the grove stands Grizzly Giant, a 2700-year-old forest denizen, as well as about 200 other trees measuring over ten feet in diameter.

YOSEMITE NATIONAL PARK LODGING

Accommodations in Yosemite are varied, plentiful and, because the park is so popular, difficult to reserve. The park provides several locations with facilities ranging from canvas tents to cabins to cottages to hotel rooms to deluxe suites. Still it is not enough. Particularly during summer months and on holidays, facilities are booked far in advance; it's not a bad idea to make reservations the year before your arrival. To make reservations, contact Yosemite Reservations, Yosemite Park and Curry Company (5410 East Home Avenue, Fresno, CA 93727; 209-252-4848).

Most facilities are located right in the valley—at the Yosemite Lodge, Curry Village and the Ahwahnee Hotel. Others—Tuolumne Meadows, White Wolf and Wawona—are situated in distant parts of the park and offer retreats from the crowds in the valley. Prices quoted below are summer rates; during the week in winter, rates are sometimes significantly lower.

Yosemite Lodge hosts moderate-priced motel-type lodge rooms; they are spacious and comfortable, and deer browse right outside. There are also cozy duplex cabins available for moderate prices. The "cottage rooms," contained in multiunit buildings nearby, are more spacious and slightly upscale (deluxe).

Over at **Curry Village**, ultra-deluxe-priced cabins are available, as well as hotel rooms (moderate) with natural wood furnishings and stall showers; some rooms have lofts for extra sleeping area. The village also contains "canvas tent cabins," which provide an excellent means to visit Yosemite at a budget price.

Tuolumne Meadows Lodge, nestled along Route 120 at 8600 feet, has tent cabins with beds, sparse furnishings and, to warm those chilly mountain nights, wood stoves. Bathrooms and showers are shared; budget.

THE AHWAHNEE

*Yosemite provides the opportunity to bivouac in a flowering meadow or rest yards away from the world's greatest geologic wonders. Nowhere, though, are the accommodations as grand and dramatic as at **The Ahwahnee** (209-252-4848). Built in 1927, the place is an architectural marvel, a multitiered building of wood and stone backdropped by rain-fluted cliffs, worth a tour even if you don't stay there. There are grand fireplaces large enough to stand inside and chandeliers that belong in a castle. Befitting the rest of the hotel, the bedrooms are spacious affairs decorated with a Native American motif. Ultra-deluxe.*

*For special occasions, there's the **Ahwahnee Dining Room** (209-372-1489). An entire wing of this grand old hotel is dedicated to the fine art of dining. Part of the experience simply involves sitting in the dining room, a high-ceilinged stone-and-glass affair with exposed-log beams. Service is impeccable. Dinner entrées include duck a l'orange, prime rib and veal marsala. Reservations required; dress code; deluxe.*

White Wolf Lodge, located midway between Yosemite Valley and Tuolumne Meadows at 7700 feet, has tent cabins (budget) as well as wood cabins with private baths (budget to moderate). With its dining room, stables and nearby hiking trails, it makes a great escape hatch.

At Wawona, the **Wawona Hotel**'s (209-252-4848) rolling lawn and white-pillared building make this century-old establishment a vision of the Old South. There's a nine-hole golf course, tennis court, inviting swimming pool and a covey of ivy-clad cottages. Rooms in this glorious old place often contain brass beds. Moderate.

Or try nearby **Camp Chilnualna** (Box 2095, Wawona Station; 209-375-6295), a privately owned facility within the park. Here are cabins set in the woods just off a side road. Accommodations range from one to five bedroom facilities and feature living rooms, fireplaces and sun porches; deluxe to ultra-deluxe.

For a closer-to-nature experience, you can camp in many spots in Yosemite Valley and throughout the park. Reservations, which are a must, can be made through Ticketron. Wilderness permits are required for back country camping.

Five High Sierra camps, open during the summer, have dormitory tents and dining facilities. For information, contact High Sierra Reservations, Yosemite Park and Curry Company (5410 East Home Avenue, Fresno, CA 93727; 209-454-2002).

For information on weather, road conditions and campground status, call 209-372-4605.

YOSEMITE NATIONAL PARK RESTAURANTS

Yosemite Village has an informal dining room called **The Loft**. Dominated by a mammoth fireplace, this oilcloth eatery boasts one of the valley's best deals. Lunch features hamburgers and sandwiches, while evening entrées include mountain trout, sirloin steak and vegetarian lasagna; moderate.

The nearby **Four Seasons Restaurant** provides a step upscale to a large but comfortable dining room where captain's chairs and an exposed-beam ceiling add a touch of class. Breakfast dishes are pretty standard; at dinner the Four Seasons features prime rib, roast pork loin and chopped steak. No lunch; moderate.

The **Mountain Broiler** is yet another step heavenward. Smaller and more intimate than its neighbors, this dining room also hosts an outdoor patio. The interior is dominated by a striking photo of a rock climber dangling upside down from a granite cliff, while outside tables face the actual rockfaces that draw such climbers. The menu features steak, steak and steak—as in sirloin and filet mignon—along with fish and chicken. Dinner only; deluxe.

Curry Village features **Curry Dining Pavilion**, open for breakfast and dinner and one of the park's best restaurant bargains. It's large, impersonal and cafeteria-style, but dinners here—ham steak, lasagna, rainbow trout—are budget-priced.

Scattered around the various corners of this expansive park are several other restaurants. Outside the valley, up on Route 120, there's a dining facility at **White Wolf Lodge**. Farther up the highway, you'll encounter surprisingly sophisticated cuisine at **Tuolumne Meadows Lodge**. This moderately priced dining room features mountain brook trout, Cajun steak and a vegetarian plate. They also serve hearty breakfasts, but no lunch.

The splendid **Wawona Hotel** (209-375-6556) contains a white-linen dining room that overlooks manicured lawns. Decorated with antique photos of Yosemite and illuminated by hooded lamps, it's a regal affair. In addition to breakfast, they feature a lunch buffet. Dinner sports a moderate to deluxe price tag and presents a Szechuan vegetable plate, trout, roast loin of pork or tournedos in cognac sauce.

YOSEMITE NATIONAL PARK NIGHTLIFE

The **Mountain Room Bar** at Yosemite Lodge is a spacious, oak-paneled lounge complete with fireplace. The perfect spot for a late-night brandy, the room is walled in glass and looks out toward Yosemite Falls.

Over at the beautiful Ahwahnee Hotel, you'll encounter the intimate **Indian Room Bar**, a plushly appointed drinking place.

Mammoth Lakes

On the eastern face of the Sierra Nevada, earthquakes and volcanic eruptions have carved a string of alpine lakes. Geysers and glacier-formed streams also reflect this area's tumultuous geology.

Mammoth Scenic Loop, branching from Minaret Road one mile outside Mammoth Lakes, contains several points of interest. **Inyo Craters** (one mile down a dirt side road and one-quarter mile up a trail) is a string of three volcanic cavities created by violent eruptions.

The facts and figures concerning Mammoth Lakes are found at two locations: the **Mammoth Visitor Center** (Route 203 just outside Mammoth Lakes; 619-934-2505) and **Mammoth Lakes Visitors Bureau** (Village Center Mall along Route 203; 619-934-2712). The latter will provide details on local hotels, restaurants and other amenities.

Lake Mary Road climbs past a chain of beautiful glacial lakes. **Twin Lakes**, a wasp-waisted body of water that was once two separate lakes, sits in a granite bowl. Just beyond here a half-mile trail leads to **Panorama Dome**, a volcanic rock with outstanding views of the surrounding lakes and the White Mountains.

The loop around **Lake Mary**, largest of this glacial group, diverts to **Lake George**, a crystal pool dominated by a single granite shaft. During early summer, meadows along the nearby hiking trails are lush with flowers.

Spilling down from **Lake Mamie** are the **Twin Falls**, which cascade 300 feet along a granite bed into Twin Lakes. **Horseshoe Lake**, the only lake where swimming is permitted, sits near the top of the road at 8950 feet elevation.

A number of sights lie along Minaret Road (Route 203), which ascends from the town of Mammoth Lakes into the mountains. Unsettling evidence of Mammoth Lakes' dramatic geology lies along the sharp walls of the **earthquake fault**. A nature trail wends along the sides of this fracture, where the earth has opened to create a deep fissure.

At Mammoth/June Lakes Ski Resort farther uphill, you can take a **gondola ride** (619-934-2571; admission) to the 11,053-foot summit of Mammoth Mountain.

Minaret Vista, with its views of the Ansel Adams Wilderness, is otherworldly. The San Joaquin River winds through the deep canyon below; and the stark peaks of the Ritter Range loom above, creating a setting in which the top of the world seems to have been ripped away, leaving a jagged line of needle-point peaks and razor-edge ridges.

At **Rainbow Falls** (off Minaret Road and along a 1.3-mile trail) the San Joaquin River plunges 100 feet over volcanic rock to an alpine pool, forming multihued patterns in the mist.

But enough mere beauty. At **Devils Postpile National Monument**, where Minaret Road (Route 203) reveals its final surprise,

---

HOT CREEK

Hot Creek, a beautiful stream set deep in a rock-rimmed canyon, is one of Mammoth Lakes most deceptive and alluring spots. One section, peaceful as a babbling brook, is popular with fly fishermen. Farther downstream, hot springs warm the water to perfect spa temperature. Then, within 100 yards of this popular bathing pool, the creek erupts in low geysers and dramatic steam vents. (Hot Creek is located six miles south of Mammoth Lakes. From Route 395 turn east on the road next to Mammoth–June Lakes Airport and follow it three and one-half miles to the parking lot; then hike down to the creek.)

physical beauty is combined with the magic of geology. Here layer on layer of angular shafts, some vertical, others twisted into curving forms, create a 60-foot-high cliff with smooth-sided columns. Volcanic forces followed by glaciers brought about these spectacular formations.

The geometric surface here resembles a tile floor (which can be viewed from atop Devils Postpile). Along the trail at the bottom you can gaze at this unique wall of polygonal pillars. Directly below them, like splinters from a magnificent sculpture, lie piles of fallen columns.

MAMMOTH LAKES LODGING

Mammoth Mountain Inn (Minaret Road outside Mammoth Lakes; 619-934-2581) is a modern hotel with a distinct Swiss atmosphere. Located across the road from Mammoth/June Lakes Ski Resort, the inn is primarily a ski lodge, but its easy proximity to Devil's Postpile and other natural features make it popular year-round. There are restaurants, spas and shops here as well as a wood-and-stone lobby. Hotel rooms and condominiums are moderate to ultra-deluxe, depending on the season.

One of the prettiest and most secluded spots in Mammoth Lakes is **Tamarack Lodge Resort** (Tamarack Lodge Road; 619-934-2442), located at 8600 feet. A classic mountain lodge with split-log walls and stone fireplace, it sits on Twin Lakes in the shadow of the mountains. There are small pine-paneled rooms in the lodge. More than 20 modern cabins, ranging from studios to four-bedroom extravaganzas, also dot the six-acre grounds. Lodge rooms are budget to moderate, cabins moderate to deluxe, also depending on the season.

MAMMOTH LAKES RESTAURANTS

Shogun Japanese Restaurant (Sierra Centre Mall, Old Mammoth Road, Mammoth Lakes; 619-934-3970) may be parked in a shopping mall, but it still provides marvelous views of the mountains. Equipped with a sushi bar and adjoining lounge, the restaurant has sukiyaki, tonkatsu and teriyaki dishes. Moderate.

With its Swiss alpine atmosphere, the **Matterhorn Restaurant** (Minaret Road; 619-934-3369) is one of Mammoth Lakes' most congenial dining places. The breakfast specialty is eggs—eggs Benedict, eggs florentine, eggs nordic (with salmon), to name a few. The continental dinner menu features entrées like champagne-poached salmon, wienerschnitzel and veal *médaillons*. Moderate to deluxe.

MAMMOTH LAKES NIGHTLIFE

During summer and winter, the bar at **Slocums Italian American Grill** (Route 203; 619-934-7647) is a popular watering hole.

The **Cactus Club** (Route 203; 619-934-2265) is a spacious Mammoth Lakes lounge where you can dance to recorded music and rock videos. During winter months there's dancing to live bands Tuesday through Sunday at **La Sierra's Mexican Restaurant and Cantina** (3789 Route 203; 619-934-8083). This club has one of the largest dancefloors in town.

Owens Valley

A land bled dry by thirsty Los Angeles, which diverted its once plentiful water supply, **Owens Valley** has become a morass of sand divided in random fashion by arroyos, a dust bowl with a rim of mountains. Today only the mountains remain—to the east the Inyos, Panamints and Whites, in the west the Sierra Nevada. From them the valley, victimized by a metropolis hundreds of miles away, derives its identity and maintains its dignity.

The backbone of this region is Route 395, which runs past black lava hills, red cinder cones and other volcanic outcroppings.

Off the highway slightly north of Bishop, the town of Laws, a major railroad stop during the 1880s, is re-created at the **Laws Railroad Museum and Historical Site** (Route 6; 619-873-5950). The general store is here with its lard buckets and spice canisters, and the surgical tools in the doctor's office look as threatening as they did back when. In addition, the original Bishop Catholic Church has been converted into a library, museum and art gallery.

But the centerpiece of the exhibit is still the railroad yard. Here the station, with its waiting room and telegraph office, has been nicely preserved. Resting just down the track is old Southern Pacific Engine Number Nine, with a line of freight cars and a bell whose clangs still echo across the valley.

Bishop is one of those towns that exist not in and for themselves but for what is around them. The **Bishop Chamber of Commerce** (690 North Main Street; 619-873-8405) serves as the local information center, a good place to plan an exploration of the area.

Dedicated to Native American traditions, the town's Paiute **Shoshone Indian Cultural Center** (2301 West Line Street; 619-873-4478) has outstanding displays of basketry, leathercrafts and petroglyphs. Centerpiece of the showroom is a circular house of straw, replicating the traditional homes of Owens Valley tribes.

In the little town of Big Pine, Route 168 connects with a side road that leads up into the White Mountains. Climb this backcountry byway and a dazzling 180° **mountain panorama** of the Sierra Nevada and Inyos will open to view. Within this ring of 13,000-foot peaks rests **Palisade Glacier,** the southernmost glacier in North America.

Then the road ascends to over 10,000 feet elevation and enters a mysterious realm where the residents are over 4000 years old, the world's most ancient living things, dating back to the days of the Egyptian pyramids. The site is an **Ancient Bristlecone Pine Forest,** where short, squat trees with needles like fox tails grow on an icy, windblown landscape. Sculpted by the elements, they resemble living driftwood.

Farther south along Route 395, with the Sierra Nevada looming in the background like an impenetrable wall, stands **Manzanar.** In 1942, when panic over Pearl Harbor pervaded the country, 10,000 Americans of Japanese ancestry were "relocated" and interred. Today little remains to commemorate their tragedy other than two guard stations, fashioned, almost insultingly, like pagodas. A plaque implores that "the injustices and humiliation suffered here as a result of hysteria, racism and economic exploitation never emerge again."

The **Eastern California Museum** (155 Grant Street; 619-878-2411; 619-878-2010 on weekends) in Independence contains photo-

---

GATEWAY TO THE CLOUDS

*In the neon town of Lone Pine you can pick up Whitney Portal Road, which climbs from 4000 to 8300 feet elevation in its 13-mile course. Passing streams shaded by cottonwood trees, it cuts through the reddish **Alabama Hills**. If they seem a bit too familiar, little wonder: they have served as the setting for countless Westerns.*

*For a close-up of cowboy country, turn right on Movie Road (off Whitney Portal Road three miles from Route 395). A network of dirt roads leads past **Movie Flat**, where many sequences were shot, and continues into this badlands of humpbacked boulders.*

Then Whitney Portal Road rides out of this rolling rangeland, trading the soft contours of the Alabamas for the cold granite world of the Sierra Nevada. These latter mountains are roughhewn, with adze-like slopes that lift away from the road in vertical lunges.

*When the road itself quits at **Whitney Portal**, base camp for climbers, you find above you Mount Whitney, at 14,495 feet the tallest mountain in the contiguous United States. In the giant's shadow stand six other peaks, all topping 14,000 feet. It is a scene of unpronounceable beauty, fashioned from dark chasms and stone minarets, almost two miles above the floor of Owens Valley.*

graphs and news clips retracing the story of Manzanar. This excellent regional facility also displays Indian artifacts. Out back, many of the town's original buildings—weatherbeaten, woodframe structures—still stand.

To understand the allure of Owens Valley, stop by the **Eastern Sierra InterAgency Visitors Council** (Route 395 one mile south of Lone Pine; 619-876-4252). A valuable resource, the information center has a good selection of maps and pamphlets and an excellent collection of books on California's mountain and desert regions.

OWENS VALLEY LODGING

The Matlick House (two miles north of Bishop on Route 395; 619-873-3133), with its porches on both floors, handmade quilts and beveled-mirror armoires, is known for miles around. Each of the five guest rooms has been decorated with a flourish: there are overhead fans, turn-of-the-century settees, Victorian love seats. Moderate to deluxe.

An extraordinary getaway set on 160 rustic acres in the Alabama Hills, **Cuffe Guest Ranch** (Whitney Portal Road about four miles west of Route 395, Lone Pine; 619-876-4161) looks so much like the Old West that movie makers have frequently used it as a location. With Mount Whitney rising in the distance, the views of basin and range are breathtaking. The housekeeping cabins are pretty basic, but there's an orchard outside your door. Rooms in the main house are appointed with antiques. Moderate.

OWENS VALLEY RESTAURANTS

Beef, barbecued beef and more beef are the order of the day at restaurants here in mountain country. **The Sportsman** (206 South Route 395, Lone Pine; 619-876-5454) serves several kinds of steak as well as beef ribs and prime rib. If you're otherwise inclined, they offer a few fish entrées plus a salad bar. For decor there are marvelous old stills from Western movies. Budget to moderate.

If local crowds are any indication, **Bishop Grill** (281 North Route 395; 619-873-3911) is the best place in Bishop to eat. It's certainly the cheapest: the low budget prices at this cafe are vintage 1960s. The cuisine is straight Americana from the ham dinners to the pork chops to the breaded trout.

Sequoia and Kings Canyon Parks

Two of California's finest parks, Sequoia and Kings Canyon, lie next to each other along the western slopes of the Sierra Nevada range. Covering more than 850,000 acres and encompassing 14,000-foot peaks, alpine lakes and stands of giant sequoia trees, they provide a lush wilderness area that remains relatively free of the crowds that gather at other California parks.

SEQUOIA NATIONAL PARK   Prelude to the park is the drive to **Mineral King**, a remote mountain hamlet that boomed as a silver mining center during the 1870s and quickly went bust. The 25-mile Mineral King Road, branching from Route 198 a few miles before the southern entrance to the park, leads to a remote and particularly pretty section of Sequoia National Park. En route are sharp canyons, switchbacks that jackknife above sheer cliffs and a lone arched bridge.

Generals Highway, the road through Sequoia and Kings Canyon, is a continuation of Route 198, which enters the park at Ash Mountain. The nearby **visitor's center** (209-565-3456) provides maps and information, but your symbolic entrance into this world of granite mountains and giant trees comes a few miles farther as you pass beneath **Tunnel Rock**. The roadway here has been cut from a monstrous boulder that serves as a stone portal.

At **Hospital Rock**, a granite outcropping near the turnoff to Buckeye Flats, there are pictographs from an early tribe of Indians. These painted designs, red stains against gray rock, were a vital element in local Native American culture.

Giant Forest Village, a mountain complex complete with lodge and restaurants, lies at the center of Sequoia National Park. **Round Meadow**, located just below the lodge, is a flowering glade with a one-mile loop trail that passes regal stands of sequoia.

A short distance from the village, Crescent Meadow Road curves through the woods past several points of interest. **Auto Log**, a giant tree that fell in 1917, has been dug out to form a driveway. If for some unspeakable reason you long to wheel your car onto a sequoia, this is your only chance. The **Parker Group**, a pretty grove of sequoias, lies farther up the road, as does **Tunnel Log**, a felled sequoia under which you can drive (having already driven *over* another of the brutes).

From here it's on to **Crescent Meadow**, an overgrown marsh surrounded by sequoias and filled in spring and summer with wildflowers. A fork from Crescent Meadow Road runs past **Hanging Rock**, a granite boulder poised uneasily above a deep chasm, and **Moro Rock**, where a steep quarter-mile staircase ascends a magnificent dome. The views from this 6725-foot summit reach along the

(Text continued on page 472.)

CALIFORNIA'S FAR NORTH

California's best-kept secret is a sprawling, thinly populated area full of history and incredible natural beauty. Much of the sector's lush terrain is virtually untouched. Reaching from Redding to Oregon and from the Coast Range to Nevada, the Far North encompasses a huge swath of California. Siskiyou, Modoc, Shasta and Lassen counties are part of this tumbling block of territory.

The Far North represents California in its truly pristine state. Thousands of lakes and rivers make it a paradise for white-water rafting. Chinook run 50 pounds and the fishing is excellent for trout and bass as well. Most of the region is preserved in a series of national forests, making it a retreat for hikers and campers. You can rent a houseboat on Lake Shasta, hike deep into the Trinity Alps or explore remote caverns and volcanoes.

A wilderness of alpine lakes and granite heights, the Far North's mountains include the Klamath, Marble, Salmon, Trinity and Warner ranges. Foremost is the Cascade Range, extending south from Washington and Oregon. Mt. Shasta, rising over 14,000 feet, is lord of the land, a white-domed figure brooding above a forested realm. Lassen Peak, its infernal cousin, is an active volcano which last erupted in 1921.

Route 5 runs like a spine through this rural region, moving north and south from Sacramento to Oregon. Redding is the closest facsimile around to a buzzing metropolis. This town of 42,000 folks is also the major jumping-off point for sightseers.

*No matter where you plan to visit, the first stop should be the **Shasta– Cascade Wonderland Association** (1250 Parkview Avenue, Redding; 916-243- 2643). The friendly staff here will provide enough maps and brochures to stuff an extra suitcase.*

*From Redding, Route 299 leads west for a few miles to the late, great gold mining outpost of **Shasta**. This brickfront ghost town was the region's "Queen City" back in the 1850s, producing over $100,000 in gold dust every week. A trail leads along a row of old ruins. At **Shasta State Historic Park** (Route 299, Shasta; 916-243-8194; admission), you'll find Indian artifacts, antique photos, wanted posters, yellowed newspapers and paintings by California artists.*

*Five miles further west lies **Whiskeytown Lake**, one of California's best boating, fishing, camping and swimming spots. With 36 miles of shoreline, green rolling hills, tiny wooded islands and dense stands of ponderosa pine, it's a paradise for backcountry explorers.*

*The historic mining town of **French Gulch**, settled in 1849, is situated off Route 299 along Trinity Mountain Road. Once an important way station on the Old Oregon Pacific Trail, it's a place where time has refused to budge for the last 100 years. From here, Route 299 winds past beautiful mountain vistas en route to **Weaverville**, a country-style Victorian town shaded by honey locusts.*

*Due north from Redding along Route 5, you'll encounter **Shasta Lake**, an extremely popular recreation area which is a paradise for naturalists and statisticians alike. Why the strange combination of interests? Because Shasta Lake, with its 370-mile shoreline and 30,000-acre expanse, is the largest manmade lake in the* *state. Its four arms stretch into the Sacramento, McCloud and Pit rivers, as well as Squaw Creek. It boasts 17 types of game fish, a colony of houseboats, miles of hiking trails, and every other outdoor diversion imaginable.*

*Then there's **Shasta Dam**, located along Shasta Dam Boulevard five miles west of Route 5. Three times taller than Niagara Falls, it measures 602 feet, making it the world's second highest dam. Eight years labor and six million cubic yards of concrete went into its completion. If those superlatives are insufficient, continue north on Route 5 a few miles and you'll cross **Bridge Bay**, the world's highest double-deck bridge.*

*From the nearby town of O'Brien, you can visit **Lake Shasta Caverns** (Shasta Caverns Road, O'Brien; 916-238-2341; admission). Guides will take you across the lake by boat, then along a picturesque road by bus, to this mazework of limestone caves. Within are strangely shaped stalactites and awesome stalagmites, dating back perhaps a million years. This natural statuary comes in the form of spires and minarets, stone curtains and Disneyesque figures.*

***Castle Crags State Park** (916-235-2684), further north along Route 5 in Castella, is a land of granite domes and startling landscapes. From the vista points, you can gaze out upon the Cascade Range.*

*Foremost among these majestic peaks is **Mt. Shasta**, a 14,162-foot giant which carries five glaciers along its flanks. Dominating the skyline, it consists of two volcanic cones and features alpine lakes, flower-choked meadows and deep forests. For a closer look at this sacred mountain, follow Route A10 through Mt. Shasta Recreation Area. The road winds to an elevation of 6800 feet and offers a different view at every hairpin turn.*

*The best way to explore California's hidden northeastern corner is along a 400-plus mile odyssey from Redding. First stop on this wilderness expedition is **Lassen Volcanic National Park** (916-595-4444), located about 50 miles from Redding off Route 44. Lassen Peak, a 10,457-foot volcano, is the highlight and highpoint of this extraordinary region. This is part of the same mountain chain which brought you the Mt. St. Helens catastrophe. Lassen's last eruptions were between 1914 and 1921. Spewing fumes and ash 30,000 feet in the air, one explosion tore away an entire side of the mountain and flicked 20-ton boulders down the hillside. Today it's still a very active volcano, and the surrounding area is filled with steam vents, mud pots and moonscape features.*

*Another of the region's amazing parks, **Lava Beds National Monument** (located off Route 139; 916-667-2283) is a land of cinder cones, craters and 30,000-year-old lava flows. It also features one of the world's finest series of lava tubes.*

*Before leaving the wilderness entirely, stop at **McArthur–Burney Falls Memorial State Park** (916-335-2777). Located midway between Mt. Shasta and Lassen Park, it features two spectacular waterfalls, fed by springs, which cascade over a 129-foot cliff. Ornamented with rainbows and an emerald pool, the twin falls were reputedly deemed the eighth wonder of the world by President Theodore Roosevelt. They are a fitting climax to this long, lonely loop into California's most secluded realm.*

Great Western Divide, a chain of 12,000-foot peaks. In the dizzying depths 4000 feet below, the Middle Fork of the Kaweah River carves a stone channel en route to the San Joaquin Valley.

During summer months one-hour tours of **Crystal Caves** are available. The hike down to these beautiful caverns is steep and requires sturdy shoes. Once beneath the earth you'll encounter temperatures of 48°, so bring along extra clothing.

Next, you can follow Generals Highway up to the central attraction of the entire park. Surrounded by conifers that appear little more than children stands the **General Sherman Tree**. The largest living thing on earth, this leviathan weighs 1385 tons, measures 102 feet around and rises 275 feet high. About 2500 years old, the tree is as tall as a 27-story building. Even statistics so overwhelming fall short in conveying the magnificence of this colossus.

KINGS CANYON NATIONAL PARK   Headquarters in Kings Canyon National Park is Grant Grove. This mountain village, a few miles from the park entrance, offers a small grocery, restaurant, lodge and gift shop. The **Grant Grove Visitor Center** (209-335-2315) provides information, maps and wilderness permits.

Pride of the park is the **General Grant Grove**, a forest of giants dating back more than 3000 years. Here a short loop leads past a **twin sequoia**, formed when two trunks grew from a single base. Nearby lies the **Fallen Monarch**, a 120-foot-long hollow log that has served as a loggers' shelter, saloon and stable.

The Civil War is still being fought here in Grant Grove. Among these sentinel-straight sequoias is the **Robert E. Lee Tree**, rising 254 feet above the forest floor. The **General Grant Tree** is a gnarly giant tattooed with woodpecker holes and adorned with thick, stubby branches that twist upward. Needless to say, the General Grant outstrips its Confederate counterpart, topping out at 267 feet and boasting a diameter (40 feet) greater than any other sequoia. In the shadow of this leviathan sits the **Gamlin Cabin**, a log house built in 1872 by an early settler.

From Grant Grove a mountain road corkscrews up to **Panoramic Point**. Situated at 7520 feet, this lookout could as soon be at sea level considering the peaks that rise above it. Stretched along the horizon in a kind of granite amphitheater is a line of bald domes, cresting at 13,000- and 14,000-foot heights. Each bears a name resonant of the simple poetry of stone—Kettle Dome, Marble Mountain, Eagle Peaks and Thunder Mountain.

Follow Route 180 from Grant Grove down into Kings Canyon itself. Along this 35-mile mountain road, which twists and curves as it descends the canyon walls, are countless vista points where you can peer down sharp rockfaces or at massive ridges.

A side road diverges to **Hume Lake**, a small mountain lake that reflects in its glassy surface the faces of surrounding peaks. Then Route 180 descends farther and farther into this shadowy canyon, where the granite walls edge closer and climb more steeply. Eventually the landscape narrows to a sharp defile and then reopens to reveal a tumbling river strewn with boulders, the South Fork of the Kings River.

Here, where road meets river, sits **Boyden Cavern** (209-736-2708; admission). Formed over a 300,000-year period, this limestone cave descends past rock pools, massive stalagmites, cave pearls and ornate stalactites with names like Upside Down City and Layer Cake.

Route 180 continues along the river past **Cedar Grove**, where civilization rises in the form of a lodge with grocery store and snack bar. Just beyond this oasis lies **Roaring River Falls**, a cascade that crashes through a granite chasm and debouches into an emerald pool.

Nearby **Zumwalt Meadow** is awash with color in spring when the wildflowers bloom. For an even more intimate view of the natural surroundings, drive or hike the **Motor Nature Trail**, which bumps for three miles along a dirt road, paralleling the river and passing rich marshland.

Here, deep in the canyon, you will find the river loud in your ears. Sounds echo off the surrounding walls, ricocheting upward along flinty rockfaces and cliffs. Vying with Yosemite in grandeur, the valley is more than 8000 feet beneath the surrounding mountains, the deepest canyon in the United States.

SEQUOIA AND KINGS CANYON LODGING

Accommodations in both Sequoia and Kings Canyon national parks fall into several categories. There are "rustic cabins," available only in summer, which lack bathrooms and decoration, utilize oil or wood stoves and price in the budget range. The "cabins" are trim woodframe structures with private baths and thermostat heaters. These are moderately priced and quite comfortable.

Both parks also offer "motel rooms." Tabbed in the moderate category, they are roadside-style accommodations with veneer furniture, wall-to-wall carpeting and private baths. The central number for reservations to all facilities is 209-561-3314. Remember, large sections of the parks are closed in winter.

The main complex in Sequoia National Park is **Giant Forest Lodge** (209-561-3314). Located along Generals Highway, it is part of a village layout that includes a restaurant, cafeteria, market and lounge. Accommodations include rustic cabins, cabins and motel rooms.

Stony Creek (209-561-3314), located on Generals Highway between Sequoia and Kings Canyon, features a lodge with motel-type accommodations. There's a dining room, gift shop and market here as well as a lobby with stone fireplace.

Grant Grove Lodge (209-561-3314), the central facility in Kings Canyon National Park, sits in a village that features a restaurant, grocery and information center. Facilities include rustic cabins and cabins.

Cedar Grove (209-561-3314), located on Route 180 deep within Kings Canyon, is a mountain lodge idyllically set in a grove of tall trees beside a river. There are motel rooms here, as well as a snack bar, market and gift shop.

SEQUOIA AND KINGS CANYON RESTAURANTS

You can scale granite cliffs in Sequoia and Kings Canyon, shoot whitewater rapids and return unscathed. What will kill you is the food. Nowhere is the "good enough for government work" philosophy more closely followed than in the kitchens of these national parks.

Adding inconvenience to insult, there aren't very many places to eat, and most are open only in summer. Probably the nicest is **Sequoia National Park's Lodge Dining Room** (Giant Forest Village; 209-565-3393). Overlooking a mountain meadow and stands of sequoia, it's an attractive dining room serving standard breakfast dishes and dinners featuring chicken Veronique, New York steak and rainbow trout; moderate.

The nearby **Village Cafeteria** (209-565-3393) ladles out steam-tray food for all three meals at budget prices. At **Lodge Pole** (209-656-3301) a deli serves up fried chicken and an assortment of sandwiches, burgers and hot dogs.

The **Grant Grove Coffee Shop** (209-335-2314) is located in Kings Canyon near park headquarters. It serves standard American fare at budget to moderate prices.

Sporting Life

FISHING

It's easy to hook a trout in the High Sierra. The Lake Tahoe area's best bets are **Hooker For Hire** (Tahoe City; 916-525-5654) and **Tahoe Sport Fishing** (968 Ski Run Boulevard, South Lake Tahoe; 916-541-5448).

The Kern and Kings rivers in Sequoia and Kings Canyon national parks offer trout fishing. The Mammoth Lakes area is also an angler's delight. For fishing gear rentals, tackle and friendly information, contact **Ernie's Tackle and Ski Shop** (June Lake; 619-648-7756).

HORSEBACK RIDING AND PACK TOURS

Horseback riding can bring you a glimpse of the mountains the way Indians and settlers first saw them. Around Lake Tahoe, call **Camp Richardson's Corral** (Emerald Bay Road, Camp Richardson; 916-

---

SKI CALIFORNIA

During winter, when rain spatters the coast and fog invades the valleys, the Golden State has one more treat in its bottomless bag—snow. No sooner has the white powder settled than skiers from around the world beeline to the region's high altitude resort areas.

The season begins in late fall and sometimes lasts until May. During those frosty months dozens of ski areas offer both downhill and cross-country skiing. In the Far North, the Shasta Cascade Wonderland Association (1250 Parkview Avenue, Redding, CA 96001; 916-243-2643) provides information on facilities. Here, 14,162-foot Mt. Shasta and 10,457-foot Mt. Lassen feature downhill skiing as well as miles of trackless wilderness.

The center of California skiing lies in the Sierra, where large resorts surround Lake Tahoe and extend south toward Yosemite National Park and beyond. The California Ski Industry Association (340 Townsend Street, Suite 407, San Francisco, CA 94107; 415-543-7036) has full information.

Many provide complete facilities for their athletic guests. Some, like Squaw Valley (Olympic Valley, CA 95730; 916-583-6985), are self-contained villages offering every facility imaginable, from boutiques to après-ski spots.

For those from Los Angeles, the Mammoth/June Lakes region represents skier heaven. Mammoth Mountain (619-934-2571), one of the largest ski areas in the United States, boasts mountain lodges, craggy peaks and enough white powder to create an aura of the Alps right in sun-drenched Southern California.

Within Los Angeles County itself, Angeles National Forest features both Kratka Ridge (818-449-1749) and Mt. Waterman (818-790-2002) ski areas plus five nordic ski trails. For further information, contact the local ranger station at 818-790-1151. One of Southern California's most popular ski areas is Mt. Baldy (714-981-3344), a 10,064-foot peak just 45 minutes from the city.

The neighboring San Bernardino Mountains, which rise to over 11,000 feet, offer several alpine ski areas, including Snow Valley (714-867-2751), Snow Summit (714-866-5766) and Bear Mountain Ski Resort (714-585-2519).

Even Palm Springs, California's vaunted warm-weather hideaway, offers skiing at 8000 feet elevation in Mount San Jacinto State Park (619-327-0222), where a nordic center rents cross-country gear and two loop trails circle through backcountry wilderness.

541-3113) or **Alpine Meadows Stable** (Alpine Meadows, Tahoe City; 916-583-3905). **Yosemite National Park** has stables in the Valley and at Wawona, White Wolf and Tuolumne Meadows; call 209-372-1000 for information.

Pack trips in the southern Sierra Nevada often combine horseback riding with fishing expeditions. If you prefer something less adventurous, most outfits offer day or half-day excursions as well as longer treks. For details contact **Schober Pack Station** (Bishop; 619-873-4785), **Red's Meadow Resort Pack Train** (Mammoth Lakes; 619-934-2345 in summer; 619-873-3928 in winter), **Frontier Pack Station** (June Lake; 619-648-7701) or **Cedar Grove Pack Station** (Three Rivers; 209-561-4621).

In Sequoia and Kings Canyon national parks there are stables at **Grant Grove** (209-335-2374), **Cedar Grove** (209-565-3464) and **Mineral King** (209-561-4142).

BOATING, WINDSURFING AND WATERSKIING

The place for recreational boating, including sailing, canoeing, ski boating and board sailing, is Lake Tahoe. For boat rentals, contact **Richardson's Marina** (Jameson Beach Road, Camp Richardson; 916-541-1777).

KAYAKING AND WHITE-WATER RAFTING

An exhilarating river sport, white-water rafting can provide recreation along scenic waterways. Around Lake Tahoe, call **Mountain Air Sports** (205 River Road, Tahoe City; 916-583-5606).

Several tour companies in the southern Sierra feature exciting adventures on rubber rafts, and some offer kayaking. Among them are **Sierra South** (Kernville; 619-376-3745), **Spirit Whitewater** (1001 Rose Avenue, Penngrove; 707-795-7305), **Zephyr River Expeditions** (P.O. Box 510, Columbia; 209-532-6249) and **Whitewater Voyages** (El Sobrante; 415-222-5994).

BALLOONING AND GLIDING

You can take a silent flight above the Sierra and Lake Tahoe areas in a glider. Call **Mountain High Balloons** (Truckee; 916-587-6922) anytime from June through September. In the Mammoth Lakes area, try **High Sierra Ballooning and Alpine Adventures** (Mammoth Lakes, 619-934-7188; Bishop; 619-873-5838).

BICYCLING

Exploring the High Sierra by bicycle can be an exhilarating experience. To enjoy touring this area, cyclists should plan their trips carefully, if possible scouting routes in advance. The mountain roads are steep and arduous, and the high altitude makes pedaling even more strenuous.

The Lake Tahoe area is best toured by physically fit folks on tenspeed bikes. Almost all roads are open for bicycling, but heavy traffic and steep grades make for an arduous journey. Check with the local chamber of commerce for bike routes. Sightseeing by bicycle is also one of the most enjoyable ways to explore Yosemite Valley.

Transportation

BY CAR

Route 80 travels northeast into the High Sierra, passing within ten miles of Lake Tahoe's North Shore. The quickest way to the South Shore is via **Route 50** from Sacramento. To reach Yosemite, follow the freeways leading east from San Francisco, then pick up either **Route 120** or **Route 140** into the Park.

Route 395 leads through the Mammoth Lakes area and runs the entire length of the Owens Valley.

Two highways lead into Sequoia and Kings Canyon national parks: **Route 198** from Visalia and **Route 180** from Fresno.

BY AIR

South Lake Tahoe Airport is serviced by American Airlines and American Eagle.

In the Mammoth Lakes area try Alpha Air, which flies into **Mammoth-June Lakes Airport**. For information about charter service, contact Mammoth Airport Information (619-934-3825).

BY BUS

Greyhound Bus Lines (916-544-2241) provides service to South Lake Tahoe.

To visit the Mammoth Lakes region and Owens Valley, try **Greyhound Bus Lines**, which stops in Lone Pine (107 North Main Street; 619-876-5300) and Mammoth Lakes (Mammoth Tavern Road).

BY TRAIN

Train aficionados can climb aboard **Amtrak** (800-872-7245) for an excursion to Lake Tahoe or Yosemite. From Oakland, the "Zephyr" carries passengers to Truckee in the Tahoe area. Those traveling to Yosemite from Oakland or Los Angeles can take Amtrak's "San Joaquin" to Merced, where **Yosemite Via Busline** (209-722-0366) provides connecting bus service into Yosemite Valley.

CAR RENTALS

At South Lake Tahoe Airport, cars are available through **Avis Rent A Car** (916-541-7800), **Hertz Rent A Car** (916-544-2327) or **Budget Rent A Car** (916-541-5777).

PUBLIC TRANSPORTATION

Tahoe Area Regional Transit (916-581-6365), or TART, services North Lake Tahoe. In South Lake Tahoe, **South Tahoe Area Ground Express** (916-573-2080), or STAGE, provides transportation around the South Shore. In Yosemite Valley, a **tram** (209-372-1240) shuttles folks back and forth between various points of interest.

Index

Also Available From Ulysses Press

DISNEY WORLD AND BEYOND
The Ultimate Family Guidebook
Unique and comprehensive, this handbook to Disney World and
its surrounding area is a must for family travelers. 200 pages. $8.95

HIDDEN HAWAII
A classic in its field, this top-selling guide captures the spirit of the
islands. 384 pages. $13.95

HIDDEN FLORIDA
From the Keys to Cape Canaveral, this award-winning guide
combs the Sunshine State. 492 pages. $13.95

HIDDEN FLORIDA KEYS AND EVERGLADES
Covers an area unlike any other in the world—the tropical Florida
Keys and mysterious Everglades. 156 pages. $7.95

HIDDEN NEW ENGLAND
A perfect companion for exploring America's birthplace. 564 pages.
$13.95

HIDDEN BOSTON AND CAPE COD
This compact guide ventures to historic Boston and the windswept
Massachusetts coastline. 228 pages. $7.95

HIDDEN COAST OF CALIFORNIA
Explores the fabled California coast from Mexico to Oregon. 468 pages. $13.95

HIDDEN SOUTHERN CALIFORNIA
The most complete guidebook to Los Angeles and Southern California in print. 516 pages. $12.95

HIDDEN SAN FRANCISCO AND NORTHERN CALIFORNIA
A major resource for travelers exploring the Bay Area and beyond. 444 pages. $13.95

HIDDEN MEXICO
Covers the entire 6000-mile Mexican coastline in the most comprehensive fashion ever. 432 pages. $12.95

TO ORDER DIRECT   For each book send an additional $2 postage and handling (California residents include 6% sales tax) to Ulysses Press, P.O. Box 3440, Berkeley, CA 94703

About the Author

Ray Riegert is the author of seven travel books, including *Hidden Coast of California*. His most popular work, *Hidden Hawaii*, won the coveted Lowell Thomas Travel Journalism Award for Best Guidebook. In addition to his role as publisher of Ulysses Press, he has written for the *Chicago Tribune, Saturday Evening Post, San Francisco Examiner & Chronicle* and *Travel & Leisure*. A member of the Society of American Travel Writers, he lives in the San Francisco Bay Area with his wife, travel publisher Leslie Henriques, and their son Keith and daughter Alice.

About the Illustrator

Timothy Carroll has worked as a graphic designer for almost a decade. He has illustrated several other Ulysses Press guidebooks, including *Hidden Florida* and *Hidden Southern California*. His artwork has also appeared in *Esquire, GQ*, the *Boston Globe, San Francisco Focus, Premiere* and the *Washington Post*.